Dictionary of Computer and Internet Terms

Eleventh Edition

Douglas A. Downing, Ph.D.
School of Business and Economics
Seattle Pacific University

Michael A. Covington, Ph.D.
Artificial Intelligence Center
The University of Georgia

Melody Mauldin Covington
Covington Innovations
Athens, Georgia

Catherine Anne Barrett, B.F.A.
University of Kentucky Law School
Lexington, Kentucky

Sharon Covington, B.A.
Covington Innovations
Athens, Georgia

BARRON'S

ABOUT THE AUTHORS

Douglas Downing teaches economics and quantitative methods at the School of Business and Economics at Seattle Pacific University. He is the author of several books in both Barron's E-Z and Business Review series. He is also the author of *Java Programming the Easy Way* and *Dictionary of Mathematics Terms*, published by Barron's Educational Series, Inc. He holds the Ph.D. degree in economics from Yale University.

Michael Covington is Associate Director of the Artificial Intelligence Institute at the University of Georgia. He is the author of several books and over 250 magazine articles. He holds the Ph.D. degree in linguistics from Yale University.

Melody Mauldin Covington is a graphic designer living in Athens, Georgia. She is the author of *Dictionary of Desktop Publishing* (published by Barron's).

Catherine Anne Barrett is a graduate of the Lamar Dodd School of Art (University of Georgia) and a student at University of Kentucky Law School.

Sharon Covington is a graduate of Emory University.

Barron's books are available at special quantity discounts to use as premiums and sales promotions, or for use in corporate training programs. For more information, please write to the Special Sales Manager, Barron's Educational Series, Inc., at the mailing address indicated below.

All inquiries should be addressed to:
Barron's Educational Series, Inc.
250 Wireless Boulevard
Hauppauge, NY 11788
www.barronseduc.com

ISBN: 978-0-7641-4755-5

Library of Congress Control Number: 2012021295

Library of Congress Cataloging-in-Publication Data
Dictionary of computer and internet terms / Douglas A. Downing . . . [et al.]. – Eleventh ed.
    p. cm.
  Includes bibliographical references and index.
  ISBN 978-0-7641-4755-5 (alk. paper)
  1. Computers–Dictionaries. 2. Internet–Dictionaries. I. Downing, Douglas.
  QA76.15.D667   2012
  004.03–dc23

                                                                    2012021295

PRINTED IN CHINA
9 8 7 6 5 4 3

CONTENTS

TO THE READER

Computers are no longer just for specialists. Today, computing is not just a profession and a hobby; it is also a tool used in virtually all human activities.

That's why we've compiled this book of background knowledge. Its purpose is to tell you the things other people think you already know.

Much has changed since the first edition of this book was published a quarter century ago. New terms are being invented every day. We regularly update the book, and this edition contains new entries on a variety of topics, including Windows 7 and 8, the iPhone and iPad, Twitter, Facebook, and cloud computing. We have also cut out material that was showing its age.

To keep the book small enough to be convenient we have had to be selective. In some ways it would have been easier to write a book five times as large, but such a book would be hard to use. To identify words that we don't cover, use the Internet and do a web search (*see* SEARCH ENGINE). For words specific to particular pieces of software, look in the documentation for that software. If you can't understand our definition of a term, try looking up the other terms used in it.

Terms are marked *slang* or *humorous* if they are seldom used in serious writing. They are marked as *jargon* if, in our estimation, they are somewhat pretentious new names for old concepts and are not likely to endure. We provide occasional *Usage notes* to explain grammar, spelling, and proper use of words, such as the exact difference between *disc* and *disk*.

Throughout, we use SMALL CAPITALS to mark important words that are defined elsewhere in this book. By following cross-references, you can quickly find many entries that pertain to whatever interests you. Here are some entries you may wish to start with to learn about particular topics:

- Internet culture: CHAT ROOM
- right and wrong: COMPUTER ETHICS
- safe computing: COMPUTER SECURITY
- solving exceptionally difficult problems: ARTIFICIAL INTELLIGENCE
- productively using computers in business and daily life: APPLICATION PROGRAM
- listening to music: DIGITAL MUSIC
- taking pictures: DIGITAL CAMERA
- creating web pages: HTML
- writing computer programs: PROGRAMMING LANGUAGE
- software that controls a computer: OPERATING SYSTEM
- how a computer works: COMPUTER ARCHITECTURE
- networking and the Internet: INTERNET
- connecting computers wirelessly: WIRELESS COMMUNICATION
- electronic components: TRANSISTOR

Be sure to notice the visual dictionary of symbols at the end of the book. If you don't know what Σ or $\approx$ or $\bullet$ is called, don't worry; you can look it up there.

All of us want to thank The University of Georgia and Seattle Pacific University for access to facilities and for accommodating us as we worked on the project. We also want to thank Robert Downing for help with 1960s data processing terminology and Brantley Coile of Coraid, Inc., for permission to adapt material from Coraid's glossary of networking and data storage.

NUMBERS

1G (first-generation wireless telephony) analog CELLULAR TELEPHONE technology, using conventional FM radio modulation to carry voice over wireless telephones. *Contrast* 2G, 3G, 4G.

1-2-3 *see* LOTUS 1-2-3.

2G (second-generation wireless telephony) the oldest type of digital CELLULAR TELEPHONE technology, using digitally encoded audio to carry voice over wireless telephones. This provides much better privacy than 1G telephony. *Contrast* 1G, 3G, 4G.

3Com a leading producer of networking hardware, mainly focusing on residential and small to medium businesses. In recent years the company has sharpened its focus in this area by acquiring U.S. Robotics but selling off Palm (see PALM). Their web address is *www.3com.com.*

3D *see* THREE-DIMENSIONAL GRAPHICS.

3G (third-generation wireless telephony) digital CELLULAR TELEPHONE technology that includes access to the Internet and to video signals through the cellular network; it is a combination of ETHERNET and previous cellular telephone technology. *Contrast* 1G, 2G, 4G.

4×, 8×, 16× . . . 64× (etc.) describing a CD or DVD drive, able to transfer data at 4, 8, 16 (etc.) times the speed of normal audio or video. For example, a 16× CD-R drive can record a full CD, equivalent to about an hour of audio, in about four minutes.

4G (fourth-generation wireless telephony) digital CELLULAR TELEPHONE technology that includes access to the Internet at full broadband speed (100 megabits per second or more); a standard adopted in 2009 as a successor to 3G. *Contrast* 1G, 2G, 3G.

5.1 a format of SURROUND SOUND with five speakers that transmit the full audio spectrum and one that transmits only bass. The five full-range speakers are positioned as front left, center, and right, and rear left and right. The bass speaker, or SUBWOOFER, is usually placed in front. *See* Fig. 253, p. 474. *Compare* 6.1, 7.1.

6.1 a format of SURROUND SOUND with six full-range speakers in the left front, center front, right front, left, right, and rear center positions, plus a SUBWOOFER for additional bass. *Compare* 5.1.

7-layer model *see* DATA COMMUNICATION.

7.1 a format of SURROUND SOUND with seven full-range speakers in the left front, center front, right front, left, right, left rear, and right rear positions, plus a SUBWOOFER for additional bass. *Compare* 5.1.

8.3 filename a filename consisting of up to 8 letters or digits, a dot (period), and up to three more letters or digits, as in DOS and Windows 3.

10/100 (describing a network adapter) capable of operating at 10 or 100 megabits per second. *See* 10BASE-T; 100BASE-T.

10/100/1000 (describing a network adapter) capable of operating at 10, 100, and 1000 megabits per second. *See* 10BASE-T; 100BASE-T; 1000BASE-T.

10base-2 thinwire Ethernet; a type of Ethernet connection using thin coaxial cable with BNC T-connectors, a bus topology, and a maximum data rate of 10 megabits per second. Cable segments can range from 2 feet (0.6 m) to 607 feet (185 m) in length. *See* ETHERNET; THINWIRE.
  Usage note: In this and similar terms, *10* stands for the data rate in megabits per second; *base* means *baseband* (not modulated on a higher-frequency carrier); and *2* is the approximate maximum cable length in hundreds of meters. The hyphen is often left out.

10base-5 thickwire Ethernet; a type of Ethernet connection using thick coaxial cable with special cable-piercing taps, a bus topology, and a maximum data rate of 10 megabits per second. Cable segments can range from 8.2 feet (2.5 m) to 1640 feet (500 m) in length. *See* ETHER-NET; THICKWIRE.

10base-F fiber-optic Ethernet; a type of Ethernet connection using fiber-optic cable and a maximum data rate of 10 megabits per second. Cables can be as long as 1.2 miles (2 km). *See* ETHERNET; FIBER OPTICS.

10base-T twisted-pair Ethernet using Category 3 or Category 5 cable and RJ-45 modular connectors, a star topology with hubs, and a maximum data rate of 10 megabits per second. Each cable can be up to 328 feet (100 m) long. However, because they are unshielded, these cables are somewhat subject to electrical noise if placed close to motors or fluorescent lights. *See* ETHERNET; CROSSOVER CABLE; CATEGORY 3 CABLE CATE-GORY 5 CABLE (ETC.).

16-bit program a program that runs on Intel microprocessors using only the features of the 8088 or 80286, with 16-bit internal registers. Most DOS applications and many earlier Windows applications are 16-bit programs. *Contrast* 32-BIT PROGRAM.

24-bit graphics graphical images that use 24 bits to represent color as a mixture of red, green, and blue. The level of each of these three colors is measured on a scale of 0 to 225 (requiring 8 bits each), and a total of 16,777,216 colors is available. Often called "millions of colors." *See* COLOR.

24 × 7 (or **24/7**, **24-7**) available 24 hours a day, 7 days a week.

32-bit program a program that uses the 32-bit internal registers and large memory capacity of the Intel 386, 486, Pentium, or other compatible microprocessor; generally faster than a 16-bit program doing the same computation on the same CPU. *Contrast* 16-BIT PROGRAM. *See also* WIN32S.

32-bit Windows Microsoft Windows 95, NT, and their successors for the Pentium and related processors, as distinct from Windows 1.0–3.1 (apart from 32-bit add-ons) or Windows CE. *See* WINDOWS (MICROSOFT).

35-mm equivalent the focal length of lens, on a 35-mm film camera, that would cover the same field of view as a particular digital camera and lens. *See* CROP FACTOR; FOCAL LENGTH; ZOOM.

47 USC 227 the 1991 U.S. law that banned "junk faxing" (unsolicited advertising by fax). *See* JUNK FAX.

100base-F fast fiber-optic Ethernet, like 10base-F but with a maximum data rate of 100 megabits per second.

100base-T fast twisted-pair Ethernet using Category 5 cable and RJ-45 modular connectors; like 10base-T but with a maximum data rate of 100 megabits per second. Many network cards and hubs are compatible with both 10base-T and 100base-T transmission. Thus, you can convert a 10base-T network to 100base-T component-by-component and switch to the higher speed when all the components have been modernized.

386 the first Intel microprocessor with 32-bit internal registers and good support for multitasking and extended memory; able to run Windows 95, but too slow for most present-day software. *See* MICROPROCESSOR.

403 FORBIDDEN HTTP error message indicating that the HTTP server is not permitted to read a file. This usually means that the owner of the web page has not set the correct permissions on the file. *See* PERMISSION.

404 NOT FOUND HTTP error message indicating that a web address is invalid. *See* DEAD LINK.

419 scam, 4-1-9 scam a form of fraud conducted through e-mail, usually from Nigeria, where it violates section 4-1-9 of the criminal code, hence the name.

The perpetrator sends out mass e-mail claiming to be a bank officer or government official who needs help sneaking some money out of the country and wants to use someone else's bank account. In return, the victim will get thousands or millions of dollars.

What actually happens is that the victim's bank account is emptied, or the victim's information is used for further fraud. Some victims have even been lured into traveling overseas without proper visas so that they could be trapped and blackmailed.

The 419 scam is so common that many active Internet users receive more than one solicitation per day. Newer versions of the scam no longer mention Nigeria, and many of them claim to offer lottery winnings, inheritances, or business deals.

See also SPAM; COMPUTER ETHICS.

486 an Intel microprocessor similar to the 386 but faster; predecessor of the Pentium. *See* MICROPROCESSOR

TABLE 1
IEEE 802.11 STANDARDS FOR WIRELESS NETWORKING

Specification	Popular name	Frequency	Speed	Compatible with
802.11a	Wireless-A	5 GHz	54 Mbps	Wireless-A
802.11b	Wireless-B	2.4 GHz	11 Mbps	Wireless-B
802.11g	Wireless-G	2.4 GHz	54 Mbps	Wireless-B, -G
802.11n	Wireless-N	2.4 GHz	100 Mbps	Wireless-B, -G, -N

802.11 (more fully, IEEE 802.11) a set of specifications for wireless networking that give performance similar to 10base-T or 100base-T and implement Wi-Fi product compatibility standards (Table 1).

Note that the three 2.4-GHz specifications are downward compatible; that is, a Wireless-B computer will work in a Wireless-G or Wireless-N network. Of course, in that case, communication takes place at the lower speed of Wireless-B.

802.16 *see* WIMAX.

1000base-T fast twisted-pair Ethernet using Category 5e or 6 cable and RJ-45 modular connectors, like 100base-T and 10base-T and largely compatible with it. *See* 10BASE-T; 100BASE-T.

1394, 1394a, 1394b *see* FIREWIRE.

2000 *see* YEAR 2000 PROBLEM.

2600 a number used as an identifying code by groups of people who exchange detailed information about how to break into computers, tamper with telephone systems, duplicate credit cards, and the like, whether for the purpose of preventing or encouraging these acts. There is a magazine (*2600: The Hacker Quarterly*), a newsgroup (alt.2600), and a variety of loosely organized local "2600" groups. *See* HACKER (definition 3); CRACKER; PHREAK.

The number 2600 is from the 2600-Hz control tone formerly used in telephone systems. The Atari 2600 video game machine is completely unrelated.

8088 the Intel microprocessor used in the original IBM PC (1981). It has 16-bit registers and an 8-bit external bus. *See* MICROPROCESSOR.

68000 the series of Motorola microprocessors originally used in the Apple Macintosh. *See* MICROPROCESSOR.

80286 the Intel microprocessor used in the IBM PC AT (1984). It is faster than the 8088 and supports extended memory but does not have 32-bit registers or the built-in ability to emulate multiple 8088s; for that reason, multitasking operating systems did not become common until the 386 was introduced. *See* MICROPROCESSOR.

80386, 80486 unofficial names for the Intel 386 and 486 microprocessors. *See* 386, 486, and references there.

A

A (on a digital camera) aperture-priority autoexposure, the mode in which the user sets the lens opening (f-ratio) and the camera chooses the exposure time; same as *Av. Contrast* P, TV, S.

A4 a size of typing paper 210×297 mm (about $8\frac{1}{4} \times 11\frac{3}{4}$ inches). *See* PAPER SIZES.

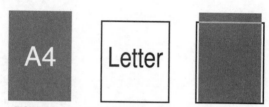

FIGURE 1. A4 paper is longer and narrower than letter size

AAC Advanced Audio Coding, an audio compression format newer and more efficient than MP3, used internally by iTunes and Nintendo Wii. *See www.mpeg.org/MPEG/aac.html.*

ABC Atanasoff Berry Computer, a machine developed in 1939 at Iowa State University by John Atanasoff and Clifford Berry for solving equation systems. Although it did not allow for stored programs, it was an important predecessor of the ENIAC and other digital computers.

abort to cancel an action or command.

abs the function that calculates absolute value in many programming languages and on scientific calculators. It converts negative numbers to positive while leaving positive numbers unchanged. For example, abs(37) = 37; abs(-37) = 37; abs(-2.5) = 2.5; abs(0) = 0.

absolute address
1. a fixed location in the computer's memory. *See* COMPUTER ARCHITECTURE; OFFSET.
2. in a spreadsheet program, a cell address that will not change when a formula is copied to another location. In Excel, absolute addresses are indicated by placing a dollar sign before the column and/or row indicator. For example, if the formula 2*D7 is entered into a cell, then D7 is an absolute address. If this formula is copied to another cell, the address D7 will not change. *Contrast* RELATIVE ADDRESS.
3. *See* ABSOLUTE URL.

absolute URL a URL that contains the full address, identifying the machine, directory, and file. For example, if a web page contains the link:

```
<a href="http://www.census.gov/2010census/about_2010_census/">
```

it will find about _2010_census in the directory 2010census at the Internet node labeled as www.census.gov. *Contrast* RELATIVE URL.

abstract
1. a summary of a document or file.
2. not tied to a specific pre-existing example. For example, an abstract data type is one that does not correspond exactly to anything in the architecture of the computer; instead, it is declared by the programmer to suit the purposes of the program.
3. In object-oriented programming, a class is declared abstract if there will not be any data or methods specific to that class; instead, it is to be used as a superclass for other classes that will have specific data. An abstract class cannot be instantiated, but other classes can extend it.

accelerator a device that makes an operation run faster. For example, a graphics accelerator is a card that contains built-in circuits for performing graphics operations, allowing the system to render graphics more quickly than would be the case if the microprocessor bore the entire load.

accelerometer a component that measures motion. For example, an accelerometer in the iPad senses when you turn the device, so it can adjust the display to be right-side up.

accents marks added to letters (as in *é è ê ë*) to indicate differences of pronunciation; said to have been introduced by Aristophanes of Byzantium c. 200 B.C. to preserve the pitch accent of ancient Greek, which was dying out. The only major languages that do not require accents are English and Latin.
    Most computer software treats a letter with an accent as a single character. More sophisticated systems represent the accent and the letter separately, so that any accent can be put on any letter.

acceptable-use policy a policy established by the owner of a computer system, or by an Internet service provider, concerning acceptable use of the computer and network facilities. Acceptable-use policies should generally include the following points:
1. Users are accountable for what they do. Deliberate snooping, harassment, or interference with other users will not be tolerated, nor will any deliberate unauthorized activity.
2. The computer shall be used only for its intended purposes. For example, you generally can't use your employer's computer to run another business on the side; nor can you run private money-making schemes on a computer owned by a state university. Employees are accountable for how they use their time at work.
3. Passwords must be kept secret. *See* PASSWORD.

4. The service provider has the right to suspend accounts that are being misused. People accused of misconduct have the right to a fair hearing.

5. Users must abide by the acceptable-use policies of newsgroups and other electronic discussion forums, which are mostly paid for by other people. On the Internet you are always someone's guest.

6. Chain letters and mass e-mailing are expensive, unwelcome, and generally not permitted.

7. Cyberspace is not above the law. Practices that are illegal in the real world, such as forgery, gambling, obscenity, and threatening or inciting violence, are still illegal when you do them on the computer.

8. Losing an account is not necessarily the only penalty for misconduct. The service provider cannot shield users from criminal or civil liability when they break laws or deliberately harm others. Really destructive computer abusers generally have several accounts and must be stopped by other means.

See also COMPUTER ETHICS; COMPUTER LAW.

Access a powerful, highly programmable RELATIONAL DATABASE marketed by Microsoft as part of the Office suite of products.

access control list in Windows, the list of which users or groups are allowed to use a file, directory, or device. *See* CACLS.

access provider *see* INTERNET SERVICE PROVIDER.

access time the amount of time needed by a memory device to transfer data to the CPU.

accessibility the measure of how fully a computer product can be used by people of varying abilities. For example, a blind computer user visiting a web page may use speech synthesis software to read the page aloud. A web site where images all have alternate text descriptions is more accessible than a web site without such tags. *See also* WAI.

account authorization to use a computer or any kind of computer service, even if free of charge. An account consists of an identifying name and other records necessary to keep track of a user. Sometimes an account belongs to another computer or a computer program rather than a human being.

accounting system software that reads in data for transactions and generates income statements, balance sheets, and related financial reports. *See also* QUICKEN.

accumulator a register where a computer retains the result of an arithmetic operation. For example, in 8086 assembly language, the instruction ADD AX,10 means "Add 10 to the number in the accumulator, and leave the result there." Some computers can use more than one register as an accumulator. *See* COMPUTER ARCHITECTURE; ASSEMBLY LANGUAGE; REGISTER.

acid2 test, acid3 test test web pages that can be used to verify that a web browser correctly implements standard features. *See www.webstandards. org/action/acid2/guide.* In chemistry, a strong acid can be applied to a metal to distinguish between precious and base metals, so the term acid test has come to have a more general meaning as a quick, decisive test.

ACL *see* ACCESS CONTROL LIST.

ACM (**A**ssociation for **C**omputing **M**achinery) a worldwide association of computer professionals headquartered in the United States (web address is *www.acm.org*).

ACPI (**A**dvanced **C**onfiguration and **P**ower **I**nterface) a set of standard hardware/software interactions that give the operating system the ability to direct power management of hardware devices. For example, a computer with ACPI can turn itself off under software control as the last step in shutting down the operating system.

acquire to obtain a file (for editing) from a scanner or a camera. Similar to IMPORT, except that the image is not coming from a file.

Acrobat software from ADOBE SYSTEMS, INC., for creating and reading PDF (**P**ortable **D**ocument **F**ormat) files. Acrobat *Reader* is a browser plug-in available free from Adobe's web site (*www.adobe.com*) that enables users to view and print PDF files that they receive from others. The full version of Acrobat is a powerful multi-use utility designed to facilitate annotation and distribution of digital documents. With Acrobat, comments and highlights can be added to documents. It's possible to perform minor text edits, although large changes to page layout are not possible. Forms can be made interactive. Multiple .pdf documents can be combined or pages may be extracted into separate files. Acrobat also includes the ability to add a secure digital signature to .pdf documents. *See* PDF.

acronym a word formed from the initial parts of other words. For example, LAN stands for **L**ocal **A**rea **N**etwork. *See also* TLA.

activate
  1. to choose a window in which you want to type. This is done by moving the mouse pointer into the window and clicking one button. In some operating systems you must click on the window's title bar. *See* WINDOW.
  2. to start a piece of software by double-clicking on its name or icon. *See* CLICK; ICON.
  3. to make a software product usable by informing the manufacturer that it has been installed and obtaining an activation code. This can be done on line or by making a telephone call. *See* REGISTRATION (definition 1).

active color the color currently selected (in a painting or drawing program). Whatever tool is being used will paint or draw in the active color.

Active Desktop in Windows, the ability to use a WEB PAGE as the desktop, i.e., the screen itself, not just as one of the programs running on it. This makes it easy to display a web page that is constantly updated, such as weather or stock price information, without having to start and run a BROWSER. *See also* DESKTOP; WORLD WIDE WEB.

active matrix a type of liquid crystal display (LCD) that produces higher contrast than earlier passive-matrix displays by incorporating transistors into the LCD matrix.

active window the window currently in use, the one in which the user is typing, drawing, or making menu choices (*see* Figure 2). There can only be one active window on a screen at one time. *See* WINDOW; ACTIVATE.

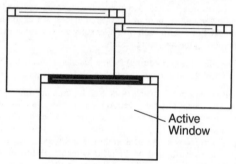

— Active Window

FIGURE 2. Active window

ActiveX a marketing name used by Microsoft for many types of software components implemented in the COM (Component Object Model) architecture (*see* COM).

actor in computer animation, any object that moves in a specified manner along a path, whether or not it represents a human being. Even a bouncing ball is an actor.

actual parameter the value actually passed to a function or procedure in a programming language. For example, if you compute ABS(1+X) and the value of X is 2.5, then 3.5 is the actual parameter of ABS. *See* FORMAL PARAMETER; PARAMETER.

A/D converter *see* ANALOG-TO-DIGITAL CONVERTER.

Ada a programming language developed in the late 1970s for the U.S. Department of Defense. It is named for Augusta Ada Byron, Countess of Lovelace, who worked with Babbage's mechanical calculator in the nineteenth century.

Ada subprograms can be compiled separately and linked together before execution. In the sample program, the with and use statements specify that this program uses a library of precompiled subroutines called I_O_PACKAGE.

Much of the original motivation for designing Ada was the need for a better language for real-time programming, that is, programming computers to control automatic or semiautomatic equipment. Toward this end, Ada allows the programmer to create multiple tasks that run concurrently (*see* TIMESHARING) to pass signals from one task to another and to introduce controlled time delays.

```
with I_O_PACKAGE;
procedure FACTORIAL is
  use I_O_PACKAGE;
  --This program reads a number and
  --computes its factorial.
  NUM, FACT, COUNT: INTEGER;
begin
  GET(NUM);
  FACT := 1;
  for COUNT in 2..NUM loop
    FACT := FACT * COUNT;
end loop;
  PUT("The factorial of ");
  PUT(NUM); PUT(" is ");
  PUT(FACT);
end;
```

FIGURE 3. Ada program

adaptive technology technology that helps people work around physical limitations. Computer-related examples include magnified screen displays, speech recognition devices, and keyboards with latching shift and control keys for people who can press only one key at a time. *See* ACCESSIBILITY.

ADC *see* ANALOG-TO-DIGITAL CONVERTER.

add-in a package providing additional features to a program such as a spreadsheet; for example, the Solver add-in for Microsoft Excel.

add noise a paint program filter that adds a speckled texture to a picture. This is done by adding noise (random variation) to the pixel values. *Compare* WHITE NOISE.

FIGURE 4. Add Noise filter adds texture to image

address

    1. a number or bit pattern that uniquely identifies a location in a computer memory. Every location has a distinct address.

    2. a letter and number identifying the column and row of a cell in a spreadsheet. *See* RELATIVE ADDRESS; ABSOLUTE ADDRESS.

    3. a set of numbers identifying a machine on the Internet. *See* IP ADDRESS.

    4. an electronic mail address. *See* ELECTRONIC MAIL.

    5. a URL identifying a web page. *See* URL.

address book a facility in an e-mail program, chat program, or web browser for storing addresses of individuals or web sites. Addresses may be added to the address book automatically when the user replies to e-mail.

ADF (**a**utomatic **d**ocument **f**eeder) a device for feeding documents into a SCANNER automatically, sheet by sheet.

admin abbreviation for ADMINISTRATOR.

Administrator the account name used by the system administrator under Windows NT and its successors. *Compare* ROOT.

Adobe Systems, Inc. (San Jose, California) the software company that developed the PDF format for distributing documents on the web and the PostScript command language for output devices. Other products include Photoshop, Illustrator, GoLive, PageMaker, Premiere for digital video production, and a library of type styles. *See* PDF and POSTSCRIPT. Web address: *www.adobe.com*

ADSL (**A**symmetric **D**igital **S**ubscriber **L**ine) a widely used way of providing a high-speed Internet connection through ordinary telephone lines; called asymmetric because the upstream and downstream data rates are different. Full-rate ADSL provides data rates of up to 8 Mbps downstream and 1.5 Mbps upstream. The variety of ADSL commonly provided to homes is called G.lite and provides data rates up to 1.5 Mbps downstream and 0.5 Mbps upstream. *See* DSL and cross-references there.

advance fee fraud scams promising you a large amount of money provided you pay some kind of fee in advance. Needless to say, do not send money to anyone that sends such an e-mail to you. *See* 419 SCAM.

adventure game a game in which the player navigates through an interactive story, solving puzzles and exploring areas. There may be multiple endings to the game, and the player's actions determine which ending is reached. Adventure games test reasoning skills instead of reflexes.

    The first adventure games, such as Zork, had no graphics, only textual descriptions:

        "You are in a maze of twisting passages, all alike..."

Some, such as Rogue, used symbols, punctuation, and other ASCII characters to draw rooms and passages on a non-graphical text-only screen. *Compare* ASCII GRAPHICS.

Other notable examples are many games produced by Sierra, such as the King's Quest series, and the Myst series from Cyan Worlds.

adware software whose main purpose is to display advertisements on the user's computer. Sometimes *adware* refers to legitimate software sent out as samples or sales presentations, but more often, the term denotes software installed without the user's full knowledge and consent. Adware of the latter type can make advertisements pop up on the screen even when the web browser is blocking pop-up ads. *See* POP-UP AD.

Software tools for detecting and removing malicious adware can be found at *www.safer-networking.org* and *www.lavasoftusa.com*. *See also* MALWARE; SPYWARE.

Aero the new window style of Windows Vista and 7, including many subtle changes from earlier versions, the most noticeable of which is that windows can have transparent borders. Compared to Windows 2000 and XP, Aero shows considerable influence from MAC OS X. Graphics features such as transparency can be turned off to improve performance on slow CPUs.

AES (**A**dvanced **E**ncryption **S**tandard) data encryption standard adopted by the U.S. government in 2002, using key sizes of 128 to 256 bits. *See* ENCRYPTION.

AF (**a**udio **f**requency) a frequency within the range of human hearing, 20 to 20,000 hertz. *Contrast* RF.

AFAIK online abbreviation for "as far as I know."

AFAIR online abbreviation for "as far as I remember."

affiliate program a promotional program whereby a business makes payments or provides free services to others who refer customers to them. For example, many web sites participate in the affiliate program of AMAZON.COM to sell books.

afk online abbreviation for "away from keyboard."

agent a piece of software that performs a service for someone, usually silently and automatically. For example, an agent might run on a CLIENT computer to keep the SERVER informed of its needs.

aggregation point a point where signals from different wireless network nodes are collected and then connected to the rest of the Internet.

AGP (**A**ccelerated **G**raphics **P**ort) a fast bus connection that allows the graphics adapter to communicate with the CPU at a higher speed than the conventional ISA, EISA, or PCI bus. AGP was introduced with Intel's Pentium II processor. *See also* PCI EXPRESS.

AH abbreviation for AMPERE-HOUR. *See also* BATTERY.

AI *see* ARTIFICIAL INTELLIGENCE.

AIM **A**OL **I**nstant **M**essenger; an application that allows computer users to correspond with friends while online. *See* INSTANT MESSAGING.

airbrush a tool available in some paint programs that simulates the effect of spraying paint; the edges are soft and the colors are translucent. The softness of the edge, size of the spray pattern, and the degree of opaqueness can be controlled (*see* Figure 5).

In bitmap-editing programs that do not offer an airbrush tool, there is usually a SPRAY CAN, which is basically a coarser version of the airbrush.

FIGURE 5. Airbrush

airplane mode a mode in which a wireless device emits no signals, so it can be used safely on an airplane.

AirPort trade name used by Apple for various wireless networking adapters for the MACINTOSH.

Ajax (**A**synchronous **J**avaScript **a**nd **X**ML) a method for providing dynamic content on web pages, often used with PHP server-side scripting.

ALGOL (**Algo**rithmic **L**anguage) a pair of programming languages that had a strong impact on programming language design. The first, ALGOL 60 (developed by an international committee around 1960), was an immediate ancestor of Pascal and introduced many Pascal-like features that have been adopted by numerous other languages, including:
- recursion;
- begin and end keywords to allow grouping statements into blocks;
- the "block if" statement, of the form:

```
if condition then
   begin
     statements
   end
else
   begin
     statements
   end
```

- the symbol := for arithmetic assignment;
- semicolons between statements, leaving the programmer free to arrange statements in any convenient layout rather than putting one statement on each line.

An ALGOL program is a set of blocks of statements embedded within larger blocks. Thus, hierarchical design is easier to establish and follow.

But the ALGOL 60 standard did not specify statements for input and output, since these were considered machine-specific, and as a result, although much admired for its design, ALGOL 60 was not widely used in practice.

ALGOL 68 (released in 1968) is a much more abstract language with a reputation for being powerful but hard to learn. It introduced widespread use of pointer variables (called *refs*) and variant types (called *unions*). An important principle of ALGOL 68 is *orthogonality*, which means that all meaningful combinations of features are allowed. (In geometry, two things are orthogonal if they meet at right angles.)

Discontent with the complexity of ALGOL 68 led Niklaus Wirth to design first ALGOL W and then Pascal (*see* PASCAL), which almost completely replaced ALGOL in practical use. *See also* RECURSION; STRUCTURED PROGRAMMING; POINTER; VARIANT.

algorithm a sequence of instructions that tells how to solve a particular problem. An algorithm must be specified exactly, so that there can be no doubt about what to do next, and it must have a finite number of steps. An algorithm might be written in a computer program, or it can be a set of instructions for a person to follow.

A set of instructions is not an algorithm if it does not have a definite stopping place, or if the instructions are too vague to be followed clearly. The stopping place may be at variable points in the general procedure, but something in the procedure must determine precisely where the stopping place is for a particular case.

There are well-understood algorithms for many common computations (for example, *see* SELECTION SORT). However, some problems are so complicated that there is no known algorithm to solve them, and in other cases, the only known algorithm takes impossibly large amounts of time. *See* HEURISTIC; LIMITS OF COMPUTER POWER.

algorithmically unsolvable problem *see* LIMITS OF COMPUTER POWER.

alias

1. (Macintosh) a copy of a file icon that provides an alternate way of starting an application program or opening a file, folder, or disk. You can place the alias anywhere that's convenient—the desktop, the Apple menu, or a special folder. The title of an alias icon is in italics and displays a small arrow in the lower left corner of the icon. In Windows, an alias is called a SHORTCUT.

2. (UNIX) an alternative way of typing a command. The `alias` command creates aliases. For example, if you execute the command alias dir ls -al

then from then on, dir will mean ls -al (the complete file listing command).

aliasing the appearance of false stairsteps or bands in an image, or false frequencies in digitized sound, due to interaction of the original signal with the sampling rate. *See* ANTIALIASING; SAMPLING RATE.

Stairsteps

FIGURE 6. Aliasing

All Your Base Are Belong To Us a phrase from a poorly translated Japanese video game (*Zero Wing*, 1989) that achieved brief but widespread popularity as a catchphrase.

allocation unit the smallest quantity of disk or memory space that can be obtained for use. For example, if memory is allocated in 1024-byte units, a program that requests just a few bytes will get a 1024-byte block. If a disk drive uses 4096-byte allocation units, the space occupied by every file will be a multiple of 4096 bytes, regardless of how small the file is. A disk allocation unit is also called a CLUSTER. *See also* FAT32.

alpha (α) a measure of the opacity, or visibility, of an object in a graphical image. A transparent object has an alpha of 0 and is invisible; most objects have an alpha of 1 and completely cover the objects behind them.

alpha channel (in paint programs) a CHANNEL that defines a selection. Instead of specifying a color of ink to print, the alpha channel marks part of the image for special treatment. An image may have multiple alpha channels. *See* SELECTION TOOLS.

alpha testing the first stage of testing of a new software product, carried out by the manufacturer's own staff. *Contrast* BETA TESTING; GAMMA TESTING.

alphabet soup (*slang*) unrecognizable abbreviations.

alphanumeric characters letters and digits (but not punctuation marks, mathematical symbols, or control codes).

alt a key on a computer keyboard that is used to give an alternate meaning to other keys. It is used like the Shift key; that is, you hold it down while pressing the other key. For example, to type Alt-P, type P while holding down Alt. In Windows, pressing and then releasing Alt (without typing anything else) often brings up a menu bar that was previously hidden. *See also* ALT GR.

Alt Gr *See* U.S. INTERNATIONAL.

Altair a pioneering microcomputer marketed to hobbyists in 1975, significant because the version of BASIC for this machine was the first Microsoft product.

aluminum chemical element (atomic number 13, symbol Al) added to silicon to create a P-type SEMICONDUCTOR.

Amazon.com the first prominent E-TAIL merchant. Established as a bookstore in 1995 in Seattle, Washington, Amazon has since expanded to sell a wide variety of products around the world, including the KINDLE. Web address: *www.amazon.com*

AMD (Advanced Micro Devices) a manufacturer of digital integrated circuits, including the Athlon and Opteron. They make chips which are compatible substitutes for Intel's Pentium. AMD is headquartered in Sunnyvale, California (web address: *www.amd.com*). *See also* FUSION; MICROPROCESSOR.

AMD64 *see* X64.

America Online (AOL) a pioneering online information service whose dial-up online service was popular before the Internet was available.

It now provides online content and services, as well as being a popular Internet service provider. In 2000, AOL merged with Time Warner, but in 2009 it became an independent company again (web address: *www.aol.com*).

AMI (American Megatrends, Inc.) a leading supplier of the BIOS software built into PC motherboards (*see* BIOS). AMI also makes diagnostic software, RAID disk array controllers, and other products. The company is headquartered in Norcross, Georgia (a suburb of Atlanta) (web address: *www.ami.com*).

Amiga a computer marketed by Commodore Business Machines in the 1980s to mid-90s. Similar in size and cost to the IBM PC, it had a quite different architecture and was ahead of its time in many ways, offering multitasking, windowing, an advanced graphics system, and MIDI music. Like the Macintosh, it used Motorola 68000-series microprocessors.

Despite being admired by knowledgeable programmers, the Amiga never achieved the popularity of the PC or Macintosh. Although Commodore went bankrupt in 1994, a new company named Amiga continued development on the Amiga platform (web address: *www.amiga.com*).

ampere, amp a unit for measuring electric current. A current of 1 ampere means that 6.25×10^{18} electrons are flowing by a point each second. A group of 6.25×10^{18} electrons has a charge of 1 coulomb, so 1 ampere = 1 coulomb per second.

ampere-hour a unit of battery capacity, indicating the ability to supply 1 ampere for 1 hour at the rated voltage, or, equivalently, 1/10 ampere for 10 hours, 1/100 ampere for 100 hours, and so forth. *See* BATTERY.

ampersand the character &, which stands for the word *and*. For an illustration of ampersands in various typefaces, *see* Figure 7.

FIGURE 7. Ampersands

amplified speaker a speaker that includes its own amplifier to produce louder sound and stronger bass. *See* SOUND CARD; MULTIMEDIA.

anacronym

1. a reinterpreted abbreviation or acronym. For example, *DVD* originally stood for *digital video disc* but is now said to stand for *digital versatile disc*. *Compare* BACKRONYM.

2. an apparent abbreviation or acronym that does not actually stand for a series of words. For example, *POSIX* is apparently a blend of the words *portable* and *UNIX* but has no exact official interpretation.

analog representing data in a form that can vary continuously along any real value in a range. The image picked up by a film camera or scanner and the sound picked up by a microphone are examples of analog data that must be digitized (converted into the computer's internal representation) in order to be stored in a computer. *See also* ANALOG COMPUTER; ANALOG-TO-DIGITAL CONVERTER. *Contrast* DIGITAL.

analog computer a computer that represents information in a form that can vary smoothly between certain limits rather than having discrete values. (*Contrast* DIGITAL COMPUTER.) An analog computer can be constructed to solve differential equations (using capacitors to determine derivatives and inductors to determine integrals, given an input waveform). A slide rule is an example of an analog computer because it represents numbers as distances along a scale.

All modern, programmable computers are digital. Analog computer circuits are used in certain kinds of automatic machinery, such as automotive cruise controls and guided missiles. Also, a fundamental analog computer circuit called an *operational amplifier* is used extensively in audio, radio, and TV equipment.

analog television transmission of television signals to the viewer as analog (non-digitized) signals in a format such as NTSC (now discontinued). *See* NTSC. *Contrast* DIGITAL TELEVISION. The ending of analog television broadcasts in 2009 made a huge chunk of spectrum available for other uses. However, most radio broadcasting remains analog.

analog-to-digital converter (ADC) a device that changes data from analog to digital form. For example, a sound card uses an analog-to-digital converter to convert audio waveforms into digital representations. Laptop computers use analog-to-digital converters to measure the voltages of their batteries. *See* ANALOG COMPUTER; SOUND CARD; CODEC.

analytic processing *See* OLAP.

Analytical Engine *see* COMPUTERS, HISTORY OF.

anchor a marked position in an HTML document (web page), to which the user can jump from elsewhere. For example, the HTML command

```
<A NAME="Elephants"/>All about Elephants
```

marks its position as an anchor named "Elephants," and if it resides in file `http://www.vet.uga.edu/animals.html`, then the full address of the anchor is

```
http://www.vet.uga.edu/animals.html#Elephants
```

See HTML; WORLD WIDE WEB.

AND gate a logic gate that produces an output of 1 only when all of its inputs are 1, as specified by this truth table for a two-input AND gate:

Inputs		Output
0	0	0
0	1	0
1	0	0
1	1	1

The symbol for an AND gate is shown in Figure 8.

AND gates are used in computer arithmetic. AND gates with more than two inputs are used to recognize signals coming in simultaneously on several wires, such as memory addresses. *See* BINARY ADDITION; DECODER; LOGIC CIRCUITS.

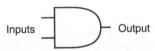

FIGURE 8. AND gate (logic symbol)

android a ROBOT (definition 1) whose shape resembles the human body.

Android a LINUX-based operating system for SMARTPHONES and similar devices, developed by Google, Inc., and largely released as freeware. Android-based smartphones are made by a number of manufacturers. *See* DROID.

angle brackets the characters < > or, more properly, ⟨ ⟩, used in mathematics to enclose ordered pairs and the like. (Strictly speaking, < and > are the less-than and greater-than signs, respectively.) *Contrast* SQUARE BRACKETS; CURLY BRACKETS; PARENTHESES.

angry birds popular game for mobile devices, involving birds shooting slingshots at pigs (web address: *www.rovio.com.*)

animated gif *see* GIF89A.

animation the simulation of motion by showing a series of still images redrawn many times per second. (*See* Figure 9.) Computers have become the primary way to create animation for theatrical releases, television programs, and commercials. Animation studios such as Pixar and Dreamworks Animation utilize custom software written by their own programmers.

Animations produced with Macromedia Flash are very popular on the World Wide Web. (*See* FLASH.) Small icons and graphics can also be animated by saving a series of images as an ANIMATED GIF file. *See* GIF89A.

FIGURE 9. Animation

anonymous FTP *see* FTP.

anonymous variable in Prolog, a variable (written _) that does not retain a value. If several anonymous variables occur in the same fact or rule, they are not the same variable. In pattern matching, anonymous variables match anything. *See* PROLOG.

ANSI (**A**merican **N**ational **S**tandards **I**nstitute) the main industrial standardization organization in the United States. There are official ANSI standards in almost all industries, and many of them have to do with computers.

antialiasing
  1. a technique for eliminating the stairstep appearance of slanted and curved lines on computer displays by using shades of gray in pixels adjacent to the line. See Figure 10.
  2. a technique for eliminating spurious tones in digitized sound by filtering out all frequencies above, or too close to, the sampling rate. *See* ALIASING.

FIGURE 10. Antialiasing

antivirus software software that protects a computer from viruses (secretly destructive software modifications), either by blocking the

TABLE 2
ANSI CHARACTER SET USED IN MICROSOFT WINDOWS

0128	€	0160		0192	À	0224	à
0129		0161	¡	0193	Á	0225	á
0130	‚	0162	¢	0194	Â	0226	â
0131	ƒ	0163	£	0195	Ã	0227	ã
0132	„	0164	¤	0196	Ä	0228	ä
0133	…	0165	¥	0197	Å	0229	å
0134	†	0166	¦	0198	Æ	0230	æ
0135	‡	0167	§	0199	Ç	0231	ç
0136	^	0168	¨	0200	È	0232	è
0137	‰	0169	©	0201	É	0233	é
0138	Š	0170	ª	0202	Ê	0234	ê
0139	‹	0171	«	0203	Ë	0235	ë
0140	Œ	0172	¬	0204	Ì	0236	ì
0141		0173	-	0205	Í	0237	í
0142		0174	®	0206	Î	0238	î
0143		0175	¯	0207	Ï	0239	ï
0144		0176	°	0208	Ð	0240	ð
0145	'	0177	±	0209	Ñ	0241	ñ
0146	'	0178	²	0210	Ò	0242	ò
0147	"	0179	³	0211	Ó	0243	ó
0148	"	0180	´	0212	Ô	0244	ô
0149	•	0181	µ	0213	Õ	0245	õ
0150	–	0182	¶	0214	Ö	0246	ö
0151	—	0183	·	0215	×	0247	÷
0152	~	0184	¸	0216	Ø	0248	ø
0153	™	0185	¹	0217	Ù	0249	ù
0154	š	0186	º	0218	Ú	0250	ú
0155	›	0187	»	0219	Û	0251	û
0156	œ	0188	¼	0220	Ü	0252	ü
0157		0189	½	0221	Ý	0253	ý
0158		0190	¾	0222	Þ	0254	þ
0159	Ÿ	0191	¿	0223	ß	0255	ÿ

modifications that a virus tries to make, or by detecting a virus as soon as possible after it enters the machine. *See also* VIRUS.

AoE (**A**TA **o**ver **E**thernet) a method of communicating with a disk drive on a server using the same protocol as if it were an internally mounted ATA drive, but sending the data back and forth as Ethernet packets. For more information, see *www.coraid.com. Compare* ISCSI.

AOL *see* AMERICA ONLINE.

Apache a web (HTTP) server program used by many web sites on a variety of computers. It is an example of open-source software, where the source code is published and a variety of people make contributions. The first version was released in 1995. Within a year, it became the leading web server software. Apache is available from the Apache Software Foundation at *www.apache.org*.

API (**A**pplication **P**rogram **I**nterface) the set of services that an operating system makes available to programs that run under it. For example, the Windows API consists of a large number of procedures and data areas that can be used by programs running under Windows. With modern operating systems, it is important for programs to use the operating system API, as far as possible, rather than manipulating hardware directly, because direct manipulation of hardware can interfere with other programs that are running concurrently and may expose your computer to being taken over by MALWARE. *See also* MACINTONSH, .NET.

APL a programming language invented by Ken Iverson in the early 1960s and still used for some kinds of mathematical work. APL stands for *A Programming Language,* the title of Iverson's 1962 book.

APL has its own character set, so that most operations are represented by special characters rather than keywords. Additionally, in APL, arrays rather than single numbers are considered the basic data type; a single number is merely a one-element array. Here is an APL program that reads a series of numbers into an array and computes their average:

$$\nabla\ AVG$$
$$[1]\ X \leftarrow \square$$
$$[2]\ K \leftarrow \rho X$$
$$[3]\ (+/X) \div K$$
$$\nabla$$

Here $X \leftarrow \square$ means "read something from the keyboard into X," and X becomes an array if the user types a series of numbers rather than just one. Then ρX is the number of elements in X, and $(+/X)$ is the operation of addition distributed over X, i.e., the sum of all the elements. The last line of the program is an expression that defines the result.

app (*informal*) APPLICATION PROGRAM, a piece of software that performs a particular function for the user. Some apps are complex pieces of software, such as spreadsheets, while others are small lifestyle aids, such as to-do-list organizers, and some are little more than special-purpose web browsers to retrieve information about particular things. The term app is particularly popular in the context of the iPod, iPad, and smartphones, referring to application software for other computers.

app store any of several online stores that sell application software (apps) by direct download, including Apple's App Store (for the iPad family), Apple's Mac App Store (for the Macintosh), and Amazon's Appstore (for Android smartphones).

append to put something at the end of something else. For example, if you append the character string `ian` to the character string `washington`, you get `washingtonian`.

Apple an influential manufacturer of personal computers and entertainment equipment. The company, located in Cupertino, California, was founded by Steve Jobs and Steve Wozniak, who began work in a garage. (Web address: *www.apple.com*.)

The Apple II, introduced in 1977, was one of the earliest popular microcomputers. It was based on the 8-bit MOS technology 6502 microprocessor. The Apple II was widely used in educational institutions, and the first microcomputer spreadsheet program (VisiCalc) ran on the Apple II.

In 1984 Apple introduced the Macintosh, which was the first widely used computer with a graphical user interface (GUI). The Macintosh became widely used for desktop publishing and artistic applications, and it became one of the two main standards for microcomputers. Apple produces both the hardware and the operating system software for the Macintosh (which is very different from the situation with Windows-based computers, the other main standard). *See* MACINTOSH. Apple also produces the QUICKTIME software for playing audio and video on microcomputers, now used on Windows computers as well as the Macintosh.

Recent big sellers include the iPod digital music player and the iPhone (which includes a portable phone, web browser, and music and video player). In 2003 Apple introduced the iTunes music store, allowing users to legally download songs for 99 cents each. *See* DIGITAL MUSIC; IWORK. In 2010, Apple introduced the IPAD. *See also* JOBS, STEVE.

Apple menu (Macintosh) the menu at the far left of the top menu bar that holds log out options, System Preferences, Recent Items list, and other controls.

applet an application program that is downloaded automatically through a World Wide Web browser and executed on the recipient's machine. Applets are normally written in Java. *See* WORLD WIDE WEB; BROWSER; JAVA.

application *see* APPLICATION PROGRAM.

application framework a set of predefined procedures or classes that saves the programmer much of the work of writing a program with a sophisticated user interface. Using an application framework, the programmer need not write code to handle menu choices, mouse movements, etc., because that work has already been done.

An important early application framework was MacApp for the Macintosh. Newer programming languages such as Delphi, Visual Basic, and Java have application frameworks built in.

application program a computer program that performs useful work not related to the computer itself. Examples include WORD PROCESSING

programs, DESKTOP PUBLISHING programs, SPREADSHEETS, DATABASE MAN-
AGEMENT programs, CAD and CAM systems, web BROWSERS, presentation
programs, such as POWER-POINT, and ACCOUNTING SYSTEMS. *Contrast*
UTILITY; OPERATING SYSTEM. *See also* APP.

applications programmer a person who writes programs that use the
computer as a tool to solve particular problems, rather than just to manage the computer itself. *Contrast* SYSTEMS PROGRAMMER.

APU (Accelerated Processing Unit) a chip containing a CPU and a unit for
accelerating other calculations, such as a GPU (**G**raphical **P**rocessing
Unit. *See* FUSION.

arc
  1. part of the circumference of a circle.
  2. a data compression program for the IBM PC formerly produced by
  System Enhancement Associates in the mid-1980s, a precursor of ZIP.
  See ZIP FILE.

arccos, arc cosine the inverse of the trigonometric cosine function. If $x =$
  cos y, then $y =$ arccos x (also sometimes written as $\cos^{-1} x$, but note that
  the exponent does not indicate "raising to the negative one power").
  Many computer languages provide the arc tangent function but not the
  arc cosine function. You can work around this by using the relation:

  $$\arccos x = \arctan \frac{\sqrt{1 - x^2}}{x}$$

  where x is positive and angles are expressed in radians. *See also* TRIGO-
  NOMETRIC FUNCTIONS.

archival storage storage for data that must be kept for a long time but will
  seldom be used, such as backup copies of working programs. Microcomputers often use CD-R, DVD-R, or external hard disks for archival
  storage.

archive
  1. a filing system for information designed to be kept for a long time.
  See ARCHIVAL STORAGE.
  2. a file containing the compressed contents of other files. The original
  files can be reconstructed from it. *See* ARC; ZIP FILE; TAR FILE; DATA
  COMPRESSION.
  3. in Windows, a file attribute that says whether or not the file has been
  backed up by copying to another disk or tape. The `attrib` command can
  be used to examine or change archive bits. The archive bit makes it possible to back up only the files that have not already been backed up. *See*
  ATTRIBUTES.

arcsin, arc sine the inverse of the trigonometric sine function. If $x = \sin y$, then $y = \arcsin x$ (also sometimes written as $\sin^{-1} x$). Many computer languages provide the arc tangent function but not the arc sine function. You can work around this by using the relation:

$$\arcsin x = \arctan \frac{x}{\sqrt{1 - x^2}}$$

in which all angles are expressed in radians. *See* TRIGONOMETRIC FUNCTIONS.

arctan, arc tangent the inverse of the trigonometric tangent function. If $x = \tan y$, then $y = \arctan x$.

Arduino an open-source hardware and software system for writing programs that run on a circuit board connected to sensors that read information about the environment, and control switches that can operate lights, motors, and other electronic devices. See *www.arduino.cc*.

arguments (actual parameters) values passed to a function or procedure by the calling program. *See* ACTUAL PARAMETER.

ARPANET a computer network originally developed for the U.S. Defense Advanced Research Projects Agency (ARPA, now known as DARPA) to link research institutions. ARPANET introduced the TCP/IP protocols and eventually developed into the Internet. *See* INTERNET; WIDE AREA NETWORK; TCP/IP; PROTOCOL.

arrange
  1. to place the icons on the screen in neat rows and columns, retrieving any that have been moved off the edge of the screen (Figure 11).
  In Windows, "Arrange Icons" is on the menu that pops up when you right-click on an empty area of the desktop; it is also on the "View" menu of individual windows.
  If you want the computer to keep the icons arranged automatically, turn on the "Auto arrange" feature; a check mark shows that it is selected. *See also* CASCADE; TILE.
  2. to place an item in relation to other items. In drawing programs, there is usually an Arrange menu that contains commands (ALIGN, SEND TO BACK; TO BACK; etc.) relating to the placement of selected objects. Objects are layered as if they were opaque pieces of paper.

FIGURE 11. "Arrange Icons"

array a collection of data items that are given a single name and distinguished by numbers (subscripts). Array elements must be of the same type (for contrast, *see* STRUCT). For example, in C and related languages, the declaration

```
int x[5];
```

creates an array of five elements that can be referred to as x[0], x[1], x[2], x[3], and x[4]. (In some languages, such as BASIC, the elements are numbered from 1 rather than from 0.)

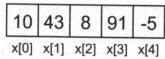

FIGURE 12. Array (one-dimensional)

You can store numbers in these elements with statements such as

```
x[0] = 10;
x[1] = 43;
x[2] = 2+9;
x[3] = 8*3;
x[4] = -5;
```

just as if each element were a separate variable. You can also perform input and output on array elements just as if they were ordinary variables.

Arrays are useful because they let you use arithmetic to decide which element to use at any particular moment. For example, you can find the total of the numbers in the five-element array x by executing the statements:

```
total = 0;
for (i=0; i<5; i++)
{
  total = total + x[i];
}
```

Here total starts out as 0 and then gets each element of x added to it.

Arrays can have more than one dimension. For example, the declaration int y[3][5] creates a 3×5 array whose elements are:

```
y[0][0]  y[0][1]  y[0][2]  y[0][3]  y[0][4]
y[1][0]  y[1][1]  y[1][2]  y[1][3]  y[1][4]
y[2][0]  y[2][1]  y[2][2]  y[2][3]  y[2][4]
```

Multidimensional arrays are useful for storing tables of data, such as three test grades for each of five students. *See also* DATA STRUCTURES; SORT.

31	17	95	43	60
32	95	86	72	40
10	43	8	91	-5

FIGURE 13. Array (two-dimensional, 3 × 5)

arrow keys a set of four keys that move the cursor up, down, left, or right. The effect of these keys depends on the software being used. In a GUI environment, the arrow keys are an alternative to a mouse. Some drawing environments let you NUDGE the selected object with the arrow keys, giving you greater precision. Touch typists sometimes prefer the arrow keys to a mouse because it allows them to keep their hands on the keyboard. *See* KEYBOARD; MOUSE; NUDGE.

artifact any unwanted part of a signal or image that results from the way it was recorded or processed. For instance, a low-level hiss is a familiar artifact of tape recording.

If you greatly increase the brightness or contrast of a JPEG image, you may see unusual stripes or blocks of color. They are artifacts of JPEG compression, in parts of the picture where the JPEG algorithm chose to sacrifice low-contrast detail in order to make the file smaller. *See* JPEG.

artificial intelligence (AI) the use of computers to simulate human thinking. Artificial intelligence is concerned with building computer programs that can solve problems creatively, rather than just working through the steps of a solution designed by the programmer.

One of the main problems of AI is how to represent knowledge in the computer in a form that can be *used* rather than merely reproduced. In fact, some workers define AI as the construction of computer programs that utilize a knowledge base. A computer that gives the call number of a library book is not displaying artificial intelligence; it is merely echoing back what was put into it. Artificial intelligence would come into play if the computer used its knowledge base to make generalizations about the library's holdings or construct bibliographies on selected subjects. *See* EXPERT SYSTEM.

Computer vision and *robotics* are important areas of AI. Although it is easy to take the image from a TV camera and store it in a computer's memory, it is hard to devise ways to make the computer recognize the objects it "sees." Likewise, there are many unsolved problems associated with getting robots to move about in three-dimensional space—to walk, for instance, and to find and grasp objects—even though human beings do these things naturally.

AI also includes *natural language processing*—getting computers to understand speech, or at least typewritten input, in a language such as English. In the late 1950s it was expected that computers would soon be programmed to accept natural-language input, translate Russian into English, and the like. But human languages have proved to be more complex than was expected, and progress has been slow. *See* NATURAL LANGUAGE PROCESSING.

Do computers really think? Artificial intelligence theorist Alan Turing proposed a criterion that has since become known as the Turing test: A computer is manifesting human-like intelligence if a person communicating with it by teletype cannot distinguish it from a human being. Critics have pointed out that it makes little sense to build a machine whose purpose is to deceive its makers. Increasing numbers of AI workers are taking the position that computers are not artificial minds, but merely tools to assist the human mind, and that this is true no matter how closely they can be made to imitate human behavior. *See also* COGNITIVE ENGINEERING; COGNITIVE PROSTHESIS; COGNITIVE SCIENCE; COMPLEXITY THEORY; ELIZA; LIMITS OF COMPUTER POWER; NEURAL NETWORK; TURING TEST.

ascender the part of a printed character that rises above the body of the letter. For instance, the letter *d* has an ascender and the letter *o* does not. *See* DESCENDER; TYPEFACE; X-HEIGHT.

FIGURE 14. Ascenders

ASCII (American Standard Code for Information Interchange) a standard code for representing characters as numbers that is used on most microcomputers, computer terminals, and printers. In addition to printable characters, the ASCII code includes control characters to indicate carriage return, backspace, etc. Table 3 (page 31) shows all the ASCII character codes as decimal numbers. For alternatives to ASCII, *see* EBCDIC and UNICODE.

ASCII file a text file on a machine that uses the ASCII character set. (*See* TEXT FILE.) In Windows, each line ends with a carriage return and line feed (code 13 and 10).

ASCII graphics an amusing technique of drawing pictures using only the standard keyboard characters (Figure 15). By making use of the intrinsic shapes of the characters, or of their relative densities, the artist can render surprisingly realistic graphics. These pictures are best when designed and displayed in a fixed-pitch font. (*See* FIXED-PITCH TYPE.) Because

TABLE 3
ASCII CHARACTER CODES (DECIMAL)

0	Ctrl-@	32	Space	64	@	96	`
1	Ctrl-A	33	!	65	A	97	a
2	Ctrl-B	34	"	66	B	98	b
3	Ctrl-C	35	#	67	C	99	c
4	Ctrl-D	36	$	68	D	100	d
5	Ctrl-E	37	%	69	E	101	e
6	Ctrl-F	38	&	70	F	102	f
7	Ctrl-G	39	'	71	G	103	g
8	Backspace	40	(	72	H	104	h
9	Tab	41	)	73	I	105	i
10	Ctrl-J	42	*	74	J	106	j
11	Ctrl-K	43	+	75	K	107	k
12	Ctrl-L	44	,	76	L	108	l
13	Return	45	-	77	M	109	m
14	Ctrl-N	46	.	78	N	110	n
15	Ctrl-O	47	/	79	O	111	o
16	Ctrl-P	48	0	80	P	112	p
17	Ctrl-Q	49	1	81	Q	113	q
18	Ctrl-R	50	2	82	R	114	r
19	Ctrl-S	51	3	83	S	115	s
20	Ctrl-T	52	4	84	T	116	t
21	Ctrl-U	53	5	85	U	117	u
22	Ctrl-V	54	6	86	V	118	v
23	Ctrl-W	55	7	87	W	119	w
24	Ctrl-X	56	8	88	X	120	x
25	Ctrl-Y	57	9	89	Y	121	y
26	Ctrl-Z	58	:	90	Z	122	z
27	Escape	59	;	91	[	123	{
28	Ctrl-\	60	<	92	\	124		
29	Ctrl-]	61	=	93	]	125	}
30	Ctrl-^	62	>	94	^	126	~
31	Ctrl-_	63	?	95	_	127	Delete

ASCII graphics uses only standard characters, these pictures can easily be transmitted by e-mail or in newsgroup postings and are popular in a SIGNATURE FILE.

FIGURE 15. ASCII graphics

ASIC (**A**pplication **S**pecific **I**ntegrated **C**ircuit) an integrated circuit (silicon chip) specifically made for a particular complete piece of electronic equipment. For example, the video controller in a typical PC is an ASIC designed specifically for use on that particular make and model of video card, whereas the memory chips are standard ICs also used in other types of computers.

Ask.com a search engine originally called "Ask Jeeves" that began in 1996 as a natural-language search engine able to understand English questions such as "what is a platypus?" In February 2005 it was reformed as a conventional search engine at *Ask.com*.

ASP

1. (**A**ctive **S**erver **P**ages) on Windows web servers, a system for generating web pages partly or completely by computation, not by launching a separate program as in CGI, but by running scripts interpretively within the web pages as they are delivered to the client. Thus, a web page can be written partly in VBscript or another programming language in order to do computation as it is being served.

The current version of ASP, using the .NET Framework, is called ASP.NET. *See* IIS. *Contrast* CGI (definition 1); PHP.

2. (**A**pplication **S**ervice **P**rovider) a network service provider that also provides application software, such as networked database programs. *Compare* INTERNET SERVICE PROVIDER, CONTENT PROVIDER.

aspect ratio the ratio of height to width. For example, some images are taller than they are wide, and others are wider than they are tall. You can hold an iPad in either orientation and it will automatically sense which way is up and display the image right side up. *See also* LANDSCAPE, PORTRAIT.

ASPI (**A**dvanced **SCSI** **P**rogramming **I**nterface) a standard way for application programs to access SCSI hardware. *See* SCSI.

assembler a computer program that translates assembly language into machine language. *See* ASSEMBLY LANGUAGE; MACHINE LANGUAGE; COMPILER.

assembly in Microsoft's .NET Framework, a set of files containing software components that work together as a single program. All the components are explicitly and uniquely identified so that accidental substitutions cannot occur. (*Assembly* in this sense has nothing to do with assembly language.) *See* .NET FRAMEWORK. *Contrast* DLL HELL.

assembly language a computer language in which each statement corresponds to one of the binary instructions recognized by the CPU. Assembly-language programs are translated into machine code by an *assembler.*

Assembly languages are more cumbersome to use than regular (or high-level) programming languages, but they are much easier to use than pure machine languages, which require that all instructions be written in binary code.

Complete computer programs are seldom written in assembly language. Instead, assembly language is used for short procedures that must run as fast as possible or must do special things to the computer hardware. For example, Figure 16 shows a short routine that takes a number, checks whether it is in the range 97 to 122 inclusive, and subtracts 32 if so, otherwise leaving the number unchanged. (That particular subtraction happens to convert all lowercase ASCII codes to their uppercase equivalents.)

This particular assembly language is for the Intel 8086 family of processors (which includes all PC-compatible computers); assembly languages for other processors are different. Everything after the semicolon in each line is a comment, ignored by the computer. Two lines (PROC and ENDP) are *pseudo instructions*; they tell the assembler how the program is organized. All the other lines translate directly into binary codes for the CPU.

Many of the most common operations in computer programming are hard to implement in assembly language. For example, there are no assembly language statements to open a file, print a number, or compute a square root. For these functions the programmer must write complicated routines from scratch, use services provided by the operating system, or call routines in a previously written library.

```
; Example of IBM PC assembly language
; Accepts a number in register AX;
; subtracts 32 if it is in the range 97-122;
; otherwise leaves it unchanged.

SUB32      PROC              ; procedure begins here
           CMP    AX,97      ; compare AX to 97
           JL     DONE       ; if less, jump to DONE
           CMP    AX,122     ; compare AX to 122
           JG     DONE       ; if greater, jump to DONE
           SUB    AX,32      ; subtract 32 from AX
DONE:      RET               ; return to main program
SUB32      ENDP              ; procedure ends here
```
FIGURE 16. Assembly language

assignment statement a statement in a computer language that calculates the value of an expression and stores that value in a variable. For example, this is an assignment statement in C:

$$y = sqrt(a*x*x + b*x + c);$$

This statement calculates the value of $\sqrt{ax^2 + bx + c}$ and then gives that value to the variable y. Another example is

$$i = i + 1;$$

which makes i take on a value 1 greater than its previous value.

associate to tell a computer that a particular file should always be processed by a particular program, so that the next time the user opens the file, that program will automatically start.

Under Windows, associations are largely based on filename extensions. (*See* EXTENSION, definition 2.) To change the association of a file extension, open any directory (folder); then select View, Folder Options, File Types. Associations can also be changed by editing the REGISTRY.

asterisk the star-shaped character *. An asterisk is usually used to mark a footnote.

In Windows, UNIX, and other operating systems, an asterisk is used as a wild card character, to match any characters occurring in a particular place in a filename. For example, if you type `dir *.exe` at a command prompt, you will get a list of all files with extension exe. *See* WILD CARD.

FIGURE 17. Asterisks

asynchronous discussion a discussion where the participants do not all have to be present at the same time. For example, in a newsgroup, participants can read comments about a particular topic that have been previously posted by other participants and then add to them. *See* NEWSGROUP.

AT (**A**dvanced **T**echnology) the class of IBM PCs originally introduced in 1984 using the 80286 microprocessor and a 16-bit bus. *See* IBM PC. *Contrast* XT.

AT command set the set of commands used to control Hayes modems; they all begin with the letters AT. *See* HAYES COMPATIBILITY.

at sign the symbol @, which stands for "at" and was originally used in price quotes (e.g., 4 items @ $3 each) and is now used in e-mail addresses (*jones@somewhere.com*). Some colorful nicknames for @ include "elephant's ear" and "cinnamon bun."

In Windows .bat files, commands beginning with @ are not displayed on the screen.

FIGURE 18. At sign

ATA *see* SATA.

ATA over Ethernet *see* AOE.

ATAPI (AT Attachment **P**acket **I**nterface) the interface used by CD-ROM drives and other devices other than hard disks that are connected to an IDE hard disk controller.

Athlon a high-speed Pentium-compatible microprocessor made by AMD.

ATM
1. online abbreviation for "**at the m**oment" (i.e., now).
2. in banking, abbreviation for **a**utomatic **t**eller **m**achine.
3. in networking, abbreviation for **A**synchronous **T**ransfer **M**ode, a set of high-speed data transmission protocols. *See* PROTOCOL. *Contrast* IPX/ SPX; NETBEUI; TCP/IP.

attachment a file transmitted as part of a piece of electronic mail. *See* ELECTRONIC MAIL.

atto- metric prefix meaning $\div 1,000,000,000,000,000,000$. *Atto-* is derived from the Danish word for "eighteen" (because it signifies 10^{-18}). *See* METRIC PREFIXES.

attributes the properties of files in Windows and similar operating systems. Files can be marked as hidden, system, read-only, and archive (which means that they have changed since last backed up). The attrib command displays and changes file attributes.

auction a sale in which buyers make bids (offers) and the highest offer is accepted. For information about online auctions *see* EBAY. *See also* DUTCH AUCTION; RESERVE PRICE; BID.

audio sound, represented by means of electronic signals. *See also* SOUND CARD; FM SYNTHESIS; WAVETABLE SYNTHESIS; MIDI; SAMPLING RATE; *Contrast* VIDEO.

FIGURE 19. Audio (sound) waveform displayed graphically

audit trail a record kept by a computer program that shows how data was entered into the computer. These records are essential for ensuring the reliability of financial data processing systems.

angmented reality adding virtual objects to a real-word scene, visible on a screen, such as smartphone. The first-down lines visible to television football viewers are an example.

AUP *see* ACCEPTABLE-USE POLICY.

autodimensioning a CAD feature that keeps imported graphics correctly scaled as the drawing or diagram is completed.

AUTOEXEC.BAT in DOS and early versions of Windows, a file that contains commands to be executed as the computer boots up.

In Windows NT, 2000, XP, and their successors, the function of AUTO-EXEC.BAT has been taken over by the Registry. However, if an AUTOEXEC.BAT file exists, Windows normally reads it and executes the SET and PATH commands in it. Whether this happens is controlled by the registry key *ParseAutoexec*. A separate file, AUTOEXEC.NT, is executed at the beginning of every DOS-mode program.

autohide when a screen component automatically disappears from view when not needed. For example, in Internet Explorer full screen view, the various buttons at the top of the window will automatically disappear from view unless you move the mouse to the top of the screen.

autojoin a feature of drawing programs that automatically joins endpoints that are within a certain distance of each other, so that you can draw a closed curve without having to come back to the exact pixel where the curve started. (*See* Figure 20.) If you are having trouble getting curves to close so you can fill them, try increasing the autojoin setting. See your software manual for details.

FIGURE 20. Autojoin

automagically (*slang, comical*) automatically, as if by magic.

AutoPlay the operation that happens automatically when a CD or DVD is inserted into the drive, unless it is disabled. Audio and video discs are played automatically; Windows software discs behave as specified in their AUTORUN.INF files.

autorun.inf the file on a CD-ROM or DVD-ROM that tells Windows how to AUTOPLAY it. The file specifies the name of a program to execute and can also specify an icon to identify the disc.

autotrace (DRAW PROGRAM) a command that instructs the computer to fit a curve to the outline of a bitmap. When the bitmap is traced (converted into VECTOR GRAPHICS), it is more easily manipulated in the drawing program.

FIGURE 21. Autotracing a bitmap

AV

1. abbreviation for *audio-visual*; pertaining to the recording and reproduction of sounds and pictures.

2. (for "aperture value," on a digital camera) aperture-priority autoexposure. *See* A. *Contrast* P, TV, S.

avatar an image representing the user of a visual chat or virtual reality program. Avatars range from simple images to complex, personalized three-dimensional models. In Hinduism, an avatar is an incarnation or materialization of a god.

AVI file (**A**udio-**V**ideo **I**nterleave file) a file containing video and audio (i.e., moving pictures with sound) in any of several formats, identified by a filename ending in `.avi`. *Compare* QUICKTIME.

AWK a programming language for scanning text files and processing lines or strings that match particular patterns, now largely superseded by Perl. AWK was developed by A. V. Aho, P. J. Weinberger, and B. W. Kernighan, and the name "AWK" is an acronym composed of their initials. *Compare* PERL; PYTHON; REXX.

AWT (**A**bstract **W**indow **T**oolkit) a set of tools provided in Java for using a graphical user interface. Crucially, AWT is not tied to Windows, Mac OS, or any other operating system; programs that use AWT are portable.

AX.25 a standard format used in amateur radio for transmitting data in packets. It is an adaptation of the ITU-T (formerly CCITT) X.25 standard. *See* PACKET RADIO; X.25.

Azure Microsoft's CLOUD COMPUTING services (web address: *www.microsoft.com/windowsazure*).

B

B-spline a smooth curve that approximately connects two points. B-splines can be joined together to make a smooth curve passing close to any number of points. For an illustration *see* SPLINE.

Each segment of a B-spline curve is influenced by four points—the two that it lies between, plus one more in each direction. This makes computation of a B-spline much quicker than computation of a cubic spline, because every part of a cubic spline is influenced by all the points to be joined.

To plot a B-spline defined by four points (x_1,y_1), (x_2,y_2), (x_3,y_3), and (x_4,y_4), let t range from 0 to 1 and compute values of x and y for each t as follows:

$$a = -t^3/6 + t^2/2 - t/2 + 1/6$$
$$b = t^3/2 - t^2 + 2/3$$
$$c = -t^3/2 + t^2/2 + t/2 + 1/6$$
$$d = t^3/6$$
$$x = ax_1 + bx_2 + cx_3 + dx_4$$
$$y = ay_1 + by_2 + cy_3 + dy_4$$

That gives you a curve that lies approximately between (x_2,y_2) and (x_3,y_3). You can then advance by one point (letting the old x_4 become the new x_3, and so on) to plot the next segment. *See also* BÉZIER SPLINE; CUBIC SPLINE.

Babbage, Charles (1791–1871) inventor of a number of computing machines, including the "Analytical Engine," which introduced concepts that were later used in electronic computers. Babbage was the first to envision a machine controlled by a program stored in its memory.

back browser command that returns you to the most recently viewed web page. *Contrast* FORWARD.

back camera a camera on a SMARTPHONE that faces away from the user, for general-purpose photography. *Contrast* FRONT CAMERA.

back door an alternate way of entering a computer system. For example, the original programmer of the system may have programmed a secret way of logging onto the system not requiring the normal password entrance. Viruses often create backdoors.

back end the part of a computer system not directly interacting with the user. For example, a database system running on a mainframe computer is the back end of a system, whereas the microcomputers used by those accessing the system are the front end of the system. *See* THREE-TIER ARCHITECTURE.

back one; send backward drawing program commands that send the selected object down one layer. For contrast, see the illustration at BRING TO FRONT; TO FRONT. *See also* ARRANGE; DRAW PROGRAM; FORWARD ONE.

backbone the main communication path in a WIDE-AREA NETWORK; the set of cables or connections that carries most of the traffic. Other data paths branch off from the backbone. *See also* T3 LINE.

background the field or color against which objects are drawn or displayed on the screen.

background execution the continued execution of a program while it is not visible on the screen (or does not occupy much of the screen) and the user is free to run other programs at the same time. Background execution is possible only in multitasking operating systems. *See* MULTITASKING; UNIX; WINDOWS (MICROSOFT).

backlit illuminated from behind (as in the liquid crystal displays on some calculators and laptop computers).

backronym an acronym that is made up by choosing the abbreviation first and then (possibly much later) finding words to fit it. The name of the programming language BASIC (said to stand for Beginner's All-purpose Symbolic Instruction Code) appears to be a backronym.

Compare ACRONYM, ANACRONYM.

backslash the character \ as opposed to the forward slash /. *See* MISFEATURE.

backtracking a method of solving problems by trying various combinations of moves until a successful combination is found.

Backtracking works as follows: First, choose a possible move and make it. Then, proceed from there by choosing a possible move, and so on, until a solution is found. If you reach a point where you have not found a solution but no more moves are possible, back up to the most recent untried alternative. That is, undo one or more moves until you get back to an alternative you did not take. Follow that different choice to see if the solution lies in that direction. If not, keep backing up until you find what you're looking for (you may have to try all possible moves).

Backtracking is built into the programming language Prolog, which uses it extensively (*see* PROLOG). In this article we will discuss how to implement backtracking in a conventional language.

For example, consider this problem: Find three whole numbers $x[1]$, $x[2]$, and $x[3]$, each between 1 and 5, such that their sum is equal to their product. While you might try to solve this problem mathematically, it is easier just to try all the combinations. One way to get all the combinations is to set up three nested loops as follows:

```
FOR x[1]:=1 to 5 DO
 FOR x[2]:=1 to 5 DO
  FOR x[3]:=1 to 5 DO
   IF x[1]+x[2]+x[3] = x[1]*x[2]*x[3] THEN
    write (x[1],x[2],x[3],' is a solution');
```

This is possible because you know in advance that the solution will take three moves (choosing one number in each move), so you can set up three loops.

Backtracking occurs in this example because if the innermost loop doesn't find a solution, control returns to the middle loop, which increments x[2] and starts the innermost loop over again. Similarly, the middle loop backtracks to the outer loop if it fails to find a solution. The loop counters keep track of untried alternatives, but it's important to understand that any method of generating alternatives one by one would work just as well.

With some problems, you don't know how many moves a solution will take. In such a case you must use recursion to nest the loops at run time. Figure 22 shows a program that solves the problem we've just discussed but uses recursion rather than nested loops.

```java
class backtrack {

/* Java program that demonstrates backtracking          */

/* This program displays all triples x[1], x[2], x[3],
   for values of the x's from 1 to 5, and displays "**"
   next to a triple if x[1]+x[2]+x[3]=x[1]*x[2]*x[3]     */

static int x[]={0,0,0};
static void choose(int n)
{
   if (n<3)
   {
     for (int i=1; i<=5; i++)
     {
       x[n]=i; choose(n+1);
     }
   }
   else
   {
   System.out.print(" ("+x[0]+","+x[1]+","+x[2]+")");
   if ((x[0]+x[1]+x[2])==(x[0]*x[1]*x[2]))
   {
     System.out.print("**");
   }
   else
   {
     System.out.print("  ");
   }
   if (x[2]==5)
   {
     System.out.println(" ");
   }
   }
}
public static void main(String args[])
{
   choose(0);
   }
}
```

FIGURE 22. Backtracking

In Prolog, where backtracking is built in, all you have to do is specify possible values for the integers and specify the condition they must meet. You can solve our example problem by typing the query:

```
?- member(X1,[1,2,3,4,5]),
   member(X2,[1,2,3,4,5]),
   member(X3,[1,2,3,4,5]),
   Sum is X1+X2+X3,
   Product is X1*X2*X3,
   Sum == Product,
   write([X1,X2,X3]).
```

Each clause in the query specifies a condition that the answer must meet. Whenever the computer encounters a clause whose condition cannot be satisfied, it backs up to an untried alternative in a previous clause and tries again.

backup copy a copy of working programs and related files that can be used to restore lost or damaged programs and files. You should have a full backup copy of your hard disk on CD-R discs, DVD-R discs, or an external hard disk. It's a good idea to also make *daily* backups of work in progress. Ideally, store some backup copies in a secure place, preferably a fireproof box, and other backup copies at another location, so they won't be affected by any event damaging the building where you normally work. Then, in case of any hardware or software problems, you will be able to restore your files. *See also* ARCHIVAL STORAGE; HARD DISK MANAGEMENT; CD-R.

Backus-Naur form (BNF) a notation used to describe the syntax of languages. BNF was devised by John Backus and Peter Naur and introduced in the first official description of ALGOL 60 (*see* ALGOL); it is sometimes referred to as Backus normal form.

Each BNF statement describes some syntactic unit by giving one or more alternative expansions of it, separated by the symbol |. For example, the following is a BNF description of the assignment statement in BASIC (we assume that <line number>, <variable name>, and <expression> have already been defined, and that <empty> stands for the absence of any written symbol):

```
<let keyword> ::= LET | <empty>
```

```
<assignment statement> ::=
   <line number> <let keyword> <variable name> = <expression>
```

The first statement defines <let keyword> as standing for either the word let or no symbol, in order to indicate that the word let is optional. The second statement defines <assignment statement> as consisting of a line number, an optional let keyword, a variable name, an equals sign, and an expression.

Many languages contain syntactic rules that cannot be expressed in BNF; for instance, BNF provides no way to say that an integer cannot exceed 32,767. Still, BNF descriptions are handy because they are concise and definitive and because parsers can be generated directly from them. *See* PARSING.

Backus normal form *see* BACKUS-NAUR FORM.

backward compatible able to substitute for an older computer or operating system. For example, Windows 7 is mostly backward compatible with Windows 2000; that is, it can run most Windows 2000 software.

bacn (*slang*; pronounced "bacon") pesky e-mail that arrives because you subscribed to it or gave permission for it to be sent to you; something resembling SPAM but slightly more desirable. *See* SPAM.

BAK chat-room abbreviation for "**b**ack **a**t **k**eyboard" and ready to resume the conversation. *Contrast* AFK.

balloon popup, balloon prompt a message that pops up on the Windows taskbar in the shape of a balloon or cartoon speech bubble (Fig. 23).

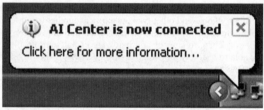

FIGURE 23. Balloon popup (balloon prompt)

banding the appearance of strips of colors in an image due to the inherent difficulty of representing gradations of tones with a limited color palette. *See* Figure 24. Increasing the number of bands gives a smoother color transition.

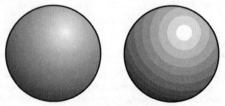

FIGURE 24. Banding (right)

bandwidth the rate at which a communication system can transmit data; more technically, the range of frequencies that an electronic system can transmit. High bandwidth allows fast transmission or the transmission of many signals at once. On a monitor screen, high bandwidth provides a sharp image. On a computer network, the bandwidth of a connection is limited by the slowest link in the chain connecting two computers.

bang (*slang*) the character !, better known as the exclamation mark.

banner
1. an area of a web page reserved for an advertisement. *See* BANNER AD.
2. a sign made by piecing together pages of computer printout.

banner ad an advertisement placed on a web page by a third party, who provides free services or payment in return. Many useful web sites, such as *www.weather.com*, are supported by banner ads. Some sites provide free web space to individuals in return for being allowed to place banner ads on the web pages.

A "banner" is an area of a web page reserved for such an ad. *Compare* POP-UP AD, POP-UNDER AD.

It is unwise to allow a third party to place on your web page ads that you cannot control. Generally, the ad resides on the advertiser's site, and the advertiser can change its content at any time. Web users have been embarrassed to find that formerly innocuous banner ads have changed into obnoxious material or even ads for their direct competitors.

bar a character consisting of a vertical line: |. In C++ and other languages, the double bar || is the operator for inclusive OR, and the single bar | indicates bitwise OR operations.

bar code a pattern of wide and narrow bars printed on paper or a similar material. A computer reads the bar code by scanning it with a laser beam or with a wand that contains a light source and a photocell. The most familiar bar code is the Universal Product Code (Figure 25), used with cash registers in supermarkets, but bar codes have been utilized to encode many kinds of data, including complete computer programs. *See also* QR CODE.

FIGURE 25. Bar code

bar graph a type of chart that displays information by representing quantities as rectangular bars of different heights. Sometimes symbols are stacked or stretched to the appropriate heights to lend some visual interest to the chart (*see* PICTOGRAPH, definition 2).

Bar graphs are usually preferred for representing and contrasting data collected over a period of time.

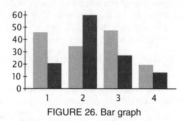

FIGURE 26. Bar graph

bare metal (*slang*) the computer hardware itself. "Programming to the bare metal" means controlling the hardware directly rather than relying on operating system services. *See* API.

barebones incomplete. A barebones computer kit only contains the bare essentials, usually a case/power supply and motherboard, with the expectation that the builder will add the other parts. In software, a barebones program is one that only has the most basic functions, without anything more advanced included.

base
   1. the middle layer of a bipolar transistor. *See* TRANSISTOR.
   2. a number raised to an exponent; for example, in $y = a^x$, a is the base.
   3. the number of digits used in a number system. For example, decimal numbers use base 10 and binary numbers use base 2. *See* BINARY NUMBER; DECIMAL NUMBER; HEXADECIMAL NUMBER; OCTAL.

base-10 (describing a number) written with the conventional digits 0 to 9 in the usual way, as opposed to binary, octal, or hexadecimal.

base-16 *see* HEXADECIMAL NUMBER.

base-2 encoded using just the digits 0 and 1; BINARY NUMBER.

base-8 *see* OCTAL.

Base64 a system, used in MIME and other contexts, for encoding any kind of data in printable, nonblank ASCII characters so that they can be sent through e-mail systems that only handle text.
   To do the encoding, every group of three 8-bit bytes is treated as a 24-bit sequence, which is split into four 6-bit fields, each of which is encoded as a base-64 number using A-Z, a-z, 0-9, +, and –, in that order as the 64 digits, and = as a padding character in unused positions at the end.
   Base64 files contain lines of equal length (usually 64 characters) consisting of seemingly random letters and digits with no spaces or punctuation. The UNIX *uuencode* and *uudecode* commmands convert to and from this format.

baseband the range of frequencies needed to convey a signal itself, without a higher-frequency carrier. For example, the video signal from a TV camera is a baseband signal. When modulated onto a radio-frequency carrier so that it can share a cable with many other TV signals, it becomes a broadband signal. Likewise, baseband Ethernet carries one packet at a time; broadband Ethernet carries many different packets, or data packets plus other types of signals, on different high-frequency carriers. *See* BROADBAND.

BASIC (**B**eginner's **A**ll-purpose **S**ymbolic **I**nstruction **C**ode) a computer language designed by John Kemeny and Thomas Kurtz in 1964 and popularized by Microsoft in the 1970s.

BASIC is good for programming simple calculations quickly, and you do not have to learn much of the language in order to begin using it. Because no declarations are required, programs can be quite short.

Figure 27 shows a simple BASIC program and the results of running it.

Usage note: Since it is an acronym, *BASIC* is usually written in all capital letters. Newer Microsoft publications, however, write *Basic* by analogy to *Pascal*. For a newer version, *see* VISUAL BASIC.

```
10 REM Temperature conversion program
20 PRINT "Temperature in Fahrenheit";
30 INPUT F
40 LET C=(F-32)*5/9
50 PRINT F;" F equals ";
60 PRINT C;" C"
70 END

Temperature in Fahrenheit? 98
98 F equals 36.66667 C
```

FIGURE 27. BASIC program and its output

BAT file (batch file) in Windows, a file whose name ends in .BAT and that contains a list of commands that could be typed in CONSOLE MODE. For example, if you store the commands

```
cls
ver
ipconfig
pause
```

on a file called INFO.BAT, then you can type INFO and the four commands in the file will all be executed in succession; in this example, they will clear the window, report the version of Windows, report the IP configuration, and wait for you to press a key. If you frequently need to execute a set of commands, combining them in a BAT file can save a lot of time. *See also* AUTOEXEC.BAT.

batch processing the noninteractive use of computers. In batch processing, the user gives the computer a "batch" of information, referred to as a *job*—for example, a program and its input data—and waits for it to be processed as a whole. Batch processing contrasts with interactive processing, in which the user communicates with the computer by means of a terminal while the program is running. The crucial difference is that with batch processing the user must put all of the data into the computer before seeing any of the results, while with interactive processing the user can decide how to handle each item on the basis of the results obtained with earlier items.

battery a device that obtains electric current from chemical reactions, taking advantage of the flow of electrons from one material to another during a chemical change. Some batteries are rechargeable, meaning that the chemical reaction can be reversed by making electricity flow through the battery from an external source.

Every battery has a voltage, which is more or less fixed by the nature of the chemical reaction (although it diminishes slightly as the battery runs down), and a capacity, measured in ampere-hours (AH) or milliampere-hours (mAH). A capacity of 1 ampere-hour means that a battery can supply a current of 1 ampere, at its rated voltage, for 1 hour, or 1/10 ampere for 10 hours, and so on. In practice, these equivalences are not perfect, and there are limits to how much current (how many amperes) a battery can supply at one time, regardless of its AH rating.

Portable computer devices often contain rechargeable lithium-ion batteries, which require safety precautions because they can catch fire and even explode if short-circuited or crushed. (*See* LI-ION.). Older rechargeable battery technologies include nickel-cadmium (NICAD) and nickel-metal-hydride (NIMH) and the lead-acid gel cells used in UPSes.

The main factors affecting battery life in a laptop computer are the CPU speed, the power required to spin a hard disk, and the power required to illuminate the screen. In cellular telephones and other mobile devices, the power needed to transmit radio signals to the tower is an important factor. When far from a tower or well shielded by buildings, a cellular telephone will automatically transmit a stronger signal and run down the battery faster.

baud a unit that measures the speed with which information is transferred. The baud rate is the maximum number of state transitions per second: for instance, a system whose shortest pulses are 1/300 second is operating at 300 baud.

On an RS-232 serial link, the baud rate is equal to the data rate in bits per second (bps). With other kinds of communication, the data rate may be considerably faster than the baud rate. For instance, a 2400-baud modem takes 2400-baud (2400-bps) serial data and encodes it into an audio signal whose true baud rate is 600, near the maximum rate at which a telephone line can transmit pulses. Each pulse carries more than one bit of information. At the receiving end, another modem transforms the signal back into 2400-baud serial data.

Modems connected to telephone lines are still used extensively, but a large amount of Internet traffic is moving to faster BROADBAND services.

bay a place provided for a disk or tape drive in a computer enclosure.

Bayer matrix (or **Bayer filter mosaic**) the pattern of alternating red, green, and blue filters placed in front of the pixels of a color CMOS or CCD image sensor (Fig. 28), invented by Bryce Bayer (pronounced BY-er) of Kodak.

The idea behind the Bayer matrix is that adjacent points in an image are likely to be the same color, even if they are not the same brightness. Thus, each pixel determines its own brightness, but its color is determined by comparing it to two adjacent pixels with differently colored filters. Green gets twice as many filters as the other two primary colors because it is in the middle of the visible spectrum.

The filters do not block complementary colors completely; they only make each pixel prefer a specific color. The process of decoding colors (DE-BAYERIZATION) is done by the CPU in the digital camera.

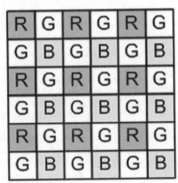

FIGURE 28. Bayer matrix of red, green, and blue filters

Bayes' theorem the formula

$$Pr(A|B) = \frac{Pr(B|A)Pr(A)}{Pr(B|A)Pr(A) + Pr(B|A')Pr(A')}$$

where A and B are two events; $Pr(A|B)$ is the conditional probability that event A happens given that event B happens; $Pr(B|A)$ is the probability of B given A, and A' is the event A complement (the event that A does not happen). The vertical line is read as "given that."

For example, if you have a jar with 2 big red marbles, 4 big blue marbles, 6 small red marbles, and 8 small blue marbles, and you randomly choose one marble, the probability that it will be a big marble given that it is a blue marble will be:

$$Pr(big|blue) = \frac{Pr(blue|big)\,Pr(big)}{Pr(blue|big)\,Pr(big) + Pr(blue|small)\,Pr(small)}$$

$$= \frac{\dfrac{4}{6} \times \dfrac{6}{20}}{\dfrac{4}{6} \times \dfrac{6}{20} + \dfrac{8}{14} \times \dfrac{14}{20}}$$

$$= \frac{\dfrac{4}{20}}{\dfrac{4}{20} + \dfrac{8}{20}} = \frac{\dfrac{4}{20}}{\dfrac{12}{20}} = \frac{4}{12} = \frac{1}{3}$$

In words: "There is a one-third probability that a marble will be big, given that it is blue"; or another way of saying it: "one-third of the blue marbles are big."

The theorem is named after Rev. Thomas Bayes, English theologian and mathematician (1702–1761).

See BAYESIAN SPAM FILTER.

Bayesian spam filter a spam filter that uses BAYES' RULE to adjust its estimate of the probability that a message is spam. Some words have a high probability of being contained in spam, and other words have a high probability of being contained in legitimate e-mail. These probabilities can be different for different users, so a Bayesian spam filter can adjust probabilities for different users as users train the system by indicating whether a particular message is spam or not. In general, the Bayesian approach to statistics views probabilities as being conditional on available information, and provides a way to revise them as more information is obtained. However, spammers can try to subvert the filter by including extraneous text in the message that the filter is likely to think is legitimate, or misspelling words that have a high probability of being contained in spam.

bbl chat-room abbreviation for "[I'll] be back later."

BBS (**b**ulletin **b**oard **s**ystem) an online message board, especially those that were run on non-networked computers with dial-up modems in the 1980s. *See* MESSAGE BOARD.

Bcc business abbreviation for "blind copies" (*compare* CC). In e-mail headers, BCC: precedes additional addresses to which copies of the message should be sent. Unlike the CC: header, the BCC: header is not sent out with the message, so the copies are "blind" (i.e., recipients of the message do not know that copies are being distributed).

Using BCC:, you can send a message to a large number of people without giving them each other's e-mail addresses, thus protecting their privacy.

BCD *see* BINARY-CODED DECIMAL.

BD *see* BLU-RAY DISC.

BD-R recordable BLU-RAY DISCS.

bells and whistles elaborate features added to a computer program. The phrase *bells and whistles* usually connotes that the features are unnecessary and confusing; it originally referred to sound effects devices on theater organs in the silent movie era.

benchmark a computer program used to test the performance of a computer or a piece of software. For example, the speed with which computers do arithmetic is often measured by running a prime-number-finding algorithm called the Sieve of Eratosthenes.

Benchmark results are always somewhat untrustworthy because no single program tests all aspects of a computer's operation. A particular benchmark may exaggerate a difference between two machines that is unimportant in practice, or it may conceal an important difference. *See also* MIPS.

Beowulf a type of cluster computing system using machines running LINUX, named for a hero of early English literature. See *www.beowulf.org*.

Berners-Lee, Tim developer of the hypertext concepts that became the World Wide Web, while he was at the European physics laboratory CERN in the early 1990s.

best practices highly recommended procedures for maintaining computer security or performing other management tasks.

beta testing the second stage of testing a new software product that is almost ready for market. Beta testing is carried out by volunteers in a wide variety of settings like those in which the finished product will be used. *Contrast* ALPHA TESTING; GAMMA TESTING.

Bézier spline a curve that connects two points smoothly and is further defined by two more points that it does not pass through. Most draw programs represent curves as Bézier splines. (Bézier is pronounced, roughly, "bay-zee-ay.")

A Bézier spline can be thought of as a gradual transition from one line to another. Call the four *control points* that define the curve P_1, P_2, P_3, and P_4. Then the curve starts out heading from P_1 toward P_2. But it curves around so that by the time it gets to P_4 it is approaching from the direction of P_3.

To plot a Bézier spline, let (x_1,y_1), (x_2,y_2), (x_3,y_3), and (x_4,y_4) be the coordinates of $P_1 \ldots P_4$ respectively, and let t range from 0 to 1. Then compute x and y from t as follows:

$$a = -t^3 + 3t^2 - 3t + 1$$
$$b = 3t^3 - 6t^2 + 3t$$
$$c = -3t^3 + 3t^2$$
$$x = ax_1 + bx_2 + cx_3 + t^3x_4$$
$$y = ay_1 + by_2 + cy_3 + t^3y_4$$

Notice that as t goes from 0 to 1, a drops from 1 to 0, and t^3 rises from 0 to 1. This computation was first described by Pierre Bézier in 1970.

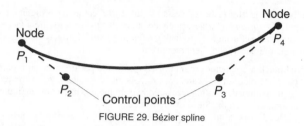

FIGURE 29. Bézier spline

BHO (**B**rowser **H**elp **O**bject) a software component that can be added to Internet Explorer to add new functions. However, BHOs have also been used as SPYWARE.

bidirectional able to transmit data in two directions. *See* PARALLEL PORT.

big-endian a system of memory addressing in which numbers that occupy more than one byte in memory are stored "big end first," with the upper-most 8 bits at the lowest address.

For example, the 16-digit binary number 1010111010110110 occupies two 8-bit bytes in memory. On a big-endian computer such as the Macintosh, the upper byte, 10101110, is stored at the first address and the lower byte, 10110110, is stored at the next higher address. On a little-endian machine, the order is reversed. *Contrast* LITTLE-ENDIAN.

The terms big-endian and little-endian are from *Gulliver's Travels*; they originally referred to the parties in a dispute over which end of a boiled egg should be broken first.

bilingual
1. using more than one language.
2. (describing FIREWIRE cables) having a Firewire 1394b 9-pin connector on one end and a Firewire 1394a 4- or 6-pin connector on the other.

Bilski *see* PATENT.

binary addition the process of calculating a sum of numbers expressed in base-2 form. It is one of the basic arithmetic operations performed by computers, and understanding it is the key to understanding how machines do arithmetic.

If each of the numbers to be added has only one digit, addition is simple:

$$0 + 0 = 00$$
$$0 + 1 = 01$$
$$1 + 0 = 01$$
$$1 + 1 = 10$$

A circuit that implements this function is called a *half adder* and can be made out of standard logic gates as shown in Figure 30. Notice that there are two digits of output; the higher digit is called the *carry bit* because it is carried to the next column when adding multi-digit numbers.

To add numbers with more than one digit, we proceed one digit at a time, starting at the right, just as with pencil-and-paper arithmetic. Each step of the addition can have three inputs: one digit from each of the numbers to be added, plus a digit carried from the previous column to the right. Accordingly, for each column except the rightmost, we need a circuit called a *full adder*, which takes three one-digit inputs. Its output still has only two digits because the largest value that can be obtained is $1 + 1 + 1 = 11$. A full adder can be built out of two half adders (Figure 31).

To add two 16-bit binary numbers, a computer needs 15 full adders and one half adder, with the carry output of each adder connected to an input of the adder to its left. All of this circuitry is part of the CPU; when the CPU receives an add instruction, it sends the contents of two registers to the inputs of the set of adders, and then stores the output in a register.

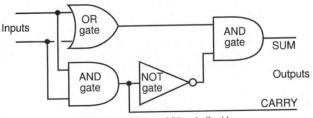

FIGURE 30. Binary addition: half adder

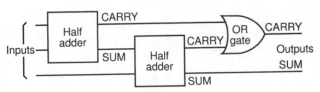

FIGURE 31. Binary addition: full adder

binary-coded decimal (BCD) a way of representing numbers by means of codes for the decimal digits. For example, consider the number 65. In binary, 65 is 01000001, and that is how most computers represent it. But some computer programs might represent it as the code for 6 followed by the code for 5 (i.e., 0110 0101).

The advantage of BCD shows up when a number has a fractional part, such as 0.1. There is no way to convert 0.1 into binary exactly; it would require an infinite number of digits, just like converting $\frac{1}{3}$ into decimal (*see* ROUNDING ERROR). But in BCD, 0.1 is represented by the code for 1 immediately after the point, and no accuracy is lost. Furthermore, BCD values convert directly to or from strings for human input or output, whereas binary conversion is slower.

BCD arithmetic is considerably slower and takes more memory than binary arithmetic. It is used primarily in financial work and other situations where rounding errors are intolerable. Pocket calculators use BCD.

binary file a file containing bits or bytes that do not represent printable characters. The term *binary file* usually denotes any file that is not a plain text file, such as executable machine language code, sound, pictures, or even documents in the format of a particular word processor. *Contrast* TEXT FILE.

binary multiplication a basic operation in computer arithmetic. For single-digit numbers, the binary multiplication table is very simple and is the same as the Boolean AND operation (*see* AND GATE):

$$0 \times 0 = 0$$
$$0 \times 1 = 0$$
$$1 \times 0 = 0$$
$$1 \times 1 = 1$$

For numbers with more than one digit, the computer does something very similar to what we do to decimal numbers in pencil-and-paper arithmetic. To find 13×21 in decimal, we proceed like this:

$$
\begin{array}{r}
21 \\
\times 13 \\
\hline
63 \\
21 \\
\hline
273
\end{array}
$$

First, find 3×21. Then, find 10×21, and add these two results together to get the final product. Note that the product has more digits than either of the two original numbers.

You can follow the same procedure to multiply two binary numbers:

$$
\begin{array}{r}
10101 \\
\times 01101 \\
\hline
10101 \\
00000 \\
10101 \\
10101 \\
00000 \\
\hline
100010001
\end{array}
$$

Notice that each of the partial products is either zero or a copy of 10101 shifted leftward some number of digits. The partial products that are zero can, of course, be skipped. Accordingly, in order to multiply in binary, the computer simply starts with 0 in the accumulator and works through the second number to be multiplied (01101 in the example), checking whether each digit of it is 1 or 0. Where it finds a 0, it does nothing; where it finds a 1, it adds to the accumulator a copy of the first number, shifted leftward the appropriate number of places.

binary number a number expressed in binary (base-2) notation, a system that uses only two digits, 0 and 1. Binary numbers are well suited for use by computers, since many electrical devices have two distinct states: on and off. Writing numbers in binary requires more digits than writing numbers in decimal, so binary numbers are cumbersome for people to use. Each digit of a binary number represents a power of 2. The right-most digit is the 1's digit, the next digit leftward is the 2's digit, then the 4's digit, and so on:

Decimal	Binary
$2^0 = 1$	1
$2^1 = 2$	10
$2^2 = 4$	100
$2^3 = 8$	1000
$2^4 = 16$	10000

Table 4 shows examples of numbers written in binary and decimal form. *See also* DECIMAL NUMBER; HEXADECIMAL NUMBER; OCTAL.

TABLE 4
DECIMAL-BINARY EQUIVALENTS

Decimal	Binary	Decimal	Binary
0	0	11	1011
1	1	12	1100
2	10	13	1101
3	11	14	1110
4	100	15	1111
5	101	16	10000
6	110	17	10001
7	111	18	10010
8	1000	19	10011
9	1001	20	10100
10	1010	21	10101

binary search a method for locating a particular item from a list of items in alphabetical or numerical order. Suppose you need to find the location of a particular word in a list of alphabetized words. To execute a binary search, look first at the word that is at the exact middle of the list. If the word you're looking for comes before the midpoint word, you know that it must be in the first half of the list (if it is in the list at all). Otherwise, it must be in the second half. Once you have determined which half of the list to search, use the same method to determine which quarter, then which eighth, and so on. At most, a binary search will take about N steps if the list contains about 2^N items.

binary subtraction a basic operation in computer arithmetic. The easiest way to subtract two binary numbers is to make one of the numbers negative and then add them. Circuits for doing binary addition are readily constructed with logic gates (*see* BINARY ADDITION). A negative binary number can be represented by its *2-complement*.

Suppose that we have a number x, represented as a binary number with k digits. The 2-complement of x (written as $\bar{x}$) is

$$\bar{x} = 2^k - x$$

Then, to find the difference $a - x$ we can compute

$$a - x = a + \bar{x} - 2^k$$

This is easier than it looks, for two reasons. First, subtracting 2^k is trivial, because 2^k is a binary number of the form 1000, 100000, and so on, with $k+1$ digits. So all we have to do is discard the leftmost digit to get our k-digit answer.

Second, finding the 2-complement of x is easy: just invert all the digits of x (changing 0's to 1's and 1's to 0's) and then add 1. *See* INVERTER.

Suppose we want to compute $5 - 2$ using 4-digit binary representations. That is, we want to compute:

$$0101 - 0010$$

First, change the second number to its complement, change the minus to a plus, and subtract 2^k:

$$0101 + \overline{0010} - 10000$$

To actually compute the complement, invert the digits of 0010 and add 1, so the whole computation becomes:

$$0101 + (1101 + 1) - 10000$$

Evaluate this expression by performing the two additions

$$0101 + 1101 + 1 = 10011$$

and then throwing away the leftmost digit, giving 0011 (=3), which is the answer.

This method for handling subtraction suggests a way to represent negative numbers. Suppose we want to represent −3. Positive 3 is binary 011. Negative 3 can be represented by the 2-complement of 3, which is the binary representation of 5: 101. However, we need an extra bit to indicate that 101 indicates −3 instead of 5. The bit indicating the sign will be included as the first digit of the number, with 1 indicating negative and 0 indicating positive.

The range of numbers that can be represented is different than before. Without the sign bit, 4 binary digits can hold numbers from 0 to 15; with the sign bit, the numbers range from −8 to 7. The table shows how.

Positive	Numbers		Negative	Numbers
Decimal	Binary		Decimal	Binary
0	0 0 0 0			
1	0 0 0 1		−1	1 1 1 1
2	0 0 1 0		−2	1 1 1 0
3	0 0 1 1		−3	1 1 0 1
4	0 1 0 0		−4	1 1 0 0
5	0 1 0 1		−5	1 0 1 1
6	0 1 1 0		−6	1 0 1 0
7	0 1 1 1		−7	1 0 0 1
			−8	1 0 0 0

On real computers it is typical to use 16 bits (2 bytes) to store integer values. Since one of these bits is the sign bit, this means that the largest positive integer that can be represented is $2^{15} - 1 = 32,767$, and the most negative number that can be represented is $-(2^{15}) = -32,768$. Some programming languages also provide an "unsigned integer" data type that ranges from 0 to 65,535.

bind to associate symbols with data, or to associate one piece of data with another, in several different ways, among them.

1. to give a variable a value.

2. to allocate a specific address in memory to a variable or to the entry point of a procedure.

3. to associate a network protocol with a particular Ethernet port or the like. *See* PROTOCOL.

4. to map an XML document onto a set of variables or objects in Java or another programming language.

5. to put together the pages of a book.

binding *see* BIND (all definitions).

Bing search engine from Microsoft (web address: *www.bing.com*)

biometrics measurable physical characteristics of the human body, used to identify an individual for security purposes. They include fingerprints, the distinctive appearance of faces and eyes, and the distinctive sound quality of one's voice. There are computer input devices to read these characteristics.

BIOS (**B**asic **I**nput **O**utput **S**ystem) a set of procedures stored on a ROM chip inside PC-compatible computers. These routines handle all input-output functions, including screen graphics, so that programs do not have to manipulate the hardware directly. This is important because if the hardware is changed (e.g., by installing a newer kind of video adapter), the BIOS can be changed to match it, and there is no need to change the application programs.

The BIOS is not re-entrant and is therefore not easily usable by multitasking programs. Windows programs do not call the BIOS; instead, they use procedures provided by the operating system.

BIOS enumerator the BIOS routine that tells a PLUG AND PLAY system what hardware is installed.

bipolar transistor a semiconductor device formed by sandwiching a thin layer of P- or N-type semiconductor between two layers of the opposite type of semiconductor. (*See* TRANSISTOR.) The other general type of transistor is the field-effect transistor (FET).

bis Latin for "a second time," used to denote revised CCITT and ITU-T standards. *See* CCITT; ITU-T.

BIST (**b**uilt-**i**n **s**elf **t**est) a feature included in newer integrated circuits and other electronic equipment. An electronic device that has BIST can test itself thoroughly whenever it is turned on. *See* INTEGRATED CIRCUIT.

bit a shorthand term for *binary digit*. There are only two possible binary digits: 0 and 1. (*See* BINARY NUMBER.) A computer memory is a collection of devices that can store bits.

A *byte* is the number of bits (usually 8) that stand for one character. Memory is usually measured in units of *megabytes*. *See* MEMORY; METRIC PREFIXES.

One important measure of the capability of a microprocessor is the number of bits that each internal register can contain. For example, the classic Z80 microprocessor had 8-bit registers. The Intel 8088, used in the original IBM PC, had 16-bit registers but only an 8-bit bus, leading to some confusion as to whether it should really have been called a 16-bit processor. Newer microprocessors have 32 or 64 bits per register. In general, a processor with a greater number of bits per instruction can process data more quickly (although there are other factors to consider that also determine a computer's speed). *See also* MICROPROCESSOR.

The number of colors that can be displayed is sometimes given by listing the number of bits used to represent a color. For example, a 24-bit color system uses 8 bits for red, 8 for green, and 8 for blue, so it can display $2^8 = 256$ different levels of each of the three primary colors, or $2^{24} = 16,777,216$ different mixtures of colors. *See* COLOR.

The term bit is also used to indicate the quality of digitized sound, as in 8 bit or 16 bit. *See* SAMPLING RATE.

bit bucket (slang) a place where data is lost. For example, under UNIX, the filename /dev/null can be used as a bit bucket; anything written to it will be ignored, but the program will think it is successfully writing to a file.

bit depth in graphics, the number of bits that are used to record the intensity and color of each pixel. For example, 1-bit graphics can distinguish only black and white; 8-bit graphics can distinguish 256 shades of gray or 256 colors; and 24-bit graphics can distinguish more than 16 million colors. Sometimes *bit depth* denotes the number of levels of each color; for example, an image in which each pixel has 8 bits each for red, green, and blue might be called either a 24-bit image or an 8-bit RGB image.

bitblt (**bit-b**lock **t**ransfer, pronounced "bitblit") the rapid copying of a block of memory or a portion of an image from one place to another. *Compare* BLIT.

bitlocker a security feature of Windows Vista and later versions that encrypts data on a hard drive, using an encryption key contained in a separate microchip in the computer, or provided on a flash drive.

bitmap
1. a graphical image represented as an array of brightness values. For example, if 0 represents white and 1 represents black, then

```
00000000
01111110
01000010
01000010
01111110
00000000
```

is a bitmap of a black rectangle on a white background. Each point for which there is a value is called a PIXEL. *See also* DIGITAL IMAGE PROCESSING.

Bitmaps can be imported into other application programs such as word processors and page layout programs, but you will not be able to edit bitmaps in those environments. You must use a PAINT PROGRAM to change bitmaps. *Contrast* VECTOR GRAPHICS. *See also* BMP; DRAW PROGRAM; PAINT PROGRAM.
2. a bitmap image (definition 1) that uses only black and white with no other colors or shades of gray.

bitmap graphics a method of displaying pictures on a computer. The picture is treated as a large array of pixels (*see* PIXEL), each of which is stored in a specific memory location. The picture is drawn by specifying the color of each pixel. *Contrast* VECTOR GRAPHICS. *See also* BITMAP; DRAW PROGRAM; PAINT PROGRAM.

bitness (*slang*) the property of using a specific number of bits. For example, a single-precision integer and a double-precision integer differ in bitness.

BITNET a wide-area network linking university computer centers all over the world. It originated in the northeastern United States in the early 1980s and was later combined with the Internet. Its most common use was to transmit electronic mail among scholars who were working together.

BitTorrent a peer-to-peer file sharing system that reduces dependency on the original host (or the SEED) by having everyone who downloads the file also offer it for anonymous upload to others. The more people who download the file (and therefore host the pieces they already have), the faster the file is downloaded. This format is especially useful for large files such as rich media (movies, music, etc.). See *www.bittorrent.com*.

black hat someone who attempts to break into computers maliciously; a villain (like the characters in old Western movies who wore black hats). *Contrast* WHITE HAT.

BlackBerry a wireless device produced by Research In Motion, Inc., which is a combination cellular telephone, PDA, and web browser. Web address: *www.blackberry.com. See also* PDA; SMARTPHONE.

Blackberry thumb an informal name for painful repetitive stress injuries caused by excessive typing on small keyboards like the ones on Blackberries or cellular phones. *See* CARPAL TUNNEL SYNDROME.

blacklist a list of senders or sites from which messages will not be accepted. *Synonyms:* IGNORE LIST; KILL FILE.

blend
1. a drawing program command that computes the intermediate shapes between two selected objects. You would use the blend command to make the smooth highlights on a rendering of a three-dimensional object.

In many ways, the blend command is like the *morphing* special effects we see on television commercials. You could make the letter C turn into a cat, for example. However, blend has practical applications as well as the playful ones. You can use it to create equally spaced objects, such as lines for a business form. Align two *identical* objects, and then set the intermediate blend steps to the desired number.
2. a paint program filter that smooths colors and removes texture over a selected area.
3. A piece of digital art where several images have been combined seamlessly into a visually interesting whole. Figures and objects are often layered so that it takes several seconds to identify what you are seeing.

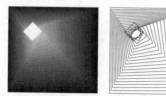

FIGURE 32. Blend (in a draw program)

blind copies *see* BCC.

blit **bl**ock **i**mage **t**ransfer, the rapid copying of a portion of an image (or, sometimes, any type of memory contents) from one place to another. *Compare* BITBLT.

blittable capable of being copied rapidly by BLIT.

bloatware (*slang*) **bloat**ed soft**ware**; inefficient, slow software that requires unreasonable amounts of disk space, memory, or CPU speed. Too many added features can make bloatware difficult to use (*see* CREEP-ING FEATURISM) and prone to crashes. Many critics claim that much modern software is designed to sell computers larger and faster than are actually needed to do the computations efficiently.

  The term also applies to software that creates bloated output files.

block move the operation of moving a section of a file from one place to another within the file. *See* EDITOR.

block protect to mark a block of text so that it will not be split across pages when printed out. This is useful to prevent a table or formula from being broken up. *Compare* NON-BREAKING SPACE.

blog a "web log"; a type of personal column posted on the Internet. Most blogs consist of small, frequent entries. Some blogs are like an individual's diary while others have a focused topic, such as recipes or political news. *See also* MICROBLOGGING; TWITTER.

Blogger a web site (*www.blogger.com*) providing one of the most popular and oldest web log services. Anyone can maintain a BLOG there and update it from any computer with an Internet connection. Blogger has been owned by GOOGLE since 2003. *Compare* LIVEJOURNAL; WORDPRESS; XANGA.

blogosphere The world of BLOGs; the very loosely-knit community of blog writers and their audiences. The blogosphere provides important forums for political discussion and news reporting separate from the established news media.

Blu-Ray disc an optical disc similar to a DVD and the same size, but read and written with a blue or violet laser, whose shorter wavelength makes a higher data density possible. Blu-Ray discs can hold 25 GB (single layer) or 50 GB (double layer). *Contrast* HD DVD.

Blue Screen of Death (*slang*) (sometimes written BSOD) in Windows, a serious error message displayed in white type on a blue screen, without any use of windows or graphics (*see* Figure 33). Windows Vista and later versions usually reboot after a serious error of this type, usually bypassing the blue screen.

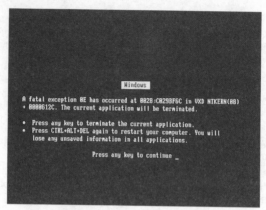

FIGURE 33. Blue Screen of Death

Bluetooth a standard for wireless networking of relatively slow devices in the same room; for details see *www.bluetooth.org*. The name alludes to a medieval Danish king. *Contrast* 802.11.

blur a paint program filter that throws the image slightly out of focus. Blur can be repeated until the desired effect is achieved. *See also* MOTION BLUR.

FIGURE 34. Blur filter

.bmp the filename extension for files in Microsoft Windows that contain bitmap representations of images. *See* BITMAP.

BNC connector a push-and-twist connector (*see* Figure 35) used to join coaxial cables in thinwire Ethernet networks and in some types of video equipment. *See* 10BASE-2; COAXIAL CABLE; ETHERNET. *Contrast* RCA PLUG.

FIGURE 35. BNC connectors

board
1. a printed circuit board for a computer, the MOTHERBOARD, or an add-on board, sometimes also called a *card.* Most computers contain *expansion slots* where you can add additional boards to enhance the capabilities of the machine.
2. a bulletin board system (BBS) or similar discussion forum. *See* BBS.

boat anchor (*slang*) obsolete, useless machine.

BOF (**b**irds **o**f a **f**eather) an informal meeting of a group of computer professionals with an interest in common, held as part of a larger convention.

bogus (*slang. obsolescent*) fake, incorrect, or useless. (In computer slang, this word covers a much wider range of meanings than in ordinary English; it can be applied to almost anything that is defective in any way.)

bold a type style that appears heavier and darker than normal type. The entry terms in this dictionary are set in **bold type**. *See* WEIGHT.

bomb (*slang*) to fail spectacularly (either computer programs or human performers); to CRASH. When a program bombs on a Macintosh, an alert box containing a picture of a bomb appears—the computer must be restarted and all changes made since the last "Save" will be lost. *Contrast* FREEZE UP; HANG.

bookmark
1. a remembered position in a file that is being edited. Some editors let the user set bookmarks in order to return quickly to specific points in the file.
2. a remembered address on the WORLD WIDE WEB. Web browsers normally let the user record the addresses of web pages in order to go directly to them in the future without having to type the address.
3. a placeholder that allows one to return to a specific point in a multimedia presentation.

Boole, George (1815–1864) the mathematician who discovered that logical reasoning can be represented in terms of mathematical formulas

(BOOLEAN ALGEBRA). Boole's work is the basis of modern digital computing.

Boolean algebra the study of operations carried out on variables that can have only two values: 1 (true) and 0 (false). Boolean algebra was developed by George Boole in the 1850s; it was useful originally in applications of the theory of logic and has become tremendously important in that area since the development of the computer.

Boolean query a query formed by joining simpler queries with *and*, *or*, and *not*. For example: "Find all books with author 'Downing' *and* subject 'Computers' *and not* published before 1987." *See also* FULL-TEXT SEARCH; SEARCH ENGINE.

Boolean variable a variable in a computer program that can have one of two possible values: true or false. *See* BOOLEAN ALGEBRA.

Boolean variables are useful when the results of a comparison must be saved for some time after the comparison is done. Also, they can be operated on repeatedly to change their values. For example, the following Java program segment reads numbers in an n-element array called a (which has already been defined) and reports whether a number over 100 was encountered; the Boolean variable is used somewhat as an integer would be used to keep a running total.

```
boolean b=false;
for (int i=0; i<=n-1; i++)
{
  b = (b | (a[i]>100)); /* vertical line means OR */
}
System.out.println("Was there a number over 100?");
if (b)
{
  System.out.println("There was a number over 100.");
}
```

FIGURE 36. Boolean variable in Java

boot to start up a computer. The term *boot* (earlier *bootstrap*) derives from the idea that the computer has to "pull itself up by the bootstraps," that is, load into memory a small program that enables it to load larger programs.

The operation of booting a computer that has been completely shut down is known as a *dead start*, *cold start*, or *cold boot*. A *warm start* or *warm boot* is a restarting operation in which some of the needed instructions are already in memory.

boot disk a disk, diskette, or CD that can be used to BOOT (start up) a computer.

boot image *see* IMAGE (definition 2).

Borland a manufacturer of microcomputer software, founded by Philippe Kahn and headquartered in Scotts Valley, California. It produced Turbo Pascal, an extremely popular Pascal compiler released in 1984, and other development tools. Borland was acquired by Micro-Focus in 2009. Web address: *www.borland.com*

boron chemical element (atomic number 5; symbol B) added to silicon to create a P-type SEMICONDUCTOR.

bot (*slang*) *see* ROBOT (definition 2).

botnet a group of computers that have been infiltrated so they act as ZOMBIES.

bottleneck the part of a computer system that slows down its performance, such as a slow disk drive, slow modem, or overloaded network. Finding and remedying bottlenecks is much more worthwhile than simply speeding up parts of the computer that are already fast.

   The *Von Neumann bottleneck* is a limit on computer speed resulting from the fact that the program and the data reside in the same memory. Thus, at any moment the CPU can be receiving a program instruction or a piece of data to work on, but not both. Newer computers mitigate the Von Neumann bottleneck by using pipelines and caches. *See* CACHE; PIPELINE; VON NEUMANN ARCHITECTURE.

bounce
   1. to return a piece of E-MAIL to its sender because of problems delivering it.
   2. to transfer a piece of incoming e-mail to another recipient without indicating who forwarded it.
   3. (*slang*) to turn a piece of equipment off and on again (to POWER-CYCLE it).

bounding box an invisible box surrounding a graphical object and determining its size. *See* Figure 37.

FIGURE 37. Bounding box

box
   1. (*slang*) a computer, especially a small one. For example, a Linux box is a computer that runs Linux.
   2. (*jargon*) a set of presumed limits. *See* THINKING OUTSIDE THE BOX.

boxing (in Microsoft .NET Framework) the automatic conversion of simple data types, such as numbers and STRUCTS, into OBJECTS (definition 1) so that they can be processed by object-oriented routines. *See* OBJECT-ORIENTED PROGRAMMING.

Bps (with capital B, **Bps**) **b**ytes **p**er **s**econd.

bps (with lowercase b, **bps**) **b**its **p**er **s**econd. *See also* BAUD.

braces the characters { and }, sometimes called CURLY BRACKETS.

brackets the characters [and], also called SQUARE BRACKETS.

brb chat-room abbreviation for "[I'll] **b**e **r**ight **b**ack."

breadcrumb menu a menu on a WEB PAGE that indicates its place in the hierarchical organization of a web site, such as:

> <u>Home</u> > <u>Products</u> > <u>Cameras</u> > DSLR cameras

This means that you are on the "DSLR cameras" page, which you probably reached from "Cameras," which you probably reached from "Products" and then from "Home." By clicking on any of these, you can go back to them.

breakpoint a place in a program where normal execution is interrupted and can be resumed after manual intervention, typically as an aid in debugging.

bridge a device that links two or more segments of a network. Unlike a hub, a bridge does not pass along all data packets that it receives. Instead, a bridge examines each packet and passes it along the path to its destination. In this way, local traffic can be prevented from flooding a larger network. *Compare* HUB; ROUTER; SWITCH (definition 2).

briefcase a feature of Windows allowing you to synchronize files that you work on using different computers, making sure that the version of the file on your main computer will include the most recent changes you made on another computer. *See* VERSION PROBLEM.

brightness
   1. a paint program filter that has the same effect as the brightness control on a TV or monitor; it lightens or darkens the entire area that it's applied to. Brightness may be combined with the contrast filter since the two attributes affect each other.
   2. a software control normally available with scanners, used to adjust the overall brightness of the image.
   3. the total amount of light emitted or reflected by a colored object.

FIGURE 38. Brightness—light, normal, and dark

bring forward; forward one comparable commands that send the selected
object down one layer. *See also* ARRANGE; BRING TO FRONT; TO FRONT;
DRAW PROGRAM; SEND BACKWARD; BACK ONE; SEND TO BACK; TO BACK.

bring to front; to front draw program commands that send the selected
object to the top layer. *See also* ARRANGE; BRING FORWARD; FORWARD ONE;
DRAW PROGRAM; SEND BACKWARD; BACK ONE; SEND TO BACK; TO BACK.

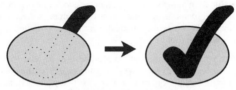

FIGURE 39. Bring to front

brittle working correctly but easily disrupted by slight changes in conditions; the opposite of ROBUST.

broadband covering a wide range of frequencies; permitting fast data
transfer. In this sense, ADSL lines, T1 lines, and all kinds of Internet
connections that are appreciably faster than a modem are often described
as broadband.

   In a narrower sense, broadband denotes systems of modulating many
signals onto different high-frequency carriers so that they can share the
same cable. Cable television is a simple example; many video signals are
delivered at once, on different frequencies. Broadband Ethernet allows
many networks, or a network and other types of signals, to coexist on the
same cable by using different high-frequency carriers. *Contrast* BASEBAND.

broadcast flag a code embedded in a DIGITAL TELEVISION broadcast that is
intended to prevent copying or recording by the recipient. In the United
States, the FCC issued a rule requiring television receivers (including
video recorders and computers) to obey the broadcast flag by July 1,
2005, but the rule was withdrawn in 2011 after widespread opposition.
It had never been enforced because the U.S. Court of Appeals ruled that
the FCC does not have the authority to regulate the use of electronic
devices when they are not receiving a broadcast signal, such as when
playing back a recording (*American Library Association, et al. v. Federal Communications Commission*).

broken hyperlink a link in a web page that points to a document that is no
longer at that address. *See also* DEAD LINK.

broken pipe a communication failure between two programs that are running concurrently. Typically, a broken pipe occurs when a network connection is lost or one of the programs terminates while the other is still
trying to communicate with it. *See* PIPE (definition 1).

brownout an extended period of insufficient power-line voltage. It can damage computer equipment. *See* POWER LINE PROTECTION.

browse
1. to explore the contents of the World Wide Web or, more generally, the Internet. *See* BROWSER.
2. to explore the contents of a disk drive or a computer network.

browse master in Windows, the computer on the local area network that tells the other computers what shared resources are available. The browse master is chosen automatically from the computers that are on the network at a particular time.

browser a computer program that enables the user to read HYPERTEXT in files or on the WORLD WIDE WEB (Figure 40). Specific World Wide Web browsers include CHROME; FIREFOX; INTERNET EXPLORER; MOSAIC; MOZILLA; NETSCAPE NAVIGATOR; OPERA, and SAFARI.

FIGURE 40. Browser displaying a web page

BSD a version of UNIX that was developed at the University of California at Berkeley (UCB). (*See* UNIX.) BSD UNIX introduced the vi full-screen editor and a number of other enhancements. SunOS (Solaris) and System V are combinations of BSD UNIX with the original AT&T UNIX.

BSOD *see* BLUE SCREEN OF DEATH.

BTW online abbreviation for "**by the way.**"

bubble sort an algorithm for arranging items in order, as follows: First, examine the first two items in the list. If they are in order, leave them alone; if not, interchange them. Do the same with the second and third items, then with the third and fourth items, until you have reached the last two. At this point you are guaranteed that the item that should come last in the list has indeed "bubbled" up to that position. Now repeat the whole process for the first $n - 1$ items in the list, then for $n - 2$, and so on.

Bubble sort is not a particularly fast sorting algorithm on conventional computers, but it works well on parallel computers that can work on different parts of the list simultaneously.

Figure 41 shows a Java program that performs a bubble sort. For clarity, this version of the algorithm does not use element 0 of the array.

```java
class bubblesort
{
  /* This Java program performs a bubble sort */
  /* Array to be sorted and number of items in it.
     Element a[0], which contains 0 here, is ignored. */
  static int a[] = {0,29,18,7,56,64,33,128,70,78,81,12,5};
  static int n=12;

  public static void main(String args[])
  {
    /* Perform the bubble sort */
    for (int i=1; i<=n; i++)
    {
      for (int j=1; j<=(n-i); j++)
      {
        if (a[j]>a[j+1])
        {
          int t=a[j];
          a[j]=a[j+1];
          a[j+1]=t;
        }
      }
    }
    /* Display the results */
    for (int i=1; i<=n; i++)
    {
      System.out.println(a[i]);
    }
  }
}
```

FIGURE 41. Bubble sort

buddy list a set of online friends, with contact information. Most instant messaging programs have buddy lists, which not only keep track of your chatting buddies but show whether or not they are presently logged in.

buffer

1. areas in memory that hold data being sent to a printer or received from a serial port. The idea here is that the printer is much slower than the computer, and it is helpful if the computer can prepare the data all at once, and then dole it out slowly from the buffer as needed. Similarly, a serial port needs a buffer because data may come in when the computer is not ready to receive it.

2. an area in memory that holds part of a file that is being edited. Some editors allow you to edit more than one file at once, and each file occupies its own buffer.

3. an area in memory that holds data being sent to, or received from, a disk. Some operating systems allow you to adjust the size or number of disk buffers to fit the speed of your disk drive. *See also* UNDERRUN.

4. an area in memory that holds signals from keys that have been pressed but have not yet been accepted by the computer.

5. an electronic device whose output is the same as its input (e.g., an amplifier for driving long cables).

bug an ERROR in a computer program. The term is somewhat misleading because it suggests that errors have a life of their own, which they do not. Bugs fall into at least three classes: *syntax errors*, where the rules of the programming language were not followed; *semantic errors*, where the programmer misunderstood the meaning of something in the programming language; and *logic errors*, where the programmer specified some detail of the computation incorrectly. Nowadays there is beginning to be a serious problem with a fourth class, which can be called *infrastructure errors*, where the programmer fell victim to something wrong with the operating system or a programming tool.

build

1. (*verb*) to put together a piece of software from its components by compiling, linking, and doing whatever else is necessary to make a working, deliverable version. *See* COMPILER; LINKER.

2. (*noun*) the result of building a piece of software on a particular occasion. Some software developers keep track of build numbers, which change much more rapidly than version numbers.

built fraction a fraction that is composed by setting the numerator and denominator as regular numerals separated by a forward slash (1/2, 1/4). *Contrast* CASE FRACTION; PIECE FRACTION.

$$^3/_4 \qquad 3/4 \qquad ^3/_4$$

Case fraction	Built fraction	Piece fraction

FIGURE 42. Built fraction (center) vs. case and piece fractions

bullet a character such as • used to mark items in a list.

bulletin board a message board; an online service where people can post messages. Bulletin boards are now accessed through the World Wide Web, but in the 1980s they originated as services to which a user's computer could connect through a telephone line modem. *See* MESSAGE BOARD.

bullying *see* CYBERBULLYING.

bundled software software that is sold in combination with hardware. For example, software for processing speech and music is often bundled with sound cards.

burn (*slang*) to record information on a CD or DVD disc or an EPROM.

bus the main communication avenue in a computer. For a diagram, *see* COMPUTER ARCHITECTURE.

The bus consists of a set of parallel wires or lines to which the CPU, the memory, and all input-output devices are connected. The bus contains one line for each bit needed to give the address of a device or a location in memory, plus one line for each bit of data to be transmitted in a single step, and additional lines that indicate what operation is being performed.

Most personal computers today use a 32-bit bus or a 64-bit bus.

Here is how an 8-bit bus works: If the CPU wants to place the value 00011001 into memory location 10100000, it places 00011001 on the data lines, places 10100000 on the address lines, and places 1 (rather than the usual 0) on the "write memory" line. The memory unit is responsible for recognizing the "write memory" request, decoding the address, and storing the data in the right location.

The bus can transmit data in either direction between any two components of the system. If the computer did not have a bus, it would need separate wires for all possible connections between components. *See also* EISA; ISA; PCI; PCMCIA; SERIAL BUS.

button a small circle or rectangular bar within a windowed DIALOG BOX that represents a choice to be made. One of the buttons in a group is normally highlighted, either by having a black circle inside of it or having a heavy black border. This represents the DEFAULT choice. You can choose any one of the buttons by clicking on it.

There are two kinds of buttons: OPTION BUTTONS (sometimes called *radio buttons*) and command buttons. Option buttons represent mutually exclusive settings; that is, you can choose only one. They are usually small and round but are sometimes diamond-shaped. If you change your mind and click on another option button, your original choice will be grayed (dimmed). *See* CLICK; DIALOG BOX; DIMMED; HIGHLIGHT.

Command buttons cause something to happen immediately when you click on them. They are usually rectangular and larger than option buttons. The most familiar examples are the OK and Cancel buttons that are in almost every dialog box. If the command button brings up another dialog box, you will see an ELLIPSIS (. . .) after its label.

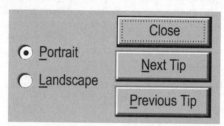

FIGURE 43. Buttons: option buttons (left)
and command buttons (right)

button bar a row of small icons usually arranged across the top of the workspace on the screen. Each icon represents a commonly used command; many programs allow you to customize your button bar to suit your taste.

FIGURE 44. Button bars

bwahahahaha typewritten representation of an evil laugh.

Byron, Augusta Ada *see* ADA.

byte the amount of memory space needed to store one character, which is normally 8 bits. A computer with 8-bit bytes can distinguish $2^8 = 256$ different characters. This is sufficient for the old ASCII character code. In various implementations of UNICODE, a character may occupy one, two, or four bytes. *Compare* OCTET. *Contrast* BIT.

The size of a computer's memory, file, or disk is measured in kilobytes (= 2^{10} = 1024 bytes), megabytes (= 2^{20} = 1,048,576 bytes), or gigabytes (= 2^{30} = 1,073,741,824) bytes. *See* METRIC PREFIXES.

bytecode the concise instructions produced by compiling a Java program. This bytecode is the same for all platforms; it is executed by a Java virtual machine. *See* JAVA; JVM. *See also* .NET FRAMEWORK.

C

C a programming language developed at Bell Laboratories in the 1970s, based on the two earlier languages B (1970) and BCPL (1967). A C compiler is provided as a part of the UNIX operating system (*see* UNIX), and C was used to write most of UNIX itself. In addition, C is popular as an alternative to assembly language for writing highly efficient micro-computer programs. There is a widespread (and often mistaken) belief that programs written in C are more efficient than programs written in any other language.

C is a general-purpose language like Pascal and ALGOL, but, unlike other general-purpose languages, it gives the programmer complete access to the machine's internal (bit-by-bit) representation of all types of data. This makes it convenient to perform tasks that would ordinarily require assembly language, and to perform computations in the most efficient way of which the machine is capable.

```
/* CHKSUM.C */
/* Sample program in C —M. Covington 1991 */
/* Based on a program by McLowery Elrod */

/* Reads a character string from the keyboard */
/* and computes a checksum for it. */

#include <stdio.h>

#define N 256

main()
{
   int i, n;
   char str[N];

   puts("Type a character string:");
   gets(str);
   printf("The checksum is %d\n",chksum(str));
}

chksum(s,n)
char* s;
int n;
{
   unsigned c;
   c = 0;
   while (n- >0) c = c + *s++;
   c = c % 256;
   return(c);
}
```

FIGURE 45. C program

In C, things that are easy for the CPU are easy for the programmer, and vice versa. For example, character string handling is somewhat clumsy because the CPU can only do it through explicit procedure calls. But integer arithmetic is very simple to program because it is simple for the CPU to execute. Most programmers who use C find themselves writing efficient programs simply because the language pushes them to do so.

Figure 45 shows a program written in C. This language encourages structured programming; the three loop constructs are `while`, `do`, and `for`. The comment delimiters are `/* */`. A semicolon comes at the end of every statement (unlike Pascal, where semicolons only come between statements).

C allows operations to be mixed with expressions in a unique way. The expression `i++` means "retrieve the value of i and then add 1 to it." So if i equals 2, the statement `j = (i++)*3` will make j equal 6 (i.e., 2 × 3) and will make i equal 3 (by adding 1 to it after its value is retrieved; but notice that its *old* value was used in the multiplication).

Another noteworthy feature of C is the `#define` statement. The sample program contains the line

```
#define N 256
```

which tells the compiler that wherever N occurs as a symbol in the program, it should be understood as the number 256. *See also* C++.

C++ an object-oriented programming language developed by Bjarne Stroustrup at Bell Laboratories in the mid-1980s as a successor to C. In C and C++, the expression c++ means "add 1 to C."

Figure 46 shows a program in C++. Comments are introduced by `//` and object types are declared as `class`. The part of an object that is accessible to the outside world is declared as `public`. For an explanation of what this program does, *see* OBJECT-ORIENTED PROGRAMMING, where the equivalent Java code is explained.

In C++, input-output devices are known as *streams*. The statement

```
cout << "The answer is " << i;
```

sends "The answer is" and the value of i to the standard output stream. This provides a convenient way to print any kind of data for which a print method is defined.

C++ lets the programmer *overload* operators (give additional meanings to them). For example, + normally stands for integer and floating-point addition. In C++, you can define it to do other things to other kinds of data, such as summing matrices or concatenating strings.

C++ is the basis of the Java and C# programming languages. *See* JAVA; C#.

```
// SAMPLE.CPP
// Sample C++ program −M. Covington 1991
// Uses Turbo C++ graphics procedures

#include <graphics.h>

class pnttype {
  public:
    int x, y;
    void draw() { putpixel(x,y,WHITE); }
};

class cirtype: public pnttype {
  public:
    int radius;
    void draw() { circle(x,y,radius); }
};

main()
{
   int driver, mode;
   driver = VGA;
   mode = VGAHI;
   initgraph(&driver,&mode,"d:\tp\bgi");

   pnttype a,b;
   cirtype c;

   a.x = 100;
   a.y = 150;
   a.draw();

   c.x = 200;
   c.y = 250;
   c.radius = 40;
   c.draw();

   closegraph;
}
```

FIGURE 46. C++ program

C# (pronounced "C sharp") a programming language developed by Anders Hejlsberg (the developer of Turbo Pascal and Delphi) for Windows programming under Microsoft's .NET Framework.

C# is similar in appearance and intent to Java, but it is more tightly tied to the object-oriented operating-system interface of the .NET Framework. In some ways it reflects the spirit of Pascal, with clean and simple design, but it is fully object-oriented. Memory allocation is automatic, and programmers do not normally manipulate pointers. Care has been taken to make common operations simple and concise, and the handling of windows is especially straightforward; programmers never have to declare handlers for events that they do not actually want to handle.

Figure 47 on page 72 shows a sample program in C#. Compare it to the sample Pascal program on page 364.

```csharp
using System;
class primecheck
{
  // Sample C# program to test whether a number is prime.
  static void Main(string[] args)
  {
    int n, i, max;
    bool cont;
    string s;

    while (true)
    {
      Console.Write("Type a number (0 to quit): ");
      n = Convert.ToInt32(Console.ReadLine());
      if (n==0) break;

      s = "prime";
      cont = (n > 2);
      i = 1;
      max = (int)Math.Sqrt(n); // largest divisor to try
      while (cont)
      {
        i++;
        Console.WriteLine("Trying divisor {0}",i);
        if (n % i == 0) //if n divisible by i
        {
          s = "not prime";
          cont = false;
        }
        else
        {
          cont = (i < max);
        }
      }
      Console.WriteLine("{0} is {1} \n",n,s);
    }
  }
}
```

FIGURE 47. C# program

CA (certificate authority) an agency that issues digital certificates. *See* CERTIFICATE, DIGITAL; DIGITAL SIGNATURE.

cable modem a MODEM that provides computer communication over television cables (either coaxial or fiber-optic) rather than telephone lines.

cache

1. a place where data can be stored to avoid having to read the data from a slower device such as a disk. For instance, a disk cache stores copies of frequently used disk sectors in RAM so that they can be read without accessing the disk.

The 486 and Pentium microprocessors have an internal instruction cache for program instructions that are being read in from RAM; an external cache is also used, consisting of RAM chips that are faster than those used in the computer's main memory. *See also* L1 CACHE; L2 CACHE.

2. a set of files kept by a WEB BROWSER to avoid having to download the same material repeatedly. Most web browsers keep copies of all the web pages that you view, up to a certain limit, so that the same pages can be redisplayed quickly when you go back to them. If a web page has been changed recently, you may have to RELOAD it to see its current contents.

cacls (presumably: **c**hange **a**ccess **c**ontrol **l**ists) a powerful console-mode command in Windows 2000 and its successors for changing permissions and security attributes of files, analogous to CHMOD in UNIX. For example, the command

```
cacls myfile.txt /g "Domain Users":R
```

gives all members of the group "Domain Users" permission to read myfile.txt. For full documentation type:

```
cacls /?
```

The cacls command is used mainly in BAT files, since you can also change permissions by right-clicking on the file or folder and following the menus. *See also* CHMOD; PERMISSION.

CAD (**C**omputer-**A**ided **D**esign) the use of a computer for design work in fields such as engineering or architecture, with the computer's graphics capabilities substituting for work that traditionally would have been done with pencil and paper.

In order to draw a building, for example, it is necessary to enter the plans by using a graphical input device, such as a mouse or graphics tablet. There are several advantages to having the plans in the computer:

1. The computer can automatically calculate dimensions. In fact, the ability to calculate dimensions is the biggest difference between CAD programs and ordinary draw programs.
2. Changes can be made easily (e.g., adding a new wall).
3. Repetitive structures can be added easily.
4. The image can be enlarged to obtain a close-up view of a particular part, or it can be shrunk to make it possible to obtain an overall view. The image can be rotated to view it from many different perspectives. For example, the Boeing 777 airplane, first rolled out in 1994, was designed entirely on computers. Previous airplanes had been designed the traditional way with paper drawings, and then a full-scale mock-up had to be constructed to make sure that the parts would fit together in reality as they did on paper. CAD made this extra work unnecessary.

CAD/CAM *see* CAD; CAM.

CAI (**c**omputer-**a**ided **i**nstruction) teaching any kind of knowledge to people with the aid of a computer.

Cairo Microsoft's code name for a version of Windows under development during the mid-1990s. As it turned out, no single version of Windows corresponds to Cairo; portions of the Cairo project appeared in versions ranging from Windows 3.1 to Windows Vista. *Compare* CHICAGO; LONG-HORN; MEMPHIS; WHISTLER.

cakebox (*humorous*) the round plastic box in which bulk recordable CDs are supplied.

calendar *see* GREGORIAN CALENDAR; JULIAN CALENDAR; JULIAN DATE; LEAP YEAR.

calibration adjustment of image values to ensure faithful rendering of colors and gray tones when output to a printer or imagesetter. The calibration loop should include your scanner, your monitor, your software, and the printer. The goal is to make sure that colors are treated identically by the scanner, the software, the screen, and the printer. *See* COLOR.

CALL
  1. a statement in FORTRAN, PL/I, some versions of BASIC, and most assembly languages, which transfers control of execution to a subprogram. When the subprogram ends, the main program resumes with the statement immediately after the CALL. In a BAT FILE, CALL calls another BAT file. Languages such as C, C#, Pascal, and Java perform calls by simply giving the name of the routine to be called. In line-numbered BASIC, subroutines are called with the GOSUB command.
  2. **c**omputer-**a**ided **l**anguage **l**earning, the teaching of foreign languages to people with the aid of a computer.

callout the line and caption marking the specific parts of a labeled illustration. For examples, *see* Figure 303 at WINDOW on page 552.

-cam abbreviation for *camera*, especially a digital or video camera whose images are made available by computer network. For instance, a camera connected to the World Wide Web is a *webcam*; a camera mounted on a tower is a *towercam*; and a camera strapped to the back of a horse might be called a *horsecam*.

CAM (**C**omputer-**A**ided **M**anufacturing) the use of computers in a manufacturing process. For example, a computer could store a three-dimensional representation of an object and then control the manufacture of the object by automated machinery. Some of the principles of CAM are the same as with computer-aided design (*see* CAD), and sometimes a system is referred to as CAD/CAM.

camel notation a way of combining words by running them together, capitalizing every word except the first: thisIsAnExample. A word written this way has a low head and one or more humps, like a camel. *Contrast* PASCAL NOTATION. *See* INTERCAPS.

camera-ready copy artwork or printed pages that are ready to be photographed and offset printed. The camera will see only black and white, not shades of gray, so the camera-ready copy must be free of smudges, dust, and stray marks. Usually, pale blue marks do not photograph, and most other colors photograph as black.

camera, digital *see* DIGITAL CAMERA.

CAN-SPAM (**C**ontrolling the **A**ssault of **N**on-**S**olicited **P**ornography and **M**arketing) a law passed by the U.S. Congress in 2003 (15 U.S.C. 7701) providing penalties for sending deceptive mass e-mails. The act required the Federal Trade Commission to investigate whether or not to establish a national Do Not E-mail registry, but the commission concluded that such a registry would not work and instead emphasized the need to establish a means to authenticate the origin of e-mail messages.

cancel
1. to stop the execution of a command. Most dialog boxes have a Cancel button. This clears the dialog box from the screen without taking any action.
2. to send a command deleting a message from a newsgroup or other public forum. (*See* NEWSGROUP.) It is important to know how to do this in case you post something that turns out to be redundant or misinformed. On Usenet, the cancellation does not take effect instantly because the cancel command has to travel to all the sites that received the original message. Normally, users can cancel only their own messages, but *see* CANCELBOT.

cancelbot (from *cancel* and *robot*; *see* BOT) a computer program that automatically cancels certain messages from a newsgroup or other public forum. Cancelbots often eliminate messages that are excessively large or are copied to excessive numbers of newsgroups (*see* SPAM).

Canon engine *see* ENGINE.

Capability Maturity Model a set of criteria developed by the Software Engineering Institute at Carnegie Mellon University for judging and improving the performance of a software development organization. The model recognizes five levels of maturity:

1. *Initial:* Developers work as rugged individualists, trying to emulate other successful software developers.
2. *Repeatable:* The work is planned and somewhat predictable.
3. *Defined:* The work is planned in some detail with a plan that can be, and is, followed.
4. *Managed:* The work is not only planned but measured; managers know whether the expected level of productivity is being achieved.

5. *Optimizing:* Based on measurements, the process is continually improved.

Many software companies never get past the initial stage, which is adequate for highly talented individuals but leaves the overall organization very dependent on their specific talent (*compare* HACKER, definition 1). *See also* SOFTWARE ENGINEERING.

caps capital letters. THIS SENTENCE IS TYPED IN ALL CAPS. *Contrast with* MIXED CASE; LOWERCASE.

Internet tip: Don't send e-mail or post to newsgroups with your message typed in all caps. Not only is it more difficult to read, but it seems as if you are shouting (all your words are emphasized).

Caps Lock a special keyboard key which acts like the Shift key for the letter keys. You do not have to hold it down; when Caps Lock is on, YOUR TYPING LOOKS LIKE THIS. A common mistake is to leave Caps Lock on when you wish to type normally. Then letters you wish to be capitalized are lowercase, but everything else is all caps lIKE tHIS. Be especially careful to avoid this problem when entering a password. Some word processors have commands to correct capitalization errors of this sort.

CAPTCHA (Completely Automatic Public Turing Test to Tell Computers and Humans Apart) an on-screen device that presents a quiz requiring a human response, to prevent an automatic BOT from gaining access to a location, such as a web page selling tickets. The CAPTCHA often appears as a graphical image of a simple arithmetic problem or a word written along a wavy curve. The automated bot only sees a graphical image and can't provide the answer to the math problem. One purpose of the CAPTCHA is to prevent ticket scalpers from using bots to purchase large amounts of tickets from Internet ticket sellers. However, software advances may allow the bot to solve the CAPTCHA quiz.

capture

1. to cause a picture or graphic to be saved as a bitmapped image. *See* FRAME GRABBER; SCREEN SHOT, SCREEN SNAPSHOT.

2. to divert data from a serial or parallel port to a networked printer, a print spooler, or the like.

Carbon application, Carbonized application (on the Macintosh) a software package written to take advantage of new features of Mac OS X, but also compatible with Mac OS 9. *Contrast* COCOA APPLICATION.

carbon copy a copy of an outgoing electronic mail message kept by the sender or forwarded to someone other than the recipient. (*See* CC; BCC; FCC.) In pre-computer days, carbon copies were made in typewriters by placing a sheet of carbon-coated paper and an extra piece of plain paper behind the main document.

card

1. a medium for storing data, such as a FLASH MEMORY CARD, SECURE DIGITAL CARD, SMARTMEDIA, or COMPACTFLASH. *See* CARD READER.

2. a printed-circuit board, especially one designed to be added to a microcomputer to provide additional functions (*see* Figure 48).

3. *see* PUNCHED CARD.

FIGURE 48. Card (definition 2)

card reader

1. a device that enables a computer to read FLASH MEMORY CARDS, (SMARTMEDIA, COMPACTFLASH, and the like).

2. a device that enabled a computer to read PUNCHED CARDS.

CardBus the 32-bit version of the PCMCIA (PC CARD) bus. *See also* EXPRESS-CARD and note there.

caret

1. The character ^ (more properly called CIRCUMFLEX or HAT), which indicates exponentiation in some programming languages.

2. ^ the proofreading symbol used to mark where something should be inserted. (*Caret* is Latin for "is missing.")

3. the INSERTION POINT (i.e., the point on the screen where characters will appear when they are typed on the keyboard).

careware SHAREWARE that requests a donation to charity rather than a monetary payment to the author. *See* FREE SOFTWARE.

carpal tunnel syndrome a repetitive-use injury of the carpal tunnel (a nerve pathway in the wrist) that afflicts some typists. The main symptoms are numbness and tingling in the hand. Stretching exercises and medication help mild cases, but sometimes surgery is necessary to relieve the pain. To prevent carpal tunnel syndrome, take a break and stretch your hands frequently. Some typists find a padded wrist support to be helpful. *See* ERGONOMICS.

carriage return *see* CR.

carrier a signal that has another signal modulated onto it. For example, a modem transmits data through a telephone line by transmitting a continuous tone as a carrier. Variations in frequency and phase of the carrier encode the binary data. DSL networks use a radio-frequency carrier to transmit data over phone lines.

cartridge a self-contained, removable part of a computer, usually small and contained in a plastic case. For example, laser printers often take *toner cartridges* (containing toner, i.e., ink). Game machines often accept software in plug-in cartridges.

cascade to arrange multiple windows so that they look like a stack of cards, with all but the top and left edges of each window hidden by the one in front of it (*see* Figure 49). When the windows on a screen are cascaded, you can see the title bar of every window. *Contrast* TILED WINDOWS; OVERLAID WINDOWS.

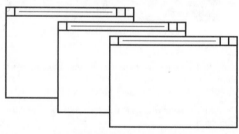

FIGURE 49. Cascaded windows

cascading menu a menu that leads to more menus. For an example, *see* START MENU.

cascading style sheet a set of HTML rules governing the appearance of a set of pages at a web site on the World Wide Web. Cascading style sheets use precedence rules to decide which of two commands should take effect in case of a conflict. *See* STYLE SHEET.

CASE (**c**omputer-**a**ided **s**oftware **e**ngineering) the use of computers to help with the process of designing software.

case

1. the property of being capitalized (uppercase, LIKE THIS) or lowercase (like this); so called because of the wooden cases in which printers' type was stored in the 1800s.

2. a keyword in Pascal and other programming languages that directs a program to choose one action from a list of alternatives, depending on the value of a given variable. Here is an example of a case statement:

```
CASE place OF
  1 : writeln('First place !!!');
  2 : writeln('Second place');
  3 : writeln('Third place')
END;
```

If the variable place has the value 1, then the first writeln statement will be executed, and so on. The switch statement in C and Java and the SELECT CASE statement in newer versions of BASIC perform similar functions.

case fraction a small fraction that is a single character in a font. *See illustration at* BUILT FRACTION, *page 66. Contrast* BUILT FRACTION; PIECE FRACTION. *See also* EXPERT SET.

case-sensitive distinguishing between upper- and lowercase letters, such as A and a. For example, UNIX filenames are case-sensitive, so that MYDATA and mydata denote two different files. DOS and Windows filenames are not case-sensitive, so that MYDATA and mydata are equivalent.

Names typed in C, C++, Java, and C# are case-sensitive; names typed in Pascal are not.

Windows preserves the case in which filenames were originally typed, but names that differ only in case are treated as matching.

Cat-3, Cat-5, Cat-5e, Cat-6, Cat-7 *see* CATEGORY 3 CABLE (etc.).

catalog an older name for a list of the contents of a disk. *See* DIRECTORY.

catch *see* TRY.

Category 3 cable, Category 5 cable (etc.) a series of standards for 8-conductor unshielded twisted-pair network cables, which can also be used for telephone wiring. They are known in brief as Cat-3, Cat-5, and so on.

Category 3 cable is for 10base-T and other networks up to 10 Mbps. Category 5 is compatible with 100base-T networking at ten times the speed, and categories 5e and up are compatible with GIGABIT ETHERNET (1000base-T). Each successive category has better high-frequency performance and lower CROSSTALK. It is always desirable to use a higher category than originally specified, since performance may improve and will certainly be no worse.

See also 10BASE-T; 100BASE-T; 1000BASE-T; RJ-45 (wiring cable); PLENUM-RATED; RISER-RATED.

catenation *see* CONCATENATION.

CAV (**c**onstant **a**ngular **v**elocity), in disk drives, a constant speed of rotation, regardless of whether the track being read is a long one (near the edge of the disk) or a short one (near the center). Hard disks, diskettes, and some of the newest CD-ROM drives use CAV. *Contrast* CLV.

Cc business abbreviation for "copies"; the double letter C indicates the plural. In e-mail headers, cc: precedes additional addresses to which copies of the message should be sent. *See also* BCC.

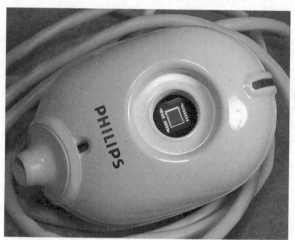

FIGURE 50. CCD image sensor (in webcam with lens removed)

CCD image sensor (charge-coupled device) the electronic image sensor most often used in digital cameras, video cameras, and scanners. A lens forms an image on an array of cells (Figure 51), each of which contains a photoconductive layer that accumulates a charge in proportion to the amount of light that falls on it. The accumulated electrons are then shifted from cell to cell until each cell's value appears at the output. Scanners often use sensors in which the cells are in a line rather than a rectangular array.

CCDs record only the intensity of the light, not the color. In scientific work, color pictures are obtained by taking a set of black-and-white images through different filters. In most color digital and video cameras, adjacent pixels on the CCD contain pale red, green, and blue filters, so that a color image can be obtained all at once; the color of each pixel is interpolated from those around it. In rare cases this gives inaccurate color, as when photographing a distant zebra whose black and white stripes hit pixels with different color filtration. *Contrast* FOVEON.

Inherently, CCDs respond strongly to infrared light, but most of them contain extra layers to increase the response across the visible spectrum and cut the response to infrared. A CCD camera can often "see" the infrared beam from a TV remote control.

The main limitation of CCDs is that the cells conduct some electrons even in the absence of light, in a highly random manner. This shows up when the exposure is longer than about 5 to 10 seconds; the image is covered with speckles. The CCDs used for long exposures in astronomy are cooled to low temperatures to reduce this problem, and a sample of the noise itself (a long exposure with the shutter closed) is often digitally subtracted from the image.

See also CMOS IMAGE SENSOR; BAYER MATRIX.

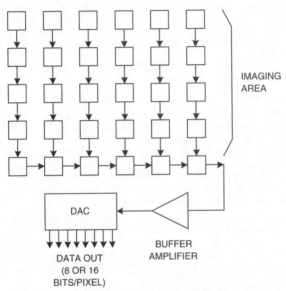

FIGURE 51. CCD image sensor

CCITT (Comité Consultatif Internationale Télegraphique et Téléphonique) former name of the international organization that sets standards for data communication, now known as ITU-T. *See* ITU-T; X.25.

ccTLD (**c**ountry **c**ode **T**op **L**evel **D**omain) a two-letter code indicating the country of an Internet address. For example, the web address for Oxford University is *www.ox.ac.uk*; here *.uk* is the country code for the United Kingdom. For a complete listing of the ccTLDs, *see* the tables on pages 580/582.

Most codes can be used only for sites in the countries to which they belong. However, some countries, such as Tuvalu, encourage the use of their country codes elsewhere, so long as the country's own registrar gets the registration fees. For examples, *see* .TV. *See also* GTLD.

CD (**C**ompact **D**isc) a type of plastic optically readable disk introduced by Philips and Sony in the 1980s to store digitized music recordings. Subsequently, CDs have become popular as a way of storing computer files (*see* CD-ROM). The data on CDs is encoded in microscopic grooves and is read by scanning the rotating disk with an infrared laser beam. Conventional CDs are 12 cm (4.7 inches) in diameter. An 8-cm (3.15-inch) size ("mini-disc") is also used; it has about 1/5 the capacity.

Unlike a diskette, a CD has its data on one long spiral track, like the groove in a phonograph record; this simplifies the design of CD players. One CD can hold 75 minutes of audio (just enough for Beethoven's *Ninth Symphony,* which was the design goal) or 680 megabytes of computer data. Newer CDs have slightly more capacity, 80 minutes or 700 MB.

Note the spellings *disc* for CDs versus *disk* for magnetic disks. *See also* RED BOOK; CD-ROM; DVD.

CD-E (**C**ompact **D**isc—**E**rasable) an older name for CD-RW.

CD-R (**C**ompact **D**isc—**R**ecordable) a type of CD (compact disc) that can be recorded by the user. CD-Rs have the same capacity and are readable in the same drives as ordinary CDs (except for DVD drives—*see* DVD). Instead of being manufactured by pressing, CD-Rs are recorded by bleaching ("burning") small areas of dyed plastic with a laser to create an appearance similar to the indentations in an ordinary CD.

CD-Rs are somewhat less durable than pressed CDs, though still more durable than most other computer media.

CD-ROM (**C**ompact **D**isc—**R**ead-**O**nly **M**emory) an optical disk like an audio compact disc, but containing computer data. Audio and computer CDs are physically the same; in fact, a single CD can contain both computer files and music. CD-ROMs can only be read, not recorded on, by the user's computer. CD-R and CD-RW are CD-ROM-compatible media that can be recorded on by the user.

CD-ROMs are not tied to the operating system of a specific computer (although the software that is on them may be). Any computer can read the data on any CD-ROM. CD-ROM drives are rated for their speed compared with the playback speed of an audio CD. For example, a 48× drive can read a CD 48 times faster than an audio CD would be played.

See also CD; CD-R; DVD; RED BOOK; GREEN BOOK; YELLOW BOOK; ORANGE BOOK; ISO 9660; HIGH SIERRA FORMAT; MPC; MULTIMEDIA; MULTI-SESSION CD; PHOTO CD.

CD-ROM XA (**CD-ROM** extended **a**rchitecture) a set of extensions to the ISO 9660 format for compact disc data, allowing sound and video to be interleaved with computer data. The earlier format required sound, video, and computer files to be on separate tracks; XA removes this restriction. Virtually all CD-ROMs are now this type.

CD-RW (**C**ompact **D**isc—**Re**Writable) a type of CD (compact disc) that can be recorded, erased, and reused by the user.

The surface of a CD-RW contains an alloy that can change back and forth between a bright crystalline state and a dark amorphous state; it can be switched from one state to the other by heating it to specific temperatures with a laser.

Because of the different material used in them, CD-RW discs cannot be read by some early-model CD-ROM or CD-R drives.

CDA *see* COMMUNICATIONS DECENCY ACT.

CDFS the CD-ROM file system under Windows 95 and later.

CE *see* WINDOWS (MICROSOFT).

Celeron a lower-cost version of the Intel Pentium II microprocessor, with less on-chip cache memory. Before its introduction, the Celeron was code-named *Covington,* to the delight of the authors of this book.

cell
   1. a unit of information that forms a building block for a chart, database, or spreadsheet.
   2. one of the sections into which a city or region is divided for cellular telephone service. Each cell is served by a different antenna tower.

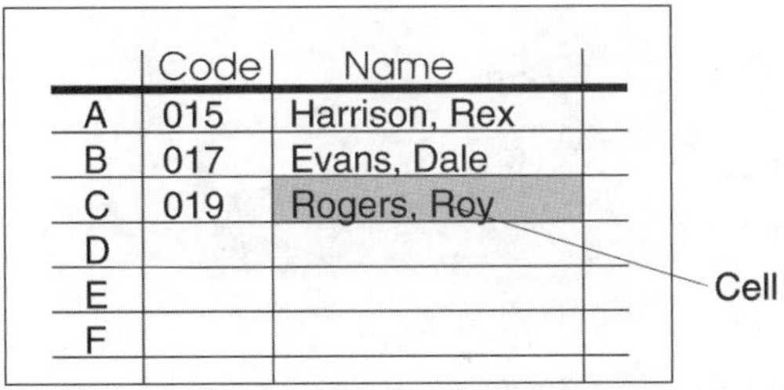

	Code	Name	
A	015	Harrison, Rex	
B	017	Evans, Dale	
C	019	Rogers, Roy	
D			
E			
F			

Cell

FIGURE 52. Cell in a spreadsheet

cellular network the wireless communication network used by cellular telephones and related wireless devices. *See* 1G, 2G, 3G, 4G.

cellular telephone a wireless telephone that communicates through any of a number of antenna towers, each serving a particular "cell" of the city. The user is automatically transferred from cell to cell as he or she moves around. This contrasts with earlier mobile telephones that had to be within range of a particular tower in order to work. *See also* DATA PLAN.

center to cause type or other objects to appear in the middle of the line with equal amounts of space to either side.

> This text
> is set centered.
> Centered text is
> considered
> formal.

Contrast FLUSH LEFT; FLUSH RIGHT; JUSTIFICATION.

centi- metric prefix meaning ÷ 100. *Centi-* is derived from the Latin word for "hundredth." *See* METRIC PREFIXES.

central processing unit *see* CPU.

Centrino a set of integrated circuits made by Intel comprising the PENTIUM M microprocessor and associated components designed for use in laptop computers with wireless networking.

Centronics interface a standard protocol for parallel data transmission to and from microcomputer equipment, especially printers. It was originally used on Centronics printers. The PARALLEL PORT of a microcomputer is normally Centronics-compatible. *See also* IEEE 1284; PROTOCOL.

The connector usually used with a Centronics interface is similar to one type of SCSI connector but has 36 connections instead of 50 (Figure 53).

FIGURE 53. Centronics interface connector

certainty factor *see* CONFIDENCE FACTOR.

certificate authority a trusted organization that issues digital certificates. (*See* CERTIFICATE, DIGITAL.) For examples, see *www.verisign.com* and *www.thawte.com*.

certificate, digital an attachment to an electronic message using public key encryption to verify that the message truly comes from the sender it claims to come from, and has not been altered in transit. To be useful, certificates must be issued by a trusted CERTIFICATE AUTHORITY so that the recipient can check on the public key. *See* ENCRYPTION.

Your operating system or browser may warn you if you try to run software that was downloaded or e-mailed through the Internet and is not signed with a digital certificate. The digital certificate would help you be sure that the software has not been altered to insert a VIRUS or other MALWARE. This is important when you are downloading software from a third party, but not when you are sure you are downloading it directly from its originator. Nor does the certificate prove that the software is reliable or works correctly—it only verifies the identity of the author.

CGI

1. (**c**omputer-**g**enerated **i**mage) a method of ANIMATION in which the computer creates two-dimensional moving images of three-dimensional objects, replacing older animation techniques that involved a series of hand-drawn or hand-edited images.

2. (**C**ommon **G**ateway **I**nterface) a standard way for computer programs to generate web pages as needed, containing current information or the results of computations. Instead of a file containing the web page itself, the server contains a program that writes the web page to standard output. This program is often called a CGI script. It can receive input from the web page that links to it, either through environment variables or on the standard input stream. *See also* PHP.

Note: The two definitions are easy to confuse, since animations on web pages can be generated by CGI programs.

CGM (**C**omputer **G**raphics **M**etafile) an ANSI standard file format for graphical data (both vector and bitmap). CGM files are used mainly for exchanging data between applications.

chad the small pieces of paper that have been punched out of a PUNCHED CARD or punched paper tape. Until the 2000 U.S. presidential election, most people had never heard of chad, but in that year, the failure of some voting machines to punch neat holes in cards may have changed the course of history.

chain letter a message that is intended to be forwarded from each recipient to as many others as possible. On the Internet, chain letters are very unwelcome because they waste money; the cost of delivering e-mail is borne by the recipient's site. Many chain letters perpetrate hoaxes or pyramid schemes (*see* HOAX; PYRAMID SCHEME).

channel

1. a radio frequency or communication path (e.g., a TV channel).

2. in desktop publishing, a set of images that will compose the final image when combined. The most common use for channels is the representation of the CMYK color separations in a paint program. Each color has its own channel. Sometimes channels can be used like layers in a DRAW PROGRAM. Selected areas can be saved to a new channel, manipulated separately from the rest of the image, and later recombined with the main channel.

3. a discussion forum in Internet Relay Chat or a similar service. *See* IRC; CHAT ROOM.

4. a web page that is constantly updated, so that viewing it is like watching a television channel. *See* PUSH (definition 2).

character any symbol that can be stored and processed by a computer. For example, A, 3, and & are characters. The ASCII coding system is one way of representing characters on a computer. *See* ASCII; EBCDIC; UNICODE.

character string a series of characters, such as "JOHN SMITH" or "R2D2." *See* STRING.

charge-coupled device *see* CCD IMAGE SENSOR.

chat room an electronic forum in which users can communicate with each other in real time. Chat rooms are found on the Internet (*see* IRC).

People in chat rooms use a lot of abbreviations so they can type as quickly as possible and to offer hints of their emotional reactions (*see also* EMOTICON). Many times the abbreviations are recognized from their context, but until you get the hang of it, a chat room can be a bewildering place. For example, the words two, too, and to are almost never written out—they are replaced by the numeral 2. The numeral 4 is used to replace four and for. See Table 5 for some common phrases. *See also* ELECTRONIC MAIL; INSTANT MESSAGE; LEETSPEAK; SOCIAL NETWORKING.

check box a small box (in a window) that the user can turn on or off by clicking with the mouse. When on, it displays an X or check mark in a square; when off, the square is blank. Unlike option buttons, check boxes do not affect each other; any check box can be on or off independently of all the others.

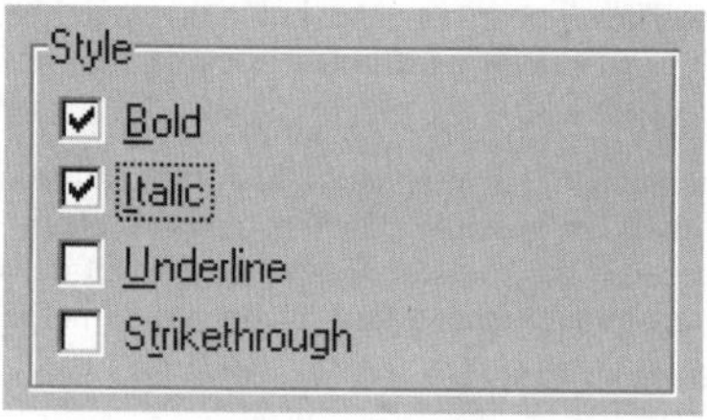

FIGURE 54. Check Box

checked (describing Windows versions) containing extra error detection and debugging code. Checked versions of Windows are used only for certain kinds of development work. *Contrast* FREE.

checksum a number that accompanies data transferred from one place to another and helps to ensure that the data was transferred correctly.

One way to ensure correct transmission would be to transmit all of the information twice; if there were an error, the two copies would almost

TABLE 5
CHAT-ROOM ABBREVIATIONS

AFAIK	as far as I know
AFAIR	as far as I remember
AFK	away from keyboard
ATM	at the moment
BAK	back at keyboard
BBL	[I'll] be back later
BRB	[I'll] be right back
BWAHAHAHAHA	(representation of evil laugh)
CUL8R	see you later
F2F	face to face
FS	for sale
FU	f. . . you (offensive word)
FWIW	for what it's worth
GR8, GR8T	great
IANAL	I am not a lawyer
IIRC	if I remember correctly
IMHO	in my humble opinion
IMO	in my opinion
IOW	in other words
IRL	in real life
ISO	in search of
ISTR	I seem to remember
J/C	just chilling
L8ER, L8TER	later
LOL	laugh(ing) out loud
MWAHAHAHAHA	(representation of evil laugh)
PMJI	pardon me for jumping in
QT	cutie
ROFL	rolling on floor, laughing
S/AC	"sex and age check" (please tell me your age and gender)
S/H	same here
SW :()	say what!? (gasp)
TIA	thanks in advance
THX, TNX	thanks
TTFN, TT4N	ta-ta (goodbye) for now
Y	why?
WAZ^	what's up?
WBASAYC	write back as soon as you can
WTF	what the f. . . (offensive word)

certainly disagree. However, this is too time-consuming to be practical. A better approach is to divide the information into small packets, such as lines of text or disk sectors, and compute a checksum for each packet. A checksum is a number that would almost certainly be different if the information were altered.

A simple way to compute a checksum is to add up the ASCII codes for all the characters of data (*see* ASCII) and take the result modulo 256. (For a program that does this, *see* C.) Since this method gives only 256 possible checksums, it is quite possible for two different data packets to have the same checksum. However, it is very unlikely that a transmission error would change a packet of information into another packet with the same checksum. Hence errors can be detected by transmitting the checksum along with each packet, and then testing whether the checksum matches the data actually received. *Compare* CYCLICAL REDUNDANCY CHECK; PARITY.

Cheetah version 10.0 of MAC OS X.

Chicago the code name by which Windows 95 was identified before its release. *Compare* CAIRO; LONGHORN; MEMPHIS; WHISTLER.

child an object which inherits the properties of another object (called the PARENT). Updating the properties of the parent object affects the children, but changing the properties of the child does not affect the parent. *See* VECTOR GRAPHICS; OBJECT-ORIENTED PROGRAMMING.

child process a process launched by and considered dependent on another process. *See* PROCESS; MULTITASKING; UNIX.

chip *see* INTEGRATED CIRCUIT.

chipset a set of integrated circuits intended to be used together. For example, many modems use a chipset made by Rockwell, and many motherboards use an Intel chipset along with a Pentium processor.

chmod UNIX command for changing file permissions. For example of its use, *see* PERMISSION.

chroma-keying the process of digitally combining video images by the use of a subtractive background. This is the method used to show a weather forecaster in front of a set of maps. The person is videotaped in front of a blue or green background. The colored background is digitally removed (hence *chroma-*, meaning color), and the desired map is put in place of it. The weather forecaster watches a monitor off-camera so he or she can point to the correct spot.

Chroma-keying is also used for a variety of special effects in movies.

Chrome a WEB BROWSER developed by GOOGLE (web address: *www.google. com/chrome*).

chromogenic print a picture printed photographically with colored dyes; a conventional color photograph or (much less often) a black-and-white photo produced with similar chemistry. *Contrast* GELATIN SILVER PRINT; GICLÉE PRINT.

Church's Thesis (*or Church-Turing Thesis*) the hypothesis that a TURING MACHINE (or any of its mathematical equivalents) is as powerful as a mechanical computing device can be; other devices are more efficient at particular tasks, but none of them can do anything fundamentally different. It was proposed, at different times and in different forms, by Alan Turing and by the logician Alonzo Church.

CIFS (**C**ommon **I**nternet **F**ile **S**ystem) the file sharing protocol that forms the basis of Microsoft Windows networking. Formerly known as SMB (Server Message Block), it is also supported by UNIX and Linux systems using the Samba software package. *See* SAMBA. *Contrast* NFS.

cinnamon bun *(slang)* the symbol @; *see* AT SIGN.

CIO Chief Information Officer, an officer of a business responsible for its computers and data processing.

CIPA (**C**hildren's **I**nternet **P**rotection **A**ct) a law passed by Congress in 2000 (47 USC 254) requiring libraries to use blocking programs to prevent access to Internet sites with objectionable content. The Supreme Court upheld this law in 2003 (*United States v. American Library Association*).

circle a group of users of GOOGLE+. *See* GOOGLE+; SOCIAL NETWORKING.

circularity the problem that arises when a computer cannot finish a task until it has already finished it—an impossible situation. For example, in a spreadsheet, a circularity problem arises if you enter the formula 2*B1 into cell A1 and then enter the formula A1/2 into cell B1. In order to evaluate each of the cells the computer needs the value of the other one. Thus, it cannot proceed, and it displays a warning message instead. *See* Figure 55.

Likewise, two tasks can never finish if each one depends upon the completion of the other one. This scheduling dilemma is known as a "deadly embrace."

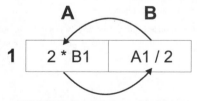

FIGURE 55. Circularity in a spreadsheet

circumflex the symbol ˆ, either written by itself as an ASCII character, or written above a letter (e.g., ê).

CISC (**C**omplex **I**nstruction **S**et **C**omputer) a computer with many different types of machine language instructions, and complex data paths within the CPU. *Contrast* RISC. CISC instructions usually include arithmetic operations that also access memory directly. RISC usually separates computation from memory access. Many CISC architectures use "microcode" to specify a list of steps to be carried out for each opcode. The IBM PC, 68000-based Macintosh, Pentium, IBM 370 mainframe, and VAX are CISC machines.

Cisco Systems, Inc. a company headquartered in San Jose, California that is the leading provider of high-speed networking hardware. The web address is *www.cisco.com*.

CISSP (**C**ertified **I**nformation **S**ystems **S**ecurity **P**rofessional), a certification achieved by passing the CISSP exam (web address: *www.cissp.com*).

class an object type in object-oriented programming. *See* OBJECT-ORIENTED PROGRAMMING.

Class A (describing computer equipment) approved by the U.S. Federal Communications Commission for use in industrial or business but not residential areas because of the risk of radio-frequency interference. *See* FCC (definition 1).

Class B (describing computer equipment) approved by the U.S. Federal Communications Commission for use in residential areas because the risk of radio-frequency interference is low. *See* FCC (definition 1).

class library a set of classes available to programmers in an object-oriented language such as Java or C++. In addition to the base classes that come with the language itself, a programmer can use and extend other classes created from other sources.

Classic mode an operating system mode which allows Macintosh computers running OS X to run older Mac OS 9 software.

clear
1. to set one or more bits to zero.
2. to make the screen go blank.

click to press one mouse button very briefly (usually the leftmost button, if there is more than one). *Contrast* PRESS; DOUBLE-CLICK. *See also* WINDOW.

FIGURE 56. Click

click path analysis the study of the sequence of web pages reached by visitors to a web site, which can be helpful in determining if visitors can find information as was intended by the web designers.

clickable image a picture on a WEB PAGE or in a HYPERTEXT document that the user can select, by clicking with the mouse, in order to call up further information. *See* IMAGE MAP.

ClickOnce deployment a method of software installation, under Microsoft .NET Framework, where a program is downloaded and installed from a web address and can automatically check the same web address for updated versions.

clickworker
1. a volunteer doing tedious computer work for scientific research, usually in short work sessions. For an example, see *clickworkers.arc.nasa.gov/top*.
2. (more generally) a worker who manages information with the aid of a computer, typically without being especially knowledgeable about or interested in computing.

client
1. a computer that receives services from another computer. For example, when you browse the World Wide Web, your computer is a client of the computer that hosts the web page.
2. an operating system component or application program that enables a computer to access a particular kind of service. For example, computers that use Remote Desktop must have Remote Desktop client software installed on them.

client area the part of a window in which editing or drawing actually takes place. It does not include the borders, the title, the menu bar across the top, or the scroll bars, if any.

client-side application a computer program that runs on a network client rather than on the server. For instance, Java applets are client-side applications; when you view a web page that contains an applet, the applet is sent to your computer and runs on it. *Contrast* SERVER-SIDE APPLICATION.

clip art artwork that can be freely reproduced. Many of the pictures in newspaper advertisements come from clip art. Many clip art collections are available on diskettes or CD-ROMs for use with various drawing, painting, and desktop publishing programs.

FIGURE 57. Clip art examples

Clipboard on the Macintosh and in Windows, a holding area to which information can be copied in order to transfer it from one application program to another. For instance, the Clipboard can be used to transfer text from a word processor into a drawing program.

The contents of the Clipboard vanish when the computer is turned off. Also, in most software, only one item at a time can be on the Clipboard; the next CUT or COPY command will replace the old item with a new one. *See also* PASTE; SCREEN SHOT; SCREEN SNAPSHOT.

clipping

1. in digital audio, chopping off the tops and bottoms of the sound waves, resulting in distorted sound.

2. (on Macintosh) a fragment of text or graphic image that can be temporarily stored on the Desktop. This provides another way (other than the Clipboard) for transferring information from one program to another.

clock

1. the circuit in a computer that generates a series of evenly spaced pulses. All the switching activity in the computer occurs while the clock is sending out a pulse. Between pulses the electronic devices in the computer are allowed to stabilize. A computer with a faster clock rate is able to perform more operations per second.

The clock speed of a computer is often given in megahertz (MHz) or gigahertz (GHz), where 1 MHz = 1,000,000 cycles per second and 1 GHz = 1000 MHz. Often, the clock speed is doubled or tripled inside the CPU so that high-speed signals do not have to be carried outside it. The original IBM PC had a clock speed of 4.77 MHz. *See* MICROPROCESSOR.

2. the circuit within a computer that keeps track of the date and time, often called a *real-time clock* or *clock/calendar*. Commonly, the real-time clock is powered by a battery and runs even when the computer is turned off.

clone

1. a computer that is an exact imitation of another (e.g., a clone of the IBM PC), or a software product that exactly imitates another. In biology, a clone is an organism that has exactly the same genetic material as another, such as a plant grown from a cutting.

2. in OBJECT-ORIENTED PROGRAMMING, to duplicate an object.

clone tool

1. a tool available in paint programs that allows you to duplicate areas. To use the clone tool, click on the center of the area you wish to copy. Move the cursor to where you want the new area to be. Press and hold down the mouse button (the leftmost button if there is more than one) while you paint in the image. The clone tool can be used to create a bunch of cherries out of a few, cover a gap left by deleting an area, or to put a third eye on someone's forehead. It is not necessary to define the outline of an area or object when using the clone tool; it works from the center out as far as needed. *See also* RUBBER STAMP.

2. (in drawing programs) a tool that copies the properties of an object to a secondary object.

FIGURE 58. Clone tool

close

1. (in electronics) to put a switch into the position that allows current to flow.

2. (in programming) to release a file when a program is finished using it.

3. (in Windows) to exit a program and clear it from the computer's memory. This is different from MINIMIZE in that a program reduced to an icon is still running and waiting for input from you, but a closed program has been put away. Most importantly, a minimized program is still being held in the computer's memory. If you close a minimized program, you will regain the memory it is taking up.

4. (on the Macintosh) to reduce a window to an icon *without* quitting the application software. The Close button is at the far left of the title bar. Click once to close the open window. This sense of *close* is analogous to

MINIMIZE in Windows. To clear the program from memory, choose Quit from the File menu.

This illustrates one of the most basic areas of confusion between Macintosh and Windows terminology. Be careful when talking to your cross-platform friends or you'll both end up confused!

5. (in Visual Basic.NET) removing a form from the screen and exiting the program.

Closed Beta a test of incomplete software that is only open to a small group, such as the developer's employees. See BETA TESTING.

cloud computing computing operations carried out on servers that are accessed through the Internet, rather than on one's own personal computer. For example, many people read their e-mail via cloud computing; that is, they connect to a web site where the server handles the mail. More recently, it has become possible to do word processing, document storage, and other kinds of work "through the cloud." The users pay for computing as a service rather than owning the machines and software to do it.

Why this is called "cloud computing" is somewhat unclear. The key concept is that the user does not know where the server is located, or whether there is one server or many; everything is "off in the clouds." On network diagrams, a cloudlike shape has long been used to indicate a large network whose internal structure is not known or does not matter. The term WIRELESS CLOUD may also play a role, although cloud computing need not be wireless.

cloud, the any CLOUD COMPUTING resource; any set of computers accessed remotely. "The cloud" is not a specific place or service. *Compare* CYBERSPACE.

cluster

1. a group of disk sectors that are treated as a unit for purposes of allocating space; an ALLOCATION UNIT. *See also* LOST CLUSTER.

2. a group of servers that function as a single system.

cluster computing using networked computers to work on computationally complicated problems, often more economically than on a traditional SUPERCOMPUTER. Software needs to be designed to distribute the tasks to the different machines. For an example, see BEOWULF. The clustered computers are part of the same organization, in contrast with GRID COMPUTING.

CLV (constant **l**inear **v**elocity) in disk drives, a speed of rotation that varies depending on whether the drive is reading a long track near the edge of the disk or a short track near the center. Thus the disk itself passes beneath the head at a constant speed. Most CD-ROM drives use CLV. *Contrast* CAV.

CMOS (**c**omplementary **m**etal-**o**xide **s**emiconductor) a type of integrated circuit noted for its extremely low power consumption and its vulnerability to damage from static electricity. CMOS devices are used in digital watches, pocket calculators, microprocessors, and computer memories. *See* FIELD-EFFECT TRANSISTOR.

CMOS image sensor an image sensor similar to a CCD, but that uses metal-oxide semiconductor (MOS) transistors for lower power consumption. *See* CCD IMAGE SENSOR; FOVEON.

CMOS RAM a special kind of low-power memory that stores information about the configuration of a computer. It is operated by a battery so that it does not go blank when the machine is turned off. *Compare* NVRAM.

CMS
    1. (**C**onversational **M**onitor **S**ystem) the interactive part of IBM's VM/SP (VM/ESA) operating system for mainframe computers.
    The key idea behind VM and CMS is that each user has a whole simulated mainframe computer all to himself. The simulated computer has a *virtual disk* (i.e., one large real disk file that simulates the function of a disk drive on which many small files can be stored). *See also* VIRTUAL MACHINE; VM/ESA.
    2. **C**ontent **M**anagement **S**ystem (also known as **C**onfiguration **M**anagement **S**ystem, or version control), software allowing an organization to manage the creation, publication, and updating of a set of web pages and other documents that have multiple authors. The system should ensure consistency (so that the web version of a document has the same content as the paper version); it should make sure that changes are only made to the most recent version (so different authors aren't making changes to different versions of the document) and it must protect the documents against any changes made by unauthorized persons. Also, authors must use LOGICAL DESIGN when creating their documents so that the actual visual appearance can be determined at the time of publication. *See also* VERSION PROBLEM.

CMYK the four standard printing inks: **c**yan, **m**agenta, **y**ellow, and blac**k**. When combined, these four colors can reproduce a full-color image. If you ask your computer to make color separations for a PROCESS COLOR job, four COLOR SEPARATIONS will be generated, one for each of the standard inks. *See also* SPOT COLOR.

coaster *(slang)* a compact disc (CD) given away free as advertising material; if you don't need the software, you can at least put the disc under your coffee cup.

coaxial cable a cable that consists of a single conductor surrounded by insulation and a conductive shield. The shield prevents the cable from picking up or emitting electrical noise. (*Contrast* TWISTED PAIR.) Coaxial cables are rated for their *impedance*, given in ohms, which indicates how the inductance and capacitance of the cable interact. For instance, RG-58 cable is rated at 52 ohms. This impedance cannot be measured with an ohmmeter.

COBOL (**C**ommon **B**usiness-**O**riented **L**anguage) a programming language for business data processing, developed in the early 1960s by several computer manufacturers and by Grace Murray Hopper and others at the U.S. Department of Defense. As the sample program in Figure 59 shows, COBOL statements resemble English sentences, and the structure of the program requires that some documentation be included. COBOL programs are long and wordy, but easy to read, making it easy for programmers other than the author to make corrections or changes.

```
IDENTIFICATION DIVISION.

PROGRAM-ID. COBOL-DEMO.
AUTHOR. M. A. COVINGTON.

ENVIRONMENT DIVISION.

CONFIGURATION SECTION.
SOURCE-COMPUTER. IBM-PC.
OBJECT-COMPUTER. IBM-PC.

DATA DIVISION.

WORKING-STORAGE SECTION.
77 SUM PICTURE IS S999999, USAGE IS COMPUTATIONAL.
77 X   PICTURE IS S999999, USAGE IS COMPUTATIONAL.

PROCEDURE DIVISION.

START-UP.
  MOVE 0 TO SUM.
GET-A-NUMBER.
  DISPLAY "TYPE A NUMBER:" UPON CONSOLE.
  ACCEPT X FROM CONSOLE.
  IF X IS EQUAL TO 0 GO TO FINISH.
  ADD X TO SUM.
  GO TO GET-A-NUMBER.
FINISH.
  DISPLAY SUM UPON CONSOLE.
  STOP RUN.
```

FIGURE 59. COBOL program

Cocoa application (on the Macintosh) a software package written specifically for Mac OS X. *Contrast* CARBON APPLICATION.

code

1. a way of encrypting information (making it unreadable). *See* ENCRYPTION.

2. a way of representing information on a machine or in some physical form. For example, the bit patterns in memory can be used as a code to stand for letters and digits.

3. computer programs, whether written in machine language (OBJECT CODE) or a programming language (SOURCE CODE).

code base the collection of computer program SOURCE CODE that constitutes a software product. For example, the code base of Windows 2000, XP, Vista 7, and 8 is derived from Windows NT.

code page the table of information, inside DOS and its derivatives, that tells it how to display characters and interpret keystrokes. Code pages other than the usual (default) one are normally used outside the United States to accommodate the characters needed for foreign languages.

code signing attaching a DIGITAL SIGNATURE to a piece of code so a person who downloads it will know its origin. If the code comes from a trusted person or organization, the user will be more likely to grant it permission to take a wider range of actions, such as writing to the local disk drive.

codec (**co**der-**dec**oder or **co**mpressor-**dec**ompressor)

1. a software component that enables a computer to play and/or record a particular audio or video file format. A common problem is that not all PCs have codecs for all popular file formats, and since codecs are usually installed with software rather than as separate items, the user does not know what is and is not present. Occasionally, a slightly corrupted audio or video file will play successfully with one codec but not with another that should also handle it.

2. an electronic circuit for converting audio or video signals into or out of digital form.

coding the process of writing an algorithm or other problem-solving procedure in a computer programming language.

cognitive computing the use of computers in COGNITIVE SCIENCE.

cognitive engineering the practical application of COGNITIVE SCIENCE, especially as it involves computers; the art of building tools to help people think. Cognitive engineering is broader than ARTIFICIAL INTELLIGENCE because its goal is to build tools, not just models.

cognitive prosthesis a tool that extends the human mind, such as a calculator or computer.

cognitive science the scientific study of intelligence (as distinct from the study of the brain), including artificial intelligence and some branches of computer science. *See* ARTIFICIAL INTELLIGENCE.

cold boot, cold start *see* BOOT.

collate to place printed pages in order. If you have three copies of a five-page document, they will be collated if the pages are arranged as

1 2 3 4 5 1 2 3 4 5 1 2 3 4 5

Collated pages can be stapled or bound to produce complete documents.

An uncollated arrangement would be

1 1 1 2 2 2 3 3 3 4 4 4 5 5 5

This arrangement is convenient if you wish to distribute the pages to a group one page at a time.

collating sequence the alphabetical order of all characters representable on a computer (including digits, punctuation marks, and other special characters). The collating sequence is important because it is often necessary to sort (alphabetize) data that includes characters other than letters. The collating sequence of a computer is usually the same as the order of the numeric codes for the characters. *See* ASCII; EBCDIC.

collector one of the three layers of a bipolar transistor. *See* TRANSISTOR.

collision the situation in which two computers are trying to transmit on the same Ethernet network segment at the same time. Each of them will try again after a random length of time (not the same length of time, or they would collide again, ad infinitum). Some collisions are normal on any busy network. Constant collisions indicate that the network is overloaded. *See* ETHERNET.

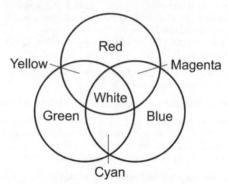

FIGURE 60. Additive color mixing

color the visible difference between different wavelengths of light. Fortunately, the human eye can be fooled—the color of any wavelength can be simulated by mixing light of other wavelengths.

Screen colors are specified as RGB (red, green, and blue) values in either of two ways. One way is to define a PALETTE (a working set of colors) and assign numbers to the colors on it. For example, a bitmap image with 4 bits per pixel can distinguish up to 16 colors. The other way is to give values of red, green, and blue for each pixel. For example, *24-bit color* uses 8 bits each for red, green, and blue, requiring a total of 24 bits per pixel.

Since 8 bits are used for each color, there are $2^8 = 256$ different levels for that color, and $2^{24} = 16,777,216$ total possible colors. Each color value is often represented as a two-digit HEXADECIMAL NUMBER, where 00 is the minimum value and FF is the maximum value. Here are some specific examples:

Hexadecimal code	Color
FF0000	red (maximum intensity)
00FF00	green (maximum intensity)
0000FF	blue (maximum intensity)
FFFF00	yellow (mixed red and green)
FF00FF	violet (mixed red and blue)
FFC800	orange
000000	black
FFFFFF	white

In general, if the red, green, and blue values are equal, the result will be a shade of gray.

Colors on paper are usually specified as CMYK (cyan, magenta, yellow, and black) or HSB (hue, saturation, and brightness). Because the pigments being mixed are completely different from the phosphor dots on the screen, printed colors do not always match screen displays, even after extensive CALIBRATION. *See also* GAMUT.

color channel a representation of color information in a color bitmap image. An RGB image has three channels: red, green, and blue. Each channel can be manipulated separately from the others.

color separations camera-ready artwork that has been broken down into individual printouts, one for each color of ink that is to be printed. All the elements that should print in black will be on one sheet, and all the elements that should print in red will be on another, and so forth. Each printout will have registration marks so that the colors can be aligned properly or registered (*see* REGISTRATION, definition 2).

color temperature a method of measuring the redness or blueness of a photographic light source by comparing it to the temperature (in degrees Kelvin) of a white-hot object that would produce the same color of light. Sunlight has a color temperature of about 5000 K; incandescent light bulbs, 2700 K to 3400 K. Color temperature measures only redness or blueness and does not account for other tints that a light source might have, such as green or purple.

color/gray map a paint program filter that allows adjustment of a picture's color balance. In grayscale mode, it can be used to adjust the exposure of an imperfect black-and-white photo.

.com
   1. a suffix indicating that a web or e-mail address belongs to a commercial entity (in any country, but mostly the United States). Along with *.edu, .gov, .int, .net, .org,* and *.mil,* this is one of the original set of Internet top-level domains. Since 2000, *.com, .net,* and *.org* have been assigned almost indiscriminately to organizations of all types. *See also* TLD; ICANN.

2. the filename extension used for small, nonrelocatable machine language programs in DOS. To execute the program, type the name of the file without the final ".COM"; for example, to execute AAA.COM, type aaa. *Contrast* EXE FILE.

COM (**C**omponent **O**bject **M**odel) Microsoft's architecture for building software components (i.e., packages of procedures and data structures ready for use by programmers). Many of these components are referred to as *ActiveX controls* (*see* ACTIVEX).

COM was introduced in the mid-1990s and provides infrastructure for OLE (Object Linking and Embedding; *see* OLE). COM components can be written in any major programming language. They can be used by the program to which they belong, other programs running concurrently on the same computer, or even programs running elsewhere and communicating through a network; the last of these is called DCOM (Distributed COM; *compare* CORBA). Though developed for Windows, COM has been ported to UNIX.

COM+ is an extended form of COM in which more of the creation and handling of components is done automatically. The .NET Framework takes the same idea even further (*see* .NET FRAMEWORK).

combine a drawing program command that merges two separate objects into one so that the whole thing can become one object. This is similar to grouping objects, but there is an important distinction. A group of objects can be treated as a single object, but the individual elements retain their separate attributes. A combined object *is* a single object; it has only *one* outline (or path) and only *one* fill. Interestingly, a combined object can have holes in it that you can see through. *See* MASK; PATH (definition 3).

comma-separated values *see* CSV FILE.

Command key the key marked with a cloverleaf-like symbol (⌘) on the Macintosh. It is used like a shift key to change the meanings of other keys or to perform special functions. For example, you can print a picture of the current screen by holding down Command and Shift and pressing 4. If you press 3 instead, a picture of the current screen will be saved as a MacPaint document.

command line the place where a user types in response to a single COMMAND PROMPT, ending by pressing Enter.

command prompt
1. the series of characters, such as c:\TEMP> (on Microsoft systems) or unix% (on Macintosh or Unix), that indicates that an operating system is ready for the user to type a command.
2. in Windows, a CONSOLE MODE window in which the user can type commands. *See also* BAT FILE.

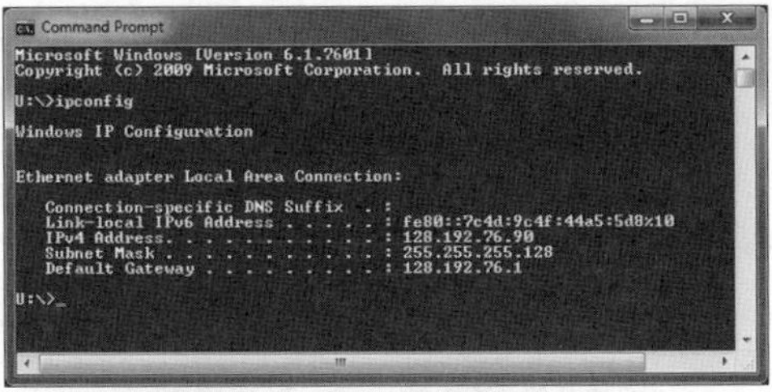

FIGURE 61. Command prompt

comment information in a computer program that is ignored by the computer and is included only for the benefit of human readers. Various computer languages identify comments with markers such as `c`, `;`, `REM`, or `/* */`.

Comments reflect the fact that programs are written to be read by human beings, not computers. If we could write in the language that best suited the computer, we would not need human-readable programming languages such as Pascal, C, and Java.

Comments can also be used to remove material from a program temporarily without deleting it. When you modify a program, it is a good idea to preserve the original form of the material you changed, in a comment, so that you can restore it or study it if the need arises. *See also* DOCUMENTATION.

common logarithm a logarithm to the base 10. *See* LOGARITHM.

Communications Decency Act a law passed by the U.S. Congress in 1996 making it illegal to transmit indecent material to children through the Internet. In 1997, the Supreme Court declared this law to be unconstitutional (*Reno v. American Civil Liberties Union*) on the ground that the Internet is inherently entitled to the same freedom of speech as printed media, and that there is no practical way to block material from reaching children while transmitting it freely to adults. *See* INDECENCY and cross-references there.

Note that the Communications Decency Act is separate from laws against pornography, including child pornography, and such laws were not affected when it was overturned.

CompactFlash a type of flash-memory non-volatile storage device commonly used in palmtop computers, Nikon digital cameras, and other portable devices. CompactFlash cards are rectangular, about 40 mm (1.6 inches) wide, and either 3.3 mm (0.13 inch) thick (Type I) or 5 mm (0.2 inch) thick (Type II) (*see* Figure 62).

Flash-memory CompactFlash cards interact with the computer like ATA hard disks. There are also CompactFlash Type II cards that contain an actual magnetic disk (the IBM Microdrive). *Compare* SMARTMEDIA;

SECURE DIGITAL CARD; MEMORYSTICK; MULTIMEDIACARD; FLASH MEMORY CARD.

FIGURE 62. CompactFlash card

Compaq a major manufacturer of IBM PC-compatible computers. Compaq's first product, released in 1983, was the first PC CLONE (i.e., the first PC-compatible computer not made by IBM). Compaq produced a portable PC, about the size and weight of a small suitcase, which became popular among professionals. In 1988 Compaq led a group of other computer companies in the development of a 32-bit PC bus (*see* EISA). In 1998, Compaq acquired Digital Equipment Corporation, manufacturers of the Alpha microprocessor. In 2002, Compaq merged with Hewlett-Packard.

compatibility mode the ability of recent versions of Microsoft Windows to simulate earlier versions in order to run older software. To set the compatibility mode for a piece of software, right-click on its icon and look for the settings under Properties.

compatible
  1. able to work together. For example, a particular brand of printer is compatible with a particular computer to which it can be connected.
  2. able to run the same software. *See* PC COMPATIBILITY.

compile-time error an error in a computer program that is caught in the process of compiling the program. For example, a compile-time error occurs if the syntax of the language has been violated. *Contrast* RUN-TIME ERROR. *See also* BUG.

compiler a computer program that translates C, C++, BASIC, Pascal, or a similar high-level programming language into machine language. The high-level language program fed into the compiler is called the *source program;* the generated machine language program is the *object program.*

complement

1. either of two ways of representing negative numbers in binary:

   a. The *1-complement* of a binary number is obtained by simply changing every 0 to 1 and every 1 to 0. For example, the 1-complement of 0001 is 1110. In this system, 0000 and its complement 1111 both represent zero (you can think of them as +0 and –0, respectively).

   b. The *2-complement* of a binary number is found by reversing all the digits and then adding 1. For example, the 2-complement of 00000001 is 11111110 + 1 = 11111111. This is the system normally used on most computers, and it has only one representation of zero (00000000) (but one negative value, −128 = [11111111] has no positive inverse). *See* BINARY SUBTRACTION.

2. the opposite of a color; the hue, which when mixed with the first hue, can give colorless gray. For example, red is the complement of green.

complex number a number consisting of two parts, called *real* and *imaginary*. Complex numbers are written in the form $a + bi$, where a is the real part, b is the size of the imaginary part, and i is the square root of -1. (If $b = 0$, the complex number is of course equal to a real number.)

Unlike real numbers, complex numbers can produce negative numbers when squared. All polynomials have complex roots even though some of them lack real roots. Another use of complex numbers is to represent vectors in two-dimensional space; the imaginary number line is thought of as running perpendicular to the real number line.

Arithmetic on complex numbers obeys the ordinary laws of algebra, as follows:

$$(a + bi) + (c + di) = (a + c) + (b + d)i$$
$$(a + bi) - (c + di) = (a - c) + (b - d)i$$
$$(a + bi) \times (c + di) = ac + adi + bci + bdi^2 = (ac - bd) + (ad + bc)i$$

Complex numbers are provided as a data type in Fortran and C++, and in mathematical packages such as Maple, but not in most other programming languages. *See also* MANDELBROT SET.

complexity theory the mathematical study of the time (number of steps) and amount of memory needed to perform a computation.

Suppose a computer is going to process n items of input. The time complexity of the calculation may be any of the following:

- *Constant* or $O(1)$ if the computation takes the same number of steps regardless of how many items are to be processed. An example is copying a diskette with a program that duplicates the entire diskette regardless of how much of it actually holds data.
- *Linear* or $O(n)$ if the number of steps is proportional to n. An example would be copying a set of n names and addresses from one file to another, or finding the sum of n numbers, or any program that contains only one loop.

- *Polynomial* or $O(n^k)$ if the number of steps is proportional to n raised to some constant power. For example, if the computation involves comparing each item of input with all of the other items, it will take n^2 steps. Many sorting algorithms are $O(n^2)$. A program that contains k nested loops, each with a number of steps proportional to n, will take time proportional to n^k.

- *Exponential* or $O(k^n)$ if the number of steps is proportional to some constant k raised to the nth power. This is what happens if the computer has to try arranging n elements in all possible sequences. Exponential-time computations are generally not practical.

There are some other possibilities; for example, Quicksort takes time proportional to $n \log n$, which is less than n^2.

In calculating complexity, we ignore factors that become insignificant as n becomes large. Suppose a computation requires $n^2 + 3n + 5$ steps. For sufficiently large n, this gets closer and closer to n^2, so we say that the complexity is $O(n^2)$.

Besides the time complexity, a computation may require constant, linear, polynomial, or exponential amounts of memory. *See also* COMPUTER SCIENCE; LIMITS OF COMPUTER POWER; QUICKSORT.

component any part of a larger system, either software or hardware. Reusable parts of programs are called software components. For examples of how software components are used, *see* ACTIVEX; COM; CORBA.

composite video the kind of video signal used in analog TV sets and still used in some types of video equipment. The whole signal is transmitted on one wire. By contrast, an RGB signal has separate wires for red, green, and blue. *See* MONITOR.

compositing the combining of bitmap images from different sources or different objects in a single image. The opacity, or ALPHA, of each object determines how it combines with objects behind it. *See also* CHROMA-KEYING.

compound a substance consisting of more than one ELEMENT; for example, a water molecule (H_2O) consists of two hydrogen atoms and one oxygen atom.

compression *see* DATA COMPRESSION.

CompuServe a pioneering online information service, which later became part of AOL.

computational linguistics the use of computers in the study of human language, and the study of how to make computers understand information expressed in human languages. *See* NATURAL LANGUAGE PROCESSING; PARSING.

computer a machine capable of executing instructions on data. The distinguishing feature of a computer is its ability to store its own instructions.

This ability makes it possible for a computer to perform many operations without the need for a person to type in new instructions each time.

Computer a link on the DESKTOP or in the START MENU of Microsoft Windows Vista and later versions that contains links to all the disk drives, the Control Panel, and other information about the system.

Ordinarily, folders are directories. The root directory of a disk drive is also a folder. "Computer" is a special folder that gives you access to the entire machine.

In previous versions of Windows, this folder was called "My Computer."

computer architecture the design and internal structure of digital computers.

Fundamentally, a computer is a machine that can store instructions and execute them. Thus, it consists of two major parts, MEMORY and the central processing unit (CPU), which communicate through a set of parallel electrical connections called the BUS (Figure 63). The bus also connects to input-output devices such as a screen, a keyboard, and disk drives.

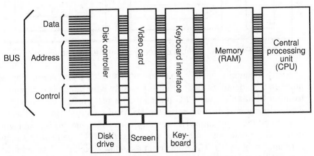

FIGURE 63. CPU communicates with memory and other devices via bus

The CPU spends its time retrieving instructions from memory and doing whatever those instructions say. Each instruction is a pattern of bits (binary ones and zeroes, represented by electrical on and off signals). When the instruction reaches the CPU, the CPU must *decode* (recognize) it and activate the appropriate *functional unit* within the CPU in order to carry out the instruction. Functional units include adders, multipliers, circuits to compare bit patterns, etc., all of which are built from logic gates (for an example, *see* BINARY ADDITION).

The CPU contains REGISTERS to hold data that is being worked on. For example, in order to add two numbers, the CPU will typically retrieve the two numbers from memory into registers, perform the addition, place the result in another register, and finally store it back into memory.

Figure 64 illustrates the parts of the CPU. In most present-day computers, the CPU is a single integrated circuit (IC) called a MICROPROCESSOR.

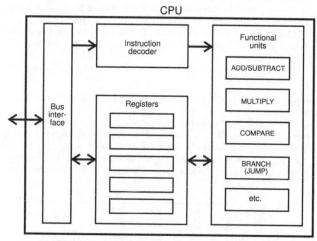

FIGURE 64. CPU (central processing unit) internal structure

Every location in memory has an ADDRESS (i.e., a bit pattern, binary number, that identifies the location). To retrieve the contents of memory location 011000011, the CPU places the bit pattern 011000011 on the address portion of the bus, activates the "read memory" line, and waits a specified length of time. The memory places the contents of that location onto the data portion of the bus so that the CPU can read it. To put data into memory, the CPU puts both the address and the data onto the bus and activates the "write memory" line. Some computers also include "read port" and "write port" lines, which are like the lines used for accessing memory except that addresses are understood as applying to input and output devices (printer ports, etc.) rather than memory.

Most computers use a VON NEUMANN ARCHITECTURE, which means that programs and data are stored in the same kind of memory. Some microcontrollers use a HARVARD ARCHITECTURE, with separate memories for program and data (mainly because programs are kept permanently recorded in ROM, but data must be changeable).

Programmers normally do not write CPU instructions. Instead, they write programs in a high-level language such as C, Java, or C#, and use a COMPILER to translate the programs into machine language. It is also possible to write programs in ASSEMBLY LANGUAGE, which translates into machine language more directly.

computer crime *see* COMPUTER SECURITY.

computer ethics the responsible use of computers and computer networks. Malicious misuse of computers is rare, but serious misjudgments by well-meaning people are unfortunately common. Some important points to remember are the following:

1. *People have the same legal and ethical responsibilities when using a computer as at any other time.*

   Slander, deception, harassment, and the like are just as wrong when done via computer as when done any other way, and they incur the same legal penalties.

   Using a computer without the owner's permission is prosecutable as theft of services (just like using any other machine without the owner's permission). Damaging property or data by releasing a computer virus is also prosecutable as a crime.

2. *Computers will not necessarily prevent all improper acts; users are responsible for what they do.*

   For example, if a computer is set up incorrectly so that it lets unauthorized people use it without a password, that does not justify the unauthorized usage, just as a defective door lock does not justify burglary.

3. *Some of the information stored in computers is private and confidential and should not be abused.*

   This applies particularly to credit records, educational records, and the like. Such information may also be incomplete or inaccurate because people did not correct errors that they considered inconsequential. If the information is later used for a completely different purpose, the errors can be damaging.

4. *Electronic communications are not guaranteed to be private.*

   You do not know what path your electronic mail follows or who may see it en route. Do not send credit card numbers or other confidential information through e-mail unless you have confirmed that it is traveling by a secure path.

   Also, be aware that e-mail can be faked; there is no guarantee that a piece of mail actually came from the person or site shown on the header.

5. *Users must respect software copyrights and licenses.*

   The price of a piece of software includes your share of the cost of developing the product. If people don't pay for software, there will be no software.

6. *Manufacturers, programmers, and independent consultants have responsibilities to their customers.*

   It's wrong to claim to be more of an expert than you really are; it's also wrong to sell a shoddy product while concealing defects in it. Admittedly, no one can ensure that any complex piece of software is 100% reliable, but common decency requires programmers and vendors to act in good faith—when there's a problem, do your best to correct it or at least warn the user about it.

In the past, many manufacturers have tried to disclaim all responsibility for the performance of their products, but there are encouraging signs that the user community will no longer tolerate this dubious practice.

7. *On the Internet, you are everyone else's guest.*

The cost of running the Internet is paid by the sites that receive messages, not just the sites that send them. Accordingly, you must be careful what you send out, and to whom.

For more about ethical aspects of computer communications *see* ACCEPTABLE-USE POLICY; COMPUTER LAW; CYBERBULLYING; DOMAIN NAME POACHING; HACKER ETHIC; INTERNET; MAIL BOMBING; NETIQUETTE; OBSCENITY; PORNOGRAPHY; SPAM; SPOOFING; USENET.

computer law laws pertaining to computers. An important principle is that computers are not exempt from the pre-existing laws. For instance, computer users must obey laws against fraud, misrepresentation, harassment, eavesdropping, theft of services, and tampering with other people's property, even if the laws do not specifically mention computers. Further, many jurisdictions have specific laws against COMPUTER TRESPASS and similar acts. *See also* ACCEPTABLE-USE POLICY; BROADCAST FLAG; CAN-SPAM; CIPA; COMMUNICATIONS DECENCY ACT; COPYRIGHT; DMCA; ECPA; GAMBLING; LICENSE; MICROSOFT ANTITRUST CHARGES; PATENT; PORNOGRAPHY; PUBLIC DOMAIN; PYRAMID SCHEME; TRADE SECRET; USC; VIRUS.

computer priesthood *(1970s slang, still used)* computer specialists; the experts on whom ordinary people rely for their access to the computers, as if they were priests with access to a secret part of the temple.

computer science the mathematical and scientific study of the possible uses of computers. Computer science is a wide-ranging field including pure mathematics (*see* COMPLEXITY THEORY; HALTING PROBLEM), engineering (*see* COMPUTER ARCHITECTURE), management (*see* SOFTWARE ENGINEERING), and even the study of the human mind (*see* ARTIFICIAL INTELLIGENCE). Indeed, computer scientists often work on problems in almost any field to which computers can be applied. Computer science is more than just training in the use of today's computers and software; it includes preparation to understand the technology of the future and its theoretical underpinnings.

computer security the protection of computers from tampering, physical danger, and unwanted disclosure of data. The advent of personal computers has made it easy for important business records or confidential data to be lost, sabotaged, or misused. Computers need protection from the following kinds of hazards:

1. *Machine failure.* Make backups of important files frequently. Every disk drive in the world will one day fail, losing all data.

2. *Physical hazards.* Protect the computer from fire, flood, and similar hazards, and store backups at a remote location. Remember, too, that the machine can be stolen. An increasing number of computer thieves are after data, not just equipment.

When traveling with a laptop computer, *never let it out of your possession.* Many thefts occur at airport check-in counters: while you are preoccupied making your arrangements, someone can quietly steal the laptop computer you placed on the floor. Keep the computer in your hand. Stay close to the computer as it goes through the airport security check. Always bring your laptop on board as carry-on luggage. Checked baggage is treated far too roughly.

3. *Operator error.* It is easy to delete information accidentally. This hazard can be minimized with software that retains original files while altered copies are being made.

4. *Computer tampering.* Can someone come in and alter your records without your knowing it? Bear in mind that large numbers of people know how to use popular business software packages. If possible, use software that keeps records of changes—recording who made them and when—and requires validation (such as a password) to make unusual changes.

5. *Malicious programming.* Some computer crimes have been perpetrated by programmers who did such things as collect all the money that was lost by rounding interest payments to the nearest penny. A clever bookkeeping system run by a dishonest programmer can easily conceal abuse.

   More recently, some people have gotten their kicks by distributing destructive computer programs over the Internet. *See* TROJAN HORSE. Even more have gotten their kicks by circulating false warnings (*see* HOAX).

6. *Malicious programs arriving in e-mail,* often falsely described as other things. Never open a file that arrives unexpectedly, even if it's from someone you know, unless you have confirmed what the file is. Never click on a link that appears in an e-mail unless you know for sure who it is from and what it is for. Never trust an e-mail asking for you to send money or reveal your password, even if it claims to be from an administrator threatening to shut down your e-mail account or from a relative in trouble. If you think such a request might actually be legitimate, be sure you verify it with a phone call. *See* WORM; PHISHING.

7. *Break-ins by modem or network.* Make sure you know all the possibilities for connecting to your computer from elsewhere, and that you've blocked all access that you don't want to allow. The UNIX operating system, designed originally for use in laboratories where no security was needed, is generally thought to be particularly vulnerable. *See* DICTIONARY ATTACK; WAR DIALING.

8. *Be especially careful with wireless networks, and make sure all communications are encrypted.* A cracker with a special antenna can access your wireless network from ten times the normal distance. *See* WAR DRIVING; WIRELESS NETWORK.

9. *Easily guessed passwords.* A computer password must never be a person's initials, nickname, child's name, birthdate, etc., nor

should it be a correctly spelled word in any language. A common way to crack accounts is to try all the words in a large dictionary, as well as all names and abbreviations that are associated with a person. Also, if a user signs onto a computer and then leaves the terminal unattended, others can tamper with it without typing the password. *See* PASSWORD.

10. *Viruses and known software defects.* Always run antivirus software, and make sure your software and operating system are kept up to date.

11. *Excessive security measures.* Excessive attempts to build security into a computer can easily make the computer so hard to use that productivity is crippled. In the final analysis, all computer security depends on human trustworthiness. Concentrate on securing the people, not the machine. That is, ensure that employees are trustworthy and that strangers have no access to the machine; then give authorized users all the access they need to do their jobs effectively.

See also 2600; BHO; COOKIE; CYBERBULLYING; DDOS; DENIAL-OF-SERVICE ATTACK; ENCRYPTION; ETHICAL HACKING; FINE-GRAINED SECURITY; HONEYPOT; MAIL BOMBING; PING FLOODING; QR CODE; VIRUS.

computer trespass the crime of using a computer without the owner's permission (*see* CRACKER). Even in jurisdictions that have no specific law against it, computer trespass is illegal under pre-existing laws that prohibit unauthorized use of other people's property.

computer virus *see* VIRUS.

computer vision *see* VISION, COMPUTER.

computers, history of a story spanning many centuries. The abacus, on which information is stored by moving beads along rods, was one of the earliest calculating devices. Blaise Pascal developed an adding machine in 1642 that used toothed wheels to handle carries from one digit to the next. Charles Babbage developed the concept of a stored program computer when he designed the "Analytical Engine" in 1833. Unfortunately, the mechanical devices of his day could not be made to work reliably, so the "Analytical Engine" was never completed.

An important data processing device, the punched card, was developed by Herman Hollerith to help the U.S. Census Bureau tabulate the census of 1890. The first electronic digital computer was the ENIAC (Electronic Numerical Integrator and Calculator), which was built for the U.S. Army in 1946, largely because of the need to calculate ballistics tables. The ENIAC was programmed by plugging in cables to connect different units. In 1945 John von Neumann introduced the modern concept of a stored-program computer, in which the computer memory could store both programs and data.

Once the concept was established, major improvements were made by developing smaller and more reliable electronic components. The

ENIAC was a huge machine made with vacuum tubes. The invention of the transistor in the late 1940s made it possible to build much smaller computers that needed less cooling. Continued improvements in integrated circuits, which were first developed in the late 1950s, made it possible to continue the miniaturization of computers.

An important advance occurred in the mid-1970s when the first microcomputers were built. Previously, all computers had been large and expensive. Microcomputers are small enough and cheap enough that they can be purchased by small businesses and individuals. A microcomputer is built around a microprocessor chip, such as the 486 or Pentium, that contains the entire central processing unit on a single crystal of silicon. The advent of powerful, low-cost microcomputers has made the computer a common household appliance. *See also* INTERNET.

concatenation the operation of joining two or more character strings together, end to end. For example, "ABC" concatenated with "DEF" equals "ABCDEF". *See* STRING OPERATIONS.

concurrent processing the apparently simultaneous execution of two programs, where a single CPU is actually switching its attention back and forth between them very rapidly. *See also* MULTITASKING; PARALLEL PROCESSING; TIMESHARING.

conferencing the use of computer networks to enable workers to communicate in real time (without delay) while working together. *See* IRC; MUD.

confidence factor (certainty factor) a truth value between 0 and 1, used to describe the reliability of a piece of information whose truth is unclear or uncertain. There are several systems of reasoning that use confidence factors; for one example, *see* FUZZY LOGIC. *Contrast* DEFAULT LOGIC, which deals with exceptions without using confidence factors.

configure to set up a computer, operating system, or program to be used in a particular way (for example, to configure Windows to work with two displays at once.)

connector *see* USB; FIREWIRE; HDMI; RS-232; RJ-11; RJ-45; PORT; PARALLEL PORT; SERAL PORT; BNC CONNECTOR; CENTRONICS INTERFACE; DB-9, DB-15, DB-25; VGA CONNECTOR; DVI; ETHERNET; IEC POWER CONNECTOR; IEEE 1284; PATA; JACK; RCA PLUG; SCSI; SOCKET.

console
1. the main keyboard and screen of a multi-user computer.
2. a keyboard and (non-graphical) screen, or a window serving the purpose of such a screen.

console application a Windows program that runs in CONSOLE MODE.

console mode a way of controlling a computer by typing commands and reading responses, rather than by clicking with a mouse and viewing graphical output. Before the Apple Macintosh (1984), personal computers used only console mode. Microsoft Windows provides a console mode that resembles DOS (Figure 65) but in fact can run 32-bit native Windows programs and supports numerous commands specific to Windows. The console mode of the current Macintosh accepts BSD UNIX commands. *See also* BAT FILE.

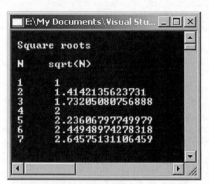

FIGURE 65. Console mode (Windows 7).

constant a value that remains unchanged during the execution of a program. Literal expressions, such as 3.5 and "DOLLY MADISON", are constants because they always stand for the same value.

constrain (in drawing programs) to restrict or limit the available movements or shapes. For example, when drawing a circle with a circle tool, you must hold down the Control key to constrain the rounded shape to a circle. If you let go of the constraining key too soon, you may get a fat oval rather than a perfect circle.

The constrain command is also used with the rectangle drawing tool (constrains to a square) and the line drawing tool (constrains to preset angles).

constructor in OBJECT-ORIENTED PROGRAMMING, a method called when a new object is created.

content provider a company or organization that provides information (*content*) online. For example, *www.cnn.com* (Cable News Network) is a content provider for world news and related information. *Contrast* ASP (definition 2); INTERNET SERVICE PROVIDER.

contention *see* DEVICE CONTENTION.

context-sensitive help information provided by a computer program when you ask for help, chosen to match what you are doing at the time. For example, a context-sensitive help key will give you information about how to edit if you press it while editing, or how to print if you press it while preparing to print.

contiguous adjacent, next to each other. For instance, the states of North
Dakota and South Dakota are contiguous, but Texas and Maine are not.

Most computers can store a disk file in either contiguous or noncon-
tiguous sectors. (*See* DISK.) Access is slowed if the sectors are not contiguous, since to get from one part of the file to another, the read/write
head must jump from one part of the disk to another. *See*
FRAGMENTATION.

continuous speech speech that is spoken without pauses between words.
See SPEECH RECOGNITION. *Contrast* DISCRETE SPEECH.

contrast the range of light and dark values in a grayscale (continuous tone)
image. A *high-contrast* image is mostly white and black with very few
intermediate gray shades. A *low-contrast* image has little difference
between the darkest darks and lightest lights. *See* Figure 66.

The contrast of an existing picture can be adjusted with picture editing software. *See* SCANNER; HISTOGRAM.

FIGURE 66. Contrast: low, normal, and high

contrast ratio the luminosity of the brightest white that can be produced
by a monitor divided by the luminosity of the darkest black.

control a reusable software component in Visual Basic, ActiveX, or a similar system. Many of the first controls were user interface components—
check boxes, sliding bars, and the like—hence the name.

control box (Windows) a small box at the left of the title bar of a window.
Clicking the control box pops up a menu for controlling the size of the
window. Double-clicking on the control box closes the window and the
application running in it.

Control key (Ctrl or Cntl key) a special key on many computer keyboards.
When it is pressed in conjunction with another key, it gives the other key
a new meaning that depends on the program in use. *See* ASCII to see
how the Control key can be used to type nonprintable control characters.
See also CTRL-ALT-DEL.

control menu (Windows) a menu that appears when the user clicks on the CONTROL BOX (the box at the left of the title bar). The control menu for each window allows you to maximize, minimize, restore, resize, or close the window. *See* Figure 67 for illustration. *See also* WINDOW.

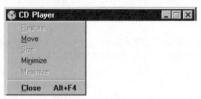

FIGURE 67. Control menu

Control Panel (in Windows) a group of utility programs for making settings that affect the computer's operation. These range from desktop color, mouse tracking, and the like, to network communication parameters and printer drivers.

control point *see* NODE.

CONUS abbreviation for **con**tinental **U**nited **S**tates, usually meaning the 48 contiguous states. (Alaska is part of the North American continent but is commonly overlooked.)

conversion program a program that is capable of changing a file from one format to another.

For example, to use a TIFF (Tagged Image File Format) file in a web page design, the image must be converted to .JPEG or .GIF format. This can be done with a separate conversion program or by using the "Save as . . . " command in the appropriate image-editing program. (*See* IMPORT; EXPORT; FILE FORMAT.)

Note that simply changing the *name* of the file from myfile.tif to myfile.jpg does *not* convert the file *type*. The data contained in the file has to be reorganized by the conversion program.

convolution an image processing computation described by a matrix. Suppose, for example, that you want to bring out fine detail in an image. One way to do this is to increase the difference between each pixel and its neighbors. Treating the pixels as numbers representing their brightnesses, you can use the following convolution matrix:

$$\begin{bmatrix} -1 & -1 & -1 \\ -1 & 9 & -1 \\ -1 & -1 & -1 \end{bmatrix}$$

That means: Work through the whole image, one pixel at a time. Whenever you get to a pixel, multiply it by 9, multiply each of the surrounding pixels by −1, and add them together. Then replace the original pixel with that value.

If all of the pixels are the same brightness, nothing changes, but if a pixel is brighter or fainter than its neighbors, the difference is exaggerated by a factor of 9. Other convolutions can perform other special effects, such as smoothing, eliminating details smaller or larger than a certain size, and even eliminating streaks in a particular direction.

When performing a convolution, the input is always from the original, unprocessed image. That is, the next pixel will not be affected by any changes made by the processing of the previous pixel.

convolve to perform a convolution. *See* CONVOLUTION.

cookie information stored on a user's computer by a WEB BROWSER at the request of software at a web site. Web sites use cookies to recognize users who have previously visited them. The next time the user accesses that site, the information in the cookie is sent back to the site so the information displayed can vary depending on the user's preferences. Cookies are not a security risk because they only store information that came from the web site or was sent to it by the user. *See also* SUPER-COOKIE; TRACKING COOKIE.

The term *cookie* comes from a 1980s prank computer program called Cookie Monster that would interrupt users and demand that they type the word "cookie" before continuing.

COPPA (**C**hildren's **O**nline **P**rivacy **P**rotection **A**ct) a law passed by Congress in 1998 (15 USC 6501-6502) making it illegal for an operator of a web site or online service to collect personal information from children without parental consent. *See* COMPUTER LAW.

copper chemical element (atomic number 29, symbol Cu) often used in electronics because it is a good conductor of electricity.

coprocessor a separate circuit inside a computer that adds additional functions to the CPU (central processing unit) or handles extra work while the CPU is doing something else.

copy

1. to duplicate information in another place, leaving the original unchanged. In many spreadsheets, editors, and drawing programs, *copy* means either of two things:
   a. to copy material from one place to another;
   b. to copy material from the document being edited into a holding area, from which you can then "paste" it elsewhere. *See* CUT; PASTE; CLIPBOARD.
2. a command that makes a copy of a disk file.

copy protection any of numerous techniques to keep a diskette, CD, or DVD from being copied with ordinary equipment. Copy-protected diskettes were common in the 1970s and 1980s but fell into disfavor because they were incompatible with newer disk drives. A number of types of copy-protected CDs have appeared recently, and similar problems may befall them. DVD technology has copy protection built in, backed up by a rather unusual copyright law (*see* DVD; DMCA). *See also* DRM.

copyleft *(humorous)* a copyright whose owner gives permission for the product to be distributed free subject to certain conditions. *See* GNU.

copyright (the *right* to *copy*) a legal restriction on the copying of books, magazines, recordings, computer programs, and other materials, in order to protect the original author's right to ownership of, and compensations for reproduction of, an original work. Most computer programs are protected not only by copyright but also by a software license (*see* SOFTWARE LICENSE; FREE SOFTWARE).

Since 1989, literary works and computer programs have been protected under U.S. copyright law from the moment they are created. It is not necessary to include a copyright notice or register the copyright with the government.

However, it is still prudent to include a notice of the form *Copyright 1996 John Doe* or © *1996 John Doe* in any work to which you claim copyright. If you think the copyright is likely to be infringed, you should also register it at the time of publication, since this increases the penalties you can collect from the infringer. In general, copies of copyrighted published works must be sent to the Library of Congress whether or not the copyright is registered. For up-to-date information see *www.copyright.gov*.

U.S. copyright law allows limited copying of books and magazines for private study or classroom use. However, this does not apply to computer programs, which can only be copied with the permission of the copyright owner, or in order to make backup copies that will not be used as long as the original copy is intact.

Do not reproduce copyrighted material on web pages or anywhere on the INTERNET without the owner's permission. Placing something on a web page constitutes republication just as if you were making printed copies. Remember that copyrights apply to sounds and pictures as well as texts. Distributing a sound bite from a movie or a picture of a cartoon character can be a copyright violation.

Copyright protects expressions of ideas, not the ideas themselves. Copyrights do not cover algorithms, mathematical methods, techniques, or the design of machines (which, however, can be patented).

The purpose of copyright is to encourage communication. It is therefore paradoxical that the Digital Millennium Copyright Act prohibits the publication of certain information about copy protection schemes. *See* DMCA. *See also* COMPUTER LAW; CSS; FAIR USE; PATENT; TRADE SECRET.

CORBA (**C**ommon **O**bject **R**equest **B**roker **A**rchitecture) a standard set of definitions for objects to interact with each other. CORBA was created by the Object Management Group (*see* OMG). CORBA defines a standard for a layer of middleware called the ORB (Object Request Broker). The way that components interact with other components is specified by IDL (Interface Definition Language). This allows client-server computing where the clients don't need to have any knowledge of the specific operation of the component they are interacting with. For example, the client doesn't need to know the language in which the component was written; it only needs to know the IDL specification of how the component interacts. For an alternative standard, *see* DCOM.

core
1. the central part of a CPU, containing the circuitry needed to execute a single series of instructions. A CPU with more than one core can run more than one series of instructions at the same time without switching back and forth between them.
2. the essential design of a CPU, in detail; thus, two different models of CPU might be described as being built on the same core.
3. an old term for RAM, especially magnetic RAM consisting of doughnut-shaped ferrite "cores" strung on a lattice of wires.

Core trade name for several varieties of Intel PENTIUM microprocessor that have more than one CPU core. *See* CORE (definition 1).

Corel a corporation headquartered in Ottawa, Ontario, that introduced one of the first successful DRAW PROGRAMS, CorelDraw, in 1989. In 1996, Corel acquired the WordPerfect Office business applications. Other Corel products include a variety of computer programs and utilities such as Corel Painter, DVD MovieFactory, and WinDVD. Their web address is *www.corel.com*.

corona wire a wire, in a laser printer, that emits a strong electric charge (a *corona discharge*) into the air and onto the adjacent drum. *See* DRUM.

correspondence points points in two objects (or images) that are associated with each other for blending or morphing. *See* BLEND; DRAW PROGRAM; MORPH.

cos, cosine the cosine trigonometric function. If A is an angle in a right triangle, then the cosine of A (written as cos A) is defined as:

$$\cos A = \frac{\text{length of adjacent side}}{\text{length of hypotenuse}}$$

The function cos(A) in many programming languages calculates the value of cos A, expressed in radians. For an illustration, *see* TRIGONOMETRIC FUNCTIONS.

coulomb a unit of electric charge equivalent to the charge of 6.25×10^{18} electrons. *See* AMPERE.

country codes *See* CCTLD.

Courier a typewriter-like typeface often used on printers. Courier has fixed pitch; that is, all characters are the same width. It was designed for IBM typewriters in the 1960s, but on modern laser printers, it is often unpleasantly light (thin).

```
Courier
a b c d e f g h i j k l m
n o p q r s t u v w x y z
A B C D E F G H I J K L M
N O P Q R S T U V W X Y Z
1 2 3 4 5 6 7 8 9 0 ! @ #
```

FIGURE 68. Courier, a fixed-pitch font

CP/M (**C**ontrol **P**rogram for **M**icrocomputers) an operating system developed by Digital Research, Inc., and used on microcomputers in the 1970s and 1980s. (*See* OPERATING SYSTEM.) The original CP/M (now called CP/M-80) was widely employed on computers that used the 8-bit Z80 processor. CP/M greatly influenced the early development of MS-DOS. *See* MS-DOS.

CPU (**C**entral **P**rocessing **U**nit) the part of a computer where arithmetic and logical operations are performed and instructions are decoded and executed. The CPU controls the operation of the computer. A microprocessor is an integrated circuit that contains a complete CPU on a single chip. *See* COMPUTER ARCHITECTURE.

CR (**c**arriage **r**eturn) the character code that tells a printer or terminal to return to the beginning of the line; ASCII code 13. On the classic Macintosh, CR indicates the end of a line in a text file; Max OSX and UNIX use LF, and Windows uses CRLF. *See* CRLF; LF.

cracker a person who "breaks into" computers via the Internet and uses them without authorization, either with malicious intent or simply to show that it can be done. *Compare* HACKER. *See also* 2600; COMPUTER TRESPASS; ETHICAL HACKING; HONEYPOT.

craplet unwelcome software pre-installed on a new computer.

crash the sudden, complete failure of a computer because of a hardware failure or program error. A well-designed operating system contains protection against inappropriate instructions so that a user's program will not be able to cause a system crash.

crawler a computer program that automatically explores the WORLD WIDE WEB and collects information; also called a *spider.*

Cray Research, Inc. a company founded by Seymour Cray, a manufacturer of supercomputers (*see* SUPERCOMPUTER). Cray's first major product was the Cray-1, introduced in 1977, a vector processor designed for repetitive numeric calculations. *See* VECTOR PROCESSOR. Web address: *www.cray.com*.

CRC *see* CYCLICAL REDUNDANCY CHECK.

creeping featurism *(slang)* the practice of trying to improve software by adding features in an unsystematic way, ultimately making it less reliable and harder to use. *Compare* BELLS AND WHISTLES.

crippleware *(slang)* software that is distributed free as an incomplete or time-limited version in the hope that the user will purchase the fully functional version. *See* FREE SOFTWARE.

CRLF (**c**arriage **r**eturn, **l**ine **f**eed) a pair of ASCII codes, 13 and 10, that tell a terminal or printer to return to the beginning of the line and advance to the next line. Under Windows, CRLF indicates the end of a line in a text. *See* CR; LF.

CRM (**c**ustomer **r**elationship **m**anagement) software for keeping track of past customers, sales prospects, and the like.

crop factor the factor by which the image sensor of a DSLR camera is smaller than the film for which the camera's lenses were designed. For example, on 35-mm film, each picture is 24 × 36 mm. If a DSLR has an image sensor half as big, 12 × 18 mm, it will have a crop factor of 2. Popular DSLRs actually have a crop factor of about 1.5.

The crop factor effectively multiplies the focal length of the lens. A 100-mm lens on a DSLR with a crop factor of 1.5 will cover the same field of view as a 150-mm lens on a 35-mm film SLR. That is, it has a "35-mm equivalent" of 150 mm.

cross-platform applicable to more than one kind of computer (e.g., PC and Macintosh).

cross-post to place a single copy of a message into two or more newsgroups at once. This is less expensive than posting separate copies of it in different newsgroups. It also ensures that all replies made in any of the newsgroups will be cross-posted to all of them. *See* NEWSGROUP.

Crossfire technology allowing the use of multiple graphics cards to enhance the computer's ability to display graphics, developed by ATI (now part of AMD). *Contrast* NVIDIA.

crossover cable a cable with RJ-45 connectors that swap the input and output lines. A crossover cable can be used to connect two computers with 10base-T networking without a hub. *See* RJ-45 (wiring table).

crosstalk one electronic signal interfering with another, such as a signal on an adjacent cable. *See* CATEGORY 3 CABLE.

crowdsourcing (*crowd* + *outsourcing*) outsourcing tasks to a crowd; that is, employing a large and often undefined group of people through an open appeal. For an example, *see* MECHANICAL TURK.

CRT (**c**athode **r**ay **t**ube) a glass tube with a screen that glows when struck by electrons. An image is formed by constantly scanning the screen with an electron beam. Examples of CRTs include older television screens and computer monitors. *See also* EYEGLASSES, COMPUTER. *Compare* LCD.

crunch mode *(slang)* a work situation in which a deadline is near and everyone is working hard, keeping extended hours. Crunch mode is usually the result of a mistaken estimate made by management, not a genuine emergency. *See* SOFTWARE ENGINEERING.

cryptography the technology of encoding information so that it cannot be read by an unauthorized person. *See* ENCRYPTION and its cross-references.

C/SC text typeset in capitals and small capitals (LIKE THIS). Sometimes written "C + SC." *See also* CAPS; SMALL CAPS; U/LC. *Contrast* EVEN SMALLS.

CSMA/CD *see* ETHERNET.

CSS
1. *See* CASCADING STYLE SHEET.
2. (**C**ontent **S**crambling **S**ystem) an encryption-based software system developed by movie studios to prevent the copying of DVDs. *See* DVD; DECSS; DMCA.

CSV file a text file of **c**omma-**s**eparated **v**alues, usually with character strings in quotes, thus:

```
"Covington, Michael A.","Valdosta",4633,2.98
"Downing, Douglas","Seattle",1234,4.23
```

Spaces after the commas are permitted but have no effect. This is a popular way of saving the contents of a SPREADSHEET as a text file that can be read back in without losing the arrangement of the data. *Compare* TAB-DELIMITED.

Ctrl *see* CONTROL KEY.

Ctrl-Alt-Del a combination of keys with a special function on PC-compatible computers, typed by holding down Ctrl and Alt while pressing Del (Delete). Under Windows, it brings up a menu that makes it possible to kill (terminate) a malfunctioning program. (To do so, in current versions, choose TASK MANAGER.)
   In Windows NT and its successors, users must also press Ctrl-Alt-Del in order to log in. For hardware reasons, only the operating system is able to respond to Ctrl-Alt-Del, so this provides assurance that when

logging in, the user is seeing a real login prompt, not a fake screen put there by a prankster wanting to collect passwords.

cubic spline a curve that connects a set of points smoothly by solving a system of cubic equations. Unlike a Bézier spline, a cubic spline is defined only by the points that the curve must pass through; it has no control points that are not on the curve.

Cubic splines are the natural shapes of bent objects that are secured at particular points and are free to bend in between. The spline goes through each point smoothly, without sharp bends.

Each segment of the spline (from one point to the next) is modeled by a third-degree (cubic) polynomial of the form $y = ax^3 + bx^2 + cx + d$, where a, b, c, and d depend on the endpoints of the segment and the slope that the segment should have at each end.

If (x_1, y_1) and (x_2, y_2) are the endpoints and y'_1 and y'_2 are the slopes, then a, b, c, and d can be found by solving the four-equation system:

$$y_1 = ax_1^3 + bx_1^2 + cx_1 + d$$
$$y_2 = ax_2^3 + bx_2^2 + cx_2 + d$$
$$y'_1 = 3ax_1^2 + 2bx_1 + c$$
$$y'_2 = 3ax_2^2 + 2bx_2 + c$$

More commonly, the slopes are not known, but the slope at the end of each segment is set equal to the slope at the beginning of the next segment. The slopes and coefficients are then found by solving a system of simultaneous linear equations (linear because x, x^2, and x^3 are known and can be treated as constants). *Compare* B-SPLINE; BÉZIER SPLINE.

FIGURE 69. Cubic spline

cue (in animation and presentation programs) an embedded code that specifies when an action is to occur.

curly brackets the characters { }, also called BRACES. *Contrast* SQUARE BRACKETS; PARENTHESES; ANGLE BRACKETS.

current the flow of electrical charge. Current is measured in amperes; 1 ampere = 6.25×10^{18} electrons per second = 1 coulomb per second.

current directory the directory in which the computer looks for files if no other directory is specified. The current directory can be changed by cd commands in Windows and UNIX. In Windows, there is a current directory on each drive, so that, for example, c:MYFILE means file MYFILE in the current directory of drive C (whereas c:\MYFILE would mean MYFILE in the root directory).

To see the current directory and current drive, type cd in Windows, or pwd in UNIX.

current drive in Windows and similar operating systems, the disk drive on which the computer looks for files if no other drive is specified. *See* CURRENT DIRECTORY.

current loop a predecessor of RS-232 serial communication; it is occasionally still seen on older equipment. (*See* RS-232.) Do not connect current loop equipment directly to RS-232 equipment; the current loop system uses voltages as high as 100 volts and can cause damage.

cursor
1. the symbol on a computer terminal that shows you where on the screen the next character you type will appear. Cursors often appear as blinking dashes or rectangles. Many computers have cursor movement (arrow) keys that allow you to move the cursor vertically or horizontally around the screen. This ability is essential for text-editing purposes such as word processing. You can use the mouse to move the cursor quickly around the screen. *Compare* INSERTION POINT.
2. the mouse pointer. *See also* HOURGLASS.

curve *see* SPLINE.

cusp node a type of NODE that marks a sudden change in the direction of the line. *See* Figure 70. *Contrast* SMOOTH NODE.

FIGURE 70. Cusp node

cut to remove material from the document you are editing and place it into a holding area. *See* COPY; PASTE; CLIPBOARD.

cyan a vivid greenish-blue color that is one of the standard printing ink colors. *See* CMYK.

cyber- *(prefix) see* CYBERNETICS.

cyber cafe an INTERNET CAFE.

Cyberabad nickname for the city of Hyderabad, India, a center of high-technology industry.

cyberbullying repeated intentional harassment using the Internet and related technologies such as texting. Recent suicides of teenagers where cyberbullying was a contributing factor have brought attention to this problem. The psychology of cyberbullying may involve failure to distinguish the Internet from a video game, or the illusion that other people on the Internet aren't real or that things done to them have no real consequences.

cybernetics the study of the processing of information by machinery, especially computers and control systems; derived from Greek *kybernetes* meaning "helmsman"; first conceived in the 1940s. Cybernetics has evolved into computer science, operations research, and a number of other fields. The prefix *cyber-* on numerous computer terms is derived from this word.

cyberpunk
  1. an antisocial person who uses computers as a means of self-expression, often performing destructive acts.
  2. a genre of science fiction dating from William Gibson's 1982 novel *Neuromancer*, with themes of pessimism and rebellion against a computer-controlled society.

cyberspace the part of human society and culture that exists in networked computer systems rather than in any particular physical location. For example, cyberspace is where most bank accounts and electronic messages reside.

cybersquatting another name for DOMAIN NAME POACHING. *See also* UDDRP; UDRP.

cyburbia (**cyber** su**burbia**) the community of computer users that exists in cyberspace. *See* CYBERSPACE; NETIZEN.

cycle one oscillation of a computer's CPU CLOCK; the shortest step into which computer actions can be divided. When two or more programs are running at once, they are said to be competing for cycles.

cyclical redundancy check an error-detecting code similar to a CHECKSUM but computed with a more elaborate algorithm. Each segment of the original message is combined with additional bits to make a binary number that is divisible by some previously chosen divisor.

  Cyclical redundancy checks are used to ensure that data is read correctly from disks and other storage media. A defective CD or DVD often causes a cyclical redundancy check failure.

cylinder *see* DISK.

Cyrillic the Russian alphabet. *Contrast* LATIN.

D

DAC, D/A converter *see* DIGITAL-TO-ANALOG CONVERTER.

daemon (under UNIX) a program that runs continuously in the background, or is waiting to be activated by a particular event. The word *daemon* is Greek for "spirit" or "soul."

dagger the character †, sometimes used to mark footnotes. *See also* FOOTNOTE. Also called an OBELISK or LONG CROSS.

daisy-chain to connect devices together in sequence with cables. For example, if four devices A, B, C, and D are daisy-chained, there will be a cable from A to B, a cable from B to C, and a cable from C to D.

DAS *see* DIRECT(LY) ATTACHED STORAGE.

dash (—) a punctuation mark similar to a hyphen, but longer. On a typewriter, a dash is typed as two hyphens.

Proportional-pitch type often includes one or more kinds of dashes, such as an em dash (—), which is as wide as the height of the font, and an en dash (–), which is two-thirds as wide as the em dash. Normally, the em dash joins sentences and the en dash joins numbers (as in "2015–2018").

data information. The word was originally the plural of *datum*, which means "a single fact," but it is now used as a collective singular.

data bits a parameter of RS-232 serial communication. Either 7 or 8 bits are used for each character, preceded by a *start bit* and followed by a *parity bit* (optional) and a *stop bit. See also* RS-232; KERMIT.

data communication the transfer of information from one computer to another. In order for communication to take place, several aspects of the communication process must be standardized. The international OSI (Open Systems Interconnection) standard (ISO Standard 7498) defines seven layers at which decisions have to be made:
1. *Physical layer.* What kind of electrical signals are sent from machine to machine? For examples of standards on this level, *see* 10BASE-T; RS-232; MODEM.
2. *Link layer.* How do the two machines coordinate the physical sending and receiving of signals? For examples, *see* HANDSHAKING; PACKET.
3. *Network layer.* How does one machine establish a connection with the other? This covers such things as telephone dialing and the routing of packets. For examples, *see* HAYES COMPATIBILITY; PACKET; COLLISION; X.25.
4. *Transport layer.* How do the computers identify each other and coordinate the sending of messages back and forth? This is the

level at which most network protocols operate. For examples, *see* TCP/IP; NETBEUI; IPX/SPX. *See also* PROTOCOL.

5. *Session layer.* How do users establish connections, log on, and identify themselves?

6. *Presentation layer.* What does the information look like when received on the user's machine? The presentation layer includes file format and filename conversions and the like.

7. *Application layer.* How does software use the network—that is, how do application programs exchange data? The application layer does not consist of the programs themselves but, rather, the communication facilities that they use.

The OSI standard does not specify what any of these layers should look like; it merely defines a framework in terms of which future standards can be expressed. In a simple system, some of the layers are handled manually or are trivially simple.

data compression the storage of data in a way that makes it occupy less space than if it were stored in its original form. For example, long sequences of repeated characters can be replaced with short codes that mean "The following character is repeated 35 times," or the like. *See* RUN LENGTH ENCODING. A more thorough form of data compression involves using codes of different lengths for different character sequences so that the most common sequences take up less space.

Most text files can be compressed to about half their normal size. Digitized images can often be compressed to 10 percent of their original size (or even more if some loss of fine detail can be tolerated), but machine-language programs sometimes cannot be compressed at all because they contain no recurrent patterns. *See also* ZIP FILE; STUFFIT; JPEG; MPEG; MP3.

data mining the exploration of DATABASES to find patterns in the data. For instance, data mining of the sales records of a supermarket chain can reveal seasonal patterns and hidden relationships between products. The classic example is the discovery that an appreciable number of customers—presumably young fathers—are likely to buy both diapers and beer on Fridays.

data processing the processing of information by computers. This term dates back to the 1960s and often describes the part of a business organization that handles repetitive computerized tasks such as billing and payroll.

Data Protection Act a British law protecting people from misuse of their personal information, enforced by the Information Commissioner's Office (web address: *www.ico.gov.uk*).

data rate *see* BAUD.

data recovery the art and technique of recovering part or all of the information lost because of accidental deletion or damage to the storage media.

The simplest kind of data recovery is to pull files back out of the Windows RECYCLE BIN or Macintosh TRASH. Special software can retrieve any deleted file that resided on an area of disk that has not yet been overwritten (*see* RECOVERING ERASED FILES).

If the disk or other storage medium has been damaged, data recovery can still be done by technicians who can replace parts of disk drives, adjust them to read poorly recorded tracks, and the like. There are also utilities for recovering lost data on FLASH MEMORY CARDS whose directories have become corrupted.

data structures ways of arranging information in the memory of a computer. In computer programming, it is often necessary to store large numbers of items in such a manner as to reflect a relationship between them. The three basic ways of doing this are the following:

1. An *array* consists of many items of the same type, identified by number. The examination scores of a college class might be represented as an array of numbers. A picture can be represented as a large array of brightness readings, one for each of the thousands of cells into which the picture is divided.

2. A *record* (in C, a struct) consists of items of different types, stored together. For example, the teacher's record of an individual student might consist of a name (character data), number of absences (an integer), and a grade average (a floating-point number). Records and arrays can be combined. The teacher's records of the entire class form an array of individual records; each record might contain, among other things, an array of test scores.

3. A *linked list* is like an array except that the physical memory locations in which the items are stored are not necessarily consecutive; instead, the location of the next item is stored alongside each item. This makes it possible to insert items in the middle of the list without moving other items to make room. More complex linked structures, such as *trees*, can be constructed by storing more than one address with each item.

4. An *object*. *See* OBJECT; OBJECT-ORIENTED PROGRAMMING.

See ARRAY; LINKED LIST; RECORD.

data type a kind of information that can be represented in a computer program, such as whole numbers, floating-point numbers, Boolean values (true and false), characters, strings, and pointers. In most programming languages, the type of each variable must be declared before the variable can be used. Some languages such as Lisp, Prolog, and Visual Basic allow some or all variables to take on values of any type.

In many programming languages, programmers can define their own types, either as subranges of existing types (e.g., numbers between 0 and 23), or as DATA STRUCTURES combining smaller units of information. In

OBJECT-ORIENTED PROGRAMMING, user-defined types can have procedures (called METHODS) associated with them.

database a collection of data stored on a computer storage medium, such as a disk, that can be used for more than one purpose. For example, a firm that maintains a database containing information on its employees will be able to use the same data for payroll, personnel, and other purposes. *See* DATABASE MANAGEMENT.

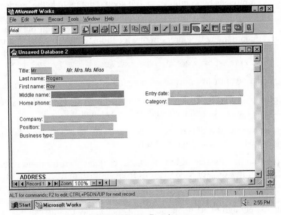

FIGURE 71. Database

database management the task of storing data in a database and retrieving information from that data. Some examples of database applications include maintaining employee lists and preparing payrolls; maintaining parts order lists and keeping track of inventories; maintaining customer lists and preparing bills for credit customers; and keeping track of the students at a school.

Information in a database system is generally stored in several different files. For example, a business will often have a file of regular customers and a file of employees. Each file consists of a series of records, each representing one person or one transaction. Each record consists of several fields, with each field containing an individual data item. For example, in an employee file there would be one record for each employee, and there would be a field containing the person's name, a field for the address, and so on.

The main purpose of a database management system is to make it possible to obtain meaningful information from the data contained in the database. Here are some general functions that a database management system should be able to fulfill:

1. Sort the records (in alphabetical order, or some other relevant order).

2. Set up selection criteria that allow you to examine only the records that meet a specific condition.
3. Count the number of records that meet a specific condition.
4. Perform calculations, such as the year-to-date pay for each employee.
5. Connect information from more than one file. A very important rule is to make sure you don't need to enter the same information in more than one place. A file of payroll transactions should list employees by id number, and it should not include the employee's address—that information should be in a separate file listing employee information. If the employee moves, you only need to update the new address in one location, and every time that information is needed it will be found by referencing the correct file.

See also ACCESS; RELATIONAL DATABASE; SQL.

datagram a PACKET of information transmitted by NETWORK.

dataplan a service from a wireless provider that includes transmittal of data, such as text messaging and web browsing.

daughterboard, daughtercard a small circuit board that plugs into a larger one. *Contrast* MOTHERBOARD.

day trading the practice of buying stocks or other securities and reselling them within a day (or less) to profit from short-term fluctuations. Before the Internet, day trading was possible only by spending all your time at a stockbroker's office; otherwise you would not see market results quickly enough to act upon them. Nowadays, day trading can be carried out online. *See* ONLINE TRADING.

Dazed and confused. . . an error message displayed by some versions of LINUX upon encountering an apparent hardware failure.

dB abbreviation for DECIBEL.

DB-9, DB-15, DB-25 designations for the kind of connectors commonly used on serial ports, video cards, and parallel ports respectively, with 9, 15, or 25 pins. The suffix P means "plug" and S means "socket;" thus a DB-25P has 25 pins and a DB-25S has 25 holes. *See* VGA CONNECTOR.

DB2 popular database management software from IBM (see *www-306.ibm.com/software/data/db2*).

dBm power level in decibels relative to a level of one milliwatt; used to measure signal strength on telephone lines. *See* DECIBEL.

DBMS (**DataBase Management System**). *See* DATABASE MANAGEMENT.

DCOM (**Distributed Component Object Model**) a Microsoft-developed standard for allowing software components to interact with each other over a network. For an alternative standard, *see* CORBA and COM.

DDoS (**D**istributed **D**enial **of** **S**ervice) a DENIAL-OF-SERVICE ATTACK conducted through a large set of attackers at widely distributed locations. This is often done by distributing a computer virus that will turn its victims into ZOMBIES that carry out the attack.

DDR
1. (describing computer memory) (**d**ouble **d**ata **r**ate) term used to describe a type of SDRAM computer memory that gives faster performance by transmitting data on both the rising and the falling edges of each clock pulse. *See* SDRAM.
2. (**D**ance **D**ance **R**evolution) a popular game for the Sony Playstation, Nintendo Wii, and other game machines, in which the player dances on a platform that senses his or her movements. Introduced in 1998, it was one of the first video games to incorporate real exercise.

DDR 2, DDR3 higher-speed versions of DDR SDRAM. *See* DDR (definition 1).

de-Bayerization, de-Bayering the act of decoding an image from a BAYER MATRIX to a full-color picture.

de facto standard a standard that is not official but is established by widespread usage.

dead link an HTML address that is no longer valid. When a dead link is selected, the browser returns an error message.
   Dead links are the result of the target web page having moved to a new location, an HTML programming error (usually a mistyped filename), or the server being overloaded. Try the link again later when the Internet is not as busy. If you still get an error message, you may want to e-mail the appropriate WEBMASTER about the dead link.

dead start *see* BOOT.

deadlock a situation in which each of two processes is waiting for the other to do something; thus, neither one can proceed. *See* MULTITASKING.

Debian a distribution of Linux and a wide variety of free application software originated by **Deb**ra and **Ia**n Murdock (hence the name). It is one of the most popular Linux distributions. For more information, or to download Debian free of charge, see *www.debian.org*. *See also* LINUX; UBUNTU.

deblurring the use of digital image processing to correct a blurred image. In order for this to be possible, the exact nature of the blur must be known; sometimes it can be inferred from the appearance of a small, bright object in the picture. *See* IMAGE PROCESSING; SHARPEN.

debug
1. to remove errors (bugs) from a computer program. *See* BUG.
2. to run a computer program one step at a time while monitoring the values of variables, in an attempt to diagnose errors. *See* DEBUGGER.

debugger a software tool for running programs one step at a time and examining the contents of memory.

DEC *see* DIGITAL EQUIPMENT CORPORATION.

deca- metric prefix meaning ×10(= 10¹). *Deca-* is derived from the Greek word for "ten." *See* METRIC PREFIXES.

deci- metric prefix meaning ÷10. *Deci-* is derived from the Latin word for "ten." *See* METRIC PREFIXES.

decibel (dB) a unit of relative loudness or power; one tenth of a *bel* (a unit named for Alexander Graham Bell and now rarely used). Decibels are used in three ways:

1. to express the ratio of two power levels:

$$dB = 10 \log_{10} \frac{\text{first power level}}{\text{second power level}}$$

For example, multiplying power by 2 is equivalent to adding about 3 decibels; multiplying power by 10 is equivalent to adding 10 decibels; and multiplying by 100 is equivalent to adding 20 decibels.

2. to express the ratio of two voltage levels:

$$dB = 20 \log_{10} \frac{\text{first voltage level}}{\text{second voltage level}}$$

Because power is proportional to the square of voltage, this is equivalent to the previous formula if both voltages are driving the same load impedance.

3. to describe the loudness of a sound, expressed in decibels relative to the threshold of human hearing. Clearly audible sounds range from about 20 to 100 dB; those much above 100 dB are painful to the ears.

decimal number a number expressed in ordinary base-10 notation, using the digits 0, 1, 2, 3, 4, 5, 6, 7, 8, 9, whether or not there are any digits to the right of the point. For example, 3.14 is a decimal number, and so is 314.

declare to state the attributes of a variable, such as its DATA TYPE.

decoder a circuit that recognizes a particular pattern of bits. Decoders are used in computers in order to recognize instructions and addresses. Figure 72 shows a decoder that recognizes the bit pattern 1101.

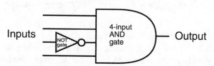

FIGURE 72. Decoder for the bit pattern 1101

decryption decoding—that is, translating information from an unreadable or secret format into a form in which it can be used. *Contrast* ENCRYPTION.

DeCSS a program making it possible to copy DVDs encrypted by CSS. It was developed by 15-year-old Norwegian Jon Johansen, working with other hackers, who was tried but acquitted of criminal charges in Norway. *See* DMCA.

dedicated assigned to only one function. For instance, a dedicated phone line is one that is always connected to the same equipment.

Deep Blue chess playing computer developed by IBM that beat grandmaster Gary Kasparov in 1997. *See* ARTIFICIAL INTELLIGENCE.

deep packet inspection the act of investigating the content of data packets sent over the Internet. For example, Internet service providers can learn more about their customers, but the process raises significant privacy concerns.

default an assumption that a computer makes unless it is given specific instructions to the contrary. For example, a word processing program may start out assuming a particular default combination of margins, page length, and so on, which the user can change by issuing specific commands.

default directory *see* CURRENT DIRECTORY.

default drive *see* CURRENT DRIVE.

default logic (defeasible logic) a formal system of reasoning in which some facts or rules have priority over others. For example, statements about ostriches might have priority over statements about birds because an ostrich is a specific kind of bird. It is then possible to say without contradiction that birds fly, but ostriches don't fly. In classical logic, "birds fly" and "ostriches are birds" together with "ostriches don't fly" is a contradiction. Default logic is often used in expert systems. *See* EXPERT SYSTEM. *Contrast* FUZZY LOGIC; CONFIDENCE FACTOR. *See also* BOOLEAN ALGEBRA.

Default.asp, Default.htm, Default.html in Microsoft's web server software, the file name that is used for a WEB PAGE when no file name is specified in the URL. It has the same role as the more common file name *index.html*. *See* INDEX.HTML.

defeasible logic *see* DEFAULT LOGIC.

deform (3D program) to digitally manipulate an on-screen object so that it is twisted or stretched. Some programs allow you to deform objects interactively; other transformations are done with FILTERS that can distort or break up the object during an animation.

degauss to demagnetize. Color CRTs need to be degaussed when they show areas of weak or incorrect color. Some monitors degauss themselves every time they are turned on.

degree measure a way of measuring the size of angles in which a complete rotation has a measure of 360 degrees (written as 360°). A right angle is 90°. *Contrast* RADIAN MEASURE.

DejaNews a SEARCH ENGINE for Usenet NEWSGROUPS, formerly located at *www.deja.com* but now incorporated into Google (*google.com*) as "Groups." It contains permanent copies of almost all newsgroup postings since 1981. The name DejaNews was a pun on French *déjà vu* "already seen."

Del the DELETE key on a computer keyboard.

delegate (in C#) a variable whose value is a METHOD; more precisely, an OBJECT that contains or points to a method, allowing one method to be passed as a parameter to another. Delegates serve the same function in C# as function pointers in C.

delete to remove an unwanted item (character, word, art, file). *See* RECOVERING ERASED FILES for help on restoring deleted files.

delimiter a character that marks the beginning or end of a special part of a computer program. For instance, /* and */ are delimiters marking the beginning and end of a comment in C. In many programming languages, quotation marks are used as delimiters to mark character strings. *See also* TEXT TO COLUMNS.

Delphi an object-oriented version of the programming language PASCAL for developing interactive programs under Windows. Delphi was designed by Anders Hejlsberg, who also developed TURBO PASCAL and C# (web address: www.embarcadero.com/products/delphi).

demibold a typeface weight between ordinary type and boldface. Sometimes just called *demi*. *See* WEIGHT.

demon *see* DAEMON.

denial-of-service attack a malicious attack on a computer whose purpose is to interfere with the computer's normal functioning, rather than to gain services for oneself or steal confidential data. Denial-of-service attacks are often launched by people who are frustrated at not being able to break into a computer, or who are angry at the target computer's users or administrators. Often the attackers do not realize they are disrupting service for everyone, not just for a single intended victim. For examples, see MAIL BOMBING; PING FLOODING. *See also* COMPUTER SECURITY; DDOS.

deployment the act of installing software on computers.

deprecated a software feature from a previous version that still exists in the current version, but the developers recommend that it no longer be used (likely because a newer feature has been introduced).

depth of field the ability of a picture to show objects at different distances in focus at the same time. Depth of field is greater at smaller apertures (higher-numbered f-ratios). *See* F-RATIO.

depth of focus tolerance of focusing errors; like DEPTH OF FIELD but referring to variation in the way the camera is focused, rather than variation in the distance of the subject.

DES (**D**igital **E**ncryption **S**tandard) an encryption system using 56-bit keys in a complicated 16-round substitution process. It was the U.S. government standard before the adoption of AES. *See* ENCRYPTION.

descender the part of a character that extends below the baseline. For instance, the letter *p* has a descender; the letter *o* does not. *See* ASCENDER; TYPEFACE.

FIGURE 73. Descenders

deselect to tell the computer you do not want to work with a particular object. There are minor differences in how different software does this, but clicking on the background or another object will usually deselect the current object. If you want to select multiple objects, you can hold down Ctrl while clicking on the desired objects. This allows you to select as many items as you want. To deselect just one item of a group, click on it again while continuing to hold Ctrl. If you are choosing between mutually exclusive options in a dialog box, choosing one button will clear the others (*see* RADIO BUTTONS; OPTION BUTTONS).

Hint: If you wish to select all but one or two objects in a drawing, the fastest way is to "Select All" (either by using the edit menu option or by MARQUEE SELECT), and then deselect the unwanted objects.

deskew to straighten; to undo the effects of a SKEW command.

desktop the whole computer screen, representing your workspace. You manipulate objects (ICONS) with the mouse in much the same way that you work with papers and other objects on your physical desktop.

On the Macintosh, the desktop is also a special file containing information about the arrangement of icons, the programs you are using, and the like. This information is saved whenever you shut the computer down and retrieved when you turn it on again.

In Windows, the desktop is a special directory for each user. It normally contains many SHORTCUTS to program files in other locations. The shortcuts are represented by files with the extension .1nk.

The desktop is not identical with the ROOT DIRECTORY of a disk; it is more like a directory containing everything on the computer, including the disk drives. In Windows, the disk drives are accessed through a desktop icon called "Computer."

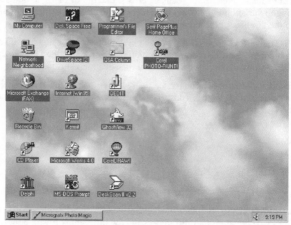

FIGURE 74. Desktop (Windows)

desktop publishing the use of personal computers to design and print professional-quality typeset documents. A desktop publishing program such as Adobe InDesign or QuarkXpress is much more versatile than a word processing program; in addition to typing documents, the user can specify the layout in great detail, use multiple input files, have comprehensive typographic control, insert pictures, and prepare the publication for printing or electronic distribution.

The distinction between word processing and desktop publishing is becoming blurred. Most word processing programs can produce elegantly typeset documents that include extensive graphics. The major difference is that desktop publishing programs allow objects to be placed in a particular location on the page, whereas word processors treat the text and graphics linearly. This gives the desktop publisher the tools necessary for handling more complex works and allows more emphasis on the publication's design.

A subcategory of desktop publishing is ELECTRONIC PUBLISHING, that is to say the production of publications that are meant to be viewed on screen rather than printed. These electronic documents are distributed by computer networks (*see* WORLD WIDE WEB), E-MAIL, or CD-ROMS. An electronic document may have sound, music, illustrations, animations, video clips, or HYPERTEXT links (special buttons or keywords that jump the reader to a new text or picture).

Desktop, Active *see* ACTIVE DESKTOP.

/dev in UNIX, the directory that contains links to specific devices such as disk drives and serial and parallel ports.

device any component of a computer that is used for input or output, such as a printer, modem, disk drive, or sound card.

device contention the situation in which several computer programs, running concurrently, are trying to use the same device (such as a modem or printer) at the same time. Multitasking operating systems handle contention in a number of different ways, such as SPOOLING output for printers, making a program wait until the requested device is available, or simply denying access to a device that is already in use.

device driver a program that extends the operating system in order to support a specific device, such as a disk or tape drive, video card, or printer.
   Device drivers are a very important part of Microsoft Windows. They insulate application programs from the hardware so that, for example, the manufacturer of a word processing program does not have to know what kind of printer you are going to be using, and if a new printer is invented in the future, you can use it even if it wasn't anticipated when the program was written. Installation of device drivers usually happens automatically when hardware or software is installed; you can also add and remove device drivers from the Control Panel (*see* CONTROL PANEL; PLUG AND PLAY).

device ID a unique name given to a hardware device for use by PLUG AND PLAY and the Windows REGISTRY.

device node a directory entry, similar to the directory entry for a file but identifying a piece of hardware. Under UNIX, device nodes are found in the directory /dev.

/dev/null in UNIX, a "device" that is actually a place for discarding data. Anything written to /dev/null is discarded, and any software that attempts to read from /dev/null is told that no data is available. You can specify /dev/null in places where a filename is required but no data will actually be read or written. *Compare* BIT BUCKET.

dewarp to straighten; to undo the effects of a WARP manipulation.

DHCP (**D**ynamic **H**ost **C**onfiguration **P**rotocol) a protocol for assigning an IP ADDRESS to each computer automatically as it joins the network, for use as long as it remains connected, rather than assigning a permanent IP address in advance. *See* LEASE; PROTOCOL.

Dhrystone *see* MIPS.

dial-up networking computer networking that relies on communication through ordinary telephone lines via MODEM.

dialog box a window that appears in order to collect information from the user. When the user has filled in the necessary information or clicked on the appropriate buttons, the dialog box disappears. Figure 75 shows a dialog box containing several different kinds of elements. There is almost always an OK button for the user to click after filling in the information. *See also* CHECK BOX; LIST BOX; OPTION BUTTONS; TEXT BOX.

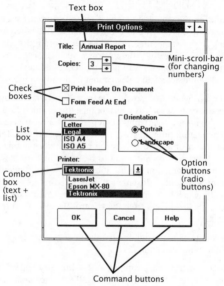

FIGURE 75. Dialog box

dictionary attack an attempt to guess a computer password by trying every word in a large dictionary and, often, every combination of letters that would make a pronounceable word.

die (plural **dice** or **die**) the individual piece of silicon containing a transistor or integrated circuit. A memory cache located "on die" is one on the same piece of silicon as the CPU.

digerati *(slang, plural)* people knowledgeable about the Web and other digital communications media. (From *digital* and Italian *litterati*.)

digital representing information as electrical "on" and "off" signals that correspond to binary digits and can be stored in computer memory. Digital electronics contrasts with analog electronics, which represents information with signals that vary within a predefined range. Digital signals have two advantages: they can be copied exactly, without even the slightest loss of quality, and they can be further processed by computer. *See also* DIGITAL COMPUTER.

digital audio sound represented in digital form. *See* DIGITAL MUSIC; MP3; SAMPLING RATE; WAVE FILE.

digital camera a camera that takes pictures with a CCD IMAGE SENSOR or CMOS image sensor and transmits them directly to a computer or records them on a memory card without using film.

The most important specification of a digital camera is the number of PIXELS in the image. To show as much detail as a good 35-mm slide, a digital image requires about 2000×3000 pixels. A much lower resolution is sufficient for snapshots. The image on a TV screen is equivalent to about 400×600 pixels. *See* MEGAPIXEL (table). *See also* AV; BAYER MATRIX; CCD IMAGE SENSOR; CMOS IMAGE SENSOR; COLOR; DEPTH OF FIELD; DEPTH OF FOCUS; DSLR; EV; FOCAL LENGTH; FOVEON; F-RATIO; IMAGE PROCESSING; PHOTOGRAPH; TV.

digital computer a computer that represents information in discrete form, as opposed to an analog computer, which allows representation to vary along a continuum. For example, the temperature of a room might be any value between $0°$ and $100°F$. An analog computer could represent this as a continuously varying voltage between 0.00 and 1.00 volts. In contrast, a digital computer would have to represent it as a decimal or binary number with a specific number of digits (e.g., 68.80 or 68.81).

All modern, general-purpose computers are digital. Analog computer circuits are, however, frequently used in industrial control equipment.

A digital computer is more accurate than an analog computer because it only needs to sense the difference between clearly distinguishable states. For example, a slight voltage fluctuation would affect the result in an analog computer, but a slight voltage fluctuation would not affect a digital computer because the computer could still easily distinguish the 0 state from the 1 state of any circuit element. For the same reason, digital music reproduction (e.g., a compact disc) is more accurate than analog reproductions (e.g., a traditional record).

digital divide the division of the world into those that have access to computers and the Internet and those that are too poor to afford that access.

Digital Equipment Corporation (DEC) a company whose products included the PDP-8, PDP-11, and VAX minicomputers, the VT-100 terminal, and the Alpha microprocessor. In 1998, Digital Equipment Corporation was acquired by Compaq, which became part of Hewlett-Packard.

digital film the memory cards or other storage devices used in digital cameras. Unlike real photographic film, the brand of digital film does not affect the quality of the picture or the amount of light required to make it. The digital memory device simply records whatever the camera gets.

digital image processing *see* IMAGE PROCESSING.

Digital Millennium Copyright Act *see* DMCA.

digital music music signals that have been converted to numbers that are stored electronically. A musical sound wave is continuous, but it can be represented by numbers that give the amplitude of the wave at each moment in time, as long as the sound is sampled often enough to seem continuous. *See* SAMPLING RATE. A music CD stores sound digitally (as opposed to a traditional vinyl record, which stored sound in analog format by the variations in the groove.) Music files can also be stored on a computer hard disk, but the file representing a song is too large to do this conveniently unless it has been compressed. The development of MP3 compression led to a boom in digital music as people stored music on computer hard disks and digital players such as the IPOD. However, rampant file sharing through services such as NAPSTER and GROKSTER led to court cases that restricted the use of these services. *See also* P2P; AAC; M4A; SOUND; CARD; WAVE FILE; WAVETABLE SYNTHESIS; MIDI; WMA; OGG VORBIS; ITUNES.

digital photo frame a device that displays one or more digital pictures in succession, over and over, without being constantly connected to a computer. The pictures are delivered to it on a memory card or by temporarily connecting to a computer using USB or network connections.

digital picture frame *see* DIGITAL PHOTO FRAME.

digital signal processing (DSP) the use of computers to process signals such as sound or video. Applications of DSP include decoding modulated signals (e.g., in modems), removing noise, and converting video to different formats.

digital signature a way of authenticating that an electronic message really came from the person it claims to have come from. A digital signature can be encrypted with your PRIVATE KEY. The recipient can decrypt the message with your PUBLIC KEY to verify that it is really you. Nobody who does not know your private key could create a signature that would correctly decrypt with your public key. However, the digital signature cannot be sent by itself, because then someone could simply copy the encrypted version. Instead, the signature needs to be sent as part of an ABSTRACT (or MANIFEST or digest) of a particular message. The recipient can check to make sure that the hash function given in the manifest matches the hash function calculated from the message. If someone tampered with the original message (so they could attach their own message to your digital signature), the mismatch would be detected.

digital television transmission of video signals to the viewer as digital data rather than as analog signals. Digital television can be delivered by cable or by antenna. In the United States, government regulators have required all full-power broadcasters to switch to digital by February 2009, although analog signals remained available in cable systems and from low-power transmitters, and older television receivers can receive digital signals by antenna through a converter box. Other countries, such as Luxembourg and the Netherlands, went all-digital as early as 2006. Analog television consumed about 6 MHz of bandwidth, so a large amount of spectrum became free when this transition happened. (Most radio signals continue to be analog.)

Digital signals can, but need not, be high-definition (*see* HDTV, SDTV). As with other kinds of digital communication, digital TV signals are almost useless if they are not strong enough to give perfect reception; it is no longer possible to make the best of a weak signal or poor antenna by tolerating a snowy picture and noisy audio. *See also* NTSC; PAL; SECAM.

digital-to-analog converter an electronic circuit that converts digital information (binary numbers) into voltages at specific levels. DACs are used to generate sound and video signals. *Contrast* ANALOG-TO-DIGITAL CONVERTER.

digital zoom a change in the field of view of a digital camera achieved by discarding outer parts of the image and using only the center. Although it is displayed enlarged, the zoomed image actually has no more resolution than if it were not zoomed, since you are still looking at the same pixels. *Contrast* OPTICAL ZOOM. *See also* RESAMPLE; INTERPOLATION (definition 2).

digitize to convert input into a form that can be processed by a computer. *See* FRAME GRABBER; OCR; SCANNER.

digitized music music represented as computer data, either by recording the sound waves themselves or by storing a musical score in digital form. *See* DIGITAL MUSIC.

dimensions (of an array) the different directions in which elements can be counted. Each dimension corresponds to one subscript. A list of objects is a one-dimensional array, while a table is a two-dimensional array. *See* ARRAY.

DIMM (**d**ual **i**nline **m**emory **m**odule) a memory module similar to a SIMM but with different signals on the two sides of the tiny circuit board. DIMMs usually have 168 pins; compared to SIMMs, they allow more memory to be installed in fewer sockets. *See* SIMM.

FIGURE 76. DIMM (dual inline memory module)

dimmed not available for selection. If a menu option appears in light gray rather than black type, it cannot be chosen. For example, if you wish to align two objects, the align command will be dimmed until you have two or more objects selected. If you click on a dimmed command, nothing happens. *See* Figure 77.

FIGURE 77. Dimmed (disabled) selections on menu

DIN paper sizes *see* PAPER SIZES.

dingbats special characters that are neither letters nor mathematical symbols, such as ‡ ♠ ♥ ◊ ♣ ↔. *See also* FLEURON.

dining philosophers a situation in which a DEADLOCK problem might arise, named after an imaginary situation with a group of philosophers at a table. Each philosopher needs to wait for another one to make resources available before being able to eat.

diode a semiconductor device that allows electric current to pass in one direction, but not in the other. Diodes are formed by joining two types of doped semiconductors: P type, with a deficiency of free electrons (and an excess of holes), and N type, with a surplus of free electrons. (*See* SEMICONDUCTOR.) The place where the two regions are joined is called the junction.

Electrons can flow from N-type to P-type material, but not the other way. The diode is said to be *forward-biased* when the voltage across it is in the right direction to make it conduct, and *reverse-biased* when the voltage is applied in the opposite direction. The diode is forward biased when a negative voltage is applied to the N region and a positive voltage to the P region; then free electrons in the N region are driven to the junction where they combine with holes from the P region. If a positive voltage is applied to the N region, electrons are pulled away from the junction and no current can flow (the diode is reverse biased).

See also ELECTRONIC CIRCUIT DIAGRAM SYMBOLS; LED; TRANSISTOR.

DIP (**d**ual **in**-line **p**ackage) a plastic case with two rows of pins (Fig. 78), the way integrated circuits (ICs) were packaged in the early days of personal computers. Most ICs now come in smaller packages which mount on the surface of a printed-circuit board rather than by placing pins into holes.

DIP switch a miniature switch or set of switches in the same size package as a DIP integrated circuit. *See* DIP.

FIGURE 78. DIP (dual in-line package) integrated circuits

dir the command, under Windows command line, that makes the computer display all the files in a particular directory. For example,

    dir

by itself lists the files in the current directory of the current disk. Here are some other examples:

dir a:	Current directory of drive A
dir a:\mystuff	Directory MYSTUFF of drive A
dir \mystuff	Directory MYSTUFF of the current disk
dir mystuff	Subdirectory MYSTUFF under the current directory of the current disk

To see a directory of all of the files on the current drive that have names ending in .doc, type

    dir *.doc

The asterisk acts as a "wild card," matching any string. *See* LS for UNIX equivalent.

direct-to-press a method of production where a machine similar to a laser printer takes data directly from a computer to produce film or plates for a printing press without the intermediate step of printing out camera-ready copy.

direct(ly) attached storage (DAS) disk drives or other storage devices that are connected directly to the computer that uses them, rather than connected through a network. *Contrast* DISK SHARING; FILE SHARING; NETWORK ATTACHED STORAGE.

directory a table where the names and locations of files are stored. A disk can, and usually does, contain more than one directory; directories can contain other directories.

On the Macintosh and in Windows, directories are called *folders*. Directories are pictured as tree structures or boxes within boxes (Figure 79).

Directories are a way of classifying files; they do not divide the disk itself into sections. Any file can use as much space as needed, anywhere on the disk, regardless of what directory it is in.

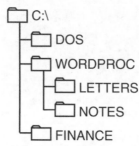

FIGURE 79. Directories (shown graphically)

DirectX an optional add-on animation and sound subsystem for Microsoft Windows, required by certain games and other software that needs higher graphics performance than can be obtained through normal operating system services. DirectX is available as a free download from Microsoft and is updated frequently. *See also* DXDIAG.

dirty *(slang)* needing to be written to disk or needing to be updated in some way.

disassembler a program that converts machine instructions into assembly language so that a human being can read them.

disc a compact disc (CD) or digital video disc (DVD). *See* DISK and usage note there.

disclaimer a statement absolving someone (or even oneself) of responsibility. The so-called "usual disclaimer" on e-mail messages is roughly, "These are not the opinions of my employer or the organization that transmits this message for me." Many people abbreviate this to "usual disclaimer applies." The disclaimer is unnecessary unless there is something about the e-mail message that would specifically cause people to misunderstand it.

discrete speech speech that is spoken with pauses between words to make it easier for a computer to recognize. *Contrast* CONTINUOUS SPEECH. *See* SPEECH RECOGNITION.

discretionary hyphen a hyphen that is used only when the word falls near the end of a line; sometimes called a SOFT HYPHEN. By specifying where you want the word to be broken, you override the word processor's automatic hyphenation. *Contrast* REQUIRED HYPHEN; HARD HYPHEN.

disk a round, flat device for storing computer data. There are three main kinds: HARD DISKS, OPTICAL DISKS (of which CD-ROMs are the most common kind), and DISKETTES.

    Hard disks are rigid disks coated with iron oxide. Microcomputers come with a hard disk permanently mounted within the computer, and external hard disks can be used to back up the internal hard disk. Hard drive capacities have increased dramatically since their introduction. Modern hard drives typically store hundreds of gigabytes.

    The iron oxide on the disk consists of microscopically small needles, each of which acts like a tiny bar magnet. Information is stored by magnetizing these needles. The read-write head, which skims the surface of the disk, can either generate a magnetic field to magnetize the needles or detect the magnetic field of needles that are already magnetized. The binary digits 0 and 1 are represented by changes in the direction of magnetization.

    Data on disks is stored in many concentric circles, each of which is called a *track*. Each track is divided into *sectors*, which are the smallest units that the computer can read into memory in a single step. On a double-sided or multilayer disk pack, the set of tracks in corresponding positions on different layers is known as a cylinder.

    The *directory* of a disk is a special area in which the computer records the names and locations of all the files on the disk. The user can create many directories on a single disk.

    Optical disks store information by etching a transparent plastic medium with a laser beam. *See* CD-ROM; CD-R; CD-RW; DVD.

    Diskettes are made of flexible plastic coated with iron oxide. They were the main storage medium during the first couple of decades of microcomputer use but they are less common now. There were two sizes: $5\frac{1}{4}$ inches and $3\frac{1}{2}$ inches.

    Usage note: This word is often spelled *disc* when referring to compact discs (CDs), DVDs, and laser discs, but is always spelled *disk* when referring to magnetic disks and diskettes. The difference in spelling probably reflects the European origin of the CD.

disk drive a device that enables a computer to read (and, in most cases, write) data on disks. Microcomputers typically contain one hard disk drive and one or more CD or DVD drives. *See* DISC and DISK.

disk farm *(slang)* a room full of disks; a large set of disk drives used by a single computer or network.

disk server a computer that performs DISK SHARING. *Contrast* FILE SERVER.

disk sharing the use of networking to allow a computer to use a disk drive that is located in another computer, and to format and control it as if it were locally attached, without relying on the server to own and manage files. Disk sharing is essentially the same thing as a storage area network (SAN). *Contrast* FILE SHARING, NAS.

diskette a removable flexible magnetic disk on which computer programs and data can be stored. *See* DISK.

diskless workstation a computer that has no disk drive of its own, downloading the operating system and all software and data files through a network.

display panel a small panel that displays information on a piece of equipment that does not have a screen. For example, a laser printer often has a display panel that can display the status of print jobs.

dissolve *see* TRANSITION EFFECT.

Distort a set of Photoshop filters that twist an image. *Glass, Ocean Ripple, Pinch*, and *Wave* are examples of effects that can be applied. *See* Figure 80 for an example.

FIGURE 80. Distort

distribute a drawing program command that places objects evenly over a defined area.

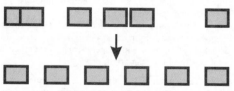

FIGURE 81. Distribute

distributed spread over more than one computer. For example, the WORLD WIDE WEB is a distributed library of information.

distro (*slang*) a distribution (a prepared, ready-to-install or ready-to-use copy) of a piece of free software such as Linux or TEX. Some free software packages are so complex that different people have prepared different ready-to-use distributions of the same software. *See* FREE SOFTWARE; LINUX; TEX.

dithering the representation of an intermediate color by mixing dots of two other colors. (*See* Figure 82.) Hardware limitations make it impossible to print or display all possible colors. Dithering is used to represent shades of gray or colors on a printer or screen that cannot produce them directly.

FIGURE 82. Dithering patterns

DL (describing a DVD or similar disc) double-layer; recorded in two layers from the same side, giving twice as much capacity as a single layer.

DLL (**D**ynamic **L**ink **L**ibrary) a file containing a library of machine-language procedures that can be linked to programs as needed at run time. *See* LINK, definition 3.

DLLs are used in Microsoft Windows. Their practical benefit is that programs don't need to include code to perform common functions because that code is available in the DLL. The program is smaller, and changes can be made once to the DLL routine instead of separately to each program.

DLL Hell (*slang*) in Windows (especially before 2000), the confusing situation that results when more than one DLL file has the same name. If the DLLs are installed in a system directory, then the most recently installed file replaces earlier ones. Since nothing prevents two programmers from choosing the same file name, the conflicting DLLs can be completely unrelated. More often, the conflicting DLLs are different versions of the same file, one newer than the other; in that case, software relying on the file will start up normally, but there will be subtle malfunctions.

In current versions of Windows, various measures are taken to separate DLLs that belong to different programs, and to undo any modifications made to system DLLs. The .NET framework eliminates DLL Hell by tying each application explicitly to its DLLs and allowing multiple versions to coexist.

DLP (**D**igital **L**ight **P**rocessing), a system developed by Texas Instruments for projectors that reflect light off an array of microscopic mirrors. By controlling the fraction of the time that a particular mirror reflects, the brightness of each pixel can be controlled. See *www.dlp.com*.

DMA (**D**irect **M**emory **A**ddressing) the ability of a peripheral device, such as a disk controller, to access the memory of a computer directly, without going through the CPU. DMA makes it possible to transfer information to or from external devices much more quickly than would be possible if the CPU had to handle every byte of information during the transfer.

DMCA (**D**igital **M**illennium **C**opyright **A**ct) a controversial law passed by the U.S. Congress in 1998 designed to secure copyright protection of digital works.

Unlike earlier copyright laws, the DMCA prohibits not only copying, but also the use of technology to get around technical measures designed to prevent copying, even when the copying itself is legal. "No person shall circumvent a technological measure that effectively controls access to a work protected under this title" (17 USC 1201). The law also makes it illegal to distribute circumvention technology but this is hard to enforce.

Critics argue that the DMCA is badly flawed. It prohibits people from experimenting to learn exactly how certain software works even when that software is running on their own computers, and unlike all earlier copyright laws, the DMCA enables copyright owners to block people from reading and viewing material that they possess, not just copying from and redistributing it. *See also* COMPUTER LAW; DECSS.

DNA
1. (**d**eoxyribo**n**ucleic **a**cid) the molecule that carries inherited information in all living things. DNA encodes the sequence of amino acids that form proteins. The data encoding within DNA is somewhat like a computer that uses three-digit base-4 numbers. In this manner, a set of DNA molecules contains the entire plans for building a plant, animal, or human being. Like computer programs, DNA uses begin and end markers to skip past some material.
2. (Windows **D**istributed **In**ternet **A**rchitecture) Microsoft's model for developing distributed computing applications with Windows.

DNG (**D**igital **Neg**ative) a standard file format for photographic images.

DNS
1. (**d**omain **n**ame **s**erver) a server responsible for translating domain addresses, such as *www.example.com*, into IP (Internet Protocol) numbers such as 127.192.92.95. Domain name servers are interconnected so that if the nearest one cannot look up a name, it will query several other servers at various locations. Normally, when a computer is attached to the Internet, the IP address of a DNS has to be given to it as part of the setup information. However, computers that receive IP addresses through DHCP are also given DNS information automatically. *See also* IANA; TLD.
2. (**D**o **N**ot **S**et) a copyediting abbreviation used to mark marginal notations or special typesetting instructions on a manuscript.

DNS prefetching when a web browser looks up the Internet address on the links on a web page as soon as the page is loaded, which saves time if the user subsequently clicks on one of those links. *See* DNS.

do the keyword, in C and related languages, to execute over and over until a condition becomes false, checking the condition at the end rather than at the beginning, so that the loop is guaranteed to execute at least once. Here is an example:

```
/* This is Java; C, C++, C# are very similar */
int i=5;
do
{
  System.out.print(i + " . . . ");
  i- -;
}
while(i > 0);
System.out.println("Finished!");
```

See WHILE for explanation of how this works; the only difference is that even if the condition of the do loop were false at the beginning, the loop would execute once, because the test is not performed until the end. *Compare* REPEAT.

Dock

1. to anchor; to fix into position. Many application programs allow the user to move subordinate windows, such as toolboxes, from their original position to a new location at the top, bottom, or side of the main window, where they snap into place. This is called docking the toolbox.

The Windows taskbar (with "Start" and icons for open applications) is normally docked at the bottom of the screen, but by dragging it with the mouse, you can dock it at the top or either side instead.

2. (in Mac OS X) a panel of animated icons at the bottom of the screen that shows the current active (running) programs, and provides a place for aliases of frequently used files and the Trash. The Dock assumes some of the functions of the Application Menu and FINDER from earlier versions of Mac OS. It is similar to the TASKBAR in Windows.

docking station an accessory that gives a laptop computer additional capabilities when it is used at a fixed location. A typical docking station will include a charger for the laptop's battery, connection to a larger monitor, and possibly additional disk drives or other peripherals.

doctor the version of ELIZA (a simulated psychotherapist) built into the Emacs editor. *See* ELIZA.

document a file containing a text to be printed (e.g., a letter, term paper, or book chapter) or a drawing or other piece of work that a human being is editing with the aid of the computer.

document mode the normal way of typing documents that are to be printed. The word processor includes codes that indicate hyphenation, page breaks, and the like, thereby producing a special word processing file rather than a text file. *See also* NONDOCUMENT MODE; TEXT FILE.

documentation written descriptions of computer programs. Documentation falls into several categories:

1. *Internal documentation*, consisting of comments within the program. (*See* COMMENT.) Internal documentation is addressed mostly to future programmers who may have to make corrections or other modifications.

2. *Online documentation*, information that is displayed as the program runs or that can be called up with a command such as `help`. The user should be able to control the amount of information displayed (more for beginners, and less as the user's experience increases). Also, help commands should be sensitive to the context in which they are invoked; for instance, typing `help` within an editor should call up information about the editor, not the whole operating system.

3. *Reference cards*, containing easily forgotten details for quick reference. A reference card assumes that the user is already familiar with the general principles of the program. Reference cards printed on paper are becoming obsolete, but the same kind of documentation is often made available online.

4. *Reference manuals*, setting out complete instructions for the program in a systematic way. Related information should be grouped together, and a good index should be provided.

5. *Tutorials*, serving as introductions for new users. Unlike a reference manual, a tutorial gives the information in the order in which the user will want to learn it; items are grouped by importance rather than by function or logical category.

Documents and Settings the directory which, in Windows 2000 and later, normally contains a directory for each user account, containing that user's "My Documents" folder and other data. In Windows Vista and later, it was renamed *Users*.

dodge/burn tool a paint program tool that simulates the effects of traditional dodging and burning methods in the photographic darkroom: the burn tool gradually increases the darkness of the area you pass the tool over; likewise, the dodge tool lightens the area.

DOM (**D**ocument **O**bject **M**odel) a system in which a web page is viewed as a collection of objects that can be manipulated by an object-oriented scripting language such as JAVASCRIPT.

domain

1. for a mathematical function, the domain is the set of all allowable values for the input for that function.

2. a portion of the Internet distinguished by a particular final part of the name. For instance, www.covingtoninnovations.com and ftp.

covingtoninnovations.com are two servers in the domain covingtonin-
novations.com, which is a subdomain of .com, its top-level domain
(TLD).

3. in Windows NT and its successors, a group of networked computers
that share a server and a set of user accounts.

domain address an Internet address in conveniently readable form, such as
jones.com, as opposed to the IP ADDRESS, which consists of numbers. *See*
INTERNET.

domain name hijacking *see* DOMAIN NAME POACHING.

domain name hoarding the practice of registering multiple domain names,
some of which will remain unused, simply to prevent a competitor from
using them.

domain name poaching the practice of registering an Internet domain
name with the intention of reselling the domain name rights to a corporation or individual. For example, you might want to register www.ford.com
for yourself in the hope that Ford Motor Company would then buy it
from you. Also called DOMAIN NAME HIJACKING and CYBERSQUATTING.
See also UDDRP, UDRP.

dongle
1. a device that attaches to a computer, typically on a USB port, and
must be present in order to run a particular piece of software, but has no
other purpose. Dongles are used to prevent unauthorized copying. *See*
COPY PROTECTION.
2. a connector that allows a network plug to be connected to a computer,
such as through a USB port.

DoS abbreviation for "Denial of Service." *See* DENIAL-OF-SERVICE ATTACK.

DOS (**D**isk **O**perating **S**ystem) the name of various operating systems
produced by various computer manufacturers, including an early operating system for the IBM 360; the disk operating system for the Apple II
(Apple DOS); MS-DOS, developed by Microsoft for 16-bit microcomputers; PC-DOS, a version of MS-DOS commonly sold with the IBM
PC; and Caldera DOS (formerly DR-DOS), a third-party substitute for
MS-DOS.
    Since 1983 the name DOS has almost always referred to MS-DOS or
equivalent operating systems, as it does throughout this book. *See*
MS-DOS.

dot
1. the character . (period), often used in filenames and Internet
addresses.
2. the decimal point. For example, "nineteen dot two" means 19.2 thousand bytes per second, a standard data transmission rate.

dot-com an Internet address ending in *.com*; more generally, a business that
operates on the Internet. *See* COM.

dots per inch *see* DPI.

double in C and related programming languages, a keyword for declaring DOUBLE PRECISION floating-point numbers.

double buffering
  1. in graphics, the practice of computing the next frame of an animation in memory while the previous frame is being displayed, and then copying the new frame to the screen quickly. That way, the process of drawing each frame on the screen does not produce flicker.
  2. more generally, the use of two buffers (memory areas) to hold data being sent to an output device. One buffer can continue to accept data while the other buffer is being copied from memory to the device.

double-byte font a FONT that uses two bytes (16 bits) to represent each character, thereby allowing more than the 256 characters that could fit into a single-byte font. *See* UNICODE. *Contrast* ASCII, and EBCDIC, which are single-byte character sets.

double-click to depress the button of a mouse twice very rapidly (if the mouse has more than one button, use the leftmost one). This is usually the shortcut to open or launch the selected file. If you find it difficult to double-click quickly enough, you can adjust the mouse's double-click speed. You'll find the mouse adjustments in the Control Panel (Macintosh and Microsoft Windows).

FIGURE 83. Double-click

double dagger the character ‡, which is sometimes used to mark footnotes. *See* FOOTNOTE for more information.

double precision a way of representing floating-point numbers with about twice the number of significant digits used in earlier implementations. Double-precision data types were first implemented in Fortran and later in BASIC and C. Today, "double" is in fact the normal floating-point type in C and its derivatives on most CPUs. *See also* ROUNDING ERROR.

double tap two taps in quick succession on a screen with a multitouch interface.

down not available for use. A computer is said to be down when it malfunctions or when it is being tested or maintained.

downlevel pertaining to an earlier version of a product. For example, Windows Server 2008 supports downlevel clients; that is, client computers attached to the server can run earlier versions of Windows. *Contrast* UPLEVEL.

download to transmit a file or program from a central computer to a smaller computer or a computer at a remote site. See KERMIT; FTP. *Contrast* UPLOAD; SIDELOAD.

downstream (describing data transmission) in a direction from the server to the client, or from the main computer to the peripheral. *Compare* DOWNLOAD. *Contrast* UPSTREAM.

downward compatibility the ability to work with older equipment and/or software than that for which a computer program or accessory was designed. *Contrast* UPWARD COMPATIBILITY.

dpi (**d**ots **p**er **i**nch) the number of pixels or printer dots per linear inch. The first generation of laser printers could print with a resolution of 300 dots per inch. 600- and 1200-dpi laser printers are now available. *See* RESOLUTION for further details.

draft quality a printout in low resolution, unsuitable for CAMERA-READY COPY, but adequate for proofing the copy and checking the placement and alignment of graphics.

drag to move an object using a mouse, touchpad, or touchscreen. To do this, move the pointer to the object, and then hold down the appropriate mouse button (usually the leftmost one) or keep your finger on the pad while moving the pointer. The object will move. When finished, drop the object by releasing the button or taking your finger off the pad.

FIGURE 84. Drag

drag and drop
 1. the ability to move text or graphics by dragging it to a new location with the mouse.
 2. a method of opening a file with a particular application program. Simply pick up a file icon and drag it to the icon of an application program that can open the file.
Compare ASSOCIATE.

drain one of the three regions in a field-effect transistor.

DRAM (**D**ynamic **R**andom-**A**ccess **M**emory, pronounced "D-ram") a computer memory that requires a refresh signal to be sent to it periodically. Almost all computers use DRAM chips for memory. *See* EDO; MEMORY; RAM; RDRAM; SDRAM. *Contrast* SRAM.

draw program a graphics program that operates in terms of lines and shapes. Unlike a paint program, a draw program treats the picture as a collection of objects, each of which will be printed as sharply as the printer can print. Thus, the sharpness of the picture is not limited by the resolution of the screen. Also, individual circles, lines, rectangles, and other shapes can be moved around without affecting other objects they overlap. However, individual pixels cannot be edited. Draw programs are sometimes called *vector graphics* or *object-oriented graphics* programs.

Draw programs are preferred for drawing diagrams, while paint programs are superior for pictorial artwork or correcting photographs. Some popular draw programs include Adobe Illustrator, CorelDraw, and Macromedia Freehand. *Contrast* PAINT PROGRAM.

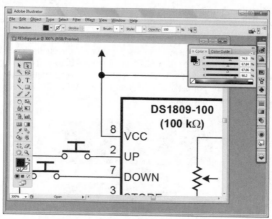

FIGURE 85. Draw program

drill down *(informal)* to follow a series of menus or otherwise reach a piece of information through a series of steps.

drive *see* DISK DRIVE.

drive bay a space in a computer enclosure that can hold a disk drive.

driver *see* DEVICE DRIVER.

drizzle an algorithm to combine digital images while resampling them to a higher resolution, invented by Andrew Fruchter and Richard Hook for processing Hubble Space Telescope data.

The drizzle algorithm gives sharper and smoother results than ordinary resampling. It is called "drizzle" because each input pixel is treated like a drop of water that is to be divided into smaller droplets. Its content is put into output pixels in proportion to the part of its area that falls on each of them.

The key step, however, is that before this is done, each drop is shrunk so that it does not cover the entire original pixel, but only its central portion. In effect, the drizzle algorithm resamples from spots rather than squares. As a result, the larger pixel size of the original images has less of a degrading effect on the output. *See* RESAMPLE.

DRM (**D**igital **R**ights **M**anagement) a system for restricting the use and copying of digital versions of intellectual property (such as music and movies). Several different systems have been used, but determined copyright infringers can find ways around them (since any digital content is subject to being copied by the right hardware). Also, DRM systems may be too restrictive by preventing content purchasers from exercising rights that are allowed under copyright law. Libraries and museums are concerned that in the future, they may not be able to play today's media, even though suitable equipment and software are available, if no one is still in business who can continue to verify the licenses. On the other hand, artists' livelihoods are at risk when their works can be freely copied. *See* COPYRIGHT; DIGITAL MUSIC.

Droid a brand of ANDROID-based smartphone made by Motorola and distributed by Verizon Wireless. *See* ANDROID; SMARTPHONE.

drop cap (drop capital) a large capital letter that occupies more than one line at the beginning of a chapter in a book.

FIGURE 86. Drop caps

drop-down menu a menu that appears when a particular item in a menu bar is selected (*see* Figure 87). Also called a pop-up menu. *See also* MENU BAR; PULL-DOWN MENU.

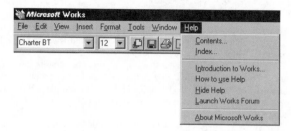

FIGURE 87. Drop-down menu

drum in a LASER PRINTER, the large photosensitive cylinder that receives the image and then transfers it to paper.

To print a page, the drum is first given an electric charge of several thousand volts from the CORONA WIRE to make it repel toner. Then it is scanned with a laser; the points hit by the laser conduct electricity and lose their charge. Finally, fine particles of TONER are applied to the drum; they stick only in the places discharged by the effect of the laser.

Then the drum rolls the image onto the transfer roller, which transfers it to the paper, and the paper is heated by the FUSER to melt the toner particles and make them stick.

Damage to the drum of a laser printer causes streaks and spots that recur on every page. Some printers include a new drum in every toner cartridge; a recycled cartridge may contain a previously used drum. Because the drum is photosensitive, it should not be exposed to bright light.

Drupal content management software for web pages (*see drupal.org/home*).

DSA (**D**igital **S**ignature **A**lgorithm) a U.S. federal standard for digital signatures using public key encryption, developed in 1991 by the National Institute of Standards and Technology. *See* DIGITAL SIGNATURE; ENCRYPTION.

DSL (**D**igital **S**ubscriber **L**ine) any of several ways of transmitting high-speed digital signals over existing telephone lines.

The DSL service usually offered to homes and small businesses provides maximum data rates of 1.5 to 6 Mbps from the Internet to the user and 0.5 Mbps from the user to the Internet.

DSL uses radio-frequency signals in wires that were designed for ordinary audio signals. This makes it possible to provide "always-on," constant network connections, and at the same time, provide ordinary telephone service on the same line.

The strength of the radio-frequency signals falls off rapidly with distance from the DSLAM (DSL Access Multiplexer) at the telephone company's central office (CO). At greater distances, or where signals are weak for other reasons, lower data rates are used, down to 384 kbps downstream. Beyond 15,000 feet from the DSLAM, DSL service is usually not available. However, as demand for DSL increases, telephone companies are quickly installing DSLAMs in wiring boxes along major roads.

The incoming phone line connects to a special DSL modem, which, in turn, is connected to a combined ROUTER and FIREWALL and then to the local area network. Ordinary telephones connect to the same line through one or more filters (*see* DSL FILTER) so that noise-reducing circuitry within the telephones will not absorb and eliminate the DSL signal.

Compare T1 LINE; T3 LINE; ISDN.

DSL filter a device that blocks high-frequency DSL signals from entering ordinary telephone equipment, where they might cause noise on the telephone, or, worse, be absorbed and weakened, interfering with DSL performance elsewhere in the building.

The best place for a DSL filter is where the phone line enters the house. The line should split there; one branch should go through a DSL filter to the rest of the ordinary telephone wiring, and a separate branch should go through high-quality Cat 5 or better cable directly to the DSL modem.

DSL filters can also be installed on individual telephones, preferably at the wall outlet.

DSLAM (DSL Access **M**ultiplexer) a device that joins a high-speed computer network to a set of ordinary telephone lines in a telephone company central office. In order to offer DSL service, a telephone company has to install a DSLAM and give it a fast connection to the Internet, which will be shared by the DSL subscribers.

DSLR (digital **s**ingle-**l**ens **r**eflex) a digital camera that is also an SLR, so that the viewfinder uses the same lens that will take the picture. The mirror that directs light to the viewfinder snaps out of the way when the picture is being taken.

Some lines of DSLRs normally take the same interchangeable lenses as the same manufacturer's film SLRs, but with a different field of view (*see* CROP FACTOR). They are designed for highest-quality professional work.

A disadvantage compared to other digital cameras is that with a DSLR, the LCD screen normally cannot display the picture until it has been taken; only the optical viewfinder works while the picture is being composed. Other digital cameras can display an electronic image continuously. Some newer DSLRs have this capability which is called live focusing or live viewing.

DSP *see* DIGITAL SIGNAL PROCESSING.

DSS (Digital **S**ignature **S**tandard) a federal standard for digital signatures using the Digital Signature Algorithm (DSA).

DTD abbreviation for "**d**ocument **t**ype **d**efinition." *See* XML.

DTMF (**d**ual-**t**one **m**ulti-**f**requency) the signaling system used on push-button telephones. Each signal consists of two tones transmitted simultaneously.

DTV *see* DIGITAL TELEVISION.

dual boot capable of running more than one operating system. Typically, the user chooses the desired operating system at boot-up time.

dual-core having two CPU cores. *See* CORE (definition 1).

dual-core processor two MICROPROCESSORS built into one, in a single package or even on a single chip. *Contrast* HYPER-THREADING, which is the ability of a single processor to follow two instruction streams. The two approaches together allow one processor to do the work of four.

dual monitor two monitors connected to a computer, usually to provide an enlarged screen area where you can drag windows from one screen to the other. Another alternative is to set up the second monitor to duplicate the display of the first monitor, which you may want to do during a presentation with a projector displaying the screen for the group, while you also have a second small monitor you can see while you are facing the group. Windows can automatically set up dual monitors under the display settings in control panel.

dump to transfer data from one place to another without regard for its significance. A dump (on paper) is a printout of the contents of a computer's memory or disk file, shown byte by byte, usually in both hexadecimal and character form. Dumps are usually very hard to read and are used only when there is no other convenient way to get access to the data. Large-scale copying of files from disk to tape, or vice versa, is sometimes referred to as dumping.

DUN *see* DIAL-UP NETWORKING.

duplex
1. printing on both sides of the paper.
2. communication in two directions. *See* HALF DUPLEX; FULL DUPLEX.

Duron a high-speed Pentium-compatible microprocessor made by AMD. *Compare* ATHLON.

dusty deck *(slang)* an ancient, poorly understood computer program that goes back to the days of punched cards; something that is obsolete but has to be kept usable because someone needs it. *Compare* LEGACY.

Dutch auction
1. an auction in which several items, all alike, are being sold at once to the highest bidders. Dutch auctions are popular on eBay and similar online auction services. *See* EBAY.

2. an auction in which, instead of asking for bids, the would-be seller gradually lowers the asking price until someone accepts it. This is rarely done online.

duty cycle the percentage of the time that a piece of equipment is in use or powered on. For example, if the lights in a room are on 8 hours out of every 24, they have a 33.3% duty cycle.

DVD (**D**igital **V**ersatile **D**isc, originally **D**igital **V**ideo **D**isc) an optical disc similar to CD-ROM but with much greater capacity (4.7 GB single-layer, 8.5 GB double-layer). Normally, DVD drives also read CDs. In 2006, an even higher-capacity disc of the same general type, the Blu-Ray disc (BD), was introduced. *See* BLU-RAY DISC.

DVD was introduced in order to store a complete, digitized feature-length movie on a single disc. However, despite "video" in the name, DVD can store any kind of computer data. *See also* CD-ROM.

DVDs can be 8 or 12 cm in diameter (the same as the two sizes of CDs), single- or double-sided, and single- or double-layered. Data DVDs store sets of computer files, which can contain any type of data. Video DVDs, playable in consumer DVD players, are the same types of disc but with a different filesystem designed specifically for video playback.

Video DVD technology includes some controversial measures to protect the copyrights of movies and music. Because movie copyrights have different owners in different countries, some discs include *region codes* to control where the disc can be played. Region codes are also built into the firmware of DVD drives, and regardless of software, most drives will not play a disc from a different region. With some drives, the region code can be changed a few times (in case the drive is sold or used in a country other than the original market), but repeated changes are not possible. Region codes are not encrypted or secret.

More controversial is the Content Scrambling System (CSS), an encryption-based security system. The effect of CSS is to make illegally copied discs unusable, because although the data can be copied, the keys needed to decrypt it do not survive the copying process. This prevents people from making backup copies of their own discs.

An unusual provision of the Digital Millennium Copyright Act makes it illegal to circumvent the CSS algorithm or provide others with tools or information to do so (*see* DMCA). Despite this, the algorithm has been cracked and posted on the Internet (*see* DECSS).

DVD-R a type of DVD designed to be recorded with studio equipment and played in ordinary DVD drives, whether or not it is compatible with home-recorded discs. DVD-R discs are not erasable or rewritable. *Compare* CD-R.

DVD-RAM an older type of recordable, erasable, rewritable DVD. DVD-RAM drives can read ordinary DVD discs, but not vice versa. *Contrast* DVD+RW; DVD-RW.

DVD-ROM a non-erasable DVD, typically one containing computer files rather than audio or video programs. *See* DVD.

DVD+R, DVD-R two types of user-recordable DVDs with similar capacity and performance but different technical specifications, designed to be readable in ordinary DVD drives. Many DVD drives record and play both. DVD+R and DVD-R discs cannot be erased or rewritten. *Compare* CD-R.

DVD+RW, DVD-RW two types of user-recordable and erasable DVDs with similar capacity and performance but different technical specifications. Like DVD+R and DVD-R discs, they are designed to be readable in ordinary DVD drives. Like CD-RW discs, DVD+RW and DVD-RW discs can be erased and rewritten. *Compare* CD-RW.

DVI

1. (**D**igital **V**isual **I**nterface) the newer type of connector for linking computers to monitors and projectors. It carries digital signals as well as the same analog signals as a VGA connector. The connector is roughly rectangular and has room for up to 29 pins, one of which is wide and flat (Fig. 88). *Contrast* VGA CONNECTOR.

2. **d**evice-**i**ndependent output from TEX or LATEX, which can be printed on any printer using the appropriate DVI program.

3. (**D**igital **V**ideo **I**nterface) Intel's file format for storing video on disk.

FIGURE 88. DVI video connector

DVR **d**igital **v**ideo **r**ecorder, a device that records video on digital media, usually DVDs.

dweeb *(slang)* an unsophisticated, untidy, obnoxious person.

dxdiag (**directx diag**nostics) a utility program for testing DirectX under Windows. To run it, go to the Start Menu, choose "Run. . ." and type dxdiag. *See* DIRECTX.

dyadic operation an operation on two numbers (operands). For example, addition, multiplication, subtraction, and division are all dyadic operations because each of them operates on two numbers. Negation is not a dyadic operation because it operates on only one number. *See also* INFIX NOTATION; POSTFIX NOTATION; PREFIX NOTATION.

dye-sublimation printer a type of color printer that gives excellent color images. Dye-sub printouts appear to be continuous-tone images like photographs. Actually they are composed of tiny dots (like laser or thermal-wax printouts), but the dots of dye have spread together. The intense colors, glossy finish, and lack of apparent halftone dots make these printouts especially suitable for fine art prints or presentations.

dynamic IP address an IP address that is assigned to a computer when it actually connects to a network and is not necessarily the same from one session to the next. *Contrast* STATIC IP ADDRESS.

dynamic link library *see* DLL.

dynamic RAM *see* DRAM.

dynamic range the ratio between the smallest and largest signals that a system can handle. For instance, if an analog-to-digital converter can digitize signals from 2 millivolts to 200 millivolts, it has a dynamic range of 100:1.

The dynamic range of an audio system or piece of music is often given in DECIBELS. Dynamic ranges that involve brightness are often given in terms of F-RATIOS or as logarithms to base 10. For instance, if a film scanner can handle a slide or negative whose dark areas transmit only 1/1000 as much light as the bright areas, then its dynamic range of 1000:1 can be described as the logarithmic value 3.0, because $\log_{10} 1000 = 3$.

E

e (in mathematics) an important number whose value is approximately 2.71828. The reason e is important is that the function e^x is its own derivative. In many programming languages, the function exp(x) computes e^x. If $y = e^x$, then x is the natural logarithm of y.

E *see* EXPONENTIAL NOTATION.

e- prefix meaning *electronic,* especially when applied to terms in the context of the Internet or World Wide Web. *See* E-MAIL and E-COMMERCE for examples.
   Usage note: Spelling of *e*-words is not yet standardized, and the new words are often spelled without hyphenation (e.g., *email, ezine*).

e-book a published book that is distributed as a computer file, for viewing on an E-BOOK READER or, sometimes, a conventional personal computer. There are a number of file formats for e-books incorporating various kinds of copy protection. *See also* PDF.

e-book reader a special-purpose TABLET COMPUTER for displaying and reading e-books: it may or may not have other computing capabilities. For example, *see* KINDLE; NOOK. *See also* ELECTRONIC PAPER.

e-commerce *see* ELECTRONIC COMMERCE.

E format *see* EXPONENTIAL NOTATION.

e-ink *see* ELECTRONIC PAPER.

e-mail ELECTRONIC MAIL.

e-mail broadcasting the sending of the same e-mail message sent to many people from one source. Newsletters and SPAM advertisements are both e-mail broadcasts. *See also* MAILING LIST. *Compare* FAX BROADCASTING.

e-paper *see* ELECTRONIC PAPER.

e-reader an E-BOOK READER.

e-tail retail sales conducted on the Internet. For an example, *see* AMAZON. COM.

e-zine, ezine *(slang)* electronically published magazine (i.e., a magazine published on a web page or the like). *See* WORLD WIDE WEB.

ear
   1. the small stroke on the right side of the letter g.
   2. a small box of information on either side of a headline or masthead. In newspapers, an ear is commonly used for the weather forecast.

(A)   (B)

FIGURE 89. (A) Ear, definition 1 (B) Ears, definition 2

Easter egg *(slang)* a hidden part of a computer program. Easter eggs are usually activated only by a bizarre series of actions—then the user is treated to an amusing presentation that usually includes the names of the development team. The actions necessary to see an egg are very complex and would never be performed by a casual user of the program; one has to be looking for the Easter egg. Information about Easter eggs is often spread on the World Wide Web.

eBay *(www.ebay.com)* an online auction house established in 1995 and headquartered in San Jose, California. By acting as an auctioneer, eBay enables individuals to buy and sell almost anything through the World Wide Web.

An online auction has several advantages over a conventional one. Bids on an item can be collected for several days, typically a week, rather than having to be delivered all at once. Perhaps more importantly, the actual bidding can be done by computer. Would-be buyers specify their maximum bids, but the computer places actual bids that are just high enough to outbid the other bidders. Finally, the computer can search quickly through thousands of item descriptions. *See also* DUTCH AUCTION; RESERVE PRICE.

EBCDIC *(pronounced "ebb-see-dik")* (**E**xtended **B**inary **C**oded **D**ecimal **I**nformation **C**ode) the numeric representation of characters on IBM mainframe computers. (*Contrast* ASCII and UNICODE, which are used on most other computers.)

ebook, e-book
  1. a book distributed electronically rather than on paper. *See* PDF.
  2. a special-purpose handheld computer for reading texts of books. *See* IPAD; KINDLE; NOOK.

EC
  1. abbreviation for ELECTRONIC COMMERCE.
  2. abbreviation for European Community.

ECC *see* ERROR-CORRECTING CODE.

ECC RAM random-access memory (RAM) that uses an ERROR-CORRECTING CODE to recover automatically from single errors in data storage, and to detect and report more serious errors.

echo to send information back to where it came from. With computers, this refers to two things:

1. When communicating by modem, a computer echoes typed characters if it sends them to its own screen as well as to the other computer. If you can't see what you're typing, turn echoing on; if what you type appears twice, turn echoing off.

2. In Windows and UNIX, the echo command sends a message to the screen; for example,

```
echo Hello there!
```

writes "Hello there!" on the screen. In a .BAT file, the command echo off tells Windows not to print commands on the screen as they are executed. You can prevent the echo off command itself from being displayed by prefixing it with @, like this:

```
@echo off
```

In fact the @ prevents display of any command, not just echo.

Eclipse a free, open-source interactive development environment (editor, compiler, and debugger) for Java and other programming languages. For further information, see *www.eclipse.org*.

ECPA (Electronic Communications Privacy Act) the main U.S. law against wiretapping and other interception of private electronic communications, whether they are transmitted by wire, radio (including wireless network), or other means. It was passed in 1986 and superseded a number of earlier laws (18 USC 2510).

Critics point out that the ECPA does not require the sender of a message to encrypt (scramble) it to make it private. Thus, private messages can still be intercepted deliberately or even by accident. For example, first-generation analog cellular telephones were assigned to frequencies formerly occupied by UHF TV channels, and they used the same kind of modulation as TV sound. Thus, telephone calls could be picked up on old television sets. Similarly, radio technicians tracking down sources of interference could find themselves hearing things that are illegal to listen to.

On the whole, however, the ECPA is an essential part of the laws protecting computer networks and communication systems from tampering and eavesdropping. It is one of the laws most commonly violated by crackers. *See* COMPUTER LAW; CRACKER; WIRELESS NETWORK.

edge detect a paint program filter or image processing technique that outlines the edges of objects. *See* Figure 90.

EDI *see* ELECTRONIC DATA INTERCHANGE.

edit to examine a file and make changes in it, usually with the aid of an EDITOR.

editor a computer program that enables the user to create, view, and modify text files.

FIGURE 90. Edge detect

EDO (**e**xtended **d**ata **o**ut) a type of dynamic random-access memory (DRAM) that holds its output on the BUS until the beginning of the next bus cycle. This enables the computer to retrieve data from memory in one bus cycle instead of two. (To further gain speed, memory is attached to a fast bus that connects directly to the CPU, rather than the slower bus that connects to expansion cards.) EDO DRAM is often used with Pentium processors. *Contrast* SDRAM.

.edu *See* TLD.

EEPROM (**E**lectrically **E**rasable **P**rogrammable **R**ead-**O**nly **M**emory) a type of memory chip whose contents can be both recorded and erased by electrical signals, but do not go blank when power is removed. (It is called "read-only" because the recording process is too slow to be used more than occasionally.) EEPROM contrasts with permanently recorded ROM chips and with EPROMs that can be programmed electrically but cannot be erased electrically. *See* EPROM; ROM.

effective megapixels the number of megapixels actually used for the image in a digital camera. *Contrast* GROSS MEGAPIXELS.

efficiency the conservation of scarce resources. In order to measure efficiency, you have to decide which resource you want to conserve. For example, one program might be more "efficient" than another if it uses less memory, and another program might be more "efficient" in terms of speed; the question is whether you would rather conserve memory or time.

With computers, some of the most important resources are:
1. computer execution time;
2. computer memory capacity;
3. auxiliary storage capacity (i.e., disk space);
4. programmer's time.

The general rule is: it is more important to work to conserve a resource if it is more scarce. With early computers, which were very slow and had limited memory (compared to computers available now), it was more important to write programs that would not require much memory and would not require as many steps for the computer to execute. Now that computers are faster and have more memory, it is often the case that the programmer's labor is the most scarce resource. This means that it is more efficient to write software in a way that simplifies the programmer's job, even if it uses more computer time and memory. An added benefit is that if the programmer's job is simplified, errors (bugs) are less likely.

egosurfing the practice of entering one's own name into a SEARCH ENGINE to see how many times it turns up. By doing this, one of the authors discovered that there is a professional boxer named Michael Covington.

EIA (Electronic Industries Alliance) an American organization that promotes industrial standards. On older computer equipment, "EIA" often marks an RS-232 or EIA-232D serial port. The EIA web site is at *www.eia.org*.

EIA-232D the new official designation for the RS-232 standard for data communication. *See* RS-232.

EICC (Electronic Industry Citizenship Coalition) a coalition of companies promoting socially responsible practices (web address: *www.eicc.info*).

EIDE (Extended Integrated Device Electronics) a newer type of IDE disk drive and controller that allows a larger number of sectors per track and thereby overcomes the original limit of 528 megabytes per drive.

EISA (Enhanced Industry-Standard Architecture) a standard 32-bit bus for IBM PC-compatible computers using the 386, 486, or Pentium microprocessor. EISA was developed by a group of competitors as an alternative to IBM's Micro Channel, retaining more compatibility with the original (ISA) bus. It has been largely superseded by PCI.

In general, EISA computers can use ISA as well as EISA cards. The extra contacts on the EISA card edge connector are in a second row above the contacts that correspond to those on ISA cards.

See ISA; BUS; PCI.

eject

1. to remove a storage device from a computer.

2. to tell a computer that a storage device is about to be removed. The Eject operation tells the computer to finish writing data to the device immediately. The drive may or may not physically eject the storage device. For example, in Windows it is a good idea to right-click on the icon for a USB flash drive and select "Eject" before removing it. That will make sure that no data is being transferred from the device while you pull it out.

electromagnetic radiation waves of electric and magnetic fields that travel through space. Visible light is one example of electromagnetic radiation, with wavelengths between 4×10^{-7} and 7×10^{-7} meters. Listed in order of decreasing wavelength, the categories of electromagnetic radiation are radio, microwave, infrared, visible light, ultraviolet, x-rays, and gamma rays. According to quantum mechanics, electromagnetic

radiation also acts as a stream of particles called *photons. See* WIRELESS
COMMUNICATION.

electronic circuit diagram symbols graphical symbols used in schematic
diagrams of electronic circuits. Examples are shown in Figure 91. *See
also* AND GATE; LOGIC CIRCUITS; NAND GATE; NOT GATE; OHM'S LAW; OR
GATE; PARALLEL; SERIAL; TRANSISTOR.

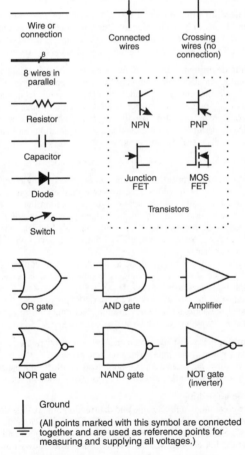

FIGURE 91. Electronic circuit diagram symbols

electronic commerce (EC) the carrying out of business transactions by computers. For example, computers at a store can monitor inventory levels and automatically order more merchandise when it is needed. Electronic commerce also includes transactions where there is a human participant, but the process is highly computerized, such as making purchases over the Internet. *See also* ELECTRONIC DATA INTERCHANGE; E-TAIL.

Electronic Communications Privacy Act *see* ECPA.

electronic data interchange (EDI) the transfer of information between organizations in machine-readable form in order to carry out business transactions. Electronic data interchange eliminates the need to type the same information into computers more than once. *See* OASIS.

electronic document a document intended to be read as it is displayed on a monitor. An electronic document can use HYPERTEXT to create an interactive environment for the reader. It can also use special effects, such as animation, sounds, and music. Unlike with traditional printed documents, there is no extra cost for full color. WEB PAGES are a type of electronic document; so are catalogs, documentation, and MULTIMEDIA presentations distributed on CD-ROM.

electronic ink *see* ELECTRONIC PAPER.

electronic mail (e-mail) the transmission of messages by computer from one person to another. Messages are saved until the recipient chooses to read them. E-mail is much more convenient than ordinary mail or telephone calls because it arrives immediately but does not require the recipient to be present, nor does it interrupt anything else the recipient may be doing. Messages are easily printed out, saved on disk, or forwarded to other people.

All users of e-mail should be aware that backup copies of the messages can be saved and forwarded to others and that perfect privacy cannot be guaranteed. *Contrast* ATTACHMENT; COMPUTER SECURITY; FLAME; IMAP; INSTANT MESSAGING; NEWSGROUP; POP; SPAM; TEXTING.

For abbreviations commonly used in electronic mail, *see* CHAT ROOM; EMOTICON. FWIW; IANAL; IMHO; IRL; RYFM; TIA; YMMV.

electronic paper a display screen that is viewed by reflected light, like ordinary paper, rather than relying on light given off by the display itself. Such displays are often used in e-book readers. Electronic paper technology is sometimes called *e-paper* or *e-ink*. *See* E-BOOK READER.

electronic publishing
1. the creation, manufacturing, and distribution of paperless documents. Examples of electronic documents are CD-ROM encyclopedias and web pages. Each of these new formats brings new challenges and technical problems, but all need the skill of someone who knows how to work with type and how to produce a pleasing combination of graphics and text.

2. the use of specialized computer-controlled equipment in the publishing and printing industries. Desktop publishing may be considered part of this trend, but electronic publishing encompasses the use of equipment not readily available to the mass market (powerful workstation class computers and digital presses, for example). Electronic publishing is superseding traditional methods of PREPRESS production.

electrostatic printer a printer that operates by using an electric charge to deposit toner on paper. Laser printers are electrostatic printers.

element

    1. one of the items in an ARRAY or LIST.

    2. a substance containing only one type of atom. Each element is specified by its atomic number, which is the number of protons contained in its nucleus. For contrast, *see* COMPOUND.

elephant's ear (*slang*) the symbol @; *see* AT SIGN.

ELIZA a computer program developed by Joseph Weizenbaum of M.I.T. in 1966 to demonstrate that it is easy to make computers *seem* intelligent. ELIZA carries on a conversation with the user in the style of a psychotherapist, but it actually responds only to certain patterns of words in the input, ignoring the rest. For example, if the user mentions "mother," ELIZA might reply, "Tell me more about your mother."

    A version of ELIZA is built into the Emacs editor (Figure 92). To run it, press Esc X and type doctor and then press Enter. *See* EMACS.

    ELIZA passes the TURING TEST in a crude way, thereby demonstrating that human-like intelligence is easily faked. *See also* ARTIFICIAL INTELLIGENCE.

```
> Hello, I am Eliza.
* I am afraid.
> How long have you been afraid?
* Since midterms.
> Tell me more...
* I am afraid that I will fail
my course.
> Do you enjoy being afraid that
you will fail your course?
```

FIGURE 92. Eliza in action

ellipsis typographic convention of using three dots (. . .) to indicate the trailing off of a thought. In Windows, the ellipsis is typed by holding down Alt while keying 133 on the numeric keypad. Macintosh users can type an ellipsis by holding down Option and typing: (colon). Note that the three dots are actually one character. The spacing is different than simply typing three consecutive periods (Ellipsis . . . ; Three periods . . .).

The ellipsis also has an important function in the menu system of Microsoft Windows. The appearance of '. . .' after a menu item means that a dialog box will appear when that command is selected.

em dash a long dash (—). *See* DASH.

EM64T *see* X64.

Emacs (originally for "editor **mac**ros") a TEXT EDITOR that originated as a set of MACROS written for another text editor by Richard M. Stallman in the 1970s. Today, Emacs is one of the most successful products of the GNU project (*see* GNU). It is distributed free of charge from *www.gnu. org/software/emacs* in versions for numerous operating systems.

Emacs is somewhat complex to use, but very powerful. It can edit files of any size, and they need not be text files, since non-text characters are represented as octal codes. Emacs features an elaborate system of context-sensitive help. A Lisp-like programming language is built in so that users can define new editing operations. *See also* ELIZA.

email ELECTRONIC MAIL.

embedded font a FONT that is included within a file to ensure faithful reproduction of the formatted document.

embedded Linux any version of Linux that is used in an embedded system.

embedded object an object included in your file that was created in another software package and that still maintains a LINK to the other software. If the object is changed in the original software, it will be updated in the second file. *See* OLE for more details.

embedded system a computer that forms part of a larger machine of some other kind. The microprocessor that controls an automobile engine is an example. Embedded systems must usually be extremely reliable. They must also respond to events in real time (i.e., as they happen) without undue delay. *See* MICROCONTROLLER; REAL-TIME PROGRAMMING.

EMC **e**lectro**m**agnetic **c**ompatibility, the protection of equipment from electromagnetic interference. *See* RFI PROTECTION.

emitter one of the three layers of a bipolar transistor. *See* TRANSISTOR.

emoticon a typewritten symbol for a facial expression, often used in electronic mail. For example, :) denotes a grin (look at it sideways), ;-) means "winking," =:-o means scared or surprised, and 8-) works if you wear glasses.

Some emoticons are written so that they are viewed upright rather than sideways.

       `ˆ-ˆ`   smile
       `0.0`   surprise
       `ˆ.ˆ;`   distress (with drops of sweat)

emulation the process of achieving the same results as if you had a different machine than the one you're actually using. For example, VT-100 emulation means making a computer act exactly like a VT-100 terminal. Emulation is different from *simulation,* which involves imitating the internal processes, not just the results, of the thing being simulated.

en dash a short dash (–). *See* DASH.

Encapsulated PostScript (EPS) a file format that is widely supported by different computers, printers, and software. Most desktop publishing software supports the importation of Encapsulated PostScript files, thus providing a common denominator for exchanging files. *See also* POSTSCRIPT.

encoding a way of interpreting binary data as representing characters. The term is used particularly in the Microsoft .NET Framework, which supports several formats of UNICODE and many national variations on ASCII.

encryption the act of converting information into a code or cipher so that people will be unable to read it. A secret key or password is required to decrypt (decode) the information. More and more confidential data is being sent along computer networks, so it is becoming increasingly important to develop ways to send information over computer networks securely.

    For example, suppose we wish to send this message:

HELLOGOODBYE

One way to encrypt it is to replace each letter with the letter that comes 10 places later in the alphabet, so that letter 1 (A) becomes letter 11 (K), letter 2 (B) becomes letter 12 (L), and so forth, starting over at A when we go past Z, like this:

Plain: ABCDEFGHIJKLMNOPQRSTUVWXYZ
Encrypted: KLMNOPQRSTUVWXYZABCDEFGHIJ

Mathematically speaking, we change letter n to $(n + 10) \bmod 26$. Here *mod* stands for *modulo* and refers to the remainder after division by 26. For example, letter 20 (T) is shifted to 30, which becomes $30 \bmod 26 = 4$, which is the letter D. Using this method, our message becomes:

ROVVYQYYNLIO

The recipients can easily decrypt the message as long as they know the algorithm (each letter is shifted by a certain number of places) and the key (in this case, 10).

    Unfortunately, this algorithm is so simple that it would be easy for a spy to crack the code. There are only 25 possible keys (a key of 26 would have no effect, and a key of 27 or higher would have the same effect as a lower one). It is easy to check all 25 possibilities:

Trying key: 1	Message decodes as:	QNUUXPXXMKHN
Trying key: 2	Message decodes as:	PMTTWOWWLJGM
Trying key: 3	Message decodes as:	OLSSVNVVKIFL
Trying key: 4	Message decodes as:	NKRRUMUUJHEK
Trying key: 5	Message decodes as:	MJQQTLTTIGDJ
Trying key: 6	Message decodes as:	LIPPSKSSHFCI
Trying key: 7	Message decodes as:	KHOORJRRGEBH
Trying key: 8	Message decodes as:	JGNNQIQQFDAG
Trying key: 9	Message decodes as:	IFMMPHPPECZF
Trying key: 10	Message decodes as:	HELLOGOODBYE

In this case the spy can stop after the tenth try.

To make the code harder to crack, we can use a longer key. For example, say that the first letter of the message will be shifted 10, the second will be shifted 8 letters, the third will be shifted 17, and so on. If you use a key with 8 numbers, then you can repeat the pattern after every 8 letters (i.e., the ninth letter will be shifted the same as the first letter, the tenth letter will be shifted the same as the second letter, and so on). The longer the key is, the harder it will be for the spy to try all possibilities. If you can design it so that the time required to check all possibilities exceeds the lifetime of the universe, you're probably safe from this kind of attack. Even if you can design it so that the expense of cracking the code is greater than the benefit the spy would receive by cracking your code, you're probably safe.

However, there are other means of attack. Not all letters of the alphabet are used with equal frequency. A spy can program a computer to make a guess for the length of the key; collect all letters encrypted with a particular part of the key; and then check the frequency of encrypted letters, guessing that the most frequently appearing letter represents E, and so on. That guess may not be right, but guessing with this system will likely proceed much faster than guessing all the possibilities. This kind of attack is easier if the message is longer, but it won't work for numerical data where the digits are equally likely to appear.

Another likely means of attack would be to attack the key itself. If the spy gets hold of the key, it will be easy to decrypt all the messages. If a lot of people are sending messages to lots of other people, it is hard for them to deliver the keys to the recipients of the messages without letting them fall into the wrong hands.

One way to solve this problem is with public key encryption. In this approach, each person has both a *public key* (which everyone knows) and a *private key* (which is kept secret). If Alice is sending a message to Bob, then the message will be encrypted using an algorithm that is based on Bob's public key. Anyone can use this key to encrypt a message to Bob, but it can only be decrypted using Bob's private key.

Here is one example of how this can work, using the algorithm developed by Whitfield Diffie and Martin Hellman in 1976. Alice and Bob agree on two numbers: $n = 37$ and $g = 7$. (In reality, n and g would be much larger than this.) Each of them has a private key, which we'll call

a and b, respectively. Alice and Bob generate their public keys A and B using the formula:

$$\text{Public key} = g^{(\text{private key})} \bmod n$$

Thus:

$$\begin{aligned}
\text{Alice's private key } a &= 8 \\
\text{Alice's public key } A &= 7^8 \bmod 37 \\
&= 5{,}764{,}801 \bmod 37 \\
&= 16 \\
\text{Bob's private key } b &= 6 \\
\text{Bob's public key } B &= 7^6 \bmod 37 \\
&= 117{,}649 \bmod 37 \\
&= 26
\end{aligned}$$

Alice now generates another key K to use for the actual message using this formula:

$$\begin{aligned}
K &= B^a \bmod n \\
&= 26^8 \bmod 37 \\
&= 208{,}827{,}064{,}576 \bmod 37 \\
&= 10
\end{aligned}$$

This key is known as the *session key*. Now she can encrypt the message. For example, if she is sending the message HELLOGOODBYE, it will be encrypted as shown at the beginning of this entry.

When Bob receives the message, he will calculate the session key using a very similar formula:

$$\begin{aligned}
K &= A^b \bmod n \\
&= 16^6 \bmod 37 \\
&= 16{,}777{,}216 \bmod 37 \\
&= 10
\end{aligned}$$

Notice that this is the same value even though it is calculated from different numbers using a different formula. This works because of the following mathematical identities:

$$\begin{aligned}
(a \times b) \bmod n &= [(a \bmod n) \times (b \bmod n)] \bmod n \\
a^c \bmod n &= (a \bmod n)^c \bmod n \\
a^{bc} &= (a^b)^c = (a^c)^b \\
a^{bc} \bmod n &= (a \bmod n)^{bc} \bmod n \\
&= [(a \bmod n)^b]^c \bmod n \\
&= [(a \bmod n)^c]^b \bmod n
\end{aligned}$$

$$a^{bc} \bmod n = (a \bmod n)^{bc} \bmod n = (a^c \bmod n)^b \bmod n$$
$$a^{bc} \bmod n = (a \bmod n)^{bc} \bmod n = (a^b \bmod n)^c \bmod n$$

To calculate the private key (equivalent to c), given the public key and the session key, you need to solve an equation of this general form:

$$k = j^x \bmod n$$

If n happens to be a large prime number, it is very difficult to discover the value of x even if you know the values of k, j, and n. Thus, large prime numbers play a crucial role in public-key encryption. In practice, when computers are used for encryption, the calculations are usually carried out directly on the binary digits of the data, using a key given as a binary number. A longer key provides greater security, but the calculation process becomes more complicated.

All this presumes that you can get people's public keys reliably so that you can be sure you're really using Bob's public key when you send messages to Bob. Since public keys are not secret, all you need is a trustworthy database in which you can look up people's public keys.

Until 2000, the U.S. government regulated the export of strong encryption software in the same way that it regulates the export of weapons. This regulation dated from the 1940s, before general-purpose digital computers existed; encryption machines at that time were considered to be military devices.

See also AES; DES; DIGITAL SIGNATURE; HASH FUNCTION; ONE-WAY FUNCTION; PGP; ROT 13; RSA ENCRYPTION; SSL.

end

1. keyword that marks the end of a particular program structure in several programming languages. In BASIC, the END keyword tells the computer to stop executing the program. In Pascal, END marks the end of blocks of statements that start with BEGIN.

2. the key on your keyboard that takes your cursor to the end of the current line. Some word processors use Ctrl-End as a keyboard shortcut to take you to the end of the document.

end-of-file mark a symbol that indicates the end of a file. For example, in CP/M, all text files ended with ASCII character 26 (Ctrl-Z) because the computer did not otherwise keep track of the exact length of the file, only the number of disk sectors. In Windows, Ctrl-Z is often used the same way even though the computer knows exactly where the file ends whether or not an end-of-file mark is present. The UNIX end-of-file mark is Ctrl-D (ASCII 4).

end user the person ultimately intended to use a product, as opposed to people involved in developing or marketing it.

Energy Star a set of guidelines proposed by the U.S. Environmental Protection Agency in 1992 to reduce the amount of electricity consumed by personal computers. An Energy Star-compliant computer consumes less than 30 watts of power when idling (i.e., when turned on but not in use) and switches automatically into low-power mode if several minutes elapse without any keyboard activity. *See* GREEN PC.

engine

1. the part of a computer program that implements a special technique; *see* INFERENCE ENGINE, MONTE CARLO ENGINE, SEARCH ENGINE.

2. the printing mechanism of a laser printer, not including the computer control circuitry. Many laser printers use an engine made by Canon in Japan.

ENIAC (**E**lectronic **N**umerical **I**ntegrator **A**nd **C**alculator) one of the first electronic computers, built at the University of Pennsylvania in the mid-1940s. It contained about 18,000 vacuum tubes. Initially, the ENIAC was programmed by plugging cables into circuit boards. Today, one of the Internet nodes at the University of Pennsylvania is named `eniac` but is, of course, not the same machine.

Enter key the key on a computer keyboard that you press at the end of each line in order to send the contents of that line into the computer. On most keyboards, the Enter key is the same as the Return key.

In windowed operating systems, pressing the Enter key is usually equivalent to clicking on the currently selected icon or other highlighted item.

entry point the address in memory where machine code begins for a SUB-ROUTINE or FUNCTION. *See* PROCEDURE.

enumerator a device driver or operating system component that identifies all hardware devices of a particular type. *See* BIOS ENUMERATOR.

envelope
  1. (in a draw program) the imaginary outline enclosing an object. You can edit the envelope, turning it from a rectangle into a curved shape, and thereby distorting everything inside it.
  2. (in engineering) the limits imposed by physical or technical constraints (called an "envelope" because they can be envisioned as surrounding an area on a graph). "Pushing the envelope" means working close to, or at, the limits.

FIGURE 93. Envelope manipulation

environment
  1. the display and human interface provided by software. On a computer, an environment defines what you can do with the computer. For instance, the operating system, a word processor, and a spreadsheet provide (at least) three different environments that respond to different commands. For example, if you type a word processing command while you are in the operating system environment, or vice versa, the command will not be understood.
  2. (in Windows and UNIX) a data area in which you can store information for use by programs. To put information there, use the `set` command; for example, under Windows,

```
set prompt=$p$g
```

tells the computer to display the current disk and directory (e.g., `c:\`
`MYDIR>`) when it is ready for a command. To see the contents of the environment area, type `set` by itself.

EPIC *see* IA-64.

EPROM (**E**rasable **P**rogrammable **R**ead-**O**nly **M**emory) a type of memory chip that can be programmed electrically and erased by exposure to ultraviolet light. *See also* ROM; PROM; EEPROM.

EPS *see* ENCAPSULATED POSTSCRIPT.

Epson a prominent Japanese manufacturer of printers and other computer peripherals, distributed in the United States by Epson America, Inc., of Torrance, California. More information about Epson can be found at *www.epson.com*.

EPUB the most widely used file format for E-BOOKS, popularized by Amazon's Kindle e-book reader. Based on XML, the EPUB format is non-proprietary.

equalize a paint program filter that adjusts the brightness range of a picture so that all levels of brightness become equally common. If some brightnesses are not used (because the picture is too bright or too dark, or because of a contrast problem), the equalized picture will often look much better. Equalizing can dramatically improve the appearance of objects that are nearly the same brightness as their background.

erase the command that erases a file or set of files from disk in Windows and other operating systems. *See also* RECOVERING ERASED FILES.

Eraser a paint program tool that removes colors from a picture, leaving the background color in its place (the background can be transparent). The eraser is used by holding down the mouse button (the leftmost if there is more than one) and dragging the eraser tool. You can adjust the size and shape of your eraser to suit your needs. Some programs will even adjust how well the eraser works; it can erase thoroughly or just lighten the color. *See* NATURAL MEDIA.

FIGURE 94. Eraser
Note: tool erases to transparent background.
(Erased material is replaced by the background color.)

ergonomics the science of designing machines and working environments to suit human needs (from the Greek words meaning "the study of work"). An ergonomically designed machine is one whose design is based on the scientific study of human requirements such as vision, posture, and health risks. After all, the most important part of a computer system is the human being who is operating the computer.

Ergonomics goes beyond considering your comfort. Smart workers know that they need to work efficiently. When you work efficiently, you can get more done. Here are some things you can do:

- *Desk.* Your computer desk should be deep enough to comfortably accommodate all of your equipment. If the system unit keeps threatening to dump the keyboard in your lap, you may not have enough room. Consider putting the system unit on the floor or to the side of the monitor.

  Check the height of your desk. Is it too tall for you to type comfortably? You may want to attach a keyboard drawer. This lowers the keyboard to a more comfortable level and gives you a storage place for the keyboard.

- *Chair.* Your chair is most vital to the health and well-being of your back. You should choose a chair that has adjustments for height and good lumbar support. Try to find a chair that lets you adjust the tilt of the seat because it helps to periodically change the seat tilt during a long work session.

- *Monitor.* The monitor is one of the big-ticket items when you purchase your computer system. Ergonomically speaking, you do not want to skimp here. LCD (Liquid Crystal Display) monitors are superior to CRT (Cathode Ray Tube) monitors because they do not flicker. If you are still using an older CRT monitor, set the refresh rate to at least 70 Hz; it may save you a headache. Make sure you are comfortable with the height and tilt of the screen. You may need a special pair of glasses for working at the computer. (*See* EYE-GLASSES, COMPUTER.)

- *Mouse and keyboard.* The big risk is CARPAL TUNNEL SYNDROME, a condition that creates numbness or a buzzing feeling in your hands. Prevention is the key. You should keep your wrists straight when typing; don't allow them to bend. Some people enjoy a cushioned wrist rest for their keyboard. If using the mouse gives you any discomfort, try using another pointing device such as a TRACKBALL.

- *Lighting.* To prevent glare on the screen, do not place your computer opposite a window. Overhead lighting should be soft (not as bright as it would be for reading).

- *Posture.* Good posture *is* important. Try to imagine that an invisible string is pulling your head up and back in line with your spine. Be relaxed rather than stiff. Sit with your feet in front of you; if they don't reach the floor, your chair is too high or you need a footrest. Take frequent stretching breaks.

error a malfunction; a situation in which a computer cannot follow its instructions, or in which recorded data cannot be retrieved correctly. In computing, *error* does not necessarily denote a mistake made by a human being. *See* ERROR MESSAGE; HARD ERROR; SOFT ERROR; EXCEPTION; RUN-TIME ERROR; COMPILE-TIME ERROR; CIRCULARITY; GPF; ILLEGAL OPERATION; TIMEOUT; ERROR-CORRECTING CODE.

error-correcting code any method of encoding data that allows small errors to be corrected. *Contrast* CHECKSUM, CYCLICAL REDUNDANCY CHECK, and PARITY, which are techniques for detecting errors but not correcting them.

A simple error-correcting code would be to send each message three times, and if some part of the message does not come out the same in all three copies, let the majority rule. In order to be uncorrectable, an error would have to corrupt two of the three copies, not just one. Even then, you would know that an error had been made.

Practical error-correcting codes are more concise and are based on binary matrix arithmetic. *See also* SECDED.

error message a message that indicates that a computer cannot do what is requested or that some part of the software or hardware is defective. Error messages range from "You can't divide by zero" to "The disk drive isn't working." They do not necessarily mean that the user of the computer has made a mistake. *See also* ERROR.

error trapping *see* TRAPPING.

eSATA (external **SATA**) a hardware implementation of the ATA disk drive protocol for connecting external disk drives to computers. It is similar to SATA but uses different connectors. *See* SATA.

escalate to transfer a customer's help request from the person who originally handled it to someone more highly trained, and/or to mark it as more urgent.

escape code a code that indicates that the following character is to be handled specially (e.g., as a printer control code), or a code that stands for a character that cannot otherwise be typed. For example, in HTML, the characters < > mark the beginning and end of a command, so if you want them to appear on the screen, you have to type them as the escape codes < and >, respectively.

Escape key a key on a computer keyboard that has a special meaning depending on what software is being used. In many programs and under Microsoft Windows, the Escape key means "get out of where you are now and get back to where you were before" (e.g., back out of a menu without making any of the choices on it). The Escape key transmits ASCII character code 27, which is a character originally used to send special messages to devices. *See also* ESCAPE SEQUENCE.

escape sequence a special sequence of character codes that cause a screen or printer to perform some action (e.g., changing type style) rather than displaying the characters.

ESDI (**E**nhanced **S**mall **D**evice **I**nterface) a standard introduced by Maxtor in 1983 as an interface for hard disks. It has largely been superseded by IDE and SCSI. *See* IDE; SCSI.

ESRB **E**ntertainment **S**oftware **R**ating **B**oard (*www.esrb.org*) a non-profit, independent organization established in 1994 that reviews entertainment software and web sites and assigns standardized ratings based on suitability for children, as well as descriptions indicating the amount of violent and/or sexual content. ESRB labels can be found on most commercial software titles. The ratings are:

EC	"Early childhood"	Age 3 and up
E	"Everyone"	Age 6 and older; comic violence, no sex
K–A	"Kids to adults"	Equivalent to E, obsolete
T	"Teen"	Age 13 and older; limited violence, suggestive themes
M	"Mature"	Age 17 and older; violence, sexual themes
AO	"Adults only"	Graphic sex and/or violence
RP	"Rating pending"	Not yet rated

See also PARENTAL CONTROLS.

/etc in UNIX, a directory that contains system configuration information; often pronounced "et-see."

Ethernet a type of local-area network originally developed by Xerox Corporation. Communication takes place by means of radio-frequency signals carried by a cable. The name "Ethernet" apparently comes from "aether," the 19th-century name for the medium through which light waves were thought to travel. Ethernet cable connectors are often built into current computers. *See* LOCAL-AREA NETWORK; DATA COMMUNICATION.

On the physical level, there are four types of Ethernet connections. Twisted-pair Ethernet uses a set of unshielded wires within a Cat-5 or similar cable; this is now the most common type of Ethernet in homes and offices. Traditional thin-wire Ethernet uses RG-58 coaxial cable. Traditional baseband Ethernet uses a thicker coaxial cable about $\frac{3}{8}$ inch (0.9 cm) in diameter, and broadband Ethernet modulates the whole Ethernet signal on a higher-frequency carrier so that several signals can be carried simultaneously on a single cable, just like cable TV channels. *See* 10BASE-2; 10BASE-T; 100BASE-T; 1000BASE-T.

The control strategy of Ethernet is called CSMA/CD (Carrier Sense, Multiple Access, Collision Detection). Each computer listens to see if another computer is transmitting. If so, it waits its turn to transmit. If two computers inadvertently transmit at the same time, the collision is detected, and they retransmit one at a time.

Ethernet systems use many software protocols, including TCP/IP, IPX/SPX, and NetBEUI. *See* MAC ADDRESS; NETBEUI; PROTOCOL; TCP/IP.

ethical hacking the practice of breaking into computers without malicious intent, simply to find security hazards and report them to the people responsible.

The concept of "ethical hacking" is questionable because most people do not want strangers trying to break into their computers, no matter how benign the motives. Malicious CRACKERS almost always claim to be "ethical hackers" when caught. We do not allow strangers to attempt "ethical burglary" or "ethical trespassing." Experiments to test the security of a system should only be done with the advance permission of the victim.

Eudora a pioneering e-mail program, widely available for PC and Macintosh computers, distributed free of charge from *www.eudora.com*. It was developed by Steve Dorner starting in 1988. He named it after the writer Eudora Welty (1909–2001), who wrote a short story, "Why I Live at the P.O.," about the importance of mail.

EULA abbreviation for end-user license agreement, the agreement that the user of a piece of software is required to accept when installing it. *See* LICENSE.

Euro the common European currency introduced in 1999 to replace national currencies in several European countries. More information about the European currency is available from the European Union at *www.europa.eu.int* and the European Central Bank, which manages the currency, at *www.ecb.int*.

The Euro symbol is shown in Figure 95. In Windows, this can be typed by holding down Alt and typing 0128 on the numeric keypad.

FIGURE 95. Euro currency symbol

European paper sizes *see* PAPER SIZES.

EV

1. (exposure value) in photography, a number that measures the effect of f-ratio and shutter speed together, as exposure adjustments. For example, an exposure of 1/250 second at $f/8$ is equivalent to 1/125 second at $f/11$; each of these is EV 14. Higher EV numbers correspond to shorter exposures or exposures at smaller apertures (higher-numbered f-stops). Adding 1 to the EV is equivalent to cutting the exposure in half. Thus, 1/250 second at $f/11$ is EV 15.

Cameras often have "EV +/–" adjustments to deliberately increase or decrease the exposure. Here +1 means to expose more than the meter indicates, and –1 means to expose less than the meter indicates.
See also F-RATIO.

2. (**E**xtended **V**alidation) a type of digital certificate with additional verification requirements to ensure that the certificate holder is really who they claim to be. (Web address: *www.cabforum.org*). *See* CERTIFICATE, DIGITAL.

EVDO (**E**volution **D**ata **O**ptimized) a system for wireless broadband (web address: *www.evdoinfo.com*). *Contrast* HSDPA.

even smalls type that is set in all small capital letters, with no lower case letters, LIKE THIS. The cross-references in this book are set in even smalls. *Contrast* C/SC.

event-driven programming programming in which the computer spends its time responding to events rather than stepping through a prearranged series of actions. Computers that control machinery are almost always event-driven. So are computer programs that run under graphical user interfaces such as the Macintosh operating system or Microsoft Windows. Such programs respond to events such as the user choosing an item on a menu or clicking the mouse on an icon. *See* GRAPHICAL USER INTERFACE; OBJECT-ORIENTED PROGRAMMING; VISUAL BASIC; WINDOW.

evil twin a malicious wireless HOT SPOT that seems legitimate, but is designed to trick unwitting users into revealing personal information.

EX (describing items for sale) "**ex**cellent," i.e., fully functional and undamaged. Particularly in the used-camera trade, EX applies to reliable, working equipment that shows some visible wear.

EX+ (describing items for sale) better than EX (i.e., fully functional and only slightly worn). *Compare* LN, LN–.

exa- metric prefix meaning ×1,000,000,000,000,000,000 (10^{18}). *Exa-* is derived from the Greek word for "beyond" or "outside." *See* METRIC PREFIXES.

Excel a popular SPREADSHEET program, originally released in 1985 by Microsoft for the Macintosh, and later adapted for Microsoft Windows.

exception a situation that prevents a computer program from running as specified, such as unexpectedly reaching the end of a file or trying to divide by zero. *See also* TRY; UNHANDLED EXCEPTION.

Exchange Server popular Microsoft software for electronic mail and other collaboration. Users run client software such as Outlook on their machines, which connect to the Exchange software on a server. See *www.microsoft.com/exchange/evaluation/whatis.mspx*.

exclusive-OR gate *see* XOR GATE.

exe file a file with EXTENSION .exe, containing an executable machine-language program for Windows. To execute it, simply double-click on it; right-click on it and choose Run; or type its name at a command prompt.

Most application programs are distributed as .EXE files. Most compilers translate source code into .EXE files. *See* COMPILER. *Contrast* BAT FILE; COM (definition 2).

Caution! Do not run .exe files received via e-mail because they are almost certainly viruses.

execute to do what an instruction says to do. A computer alternates between a fetch cycle, when it locates the next instruction, and an execute cycle, when it carries the instruction out. *See* COMPUTER ARCHITECTURE.

executive size a size of paper sometimes used for stationery in the United States, $7\frac{1}{4} \times 10\frac{1}{2}$ inches (18.4 cm × 26.7 cm).

EXIF (**ex**changeable **i**mage **f**ile format) a standard way of including META-DATA in JPEG and some other file formats, mainly to preserve information about the digital camera and the camera settings used to create an image. The EXIF standard is maintained by the Japan Electronics and Information Technology Association (JEITA, *www.jeita.or.jp*). Unofficial but useful information about EXIF is maintained at *www.exif.org*.

exit to clear an application program from memory; to QUIT. Most software prompts you to save changes to disk before exiting. Read all message boxes carefully. *Compare* CLOSE.

exp the function, in many programming languages, that calculates the value of e^x. *See* E.

expand
   1. to return a compressed file to its original size. *See* DATA COMPRESSION.
   2. to make an object or image larger; to zoom in. As a touchpad or touchscreen gesture, this is done by putting two fingers in contact with the screen and moving them apart.

FIGURE 96. Expand (gesture on a touchpad or touchscreen)

Expansion in computer games, a supplement to the original game that adds features and content. It is important to note that expansions usually do not include the original game software, which must be purchased separately.

expert set a FONT that includes a full set of accented vowels, ligatures, small caps, and other special characters (such as an extended group of CASE FRACTIONS). It is assumed that someone using such a font will have the know-how and the software to be able to set the special characters. Not every typeface has a matching expert set; you may have to take this into consideration when selecting a typeface for a particular job or when purchasing fonts.

1234567890

abd123₁₂₃ ff fi fl ffi ffl ¢ Ł ¿

¼ ½ ¾ ⅛ ⅜ ⅝ ⅞ ⅓ ⅔

ABCDEFGHIJKLMNOPQRSTUVWXYZ

FIGURE 97. Expert set (Minion typeface, partial font)

expert system a computer program that uses stored information to draw conclusions about a particular case. It differs from a database, which merely calls up stored information and presents it to the user unchanged. Expert systems are widely used to troubleshoot defects in machines; they have also been used successfully to diagnose diseases or recommend manufactured products.

Every expert system consists of three parts: (1) a user interface, which is a way of communicating with the user through such devices as menus, commands, or short-answer questions (*see* USER INTERFACE); (2) a knowledge base containing stored expertise; and (3) an inference engine, which draws conclusions by performing simple logical operations on the knowledge base and the information supplied by the user. *See also* ARTIFICIAL INTELLIGENCE; DEFAULT LOGIC; FUZZY LOGIC; PROLOG.

exploit
1. *(noun)* a way of breaching the security of a system or using features that should be inaccessible. Often written and pronounced *sploit*.
2. A piece of software designed to make it easy for a large number of would-be hackers to take advantage of such a software flaw.

exponent a number or letter or expression that indicates repeated multiplication. Thus the exponent n in the expression a^n means to multiply n number of a's together. For example:

$$3^2 = 3 \times 3 = 9$$
$$4^5 = 4 \times 4 \times 4 \times 4 \times 4 = 1,024$$
$$10^6 = 10 \times 10 \times 10 \times 10 \times 10 \times 10 = 1,000,000$$

Also, $a^2 = a \times a$ is called a to the second power, or a *squared*. The number that when multiplied by itself gives a is called the *square root* of a (written as $\sqrt{a}$). That means $\sqrt{a} \times \sqrt{a} = a$. For example, $\sqrt{9} = 3$, since $3 \times 3 = 9$.

FIGURE 98. Explorer (Windows)

exponential function a function of the form $y = a^x$, where a can be any positive number except 1 and is called the *base* of the function. The most commonly used exponential function is e^x. *See* E.

exponential notation (scientific notation, E format) a way of writing very large or very small numbers conveniently. For example, 2,500,000 can be written as 2.5×10^6 or (in E format) `2.5E6` or `2.5E+6`. For very small numbers, the exponent is negative; thus $0.003 = 3.0 \times 10^{-3} =$ `3.0E-3`.

export to save a file in a format other than the application program's native format. Many word processing and graphics programs have the ability to export to several different formats. Look under the "Save As . . ." dialog box for the available file formats.

 Because the export process is a type of file conversion (instead of a simple copy operation) there is the possibility of a loss of image quality or text formatting.

ExpressCard a type of add-on card for laptop computers introduced by the Personal Computer Memory Card International Association (PCMCIA) in 2003 to replace the earlier CardBus (PC Card, PCMCIA Card) standard. ExpressCards are much faster, since they combine USB 2.0 and PCI Express communication.
 Note: An ExpressCard slot and a CardBus (PC Card) slot look alike from outside the computer, but if you insert the wrong kind of card, no connection is made (and no damage occurs). A CardBus card is 2.1 inches (54 mm) wide. An ExpressCard can be the same width, but it narrows to 1.6 inches (34 mm) at the connector end, and many Express-Cards are that width along their entire length.

expression a series of symbols that can be evaluated to have a particular value. For example, $2 + 3$ is an expression that evaluates to 5.

Extended Industry Standard Architecture *see* EISA.

extends in C++ and Java, a keyword indicating that a class inherits all of the functionality of another class, and then adds additional data or methods. Instead of extends, C# uses a colon (:). For example, all programmer-defined Java applet classes include a declaration similar to this:

```
class myapplet extends Applet
```

This allows the class you write (myapplet) to include all of the features defined in the standard class Applet.

extension

1. anything that adds capabilities to an existing system. For example, optional components of the Macintosh operating system are called extensions.

2. the part of a filename following the period, in Windows and other operating systems. For example, the filename myfile.txt has .txt as its extension.

The purpose of extensions is to indicate the type of file, but it is important to realize that the extension does not actually cause the file to be of a particular type; you can rename any file to have any extension, but when you do, your software may no longer recognize it for what it is.

Some file extensions have standard meanings; *see* Table 6. See the individual entries in this book for more information on some of the more important types.

A practical problem arises when the same extension is used by different software packages for different purposes. For example, .tex denotes both a TeX word processing document and a Corel Draw texture. When this happens, an extension may end up associated with the wrong piece of software. See ASSOCIATE for information on how to change the software that is associated with a particular extension.

Prior to Windows 95, all extensions in MS-DOS could be no more than three characters. Newer file extensions can be longer.

In Windows, it is up to the user whether extensions are displayed or hidden (Fig. 99). The choice is under Tools, Folder Options, in any window displaying files or folders. Leaving extensions hidden is risky.

FIGURE 99. Extensions, hidden (top) and visible (bottom)

You can be tricked by a filename with two extensions. If someone sends you a file named `virus.txt.exe` and extensions are hidden, you will see the name as `virus.txt` and think it is a text file, but if you open it, it will actually execute as a program.

external viewer *see* VIEWER.

extranet a network using Internet protocols that allows a company to share information with other companies (such as suppliers and customers) but with security features preventing access to others. *See* VPN; PROTOCOL. *Contrast* INTRANET.

Extreme Programming (or **eXtreme Programming**, abbreviated **XP**) a programming methodology introduced by Kent Beck and others in 1999.

The key idea is never to write a long computer program without knowing whether it will work. Instead, build every program out of small pieces that can be tested individually. This often requires writing substitutes (STUBS) for unfinished routines so that the rest of the program can be tested.

Extreme Programming also includes other good management practices, such as encouraging teamwork and keeping working hours reasonable. Nothing in Extreme Programming is radically new or "extreme;" much of it reflects the way the best programmers have always worked. *See* SOFTWARE ENGINEERING.

Despite the abbreviation XP, Extreme Programming has no specific connection to Microsoft Windows XP, as far as we can determine.

extrude a special effect provided by drawing programs that creates a three-dimensional shadow. It looks as if the type (actually any object) has been squeezed out from a cookie gun.

FIGURE 100. Extruded type

eyedropper a tool available in paint programs that allows you to match a color in the existing picture, and cause it to become the active color (Figure 101). All you have to do is click the eyedropper on the area of color you desire and *that* becomes the selected color. You can sample for your primary, secondary, and background colors.

FIGURE 101. Eyedropper tool

TABLE 6
COMMON WINDOWS FILENAME EXTENSIONS

.ai	Adobe Illustrator subset of .eps
.asc	ASCII text file
.bak, .bk	Backup copy of a file that has been edited
.bas	BASIC program file
.bat	Batch job (file of commands, DOS or Windows)
.bmp	Bitmap graphics file
.c	C program file
.cdr	Vector graphics (CorelDraw)
.class	Java bytecode file
.com	Command file (smaller version of .exe)
.cpp	C++ program file
.cs	C# program file
.doc, docx	Document file (ASCII or Microsoft Word)
.dll	Dynamic link library
.eps	Encapsulated PostScript graphics
.exe	Executable file (machine-language program)
.gif	Bitmap graphics file (GIF format)
.hlp	Help file
.htm, .html	Hypertext Markup Language
.ico	Icon (Windows)
.ini	Initialization file (configuration settings)
.java	Java program source file
.jpeg, .jpg	Compressed graphics (popular on the Web)
.log	Log of installation or usage (various software)
.mak	Makefile (Visual Basic and other environments)
.lnk	Windows shortcut
.mid, .midi	MIDI digitized music file
.mp3	MP3 digitized audio file
.pas	Pascal program file
.pdf	Portable Document Format (images of printed pages)
.prj	Project file (various compilers)
.pl	Perl or Prolog program
.ppt, .pptx	PowerPoint presentation
.ps	PostScript printable file
.pst	Outlook e-mail archive file
.raw	Image file
.rtf	Rich Text Format word processing file
.scr	Screen saver (in .exe format)
.swf	Shockwave file
.tex	TeX document
.tif, .tiff	Bitmap graphics file (TIFF format)
.ttf	TrueType font
.tmp	Temporary file
.txt	ASCII text file
.wav	Sound wave file
.wks, .wk2, .wk3	Lotus 1-2-3 or Microsoft Works worksheet
.wma	Windows Media audio (music)
.wp, .wpd, .wp6	WordPerfect document
.xls, .xlsx	Excel worksheet file
.zip	ZIP compressed file

If at first this tool seems senseless, consider what would happen if you were working on a digitized 24-bit color photograph. There are literally millions of colors available in this format—how are you going to find the right one to extend that background shade over that telephone line? Or how are you going to remember which of those colors you were using yesterday? The eyedropper will let you pick up the right color to use. *See* 24-BIT GRAPHICS; COLOR.

eyeglasses, computer eyeglasses for viewing a computer screen two or three feet away. Most eyeglasses are designed for vision at a great distance or for reading at about 18 inches (46 cm). Neither of these is suitable for looking at a computer screen. Moreover, the screen cannot be seen properly through the dividing line or transition region of bifocals. In addition, the slight fuzziness of screen images causes some people's eyes to strain as they try to focus. As a result, many eyeglass wearers think the computer has harmed their vision, although in fact there is no evidence that computer work (or any other kind of close work) harms the eyes.

Computer screens emit tiny amounts of ultraviolet (UV) light, and special glasses are available that block this. However, there is much more UV in ordinary sunlight than in the image on a computer screen, so UV-blocking glasses are probably more beneficial outdoors than in the office.

F

F keys *see* FUNCTION KEYS.

f-ratio the focal length of a lens divided by the clear aperture (diameter) through which light enters. The adjustment for f-ratio is called the F-STOP.

The f-ratio determines the brightness of the image formed by the lens; lower f-ratios produce brighter images. Thus, a camera with an f/1.8 lens requires much less light to take a picture than a camera with an f/8 lens, even with the same film or electronic image sensor.

The brightness of the image is inversely proportional to the square of the f-ratio. That is why f-stops on lenses are often numbered as powers of $\sqrt{2}$: f/2, 2.8, 4, 5.6, 8, and so on. Each f-stop gives half as bright an image as the next larger (lower-numbered) one.

To increase or decrease exposure n "stops" means to increase it or decrease it by 2^n. Thus a one-stop decrease means to cut the exposure in half, and a two-stop decrease means to cut it to $\frac{1}{4}$ of its original value.

The rated f-ratio of a lens refers to its widest opening; smaller openings (higher f-ratios) are provided as an automatic or manual adjustment. The actual front glass element is much larger than the opening that the light must pass through. The f-ratio of a ZOOM lens generally varies as the focal length is changed.

See also A; DEPTH OF FIELD; EV; FOCAL LENGTH; P; S; TV.

f-stop the adjustment for selecting the F-RATIO of a lens. Choose a smaller aperture (higher-numbered f-stop) for greater DEPTH OF FIELD.

fabric network interconnections.

Facebook a social networking site (*www.facebook.com*), founded by Mark Zuckerberg and other Harvard computer science students in 2004. Initially restricted to students, membership was opened to all of the public as Facebook rose in popularity. Users can join groups organized by workplace, school or college, or other common interests. Facebook is currently the most popular social network. It provides a somewhat safer, more secure substitute for e-mail and the World Wide Web as a whole. *See also* ZUCKERBERG, MARK.

facetime Apple's system for video conferencing (so you can see as well as hear the person you are calling).

facsimile *see* FAX.

factorial the product of all the integers from 1 up to a specified number. The factorial of a number n is symbolized by an exclamation point: $n!$. For example:

$$2! = 2 \times 1 \qquad\qquad = 2$$
$$3! = 3 \times 2 \times 1 \qquad\quad = 6$$
$$4! = 4 \times 3 \times 2 \times 1 \quad = 24$$
$$5! = 5 \times 4 \times 3 \times 2 \times 1 = 120$$

The factorial function can be defined by recursion: $n! = n \times (n - 1)!$. A group of n objects can be arranged in $n!$ different orderings. *See* LIMITS OF COMPUTER POWER.

fade *see* TRANSITION EFFECT.

fair use in copyright law, a limited kind of use of copyrighted material that does not require the copyright holder's permission. For example, quoting a few sentences from a book and acknowledging the source is fair use.

The essential characteristic of fair use is that it does not decrease the market for the original; it may in fact increase it. Fair use does not permit reproduction of a complete essay, poem, or other copyrighted work, nor does it extend to music, artwork, or software. *See* COPYRIGHT.

fanfic (fan fiction) stories written by fans of a television series, movie, or book. Fanfic makes use of the established fictional world, expanding or enriching the original story so that it more closely matches the author's interpretation and imagination. The tradition emerged as soon as there were stories to fuel imaginations, and fan fiction is now widely published on the Internet.

FAQ (**F**requently **A**sked **Q**uestions) a file of often-needed information in question-and-answer format. Many Usenet NEWSGROUPS have, or formerly had, their own FAQ files. These are collected at *www.faqs.org* and other sites and can easily be found by using a SEARCH ENGINE.

FAT (**F**ile **A**llocation **T**able) the part of the disk that contains information about the sizes and locations of the files. In Windows, a FAT file system is a file system that is compatible with DOS, as opposed to a Windows NT native file system (NTFS). *See also* FAT32.

FAT16 the original form of the FAT file system used by DOS and by Windows 95 and its predecessors. *Contrast* FAT32.

FAT32 (**F**ile **A**llocation **T**able, 32 bits) a modified form of the FAT file system that was introduced in Windows 98 and some late releases of Windows 95. FAT32 allows each disk to be divided into a larger number of clusters (allocation units); thus, space can be allocated in smaller units and used more efficiently. More importantly, FAT32 supports disk drives larger than 2 gigabytes.

favorites recorded addresses on the WORLD WIDE WEB. Web browsers normally let the user record the addresses of frequently visited web pages in order to go directly to them in the future without having to type the full web address or use a search engine. Also called *bookmarks*.

fax (originally an abbreviation for *facsimile*) a method of transmitting copies of paper documents over telephone lines by converting the appearance of the document into an electronic signal. The output looks much like a photocopy. Computers can send and receive fax signals by using suitable software and a fax modem. A fax document consists of a BITMAP image, not a file of characters.

fax broadcasting sending the same message by fax to multiple recipients, one after another. *Compare* E-MAIL BROADCASTING. *See also* JUNK FAX; SPAM.

FCC
1. (Federal Communications Commission) (web address: *www.fcc.gov*) the agency of the U.S. government that regulates all equipment that produces radio-frequency signals, including computers. The FCC issues two levels of approval for computers: Class A (suitable for use in industrial or business areas) and Class B (suitable for use in the home). *See* RFI PROTECTION. *See also* NET NEUTRALITY; BROADCAST FLAG.
2. business abbreviation for file carbon copies, a copy of an electronic mail message that is kept by the sender. *Compare* BCC; CC.

FCS (Final Customer Shipment) the stage at which a product has completed the beta-testing phase and is available to be shipped to customers.

Fedora the continuing freeware project derived from Red Hat Linux. *See* RED HAT.

feedback
1. a rating and/or comment given to help members of an online community determine if the rated member is trustworthy. Auction sites such as eBay or review sites like Epinions depend on user feedback to function effectively.
2. a phenomenon that occurs when a control device uses information about the current state of the system to determine the next control action. For example, when a thermostat controls the temperature in a house, it needs to know the current temperature in the house before it decides whether to turn on the furnace. Thus, information about the temperature "feeds back" into the device that controls the temperature. The thermostat, heater, and air temperature form a *feedback loop*. *See* LOOP (definition 2).
3. an unwanted squeal that occurs when a microphone picks up its own output from speakers. A single vibration can be amplified by the system over and over, producing an endless, raucous tone.

femto- metric prefix meaning ÷1,000,000,000,000,000. *Femto-* is derived from the Danish word for "fifteen" (because it signifies 10^{-15}). *See* METRIC PREFIXES.

fencepost error an OFF-BY-ONE ERROR; a programming error caused by doing something one less, or one more, time than necessary. So called because a person who is asked how many fenceposts, one foot apart, are needed to build a 10-foot fence, is likely to answer "ten" rather than the correct "eleven."

FET *see* FIELD-EFFECT TRANSISTOR.

FF (form feed) the character code (ASCII decimal 12, Ctrl-L) that causes a printer to eject the current sheet of paper and start a new one. *Compare* LF (line feed).

fiber optics cables that carry light rather than electrical energy. Fiber-optic cables are made of thin fibers of glass. Large amounts of data can be carried by a single fiber-optic cable. Unlike wire cables, fiber-optic cables are not subject to crosstalk or electromagnetic noise, and they cannot be tapped into (e.g., by an eavesdropper) without producing a noticeable drop in signal level.

field
1. a portion of a record in a database, containing one piece of information. For instance, in an address list, the zip code might be stored in a 10-character field. *See also* DATABASE; RECORD.
2. a place where information can be typed on the screen, such as one of the cells in a spreadsheet. *See* SPREADSHEET.
3. a region of space where an electrical, magnetic, or gravitational effect is present.

field-effect transistor (FET) a transistor in which the flow of current from source to drain is controlled by a charge applied to the gate. This charge attracts electrons into the area between source and drain or repels them away from it, thus changing its semiconductor properties. No current actually flows into the gate (in practice, there is a tiny current, on the order of 10^{-12} ampere). Thus, field-effect transistors consume little power and can be packed very densely on integrated circuit chips.

MOSFETs (metal-oxide-semiconductor FETs) have an insulating layer of metal oxide between the gate and the rest of the transistor. They consume the least power of all kinds of transistors. *See* CMOS; INTEGRATED CIRCUIT; TRANSISTOR.

FIFO (first-in-first-out) a QUEUE (definition 1); a data structure or memory device from which items are retrieved in the order in which they were stored. *Contrast* LIFO; STACK.

fifth-generation computers computers built with advanced large-scale integrated circuits that break out of the traditional Von Neumann architecture by making extensive use of pipelining and/or vector processing. This includes the current Pentium microprocessor, but the term "fifth generation" is no longer widely used. It was popular in the 1980s when powerful computers were foreseen but not yet built.

file a block of information stored on disk, tape, or similar media. A file may contain a program, a document, an image, a song, or a collection of data (such as a mailing list). A file need not occupy a contiguous block of disk space. *See* BINARY FILE; DATABASE MANAGEMENT; DISK; EXTENSION; RECORD; TEXT FILE.

file compression *see* DATA COMPRESSION.

file format a way of arranging information in a file. Almost every computer program has one or more file formats of its own; for example, WordPerfect documents are not in the same format as Microsoft Word documents, and similar programs from different manufacturers cannot necessarily process each other's files. There are three reasons why file formats are diverse:

1. Different programs handle different kinds of data (text vs. pictures vs. spreadsheets, for example).
2. Different programmers simply pick different ways of doing the same thing. Sometimes, inventing a new format is a point of pride, or is necessary to avoid infringing someone else's copyright or patent.
3. Even when the end result is the same, the way different programs achieve it may be very different. For example, a Windows Paintbrush picture is a *bitmap* (a large grid of dots), but a CorelDraw picture consists of *vector graphics* (instructions to draw lines or shapes in particular positions). The two kinds of pictures are very different from the computer's point of view.

   Many programs have the ability to *import* (bring in) files that are not in their own format. But the format of the imported file may not be very well suited to the way the program works, resulting in a loss of quality or partial loss of information (disappearance of italics or footnotes, loss of graphics resolution, inability to edit the imported material, or the like). It is also possible to *export* files to a format other than the usual one, but again, loss of information may occur. *See* SAVE AS. . . . *See also* CONVERSION PROGRAM; EXTENSION.

file management system software allowing you to keep track of your computer files. The term is typically used to refer to products that include features that go beyond the file management capabilities provided with the operating system. The system should keep track of when changes are made and who makes them; make sure that you don't have two people trying to make changes to a file at the same time; and provide ways of indexing and searching so a specific file can be found easily. *See also* CMS.

file permissions *see* PERMISSION.

file server a computer that performs FILE SHARING. *Contrast* DISK SERVER.

file sharing the use of networking to make files available to computers other than the one that owns and manages them. With file sharing, every file exists on the server, which knows it by file name and manages its space. File sharing is essentially the same thing as NETWORK ATTACHED STORAGE (NAS). *Contrast* DISK SHARING, STORAGE AREA NETWORK.

filename *See* 8.3 FILENAME; EXTENSION; FILE.

> *Usage note:* Many publishers prefer to write *file name* as two words.

filesystem a method of using a disk, optical disc, or tape to store data in files. Different filesystems are used for different operating systems and media. For examples *see* CDFS; FAT32; NTFS.

fill (in graphics programs) the color of an object. Fills may be of a uniform tone, or they may contain shades that gradually change from one color to another. A fill may even be a pattern. *See also* LINEAR FILL; UNIFORM FILL.

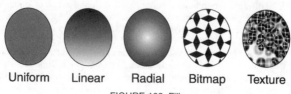

Uniform   Linear   Radial   Bitmap   Texture

FIGURE 102. Fills

film, digital *see* DIGITAL FILM.

filter

1. in paint programs, a tool for modifying the image. *See* IMAGE PROCESSING and its cross-references.

2. a program that reads a file, byte by byte, and creates another file from it in some way. For example, the Windows sort command can be used as a filter. If you type

                    dir | sort | more

you are sending the output of the dir command through the sort command, which acts as a filter to put the lines in alphabetical order; then the result is sent to the more command to be displayed on the screen. This technique originated in UNIX. *See* UNIX; PIPE.

3. a program that intercepts incoming e-mail, newsgroup messages, web connections, and so on, and blocks those with objectionable or unwanted content. *Compare* KILL FILE. *See* PARENTAL CONTROLS; SPAM FILTER.

4. a program that translates files from one format to another when called by the import or export command in a word processor or graphics program. *See* CONVERSION PROGRAM; DSL FILTER; EXPORT; IMPORT.

5. in electronics, a device that blocks certain signals or frequencies. *See* ANTIALIASING; RFI PROTECTION.

6. a device that blocks light of certain wavelengths or polarizations. Filters are used in front of computer screens to reduce glare. *See also* BAYER MATRIX.

7. a material that removes dust particles from air, sometimes used in front of a computer's cooling fan.

8. in Windows programming, a set of patterns that match desired file-names. For example, `*.c;*.h` is a filter that picks out files whose names end in `.c` and `.h`.

finally *see* TRY.

find

1. the operation of searching a file or web page for a particular word or string of characters. In many editors and web browsers, this is done by typing Ctrl-F.

2. a UNIX command that searches directories to find files with particular attributes. For example, this command starts in the current directory and searches all subdirectories to find files whose name starts with *pas*:

```
find . -name "pas*" -ls
```

In Windows, a similar function is available by choosing Search on the start menu.

3. a Windows command that finds all lines in a text file that contain a particular character string; a less powerful version of the UNIX `grep` command. For example, this command will display all the lines in `myfile.txt` that contain the word *birthday*:

```
find "birthday" <myfile.txt
```

To find the lines that do *not* contain *birthday*, add the option `/v` immediately after `find`. *Compare* GREP.

find and change, find and replace *see* SEARCH AND REPLACE.

Finder the part of MOS that enables the user to explore the contents of disk drives, launch programs, and open files.

fine-grained security a security model allowing the user to control the specific level of access that a particular program has to the computer. For example, a fine-grained security system would allow downloaded programs from certain providers to have read/write access to specified directories; read only access to other directories; and no access to other directories. This is generally better than an all-or-nothing approach to security, which forces the user to choose between crippling the functionality of a downloaded program by preventing it from having any access to the local machine, or else risking a breach of security by giving the downloaded program complete access. *See also* SANDBOX.

finger a UNIX command that provides you with information about users of your own or other machines. For example, if you type `fingersmith@gizmo1.ai.uga.edu` your computer will connect with GIZMO1 (the host computer's name) at the University of Georgia and look for a user named Smith; if one exists, you will get that person's full name and e-mail address, along with some other information depending on the exact version of the operating system.

Because the finger command has been abused (to collect addresses for junk e-mailing or even to deliberately overload a machine with requests), many larger UNIX systems no longer answer finger queries. *See* COMPUTER SECURITY.

fingerprint reader a device that identifies a computer user by detecting the person's fingerprint pattern, and can be used instead of passwords to allow access to computer services. Microsoft sells one such device for use with Windows.

FiOS a service from Verizon providing high-speed fiber optic connections to homes.

FIPS (Federal Information Processing Standard), web address: *www.nist. gov/itl/fips.cfm. See also* NIST.

Firefox a popular free Web browser introduced in 2004 by Mozilla (*www. mozilla.com/firefox*). On June 17–18, 2008, version 3 of Firefox set a world record for most number of downloads of a piece of software in a 24-hour period, and it continues to gain popularity. *See* BROWSER.

firewall a link in a network that relays only data packets clearly intended and authorized to reach the other side. Firewalls are helpful in keeping computers safe from intentional hacker attacks and from hardware failures occurring elsewhere. They can be implemented in hardware or software.

Since 2005, a software firewall has been built into Windows. Software firewalls are also included with many ANTIVIRUS SOFTWARE packages.

FireWire a high-speed serial bus standard more formally known as IEEE 1394, and similar in function to USB, but faster. The name FireWire is a trademark of Apple; the same bus is sometimes known as i.Link, a Sony trademark.

FireWire is most often used to interface video cameras to computers, but it has many other uses. The original version (IEEE 1394 and, with an improved software interface, 1394a) had a maximum speed of 400 megabits per second. The newer version, IEEE 1394b, achieves 800 to 3200 megabits per second. FireWire ports on computers look a lot like the miniature USB ports used on cameras; they are often labelled "1394" (for IEEE 1394) to identify them.

See also BILINGUAL (definition 2).

firmware software (i.e., computer programs) that is stored in some fixed form, such as read-only memory (ROM) or FLASH MEMORY. *Contrast* SOFTWARE; HARDWARE.

first-generation computers the computers that were built in the late 1940s and early 1950s, using vacuum tubes as switching elements.

first-person shooter a type of computer game in which the player pretends to shoot a gun from the perspective of the person doing the shooting.

fish tape a tool for pulling cables through inaccessible spaces. A fish tape is a very long metal strip with a hook at the end which can be used to grab a wire or another fish tape, somewhat like catching fish with a hook on a line.

fishing
1. the act of pulling a cable through the interior of a wall, or through some other inaccessible space, by using a FISH TAPE; more precisely, the act of moving a fish tape around to try to catch a cable or another fish tape.
2. the act of trying to obtain personal information by setting up a fake version of a trusted web site; normally spelled PHISHING.

fit text to path a draw program command that warps the baseline of a line of text so that it follows the shape of a specified line (PATH). *See* Figure 103 for an example.

fix a solution to a software defect; typically a new version of a program issued in order to correct a problem. *Compare* PATCH.

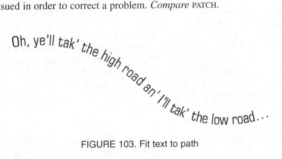

FIGURE 103. Fit text to path

fixed disk a disk drive that cannot be removed from the computer in normal use. *See* HARD DISK.

fixed-pitch type type in which all letters are the same width (e.g., I is the same width as M). Most typewriters and older printers and computer screens use fixed-pitch type. Also called MONOSPACE.
  Contrast PROPORTIONAL PITCH.

Fixed pitch

Proportional pitch

FIGURE 104. Fixed pitch vs. proportional pitch

fixed-point number a number in which the position of the decimal point is fixed. For example, amounts of money in U.S. currency can always be represented as numbers with exactly two digits to the right of the point (1.00, 123.45, 0.76, etc.). *Contrast* FLOATING-POINT NUMBER.

flame *(slang)* an angry, ill-considered e-mail message or newsgroup posting. *See* ELECTRONIC MAIL; NEWSGROUP.

flame war *(slang)* an angry, uninformative quarrel in a NEWSGROUP or other electronic discussion forum.

Flash a program developed by Macromedia, Inc. (now part of Adobe) to produce multimedia web content and presentations. To see Flash animations, viewers must first download the Flash player (*www.adobe.com/downloads*). However, Apple decided not to include Flash support on its iOS devices, such as the iPhone, making it harder for webmasters to rely on it. In 2011, Adobe announced it will no longer push the use of Flash on mobile devices and instead will concentrate on using HTML 5.

flash crowd, flash mob the sudden gathering of many people in a single place, in the real world or online.

The term *flash crowd* was introduced by science fiction writer Larry Niven to describe an imaginary world in which transportation was very fast and very inexpensive, leading huge numbers of people to congregate at any interesting event as soon as they heard about it through the news media. Today, flash crowds comprise gatherings of real people (organized using Internet and text messaging technology) as well as sudden overcrowding of online facilities such as web sites in response to an event.

flash drive a device that works like a disk drive but uses FLASH MEMORY as the storage medium. For the most common type *see* USB FLASH DRIVE.

flash memory a type of EEPROM that can only be erased in blocks; it cannot be erased one byte at a time. In this regard it resembles a disk drive that is divided into sectors. Flash memory is usually used for storing larger amounts of data, like a disk; EEPROM is used for small amounts of data, such as machine configuration. *Contrast* EEPROM. *See also* FLASH MEMORY CARD and references there.

flash memory card (flash card) generic term for a card containing flash memory for non-volatile storage. For examples *see* COMPACTFLASH; MEMORY STICK; MULTIMEDIACARD; SECURE DIGITAL CARD; SMARTMEDIA.

flat-file database a database like a relational database except that it has only one table. *See* RELATIONAL DATABASE.

flat-panel monitor a flat, thin computer screen like that of a laptop computer, using LCD technology. *Contrast* FLAT-SCREEN MONITOR.

flat-screen monitor a computer screen that is flat. Normally, flat-screen monitor denotes a conventional cathode-ray tube with a flat front, as opposed to a thin LCD panel, which is called a FLAT-PANEL MONITOR.

flatbed scanner a scanner in which the object to be scanned is held flat against a piece of glass. *See* SCANNER.

flavor
1. (*slang*) a variety or type of something. For example, CD-ROM, CD-R, and CD-RW might be described as three "flavors" of compact disc.
2. (in early object-oriented programming experiments at MIT) an inheritable object class.

fleuron a decorative typographic ornament. See Figure 105 for examples. Fleurons may be used for purely decorative purposes or to mark the beginnings of paragraphs.

FIGURE 105. Fleurons

flick brushing your finger across the screen with a multitouch interface, causing the display to scroll in that direction. When you flick, it is like you are pushing a paper, so that the screen display moves in the direction you push it. By contrast, when you move a scroll bar, it is like you are moving a window over the document, so when you move the scroll bar down, the screen display moves up. *See* SCROLL.

flip-flop an electronic circuit that can switch back and forth between two states (called 0 and 1) and will remain in either state until changed. Flip-flops are the basic component of which CPU registers are composed.

Figure 106 shows how to construct a flip-flop from two NAND gates. It has two possible states: state 1 (in which output 1 = 1) and state 0 (in which output 1 = 0). (Output 0 is always the opposite of output 1.)

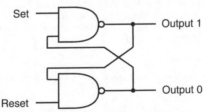

FIGURE 106. Flip-flop constructed from NAND gates

If both inputs are 1 when the flip-flop is first powered up, it will settle into one state or the other, at random. Bringing the "set" input momentarily to 0 will put the flip-flop into state 1, and bringing the "reset" input to 0 will put the flip-flop into state 0. Whenever both inputs are 1, the flip-flop stays in whatever state it was already in. Thus, a flip-flop is a 1-bit memory.

More elaborate flip-flops include control circuitry so that the data to be stored in them can be delivered through a single input. A 16-bit CPU register consists of 16 flip-flops side by side.

flip horizontal a command that creates a mirror image of the original object. The image still appears right-side-up, but left and right are reversed.

FIGURE 107. Flip horizontal; flip vertical

flip vertical a command that turns an image upside down, but maintains the image's left-right orientation, just like a reflection in still water. This is *not* equivalent to rotating the object or defined area 180 degrees. (Try it and see.)

floating illustrations illustrations that should appear near, but not necessarily at, specified positions in a text. For instance, many of the tables in this book are floating illustrations; they appear near the articles that refer to them, but not between particular words. The page-layout software places the illustrations wherever it is convenient to put them.

floating-point number a number in which the decimal point can be in any position. For instance, a memory location set aside for a floating-point number can store 0.735, 62.3, or 1200. By contrast, a fixed-point memory location can only accommodate a specific number of decimal places, usually 2 (for currency) or none (for integers). Floating-point numbers are often written in scientific notation, such as 4.65E4, which means $4.65 \times 10^4 = 46,500$. *See* DOUBLE PRECISION; REAL NUMBER; ROUNDING ERROR. *Contrast* FIXED-POINT NUMBER.

floppy disk *see* DISKETTE.

FLOPS **fl**oating-point **o**perations **p**er **s**econd, a measure of computer speed.

flowchart a chart consisting of symbols and words that completely describe an algorithm (i.e., how to solve a problem). Each step in the flowchart is followed by an arrow that indicates which step to do next.

The flowchart in Figure 108 shows how to calculate the cube root of a number a using Newton's method, where x is the guess for the cube root of a, and δ indicates how accurate the result must be. The procedure will follow around the loop until $|x^3 - a| < \delta$.

"Start" and "stop" statements are written with ovals, action statements are written with squares, and decision statements are written in diamonds. A decision statement asks a yes-or-no question. If the answer is yes, the path labeled "yes" is followed; otherwise, the other path is followed.

Writing a flowchart might help to solve a complex programming problem, although flowcharts are seldom used now that structured programming has become popular. A flowchart is often much bulkier than the program it describes. *See* STRUCTURED PROGRAMMING.

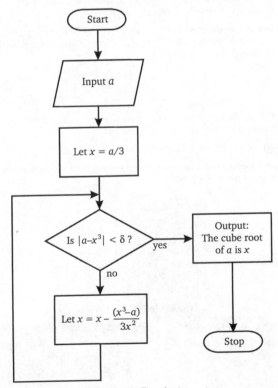

FIGURE 108. Flowchart

flush

1. flat against a margin, as in FLUSH RIGHT and FLUSH LEFT.

2. to finish an output operation by emptying the buffer in which the information is stored while waiting to be output.

flush left an arrangement of text with each line starting at the same horizontal position, making a neat left edge. *Flush left, ragged right* means that the length of the lines are allowed to vary. The right edge looks like a torn piece of paper—in other words, *ragged*.

This is
an example of some
flush-left type.

Flush left is how type is ordinarily arranged on a typewriter.
Contrast CENTER; FLUSH RIGHT; JUSTIFICATION.

flush right an arrangement of text with each line of type ending at the same horizontal position. The beginnings of the lines are irregular, but the right margin is smooth.

This is
an example of
flush-right type.

Flush-right alignment is seldom used except in charts or tables.
Contrast CENTER; FLUSH LEFT; JUSTIFICATION.

fly-in *see* TRANSITION EFFECT.

fly-out menu a secondary menu that appears to the side when you select an item on the primary menu.

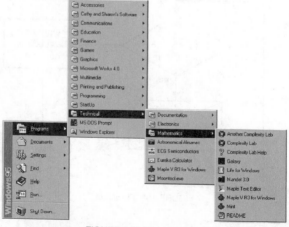

FIGURE 109. Fly-out menus

FM synthesis (frequency modulation synthesis) a technique of synthesizing musical sounds by using one waveform to modulate (vary) the frequency of another waveform. FM synthesis is an older technique for generating electronic music. It produces a wide variety of sounds, but it does not imitate conventional musical instruments as closely as WAVETABLE SYNTHESIS does. *Contrast* WAVETABLE SYNTHESIS.

FOAF *(slang)* friend of a friend, an unidentified source of a piece of information. *See* HOAX.

focal length the distance from a lens to the focal plane, or in the case of a multi-element lens, the focal length of a simple lens that would form the same size image.

A longer focal length produces a larger image and covers a narrower field. On a 35-mm camera, a "normal" lens has a focal length of about 50 mm; wide-angle lenses are 20 to 40 mm, and telephoto lenses are 80 to 200 mm or longer.

Electronic image sensors are usually much smaller than film, and they require shorter-focal-length lenses to cover the same field. The focal length of such lenses is sometimes specified as "35-mm equivalent," (i.e., the focal length that would cover the same field of view on 35-mm film). Typically, the true focal length is written on the lens, and the 35-mm equivalent is used in advertising.

The focal length of a ZOOM lens is variable (Figure 110). A lens marked "3× zoom" has a focal length that is three times as long at maximum as at minimum.

See also CROP FACTOR; F-STOP; ZOOM (definition 2).

FIGURE 110. Focal length (7–14 mm) and f-ratio ($f/3.5$–$f/4.8$) (both variable on this zoom lens)

focus the part of a WINDOW that is ready to receive input from the keyboard. The focus is generally indicated by highlighting with a special color or with an extra dotted line around a BUTTON. Usually, clicking on a location will move the focus to that location, and pressing the tab key will move the focus to the next location.

folder a directory of files (on the Macintosh or in Windows). *See* DIRECTORY.

font a complete collection of characters (including upper- and lowercase letters, numerals, punctuation, ligatures, reference marks, etc.) in a consistent style and size. Desktop publishing programs and word processors let you use more than one font in a single document. When you switch to italics or to bold or to a larger size, you are changing the *font* even though you may still be in the same TYPEFACE. *See also* TRUETYPE FONT; TYPE 1 FONT.

ABCDEFGHIJKLMNOPQRSTUVWXYZ
abcdefghijklmnopqrstuvwxyz
!"#$%&'()*+,-./0123456789:;<=>?
@[\]^_`~,ƒ„…†‡ˆ‰Š‹Œ''""•——˜™š›œŸ¡¢
£¤¥¦§¨ª«¬-®¯°±²³´µ¶·¸¹º»¼½¾¿
ÀÁÂÃÄÅÆÇÈÉÊËÌÍÎÏÐÑ
ÒÓÔÕÖ×ØÙÚÛÜÝÞß
àáâãäåæçèéêëìíîïðñòóôõö÷øùúûüýþÿ

FIGURE 111. Font (Times New Roman)

foot the bottom of the page. *Contrast* HEAD.

footer text that is placed at the bottom of each page of a printed document. *Contrast* HEAD (definition 2).

footnote a short comment placed at the bottom (FOOT) of a page that provides a citation or insightful comment to the text.* Some word processors cannot handle footnotes properly, placing them at the end of the chapter or article rather than at the foot of the page where they belong.

Footnotes should be numbered consecutively throughout an entire book, or beginning again for each chapter or page. Sometimes footnotes are not numbered, but are referenced by a traditional set of symbols. They should be used in this order: ASTERISK (*), DAGGER (†), DOUBLE DAGGER (‡), SECTION SIGN (§), and PILCROW (¶).

footprint the amount of space on a desk that a device takes up. For example, a laptop computer has a smaller footprint than a full-size PC. A smaller footprint is desirable because it leaves more space for other items on your desk. *See also* REAL ESTATE.

---

*This is a footnote. Notice that the asterisk in the footnote matches the asterisk in the text. The typeface used for the footnote is smaller than the font used for the body copy. A horizontal rule or extra vertical space should be used to separate the footnote from the text.

for a keyword that identifies one type of loop in several programming languages. A for loop causes a certain variable, known as the loop variable, to take on several values in sequence. For example, this Java code prints out the whole numbers from 1 to 10:

```
/* This is Java: */
for (int i=1; i<=10; i++)
{
  System.out.println(i);
}
```

A for loop can be used either to obtain repetition or to make the values of the variable available for some purpose. For example, here is how to calculate the sum of the whole numbers from 1 to 100 in Java:

```
int t=0;
for (int i=1; i<=100; i++)
{
  t=t+i;
}
System.out.println(t);
```

Although the statements within the loop can examine the value of the loop variable, they should not attempt to change it, since the result of doing so is unpredictable.

In C, C++, Java, and C#, the for statement is more general; it takes the form

```
for (init; test; step) {statements}
```

where *init* is a statement that is executed once, before beginning the loop; *test* is a condition that must be true at the beginning of every pass through the loop; *step* is a statement executed at the end of each pass; and *statements* are the statements within the loop, if any. Unlike its BASIC and Pascal counterparts, this kind of for statement need not step a number through a series of values; it can be used for many other kinds of repeated actions, because *init*, *test*, and *step* can be statements and tests of any kind. *Compare* DO; WHILE.

force quit (Macintosh) to escape from a frozen or hung program by pressing the Option, Command (⌘), and Escape keys simultaneously. This brings up a dialog box listing all active applications. Choose the name of the frozen program and click "Force Quit."

See FREEZE UP; HANG; CRASH. *Compare* TASK MANAGER.

form a screen display in which the user is expected to type in information and then press Enter or click OK. Forms enable readers of WEB PAGES to send information to the host site. *See* FORM, HTML.

form factor the size and shape of a piece of equipment or material. For example, motherboard form factors include AT (like the original PC AT),

"Baby AT" (a smaller board that mounts in the same case), and ATX (a newer type of motherboard introduced by Intel and others in 1996).

form feed the character code (ASCII decimal 12, Ctrl-L) that causes a printer to eject the current sheet of paper and start a new one. *Compare* LF (line feed).

form, HTML part of a web page that allows users to enter data, which can then be sent back to the server. Here is an example of the HTML code for a form where users can enter an e-mail address into a text field, use a list box to select either the deluxe, special, or standard version; use radio buttons to indicate which region they are from; use a check box to

```
<HTML>
<HEAD>
<TITLE>Form Example</TITLE>
</HEAD>
<BODY>
<H2>Example of an HTML Form</H2>
<FORM METHOD=POST ACTION="MAILTO:yourcompany@xyz.com">
Enter your e-mail address:
<INPUT TYPE="TEXT" NAME="EMAIL" WIDTH=25>
<BR>
Choose which version you prefer:
<SELECT NAME="VERSION">
<OPTION SELECTED> Standard
<OPTION> Special
<OPTION> Deluxe
</SELECT>
<BR>
Indicate which region you are from:<BR>
<INPUT NAME="REGION" TYPE="RADIO" VALUE="North">North
<INPUT NAME="REGION" TYPE="RADIO" VALUE="South">South
<INPUT NAME="REGION" TYPE="RADIO" VALUE="East">East
<INPUT NAME="REGION" TYPE="RADIO" VALUE="West">West
<BR>
Are you a new visitor?
<INPUT TYPE="CHECKBOX" NAME="NEWVIS" VALUE="yes">
<BR>
<TEXTAREA COLS=40 ROWS=5 NAME="MESSAGETEXT">
Type your message here,
as many lines as you want...
</TEXTAREA>
<BR>
<INPUT TYPE="SUBMIT"
    VALUE="Click here to submit message">
<INPUT TYPE="RESET"
    VALUE="Click here to clear all data">
</FORM>
</BODY>
</HTML>
```

FIGURE 112. Form, HTML (source code)

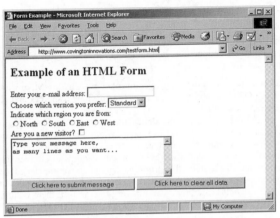

FIGURE 113. Form, HTML (as displayed on screen)

indicate whether they are a first-time visitor or not; and enter a brief message into a text area.

The ACTION command of this form will simply e-mail the result of the form to the specified address. It is also possible to specify a CGI script as the ACTION. This script needs to be specially written to process the results of the form once they are sent back to the server. The text that is not enclosed by < > are labels; see Figure 113, which shows how this form appears on the screen. Each element of the form needs to have a name by which it is identified to the server; in this example, the names are EMAIL, VERSION, NEWVISITOR, REGION, and MESSAGETEXT. Finally, the form has a submit button for the user to click when ready to send the information, and a reset button to clear information if desired.

For another example of an HTML form, *see* JAVASCRIPT.

formal parameter a name used within a function or subroutine for a value that will be passed to it from the calling program. *Contrast* ACTUAL PARAMETER.

format any method of arranging information that is to be stored or displayed. The word *format* can therefore refer to many different things relating to computers. Three of its most common uses are as follows:

1. The format of a file (or of any storage medium) refers to the way the information is stored in it. *See* FILE FORMAT.
2. To format a disk is to make the computer record a pattern of reference marks on it, which is usually done at the factory. Formatting a disk erases any information previously recorded on it.
3. In spreadsheets and programming languages, the format of a data item determines its appearance (how many digits are displayed,

whether there is a dollar sign, etc. whether to use italics, etc.). *See* LOGICAL DESIGN; WYSIWYG).

formatting the special codes in a document that indicate italics, underlining, boldface, and the like. Formatting information is lost when a file is saved as ASCII text.

FORTH a programming language invented by Charles Moore around 1970. FORTH is noted for requiring few machine resources and giving very rapid execution.

In FORTH, programmers define their own statements in terms of simpler statements. FORTH is a *threaded interpretive language,* meaning that a program is represented in the computer as a list of addresses of subroutines, each of which is composed of addresses of other subroutines, and so on until the primitive operations of the language are reached. Because it has little to do except read addresses and jump to them, a FORTH interpreter can run very fast; in fact, there is little difference between an interpreter and a compiler for FORTH.

```
C FORTRAN IV program to
C find sum of integers 1-100
      INTEGER I, SUM
      SUM=0
      DO 1 I=1, 100
    1 SUM =SUM + I
      WRITE (6,2) SUM
    2 FORMAT(1X,I5)
      STOP
      END
```

FIGURE 114. FORTRAN IV program

FORTRAN (Formula Translation) a programming language developed by IBM in the late 1950s. It was the first major programming language that allowed programmers to describe calculations by means of mathematical formulas, such as

D = (A+B)*C

where * is the symbol for multiplication.

forward to send a piece of e-mail on to another person, with an indication that you received it and forwarded it. *Contrast* BOUNCE (definition 2).

forward button on a web browser, the button that returns you to where you were before you clicked on the "back" button.

forward one a graphics program command that moves the selected object up one in the stacking order. *See also* BACK ONE; DRAW PROGRAM; SEND TO BACK; SEND TO FRONT; VECTOR GRAPHICS.

forward one; bring forward comparable commands that send the selected object down one layer. *See also* ARRANGE; BACK ONE; BRING FORWARD;

BRING TO FRONT; DRAW PROGRAM; SEND BACKWARD; SEND TO BACK; TO BACK; TO FRONT.

FOSI (Family Online Safety Institute) an organization trying to promote standards for safe online activities for children and families (web address: *www.fosi.org*).

fountain fill a fill that is composed of two or more colors. In between the colors is a smooth blending. You are able to rotate the angle of the fill (linear) or have the blend radiate from a central point (radial). Figure 115 shows a sampling of different fountain fills. *See also* UNIFORM FILL. Also called a GRADIENT FILL.

FIGURE 115. Fountain fills

fourth-generation computers computers built around integrated circuits with large-scale integration. Some people view these computers as being advanced third-generation computers.

Foveon a type of high-resolution CMOS image sensor developed by Foveon, Inc. (*www.foveon.com*) and National Semiconductor Corporation. Unlike earlier color image sensors, the Foveon has separate layers sensitive to red, green, and blue light, so the image color is sensed accurately in every pixel, and no light is discarded in colored filters. *See* CCD IMAGE SENSOR; CMOS IMAGE SENSOR. *Contrast* BAYER MATRIX.

    The name Foveon presumably alludes to *fovea,* the Latin name for the central, color-sensitive part of the retina of the human eye.

FPS
  1. (**F**rames **P**er **S**econd) the rate at which a moving image is generated or transmitted. All moving images are actually sequences of still pictures. *See* ANIMATION.
  2. abbreviation for FIRST PERSON SHOOTER.

fractal a shape that contains an infinite amount of fine detail. That is, no matter how much a fractal is enlarged, there is still more detail to be revealed by enlarging it further. Fractals are common in nature; they are the shapes of clouds, coastlines, broken rocks, the edges of torn pieces of paper, and the like. Fractals are important in generating realistic images of everyday objects on the computer.

    Figure 116 shows how to construct a fractal called a Koch snowflake. Start with a triangle and repeatedly replace every straight line with a bent line of the form:

The picture shows the result of doing this 0, 1, 2, and 3 times. If this were done an infinite number of times, the result would be a fractal.

See also MANDELBROT SET.

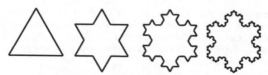

FIGURE 116. Fractal built from a triangle
(the Koch snowflake)

fragmentation a situation in which many files on a hard disk are broken into little chunks and stored in physically different areas of the disk platter. This can dramatically slow down access time and create long waits while files are being read or written.

A disk becomes fragmented when many files are created and erased on it over a long period of time. Files are recorded contiguously on an empty disk, but as files of various sizes get erased, empty spots develop that gradually become filled in with parts of newly recorded files. Eventually, when the user creates a large file, the file will be given space in many disconnected places all over the disk (*see* Figure 117 for an illustration).

To defragment a disk in Microsoft Windows, open "Computer," right-click on the disk, and choose Properties and then Tools.

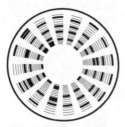

Fragmented disk   Defragmented disk

FIGURE 117. Fragmentation
(dark areas show sectors occupied by one file)

frame

    1. one in a succession of pictures in a video or animation. When displayed rapidly one after the other, successive frames give the impression of movement. *See* ANIMATION.

    2. a boxed area in a web page. *See* FRAME, HTML.

    3. a boxed area that is to contain text or a graphic (WORD PROCESSING, PAGE LAYOUT SOFTWARE).

frame grabber an accessory device that takes an image from a video camera, VCR, or other video input and digitizes it, creating a bitmap image. A video image consists of *frames* (successive pictures) transmitted at the rate of 30 per second, and the frame grabber must *grab* and digitize one of them.

frame, HTML an area in a web page that scrolls independently of the rest of the web page. A web page can be divided into multiple frames. For example, one frame can include a navigation bar that always stays on the screen as the user moves around the text of the page that appears in the other frame.

    Here is an HTML file that divides the browser window into two frames. The two files mentioned in it, navbar.html and main.html, are the source files for the separate frames.

```
<html>
<frameset rows="100%, *" cols="35%,100%">
<frame src="navbar.html" name="NavigationBar"
   scrolling=auto />
<frame src="main.html" name="main"
   scrolling=auto />
</frameset>
</html>
```

Here is file navbar.html, which produces the navigation bar in the left-hand frame:

```
<html><body>
<p><a TARGET="main" HREF="main.html#sec1">
      Section 1</a></p>
<p><a TARGET="main" HREF="main.html#sec2">
      Section 2</a></p>
<p><a TARGET="main" HREF="main.html#sec3">
      Section 3</a>
</body></html>
```

The following file, main.html, produces the main frame:

```
<html><body>
<h1><a name="sec1"> Section 1</a></h1>
The rest of the text for section 1 would go here
<h1><a name="sec2"> Section 2</a> </h1>
The rest of the text for section 2 would go here
```

```
<h1><a name="sec3"> Section 3</a></h1>
The rest of the text for section 3 would go here
</html></body>
```

Figure 118 shows the appearance of this page when displayed by the browser. If the right-hand frame did contain a large amount of text, the user could scroll through it while the links on the left-hand side always stayed in the same place, making it easier to jump to other sections of the document.

FIGURE 118. Frames, HTML

free (describing Windows versions) not containing the extra error checking and debugging code that would be in a CHECKED version. Most computers run a "uniprocessor free" version of Windows, which is a version that runs on a single CPU and does not contain extra error checking. *Contrast* CHECKED.

free software several kinds of computer software that can legally be copied and given free of charge to other users:

1. *Public-domain software.* This is software that is not covered by any kind of copyright. Few substantial public-domain programs exist, but the term public-domain is often used incorrectly to refer to other kinds of free software.

2. *Software that is copyrighted but is distributed free with permission of the copyright owner.* Two famous examples are the Linux operating system and the TEX typesetting program (*see* LINUX; TEX). Many UNIX utilities are also in this category.

3. *Shareware.* This is copyrighted software that can be distributed free to anyone, but that requests or requires a payment from satisfied users directly to the author. Shareware is often misleadingly described as "free."

Free Software Foundation *see* GNU.

free-to-play a game where there is no up-front cost to play (compare FREE-MIUM). Usually these are large multiplayer games. The company makes money by either restricting users and letting them pay for full access, and/or letting them purchase upgrades and special items for the game.

freemium (*free* + *premium*) a method of marketing games, entertainment, and communication services where the basic or entry-level service is free, but users, once they get involved, are likely to be willing to pay a fee for upgraded service or functionality.

freeware *see* FREE SOFTWARE.

freeze date a date after which the specifications for a software project cannot be changed. *See* SOFTWARE ENGINEERING.

freeze up to stop responding to input; to HANG. A frozen computer shows no activity on screen or on the front panel of the computer system and will not respond to the keyboard. Many times, the mouse cursor disappears. In Windows, control can often be regained by pressing Ctrl-Alt-Del and letting the operating system close the offending software. Macintosh users can often escape from a frozen program by pressing Option-Command-Esc and then selecting the FORCE QUIT button.

friend
  1. (*noun*) on a SOCIAL NETWORKING SITE, a person with whom you are in regular communication; friends typically see each other's postings and can communicate in other ways.
     Often no real friendship is implied; "friends" are simply people who have chosen to make their postings visible to each other.
  2. (*verb*) to make someone a friend (definition 1). *Contrast* UNFRIEND.

friendly name the most familiar or meaningful of several names denoting the same thing. For example, a networked printer might be known as \\ gizmo1\ttya-lj4 and as office Printer. The latter is its friendly name.

front camera a camera on a SMARTPHONE that faces the user, for use in video conversations. *Contrast* BACK CAMERA.

front end a computer or a program that helps you communicate with another computer or program. For example, supercomputers usually do not communicate with their users directly; instead users submit programs through another computer called the front end.

front side bus *see* FSB.

FS online abbreviation for "for sale."

FSB (**f**ront **s**ide **b**us) the BUS by which a CPU communicates with its fastest input-output devices. It is rated for speed in megahertz (MHz) or million transfers per second (MT/s). The latter rating is higher because there is usually more than one data transfer per clock cycle.

FTP (File Transfer Protocol) a standard way of transferring files from one computer to another on the Internet and on other TCP/IP networks. (*See* TCP/IP.) FTP is also the name of any of various computer programs that implement the file transfer protocol.

When you connect to a remote computer, the FTP program asks you for your user name and password. If you do not have an account on the computer that you have connected to, you can use *anonymous FTP* to retrieve files that are available to the general public. In that case the procedure is to give *anonymous* as your user name and then type your e-mail address in place of the password. Also remember to use the command binary if the file you are transferring is anything other than plain ASCII text. Figure 119 shows an example of an anonymous FTP session.

You can also retrieve files by FTP using a web browser. For example, to retrieve the file whose name is filename in directory pub/directory-name on host ftp.cdrom.com, give the URL as:

```
ftp://ftp.cdrom.com/pub/directoryname/filename
```

If you need to specify an account name and password, do this:

```
ftp://userid:password@zzzzz.com/directoryname/filename
```

Most browsers will prompt you for the password if you leave it out.

Ordinarily, FTP does not work through certain routers and firewalls. For the solution, *see* PASSIVE FTP.

See also INTERNET; PROTOCOL; WORLD WIDE WEB.

```
C:\> ftp
ftp> open ai.uga.edu
Connected to ai.uga.edu FTP server.
ftp> user
User name: anonymous
Password: yourname@your.site.address
User 'anonymous' logged in.
ftp> cd /pub/pc.utilities
ftp> binary
ftp> dir
pkzip.exe
ahed.zip
pred.zip
ftp> get pred.zip
pred.zip transferred, 17895 bytes in 2.5 seconds
ftp> quit
```
FIGURE 119. FTP session (user's commands are in italics)

FTP site a computer that makes files available for downloading by FTP.

FUD *(slang)* (**f**ear, **u**ncertainty, and **d**oubt) the tactic of trying to make customers afraid of adopting a rival product by creating doubts about its future.

full adder a logic circuit that accepts three one-digit binary numbers (two addends and one digit carried from the previous column) and produces two outputs, a sum output and a carry output. *See* BINARY ADDITION.

full duplex communication in two directions at the same time. For instance, an ordinary telephone is a full duplex device; you can hear the other person while you are talking. *Contrast* HALF DUPLEX.

full-text search the act of searching through every word in a set of documents to retrieve information you are interested in. This is a slow but thorough way to use a computer to search through web pages, court records, scholarly journals, or other material to retrieve items that you are interested in. *See also* BOOLEAN QUERY; SEARCH ENGINE.

function
1. (in mathematics) a value that depends on one or more *arguments* in such a way that, for any particular set of arguments, the function has only one value. For example, the positive real square root of a number is a function of that number. The sum of two numbers is a function of the two numbers. A function need not exist for all possible arguments; for example, negative numbers have no (real) square roots.
2. (in computer programming) a subprogram that acts like a mathematical function: given a particular set of argument values, the function returns a unique result.

In C, C++, and Lisp, all procedures (subroutines) are called functions, though they need not return a value (*see* PROCEDURE; VOID). In Java and C#, procedures and functions are called METHODS and are always attached to classes, though not always to specific objects.

function keys (F keys) keys labeled F1 to F12 on PC keyboards, and similar keys on other kinds of computers. Their function depends on the software being run. *See also* PROGRAMMABLE FUNCTION KEY.

fuser in a laser printer, the hot roller that warms the toner particles that have been deposited on the paper, to melt them and make them stick. *See* DRUM.

Fusion a line of APU (**A**ccelerated **P**rocessing **U**nit) chips introduced by AMD in 2010.

fuzzy logic a formal system of reasoning developed by Lotfi Zadeh in which the values "true" and "false" are replaced by numbers on a scale from 0 to 1. The operators *and*, *or*, and the like are replaced by procedures for combining these numbers. *See* BOOLEAN ALGEBRA.

Fuzzy logic captures the fact that some questions do not have a simple yes-or-no answer. For example, in ordinary English a 6-foot-high man might or might not be described as tall. In fuzzy logic, a 6-foot man might be tall with a truth value of 0.7, and a 7-foot man might be tall with a truth value of 1.0. A problem with fuzzy logic is that there is often no clear way to come up with the numbers that are used as truth values. For an alternative, *see* DEFAULT LOGIC.

Fuzzy logic is often used in expert systems; it nicely bridges the gap between logical inference and mathematical modeling. *See* CONFIDENCE FACTOR; EXPERT SYSTEM.

FWIW online abbreviation for "for what it's worth."

G

<g>, *g* e-mail abbreviation indicating a grin.

g2g chat-room abbreviation for "[I've] got to go."

gadgets in Windows Vista and in Google Desktop, add-ons to the desktop often created by developers other than Microsoft or Google, which provide additional functions such as displaying the weather in your area or providing a place for notes. Gadgets were de-emphasized in Windows 7 and 8, although they still work.

gain the amount of amplification in an audio amplifier or similar circuit. Adjusting the gain is one way to control the loudness of the sound from a sound card.

gambling a popular, but often illegal, online form of recreation. *Internet casinos* are World Wide Web sites that offer games of chance, with the ability to place bets and receive money. Users are often under the impression that this activity is beyond the reach of local laws, but actually gambling laws do not make any exemption for computers. U.S. federal law prohibiting placing bets "by wire" was revised by the "Unlawful Internet Gambling Enforcement Act of 2006" (part of public law 109-347) to make it illegal to use the Internet to place bets if that bet would be illegal at the location where it is initiated or received (31 USC 5362).

A further difficulty is that there is no way for the casino operator to tell whether the players are human beings. Some of them could be computer programs, simulating the behavior of a human being at a web browser, and meanwhile collecting detailed information about the workings of the casino—the ultimate card sharp, so to speak. The feasibility of doing this has been demonstrated by Paul Apostolik at The University of Georgia, although, for legal reasons, no actual money was wagered. *See* COMPUTER LAW.

Usage note: In the computer world, *gaming* does not mean *gambling*. It means playing computer games for recreation.

gamer a devoted fan of computer games. Gamers and the software they love best are responsible for pushing the limits of computer hardware further than most other groups.

gaming playing computer games for recreation (*contrast* GAMBLING).

gaming cafe a small business resembling an INTERNET CAFE but with an emphasis on computer games. Games are often networked and visitors can play against each other.

gamma (γ)
  1. in computer graphics, a measure of the nonlinear response of a video screen. The brightness of a pixel on the screen is not proportional to the

brightness value sent to it from software. Instead, the actual brightness B is

$$B = aV^t$$

where a is a constant, V is the brightness value, and the exponent γ is usually about 2 to 2.5. If gamma is known, it can be corrected so that all parts of the image are displayed with the specified brightness.

2. in photography, a measure of contrast. Normally, the gamma of film is about 0.7 and the gamma of photographic paper is about 1.4. When multiplied together, the two give a gamma of 1 so that the picture has the same contrast as the original subject. *See* IMAGE PROCESSING.

gamma testing a third stage of software testing sometimes performed after beta testing but before commercial release. In gamma testing, the software is believed to be complete and free of errors, but the manuals and packaging may not yet be in final form. *See also* ALPHA TESTING and BETA TESTING.

gamut

1. in music, the range of notes in the scale.

2. the range of colors that can be reproduced by a screen, printer, or other device.

There is no way to reproduce all visible colors with a finite number of inks or phosphors. Properly mixed primary colors will give all hues, but not all at high saturation. A color is "out of gamut" if it is more saturated (brilliant) than the available inks can reproduce.

The gamut of an RGB computer monitor is very different from that of a CMYK printer (*see* CMYK). Vivid reds and blues on the screen are often unprintable with cyan, magenta, and yellow ink; other purples and ruby-reds are printable but not displayable on the screen.

See COLOR and cross-references there. *See also* HSB; CMYK.

Gantt chart a diagram that shows the schedule for a series of tasks. *See* example at PROJECT MANAGEMENT.

garbage collection clearing out objects that are taking up space in memory but are no longer in use by a program. In Lisp, Prolog, Java, and C#, garbage collection happens automatically. In C++, there is no garbage collection; the programmer must specifically release the memory taken up by an object when it is no longer needed.

gate

1. one of the three parts of a field-effect transistor. *See* FIELD-EFFECT TRANSISTOR.

2. any of several logic circuits. *See* AND GATE; LOGIC CIRCUITS; NAND GATE; NOR GATE; NOT GATE; OR GATE.

Gates, Bill co-founder of MICROSOFT. He worked on the version of BASIC for the Altair microcomputer that was the first Microsoft product in 1975, and he led the company as its largest shareholder as it developed

MS-DOS, Windows, Microsoft Office (including Excel, Word, and PowerPoint), Internet Explorer, and a variety of other products. After the Microsoft IPO his large ownership share in the company has been enough to put him at or near the top of the list of the world's richest people.

In 2008 he left full-time Microsoft employment to concentrate on philanthropy with the Bill and Melinda Gates foundation (web address: *www.gatesfoundation.org/Pages/home.aspx*). He continues to serve as chairman of Microsoft.

gateway a link between different computer networks.

GB *see* GIGABYTE; METRIC PREFIXES.

gcc *see* CC.

geek *(slang)* an enthusiastic computer specialist; a person with an intense interest in computers to the exclusion of other human activities. The term is not normally an insult. *Compare* NERD.

gelatin silver print a conventional black-and-white photograph. (Black-and-white photographic paper uses a gelatin emulsion containing silver compounds that need not be replaced with colored dyes, though they can be.) *Contrast* CHROMOGENIC PRINT; GICLÉE PRINT.

genetic algorithm a problem-solving procedure where a new attempt is a slight modification of a previous attempt, and a fitness measurement determines if the new attempt is closer to the solution (similar to biological genetic modification and natural selection).

genius mix an iTunes feature that will automatically generate playlists of songs in your iTunes library that go well together.

Genuine Advantage a Microsoft anti-piracy program requiring users to validate their software. A key for the copy of the software is matched with a key for the hardware in an online database to prevent that copy from being used on other computers. The system will let people know if they have unknowingly bought counterfeit software, but a validation failure due to a network outage disables genuine copies of the software.

geolocation the measurement of the position of objects on earth. Geolocation can be done by receiving signals from GPS satellites, cellular telephone towers, and/or Wi-Fi access points at known locations. Many digital cameras automatically record the approximate location as part of the information stored with each picture. *See* GPS.

Less precise geolocation can be done by looking up the registered physical address of an Internet address. Web sites often use this latter kind of geolocation to deliver advertising that is targeted to viewers in a particular area.

gesture any action with a mouse, touchpad, or other pointing device that involves moving the pointer while holding a button down or holding a finger in contact with the pad. Gestures on a touchpad often involve more than one finger. For examples *see* DRAG; EXPAND (definition 2); PINCH; ROTATE; FLICK; MULTITOUCH INTERFACE.

GiB abbreviation for GIBIBYTE (1,073,741,824 bytes).

gibi- metric prefix meaning ×1,073,741,824 (2^{30}), the binary counterpart of *giga-. See* METRIC PREFIXES.

gibibyte 1,073,741,824 bytes. *See* METRIC PREFIXES.

giclée print a picture printed on an inkjet printer, usually on coated paper to resemble a photograph. (In French, *giclée* means "sprayed.") *Contrast* CHROMOGENIC PRINT; GELATIN SILVER PRINT.

GIF (**G**raphics **I**nterchange **F**ormat) a file format developed by CompuServe for storing bitmap images on disk. (*See* BITMAP.) GIF images can have up to $65,536 \times 65,536$ pixels and 256 colors. GIF is a common format for images on the World Wide Web. *Compare* JPEG; TIFF.

gif89a a GIF with the ability to play a short animation. They are very popular on web pages because, unlike FLASH, gif89a's don't require a plug-in for the animation to play. Many programs can save a series of drawings to be an animated gif. One such is Adobe's Image Ready.

You can have too much of a good thing, however. Esthetically speaking, a web page with too many animated gifs is confusing and way too busy.

giga- metric prefix meaning ×1,000,000,000 (10^9) or, in rating computer memories and disks, ×1,073,741,824 (= 1024^3). *Giga-* is derived from the Greek word for "giant." *See* METRIC PREFIXES.

Gigabit Ethernet *see* 1000BASE-T; ETHERNET.

gigabyte (GB) approximately one billion bytes. With computer memories, one gigabyte is always $2^{30} = 1,073,741,824$ bytes = 1024 megabytes. With disk drives, a gigabyte is sometimes understood as 1000 megabytes. *See also* MEGABYTE; METRIC PREFERENCES.

gigahertz (GHz) one billion cycles per second, a unit of frequency equal to 1000 megahertz; a measure of the frequency of a radio signal or the clock speed of a computer. *See* CLOCK; HERTZ; MEGAHERTZ; MICROPROCESSOR; RF; WIRELESS COMMUNICATION.

GIMP (**G**nu **I**mage **M**anipulation **P**rogram) a freely distributed paint program for UNIX and Windows, distributed from *www.gimp.org. See also* GNU.

Glide a service providing online software allowing users to access their data from any machine (web address: *www.transmediacorp.com*).

glitch erroneous response that occurs inside a computer because signals that are supposed to be simultaneous actually arrive at slightly different times. Software errors are occasionally called glitches. *See* BUG.

G.lite a popular, inexpensive type of ADSL telephone-line Internet connection that provides data rates up to 1.5 Mbps downstream and 0.5 Mbps upstream. *See* ADSL; DSL; and cross-references there. The name is a nickname for the standard's official designation, G.992.2.

glob a command in some programming languages to perform pattern matching, such as "glob *.doc" to list all files with extension ".doc". *See also* WILD CARD; REGULAR EXPRESSION.

Global Positioning System *see* GPS.

global variable a variable that can be recognized anywhere in a program. *Contrast* LOCAL VARIABLE.

glue logic additional, relatively simple logic circuits needed to connect one major part of a computer to another. For example, many microprocessors require some glue logic between the CPU and the memory. *See* LOGIC CIRCUITS.

glyph any printable character; the printed appearance of a character.

Gmail a free e-mail service provided by Google, with a large amount of space for messages and the ability to search through past messages.

GNOME (**G**NU **N**etwork **O**bject **M**odel **E**nvironment; the *g* is usually pronounced, like "g'nome") the most popular graphical desktop environment for Linux, based on the X WINDOW SYSTEM and similar in look and feel to Windows 95 and 2000. GNOME is part of the GNU project. *See* GNU. *Compare* KDE.

GNU a project led by Richard Stallman of the Free Software Foundation. *GNU* stands for "**G**nu is **N**ot **U**NIX"; the *g* is usually pronounced, like "g'noo." The GNU project's original goal was to develop a freely distributed substitute for UNIX, but Linux (the leading free UNIX) evolved into a somewhat separate project. The most important GNU products are the Emacs editor and the GNU C Compiler.

GNU software is copyrighted and is distributed free subject to certain conditions (typically, you must distribute it complete and intact, with source code). This set of conditions is sometimes called "copyleft" (i.e., a copyright with the opposite of its usual function) and also applies to some other free software, such as Linux. *See also* FREE SOFTWARE; EMACS.

GO TO, GOTO a statement in Fortran, BASIC, and other programming languages that transfers execution to another place in the program. For example, here is a BASIC program that prints "Hello" 1000 times:

```
10 LET X=0
20 PRINT "HELLO"
30 LET X=X+1
40 IF X<1000 THEN GO TO 20
```

Use of the GO TO statement has been strongly discouraged since the 1970s, when E. W. Dijkstra and others discovered that it was very error-prone. If a program contains GO TO statements, it's hard to tell, by looking at it, exactly how it will work, because execution can jump from any point to any other point. Instead, statements such as for, while, and repeat are much easier for the programmer to get correct. *See* STRUCTURED PROGRAMMING.

gold rare chemical element (atomic number 79, symbol Au) used in electronics because it is a good conductor of electricity.

gold, golden
1. (describing a disk or CD) ready to be duplicated and sold to the public.
2. (describing a software product) in its original manufactured state; thus "Windows 2000 Gold" is Windows 2000 as supplied on CD-ROM, without any subsequent updates downloaded.

gooey pronunciation of *GUI. See* GRAPHICAL USER INTERFACE.

Google a popular web search service, founded by Larry Page and Sergey Brin in 1998, that has expanded into many other areas (web address: *www.google.com*). Other search engines preceded Google in sending software SPIDERS (or webcrawlers) to automatically look at the text of a web page, and then follow all the links on each page to find other pages. In this way the search engine could create an index to the web, allowing people to enter words and then find a list of web pages including those words. However, that list might be very long, and it might contain irrelevant results. One reason Google became popular is because it developed a system to rank pages, based on the number of other pages that link to them. Also, it attempts to determine the relevance of the text on a page to the user's query, so that more relevant results will be placed near the top of the list. Another reason for Google's success is its large investment in computer hardware so its searches operate with great speed.

Google raises revenue largely through advertising, particularly because of its ability to offer customized ads based on what the user is searching for.

Google has expanded into other services, such as the CHROME web browser; YOUTUBE videos; the ANDROID mobile operating system; GOOGLE+ social networking; Google docs for documents, spreadsheets, and presentations; Gmail e-mail service; and Google Earth and Google maps to provide maps and images of the Earth's surface.

The word *Google* is also now used as a verb. For example, "I'll Google that" means "I'll search for that on the Web."

Google Desktop a program provided by Google that allows the user to easily search through files, and provides a sidebar where gadgets can be installed. *See* GADGETS.

Google Docs a service provided by Google to easily share information that includes spreadsheets and presentations that can be edited by a group of people, such as co-workers.

Google Earth an application provided by Google that allows the user to browse satellite images of the world by street address.

Google maps a global mapping service offering a choice of road maps, terrain maps, or satellite images (web address: *http://maps.google.com/maps*).

Google whacking *(slang, humorous)* the sport of trying to find a word so obscure that it occurs on just one of the many web pages indexed by Google.

Google+ (Google Plus) Google's social network, which opened to the public at large in September 2011. Unlike Facebook there is an emphasis on integration with other Google services, and greater privacy with organization of friends and contacts into circles. Users may choose which circles to share content (such as status updates and pictures) with.

Googlet *(slang)* GOOGLE+ (from misreading the plus sign as the letter t).

Gopher a hypertext protocol that was used in the early 1990s, before HTTP. The name "gopher" is a pun on "go for" (i.e., go and get things). *See* PROTOCOL; WORLD WIDE WEB.

gotcha *(slang)* a pitfall; a feature that leads to mistakes. *Compare* MISFEATURE.

.gov *see* TLD.

GPF (**G**eneral **P**rotection **F**ault) an error that arises in Microsoft Windows when a program tries to access a location in memory that is not allocated to it. GPFs are usually caused by programming errors such as uninitialized pointers. Software that produces GPFs is defective or improperly configured. *See also* ILLEGAL OPERATION.

GPS (**G**lobal **P**ositioning **S**ystem) a network of satellites allowing users with portable GPS devices to determine precise locations on the surface of the Earth. The portable GPS device measures the exact time taken for signals to reach it from at least four different satellites; from this, the instrument can compute its location.

   GPS was developed by the U.S. Department of Defense for military purposes, but it has plenty of civilian applications. Hikers and campers can use it to plot their position on maps. GPS-equipped automobiles can call up computerized maps showing their exact position. Police cars can transmit their exact position to the dispatcher automatically. Boats and ships can use GPS for practically effortless navigation.

   It is important to note that GPS satellites do not receive any information from navigational devices on the ground. If a tracking device wants to report its GPS-determined position to someone, it must use the CEL-LULAR NETWORK. *See* GEOLOCATION.

GPU (**G**raphical **P**rocessing **U**nit) an integrated circuit that assists the CPU with graphics-intensive calculations.

gradient fill a fill that is composed of two or more colors. In between the colors is a smooth blending. You are able to rotate the angle of the fill (linear) or have the blend radiate from a central point (radial). *See also* FOUNTAIN FILL; UNIFORM FILL.

FIGURE 120. Gradient fill tool (from Adobe PhotoShop)

grammar checker a part of a word processing program that flags sentences that violate rules of grammar. For example, in Microsoft Word, if you type "They is happy," the word "is" will be marked with a wavy green underline to indicate that it is not grammatical. However, grammar checkers are not always right; they sometimes make mistakes recognizing complex sentence structure, and they never know what you actually meant to say.

See also PARSING, SPELL CHECKER.

graph
1. a visual, two-dimensional display of information, designed to make it easier for the reader to interpret and understand numerical data. *See* BAR GRAPH and PIE CHART for examples.
2. in mathematics, a set of points connected together in a specific way. *See* TOPOLOGY.

graphical user interface (**GUI**) a way of communicating with the computer by manipulating icons (pictures) and windows with a mouse. Before GUIs became widespread, it was common for computers to operate in a mode where only text (no graphics) could be displayed on the screen.

Xerox developed a machine with a graphical user interface in the 1970s, but the first widely used GUI machine was the Apple Macintosh in 1984. The release of Microsoft Windows 3.0 in 1990 led to widespread use of a graphical user interface on IBM PC-compatible computers. For examples, *see* MACINTOSH; WINDOWS (MICROSOFT). *Contrast* COMMAND PROMPT.

graphics the use of computer output devices, such as screens, printers, and plotters, to produce pictures. The applications of computer graphics include publishing, education, entertainment, and the visualization of computed data (e.g., graphs of mathematical functions).

There are two basic ways to tell a computer how to draw a picture. In *vector graphics,* the computer is told to put a real or imaginary pen in a particular position and then draw a line a certain distance in a certain direction (or draw a line to another specific point). The alternative is *raster graphics* or *bitmap graphics,* in which the screen or plotting area is divided into a rectangular array of points (called *pixels,* from "picture cells"), and the computer is told what color each point should be. Computer screens and printers are raster devices, but some graphics software uses vector-style instructions internally so that all lines will appear as sharp as possible on the device actually used to display them.

The amount of fine detail that a particular graphics device can show is called the *resolution*. The resolution of a printer is usually given in dots per inch; the resolution of a screen is given as the size of the whole image. A good laser printer can print 1200 dots (pixels) per inch, so that an 8×10-inch picture is a $9600 \times 12,000$ array of pixels and contains far more detail than the screen can display.

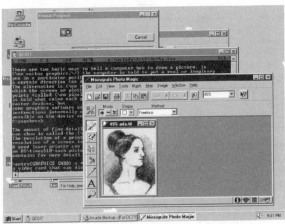

FIGURE 121. Graphical user interface (Windows)

graphics tablet an alternative to a mouse. A graphics tablet consists of a pressure-sensitive pad on which you draw with a special pen called a STYLUS. This is much more natural than attempting to draw with a mouse. *See* DRAW PROGRAM; PAINT PROGRAM.

grayed displayed in gray type and not available for selection. If a menu option appears in light gray rather than black type, it cannot be chosen (*see* Figure 78 on page 141). Menu selections are grayed whenever it is impossible to do the thing they call for (e.g., "Save" may be grayed if there is no data to be saved). *See* DIMMED.

graylist a spam filtering method in which message delivery is delayed for senders not on the WHITELIST or BLACKLIST. The message is delivered if it is re-sent (in the hope that spammers won't re-send and legitimate senders will).

FIGURE 122. Graphics tablet
(Photo courtesy of Wacom Technology)

grayscale
1. a series of boxes filled with a range of black tints from pure white to 100% black. A grayscale is used to test a printer, monitor, scanner, or printing press.
2. (scanner terminology) the range of grays in an image as measured by the scanner.
3. a description of any image that contains shades of gray as well as black and white.

Greek the alphabet used in ancient and modern Greece, A B Γ Δ . . . Ω and α β γ δ . . . ω. Greek letters are often used as mathematical symbols. For the complete Greek alphabet, see page 6. *Contrast* CYRILLIC; LATIN.

greeking the use of random letters or marks to show the overall appearance of a printed page without showing the actual text. With computers, greeking is used when the page is displayed too small for the text to be readable on the screen. *Compare* LOREM IPSUM.

Green Book the Philips/Sony standard for multimedia interactive compact discs (not including personal computer software).

Green PC a personal computer that draws little electrical power when idle, even though still turned on. A Green PC typically stops spinning its hard disk and shuts down power to the monitor if several minutes elapse with no keyboard activity. *See also* ENERGY STAR.

FIGURE 123. Greeking

Gregorian calendar the calendar system presently in use, introduced by Pope Gregory in 1582 and adopted in England in 1752 and in Russia in 1918. *See* LEAP YEAR.

grep the UNIX command that reads a text file and outputs all the lines that contain a particular series of characters. For example, the command

```
grep abc myfile
```

reads the file *myfile* and outputs every line that contains "abc."

Instead of specifying the exact characters to be searched for, you can give a regular expression that defines them. For example,

```
grep [bB]ill myfile
```

outputs all the lines that contain either "bill" or "Bill." *See* REGULAR EXPRESSION.

The origin of the word *grep* is disputed, but it may be an abbreviated editing command, g/*re*/p, where *re* stands for "regular expression," g means "global search," and p means "print" (i.e., display all lines that match the search criteria). Grep programs have been written for other operating systems, such as Windows. *Compare* FIND.

grid a feature of various draw programs and paint programs that allows lines to be drawn only in certain positions, as if they were drawn on the lines of graph paper. The grid makes it much easier to draw parallel and perpendicular lines, lay out diagrams, and avoid irregular breaks. However, when the grid is turned on, there are positions in which you cannot draw. *See also* DRAW PROGRAM; PAINT PROGRAM.

grid computing the process of solving computationally complicated problems by distributing parts of the problem to unused capacity on a widely dispersed set of machines that are connected to the Internet.

For examples, *see* SETI@HOME. *Contrast* CLUSTER COMPUTING.

grid system a way of standardizing the layout of many related pages, such as the pages of a multipage document. The designer first draws a grid that will define the possible positions of columns, horizontal divisions, and pictures. Not all the possibilities of the grid are used on any single page, but the grid ensures that column positions do not vary haphazardly, and thereby makes the pages look related.

griefer *(slang)* a person who plays a multiplayer game or participates in other online group activities for the purpose of making other people miserable. Griefers do not play to win; they do not defeat their opponents fairly. They play to lose, and they dish out insults, misinformation, and harassment in the process.

Grokster a file sharing service found liable for inducing its users to violate copyright law, in the case *Metro-Goldwyn-Mayer Studios et al. v. Grokster* (545 U.S. 913 (2005)), decided by the Supreme Court in 2005. *See also* NAPSTER.

gross megapixels the total number of megapixels on an image sensor, whether or not all of them are actually used in taking pictures. *Contrast* EFFECTIVE MEGAPIXELS.

grounding the establishment of a uniform reference voltage level across several pieces of electrical equipment that are connected together.

In any electrical device, "ground level" is the voltage level to which all other voltages are compared. In most computers, the ground level is connected to the ground pin (the third, rounded pin) of the power plug, and the power line then connects it to the earth itself, thereby assuring that the ground level for all machines is the same. This helps prevent cables from picking up noise or emitting radio-frequency interference. It also reduces the danger of damage from lightning. *See* ELECTRONIC CIRCUIT DIAGRAM SYMBOLS; POWER LINE PROTECTION; RFI PROTECTION.

Groupon a web service providing a variety of coupons for local businesses (web address *www.groupon.com*).

groupware software that makes it easy for a group of people to work on the same data through a network, by facilitating file sharing and other forms of communication.

GTG chat-room abbreviation for "[I've] **g**ot **t**o **g**o."

gTLD (**g**eneric **T**op **L**evel **D**omain) *see* TLD.

GUI *see* GRAPHICAL USER INTERFACE.

GUID (**G**lobally **U**nique **Id**entifier) a 128-bit number used by Microsoft WINDOWS to identify a user, software component, or other entity.

GUIDs are most often written as groups of hexadecimal digits in braces, such as:

```
{79376820-07D0-11CF-A24D-0020AFD79767}
```

Windows includes an algorithm to generate GUIDs based on an encrypted version of the user's MAC ADDRESS, which in turn is guaranteed to be unique. (*See* MAC ADDRESS.) Thus, anyone running Windows who has an Ethernet adapter can create GUIDs that are known to be unique in the entire world. Computers without an Ethernet adapter can generate GUIDs that are likely to be unique but not guaranteed to be.

guideline a nonprinting line that aids in aligning text and other objects in a draw program or page layout program. Some programs allow you to turn on a *snap-to-guidelines* feature that causes the guidelines and objects to have a magnetic attraction for each other. *See also* SNAP-TO-GRID.

guiltware persistent NAGWARE; software that repeatedly asks for a monetary contribution and tries to make you feel guilty if you don't pay. *Contrast* CAREWARE; FREEWARE.

gunk *(slang)* any undesirable thing that degrades the performance of a computer, such as physical dust, obsolete software, or spyware. Gunk includes well-intentioned utilities that waste CPU time constantly monitoring the status of a modem, network card, or disk drive, as well as VIRUSes, ADWARE, and other MALWARE.

gutter the blank space between columns of type or between pages of a book.

gyroscope a spinning device, free to pivot, that will always point in the same direction, due to the conservation of angular momentum. A gyroscope is included in the iPad so it can sense which direction it is pointing.

H

h4x LEETSPEAK for "hacks." *See* HACK, especially definition 4.

hack

  1. to modify, especially in an improvised way: "This version of the program has been hacked to run under UNIX instead of Windows."
  2. to program a computer, either tediously or enthusiastically: "We spent the whole night hacking."
  3. to break into a computer system or otherwise do mischief: "We've been hacked." *See also* ETHICAL HACKING.
  4. a clever programming technique: "This hack enables a console-mode program to change the title bar of its window."
  When someone in an online game is accused of "hacks," it means that he or she is suspected of using software bugs or a third-party program to achieve results that the game designers did not intend.

hack attack *(slang)* a sudden inspiration or compulsion to work on a computer program. Despite what it sounds like, a "hack attack" has nothing to do with computer security violations.

hacker

  1. an exceptionally skilled computer programmer.
  2. a person who programs computers for recreation or as a hobby.
  3. a person who "breaks into" computers without authorization, either for malicious reasons or just to prove it can be done; a CRACKER. *See* 2600; COMPUTER SECURITY.

hacker ethic the value system of computer enthusiasts who believe in helping each other advance technology by sharing knowledge without immediate concern for making money. *See* HACKER (definition 2). The hacker ethic has led to valuable cooperative projects such as GNU, LINUX, TEX, USENET, and the INTERNET.
  Usage note: The term *hacker ethic* is sometimes misappropriated by malicious individuals who believe they are somehow exempt from ordinary rules of ethics (*see* HACKER, definition 3). In its proper sense, the hacker ethic is an extension of ordinary ethics, not an exemption or loophole.

Hacker Safe *see* SCANALTERT.

hackish *(slang)* pertaining to the culture of HACKERs (definitions 1 and 2 and sometimes 3). For instance, using binary numbers on a birthday cake is a hackish thing to do.

Hadoop software from APACHE for processing large data sets on distributed computer networks (see *hadoop.apache.org*).

hafnium chemical element (atomic number 72; symbol Hf) used as an insulator in integrated circuit transistors.

hairline a very thin line, usually about .003 inch wide.

hairline	——————————
½ point	——————————
1 point	——————————
2 points	——————————
4 points	——————————

FIGURE 124. Hairline and other line widths

HAL

1. in Windows NT and its derivatives, the **H**ardware **A**bstraction **L**ayer, the component of the operating system responsible for low-level interaction with the CPU and closely related hardware.

2. the fictional computer in the movie *2001: A Space Odyssey* (1968). Replace each letter of HAL with the next letter in the alphabet to see an amusing coincidence.

half adder a logic circuit that adds two one-digit binary numbers, producing two digits of output. *See* BINARY ADDITION.

half duplex communication in two directions, but not at the same time. For instance, a two-way radio with a push-to-talk switch is a half duplex device; you cannot hear the other person while you are talking. *Contrast* FULL DUPLEX.

halftone the reproduction of a *continuous-tone* image (containing shades of gray or colors) by converting it into a pattern of very small dots of various sizes. (For an example, look closely at a picture in a newspaper or magazine.) Laser printers and printing presses can print shades of gray only as halftones. *See also* GRAYSCALE; PHOTOGRAPH.

FIGURE 125. Halftone image (enlarged)

halting problem the problem of determining whether a particular computer program will terminate or will continue forever in an endless loop; a famous theoretical result in computer science.

Consider a computer program *A* that analyzes other programs; call the analyzed program *B*. Suppose *A* can always determine, with complete certainty, whether B will ever terminate. You could arrange for A to repeat endlessly if it finds that B terminates, and terminate if it finds that B repeats endlessly.

You could then feed A a copy of itself (i.e., let $B = A$), and you'd have a program that terminates if and only if it does not terminate. This is a contradiction, proving that A, as described, cannot exist.

hand tool a tool available in some graphical environments that looks like a human hand and allows you to move the picture around the screen. If there is a hand tool provided, there will usually not be a SCROLL BAR at the side and bottom of the viewing window.

handle
1. a nickname used in online communication.
2. in Windows systems programming, a POINTER to a window or other system resource.
3. (in programs with a graphical user interface) the little black boxes at the corners and midpoints of an object that has been selected for editing. As the name suggests, handles give you a place to "grab" onto an object with the mouse and manipulate it. Dragging a corner handle (any one of the four) will change the size of the object. Dragging a midpoint handle will stretch or shrink the object in one dimension.

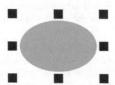

FIGURE 126. Handles (definition 3) on selected object

handshaking the exchange of signals between two computers to indicate that data transmission is proceeding successfully.

hang
1. to make a computer stop functioning because of a software bug or hardware failure.
2. (on a modem) to disconnect from the telephone line (hang up).

hanging indent, hanging tab a new paragraph indicated by letting the first word extend to the left past the normal margin into the gutter. Also called OUTDENT. Each entry in this dictionary begins with a hanging indent.

haptics human-machine interaction involving the sense of touch. Examples include touchscreens that vibrate or make a slight clicking movement in response to the user's actions, and joysticks and similar controls that give information to the user by altering their stiffness or movability.

hard-coded written into a computer program; not easily alterable. For instance, the location of video memory was hard-coded into the BIOS of the original IBM PC.

hard copy a printout on paper of computer output. *Contrast* SOFT COPY, which is a copy that is only viewable on the screen.

hard disk a data storage medium using rigid disks coated with magnetizable material. The read-write head travels across the disk on a thin cushion of air without ever actually touching the disk.

    The storage capacity of today's disks is measured in hundreds of gigabytes. To see the size of your hard disk under Windows, click on "Computer," right-click on the disk's icon, and click "Properties."

    See also DISK; DISKETTE; HARD DISK MANAGEMENT. On the interface between the hard disk and the computer, *see* ESATA; ESDI; IDE; PATA; SATA; SCSI.

hard disk management a task faced by all computer users. Modern hard disks are so large that it is easy to lose track of what you have stored on them. Here are some tips:

1. Be systematic. Choose a place to put files whenever there isn't a good reason to put them elsewhere. In Windows, the Documents folder serves this purpose.
2. Use meaningful filenames. For example, a paper about African violets should be named `Africanviolets` rather than `av9247` or `Mypaper`. Add "-old," "-previous," or the like when you need to keep more than one version of the same file.
3. Group files by project, not by software. For example, if you are writing a magazine article that consists of a word processing document and three pictures, create a folder for the project and put all four files in it.
4. Make backups. Your disk drive *will* fail one day, probably when you least expect it.
5. Learn how to search for misplaced files. In Windows, go to the Start Menu and choose Search or Find.
6. Defragment your hard disk every few weeks or months, unless your operating system does this for you automatically, as newer versions of Windows do.

hard drive a HARD DISK.

hard drive enclosure a box in which a hard disk drive can be mounted instead of mounting it in the computer's case.

hard edge in an image, an edge that is smooth and sharp, with no blending or blurring of the boundary. *See* Figure 127. *Contrast* SOFT EDGE.

FIGURE 127. Hard edge, left; Soft edge on right

hard error a persistent, reproducible error (defect) on a data storage device. *Contrast* SOFT ERROR.

hard hyphen *see* REQUIRED HYPHEN.

hard page a forced page break; a place where the word processor must begin a new page whether or not the previous page was full. In many PC word processors, the way to type a hard page is to hold down the Ctrl key while pressing Enter.

hardware the physical elements of a computer system; the computer equipment as opposed to the programs or information stored in the machine. *Contrast* SOFTWARE.

hardware interrupt a CPU interrupt triggered by a hardware event, such as pressing a key. *See* INTERRUPT.

hardware key a device that attaches to a computer to prove that it is licensed to run a particular piece of software; a dongle. *See* DONGLE.

Harvard architecture a type of computer design in which the program and the data are stored in separate memories. *Contrast* VON NEUMANN ARCHITECTURE. *See* COMPUTER ARCHITECTURE.

hash function a function that converts a string of characters to a number or a shorter string. During data transmission, the value of an agreed-upon hash function can be transmitted along with the data so it can be verified if the data has been transmitted correctly. For example, *see* CHECKSUM. A one-way hash function is a hash function that is also a one-way function. *See* ENCRYPTION; ONE-WAY FUNCTION.

hashing a storage mechanism where data items are stored at locations that are determined by a mathematical function of the data. For example, suppose you need to store a set of numbers in memory locations whose addresses run from 1 to 100. One example of a hashing function is to divide each number by 100 and use the remainder as the storage address. For example, the number 538 would be stored at memory location 38, and 1124 would be stored at location 24.

    The use of hashing makes it possible to store and retrieve the data items quickly, since it is not necessary to search through the list in order to find the item. However, there is one complication: A hashing function will sometimes assign more than one data item to the same address. For example, using the rule given, the number 638 would also be stored in location 38. To avoid that problem, a hashing system needs to be able to resolve collisions by storing the new data item in a separate place.

hashtag on Twitter and other social networking and microblogging sites, a label beginning with the hash character # to indicate words one might use to search for a message. For example, the hashtag `#computers` could be included in messages about computers.

hat
1. the character ^ (circumflex).
2. *See* BLACK HAT; RED HAT; WHITE HAT.

Hayes compatibility the ability of a telephone line modem to respond to the same set of autodialing commands as the Hayes Smartmodem (the AT COMMAND SET). Almost all modems nowadays are Hayes compatible.
 Modems do not have to be Hayes compatible to communicate with each other.
 See also MODEM; RS-232.

HCL Hardware Compatibility List.

HD DVD (high-density DVD) a high-density optical disc similar to, but not compatible with, BLU-RAY DISC, formerly marketed by Toshiba but discontinued in 2008.

HDD **h**ard **d**isk **d**rive.

HDMI (**H**igh **D**efinition **M**ultimedia **I**nterface) a standard interface and cable connector for carrying digitized audio and video. The connector is small and flat, like a USB connector, but is even smaller and contains 19 pins. *Compare* DVI (definition 1). For more information see *www.hdmi.org*.

HDR (**H**igh **D**ynamic **R**ange) an image capable of displaying a wide range of values, from the brightest whites to the darkest blacks.

HDTV **h**igh-**d**efinition **t**elevision; television with a resolution of 1280 × 720 pixels or more and, normally, a widescreen format with an aspect ratio of 16:9. Although analog HDTV was attempted in the 1990s, HDTV is now broadcast digitally because digital data compression is essential to its success. *Contrast* SDTV. *See also* DIGITAL TELEVISION.

head
1. the part of a disk drive that reads and writes information magnetically. A double-sided disk drive or multilayered hard disk has a head for each side of each layer. (*See* DISK.)
2. the top of a page or printed piece (such as a newsletter).
3. short for headline.

headless term describing a computer that lacks a keyboard, screen, and a mouse.

headset speakers (or rather earphones) and (usually) a microphone worn on a person's head.

heap a block of memory that belongs to a program but has not yet been given a specific use. For example, when a C# program creates character strings, it typically places them in space obtained from its heap.

heat sink a device to carry heat away from an electronic component. The heat sink for a CPU is typically a chunk of metal with fins or fingers, accompanied by a cooling fan. A vital part of the system is a thin layer of thermally conductive paste that conducts heat from the CPU to the metal heat sink. If this paste deteriorates or is missing, the CPU will run hot no matter how good the heat sink. *See also* OVERCLOCKING.

hecta- metric prefix meaning ×100 (10^2). *Hecta-* is derived from the Greek word for "hundred." *See* METRIC PREFIXES.

Heisenbug *(humorous)* a bug (error) in a computer program that goes away or radically changes its behavior when attempts are made to investigate it.

This is a common phenomenon. If the bug involves an UNINITIALIZED VARIABLE, the contents of the variable will be affected by other programs that have run recently. Thus, any attempt to investigate the bug will change its behavior. (From Heisenberg's uncertainty principle in physics, which states that it is impossible to determine the exact position and the exact momentum of an object at the same time; any attempt to measure one will change the other.)

See also BUG.

Hejlsberg, Anders *see* C#; DELPHI.

hello-world program a program that simply writes "Hello, world" on the most convenient output device, and terminates. Hello-world programs are the traditional way to verify that programming languages and output devices are working, at least to a minimal degree.

help information provided by a computer program to assist the user. Many computer programs contain an on-screen help facility that a user can turn to when questions arise. For example, if you have forgotten how a particular command works, you can consult a help facility (if one is available) to refresh your memory. Help might be available by telephone or at a store (such as an Apple store "Genius Bar.")

In Windows programs, one of the menu choices is usually *Help*. Windows has an elaborate help system accessible from the Start button. *See also* CONTEXT-SENSITIVE HELP; DOCUMENTATION; FAQ; HELP DESK.

help desk, helpdesk a place where people who use computers can go for assistance. It may be a single desk or a whole department of a large organization, or it may be a telephone help line (live or automated).

Helvetica a popular sans-serif typeface designed around 1957 by M. Miedinger. *See* Figure 128.

Helvetica

a b c d e f g h i j k l m
n o p q r s t u v w x y z
A B C D E F G H I J K L M
N O P Q R S T U V W X Y Z
1 2 3 4 5 6 7 8 9 0 ! @ #

FIGURE 128. Helvetica (normal weight)

hertz the number of times something is repeated per second; a unit of frequency, abbreviated Hz and named for Heinrich Hertz, discoverer of radio waves. *See also* CLOCK; GIGAHERTZ; MEGAHERTZ.

heuristic a method of solving problems that involves intelligent trial and error. By contrast, an algorithmic solution method is a clearly specified procedure that is guaranteed to give the correct answer. (*See* ALGORITHM.) For example, there is no known algorithm that tells how to play a perfect game of chess, so computer chess-playing programs must use a heuristic method of solution, using methods that are likely but not certain to give good results in any particular case.

Hewlett-Packard (HP) a leading manufacturer of computers and printers. Hewlett-Packard is headquartered in Palo Alto, California, and can be reached on the web at *www.hp.com*. The electronic test equipment division of HP is now a separate company known as Agilent (*www.agilent.com*).

TABLE 7
HEXADECIMAL EQUIVALENTS OF BINARY NUMBERS

Binary	Hex	Binary	Hex
0000	0	1000	8
0001	1	1001	9
0010	2	1010	A
0011	3	1011	B
0100	4	1100	C
0101	5	1101	D
0110	6	1110	E
0111	7	1111	F

hexadecimal number a number written in base 16. Hexadecimal numbers use 16 possible digits, written 0, 1, 2, 3, 4, 5, 6, 7, 8, 9, A (= 10), B (= 11), C (= 12), D (= 13), E (= 14), and F (= 15). For an example, the number A4C2 in hexadecimal means:

$$10 \times 16^3 + 4 \times 16^2 + 12 \times 16^1 + 2 \times 16^0 = 42,178$$

Hexadecimal numbers provide a good shorthand way of representing binary numbers, since binary numbers can be converted to hexadecimal numbers by looking at only four digits at a time. For example, binary 1111 equals hexadecimal F, binary 0100 equals hexadecimal 4, and binary 11110100 equals hexadecimal F4:

$$\underset{F}{\underline{1111}}\,\underset{4}{\underline{0100}}$$

When converting a binary number to hexadecimal by this method, start by adding zeros at the left if needed to make the number of digits a multiple of 4.

Table 7 shows the hexadecimal equivalents of the four-digit binary numbers, and Table 8 shows the decimal equivalents of the hexadecimal numbers from 00 to FF. *See also* COLOR.

TABLE 8
HEXADECIMAL NUMBERS AND DECIMAL EQUIVALENTS
(Part 1)

00 =	0	20 =	32	40 =	64	60 =	96
01 =	1	21 =	33	41 =	65	61 =	97
02 =	2	22 =	34	42 =	66	62 =	98
03 =	3	23 =	35	43 =	67	63 =	99
04 =	4	24 =	36	44 =	68	64 =	100
05 =	5	25 =	37	45 =	69	65 =	101
06 =	6	26 =	38	46 =	70	66 =	102
07 =	7	27 =	39	47 =	71	67 =	103
08 =	8	28 =	40	48 =	72	68 =	104
09 =	9	29 =	41	49 =	73	69 =	105
0A =	10	2A =	42	4A =	74	6A =	106
0B =	11	2B =	43	4B =	75	6B =	107
0C =	12	2C =	44	4C =	76	6C =	108
0D =	13	2D =	45	4D =	77	6D =	109
0E =	14	2E =	46	4E =	78	6E =	110
0F =	15	2F =	47	4F =	79	6F =	111
10 =	16	30 =	48	50 =	80	70 =	112
11 =	17	31 =	49	51 =	81	71 =	113
12 =	18	32 =	50	52 =	82	72 =	114
13 =	19	33 =	51	53 =	83	73 =	115
14 =	20	34 =	52	54 =	84	74 =	116
15 =	21	35 =	53	55 =	85	75 =	117
16 =	22	36 =	54	56 =	86	76 =	118
17 =	23	37 =	55	57 =	87	77 =	119
18 =	24	38 =	56	58 =	88	78 =	120
19 =	25	39 =	57	59 =	89	79 =	121
1A =	26	3A =	58	5A =	90	7A =	122
1B =	27	3B =	59	5B =	91	7B =	123
1C =	28	3C =	60	5C =	92	7C =	124
1D =	29	3D =	61	5D =	93	7D =	125
1E =	30	3E =	62	5E =	94	7E =	126
1F =	31	3F =	63	5F =	95	7F =	127

TABLE 8
HEXADECIMAL NUMBERS AND DECIMAL EQUIVALENTS
(Part 2)

80 = 128	A0 = 160	C0 = 192	E0 = 224
81 = 129	A1 = 161	C1 = 193	E1 = 225
82 = 130	A2 = 162	C2 = 194	E2 = 226
83 = 131	A3 = 163	C3 = 195	E3 = 227
84 = 132	A4 = 164	C4 = 196	E4 = 228
85 = 133	A5 = 165	C5 = 197	E5 = 229
86 = 134	A6 = 166	C6 = 198	E6 = 230
87 = 135	A7 = 167	C7 = 199	E7 = 231
88 = 136	A8 = 168	C8 = 200	E8 = 232
89 = 137	A9 = 169	C9 = 201	E9 = 233
8A = 138	AA = 170	CA = 202	EA = 234
8B = 139	AB = 171	CB = 203	EB = 235
8C = 140	AC = 172	CC = 204	EC = 236
8D = 141	AD = 173	CD = 205	ED = 237
8E = 142	AE = 174	CE = 206	EE = 238
8F = 143	AF = 175	CF = 207	EF = 239
90 = 144	B0 = 176	D0 = 208	F0 = 240
91 = 145	B1 = 177	D1 = 209	F1 = 241
92 = 146	B2 = 178	D2 = 210	F2 = 242
93 = 147	B3 = 179	D3 = 211	F3 = 243
94 = 148	B4 = 180	D4 = 212	F4 = 244
95 = 149	B5 = 181	D5 = 213	F5 = 245
96 = 150	B6 = 182	D6 = 214	F6 = 246
97 = 151	B7 = 183	D7 = 215	F7 = 247
98 = 152	B8 = 184	D8 = 216	F8 = 248
99 = 153	B9 = 185	D9 = 217	F9 = 249
9A = 154	BA = 186	DA = 218	FA = 250
9B = 155	BB = 187	DB = 219	FB = 251
9C = 156	BC = 188	DC = 220	FC = 252
9D = 157	BD = 189	DD = 221	FD = 253
9E = 158	BE = 190	DE = 222	FE = 254
9F = 159	BF = 191	DF = 223	FF = 255

HFS *see* HIERARCHICAL FILE SYSTEM (definition 2).

hibernate to suspend the operation of a computer by copying the entire contents of memory to a disk file, so that the computer can be powered off, then turned on again to resume where it left off, without rebooting. While hibernating, a computer consumes no electric power. *Contrast* SUSPEND.

hibernation file the data file on which the contents of memory are written when a computer hibernates. *See* HIBERNATE.

hidden file a file whose presence is normally concealed from the user to keep it from being deleted or moved. Hidden files contain information used by the operating system. Under Windows, hidden files in a folder can be viewed by making the appropriate choice under "Tools, Folder Options" on the menu bar.

hierarchical arranged in such a way that some items are above or below others in a tree-like structure. Examples of hierarchies include the organizational chart of a corporation, the arrangement of directories on a disk, and the arrangement of windows on a screen (because some of the windows are within others).

The *root* of the hierarchy is the main item that is above all of the others, such as the CEO of a corporation, the root directory of a disk, or the window that comprises the whole screen.

Many menu systems are arranged hierarchically, as menus within menus. For other examples of hierarchical data structures, *see* DIRECTORY; OUTLINE; TREE.

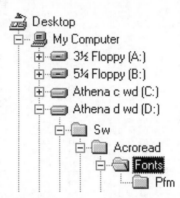

FIGURE 129. Hierarchical file system

hierarchical file system
  1. a file system that allows subdirectories or folders to belong to a higher-level subdirectory or folder (Figure 129). *See* DIRECTORY.
  2. (capitalized, Hierarchical File System, abbreviated HFS) the file system of the Macintosh. Besides disk drives, HFS is sometimes used on CDs, rendering them unreadable on computers other than the Macintosh. *Compare* JOLIET FILE SYSTEM; ROCK RIDGE.

hierarchical menu a menu with other menus under it; a CASCADING MENU. For an example, *see* START BUTTON.

high-level language a computer programming language designed to allow people to write programs without having to understand the inner workings of the computer. BASIC, C, Pascal, and Java are examples of high-level languages. By contrast, a *machine language* is at the lowest level, since machine language programming requires detailed knowledge of the computer's inner workings. An *assembly language* is at a slightly higher level than a machine language, since it uses a notation more convenient for the programmer.

High Sierra format a standard format for recording files and directories on CD-ROMs, now superseded by ISO 9660. The two formats are closely compatible, but some of the earliest CD-ROM software could read only High Sierra format disks.

highlight
1. to make a menu item prominent (either lighter or darker than the others) to show that it is selected. In most graphical user interfaces, you can choose the highlighted item by pressing Enter.
2. the lightest part of an image. In artwork, highlights show texture, shape, and the direction of the source of light.

HighMAT (**High**-performance **M**edia **A**ccess **T**echnology) a set of standards co-developed by Microsoft and Matsushita (Panasonic) for CDs and DVDs that are created on personal computers but played back on consumer electronic devices such as CD players and DVD-equipped television sets. HighMAT provides a standard way for the user to organize the files and select them for playback.

hinting additional information encoded into a digital font to help the computer software correctly display and print the letters at different sizes and resolutions.

HIPAA compliant meeting the standards set by the **H**ealth **I**nsurance **P**ortability and **A**ccountability **A**ct of 1996 for electronic data interchange. See *aspe.hhs.gov/admnsimp*.

hiragana *see* KANA.

histogram a bar graph in which the bars represent how many times something occurs (Figure 130). Histograms are often used in paint programs and scanner software to allow direct manipulation of the image characteristics. Each bar represents the total number of pixels of a particular shade of gray. By sliding the endpoints closer together, you decrease the image contrast; sliding the endpoints apart increases contrast. *See also* BRIGHTNESS; CONTRAST.

FIGURE 130. Histogram

history folder a folder that contains a list of the locations you have visited on the Internet.

hit

   1. something found by a searching. For instance, if you search the Web for instances of the word "aardvark" and find 250 of them, you've found 250 hits.

   2. on the World Wide Web, an instance of someone elsewhere calling up the web page and viewing it. The popularity of a web site is measured in hits per day.

hive a major section of the Windows REGISTRY that is automatically backed up on an external file. Examples of hives include HKEY_CURRENT_USER, HKEY_CURRENT_CONFIG, AND HKEY_LOCAL_MACHINE\SYSTEM. Not all of the top-level branches of the registry are hives.

hoax misinformation circulated as a deliberate prank; common on the Internet. (*Compare* MEME virus.) Hoaxes usually arrive in e-mail messages that say "mail this to all your friends"—that is, the hoaxer does not want you to post the message in a public forum where knowledgeable people might debunk it. Some common Internet hoaxes are the following:

   1. "A dying child (or maybe a charity) wants a gigantic number of postcards or a gigantic amount of e-mail." Nobody wants a gigantic amount of e-mail; e-mail costs money to receive.

      One young cancer victim, Craig Shergold, did appeal for postcards in 1989; his story is told in the *Guinness Book of World Records*, and his family is begging for the flood of postcards to stop. Unfortunately, his story is still circulating, often with altered names and addresses.

   2. "Some branch of government, such as the FCC, is about to do something outlandish."

      Sometimes these warnings come from well-meaning activists; more often they are pranks. In the 1970s a disgruntled license applicant started a rumor that the FCC was about to ban all religious broadcasting; the story is still circulating and the FCC can't afford to answer the flood of correspondence that it has generated. Newer hoaxes include a "modem tax" or bans on various uses of the Internet.

   3. "If you get e-mail titled 'Good times' (or 'Happy birthday' or 'Deeyenda' or something else), it will erase your hard disk (or do other great harm)."

      Any file attached to e-mail could easily contain a virus or destructive program; do not open such files unless you are sure of their origin. However, the viruses described in these particular hoaxes apparently do not exist.

Any piece of e-mail that is designed to spur you to immediate action is likely to be a hoax; before passing it on, you should check it out with your system administrator, your local computer security team, or another knowledgeable person. Better yet, do a web search to see what you can find out about it. The web site *www.snopes.com* specializes in debunking hoaxes and revealing the real facts. *See also* ADVANCE FEE FRAUD; FOAF; PYRAMID SCHEME. *Compare* URBAN LEGEND.

hole a place where an electron is missing from the atoms of a P-type semiconductor. A hole acts as a moving positive charge. *See* SEMICONDUCTOR.

/home in UNIX, a directory that contains individual users' home directories.

home directory the main directory belonging to a particular user of a UNIX system or of a file server shared by multiple users.

home page
1. the main WEB PAGE for a person or organization; the page that users are expected to read first in order to access other pages.
2. the WEB PAGE that a person sees first, immediately after starting up the BROWSER. Most browsers let you choose what web page this will be.
  See also HTML; WORLD WIDE WEB.

honeypot a trap for people who tamper with computers maliciously through the Internet, just as a pot of honey traps flies.
  A honeypot is generally a computer that is rigged to look more vulnerable than it really is, and to keep records of everything that happens to it. Honeypots serve several purposes: to catch individual crackers, to determine whether they can get into a network, and to observe how they carry out their attacks. *See* COMPUTER SECURITY; CRACKER.

hook a provision, in a computer program, for interaction with other programs that have yet to be written. For example, Adobe Photoshop and many web browsers provide hooks for plug-ins that add additional features. *See* PLUG-IN.

Hopper, Grace (1906–1992), mathematician and U.S. naval officer (later admiral) who worked on the first electronic computers. She developed the first compiler and contributed to the development of COBOL. For many years, she was the highest-ranking woman in the U.S. Navy.

horizontal side to side; across.

host computer a computer that provides services to others that are linked to it by a network; generally, the more remote of two or more computers that a person is using at once. For example, when a user in Florida accesses a computer in New York, the New York computer is considered the host.

hot list a list of bookmarks or favorites; a stored list of web addresses, filenames, or other data of immediate interest to the user. *See* BOOKMARK; FAVORITES.

hot-pluggable able to be plugged in and unplugged while a computer is powered on and running.

hot spot
1. (sometimes **hotspot**) a place where wireless access to the Internet is offered, such as for customers bringing their laptops into a coffee shop.
2. a place in a hypertext document where a user can click to call up further information. Hot spots are generally highlighted words or small pictures. Some large graphics can have multiple hot spots. *See* ANCHOR; HYPERLINK; IMAGE MAP.
3. the exact spot of a pointer (or any mouse cursor) that must touch an object in order to select it. The very tip of the arrow is the hot spot for the pointer.

hot-swappable able to be replaced (swapped out) while a computer is powered on and running.

hot zone the area at the end of a line of type that triggers the computer to hyphenate words. If a word extends into the hot zone, it will be hyphenated to make it fit on the line. *See* HYPHENATION.

hotfix a PATCH or rapidly distributed update for a piece of software. The term is used particularly with Microsoft Windows.

hourglass (in Microsoft Windows XP and earlier) the shape of the mouse pointer while the computer is too busy to accept any input from the keyboard or mouse. The pointer returns to its usual shape when the wait is over.

FIGURE 131. Hourglass

hover to leave the mouse cursor at a particular location more than momentarily, without clicking it. *See* ROLLOVER (definition 2).

HSB (**h**ue, **s**aturation, **b**rightness) a way of describing colors by means of numbers in some computer programs. HSB descriptions are especially convenient for artists who are accustomed to mixing paint. The first number, *hue,* describes the color itself (red, green, blue, yellow, etc., along a continuum).

The *saturation* is the vividness of the color, from maximum (extremely vivid) through paler colors all the way down to gray or white. For example, going from red to pale red to gray is a change of saturation.

The *brightness* is the amount of light emitted from patches of the color on the screen, from maximum brightness down to black.

HSDPA (**H**igh-**S**peed **D**ownlink **P**acket **A**ccess) a system for wireless broadband. Information available at *www.3gpp.org. Contrast* EVDO.

HTML (**H**ypertext **M**arkup **L**anguage) a set of codes that can be inserted into text files to indicate special typefaces, inserted images, and links to other hypertext documents.

The main use of HTML is to publish information on the Internet (*see* WORLD WIDE WEB). Here is a simple example of an HTML document.

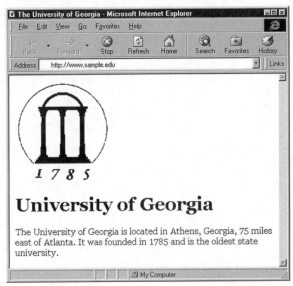

FIGURE 132. HTML example as displayed by browser

```
<html>
<head>
<title>The University of Georgia</title>
</head>
<body>
<p>
<img src="ugaseal.gif">
<h1>University of Georgia</h1>
The University of Georgia is located in
Athens, Georgia, 75 miles east of Atlanta.
It was founded in 1785 and is the oldest
state university.</p>
</body>
</html>
```

Figure 132 shows how this looks when displayed by a web browser. HTML features are indicated by special character sequences, called *tags*, enclosed with angle brackets < and >. If there were an HTML tag called xxx, then the characters <xxx> would mark the beginning of this feature, and </xxx> would mark the end. For example, the keywords <title> and </title> mark the beginning and end of the title. <p> marks a paragraph, and <img src=*filename*/> embeds an image in the document; many image formats are supported. Codes for special typefaces include the following:

opening tag		closing tag	
<h1>	. . .	</h1>	Heading, size 1 (largest)
<h6>	. . .	</h6>	Heading, size 6 (smallest)
<b>	. . .	</b>	Boldface
<i>	. . .	</i>	Italics
<u>	. . .	</u>	Underline
<t>	. . .	</t>	Typewriter type (like this)

The tag <br/> inserts a line break; note that the line breaks on the displayed web page will not necessarily match the line breaks on the original HTML text. The tag <hr/> inserts a horizontal rule.

An unnumbered list of items can be inserted as follows:

```
<ul>
<li> put first item in list here </li>
<li> put second item here </li>
<li> put third item here </li>
</ul>
```

An ordered (numbered) list is created in the same manner, except with <ol> used in place of <ul>.

A link to another document looks like this:

```
<a href="xxxx.html"> Click here.</a>
```

That means "Jump to file XXXX.HTML (another HTML document) if the user clicks on the words 'Click here.'" A URL can appear in place of the filename. A link to another place in the same document looks like this:

```
<a href="#xxxx">
This is the text that will display the link</a>
```

When the user clicks on this link, the browser will jump to the location in the current document marked with

```
<a name="xxxx"> This is the target of the link</a>
```

Comments (to be ignored by the HTML system) look like this:

```
<!-This is a comment ->
```

You can create HTML documents with any text editor, but it is more convenient to use web publishing software such as Adobe DreamWeaver to generate the HTML codes automatically as you edit the document in a WYSIWYG graphical environment.

For other examples of HTML, *see* FORM; FRAME; JAVA; JAVASCRIPT; REDIRECT; TABLE. *See also* CGI; WEB PAGE DESIGN.

HTML5 the current version of HTML, introduced in 2010. It includes many new features to reduce the need for other programming languages (JavaScript and the like) on web pages. HTML5 is still being developed (see *www.w3.org/TR/html5*).

HTTP (**H**ypertext **T**ransfer **P**rotocol) a standard method of publishing information as hypertext in HTML format on the Internet. URLs (addresses) for web sites usually begin with http:. *See* HTML; HYPERTEXT; INTERNET; URL; WORLD WIDE WEB.

HTTPS a variation of HTTP that uses SSL encryption for security.

hub a device for joining multiple Ethernet cables by copying all the data packets onto all the cables. Hubs are only suitable for use with very lightly loaded networks. *Compare* SWITCH (definition 2); ROUTER.

hue color (red vs. green vs. orange, etc.). *See* HSB.

hunt and peck *(slang)* to type by gazing at the keyboard, hunting for the letters, and pressing them one by one with one finger, rather like a trained chicken.

Hyper-Threading the ability of some microprocessors to follow two sequences of instructions at once. The central core of the microprocessor switches back and forth between the two threads, and some of the circuitry is duplicated in order to keep track of two tasks at once. *Contrast* DUAL-CORE PROCESSOR.

hyperdocument *see* HYPERTEXT.

hyperlink an item on a WEB PAGE which, when selected, transfers the user directly to another location in a hypertext document or to some other web page, perhaps on a different machine. Also simply called a LINK. For an example, *see* HTML.

hypertext (hyperdocuments) electronic documents that present information that can be read by clicking on links that lead in many directions, instead of just sequentially like reading a book. The World Wide Web is an example of hypertext, as are the help files of many software packages.

A large hyperdocument (e.g., an encyclopedia) requires large amounts of storage such as provided by a CD-ROM. The World Wide Web is a way of publishing hypertext on the Internet, using many different computers as servers for different parts of the information. *See* WORLD WIDE WEB; HTML; BROWSER.

hyphenation the practice of breaking words between syllables at the end
of a line so that the lines will be more nearly the same length.

Most desktop publishing software can automatically hyphenate text.
The computer tries to put as many words as possible on one line. When
it enters the last half inch of the line (the HOT ZONE), it calculates whether
the next word will fit; if not, the word is looked up in the hyphenation
dictionary, or hyphenated according to phonetic rules. The basic idea is
that both parts of the word should be pronounceable. There is often more
than one acceptable way to hyphenate a word, and dictionaries sometimes disagree with each other. The most basic rule is, "Make both
pieces pronounceable."

Fully justified type will always look better when hyphenated; otherwise loose lines (lines with big gaps between the words) become a
problem. If you are setting type flush left, ragged right, be aware that the
size of the hot zone will affect how ragged the right margin is.

Proofread carefully for unfortunate line breaks. The traditional
example is the word "therapist"—don't let the computer hyphenate it as
"the-rapist." Learn how to mark required hyphens so that hyphenated
names and phone numbers won't be broken across lines.

See also DISCRETIONARY HYPHEN; REQUIRED HYPHEN.

Hz *see* HERTZ.

I

I-bar, I-beam the shape of the mouse pointer in a text editing environment.
See CURSOR; INSERTION POINT.

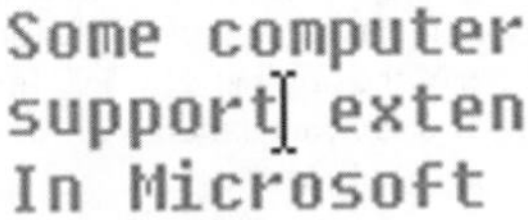

```
Some computer
support[ exten
In Microsoft
```

FIGURE 133. I-bar (I-beam) cursor

I-triple-E *see* IEEE.

I2 *see* INTERNET 2.

IA-32 (Intel Architecture-32) the architecture of the Intel 80386, 80486, and Pentium microprocessors, used on most personal computers a few years ago and now being displaced by X64. *Contrast also* IA-64.

IA-64 (Intel Architecture-64) the architecture of the 64-bit Intel microprocessors, such as the ITANIUM, that were intended to be the successor to the Pentium family (IA-32). IA-64 microprocessors can switch into IA-32 mode for compatibility with older software.

In actual use, the x64 (x86-64) architecture, introduced by AMD but also adopted by Intel, has proved considerably more popular than IA-64 and is usually used on 64-bit PCs today. *See* ITANIUM; PARALLEL PROCESSING. *Contrast* X64.

IANA (Internet Assigned Numbers Authority) an organization based at the University of Southern California with the responsibility to make sure all IP addresses are unique. Their web address is *www.iana.org*. *See* IP ADDRESS; TLD.

IBM (International Business Machines) manufacturer of computers and other office equipment. The company was formed in 1911 by the merger of three companies that made record-keeping equipment for businesses, one of which was the PUNCHED CARD company founded by Herman Hollerith.

IBM started manufacturing mainframe computers in the 1950s. By the late 1960s, IBM controlled about 80 percent of the computer market with models such as the IBM System/360, and the name IBM was practically synonymous with computing. Today, the company continues to make mainframe computers.

In 1981 IBM introduced the IBM Personal Computer (PC), which quickly became one of the most popular microcomputers. Users felt that with IBM behind it, the personal computer had come of age as a practical business machine, not just an experimental machine for laboratories or hobbyists. The IBM PC was designed in some haste, and very little of its design was patented; as a result, other companies (beginning with Compaq in 1983) were able to produce *clones* (compatible imitations) of it. The IBM PC became the most popular standard for microcomputers, even though most of the computers were produced by other companies, and Intel microprocessors and Microsoft operating system software became the defining elements of the standard. Today's "PC" computers are distant descendents of the original IBM PC. In 2005 IBM sold its PC business to Lenovo. IBM is headquartered in Armonk, New York (web address: *www.ibm.com*). See also IBM PC.

IBM PC popular lines of microcomputers manufactured by IBM. There are many variations of each; this article will mention only the most histori-cally important.

The IBM Personal Computer (PC), introduced in 1981, was the first of a family of very popular microcomputers, including not only IBM products but also "clones" (imitations) made by other companies. The original IBM PC used very little proprietary technology. Thus, it was easy for competitors to build compatible machines without violating patents. *See* CLONE; PC COMPATIBILITY.

IBM maintained a high level of upward compatibility within the PC and PS/2 line. This means that later-model machines would run virtually all software written for earlier models.

FIGURE 134. IBM PC (1981)

IBM's two original machines, the PC and PC XT, are virtually identi-cal, featuring 4.77-MHz 8088 microprocessors with an 8-bit bus. The only difference was that the XT had a 10-megabyte hard disk and had eight expansion slots instead of five. The PC AT, introduced in 1984, was the first PC to use the 80286 microprocessor, enabling programs to run much faster. The PC AT had what is now known as the ISA (Industry Standard Architecture) bus; it accepted both 8-bit (XT-style) and 16-bit plug-in cards.

The PS/2 machines were introduced in 1987 and discontinued in 1995. They were more compact than comparably configured PCs or ATs, and all but the lowest models used the Micro Channel bus, which made it possible in some situations to use more than one CPU in a single machine.

These computers use the ASCII character set (*see* ASCII). In addition, they define printed representations for all character codes from 0 to 255.

Figure 135 shows the printable part of the special character set. At a Windows COMMAND PROMPT, these characters are typed by holding down the Alt key and typing the appropriate number on the numeric keypad at the right side of the keyboard. For example, to type a shaded block, hold down Alt, type 178, and then release Alt.

(Note the arrangement: these are not in numerical order. 218 is the upper left corner box-drawing character; 192 is the lower left corner, and so on.)

á	160	é	130	í	161	ó	162	ú	163
à	133	è	138	ì	141	ò	149	ù	151
â	131	ê	136	î	140	ô	147	û	150
ä	132	ë	137	ï	139	ö	148	ü	129
å	134	É	144			ö	153	Ü	154
Ä	142			æ	145				
Å	143			Æ	146			ÿ	152

ç	135	¢	155	α	224	Ω	234	∫	244
Ç	128	£	156	ß	225	δ	235		245
ñ	164	¥	157	Γ	226	∞	236	÷	246
Ñ	165	₧	158	π	227	ø	237	≈	247
		ƒ	159	∑	228	ε	238	°	248
¿	168			σ	229	∩	239	•	249
¡	173	ª	166	μ	230	≡	240	·	250
«	174	°	167	τ	231	±	241	√	251
»	175	⌐	169	Φ	232	≥	242	ⁿ	252
		¬	170	Θ	233	≤	243	²	253

| 218 | 191 | 201 | 187 | 213 | 184 |
| 192 | 217 | 200 | 188 | 212 | 190 |

214	183	220	220	219	177
211	189	221	222		
		223	223	178	176

	179	┤	180	‖	186	╣	185	╫	215
─	196	├	195	=	205	╠	204		
┼	197	┴	194	╬	206	╦	203	╪	216
		┬	193			╩	202		

FIGURE 135. IBM PC special characters
(also used in Windows console mode)

IBM RS/6000 *see* WORKSTATION.

IC

1. *See* INTEGRATED CIRCUIT.

2. abbreviation for "**i**n **c**haracter," used in role playing games and the like to indicate a return to the imaginary situation after an out of

character (OOC) conversation. When IC, all replies are from the user's imaginary alter ego. Example: "Enough talk about iguanas. IC: This dragon is dangerous." *Contrast* OOC; see example there.

ICANN (**I**nternet **C**orporation of **A**ssigned **N**ames and **N**umbers) a nonprofit corporation established in 1998 to oversee the assignment of Internet domain names and addresses. *See also* IANA; TLD; UDDRP; UDRP. Web address: *www.icann.org*.

iCloud Apple's CLOUD COMPUTING service (web address: *www.apple.com/icloud*).

icon a small picture on a computer screen that represents a particular object, operation, or group of files. Icons are used extensively in graphical user interfaces such as Microsoft Windows and the Macintosh. *See* GRAPHICAL USER INTERFACE; MOUSE; WINDOW; WINDOWS (MICROSOFT).

Computer   User's Guide   Ulead DVD MovieFact...   Picasa2

Network   Games   Adobe Acrobat 7....   TOSHIBA Assist

FIGURE 136. Icons representing system components, files, folders, programs, and Internet connections

iconify to turn a window into an icon (same as MINIMIZE).

ICQ a widely used Internet chat program distributed free of charge from *www.icq.com*, which also gives an index of users and topics. The name is short for "I seek you." *Compare* AIM; IRC.

IDE

1. (**i**ntegrated **d**evelopment **e**nvironment) a software package for editing and compiling programs and, often, designing the program's windows graphically. Popular examples are Delphi, Visual Basic, and Visual Studio. *See* ECLIPSE.

2. (**I**ntegrated **D**evice **E**lectronics) a type of hard disk that has most of the controller circuitry built into it, to save space. *See also* ATA; ATAPI; SATA. *Contrast* SCSI.

identifier a symbolic name used in a program and defined by the programmer. Identifiers can stand for variables, constants, methods, or objects. In most programming languages, an identifier must begin with a letter, which may be followed by letters, numbers, and sometimes a few other characters (such as underscore "_"). In Perl, identifiers begin with a symbol (such as $, #, or @) that indicates a type of data structure.

identity in Outlook Express or similar mail-reading programs, a setting that determines which of several individuals is using the computer. This enables several people to share a computer and keep their e-mail separate even though the operating system is not set up for multiple users.

identity theft the crime of impersonation (i.e., pretending to be someone else), using forged documents of various kinds. Crucially, identity theft goes beyond the theft of a single credit card number or the forgery of a single document. It is an attempt to assume a person's entire identity, including name and credit rating, in order to create new accounts under the victim's name.

Identity theft often involves electronic communications media by taking advantage of the fact that online and mail-order merchants are often not very thorough in checking credit card users. *See also* COMPUTER ETHICS; EVIL TWIN; PHISHING.

ideogram, ideograph a written symbol that represents an idea rather than the pronunciation of a word. Symbols such as &, $, numerals, and computer icons are ideograms.

IDL (Interface Definition Language) *see* CORBA.

IE abbreviation for the INTERNET EXPLORER.

IEC (International Electrotechnical Commission) an organization that sets numerous standards for the electronics industry. Web address: *www.iec.ch*.

IEC power connector the type of connector commonly used to attach a PC's power cord to the computer, using three prongs oriented in the same direction.

FIGURE 137. IEC power connector

IEEE (**I**nstitute of **E**lectrical and **E**lectronics **E**ngineers) the leading professional society for electrical and computer engineers in the United States. It publishes journals, holds conferences, and publishes many standards applicable to computer equipment. The IEEE is head-quartered in Piscataway, New Jersey, and can be reached on the Web at *www.ieee.org.*

IEEE 1284 an IEEE standard for PC parallel ports, compatible with the designs used previously, but including provision for high-performance bidirectional communication with tape drives, disk drives, and other devices, not just printers. It is fully compatible with earlier EPP and ECP standards.

   The IEEE 1284 standard defines three connectors: the traditional 25-pin socket on the PC (IEEE 1284A), the 36-pin Centronics connector on the printer (IEEE 1284B), and a new miniature connector (IEEE 1284C).

   Parallel ports are IEEE 1284 *compliant* if they implement the whole IEEE 1284 standard; they are IEEE 1284 *compatible* if they implement one or more of the older standards of which IEEE 1284 is a superset.

   See CENTRONICS INTERFACE; PARALLEL PORT.

IEEE 1394, 1394a, 1394b *see* FIREWIRE.

IEEE 802.11 *see* 802.11.

IETF (**I**nternet **E**ngineering **T**ask **F**orce) an international group of network professionals who work on advances in Internet architecture and work to ensure smooth operation of the Internet. The IETF is orga-nized into several working groups on specific topics. Their web address is *www.ietf.org.*

if a keyword in many programming languages that specifies that different actions are to be performed depending on the result of some test. Here is a simple example of an if statement in Java:

```
if (price == 0)
{
  System.out.println
      ("Price can't be equal to zero!");
}
```

Here is a more practical example:

```
if (hours<=40)
{
  pay=hours*wage;
  System.out.println("No overtime hours");
}
else
{
```

```
   overtime = hours-40;
   pay= wage*40 + 1.5*wage*overtime;
   System.out.println("Overtime paid");
 }
```

In C, C++, Java, and C#, a very common error is to write if (x=5) when you mean if (x==5) or the like. Here x=5 is a command to assign the value 5 to the variable x. Some compilers will object when you embed the command in an if statement, but in C, doing so is legal (and always comes out true if the value assigned is nonzero).

ignore list a list of users you have blocked in a chat or instant messaging program. When another user is on your ignore list, your software will ignore messages from them. *Synonyms:* BLACKLIST; KILL FILE.

IIOP (**I**nternet **I**nter-**ORB** **P**rotocol) a protocol that extends TCP/IP by adding CORBA defined messages for objects to connect to each other over the network. *See* CORBA; PROTOCOL.

IIRC online abbreviation for "**if I** **r**emember **c**orrectly."

IIS (**I**nternet **I**nformation **S**ervices) the component of Microsoft Windows (professional and server editions only) that enables the computer to work as a web, FTP, and e-mail server.

i.LINK *see* FIREWIRE.

illegal operation an operation that a program is not permitted to perform, such as writing on a read-only disk or using memory allocated to some other program. Illegal operations are almost invariably the result of errors in programming. In some cases, a program can "catch" an illegal operation and perform specified actions instead. *See* TRY.

IM **I**nstant **M**essage or **M**essenger; *see* AIM; LIVE MESSENGER.

iMac a line of Apple Macintosh computers with a distinctive streamlined design introduced in 1998. The current iMac computer is built entirely within the enclosure containing its flat-screen monitor. *See also* APPLE; MACINTOSH.

image
1. a picture, represented in a computer's memory. *See* GRAPHICS.
2. a copy, on a disk, of the contents of a computer's memory. A BOOT DISK may contain an image in this sense, i.e., a large block of data that can be copied directly into memory.

image map a web page graphic to which multiple links have been assigned. It is possible to click on different parts of the picture and activate different links. For example, you might create a map of your community that appears on the web page; if the user clicks on the part of the map representing one neighborhood, then the browser will jump to a link providing information about that neighborhood. This gives the links a visual meaning that would not be there in a list of text-only links. Image maps can be created with some web-creation software programs, or they can be defined directly by hand-coding the proper HTML, using tags such as <map> and <area>.

image processing the use of a computer to modify pictures (usually bitmap images). Applications of image processing include computer vision, enhancement of photographs, and creation of works of art. Many image processing functions are built into PAINT PROGRAMS as FILTERS (definition 1). For examples, *see* ADD NOISE; BLEND; BLUR; BRIGHTNESS; COLOR/GRAY MAP; EDGE DETECT; EQUALIZE; HISTOGRAM; MOTION BLUR; PIXELATE, PIXEL-IZE; REMOVE SPOTS; SHARPEN; UNSHARP MASKING. *See also* COLOR; COM-PUTER; CONVOLUTION; DEBLURRING; GAMMA; RETOUCHING; VISION.

imagesetter a high-quality output device. Imagesetters can deliver up to 2400 DPI (dots per inch) instead of the 300 to 1200 DPI of ordinary laser printers.

IMAP (Internet Mail Access Protocol) a protocol for viewing e-mail on a personal computer while leaving it in place on the host system. *Contrast* POP, which delivers the mail and deletes it from the server. *See* PROTOCOL.

IMHO online abbreviation for "in my humble opinion."

IMO online abbreviation for "in my opinion."

impact printer a printer that prints on paper by impacting a cloth ribbon coated with ink, thus transferring ink to the paper. Dot-matrix printers are the most common type of impact printer. Today, impact printers are used mainly for business forms that involve carbon paper or carbonless copy paper.

impedance a measure of how easily an alternating current can pass through an electrical circuit. The impedance of a resistor is the same as its resistance. Capacitors and inductors also affect impedance, depending on the frequency of the current. The impedance of a capacitor decreases as the frequency increases; the impedance of an inductor increases as the frequency increases. The characteristic impedance of coaxial cable results from the interaction of its inductance and capacitance. It is not a resistance and cannot be measured with an ohmmeter. *See* COAXIAL CABLE.

import to load a file from a format other than the application program's native format. Many word processing and graphics programs have the ability to import text and graphics from several different file formats. Because importing is a type of file conversion, formatting and image detail may be lost in the process. *See* CONVERSION PROGRAM.

in the loop (*jargon*) involved in decision-making or control, like an automatic control system that uses feedback. *See* LOOP (definition 2).

incremental backup a backup operation that only copies files that have changed since the last backup. *See* BACKUP COPY.

incremental compiler a compiler that compiles the lines of a program as they are typed into the computer, rather than compiling the whole program at once. The purpose is to keep the programmer from having to wait a long time for the complete program to be compiled when it is finished. *See* COMPILER.

indecency material that offends ordinary people but does not meet the legal criterion of obscenity. In the United States, indecent material is protected by the First Amendment (freedom of speech) and is legal in printed publications, cable TV, and the Internet, but not on radio and TV broadcasts that use publicly available channels. *See also* OBSCENITY; PORNOGRAPHY.

indent to leave a tab and/or blank characters at the beginning of the first line of a paragraph. Indented margins are also used to set off long quotations. *See also* HANGING INDENT, HANGING TAB.

index
   1. an alphabetical listing of important words and concepts found in a book and the pages on which these terms may be found. Many page layout and word processing programs have the ability to automatically generate indexes from properly tagged terms (*see* DESKTOP PUBLISHING; TAG). Note that the process is not wholly automatic; the human still has to specify which words should be indexed.
   2. a pictograph of a pointing hand. Sometimes called a *fist*.
   3. the number that picks out an element of an array. For example, in A[2], 2 is the index. *See* ARRAY; SUBSCRIPT.

FIGURE 138. Index (definition 2)

indexed file a file in which the order of the items is recorded in a separate file called the index. For example, if the computer is looking for John Smith's billing records, it first looks up "Smith, John" in the index, and then the index tells it where to look in the billing record file.

index.htm, index.html on many web servers, the file name that is used for a WEB PAGE when no file name is specified in the URL. Thus, *index.html* is usually the main page of a web site (hence its name). *Compare* DEFAULT.ASP.

Industry Standard Architecture *see* ISA.

INF file a type of file, with extension `.inf`, that tells the Windows Setup program how to install a particular piece of hardware or software.

inference engine the part of an EXPERT SYSTEM that draws conclusions by reasoning logically from information. *See also* ARTIFICIAL INTELLIGENCE; PROLOG.

inferior character a subscript; small letters and numbers set on or below the baseline ₗᵢₖₑ ₜₕᵢₛ. Used mainly in mathematical typesetting. *See* SUBSCRIPT. *Contrast* SUPERIOR CHARACTER; SUPERSCRIPT.

infix notation including an operator symbol between the operands, as in ordinary arithmetic notation such as $2 + 3$. *Contrast* PREFIX NOTATION; POSTFIX NOTATION.

infix operator an operator placed between its operands, as is the plus sign in the expression $2 + 3$.

Infobahn German for INFORMATION SUPERHIGHWAY.

informatics the study of information and computation; a European name for computer science. *See* COMPUTER SCIENCE.

information extraction the act of extracting, by computer, recognizable information from documents written in a human language; an example would be reading weather reports in English and constructing a table of dates and temperatures. *Compare* INFORMATION RETRIEVAL.

information hiding *see* STRUCTURED PROGRAMMING.

information retrieval the act of identifying, by computer, documents written in a human language that are relevant to some specific question. This goes beyond simply searching for words and phrases and often includes statistical analysis of vocabulary (to determine subject matter) and a considerable amount of NATURAL LANGUAGE PROCESSING.

Information Superhighway a network of electronic and digital communication equipment that is quietly revolutionizing businesses and our private lives (*see* INTERNET).

Not only is information being disseminated faster than ever, but worldwide electronic communication is creating a unique community—one that does not have a physical location, but rather exists in what is called CYBERSPACE. Some portions of cyberspace are rather lawless right now; an ill-considered message may bring down an avalanche of angry messages (called FLAMES) upon your e-mail account. However, some standards of ethics and personal behavior are being worked out. *See* COMPUTER ETHICS.

The term *information superhighway* is also used to refer to a system of fiber-optic cables that may one day link every home to the Internet, replacing the current television and telephone cables.

infrared a kind of electromagnetic radiation similar to visible light but at a slightly longer wavelength, used to transmit data through the air in TV remote controls, wireless mice, wireless keyboards, and the like, and occasionally for short-distance computer-to-computer links. Like light, infrared signals require a clear line of sight and cannot go through walls.

Infrared radiation is abundant in ordinary sunlight and, at the levels used for communication, is not hazardous.

inheritance the process by which one object is defined to be just like another except for some specified differences. The second type of object then "inherits" the properties of the first. *See* OBJECT-ORIENTED PROGRAMMING.

INI file a file (with the extension .ini) that stores initialization information for Microsoft Windows or a specific piece of software. Windows INI files consist of editable text.

initialize
1. to store a value in a variable for the first time. If a program tries to use a variable that has not been initialized, it will get a random value, and the results will be unpredictable. Some programming languages, such as C#, automatically initialize all variables to zero or its equivalent.
2. to prepare a disk or other storage medium for use, erasing any data that may already be on it.

inkjet printer a printer that forms characters by shooting tiny droplets of ink at the paper. Advantages include speed, high resolution, and quiet operation. An ink jet printer is often an economical alternative to a laser printer; in black and white, the image quality is comparable, but printing is slower. Many color inkjet printers can print photo-quality pictures on special glossy paper; with ordinary paper, the picture quality is lower. *Contrast* LASER PRINTER. *See also* GICLÉE; SEPARATOR PAD.

inlining the conversion of a FUNCTION or PROCEDURE into machine instructions that perform the computation directly, without jumping to the procedure. In effect, the statement that calls the procedure is replaced by a copy of the procedure itself. This speeds up execution but requires slightly more memory. *See* COMPILER; FUNCTION; PROCEDURE.

input information that is given to a computer; the act of giving information to a computer. (Note that the terms *input* and *output* are always used from the computer's point of view.) The input data may be either numbers or character strings (e.g., a list of names). The computer receives input through an input device, such as a keyboard, or from a storage device, such as a disk drive.

insertion point the place, in a full-screen editor or drawing program, where characters will appear if you start typing. The insertion point, which is different from the mouse pointer, looks like a thin vertical bar or, in some contexts, a tall, thin letter "I"; it is relocated by clicking at the desired location. *See* CARET (definition 3); I-BAR, I-BEAM.

insertion sort an algorithm for placing the elements of an array in ascending or descending order. This method is efficient if the list is already close to being in order.

To perform an insertion sort, examine every item in the list except the first. Whenever you find an item that should come before the item that immediately precedes it, pick up the current item, shift its neighbor on the left one space to the right, and see whether you can put the current item in the space thus vacated. If not, shift that item to the right and try again.

Consider for example the following list:

> 2404 8653 1354 5781

The steps of the insertion sort are the following:

1. 2404 and 8653 are in the right order, so proceed to the next pair.
2. 8653 and 1354 are in the wrong order, so pick up 1354:

> 2404 8653 5781

Shift 8653 one space to the right:

> 2404 . . . . . 8653 5781

```
class insertionsort
{
/* Java example of insertion sort */
/* Array to be sorted, and number of items in it: */
static int a[] = {29,18,7,56,64,33,128,70,78,81,12,5};
static int num=12;

public static void main(String args[])
{
 /* Perform the insertion sort */
 for (int i=1; i<=num-1; i++)
 {
  int value = a[i];
  int position = i;
  while ( (position > 0) && (a[position-1] > value) )
   {
    a[position] = a[position-1];
    position--;
   }
  a[position]=value;
 }
 /* Display the results */
 for (int i=0; i<=num-1; i++)
 {
   System.out.println(a[i]);
 }
 }
}
```

FIGURE 139. Insertion sort

Can 1354 be put into the empty space? No; its neighbor on the left would be 2404, a larger number. So shift 2404 one space to the right:

> 2404 8653 5781

Now you can put 1354 into the empty space:

> 1354 2404 8653 5781

3. Now examine 8653 and 5781. They are in the wrong order, so pick up 8653 and shift it one space to the right, then put 5781 into the empty space:

> 1354 2404 8653 . . . .
> 1354 2404 8653
> 1354 2404 5781 8653

Now all the elements are in order, and the process is complete. Figure 139 shows a program that performs an insertion sort. *See also* SHELL SORT.

instance variables the variables (*fields*) that contain data unique to each object in OBJECT-ORIENTED PROGRAMMING.

instant messaging the sending of brief text messages instantly to other users of a network through software such as AOL Instant Messenger, Microsoft MSN messaging, ICQ, or (originally) the talk command in UNIX. Besides computers, instant messages can be sent to and from pagers and cellular telephones. *See also* TEXT MESSAGE.

A key feature of IM programs is their ability to display your status, whether "Online" or "Away," to your regular contacts. IM programs also allow you to designate "Friends" and provide the ability to block communication with unwanted persons. IM messages are typically brief and heavily abbreviated (*see* CHAT ROOM). Icons are sometimes used to express emotions.

Messaging programs are also becoming popular with businesses, especially when members of a tight-knit workgroup are traveling.

instantiated created or initialized. Once a new instance of a particular object type is created, it is said to be instantiated. In Prolog, a variable is said to be instantiated when it is given a value. *See* INSTANCE VARIABLES; OBJECT-ORIENTED PROGRAMMING; PROLOG.

.int *see* TLD.

int data type representing an integer in Java and other languages. Occupying 32 bits of memory, a Java variable of type int can hold values from $-2^{31} = -2, 147, 483, 648$ to $2^{31} - 1 = 2, 147, 483, 647$.

integers whole numbers and negated whole numbers, such as 1, 2, 3, 0, -10, -26, 157, 567, and -2397. An integer does not contain a fractional part. Thus, 3.4 and $2\frac{2}{3}$ are not integers.

integrated circuit (**IC**) an electronic device consisting of many miniature transistors and other circuit elements on a single silicon chip. The first integrated circuits were developed in the late 1950s, and since then there has been continued improvement. The number of components that can be placed on a single chip has been steadily rising. *See* Figure 79, page 142.

The advantages of integrated circuits over discrete components include the facts that they are very small (most are less than $\frac{1}{4}$ inch [6 mm] square), their internal connections are more reliable, they consume much less power, they generate much less heat, and they cost less than similar circuits made with separate components.

Integrated circuits are classified by their level of complexity. *Small-scale integration* describes circuits containing fewer than 10 logic gates; *medium-scale integration,* circuits containing hundreds of gates; *large-scale integration,* circuits with thousands of gates, *very-large-scale integration,* circuits with over tens of thousands of gates. The term *ultra-large-scale integration* has been proposed for circuits with over one million gates.

An integrated circuit is made by adding impurities to a silicon crystal in specific places to create P-type and N-type regions, and adding metal conductive paths to serve as wires. (*See* SEMICONDUCTOR.) The whole process uses light-sensitive chemicals whose action is controlled by a tiny image projected through a device that is like a microscope working backward; thus, tiny regions on the IC can be created from a much larger picture of the desired layout.

Integrated circuits are mass produced by making many identical circuits at the same time from a single wafer of silicon. Each circuit must be individually tested, because a single defect in the crystal can completely ruin the circuit.

The ultimate integrated circuit is the microprocessor, which is a single chip that contains the complete arithmetic and logic unit of a computer, and sometimes other parts of the computer as well. *See* MICROPROCESSOR.

Intel the manufacturer of the microprocessors used in PC-compatible computers, although other companies also make compatible equivalents. Intel products include the 8088, 80286, 386, 486, Pentium and its descendents, Itanium, Celeron, Xeon, and Core. *See* MICROPROCESSOR. Earlier, Intel developed the first microprocessors (4004, 8008) and the microprocessor for which CP/M was developed (the 8080, soon superseded by Zilog's Z80). Intel Corporation is headquartered in Santa Clara, California. Its web address is *www.intel.com.*

interactive system a computer system in which the user communicates with the computer through a keyboard and screen. Nowadays, almost all computing is interactive. *Contrast* BATCH PROCESSING.

intercaps capitalized letters in the middle of a word. The word *PostScript* contains an example. *See also* CAMEL NOTATION; PASCAL NOTATION. The companies that have coined such trademarks contend that the unusual capitalization is part of the correct spelling.

Not everybody accepts these unusual spellings. At one time there was a company that claimed the only correct spelling of its name was "en•vōs." Almost everyone printed it as Envos. The moral of the story is that names need not reproduce trademarks and logos. In fact, a company can be at a real disadvantage if it makes its name too hard to print—journalists may simply ignore it.

intercharacter spacing the spacing in between characters within words. Also called LETTERSPACING. *See* KERNING; PROPORTIONAL PITCH; TRACKING.

interface the connection between two systems through which information is exchanged. For example, in computer hardware, an interface is an electrical connection of the proper type. In software, it is a standard format for exchanging data. The USER INTERFACE of a piece of software is the way it interacts with the human being who is using it. *See also* DATA COMMUNICATION; USER INTERFACE.

interlaced GIF a BITMAP file that has been optimized for downloading to a remote site. An interlaced GIF displays faster because it can be displayed in rough form before all the information has been received. The picture initially appears in coarse blocks, which refine themselves into finer detail as the complete file is downloaded. *See* GIF.

Internet a cooperative message-forwarding system linking computer networks all over the world. Users of the Internet can view information on the World Wide Web, exchange electronic mail, participate in electronic discussion forums (newsgroups), send files from any computer to any other via FTP, or HTTP, and even use each other's computers directly if they have appropriate passwords. *See* ELECTRONIC MAIL; FINGER; FTP; HTTP; NEWSGROUP; RLOGIN; TELNET; TLD; URL; WORLD WIDE WEB.

Every machine on the Internet has an address. For example, the address

```
beetle.ai.uga.edu
```

means:

beetle	machine ("beetle")
ai	subnetwork (Artificial Intelligence Lab)
uga	site (University of Georgia)
edu	type of site (U.S. educational)

Here beetle.ai.uga.edu is a domain address that gets translated into a numeric IP address, such as 128.192.12.9, by the network itself. *See* IP ADDRESS; TCP/IP.

The cost of running the Internet is paid largely by the sites that receive messages, and the sites that pass them along, not by the sites that send messages out. This has important legal and ethical implications. *Unsolicited advertising via e-mail or in newsgroups is almost always unwelcome*, as is any self-serving misuse of electronic communications, because the sender of the material is not paying the cost of distributing it. For further ethical guidelines *see* COMPUTER ETHICS; SPAM; USENET.

The Internet grew out of the ARPAnet (a U.S. Defense Department experimental network) as well as BITNET, Usenet, and other wide area networks. *See* WIDE-AREA NETWORK. *Contrast* INTRANET.

Tim Berners-Lee developed HTML in the early 1990s while working at the scientific laboratory CERN near Geneva, Switzerland. The World Wide Web, which grew out of this work, proved to be a tremendously useful way to publish and find information on the Internet.

Mark Andreessen developed the web browser Mosaic at the University of Illinois, and then founded the company Netscape to distribute the browser (renamed Netscape Navigator) in 1994. The World Wide Web became widely popular during 1995, as more and more web pages were placed online and more and more people accessed them through their browsers. The launch of Google in 1998 provided an improved way to find information available on the web. The launch of Facebook in 2004 provided another means for people to connect to each other using the Internet.

There are some risks that come from using the Internet. See the page on "How to Be Safe on the Internet" at the very back of the book.

Usage note: Many people confuse the Internet with the World Wide Web, which is only one of several forms of communication that take place on the Internet.

Internet 2 a consortium of universities working with business and government to create a high-performance successor to the original INTERNET. For more information see *www.internet2.org*.

Internet cafe a small business selling Internet and computer use by the minute or hour. Most Internet cafes also offer other services including everything from food to live musical performances.

Internet casino *see* GAMBLING.

Internet Explorer the World Wide Web browser included in Microsoft Windows; a derivative of MOSAIC. *See* BROWSER.

Internet gambling *see* GAMBLING.

Internet radio the transmission of sound from a radio station, or similar real-time audio programs, to computer users over the Internet. This makes hearing distant and specialized radio stations possible. However, it can clog up networks because a separate copy of each data packet has to be sent to each computer. (Real radios all pick up the same signal at the same time.) The BBC World Service can be heard by Internet radio at *www.bbc.co.uk. See also* IPTV.

Internet service provider (ISP) (access provider) a company that provides its customers with access to the INTERNET, typically through DSL, a CABLE MODEM, or DIAL-UP NETWORKING. Major service providers in the United

States include Microsoft, Comcast, Earthlink, America Online, and various phone companies and cable television companies. Typically, the customer pays a monthly fee, and the Internet service provider supplies software that enables the customer to connect to the Internet. Some ISPs also provide file space for pages on the WORLD WIDE WEB and FTP file storage.

Internet telephony the making of telephone calls by digitizing the sound and transmitting it through the Internet. This is often a much cheaper alternative to conventional long-distance or international calling, but there can be delays or loss of quality when the requisite parts of the Internet are congested with heavy traffic.

Originally, Internet telephony was only possible when the people on both ends were using computers with soundcards, microphones, and special software. More recently, Internet telephony gateways have been established that allow calling from and to ordinary telephones. *See also* VOIP, SKYPE.

Internet television *see* IPTV.

interoperability the ability of machines or programs to work together. Two computers are interoperable if they can be used together in some useful way, working on the same files or sharing data through a network.

interpolation

1. in mathematics, the process of estimating an unknown value of a function in between two known values. For example, if it takes 18 minutes to cook a 1-inch-thick steak and 40 minutes to cook a 2-inch steak, you can interpolate and find that it should take about 30 minutes to cook a 1½-inch steak.

2. in computer graphics, the process of smoothing the pixels in an image that has been enlarged by filling in intermediate colors or shades of gray, thus reducing the stairstep appearance that would otherwise result from enlarging a small bitmap; also known as resampling. *See* RESAMPLE.

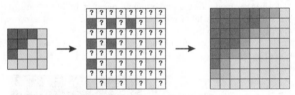

FIGURE 140. Interpolation (resampling) to enlarge an image

interpreter a program that executes a source program by reading it one line at a time and performing the specified operations immediately. Most Perl and Python systems are interpreters. *Contrast* COMPILER.

interrupt an instruction that tells a microprocessor to put aside what it is doing and call a specified routine. The processor resumes its original work when the interrupt service routine finishes. Interrupts can be caused by hardware (through input on specific pins of the microprocessor) or by software (by performing an instruction to generate an interrupt).

interrupt service routine *see* INTERRUPT.

intersection the set of elements that are in both of two other sets. For example, the intersection of {*a, b, c*} with {*c, b, r*} is {*b, c*}.

interwebs, interwebz (*slang*) the INTERNET and the WORLD WIDE WEB.

interword spacing the spacing between words, sometimes called WORD-SPACING. *Contrast* LETTERSPACING.

intranet a network confined to a single organization (but not necessarily a single site). Intranets often include web pages, so a web browser can be used to view the content. This makes the intranet appear just the same as part of the World Wide Web; the only difference is that it is not accessible to those outside the organization. Keeping it separate from the outside world is essential if it carries confidential data, such as internal business records. *Contrast* EXTRANET.

Intuit a leading producer of personal financial software (the program Quicken). Web address: *www.intuit.com*.

intuitive obvious without conscious thought. The operation of a piece of software is said to be *intuitive* if the operation fits the task so well that the user can guess how to perform common operations without consulting manuals or pausing to figure things out. *Compare* USER-FRIENDLY.

invalid media disks or tapes that cannot be used because of physical defects or because they have been partly erased by a magnetic field. In the latter case the media can be formatted (erased) and used again.

invert
1. to turn an image into a photographic negative of itself, substituting black for white and white for black, and changing colors to their complements. *Compare* REVERSE.
2. (less commonly) to turn an image upside down. For other senses, *see* INVERTER.

FIGURE 141. Inverted photograph

inverter

    1. a NOT gate. *See* NOT GATE.

    2. a device that converts direct current to alternating current for power supply purposes (e.g., to power a computer from a car battery).

invisible watermark a code secretly hidden in a picture to carry copyright information or other secret messages. An invisible watermark consists of a very slight change of contrast over large areas of the picture, invisible to the human eye, even fainter than the watermark on a piece of paper. Suitable software can recover the invisible watermark even if the image has been printed out, photographed, and scanned in again. *See* STEGANOGRAPHY.

Iomega manufacturer of Zip drives and other portable storage devices. Their corporate web site is at *www.iomega.com.*

iOS the MacOS-based operating system of the IPOD, IPAD, IPHONE, and other Apple products. The user accesses application software by touching icons on the screen. See MULTITOUCH INTERFACE. There is no file system visible to the user; instead, some application programs have their own file space.

    iOS is designed to be extremely resistant to viruses, at the expense of versatility. Software can only be obtained through Apple's "App Store" and not from other sources. This enables Apple to block viruses, malware, pornography and other software that is, in their judgment, offensive, but it denies the user a level of freedom enjoyed by users of almost all other computers throughout history. *See* JAILBREAK.

IOW online abbreviation for "**i**n **o**ther **w**ords."

IP

    1. **I**nternet **P**rotocol. *See* IP ADDRESS; IPV4; IPV6; TCP/IP.

    2. **i**ntellectual **p**roperty (i.e., patents, copyrights, and trademarks, especially patented or copyrighted designs for components of equipment or software).

IP address (**I**nternet **P**rotocol address, or IP number) the numeric address of a machine, in the format used on the Internet (IPv4 or IPv6). For example, the IPv4 address of one of the University of Georgia's computers is 128.192.76.80. Convert each of the four numbers into binary, and you get the true 32-bit binary address, which can also be written as an 8-digit hexadecimal number.

    Three blocks of IPv4 addresses are reserved for private networks and will never be officially assigned. Therefore, if you must make up an unofficial IP address, you should choose it from one of these blocks. They are 10.0.0.0–10.255.255.255, 172.16.0.0–172.16.255.255, and 192.168.0.0–192.168.255.255. The address 127.0.0.1 on any machine connects it back to itself.

    IPv6, a newer version of the protocol, uses 128-bit instead of 32-bit addresses, so that a much larger number of addresses is available. The packet format is different in a number of ways that make routing more efficient.

Contrast DOMAIN ADDRESS; MAC ADDRESS. *See also* INTERNET; STATIC IP ADDRESS; DYNAMIC IP ADDRESS.

IP spoofing *see* SPOOFING.

IP telephony *see* INTERNET TELEPHONY.

iPad a TABLET COMPUTER introduced by Apple in 2010, based on the iOS operating system and largely similar to the iPhone and iPod except for the larger screen. *See* IOS; TABLET COMPUTER; MULTITOUCH INTERFACE.

iPhone a SMARTPHONE. The iPhone runs the iOS operating system and can run largely the same apps as the iPad and iPod. *See* IOS; JAILBREAK.

IPO (Initial Public Offering) the first sale of a corporation's stock to the public. Innovative computer companies have often begun as privately held corporations, motivating employees by offering stock options that become valuable after the IPO if the market price rises. Outside investors who buy stock soon after the IPO will profit from further increases in the stock price. However, this type of investment is very risky because there is no guarantee the stock price will rise.

iPod a line of Apple products that were originally music players but have evolved into full-featured PDAs (pocket-size computers) that run the IOS operating system and include cameras, microphones, web browsers, and WiFi network access, but lack access to the cellular telephone network. Much of the application software for the iPhone and iPad also runs on the latest models of iPod.

IPTV (Internet Protocol Television) a system for transmitting television signals on request. Unlike traditional broadcast signals, which send all channels to all customers, an IPTV system conserves bandwidth by only sending signals for channels that customers have requested. However, traditional Internet transmission sends a separate signal for each user, so broadcast television signals would consume excessive bandwidth if they were sent this way. Instead, IPTV signals for multiple users are combined into a multicast signal, which contains one copy of the broadcast signal as well as the addresses of those users to whom the signal is to be sent. As the signal gets closer to the users it is split into separate signals for each user.

IPv4 the older version of the Internet Protocol, the protocol for routing traffic through large networks, introduced in 1981. *Contrast* IPV6.

IPv6 version 6 of the Internet Protocol, which provides improvements in routing network traffic and increases the number of available network addresses. Currently, the Internet is making a slow transition between IPv4 (in which addresses look like "128.192.76.90") and IPv6 (in which addresses look like "fe80:0000:7c4d:9c4f:44a5:5d80:0000:0000" and fields of all zeroes can be omitted). Many networked computers have addresses of both types. This is transparent to the user, and URLs such as *http://www.ai.uga.edu* are automatically translated into whichever kind of IP address is in use. See *www.ipv6.org. See also* PROTOCOL.

IPX/SPX (**I**nternetwork **P**acket E**x**change/**S**equenced **P**acket E**x**change) a data transmission protocol developed by Novell and widely used in local-area networking. *See* PROTOCOL. *Contrast* ATM; NETBEUI; TCP/IP.

```
<JohnBoy> Does anybody know where I can
get some information about SCSI?
<Gweep> Hello, John Boy!
<JohnBoy> Hello, Gweep!
<Hermes> There's a newsgroup called
comp.periphs.scsi. Look there.
<JohnBoy> Thanks, Hermes.
<Gweep> What's a newsgroup?
```
FIGURE 142. IRC session

IRC (**I**nternet **R**elay **C**hat) a multi-user conversation conducted over the Internet in real time. Figure 142 shows what a chat session looks like. Numerous CHANNELS (conversation forums) exist. Participants normally identify themselves by nicknames.

In addition to typing remarks for transmission to the other participants, the IRC user can type commands such as /list to see what channels are available, /join #frogs to join a channel called frogs or create it if it doesn't exist, and /bye to sign off. *See also* AIM; CHAT ROOM.

IRL online abbreviation for "**i**n **r**eal **l**ife," meaning the mundane, real, physical world as opposed to the glamorous exciting life in CYBERSPACE.

IRQ (**I**nterrupt **R**e**q**uest) a type of bus signal used on PC-compatible computers to allow input-output devices to interrupt the CPU.

ISA (**I**ndustry-**S**tandard **A**rchitecture) a term often used to describe the conventional IBM PC AT (16-bit) bus and the associated card edge connector, as opposed to EISA. *See* BUS; EISA.

ISA slot a slot in a computer where ISA accessories can be added.

iSCSI (**I**nternet **SCSI**) a method of communicating with a disk drive on a server using the same protocol as if it were attached to a SCSI port, but wrapping the SCSI data in Ethernet packets. *Compare* SCSI.

ISDN (**I**ntegrated **S**ervices **D**igital **N**etwork) a type of all-digital telephone service that can transmit computer data (e.g., for Internet connections) as well as voice, with a maximum speed of 128 kbps. ISDN service began in the United States in 1988 but has largely been superseded by DSL, which obtains higher communication speeds over conventional telephone lines. *See* DSL; T1 LINE; T3 LINE.

ISO

   1. International Organization for Standardization (abbreviated ISO in all languages), an organization that sets standards for many industries. For example, there are ISO standards for the Pascal and Prolog programming languages and for sizes of printer paper. *See also* ANSI; PAPER SIZES.
   2. online abbreviation for "**in s**earch **of**."
   3. a system for rating the sensitivity (speed) of photographic film or CCDs, based on an ISO standard, equivalent to the older ASA system. An ISO 100 film or CCD will make a correctly exposed picture of a sunlit landscape when exposed for 1/100 second at *f*/16.

ISO 9000 an ISO standard specifying various ways of ensuring the quality of manufactured products. It does not denote any specific computer technology.

ISO 9660 the basic standard format for recording computer data on compact discs (CD-ROMs). Unlike most disk formats, CD-ROMs are not tied to the operating system of a particular computer; any computer can read the data files from any standard CD-ROM. (Software recorded on the CD-ROM may of course require a specific computer in order to run.) ISO 9660 format supersedes the earlier High Sierra format, with which it is closely compatible. *See* JOLIET FILE SYSTEM; ROCK RIDGE.

ISO paper sizes *see* PAPER SIZES.

ISP (**I**nternet **s**ervice **p**rovider) a company that provides accounts allowing customers to access the Internet. *See* ACCESS PROVIDER; INTERNET SERVICE PROVIDER.

ISV (**i**ndependent **s**oftware **v**endor) a company that writes software independently of the company selling the hardware.

IT (**i**nformation **t**echnology) computers and electronic communication.

italics letters slanted to the right and designed with a more calligraphic feel than their roman counterparts. *This sentence is set in italics.* Italics are used for emphasis, for setting the titles of books and articles, and for foreign words. Italic type corresponds to underlining in handwriting or on a typewriter.

Itanium a family of Intel 64-bit microprocessors implementing the IA-64 architecture, introduced in 2001. *See* IA-64.

iteration the process of repeating a particular action. For examples *see* FOR; WHILE. *Contrast* RECURSION, in which instead of merely being repeated, the action creates another action of the same type within itself.

ITU (**I**nternational **T**elecommunication **U**nion) an organization headquartered in Geneva, Switzerland, that sets standards for electronic communication technology. For more information see the web page *www.itu.int*.

ITU-T the telecommunication section of the ITU, formerly known as the CCITT.

iTunes an online service operated by Apple to sell music and videos, mainly for use on the iPod and its relatives, and also to sell application software for iOS devices. iTunes is also the name of Apple's software for the Macintosh and PC for making purchases of music and videos, playing them on the Macintosh or PC, and downloading them to an attached iPod or other iOS device. Web address: *www.apple.com/itunes*.

iWork a suite of office software applications (word processing, spreadsheets, and presentation graphics) supplied by Apple for the Macintosh, iPad, and related computers.

J

J# (pronounced "J sharp") a programming language very similar to JAVA but implemented in the Microsoft .NET Framework; essentially a combination of Java and C#. Most Java 1.1 programs will run unaltered in J#, and in addition, the full functionality of the .NET Framework is available. *See* C#; .NET FRAMEWORK.

jack a connector into which a plug can be inserted.

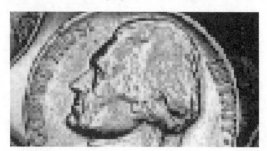

FIGURE 143. Jaggies (stairsteps) in an improperly sized bitmap

jaggies the property of an improperly sized bitmap that shows the image broken into blocky squares. *See* ANTIALIASING; BITMAP; PIXELATE; RESOLUTION.

Jaguar version 10.2 of MAC OS X.

jailbreak (*slang*) to configure an iPhone, iPod, iPad, or other iOS device so that it can work with cellular carriers other than the original one and can install software not supplied by Apple. In the United States, jailbreaking is legal but can void the Apple warranty.

Japanese writing *see* KANA.

JAR file (Java Archive) a file containing a collection of Java class files that can be downloaded more efficiently than would be possible if each file were downloaded separately.

Jargon File a glossary of computer terms begun at Stanford University in 1975, extensively enlarged at MIT, and eventually published, in highly revised form, as *The New Hacker's Dictionary*, by Eric S. Raymond (MIT Press, 3rd edition, 1996). Versions are also available on the World Wide Web. The Jargon File is important because it is one of the first instances of computer enthusiasts functioning as a cultural movement.

Java a programming language developed at Sun Microsystems in the mid-1990s to enable networked computers to transmit computations to each other, not just data. For example, an Internet user can connect to a Java APPLET (program) on the World Wide Web, download it, and run it, all at the click of a mouse, using a Java-compatible WEB BROWSER. Applets can include features, such as animation. Figure 144 shows an example of a Java program.

Java is designed for OBJECT-ORIENTED PROGRAMMING. The language is extensible: classes are defined in terms of other more general classes, and they inherit their properties. It is closely based on C++ but is fundamentally different in a number of ways that make it easier to use. Its special features include:

- architecture neutrality (a Java program can, in principle, run under any windowed operating system);
- garbage collection (memory is cleared automatically when objects no longer need it, eliminating one of the major headaches of C++ programming);
- security (Java applets downloaded from the web are restricted in their access to the machine's files and operating system; this is an essential feature of programs loaded through the Internet from a possibly untrustworthy source);
- uniform support for windowing environments (programs produce similar screen displays no matter where they are run);
- support for multiple threads of program action (concurrency).

Various Java development environments are available. Java software can be downloaded free of charge from *www.java.com*.

To compile a program, type a command such as

```
javac program1.java
```

where program1.java is the program to be compiled. This command will create the file program1.class.

Java programs are compiled not into machine code, which would not be portable, but into a concise code known as Java bytecode. How to run the bytecode depends on the type of Java program, since there are two kinds, applications (stand-alone programs) and applets. If the program is an application, it can be executed with this command:

```
java program1
```

If the program is an applet, it can be included in a web page through HTML statements such as

```
<applet code="program1.class" width=200 height=200>
</applet>
```

The applet will be executed by the browser's Java virtual machine whenever anyone views the web page. The user does not need to have the Java compiler, only the run-time support for Java that is provided by most web browsers.

Java is important not only because it allows computations to be downloaded through web pages, but also because it is the first portable

```java
/* File showball.java */
/* Displays red or blue circles when user clicks mouse */
import java.awt.*;
import java.applet.*;
public class showball extends Applet {
  Graphics g; int rc,gc,bc; ball ballobject;
  public void init() {
    setLayout(null);
    Button bluebutton = new Button("Blue");
    add(bluebutton);
    bluebutton.reshape(0,0,100,20);
    Button redbutton = new Button("Red");
    add(redbutton);
    redbutton.reshape(110,0,100,20);
    ballobject = new ball();
}

  public boolean action(Event e, Object o) {
        if ("Red".equals(o))
            {rc=255; gc=0; bc=0;}
    else if ("Blue".equals(o))
            {rc=0; gc=0; bc=255;}
     return false;
  }
  public boolean mouseDown(Event e, int x, int y) {
    ballobject.xc = x; ballobject.yc = y;
    ballobject.redcode = rc; ballobject.greencode = gc;
    ballobject.bluecode = bc;
    repaint();       return false;
  }
  public void paint(Graphics g) {
    ballobject.drawball(g);
  }
}
```

```java
/* File ball.java */
import java.awt.*;
import java.applet.*;
public class ball {
    int xc,yc,redcode,greencode,bluecode;
  public void drawball(Graphics g2) {
      Color  rgbcolor  =  new  Color (redcode,   greencode,
      bluecode);
      g2.setColor(rgbcolor);
      g2.fillArc(xc,yc,25,25,0,360);
      /* fillArc is included with the class applet*/
  }
}
```

FIGURE 144. Java program (comprising 2 files)

programming language for windowed operating systems. It does for windowing what BASIC did for the keyboard and screen, making it possible to write programs that run the same way regardless of the kind of machine. *See also* HTML; WORLD WIDE WEB.

JavaScript a language that allows a web page to include commands to be executed by the web browser. For example, you may wish your web page to have dialog boxes that appear when the user clicks on certain places. Or, if your web page will send information back to the server, you can use JavaScript to catch some common data entry errors before it is sent. This will save work for the server.

JavaScript was originally developed by Netscape. The name comes from the fact that JavaScript shares some syntax and object-oriented features with Java, but they are actually quite different languages. JavaScript commands are interpreted by the web browser (*see* INTERPRETER), rather than being compiled into bytecode as Java programs are. JavaScript is easier to learn than Java, particularly if you already know HTML, but, unlike Java, it does not have the features of a complete programming language.

Figure 145 is an example of how JavaScript can be used together with an HTML form to receive information from a customer. In this example, the user enters the item number, price, and quantity for two different items into the form. Two different JavaScript functions are defined. The function *addup* is called by the event handler onChange that is located in the HTML code for the form. Whenever one of these fields is changed, JavaScript checks for negative values and then multiplies the price times the quantity and adds up the total dollar amount.

Figure 146 shows the appearance of the screen when this web page is loaded.

For another example of programming in JavaScript, *see* ROLLOVER.

JBOD (**j**ust **a** **b**unch **o**f **d**isks) DISK SHARING in which the disks are treated separately, not organized into a RAID system. *See* RAID.

JCL (**J**ob **C**ontrol **L**anguage) the command language used in batch jobs to tell a computer what to do. (*See* BATCH PROCESSING.) The acronym JCL usually refers to the job control language used on large IBM computers, but sometimes designates very different languages used for the same purpose on other computers.

The following is an example of JCL for an IBM 360; the language is the same for all IBM mainframe computers running operating systems derived from OS/360, such as OS/VS2, and MVS:

```
//JONES JOB 123456,TIME=5
// EXEC PLIXCG
//PLI.SYSIN DD DSN=JONES.SAMPL.PLI,DISP=SHR
//GO.SYSIN DD *
1 2 3 4
/*
//
```

```
<HTML>
<HEAD><TITLE> JavaScript Example</TITLE>
<SCRIPT LANGUAGE="JavaScript">

function multiply(a,b) {
  if ((a>=0)&(b>=0)) {return a*b;}
  else {window.alert("Value can't be negative");
    return "invalid";}
      }

function addup() {
  var totalamount=0; var amount=0;
    for (i=1; i<=2; i++) {
      amount=
        multiply
        (document.orderform.elements[i*4-2].value,
        document.orderform.elements[i*4-1].value);
      document.orderform.elements[i*4].value=amount;
      totalamount+=amount;
              }
  document.orderform.total.value=totalamount;
      }
</SCRIPT>
</HEAD>

<BODY>

<H1> Order Form Example </H1>

<FORM NAME="orderform">
<ACTION "mailto:youraddress@xyz.com">
Your Name: <INPUT TYPE= "text" NAME="customername"
  SIZE=20><br>

Item Number:<INPUT TYPE="text" NAME="item1" SIZE=5>
Price:<INPUT TYPE="text" NAME="price1"
  SIZE=5 onChange="addup();">
Quantity:<INPUT TYPE="text" NAME="quant1"
  SIZE=5 onChange="addup();">
  Value: $<INPUT TYPE="text" NAME="value1"
  SIZE=8 onChange="addup();"><BR>

Item Number:<INPUT TYPE="text" NAME="item2" SIZE=5>
Price:<INPUT TYPE="text" NAME="price2"
  SIZE=5 onChange="addup();">
Quantity:<INPUT TYPE="text" NAME="quant2"
  SIZE=5 onChange="addup();">
Value: $<INPUT TYPE="text" NAME="value2"
  SIZE=8 onChange="addup();"><BR>

Total Value: $<INPUT TYPE="text" NAME="total"
  SIZE=8 onChange="addup();"><BR>

<INPUT TYPE="SUBMIT" NAME="submit"
  VALUE="E-Mail your order" SIZE=40>
</FORM>
</BODY>
</HTML>
```

FIGURE 145. JavaScript example

FIGURE 146. JavaScript in action

The first statement is the JOB card, which gives the job a name, specifies the user's account number, and establishes a CPU time limit of 5 minutes for the whole job. The EXEC PLIXCG statement calls up the procedure to compile and execute a PL/1 program; its operation happens to consist of two steps, PLI (compile) and GO (execute).

The DD (data definition) statements define files. SYSIN (standard system input) for the PLI step is defined as a cataloged disk data set named JONES.SAMPL.PLI; SYSIN for the GO step is given in the job itself, beginning after DD * and ending with /*. The // card marks the end of the job.

JDK (**J**ava **D**evelopment **K**it) a system that can be used to write Java programs. It comes with a Java compiler, standard class library, and an applet viewer. See *http://www.java.com/en*.

jewel case a rigid clear-plastic case that protects compact discs (CDs). The paper insert for the face of a jewel case is 120 mm (4.7 inches) square.

JIT compiler (**j**ust-**i**n-**t**ime compiler) a compiler that converts intermediate code into native machine language the first time it is encountered; this allows subsequent execution of that code to occur faster.

job *see* BATCH PROCESSING.

Jobs, Steve co-founder and longtime leader of APPLE. Jobs joined with Steve Wozniak in 1976 to start their company in a garage. The Apple 2 computer became widely used in the late 1970s, and the Macintosh (introduced in 1984) became the first widely used computer with a graphical user interface. However, Jobs did not have a controlling interest in the company by that time, and during a tense dispute over the future of the company he was forced out of management of the company in 1985. He then worked on founding a new company, Next, which made powerful computers which were too expensive to sell well. He also invested in the animated movie studio Pixar, an investment that finally paid off with the release of "Toy Story" in 1995.

In 1997 Apple, in serious financial trouble, hired Jobs to return as CEO. He led the company as it developed the iMac computer, the Mac

OS X operating system, the iTunes music store, the iPod, iPhone, and iPad. Jobs was particularly known for insisting on aesthetically pleasing designs.

In 2003 Jobs was diagnosed with pancreatic cancer. Except for medical leaves he continued as CEO of Apple almost until his death in 2011 at age 56.

join *see* RELATIONAL DATABASE.

Joliet file system an extension to the ISO 9660 format for recording CD-ROMs, created by Microsoft in order to support long filenames and long directory names. It is the usual format for CD-ROMs to be used under Windows 95 and later. *See also* ROCK RIDGE.

joule a unit for measuring amounts of energy. 1 joule equals 1 kilogram-meter^2/second^2. One watt is equivalent to one joule per second. *See* VOLT; WATT; WATT-HOUR.

joystick a computer input device especially helpful when playing computer games. The joystick consists of a handle that can be pointed in different directions. Because the computer can sense in which direction the joystick is pointed, the joystick can be used to control the movements of objects displayed on the computer screen.

JPEG (**J**oint **P**hotographic **E**xperts **G**roup) a file format for storing bitmap images, including lossy compression (i.e., a file can be compressed to a very small size if some blurring of detail is tolerable). JPEG file format is often used for high-quality photographic images. Filenames usually end in .jpeg or .jpg.

JScript a variant of JAVASCRIPT developed by Microsoft. JScript is not fully compatible with JavaScript.

jukebox a device for automatically selecting disks (usually CD-ROMs) from a library and inserting the desired one into the disk drive.

Julian calendar the calendar introduced in 46 B.C. by Julius Caesar, with a leap year every four years. *See* GREGORIAN CALENDAR; LEAP YEAR.

Julian date
1. the number of days elapsed since January 1, 4713 B.C., counting that date as day 1. The Julian date is now used primarily by astronomers. It is unrelated to the Julian calendar. The Julian date was introduced in 1582 A.D. by J. J. Scaliger, who named it for his father Julius. Its original purpose was to convert dates between various ancient calendars without using negative numbers. The Julian date of January 1, 2000 is 2,451,544.
2. more loosely, any date expressed as a day count rather than as year, month, and day.

jump list a WEB PAGE consisting mostly of links to other web pages. *See* HTML; INTERNET; LINK (definition 3); WORLD WIDE WEB.

JumpDrive Lexar's trademark for a brand of USB FLASH DRIVE. *See* Figure 290, page 530.

jumper a removable electrical connector that joins two pins on a circuit board. Many of the internal settings in computers are made by moving or removing jumpers.

junction the part of a diode or transistor where two opposite types of semi-conductor material meet. *See* DIODE; TRANSISTOR.

junk e-mail unsolicited electronic mail, usually containing advertisements. *See* SPAM.

junk fax an unsolicited advertisement transmitted by fax. In 1991, sending junk faxes was made illegal in the United States because it imposes an expense on the recipient (who has to pay for the paper) and ties up machines that are needed for more important messages. This law (47 USC 227) was overturned by a district court in 2002 (*Missouri v. American Blast Fax*), but the law was reinstated by an appeals court in 2003. In 2005, Congress revised this law by allowing unsolicited faxes if you previously had a business relationship with the sender (public law 109-21, the "Junk Fax Prevention Act of 2005").

junkware unwanted demonstration software added to a new computer by the seller.

justification the insertion of extra space between words in lines of type so that the left and right margins are even and smooth. Most of the type in this book is justified.

Most word processors and desktop publishing programs can automatically do the computations necessary to justify type. Problems generally arise only when the column width is too narrow, or too large a HOT ZONE has been specified. Then you will get rivers of white space running down the column (not too attractive). To cure this, make sure hyphenation is enabled, shrink the hot zone, go to a smaller type size, or increase the column width. *See* RIVER.

JVM (**J**ava **V**irtual **M**achine) software that executes Java bytecode. A program written in Java is first compiled into class files, written in bytecode. To execute these files, the computer needs to use the JVM to interpret the code. The JVM is built into web browsers that are capable of executing Java applets. The bytecode is the same for all platforms, but the JVM will be different on different platforms because it needs to execute using the native code of the machine it is running on.

Jython an implementation of PYTHON based on JAVA. See *www.jython.org*.

K

k, K abbreviation for KILOBYTE (or, less commonly, *kilohm* or other metric units). By convention, a capital K stands for a factor of 1,024, and a lowercase k stands for a factor of 1000, as in the metric system (kilograms, kilometers, etc.). *See also* BYTE; MEGABYTE; MEMORY; METRIC PREFIXES.

K6 chip microprocessor introduced by AMD in 1997 as a competitor to the Intel Pentium.

kana the Japanese phonetic writing system. There are two styles, *hiragana* and *katakana*. Kana contrasts with *kanji*, the Chinese-derived symbols for whole words. Written Japanese uses a mixture of kana and kanji.

kanji *see* KANA.

katakana *see* KANA.

KB abbreviation for KILOBYTE.

kBps kiloBytes per second. *See also* BAUD; KILOBYTE. Note the uppercase B.

kbps kilobits per second. *See* BIT. Note the lowercase b.

KDE (**KD**esktop **E**nvironment) a widely used graphical desktop environment for Linux and UNIX systems, based on the X WINDOW SYSTEM and originated by Matthias Ettrich in 1996. *Compare* GNOME.

Kerberos an authentication protocol that allows users and computers to identify each other without risk of impersonation and to communicate securely by encrypting their data. A Kerberos system uses a central authentication server to issue *tickets,* which are temporary authorizations to communicate. Each ticket is valid only for a specific user and for a limited length of time. Thus, an intercepted or stolen ticket is of little use. Because of the encryption used, forged tickets are virtually impossible to produce.

Kerberos was developed at the Massachusetts Institute of Technology, which distributes an implementation of it free of charge (*web.mit.edu/ kerberos/www*). Kerberos has many commercial implementations. *See* PROTOCOL. In Greek mythology, Kerberos (in Latin, Cerberus) is the dog that guards the gate of Hades.

Kermit a protocol for transferring files between dissimilar computers via modem or other connections (without requiring an Internet connection).

kernel the central part of an OPERATING SYSTEM. In many layered operating systems, only the kernel can access hardware directly. *Compare* BIOS.

Usage note: For obscure reasons this term is often spelled *kernal.* This may be nothing more than a typing error that appeared in an influential manual and caught on.

kerning adjustment of the amount of space between certain combinations of letters in proportional-pitch type. If the combination "To" is typeset with the same letter spacing as "Th," the letters seem to be too widely spaced. "To" looks better if the top of the "T" is allowed to overhang the "o" slightly. *See* Figure 147. *Compare* TRACKING.

To   Without kerning

To   With exaggerated kerning

FIGURE 147. Kerning

key
  1. a button on a computer keyboard.
  2. the item by which a data file is sorted or searched. For instance, if a file of names and addresses is sorted by zip codes, then the zip code is the key.
  3. the password or other secret information needed to decode an encrypted message. *See* ENCRYPTION.

keyboard the primary computer input device for alphanumeric data. There are many different types of keyboard layouts; for the most part the alphabet and numbers are consistently placed, but there is considerable variation in the placement of the auxiliary characters, editing keys, and function keys. Most keyboards have a numeric keypad (for typing digits) at the right; if you use a mouse a lot, but don't type many numbers, you may prefer a narrower keyboard that omits the keypad and lets you put your mouse closer to where you sit. Some keyboards have a mouse-like pointing device built in; these are generally fine for menu selection but not precise enough for drawing.

  When buying a new computer, be sure to evaluate the keyboard carefully. A keyboard that feels "dead" can be tiring to use. Practice typing on several different models to find one that feels good to you. Spending a few extra dollars for a good keyboard can be a wise investment; after all, it is the part of your computer that you are in contact with constantly. *See also* U.S. INTERNATIONAL; VIRTUAL KEYBOARD; WIRELESS KEYBOARD.

keyboard shortcut *see* SHORTCUT.

Keyboard viewer a screen showing how to type special characters on a Macintosh.

keyboarding entering data through the keyboard; typing.

keying
  1. typing; inputting information into the computer by means of the keyboard.

2. the process of digitally combining video images by using a subtractive background. *See* CHROMA-KEYING.

keylogging *see* KEYSTROKE LOGGING.

keystroke logging the act of recording the keys that a person presses as he or she uses a computer. Keystroke logging is often done surreptitiously by malicious SPYWARE in an attempt to capture passwords.

keyword
1. a word that has a special meaning in a particular programming language. For example, for is a keyword in C, and BEGIN is a keyword in Pascal. *Compare* RESERVED WORD.
2. words or phrases that, when included in the META tag of an HTML document, help SEARCH ENGINES catalog the contents of that web page.

KiB abbreviation for KIBIBYTE (1024 bytes).

kibi- metric prefix meaning ×1024 (2^{10}), the binary counterpart of *kilo-*. *See* METRIC PREFIXES.

kibibyte 1024 bytes.

kill file a list of people whose incoming e-mail messages or newsgroup postings are automatically deleted or hidden from view. Many mail and news reading programs allow you to set up a kill file so that obnoxious messages from known senders can be avoided. It is hard to avoid SPAM this way because spammers constantly change their names. *Compare* BLACKLIST; IGNORE LIST.

killer app *(slang)* a software application that becomes so desirable that it is the reason people purchase a computer, computer peripheral, or operating system. For example, Visicalc was a killer app for the Apple II, and Lotus 1-2-3 was a killer app for the original IBM PC. Some operating systems, such as OS/2, have failed to become popular because of the lack of a killer app.

kilo- metric prefix meaning ×1000 (10^{3}) or, in rating computer memories and disks, ×1024. *Kilo-* is derived from the Greek word for "thousand." *See* METRIC PREFIXES.

kilobyte a unit of computer memory capacity equal to 1024 characters. The number 1024 is significant because $2^{10} = 1024$.
See also BYTE; MEGABYTE; MEMORY; METRIC PREFIXES.

kilowatt-hour a unit of electrical energy consumption equal to 1000 watt-hours. *See* WATT-HOUR.

Kindle a line of e-book reader products introduced by Amazon in 2007 and relying on Wi-Fi and 3G wireless connections to download books. There is also Kindle software for Windows, the Macintosh, and iOS. *See* E-BOOK READER.

Kinect a device introduced by Microsoft in 2010 to connect to Xbox which uses an infrared camera to sense the movement of people in the room so people can control the actions on the screen with their motion.

kiosk a small stand containing a computer that people can walk up to and use to retrieve information. Kiosks often display current information about local events. They are used in museums, airports, and other public places.

kluge (pronounced "klooge") an improvised, jury-rigged, and poorly thought-out solution to a problem, usually intended only for temporary use. The word *kluge* may be derived from German *klug,* which means "clever." In Britain it is sometimes spelled *kludge* and pronounced to rhyme with "sludge."

knife (drawing program) a tool that cuts an object into pieces, defining a new outline along the cut edge and thus preserving the fill attributes of the original object.

knockout an area where an underlying color has been cut out so that the overprinting color can remain pure. Some DESKTOP PUBLISHING software automatically creates knockouts and TRAPS when preparing files for duplication on a printing press (*see* PREPRESS).

   (*Knockout* applies to mass production printing with a printing press, not to inkjet or laser printers attached directly to computers.)

knowledge base a collection of knowledge that is used as the basis for solving problems or making recommendations. *See* EXPERT SYSTEM.

knowledge representation *see* ARTIFICIAL INTELLIGENCE.

Koch snowflake *see* FRACTAL.

KVM switch (**K**eyboard-**V**ideo-**M**ouse **s**witch) a device that allows several computers to share a single keyboard, screen, and mouse. By pressing a button on the KVM switch or by typing special keystrokes, the user can connect the keyboard, screen, and mouse to any of the computers.

L

L1 cache (level-1 cache) the memory cache that is closest to the CPU or included within it.

L2 cache (level-2 cache) a memory cache outside the CPU. *Contrast* L1 CACHE.

L33T, L33TSPEAK *see* LEETSPEAK.

label
1. an identifying name or number attached to a particular statement in a computer program.
2. an identifying name recorded on a disk or other storage device and displayed with the icon representing that device on the screen.

lag the delay in transmitting data over a network. In online video, lag may be experienced as choppy movement or images freezing for several seconds. In online games, lag can cause a significant problem for players who cannot see an attack in time to respond to it.

lambda calculus the use of LAMBDA EXPRESSIONS to define functions.

lambda expression a formula that defines a function, originally using the Greek letter lambda (λ) to mark arguments.

Lambda expressions were introduced into formal logic by Alonzo Church in the 1930s. The key idea is that when a mathematician says, "Let $f(x) = x + 2$," this is really a definition of f for any argument, not just x. To make this explicit, one can say, "Let $f = (\lambda x)\ x + 2$," where (λx) indicates that x is not part of the function, but merely stands for an argument value.

In C#, the same lambda expression is written (x) =>x+ 2 and can be used in place of a DELEGATE (function pointer).

LAMP (**L**inux, **A**pache, **M**ySQL, **P**ython) term for a group of open-source software applications that can be used in developing a web server. (Sometimes PHP or Perl are used in place of Python).

LAN *see* LOCAL-AREA NETWORK.

landscape a way of orienting paper so that it is wider than it is high, like a landscape painting. That is, the paper is positioned sideways compared to the way it would otherwise be used ("portrait orientation").

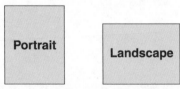

FIGURE 148. Landscape vs. portrait orientation

laptop a small, lightweight computer (under 8 pounds) with a flip-up screen. Such a computer is powered by rechargeable batteries and is easily portable. Laptops are especially valuable for people who travel frequently and need to be able to work on a computer while on the road. *See also* DOCKING STATION; PCMCIA. Because of their portability, laptops need special precautions against theft. *See* COMPUTER SECURITY. *Compare* NOTEBOOK; PALMTOP; TABLET COMPUTER.

Usage note: The distinction between "laptop" and "notebook" has become blurred; some vendors call all their portable computers notebooks.

large-scale integration (LSI) the construction of integrated circuits that contain thousands of logic gates. *See* INTEGRATED CIRCUIT.

laser (**l**ight **a**mplification by **s**timulated **e**mission of **r**adiation) an electronic device that produces rays of light that are exactly matched in wavelength and phase. Laser beams can be used to detect microscopically tiny detail (such as the pattern on a CD-ROM) and to concentrate energy in a small, precisely located space (as in a laser printer).

laser printer a computer printer that generates an image by scanning a photoconductive drum with a laser beam and then transferring the image to paper by means of electrostatic toner. Laser printers provide high-quality output of text and graphics; they are quiet and run fast. *Contrast* INKJET PRINTER. *See also* CORONA WIRE; DRUM; FUSER; PICKUP ROLLER; SEPARATOR PAD; TRANSFER ROLLER.

lasso a selection tool commonly found in PAINT PROGRAMS; it looks like a rope lariat, and you use it to define an area that you wish to work with. Crucially, the area need not be rectangular; it can be any shape. After selecting the lasso icon, you drag the mouse *freehand* around the desired area. Once the area is defined, you can scale, move, rotate, change color, apply filters, or perform any operation that is available.

Because the lasso is a freehand tool, it is dependent upon your skill as a mouse operator. Knowing how difficult it is to draw accurately with a mouse, you may want to see if your paint program has other selection tools (such as a MAGIC WAND) that would suit your needs better. *See* SELECT.

FIGURE 149. Lasso tool

last known good describing the configuration of a computer the last time it was used successfully, before changes. If you disrupt Microsoft Windows while installing patches or drivers, you can, in most cases, use the System Restore feature to boot from the last known good configuration.

last mile the connection of individual homes or businesses to a communication network. For examples *see* DSL; WIMAX.

latency a delay in processing network data.

LaTeX (pronounced "la-tekh" or "lay-tekh"; alternatively written L^{A}T$_E$X) a typesetting system designed by Leslie Lamport and implemented as a set of macros for Donald Knuth's TeX (*see* TEX). There are two versions in wide use, LaTeX 2.09 and LaTeX 2$_\varepsilon$; LaTeX 3 is planned for the future.

The key idea of LaTeX is to separate the job of the author from that of the publication designer. (*See* LOGICAL DESIGN.) The author uses commands such as \chapter{...} and \section{...} to mark chapter and section titles, figures, quotations, and the like. (Figure 150 shows an example.) Separately, a file called a *style sheet* specifies how these things should be printed and keeps them consistent. So, while other word processing programs work like a computerized typewriter, LaTeX does the job of an expert typist and layout artist.

LaTeX is especially popular for typesetting scientific and mathematical books because the full power of the TeX mathematical typesetting system is available. Many scholarly journals are typeset with LaTeX, as are most of the books published by several major publishers. LaTeX is also popular with graduate students writing theses and dissertations because it is easy to conform to standard formats—just use your university's official style sheet.

Implementations of LaTeX are available for a wide range of computers. The text of this book is written using LaTeX.

Latin the language of the ancient Romans; the Roman alphabet (including j, v, and w, which were added to it in modern times). This alphabet is used in English and several other languages. *Compare* to the Greek alphabet (page 574) or the Cyrillic (Russian) alphabet.

laumchpad an optional user interface under MacOS X Lion similar to IOS.

launch
    1. to advertise and release a new product.
    2. to start a computer program, especially in a multitasking operating system.

law *see* COMPUTER LAW.

LCD (**L**iquid **C**rystal **D**isplay) the type of display used on most digital watches, calculators, and laptop computers, and in many flat-panel computer and video displays.

   LCDs use liquid crystals, which are chemicals whose response to polarized light can be controlled by an electric field. A polarizing filter is built into the LCD; through this filter, the liquid crystal compound looks light or dark depending on its electrical state.

lead element (atomic number 82, symbol Pb), found in electronic equipment, in lead-acid batteries, and formerly in SOLDER. Lead is a metal that forms poisonous compounds and should be kept out of landfills and public water supplies. *See* ROHS.

leader a line of dots that connects one side of the page with another, often used in tables of contents, like .... this.

```
\documentclass{article}

\title{An Example}
\author{Michael A. Covington}
\date{June 27, 2008}

\begin{document}
\maketitle

\section{Overview}
This is a sample of a short paper typed with \LaTeX.
Notice the commands I use to get \emph{italics} and
\textbf{boldface}. I can also typeset mathematical formulas
such as $\sum_{x=1}^{5} A_x$.

Notice that I skip lines between paragraphs in the input.
This is the second paragraph.

\section{Another section}
This is the second section. It is very short.

\end{document}
```

An Example

Michael A. Covington

June 27, 2008

1. Overview

This is a sample of a short paper typed with L^AT_EX. Notice the commands I use to get *italics* and **boldface**. I can also typeset math-

ematical formulas such as $\sum_{x=j}^{5} Ax$.

   Notice that I skip lines between paragraphs in the input. This is the second paragraph.

2. Another section

This is the second section. It is very short.

FIGURE 150. L^AT_EX input and output

leading (pronounced "ledding") the insertion of extra space between lines of type. On old printing presses, this was originally done by inserting strips of lead between rows of type cast in lead. *See* TYPEFACE.

These lines
are typeset with
extra leading.

In some cases, it is actually beneficial to use *negative leading*—for instance, when setting type in all caps, it is not necessary to allow space for descenders. Such headlines usually look best with negative leading.

THESE LINES ARE TYPESET
WITH NEGATIVE LEADING.

leak MEMORY LEAK.

leap second an extra second added periodically to official clocks, since very precise modern clocks have shown that the Earth's rotation is slowing down so the average day length is slightly longer than 24 hours.

leap year a year in which an extra day, February 29, is added to keep the calendar year in step with the Earth's revolution around the sun. If there were no leap years, the calendar would get out of step with the Earth's motion, so that after many centuries, January 1 would occur in the summer instead of the winter. Julius Caesar introduced the JULIAN CALENDAR with a leap year every four years. The current GREGORIAN CALENDAR was adopted so that the calendar would more accurately represent the Earth's orbit around the sun.

The current rule for identifying leap years is as follows:

- Years divisible by 400 are always leap years. Thus, 2000 and 2400 are leap years.
- Years divisible by 100, but not by 400, are not leap years. Thus, 1900 and 2100 are not leap years.
- Otherwise, years divisible by 4 are leap years. Thus, 2004, 2008, 2012, 2016, and so on, are leap years.

There are 97 leap years in 400 years, so the average length of a year in the Gregorian calendar is

$$\frac{365 \times 400 + 97}{400} = \frac{146,097}{400} = 365.2425 \text{ days}$$

The actual time taken for a cycle of the seasons is 365.24219 days, so after several more centuries, a further correction will be needed. *See also* LEAP SECOND.

learning curve a graph representing mastery of a skill plotted against the time spent on learning it. If something is hard to learn to use, it is sometimes described as having a steep learning curve (although, logically, a steep curve should indicate rapid learning).

The term originated in behaviorist psychology but is now used very imprecisely.

lease the right to use an IP ADDRESS temporarily assigned by DHCP. If a lease runs out while the computer is still connected to the network, DHCP automatically renews it or assigns a new address.

LED (**l**ight-**e**mitting **d**iode) a semiconductor device that emits light when an electric current passes through it.

They are a very efficient source of illumination because nearly all the electricity is turned into light, unlike a traditional incandescent light bulb, which turns most of its incoming energy into heat.

LEd LaTeX editor. *See* LATEX.

leetspeak (from "elite speak") written slang that modifies words by replacing letters with symbols or digits to make them look more computerish, using phonetic spellings, and adopting common typing errors as conventions.

A familiar example is the spelling of *elite* as 1eet or |33t. It is common to see 3 for E, 1 for I, and @ or 4 for A. There is almost infinite variation in the ways that ASCII characters can be used creatively to form letters, and so there is no official dictionary of leetspeak; people make it up as they go.

Although leetspeak was originally used to exclude the uninitiated and to bypass chat room filters that block dirty words, it is now most frequently seen in jokes.

left-click to CLICK with the left-hand mouse button (or the right-hand button if the mouse is set up for a left-handed person).

legacy anything left over from a previous version of the hardware or software. For example, *legacy applications* are applications from earlier versions of DOS or Windows; *legacy hardware* is hardware that does not support PLUG AND PLAY.

legacy-free not burdened by the need for compatibility with substantially older equipment or software. Microsoft is promoting legacy-free PC design as a way to make PCs more reliable and easier to upgrade.

Instead of imitating the architecture of the IBM PC AT or some other earlier machine exactly, a legacy-free PC relies on software control of hardware IRQ numbers and the like. *Legacy-free PCs* are intermediates between legacy-free and conventional PCs. *See also* IRQ; PC 2001; PLUG AND PLAY.

legal size the size of paper used for legal documents in the United States, $8^{1}/_{2} \times 14$ inches. *See* PAPER SIZES.

Lenovo company that bought IBM's personal computer division in 2005 (web address: *www.lenovo.com/us/en*). Lenovo is a global company that began in China.

Leopard version 10.5 of MAC OS X.

letter size the size of paper used for business letters in the United States, $8\frac{1}{2} \times 11$ inches. Elsewhere, ISO size A4 is the nearest equivalent. *See* PAPER SIZES.

FIGURE 151. Legal- and letter-sized paper

letterspacing the space between letters (characters). *See* Figure 152. Look for the letterspacing controls with other FRAME attribute commands (letterspacing is sometimes called TRACKING).

v e r y l o o s e

l o o s e

normal

tight

touching

FIGURE 152. Letterspacing

LF (line feed) the character code that tells a printer or terminal to advance to the next line; ASCII code 10. *See* CRLF.

Li-ion (**Lithium-ion**) a type of rechargeable battery widely used in portable computers. They have high-energy density and slow loss of charge. During use, current is created by the movement of lithium ions to the positive electrode, through a non-aqueous separator. *See* BATTERY.

library

1. a collection of files, computer programs, or subroutines. A loader library is a file containing subroutines that can be linked into a machine language program.

2. a collection of reference materials and software tools, such as clip art, prerecorded sounds, and predefined objects.

license permission to use patented or copyrighted material. *See* PER COMPUTER; PER SEAT; PER USER; SHRINKWRAP LICENSE; SOFTWARE LICENSE.

LIFO (last-in-first-out) a STACK (definition 1); a data structure or memory device from which items are retrieved in the opposite of the order in which they were stored. *Contrast* FIFO.

ligature a printed character representing a combination of two or three letters (Figure 153). Some of the most sophisticated word processing programs, such as TeX, change pairs of letters into ligatures automatically.

ff fi fl ffi ffl
FIGURE 153. Ligatures

light
1. visible electromagnetic radiation, with wavelength between about 400 nanometers (4×10^{-7} meters) (the color violet) and 700 nanometers (red).
2. type that is designed and drawn with very fine strokes; the opposite of BOLD.
3. (in 3D and animation software) a virtual device that mimics the effect of real light upon the computer-generated scene. Computer lights can be adjusted in many of the same ways as their real-life counterparts: intensity, position, direction, and color.

light-emitting diode *see* LED.

light pen a pen-like light-sensitive device that can be used like a mouse to communicate with a computer. The operator holds the pen up to the screen, and the computer can sense what point on the screen the pen is touching. Light pens were popular in the 1970s but have largely been replaced by mice or touch screens.

Lightscribe a method for writing a visible label directly to a disc (on the opposite side of the disc from where the data is written). See *www.lightscribe.com*.

limitcheck PostScript error that occurs when a drawing is too complex to be printed.

limits of computer power things that computers cannot do, which is a subject of continuing theoretical study.

Computers can perform only tasks that can be reduced to mechanical procedures (algorithms). They are therefore inapplicable to tasks that cannot or should not be reduced to mechanical form, such as judging the greatness of a work of art or administering psychotherapy. Rather surprisingly, however, there are some tasks that are mathematically precise but that present-day computers cannot perform. These fall into two major types: (1) problems with no known algorithmic solution, and (2) problems whose best known algorithmic solutions require unreasonable amounts of time.

An example of a problem of the first type (one with no presently known algorithmic solution) is how to get a computer to recognize the structures of sentences in a human language such as English. Obviously, this is something computers will have to be able to do if we are ever to be able to communicate with them in English, and there is no reason to think it impossible. The difficulty is simply that English (and all other human languages) are so complicated that complete algorithms for processing them have not yet been discovered.

A good example of the second type of problem, one that takes an unreasonable amount of time to solve, is the so-called traveling salesman problem. The task is to find the shortest route by which a salesman can visit a particular set of cities (in any order). The only known way to solve this problem is to try all possible routes. A few shortcuts are possible—for instance, the testing of each route can be abandoned as soon as its length exceeds the shortest length already found, without pursuing it to the end—but the number of steps is never substantially fewer than N factorial, where N is the number of cities (*see* FACTORIAL). Suppose the fastest imaginable computer could perform one step in this algorithm by moving an electric charge a distance of 1 millimeter at the speed of light. This would mean that it could perform 3×10^{11} steps per second. Then the times required to solve the traveling salesman problem (in $N!$ steps) would work out as follows:

Number of Cities	Number of Steps	Time Required
5	120	0.36 picosecond
10	3,628,800	12 microseconds
15	1.3×10^{12}	4.4 seconds
20	2.4×10^{18}	94 days
25	1.6×10^{25}	1.6 million years
30	2.7×10^{32}	2.8×10^{13} years

And this is with a computer millions of times faster than any that presently exist. Obviously, it will never be feasible to solve the traveling salesman problem for more than a few cities unless a much better algorithm is found.

Another interesting class of computational problems, known as *NP-complete* problems, has been proved to be equivalent to the traveling salesman problem; if a better algorithm is found for any NP-complete problem, it will be applicable to all of them.

See also CHURCH'S THESIS; COMPLEXITY THEORY.

Lindows, LindowsOS the original name of LINSPIRE; it was changed to avoid infringing Microsoft's trademark rights to the name *Windows*.

line

1. in geometry, the shortest path connecting two points. A geometric line is always perfectly straight and has no width.

2. in graphics, a visible representation of a geometric line. A line in this sense has a definite color and width (normally at least 0.5-point for good visibility on paper; *see* HAIRLINE) and may be continuous, dashed, or dotted.

3. a printed line of type. Text is most readable with a line length of about 65 characters. *See also* LINESPACING; WORD WRAP.

4. an electronic communication path, such as a telephone line. *See* T1 LINE; T3 LINE.

line cap the end of a drawn line. In most DRAW PROGRAMS, you can choose square or rounded ends, or even arrowheads.

line drawing an illustration that can be represented as a series of hard-edged black lines and black areas on a white background. Line drawings are easily converted to vector images by tracing them. *Contrast* GRAYSCALE and PHOTOGRAPH.

line feed the character code that tells a printer or terminal to advance to the next line; ASCII code 10. *See* CRLF.

line in (on a sound card) line-level audio input. *See* LINE-LEVEL.

line-level (describing an audio signal) a signal level of about 0.1 to 1 volt, designed to connect to the input of another amplifier. Some line-level outputs can drive headphones; others cannot.

Speaker-level audio is a slightly higher voltage, but the main difference is that speaker-level outputs can deliver much greater current (amperage) in order to drive speakers. Microphone-level audio is a much lower level, about 0.001 volt.

line out (on a sound card) line-level audio output. *See* LINE-LEVEL.

line printer a type of IMPACT PRINTER that prints an entire line of type at once, formerly used on mainframe computers.

line spacing the spacing in between lines of type. Also called LEADING.

linear fill a way of filling an object with color so that it makes a smooth transition from one color at one side of the object to another color at the other side. The gradient need not be horizontal; it can be vertical or at any angle you specify. *Contrast* RADIAL FILL.

FIGURE 154. Linear fill

link

1. any kind of communication path between two computers.
2. an entry in one directory or menu that points directly to something in some other directory or menu; a SHORTCUT. Links can be used to make the same file accessible from more than one directory or to put the same program on more than one menu.
3. an item on a WEB PAGE which, when selected, transfers the user directly to some other web page, perhaps on a different machine. Also called a HYPERLINK. For example *see* HTML.
4. in Windows, an OLE communication path between programs. *See* OLE.
5. to combine the machine instructions for a program with the machine instructions for any predefined procedures that it uses. For example, a program that does trigonometric calculation might use predefined procedures to find sines, cosines, and tangents. Some compilers perform linking automatically; others require you to execute a linker as a separate command.
6. a pointer in a linked list or tree. *See* LINKED LIST; TREE.

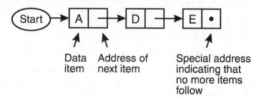

FIGURE 155. Linked list

linked list a way of organizing data items in a computer so that they are retrievable in a particular order that is not necessarily the same order as the physical locations in which they are stored. Each data item consists of two parts: the data itself, and a number giving the location of the next item. Figure 155 shows how this is usually diagrammed. To read the items in order, you need only know which item is in the beginning (the head) of the list; having located it, you can go next to the item whose address was stored with it; and so on.

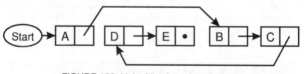

FIGURE 156. Linked list: inserting elements

Linked lists allow items to be added or removed without requiring that other items be moved to make room. For instance, the list A–D–E of Figure 155 can be changed into A–B–C–D–E by adding two items. As Figure 156 shows, the newly added items B and C can be placed in the unused area after the E, and *inserted* into the list by changing the address associated with item A.

Figure 157 shows that an item can be *deleted* by changing the addresses so that there is no longer a path to that item. In either case, using linked lists can eliminate the need to move hundreds or thousands of data items whenever an insertion or deletion takes place.

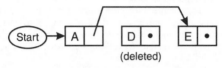

FIGURE 157. Linked list: deleting an element

Figure 158 shows a way to construct a linked list in an ordinary two-dimensional array; this can be done in practically any programming language. Each row of the array contains a data item and an integer indicating which row the next item is on (or zero, to indicate that there are no more items). In the example, it is assumed that the first item in the list will always be in row 1; if you wish to be able to delete the first item, you can use a separate integer, outside the array, to keep track of where the list starts. *See also* DATA STRUCTURES.

Item No.	Data item	Address of next item
1	A	4
2	D	3
3	E	0
4	B	5
5	C	2

FIGURE 158. Linked list stored in an array

LinkedIn a social network for business professionals (*www.linkedin.com*). Unlike Facebook or MySpace, LinkedIn focuses on business and academic connections instead of purely social ones. Users are encouraged to upload résumés and/or CVs to complete their profiles.

linker a program that puts separately compiled routines together to make a complete, working program. *See* LINK (definition 5).

Links a very fast simplified browser that provides text and limited graphical support. (Not to be confused with the "Lynx" browser.)

Linspire a commercial distribution of Linux, based on Debian and later Ubuntu, that was marketed by Linspire, Inc. (*www.linspire.com*). In 2008, the company's name changed to Digital Cornerstone. *See* DEBIAN; LINUX; UBUNTU.

Linux (usually understood as "**Lin**us' **UNIX**") a freely distributed UNIX-compatible operating system for PCs and a number of other processors.

Linux was developed by Linus Torvalds and others and is distributed under terms similar to those of Gnu's "copyleft" (*see* GNU). Copies can be given away free provided they are complete and intact, but most users prefer to purchase commercially produced CD-ROMs containing Linux together with application software.

Linux is quite reliable and highly compatible with UNIX; as a result, it is very popular with universities, Internet service providers, and small businesses that need multi-user computing at minimum cost. More information can be found on the World Wide Web at *www.linux.org*. *See also* DEBIAN; LINSPIRE; RED HAT; UBUNTU.

Linux box *(slang)* a small computer running Linux.

Lion version 10.7 of MAC OS X, released in 2011 and incorporating some features of IOS.

liquid crystal display *see* LCD.

Lisp (**List P**rocessor) a programming language developed in the late 1950s at MIT under the direction of John McCarthy. Because of the ease with which it can handle complex data structures, Lisp is used for artificial intelligence research and for writing programs whose complexity would render them unmanageable in other languages.

A Lisp program is easy to recognize because of the accumulation of closing parentheses at the end of the program. All Lisp statements and most Lisp data structures are linked lists, written as lists of elements in parentheses (*see* LINKED LIST). Programmers build a complete program by defining their own statements (actually functions) in terms of those previously defined. For example, a function that computes the factorial of X is:

```
(DEFUN FACTORIAL (X)
  (IF (= X0)
      1
      (* FACTORIAL(-X 1))))
```

Translating into English: "This is the definition of a function called FAC-TORIAL whose parameter is X. If X is zero, its factorial is 1; otherwise, its factorial is equal to X times the factorial of $X - 1$." The IF keyword works like a Pascal if-then-else statement. This function calls itself recursively; recursion is a normal way of expressing repetition in Lisp.

list

1. a set of data items that are to be accessed in a particular order; for instance, a list of the students in a class might be accessed in alphabetical order. Lists are stored in arrays or linked lists. *See* ARRAY; LINKED LIST.
2. a MAILING LIST to which messages are distributed by e-mail.
3. to display a program line by line, especially in early versions of BASIC.

list administrator the person responsible for maintaining a MAILING LIST.

list box an area in a dialog box where the user can choose among a list of items, such as files, directories, printers, or the like. For an illustration, *see* DIALOG BOX.

list processing
1. the manipulation of linked lists. *See* LINKED LIST; LISP.
2. the processing of mailing lists and similar data. *See* DATABASE MANAGEMENT.

LISTSERV a commercial software package for operating e-mail mailing lists and discussion groups, produced by L-Soft International (*www. lsoft.com*). LISTSERV runs on a server, which can be a mainframe or microcomputer. The first version of LISTSERV was implemented by Eric Thomas on BITNET in 1986. The current version includes the ability to filter out spam and viruses. *Compare* MAJORDOMO.
Usage note: "LISTSERV" does not mean "e-mail list." Not all e-mail mailing lists use LISTSERV software.

literal in a programming language, a written representation that always represents the same value. For example, the literal 2.5 always stands for the number 2.5, and the literal "abc" always stands for the character string *abc*. Names defined by the programmer, such as variable and function names, are not literals. *Contrast* CONSTANT.

little-endian a system of memory addressing in which numbers that occupy more than one byte in memory are stored "little-end-first," with the lowest 8 bits at the lowest address.
Contrast BIG-ENDIAN.

Live Microsoft's collection of online services (e-mail, photo sharing, etc.; web address: *www.windowslive.com/Home*).

Live Messenger an INSTANT MESSAGING application provided by Microsoft.

LiveJournal a web site (*www.livejournal.com*) providing a popular web log service (see BLOG) that also provides basic SOCIAL NETWORKING features. Users can control whether their posts are public or only visible to defined FRIENDS. *Compare* BLOGGER; WORDPRESS; XANGA.

ln the function, in several programming languages, that calculates the natural (base *e*) logarithm of its argument. For example, ln(x) finds the natural logarithm of x. *See* LOGARITHM; E.

LN abbreviation for "like new" (describing items for sale).

LN– abbreviation for "like new minus" (i.e., almost new, almost unused, showing only slight wear). *Contrast* EX+.

LNIB abbreviation for "like new, in box" (i.e., slightly used but supplied with original packaging). *Compare* NOS (definition 2).

load to transfer information from a disk or other outside device into the memory of a computer. *Contrast* SAVE. *See also* LOADER.

loader a computer program whose function is to load another program into memory and transfer control to it. All operating systems include loaders. For example, in Windows, if you have a program named myfile.exe and you type the command

```
C:\> myfile
```

you are telling the loader to find myfile.exe and load it.

local located at the user's computer or site. *Contrast* REMOTE.

local-area network (LAN) a network that connects several computers that are located nearby (in the same room or building), allowing them to share files and devices such as printers. *See* ETHERNET. *Contrast* WIDE-AREA NETWORK.

local bus a separate bus in a computer, designed to provide extra-fast access to the CPU for specific devices, such as video cards. It contrasts with the main bus, which connects to most other parts of the computer. For examples *see* PCI, AGP.

local variable a variable that has meaning only within a particular function, subroutine, or other program unit. The name of a local variable can be used in another subroutine elsewhere in the program, where it will refer to an entirely different variable. Local variables contrast with *global variables*, which are recognized throughout the program.

The advantage of using local variables is not obvious in short programs. However, it is a good idea when writing a long program to make as many variables as possible local, because then there will be no problem if you wish to use the same name to mean something else elsewhere in the program. This rule is even more important if several different people are writing subroutines that will be combined into one main program. *See also* SCOPE; SIDE EFFECT.

localization the process of adapting software to run and be understood in a particular culture or part of the world. Localization might involve translating screen displays into French or German, adapting to a foreign-language keyboard, printing the date differently (e.g., 2012 Oct 21 in Japan vs. 21 Oct 2012 in Britain and Oct. 21, 2012 in the United States), setting the clock for daylight saving time on different dates, or even reading or writing numbers differently (3,000.95 vs. 3 000.95 or even 3.000,95).

location the address in memory of a piece of data or the ENTRY POINT of a subroutine.

lock

1. to configure a CELLULAR TELEPHONE (or other wireless device that uses the cellular network) so that it will only connect to one company's cellular service. Many cellular telephones are supplied locked to the company that provided them but can be unlocked to work with other companies. *See also* JAILBREAK.

2. to mark a file "read-only" so that software cannot change it. In the Macintosh, this is done by checking the "Locked" box in the "Get Info" window.

3. to mark a variable, an open file, or other resource so that other concurrent tasks cannot use it. *See* MULTITASKING.

log abbreviation for LOGARITHM. In some languages and spreadsheets, $\log(x)$ is the common (base-10) logarithm and $\ln(x)$ is the natural (base-e) logarithm. In other languages, $\log(x)$ calculates the natural logarithm and $\log10(x)$ calculates the common logarithm.

log in *see* LOG ON.

log on (or log in) to identify yourself as an authorized user of a computer or a network at the beginning of a work session.

logarithm the power to which a number must be raised in order to give another number.

If $y = a^x$, then x is the logarithm of y to the base a (written as $x = \log_a y$). The most commonly used bases for logarithm functions are 10 and e (approximately 2.718). Base-10 logarithms are called *common logarithms;* base-e logarithms, *natural logarithms* (because integrals and derivatives are simpler with base e than with any other base). For example, the common logarithm of 10,000 is 4 ($\log_{10} 10,000 = 4$) because $10^4 = 10,000$.

If no base is specified in the expression $\log a$, then usually base 10 is meant; the natural logarithm of a is written $\log_e a$ or $\ln a$.

logged drive *see* CURRENT DRIVE.

logic circuits electronic circuits that accept binary digits (bits) as inputs and produce an output bit according to a specified rule. For examples *see* AND GATE; OR GATE; NAND GATE; NOR GATE; NOT GATE; FLIP-FLOP. For information on how logic circuits are used, *see* BINARY ADDITION; COMPUTER ARCHITECTURE; DECODER; XOR GATE.

A typical computer represents 1 (logic "true") as +5 volts and 0 as 0 volts. More precisely, 1 is represented by a connection to the +5-volt power supply (directly or through a resistance), and 0 is represented by a connection to ground. Note that 0 is not merely the absence of a voltage; logic circuits differ as to how they handle an unconnected input.

Basically, logic circuits are switching circuits. Figure 159(A) shows a NOT gate implemented as a switch. The output is +5 volts (binary 1, logic "true") whenever the switch is *not* closed. (When the switch is closed, the resistor dissipates the voltage and the output is connected to ground.) That is, the output is the negation of the state of the switch.

For this to be usable in a computer, the switching has to be controlled by an electrical signal. Figure 159(B) shows what happens when the switch is replaced by a switching transistor. The transistor conducts when its base is at least 0.6 volts above ground (i.e., when its input is binary 1). When the transistor is conducting, the effect is the same as the closed switch, and the output is 0. Thus, the output is the negation of the input, and the NOT gate works correctly.

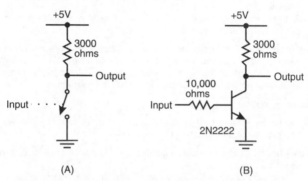

(A)   (B)

FIGURE 159. NOT gate built with a switch (A) and a transistor (B)

Figure 160 shows how to build a NAND gate out of two diodes, two resistors, and a transistor. This circuit is very similar to what is used inside TTL integrated circuits. The output is 0 ("false") if and only if both of the inputs are binary 1 (+5 volts). In that situation, the diodes do not conduct, the base of the transistor receives current through the resistor, and the transistor conducts. But if even one of the inputs is binary 0 (connected to ground), the base of the transistor is held low and the transistor does not conduct, so the output is binary 1. To understand this circuit, it is very important to remember that binary 0 is represented by a connection to ground, not merely the absence of a voltage. Like real TTL ICs, this circuit happens to treat disconnected inputs as binary 1.

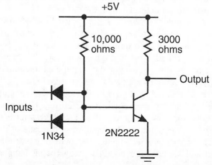

FIGURE 160. NAND gate built with transistors and diodes

NAND gates are important because all the other gates can be built from them (Figure 161). A NOT gate is simply a NAND gate with only one input, or with all its inputs tied together; an AND gate is a NAND gate followed by a NOT gate; and so on. In a similar way, all the types of gates can be built from NOR gates.

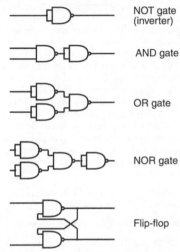

NOT gate
(inverter)

AND gate

OR gate

NOR gate

Flip-flop

FIGURE 161. Logic circuits made from NAND gates

Instead of TTL circuits, newer ICs use CMOS (complementary metal-oxide semiconductor) switching transistors, which come in pairs that respond to opposite polarities, so that one switches off whenever the other switches on. This makes it easy to connect the output either to +5 volts or to ground depending on the input. However, the circuits inside practical CMOS gates are too complicated to diagram here.

logic diagram an electronic circuit diagram that shows gates and other components that affect logic signals, but does not show the power supply or other non-digital electronic subsystems. *See* ELECTRONIC CIRCUIT DIAGRAM SYMBOLS.

logic programming a method of writing computer programs based on the mathematical study of logical reasoning. Logic programming is used in the computer modeling of human thinking. For examples, *see* PROLOG.

logical

1. possessing or pertaining to logic (in any of various senses).

2. described from the viewpoint of software. For example, if a single disk drive is divided into two partitions which the computer handles separately, it can be said to comprise two logical disk drives.

logical design

1. the design of an electronic circuit using logic gates. *See* GATE and cross-references there.

2. the design of the logic of a computer program (as opposed to its user interface or data files).

3. the practice of designing a document by using tags to indicate the function rather than the appearance of each element. For example, chapters are labeled as such rather than just being indicated by words typed in a particular arrangement on the page.

Logical design is the approach followed by LATEX, SGML, and XML; it is not followed by WYSIWYG word processors. Logical design is generally superior for complicated documents because decisions about the appearance of elements of the document can be made independently of the text. If you want to change the appearance of chapter headings, for instance, you need to make the change in only one place because all chapter headings are recognized as instances of the same unit. In a WYSIWYG system, you would need to change each heading individually because the computer does not know that they are alike. Documents with tags specifying the logical design are also easier to handle effectively in computer databases.

logical drive one of several divisions of a single partition on a hard disk. Logical drives are treated as separate disk drives.

logo a trademark or printed emblem; short for *logotype.*

LOGO a programming language developed by Seymour Papert of MIT for use in teaching programming to children. Papert's fundamental insight was that computer-aided instruction is of little use unless the pupil can control the computer, rather than the other way around. To experiment with this idea, he designed a language that is markedly easier to use than BASIC and does not share BASIC's preoccupation with numerical calculation.

Although LOGO offers a full range of computer functions, most elementary LOGO exercises revolve around the "turtle," originally a robot that rolled around on a sheet of paper making marks by lowering its "tail" and dragging it around on the paper. (The present-day turtle is a triangle that moves around the screen, drawing a line if told to do so.) Drawing shapes with the turtle appeals to children who would not be attracted to mathematical calculation or verbal input-output; at the same time, it serves as a good medium for teaching geometry and logical problem solving.

LOGO is an extensible language; that is, programs are constructed by defining statements in terms of previously defined statements. For example, the following procedure draws a square:

```
TO SQUARE
  CLEARSCREEN
  FORWARD 50
  RIGHT 90
  FORWARD 50
  RIGHT 90
  FORWARD 50
  RIGHT 90
  FORWARD 50
END
```

That is: "Clear the screen (and put the turtle in the center), go forward (up) 50 units, do a 90-degree right turn, go forward 50 units, do a 90-degree right turn," and so forth. Since LOGO procedures can call themselves recursively, complicated snowflake-like patterns are relatively easy to generate. *See also* KOCH SNOWFLAKE.

lol, LOL online abbreviation for "laugh out loud."

long in many programming languages long is a declaration indicating that a variable needs more than the normal memory for that type of variable, either because of greater range or higher precision. For example, in Java, a variable of type int fills 32 bits; a variable of type long fills 64 bits (allowing 2^{64} different values, ranging from -2^{63} to $2^{63} - 1$ (approximately $\pm 9 \times 10^{18}$).

long cross the character †, a symbol used to mark footnotes. *See also* FOOTNOTE. Also called a DAGGER or OBELISK.

Longhorn internal code name used for Windows Vista (Windows 6.0) before its release. *See* WINDOWS (MICROSOFT). *Compare* CAIRO; CHICAGO; MEMPHIS; WHISTLER.

look and feel the overall visual appearance and USER INTERFACE of a computer program. *See* COPYRIGHT.

loop
1. a series of statements in a computer program that are to be executed repeatedly. For examples *see* FOR and WHILE.
2. anything that receives electrical energy from a POWER SUPPLY.
3. (more fully, *feedback loop*) a control system in which one thing affects another, and its effect is sensed in order to make control decisions. For example, a heater, the air temperature, and a thermostat form a feedback loop. *See also* FEEDBACK; IN THE LOOP.

loose letterspacing that has been adjusted to increase the space between the letters. *Contrast* TIGHT. *See* LETTERSPACING for an illustration.

lorem ipsum meaningless filler text, often used as a placeholder in layout or mockup of documents, web pages, etc. This particular text, from the works of Cicero in Latin, begins *Lorem ipsum dotlor sit amet, consectetur adipisicing elit, sed do eiusmod tempor incidunt.*

lost cluster a group of disk sectors that are not marked as free but are not allocated to a file. Lost clusters result when the operation of creating a file is interrupted.

Lotus 1-2-3 a popular SPREADSHEET program, widely used on IBM PCs since its introduction in 1983 by Lotus Development Corporation. Lotus is now part of IBM (web address: *www-306.ibm.com/software/lotus*). The original Lotus 1-2-3 contained significant innovations in graphing and data handling ability.

lowercase the "small" letters a, b, c, d, and so on, as opposed to uppercase or capital letters, A, B, C, D, and so on. The term *lowercase* goes back to the early days of letterpress printing. The metal type was kept in divided drawers called cases; the capital letters were traditionally kept in the upper case, and the small letters in the lower.

LPI (**l**ines **p**er **i**nch) a measure of the resolution of a halftone screen (*see* HALFTONE). Most newspaper screens are 85 LPI; good quality magazines use 150 LPI. 300-DPI screened output is roughly equivalent to a 50-LPI screen (draft quality). 600 DPI on a plain paper typesetter should be acceptable for most work; it can produce the equivalent of a 100-LPI halftone. When higher resolutions are needed, the file should be output to a 2400-DPI imagesetter.

ls the Unix command to list all files in a directory. *Compare* DIR.

luminosity brightness; the property of glowing with light. Some 3D programs can render objects that seem to be emitting light by setting a high luminosity level.

lurk *(slang)* to read an online forum regularly without contributing any messages of your own. It's advisable to lurk for a while before posting any messages in order to make sure you understand the purpose and nature of the discussion. Most forums have more lurkers than the participants realize.

M

M4A (MPEG-4) a file format for audio and video files, the successor to MP3. iTunes typically uses this audio file format.

mA abbreviation for *milliampere*, 1/1000 of an AMPERE.

Mac nickname for MACINTOSH.

MAC address (**M**edia **A**ccess **C**ontrol address) a built-in number that uniquely and permanently identifies a network adapter, such as the Ethernet card in a PC. It consists of 12 hexadecimal digits, which may be written with or without hyphens, such as 13-24-6C-2D-FF-3A or 13246C2DFF3A.

Under Windows 2000 and later, the MAC address can be displayed by typing `ipconfig /all` at a COMMAND PROMPT.

Contrast IP ADDRESS, which is assigned manually or automatically by network administrators. *See also* GUID.

Mac OS X the operating system for Macintosh computers; the current version, since 2001, is version X (ten). Mac OS X is based, in part, on the UNIX operating system and has a BSD UNIX command line window. As in earlier Macintosh operating systems, the user interface is still uncluttered, consistent, and easy to use. The elegantly simple idea of *choosing* an object and then telling the computer what to do with it has been carried through all versions of the Mac operating system, desktop accessories, and third-party applications and has been adopted by other operating systems (*see* WINDOWS (MICROSOFT)).

The minor updates to OS X have been given the names of members of the big cat family:

Cheetah	v10.0
Puma	v10.1
Jaguar	v10.2
Panther	v10.3
Tiger	v10.4
Leopard	v10.5
Snow Leopard	v10.6
Lion	v10.7

See APPLE MENU; CLASSIC MODE; DOCK; FINDER; IOS.

machine-dependent program a program that works on only one particular type of computer.

machine-independent program a program that can be used on many different types of computers. The usual way to make a program machine-independent is to write it in a widely used programming language, such as C or C++, and compile it separately for each machine. A Java program is machine-independent because it is compiled to a standard bytecode, which can be run using the Java virtual machine (JVM) available for each specific machine.

machine language instructions that a computer can execute directly. Machine language statements are written in a binary code, and each statement corresponds to one machine action.

The difference between machine language and assembly language is that each assembly-language statement corresponds to one machine-language statement, but the statements themselves are written in a symbolic code that is easier for people to read. (*See* ASSEMBLY LANGUAGE.) A single statement in a high-level language such as C may contain many machine instructions.

machine learning *see* ARTIFICIAL INTELLIGENCE.

Macintosh a family of personal computers introduced by Apple in 1984; the first widely used computers with a graphical user interface, windowing, and a mouse. The Macintosh user interface was derived from that of Xerox workstations; it has been imitated by a number of other operating systems, including Microsoft Windows.

The mechanisms for using windows, icons, and mouse menus are provided by the operating system, which means they look virtually the same in all programs. Thus, anyone who knows how to use any Macintosh software package will also know how to perform similar operations in any other software package. Macintosh hardware is simple to set up because of Apple's early commitment to widely recognized standards such as PostScript, PDF, and SCSI.

There have been three generations of Macintosh hardware. The original Macintosh used the Motorola 68000 family of microprocessors. In 1994, Apple changed to the PowerPC microprocessor, and in 2006, to the Intel Pentium.

Macintoshes have always been on the forefront of practical computer graphics and related technology (for example, TrueType scalable fonts and QuickTime video), thus making them the preferred platform for the commercial arts.

The Macintosh uses BSD UNIX as its command-line mode and can run UNIX software without modification. This makes the Macintosh popular with scientists and programmers, which complements Apple's original markets of graphic designers and office workers.

Although the selection of available software is smaller than with PCs, Apple maintains a loyal and vocal following for the Macintosh. The computers perform well and the Mac user community is close-knit.

Unlike Windows applications, user programs on the Macintosh are not given privileged access (i.e., they are not allowed to bypass the API of the layered operating system); this may be why the type of viruses common to Windows are rarely it ever found on the Macintosh.

Apple currently offers a variety of Macintosh computers, giving their customers a wide variety of solutions for their computing needs. There are two basic lines of laptops: iBooks and Powerbooks (student versus professional models, respectively). As for desktop-style computers, Apple offers a traditional high-end line of computers called Power Macs, but also offers the iMac, eMac, and Mac mini. The iMac is a very elegantly designed multi-use computer. eMacs were designed as a lower-cost option to the iMac, but are adequate for most computing tasks. The Mac mini is very small and easily transported. It can quickly hook up to any available monitor, mouse, and keyboard. The Mac mini is ideal for PC-users who also need access to a Macintosh computer.

The current version of the Macintosh operating system is MAC OS X (read "ten," not "x"). *See also* MICROPROCESSOR; POSTSCRIPT; POWERPC; QUICKTIME; SCSI; TRUETYPE FONT.

macro a user-defined sequence of instructions for a computer.

In assembly language and in programming languages such as C, macros are user-defined abbreviations for sequences of program statements. When the program is compiled, each occurrence of the macro is replaced by the instructions for which it stands. This contrasts with a FUNCTION, PROCEDURE, or METHOD, which is stored in one place in memory and called by the main program every time it is needed.

In application programs, macros are user-defined sequences of operations, which can be assigned to specific keys, placed on menus, or combined with pre-existing operations such as Open and Close. In Microsoft Office applications, you can use the Macro Recorder to save a sequence of keystrokes or mouseclicks as a macro, or you can program a macro in VISUAL BASIC.

macro assembler any program that translates assembly language programs into machine code (*see* ASSEMBLY LANGUAGE) and allows the programmer to define macro instructions (*see* MACRO).

macro virus a virus written using the macro language of a particular application. For example, if a Microsoft Word document contains a macro virus that is designed to execute when the file is opened, an unsuspecting user who downloads the file and then opens it with Word will suffer the consequences of whatever the virus is programmed to do. Macro viruses are particularly dangerous because they can hide in word processing documents. Formerly, viruses could only be placed in executable code. *Contrast* TROJAN HORSE; VIRUS.

Macromedia producer of software to enhance the audiovisual content of web pages, including Dreamweaver, Flash, and Freehand. Macromedia was acquired by Adobe in 2005.

MAE (**M**etropolitan **A**rea **E**xchange) a major connecting point where Internet service providers connect to the Internet. There are several MAEs in the U.S., divided into regions (MAE East, MAE Central, and MAE West). Web address: *www.mae.net.*

magenta a purplish-red color that is one of the standard printing ink colors. *See* CMYK.

magic number *(slang)* an important number (such as an interest rate or a file size limit) buried deep within a computer program where those revising the program are likely to overlook it.

This is a bad programming practice; instead, important numbers should be defined prominently near the beginning of the program.

magic wand an editing tool that selects an entire area of a particular color, regardless of its shape; magic wands are found in many photo editing programs (Adobe Photoshop, Aldus Photostyler, Corel PhotoPaint). You use the magic wand to select an area for editing. Its power lies in its ability to do a lot of tedious work for you. When you click on a pixel, the magic wand selects an area of the same or nearly the same color, no matter how jagged the edges. You can then copy, delete, move, rotate, flip, shrink, stretch, or apply filters to this area as if it were a single object. *See also* BITMAP; PAINT PROGRAM; SELECT; SELECTION TOOLS.

FIGURE 162. Magic wand selection tool

mAH abbreviation for MILLIAMPERE-HOUR. *See also* BATTERY.

mail *see* ELECTRONIC MAIL.

mail bombing the practice of trying to flood an obnoxious person with gigantic amounts of e-mail. This is a very bad idea for several reasons. It clogs up facilities needed by other people, not just the intended recipient. More importantly, people who act obnoxiously on the Internet generally falsify their addresses, thereby bringing down floods of wrath upon innocent victims. *See* DENIAL-OF-SERVICE ATTACK.

mail merge *see* MERGE.

mailing list an online discussion conducted by relaying copies of all messages to all the participants by ELECTRONIC MAIL. Mailing lists are preferable to NEWSGROUPS when the group of interested people is relatively small or the discussion would be heckled if it were open to the general public. *See* LISTSERV; MAJORDOMO. *See also* NETIQUETTE.

mainframe computer a large computer occupying a specially air-conditioned room and supporting hundreds of users at one time. The IBM 370 and IBM 3090 are examples of mainframe computers. *Contrast* MINI-COMPUTER; PERSONAL COMPUTER.

Majordomo a free, open-source software package for operating e-mail mailing lists and discussion groups, distributed from *www.greatcircle.com*. Majordomo is written in Perl and runs primarily on UNIX systems. (The major-domo is the head servant in an aristocratic household.) *Compare* LISTSERV.

make a command, in UNIX and similar operating systems, that manages the steps of creating a machine-language program or some other complex product of computation.

Typically, a large machine-language program is made by compiling several different source files, producing a group of object files, and then linking the object files together. (*See* SOURCE CODE; OBJECT CODE.) The make command manages this process. It looks at a makefile (Figure 163) that tells it how to create each of the files needed to generate the complete program. Then it looks at the date on which each file was last modified. If any file is newer than the other files made from it, make will do whatever is needed to update those files (typically compiling or linking). By using make, the programmer avoids recompiling anything that has not been changed.

The make command can actually manage any process in which files are made from other files. All it needs is a makefile containing the appropriate commands.

```
# Each entry consists of:
# A file
# A list of other files that file depends on
# A command to generate it from them
# Each indented line must actually begin with
# the Tab character (ASCII 9), not spaces.
#
myprog:      myprog1.o myprog2.o
             cc myprog1.o myprog2.o -o myprog
#
myprog1.o:   myprog1.c
             cc -c myprog1.c
#
myprog2.o:   myprog2.c
             cc -c myprog2.c
```
FIGURE 163. Makefile

makefile a file that controls the operation of the MAKE command. Under UNIX, by default, it is named makefile or Makefile and resides in the current directory.

malware malicious software. For examples *see* ADWARE; SPYWARE; VIRUS.

man pages (**m**anual **p**ages) the online documentation built into UNIX and accessed by the command.

    man *command*

where *command* is the command or system function you want to know about. A selling point of UNIX since the earliest days has been that its manuals are online. *See* UNIX.

management information systems (MIS) a field of study that deals with effective systems for the development and use of information in an organization. The complete information system includes not just the computers but also the people. Any effective information system must determine:

1. what the goals of the organization are;
2. what information is needed to accomplish those goals;
3. how that information is originated;
4. how the information needs to be stored and transferred to accomplish those goals.

Mandelbrot set a famous fractal (i.e., a shape containing an infinite amount of fine detail). It was discovered by Benoit Mandelbrot. The Mandelbrot set is the set of values of c for which the series $z_{n+1} = (z_n)^2 + c$ converges, where z and c are complex numbers and z is initially $(0, 0)$. *See* COMPLEX NUMBER.

The detail in the Mandelbrot set fascinates mathematicians. In Figure 164, the x and y axes are the real and imaginary parts of c. The Mandelbrot set is the black bulbous object in the middle; elsewhere, the stripes indicate the number of iterations needed to make $|z|$ exceed 2.

FIGURE 164. Mandelbrot set

manifest a list of the contents of a shipment; a list of files transmitted as a group; also used with messages containing a DIGITAL SIGNATURE to be validated with a HASH FUNCTION.

Map Network Drive the operation, in Windows, that makes a directory on another computer act as if it were a local disk drive. To map a network drive, right-click on the Computer icon and select the Map Network

Drive menu item. You will need to specify the server name, directory to map, and the drive letter to use. *See also* UNC.

Mapquest a web site (*www.mapquest.com*) that allows users to create customized maps or find directions to specific addresses. Mapquest is now a subsidiary of AOL. *Compare* GOOGLE MAPS.

marching ants *(slang)* the moving dashed lines that indicate the borders of a selected object in a paint or draw program (*see* MARQUEE SELECT). Some programs allow you to hide the ants if they distract you.

markup language any language that provides ways to indicate underlining, italics, paragraph breaks, section headings, and so on, in text. For examples *see* HTML; SGML; TEX.

marquee select a method of selecting more than one object at a time in a graphical user interface (GUI). It gets its name from the animated effect of the dashed line of the bounding box—it resembles a theater marquee.

    To marquee-select items, sight along the top and the left edge of the group of items you wish to select. Position the mouse cursor there. While holding down the mouse button, pull diagonally down and to the right. When the marquee encloses all the items, release the mouse button. *See also* GUI; MOUSE; SELECT.

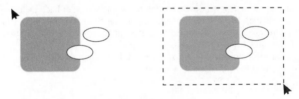

FIGURE 165. Marquee select

mashup a combination of two or more works to create an original derivative work. They are most commonly seen in music, where a famous example is DJ Danger Mouse's Grey Album, a mashup of the Beatles' "White Album" and Jay-Z's "Black Album."

mask
    1. (in draw programs) to create an object with a hole in it, so that the view of an underlying object is controlled.
    2. (in paint programs) to mark an area of the drawing as protected from the drawing tools. The mask can be removed as the drawing progresses. This is analogous to the masking used in watercolor painting.
    3. (in programming) to isolate part of a binary number by ANDing it with another binary number. For example, the first four bits of any byte can be isolated by ANDing the byte with 11110000. *See* AND GATE; SUBNET MASK.

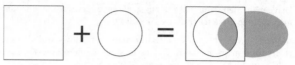

FIGURE 166. Mask

master

1. the controlling unit in a pair of linked machines. *Contrast* SLAVE (definition 1).

2. one of a pair of IDE hard disks or other devices connected to the same IDE cable. Generally, jumpers have to be set on IDE devices to identify them as master and slave. *Contrast* SLAVE (definition 2).

master browser *see* BROWSE MASTER.

master page a design template that defines the overall appearance of every page of a printed document. *See also* GRID SYSTEM.

MathML (**Math**ematics **M**arkup **L**anguage) an extension of HTML designed to facilitate the display of mathematical expressions. (See the W3C web site at *www.w3.org*.)

matrix *see* ARRAY.

maximize to make a window take over the whole screen or become as large as possible. To do this, click the mouse on the maximize button (*see* picture at WINDOW). *See also* MINIMIZE; RESTORE. Maximize is also an option under the CONTROL MENU.

    On a Macintosh, use the ZOOM box (at the far right side of the window's title bar) to enlarge a window.

MB abbreviation for MEGABYTE.

MBps **m**egabytes **p**er **s**econd. *See also* BAUD; MEGABYTE. Note the uppercase B.

Mbps **m**egabits **p**er **s**econd. *See* BIT. Note the lowercase b.

MCSE (**M**icrosoft **C**ertified **S**oftware **E**ngineer) a credential for computer professionals who pass a series of proficiency exams from Microsoft.

MDI (**m**ultiple **d**ocument **i**nterface) the ability to edit more than one file or drawing with a single copy of a Windows program.

meatware *(slang, humorous)* computer users (the parts of a computer system that are made of meat). *Compare* PEBKAC.

mebi- metric prefix meaning ×1,048,576 (2^{20}), the binary counterpart of *mega-*. *See* METRIC PREFIXES.

mebibyte 1,048,576 bytes.

Mechanical Turk Amazon's crowdsourcing marketplace that connects people willing to do small tasks (proofreading, transcribing, etc.) to those wanting to employ them. *See* CROWDSOURCING. The name comes from an 18th-century chess-playing machine, the "mechanical Turk," which appeared to be a robot but actually had a person inside.

media plural of MEDIUM.

Media Center Edition *see* WINDOWS (MICROSOFT).

media error a defect in the surface of a disk or tape, sometimes curable by formatting the disk or tape again.

medium (plural *media*)
  1. material used for storage of information. Magnetic disks, tapes, and optical disks are examples of storage media.
  2. a way of presenting information to the computer user. Vision is one medium; sound is another. Multimedia computing uses visible displays of several types together with sound.
  3. a means of mass communication, such as television.

medium-scale integration the construction of integrated circuits that contains hundreds of logic gates. *See* INTEGRATED CIRCUIT.

meg short for MEGABYTE.

mega- (**m**) metric prefix meaning ×1,000,000. *Mega-* is derived from the Greek word for "big." *See* METRIC PREFIXES.

megabyte (**MB**) $2^{20} = 1,048,576$ bytes = 1,024 kilobytes. *See* METRIC PREFIXES.

megahertz (**MHz**) million hertz or million cycles per second, a measure of the clock speed of a computer or the frequency of a radio signal. *See* CLOCK; MICROPROCESSOR.

megapixel one million PIXELS, a measure of the size of a graphical image. For example, a 1024 × 1024-pixel image is often referred to as a megapixel. Table 9 shows how many megapixels are needed for various levels of image quality. *See also* DIGITAL CAMERA; EFFECTIVE MEGAPIXELS; GROSS MEGAPIXELS; PAINT PROGRAM.

TABLE 9
MEGAPIXELS AND IMAGE QUALITY

Megapixels	Typical use
0.2–0.5	Picture on a web page
0.5–1.5	Snapshot or small photograph
1.5–3.0	Sharp full-page photographic print
3.0–8.0	Image sharp enough that portions of it will remain sharp when extracted and enlarged
16	Equal to the very sharpest photographs

meme an idea that spreads quickly from person to person. Often, on the Internet, a meme is a visual or textual joke, similar to a recurring gag in a movie or book. An example of a meme would be "Rickrolling," the practice of tricking someone into clicking on a link to listen to Rick Astley's "Never Gonna Give You Up" on the pretext of directing them to something else.

The term *meme* (from *memory* + *gene*) was introduced by evolutionary biologist Richard Dawkins in 1976 to denote important ideas, skills, or habits that are passed along from person to person almost like genes. On the Internet, however, the term is usually applied to sweeping fads.

memory the component within a computer where information is stored while being actively worked on. Most microcomputers have a small amount of read-only memory (ROM), containing the built-in programs that start the operation of the computer when it is turned on, and a large amount of random-access memory (RAM) for user's programs and data. Except for ROM, memory goes blank when the computer is turned off; any data in it must be copied to the hard disk, a CD, or a USB flash drive in order to be saved.

See also CORE (definition 3). DRAM; EDO; RDRAM; SDRAM; SIMM.

memory leak an error in a program that makes it fail to release memory or other system resources when it terminates. Thus, the available memory, disk space, or other resources are gradually eaten up until the computer is rebooted. Memory leaks are a common error in Windows programs.

Java and .NET programs avoid this problem by using a garbage collection process, which automatically releases memory locations that are no longer being referenced by the program.

MemoryStick a type of flash-memory non-volatile storage device similar to CompactFlash but physically long and thin, developed by Sony Corporation. *Compare* COMPACTFLASH; FLASH MEMORY CARD; MULTI-MEDIA-CARD; SECURE DIGITAL CARD; SMARTMEDIA.

Memphis Microsoft's internal code name for the Windows 98 development project. *Compare* CAIRO; CHICAGO; LONGHORN; WHISTLER.

menu a list of choices that appears on the screen in response to your actions. Most windows have a MENU BAR just under the title bar. When you click on an item in the menu bar, its corresponding menu will appear. You select the command you want by moving the mouse pointer to it. Commands with ellipsis dots (. . .) after them will pop up a dialog box for you to give the computer further instructions before executing the command. If there are keyboard shortcuts for any command, they will often be listed to the right of the command.

menu bar a horizontal menu across the top of the screen or window. Depending on the software, the items in the menu bar are chosen by clicking on them with a mouse, or by typing the first letter of each item, or possibly by typing the first letter while holding down Alt. Usually each item is a further menu. For an illustration, *see* MENU.

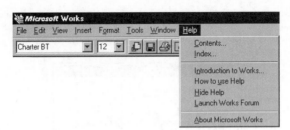

FIGURE 167. Menu

merge to insert data (e.g., names and addresses) from one file into a document that resides in another file (e.g., the text of a form letter).

merge sort an algorithm for sorting data (*see* SORT). Merge sort takes advantage of the fact that it is easy to combine two lists that are already sorted; just keep looking at the first element of each list and taking whichever element comes first. For example, to combine the lists

Adams	Bush
Buchanan	Clinton
Lincoln	Kennedy

do the following: Compare Adams to Bush; take Adams. Then compare Buchanan to Bush and take Buchanan. Then compare Lincoln to Bush and take Bush, and so on. This will give you a list of all six names in alphabetical order.

To perform a complete merge sort, first divide your data into several small sorted lists. These can be sorted with some other sorting algorithm; or they can be two-element lists which are sorted by swapping the two elements where needed; or they can even be one-element lists, which do not need sorting. Then combine these lists, two at a time, until they all have been put together into a single sorted list.

A big advantage of merge sort is that you never need to see more than the first element of any list. Thus, merge sort can take its data from tapes or from linked lists, which cannot easily be sorted by any other algorithm. *See* LINKED LIST; SEQUENTIAL-ACCESS DEVICE.

mesh network a network with multiple paths connecting nodes. Devices on the network cooperate to determine routing of messages. It can function when a node fails by rerouting messages along paths that bypass the failed node. The Internet is one example.

message board a web page, NEWSGROUP, or dial-up computer system where users can post messages and reply to messages posted by others. Messages are usually public and visible to all users. Most bulletin boards associate replies with the original messages, creating threads. *See also* FLAME; NEWSGROUP; POST; THREAD.

message box a small window that appears to present information to the user (Figure 168). When the user acknowledges reading the message by pressing a mouse button, the message box disappears.

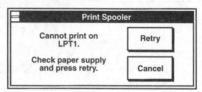

FIGURE 168. Message box

message sending one way of describing object-oriented programming: objects receive "messages," which are calls to procedures associated with them. *See* OBJECT-ORIENTED PROGRAMMING.

meta tag a piece of information added to a WEB PAGE for the benefit of indexers, SEARCH ENGINES, web page creation software, or other purposes. Meta tags are not displayed when the page is viewed.

Most meta tags consist of a name and a content field. Some names are widely recognized. Here are some examples:

```
<meta name="author" content="Catherine Anne Covington">
<meta name="keywords" content="oranges, apples, lemons">
<meta name="robots" content="noindex, nofollow">
```

The first identifies the author as Catherine Anne Covington; the second asks search engines to index the page under *oranges, apples,* and *lemons;* and the third asks search engines not to index the page at all, nor follow its links.

It is entirely up to a search engine to decide whether or not to comply with these requests. Also, meta tags are often used deceptively to bring in additional visitors to a site by making it come up when they search for something else. In a few extreme cases, pornography sites have been known to put an entire dictionary of the English language in the *keywords* meta tag.

Another type of meta tag adds information to the header sent with the HTTP file; this information helps control the browser. For example,

```
<meta http-equiv="charset" content="iso-8859-1">
```

tells the browser to use the ISO-8859-1 character set, and

```
<meta http-equiv="Refresh" content="15">
<meta http-equiv="Refresh" content="15;
    URL=http://www.xyz.org">
```

say, respectively, to refresh (reload) the web page after 15 seconds and to jump to *www.xyz.org* after 15 seconds.

metacrawler a program that submits search queries to the major Internet indexes (such as Google, Yahoo, or Lycos) and creates a summary of the results, thus giving the searcher the benefit of using all the SEARCH ENGINES simultaneously.

metadata information about information, such as information about the origin, format, or ownership of a data file.

metafile a file format that provides a common ground between two or more proprietary formats, and thus a translation path from one piece of software to another. For example, a Windows Metafile (.wmf) is a vector-based drawing format that is recognized by most drawing, page-layout, and word-processing programs. *See also* CGM.

metal *see* BARE METAL.

meta language any language used to describe another language. For example, Backus-Naur Form can be used as a metalanguage to describe the syntax of programming languages. Lisp and Prolog have the interesting property that the programs can read and modify themselves, so these programming languages can be put to practical use as metalanguages for themselves. *See* BACKUS-NAUR FORM; LISP; PROLOG.

method (in object-oriented programming) a procedure associated with an object type. *See* OBJECT-ORIENTED PROGRAMMING.

metric prefixes the prefixes used in the metric system to denote multiplication of units, such as *kilo-* meaning "thousand." The complete set is shown in Table 10.

   When measuring computer memory or disk capacity, *kilo-*, *mega-*, *giga-*, and *tera-* often stand for powers of 1024 ($= 2^{10}$) rather than powers of 1000. Even more confusingly, *mega-* occasionally means $1000 \times 1024 = 1,024,000$.

   In 1998, the International Electrotechnical Commission (IEC) proposed the "binary" metric prefixes KIBI- (2^{10}), MEBI- (2^{20}), GIBI- (2^{30}), TEBI- (2^{40}), and PEBI- (2^{50}) to be used in place of *kilo-*, *mega-*, *giga-*, and *tera-* where powers of $2^{10} = 1024$ rather than powers of 1000 are meant.

   In Greek, *kilo-*, *mega-*, *giga-*, and *tera-*, mean, respectively, "thousand," "big," "giant," and "monster."

Metro a new user interface style introduced with Windows 8 and strongly influenced by Apple's IOS. The screen is divided into panels that pictorially represent application software, and each piece of software has an entirely different look, rather than residing in a standard window.

mezzanine bus a special bus that connects the CPU to some of the faster peripherals, such as memory modules, and is separate from the slower bus used for slower peripherals. *See* BUS.

TABLE 10
METRIC PREFIXES

Prefix	Abbreviation	Meaning
yotta-	Y	$\times 10^{24} = 1{,}000{,}000{,}000{,}000{,}000{,}000{,}000{,}000$
zetta-	Z	$\times 10^{21} = 1{,}000{,}000{,}000{,}000{,}000{,}000{,}000$
exa-	E	$\times 10^{18} = 1{,}000{,}000{,}000{,}000{,}000{,}000$
peta-	P	$\times 10^{15} = 1{,}000{,}000{,}000{,}000{,}000$
tera-	T	$\times 10^{12} = 1{,}000{,}000{,}000{,}000$
giga-	G	$\times 10^{9} = 1{,}000{,}000{,}000$
mega-	M (not m)	$\times 10^{6} = 1{,}000{,}000$
kilo-	k	$\times 10^{3} = 1000$
hecta-	h	$\times 10^{2} = 100$
deca-	da	$\times 10^{1} = 10$
deci-	d	$10^{-1} = \div 10$
centi-	c	$10^{-2} = \div 100$
milli-	m (not M)	$10^{-3} = \div 1000$
micro-	μ	$10^{-6} = \div 1{,}000{,}000$ (unofficially abbreviated u)
nano-	n	$10^{-9} = \div 1{,}000{,}000{,}000$
pico-	p	$10^{-12} = \div 1{,}000{,}000{,}000{,}000$
femto-	f	$10^{-15} = \div 1{,}000{,}000{,}000{,}000{,}000$
atto-	a	$10^{-18} = \div 1{,}000{,}000{,}000{,}000{,}000{,}000$
zepto-	z	$10^{-21} = \div 1{,}000{,}000{,}000{,}000{,}000{,}000{,}000$
yocto-	y	$10^{-24} = \div 1{,}000{,}000{,}000{,}000{,}000{,}000{,}000{,}000$

MFP (**M**ulti **F**unction **P**rinter) a printer that also performs other functions such as faxing and scanning.

MHz *see* MEGAHERTZ.

MIB (describing items for sale) **m**int **i**n **b**ox (i.e., new and never unpacked). *See also* EBAY; NRFB.

MiB abbreviation for MEBIBYTE (1,048,576 bytes).

micro- metric prefix meaning ÷1,000,000 (one millionth). For example, a microsecond is one millionth of a second (0.000001 second), and a microfarad is one millionth of a farad. "Micro-" is abbreviated with the Greek letter mu (μ) or by the letter *u. Micro-* is derived from the Greek word for "small." *See* METRIC PREFIXES.

microblogging the practice of publishing short personal messages, like the entries in a BLOG but much shorter. For examples, *see* TWITTER, TUMBLR.

microbrowser a web browser using less memory than a conventional browser so it can be used on a small device such as a palmtop. *See* LINKS.

microcomputer a computer whose CPU consists of a single integrated circuit known as a microprocessor. Commonly, a microcomputer is used by only one person at a time. All home computers are microcomputers. *See* INTEGRATED CIRCUIT; MICROPROCESSOR.

microcontroller a microprocessor designed specifically for controlling equipment. Microcontrollers usually contain some memory and input-output circuitry on the same chip with the microprocessor. This enables the microcontroller to work as a self-contained unit. Microcontrollers are used in consumer products such as telephones, automobiles, and microwave ovens, as well as in industrial equipment. *See also* EMBEDDED SYSTEM.

Microdrive *see* COMPACTFLASH.

microprocessor an integrated circuit containing the entire CPU of a computer, all on one silicon chip, so that only the memory and input-output devices need to be added. The first popular microprocessor, the Intel 8080, came out in 1973 and cost approximately $400.

Microprocessors are commonly described as 16-bit, 32-bit, or the like. The number can refer either to the number of bits in each internal data register, or to the number of bits on the data bus (*see* BUS); these two numbers are usually the same. Other things being equal, larger registers and a larger bus enable the processor to do its work faster.

Clock speed is also important. The clock is the oscillator that causes the microprocessor to proceed from one step to the next in executing instructions. (Each machine instruction takes several clock cycles.) Clock speed is measured in megahertz (MHz) or gigahertz (GHz): 1 MHz is 1 million cycles per second, and 1 GHz = 1000 MHz. Higher clock speeds result in faster computation, but only if exactly the same machine instructions are being executed; it is misleading to compare the clock speeds of processors of different types. It is even possible for two microprocessors with the same instruction set and clock speed to perform computations at different rates because of differences in internal design. A 100-MHz Pentium II, for example, is faster than a 100-MHz Pentium.

microSD *see* SECURE DIGITAL CARD.

Microsoft a leading software-producing company, headquartered in Redmond, Washington, and founded by Bill Gates and Paul Allen in 1975 when they wrote a version of BASIC for an early hobbyist microcomputer, the Altair. In the late 1970s the company grew as it sold versions of BASIC to other computer makers, but it was still fairly small when it was approached by IBM to design the operating system for the IBM PC (released in 1981).

This operating system (known as PC-DOS, MS-DOS, or simply DOS) became a huge seller, since almost all PC and PC clones used it. In 1990 Microsoft released version 3.0 of Windows, providing a graphical user interface for the PC. Updated versions of Windows continue to be the most common operating system on the PC (*see* WINDOWS (MICROSOFT)).

Microsoft is also a big seller of applications software for both PCs and Macintoshes. The suite Microsoft Office includes the word processing program Microsoft Word, the spreadsheet Excel, the database program Access, and the presentation program Powerpoint. In 1991 Microsoft introduced Visual Basic, an advanced version of BASIC that allows the programmer to take advantage of the graphical environment of Windows. It now provides development environments for other languages in the Visual Studio series. Other products include the Bing search engine, the web browser Internet Explorer, and X-box game machines.

For further information about Microsoft and its products, see *www. microsoft.com. See also* GATES, BILL.

Microsoft antitrust charges a series of official accusations that Microsoft has violated U.S. antitrust laws (laws that prohibit businesses from monopolizing a market or conspiring to stifle competition).

In 1998, the U.S. Department of Justice filed a broad antitrust case against Microsoft. Among other accusations, they charged that Microsoft violated antitrust laws by including its Internet Explorer browser free with Windows, because this killed off the market for other browsers (e.g., Netscape) that were available commercially. The company was found guilty, but an appeals overturned the order that they should be broken up. The company and the U.S. Justice Department reached a negotiated settlement in November 2001. In the settlement, Microsoft agreed not to retaliate against hardware makers that worked with other software makers, and Microsoft's behavior would be subject to monitoring.

Microsoft has also been fined by the European Union for antitrust violations.

Microsoft Windows *see* WINDOWS (MICROSOFT).

middleware

1. in a three-tier system, the system that is between the user interface and the database access software. *See* THREE-TIER ARCHITECTURE.

2. software that occupies a middle position between application software and the operating system, so that programs written for the compatible middleware can run under different operating systems without change. Examples of middleware include web browsers and well-standardized programming languages (such as Fortran and Java). Because of middleware, programs and web pages can be written so that they run identically on completely different computers.

MIDI (**M**usical **I**nstrument **D**igital **I**nterface) a standard way for communicating information about music between different electronic devices, such as computers and sound synthesizers.

MIDI comprises two things: an electrical connection between musical instruments and computers, and a file format for representing musical sounds. MIDI files are more like musical scores than digitized audio; they represent notes and instrumentation, not sound waves, and the computer must "play" them like a musician. Thus, MIDI files are much more compact than WAVE FILES.

.mil *see* TLD.

millennium bug a software defect reflecting the Year 2000 Problem. *See* YEAR 2000 PROBLEM.

milli- metric prefix meaning ÷1000 (one thousandth). For example, one millisecond is one thousandth of a second (0.001 second), and a millimeter is one thousandth of a meter. *Milli-* is derived from the Latin word for "thousandth." *See* METRIC PREFIXES.

milliampere-hour a unit of battery capacity, $\frac{1}{1,000}$ of an ampere-hour. *See* BATTERY.

MIME (**M**ultipurpose **I**nternet **M**ail **E**xtensions) a standard proposed by N. Borenstein and N. Freed for including material other than ASCII text in e-mail messages. MIME messages can be recognized by the "Content-Type" declaration in the header, and the range of content types is potentially unlimited. Most e-mail software now supports MIME encoding. *See also* CGI.

mind virus *see* MEME.

mini-CD, mini-DVD a CD or DVD that is 8 cm in diameter (about 3 inches) instead of the usual 12 cm ($4\frac{3}{4}$ inches).

minicomputer a computer intermediate in size between a mainframe computer and a microcomputer; two classic examples were the Digital Equipment Corporation VAX and the IBM AS/400. A minicomputer typically occupied a large area within a room and supported 10 to 100 users at a time. In recent years minicomputers have been replaced by networks of microcomputers. *Contrast* MAINFRAME COMPUTER; PERSONAL COMPUTER.

minimize to make a window as small as possible; usually this means it becomes an icon rather than a window. In Windows minimized icons go to the taskbar at the bottom of the screen.

To minimize a window, click on the minimize button (*see* WINDOW). This is a handy way to get one piece of software out of the way temporarily while you turn your attention to something else. You can then RESTORE the window when you want to resume working with it.

Caution: the minimized program is still taking up memory and you'll find that graphics intensive programs (such as paint programs) need all the memory you can give them. You should CLOSE all minimized programs before launching a program that needs lots of memory. Some utilities can run minimized in the background (e.g., print spoolers). *See also* LAUNCH; MAXIMIZE; RESTORE.

miniSD *see* SECURE DIGITAL CARD.

mint (describing items for sale) perfectly preserved, in new condition.

minty (describing items for sale) almost, but not quite, MINT—a vague term that encourages optimism but makes no precise claims.

MIPS (**M**illion **I**nstructions **P**er **S**econd) a measurement of the speed with which computer programs are run. Because different instructions take different amounts of time, speed measured in MIPS depends on the exact program that the computer is running. For this reason, speed tests are usually done with standard programs such as Whetstone and Dhrystone.

Another problem is that equivalent programs take different numbers of instructions on different CPUs. To compare different computers meaningfully, it is common practice to calculate MIPS using the number of instructions that a program would require on a VAX rather than on the computer actually being tested. This way, equivalent programs are always viewed as having the same number of instructions and the speed of the computer under test is the only variable.

mirror

1. to flip an image so that the resulting image is a mirror image of the original.

2. to reproduce the entire contents of an FTP or WEB SITE so that the same files are available from more than one location.

3. to maintain an extra copy of a disk drive on a second disk drive automatically. *See* RAID.

FIGURE 169. Mirror, definition 1

mirroring the practice of maintaining a copy of data that is automatically kept up to date. For an example *see* RAID.

MIS *see* MANAGEMENT INFORMATION SYSTEMS.

misfeature *(slang)* an ill-conceived feature; a feature with unforeseen and unfortunate effects. For example, the choice of / as the option character in DOS 1.0 was a misfeature because it made it impossible to use / as the directory separator when DOS 2.0 introduced directories. As a result, DOS and Windows use \ where UNIX uses /, to the annoyance of programmers everywhere.

Mission Control user interface under Mac OS X Lion.

miter to cut at an angle. A way of specifying how lines should intersect; *mitered* joints come to neat points. If intersecting lines are not properly mitered, there are ugly gaps at the intersection, or the square endpoints of the lines overlap.

Most drawing programs let you set the *miter limit*; the threshold at which the computer bevels a sharp angle when two lines have a narrow angle of intersection. This prevents the pointed joint from extending way past the end of the line.

FIGURE 170. Mitered vs. unmitered joint

mixed case type set with normal capitalization, neither all caps nor all lowercase. *Contrast* CAMEL NOTATION; EVEN SMALLS.

mixed-signal handling both ANALOG and DIGITAL signals. For example, a sound card is a mixed-signal device.

mixer a software control that determines the relative loudness of various kinds of sound produced by a SOUND CARD, such as MIDI music, wave file playback, and synthesized speech.

MMO (**m**assive **m**ultiplayer **o**nline) a term describing game software that lets hundreds of users participate simultaneously. MMO is usually prefixed to another abbreviation to describe the type of game more precisely (for example, *see* MMORPG).

MMORPG abbreviation for **m**assive **m**ultiplayer **o**nline **r**ole-**p**laying **g**ame, such as World of Warcraft. *See* ROLE-PLAYING GAME.

MMX (**m**ultimedia **e**xtensions) a set of additional instructions added to the later models of the Pentium microprocessor and its successors to support high-speed processing of animation and sound. The MMX instructions support a limited form of vector processing. *See* VECTOR PROCESSOR.

mnemonic a symbol or expression that helps you remember something. For example, the expression "Spring forward, fall back" helps you remember which way to adjust your clocks in the spring and fall for daylight saving time.

A mnemonic variable name is a variable name that helps the programmer remember what the variable means. For example, in a payroll program the variable to represent the hours worked could be given the mnemonic name HOURS.

MO (**m**ega-**o**ctet) French abbreviation for MEGABYTE.

moblog (**mo**bile **blog**ing) posting to a blog from a mobile device such as a smartphone.

mobo *(slang)* **mo**ther**bo**ard.

mod

1. abbreviation for *modulo,* used to refer to the remainder in integer division. For example, in Pascal, the expression 38 mod 7 has the value 3, since 3 is the remainder when 38 is divided by 7. In C, C++, C#, and Java, this operation is symbolized by %.

2. abbreviation for *modification* (a change to a piece of hardware or software).

modal dialog box a dialog box that requires an immediate response from the user; other windows cannot be used until the modal dialog box has been dealt with. Modal dialog boxes generally warn of problems such as running out of printer paper or losing a network connection. *See* DIALOG BOX.

mode the state that a piece of hardware or software is in, defining the way it can be used.

modem (**mo**dulator-**dem**odulator) a device that encodes data for transmission over a particular medium, such as telephone lines, coaxial cables, fiber optics, or microwaves.

modifier key a key that changes or extends the meaning of a keyboard key. Examples of modifier keys are Shift, CTRL, and ALT.

Modula-2 a programming language developed by Niklaus Wirth in the late 1970s as a replacement for Pascal, which Wirth had developed some 10 years earlier. As its name suggests, Modula-2 is designed to encourage modularity (*see* STRUCTURED PROGRAMMING). Modula-2 is very similar to the extended versions of Pascal that most compilers now implement.

module a part of a larger system. A module in a computer program is a part of the program that is written and tested separately and then is combined with other modules to form the complete program. *See* TOP-DOWN PROGRAMMING.

modulo the remainder in a division problem. For computer programming examples, *see* MOD.

moiré an unintended and distracting pattern that occurs when two or more halftone screens are overprinted at the wrong angle. *See* Figure 171.

FIGURE 171. Moiré

monadic operation an operation on one piece of data. For example, negation (finding the negative of a number) is an operation that requires only
one operand and is therefore monadic. Addition is not monadic because
it requires two numbers to be added. *Contrast* DYADIC OPERATION.

monetize the process of converting a web page or other digital content so
that it earns revenue. For example, see the Amazon Associates program
affiliate-program.amazon.com/gp/associates/join.

monitor
1. a computer program that supervises the activity of other programs.
2. a device similar to a television set that accepts video signals from a
computer and displays information on its screen. *See also* CRT; EYE-
GLASSES, COMPUTER; LCD; SVGA; VGA.

monospace a typeface design that gives each letter the same width, like
this. *See* Figure 104, page 195. *See also* COURIER; FIXED-PITCH TYPE;
TYPEFACE.

Monte Carlo engine a computer or program used for MONTE CARLO
SIMULATION.

Monte Carlo simulation a simulation method that uses random numbers
to estimate complex probabilities.
   Suppose that you know the probability that a particular event will
happen, but it is too difficult to calculate the probability that a complicated combination of events will occur. In the Monte Carlo method you
use a random number generator to calculate a random number between
0 and 1, and then compare that number with the probability of the event.
For example, if the probability of the event is .62, and the random number generated is .58, then the program will simulate that the event has
occurred. You can simulate thousands of such events and look at how the
combinations of them add up. The name Monte Carlo comes from the
fact that this method is a bit like a game of chance.

MOO (**M**UD, **O**bject **O**riented) a type of MUD (Internet game or interaction environment). *See* MUD.

Moore's Law the prediction that the number of transistors that can be
placed in an INTEGRATED CIRCUIT of any given size will double every two
years. That is why microprocessors and other integrated circuits become
cheaper and more efficient year by year.
   Moore's Law was first expressed in 1967 by Gordon Moore, co-
founder of Intel, and has proved accurate so far, but it is not guaranteed
to always continue to be true.

morph to transform one image gradually into another. A *moving morph* is
an animation of the morphing process; a *still morph* is a single image of
the transition in progress. *See also* ANIMATION; COMPOSITING.

FIGURE 172. Morph

Mosaic one of the first graphical BROWSERS for the World Wide Web, distributed free by the National Center for Supercomputer Applications (*www.ncsa.uiuc.edu*) and later incorporated into Microsoft Internet Explorer and other products.

motherboard the main circuit board of a computer, containing the CPU and memory.

motion blur (paint, 3-d programs) a filter that blurs the image along a specified axis to give the effect of motion.

FIGURE 173. Motion blur

Motorola a major manufacturer of electronic equipment and parts, headquartered in Schaumburg, Illinois. Motorola makes a number of microprocessors, including the 68000 series used in the original Apple Macintosh, the PowerPC, and the 6800, used in some early microcomputers in the 1970s.

In 2004, Motorola spun off its microprocessor division as Freescale Semiconductor, Inc., headquartered in Austin, Texas. Web address: *www. freescale.com*. In 2011 Motorola was acquired by Google.

mount to put a disk or tape into a computer and make it known to the operating system. Under UNIX, a list of all currently mounted file systems can be displayed by typing the command mount. Windows shows all mounted drives under COMPUTER; Macintosh computers display mounted drives on the DESKTOP.

mount point a directory that is actually a separate disk drive. For example, if a UNIX system has two disks, one of them will likely be mounted as / (the root directory) and the other as /home. Then the second disk drive will function as if it were a subdirectory of the first one.

mouse a computer input device that is used by moving it around on your desk and pressing one or more buttons. Moving the mouse moves a pointer on the screen (*see* MOUSE POINTER). Graphical user interfaces such as Microsoft Windows and the Apple Macintosh operating system are built around the mouse. So are paint and draw programs. *See* DRAW PROGRAM; GRAPHICAL USER INTERFACE; MACINTOSH; PAINT PROGRAM; TRACKBALL; WINDOWS (MICROSOFT). *Compare* MULTITOUCH INTERFACE.

mouse pointer a small symbol on the screen that indicates what the mouse is pointing to, and moves whenever the mouse is moved. The shape of the pointer may change to indicate what it is pointing to. It may be an arrow, an I-beam, a cross, or others. Also called *mouse cursor*.

mouse potato *(slang)* a computer user who is addicted to web-surfing and other computer-related activities. Obviously adapted from *couch potato*, a person who incessantly views television.

mouseover *see* ROLLOVER (definition 2).

mousetrap a web page that is programmed, using JavaScript or another scripting language, so that the "back" button on the browser no longer works as intended. That is, once you go to such a web page, you cannot back out of it. In 2001 the U.S. Federal Trade Commission took action against an advertiser who used mousetraps on thousands of web sites to compel viewers to view a barrage of obnoxious advertisements.

MOV
  1. (**m**etal **o**xide **v**aristor) an electronic component used to protect electronic equipment from momentary voltage spikes. *See* POWER LINE PROTECTION; SURGE PROTECTOR.
  2. abbreviation for "move" in most ASSEMBLY LANGUAGES. The direction of the arguments depends on the language. On Intel processors, MOV 7,8 means move the value 8 into location 7; on Motorola processors it means move the value 7 into location 8.
  3. file format used by QUICKTIME for movies and other media types.

Mozilla an open-source web BROWSER established by Netscape; also the name of a lizard used as Mozilla's mascot. Their web site is *www. mozilla.org*.

MP3 a file compression format for music that allows users to download music over the web. MP3 is short for MPEG, layer 3 (layer 1 and layer 2 refer to previous, less-advanced compression formats) and is promoted by the Motion Picture Experts Group (*see* MPEG).
  Sound waves can be represented as numbers indicating the amplitude of the wave at each moment in time. High-fidelity sound requires storing a 16-bit number 44,100 times per second (a sampling rate of 44.1 kilohertz). This means that one minute of stereo music requires over 10 megabytes of disk space. This is generally too large to be practical, but MP3 compression reduces the file size to about 1 megabyte per minute. The compression method was developed after carefully studying human auditory perception and then designing the compression algorithm so that the information lost is imperceptible.
  MP3 format now allows many artists to make samples of their work available to the general public over the web, but the ease of copying music in MP3 format raises concerns about piracy. *See also* DIGITAL MUSIC.

MP3 player
1. a small portable device that stores and plays music in the form of MP3 files. *See* DIGITAL MUSIC. *Compare* IPOD.
2. a computer program that plays music from MP3 files.

MPC (**m**ultimedia **p**ersonal **c**omputer) a personal computer that meets requirements specified by the MPC Marketing Council for compact disc, sound, and graphics capabilities. These requirements are revised frequently.

MPEG (**M**otion **P**icture **E**xperts **G**roup) an ISO working group that sets standards for digital sound and video and the associated data compression requirements. Web address: *www.mpeg.org*.

ms (**m**illisecond) one thousandth of a second. *See* ACCESS TIME.

MS a common abbreviation for Microsoft. *See* MICROSOFT; MS-DOS.

MS-DOS Microsoft Disk Operating System, the original operating system for IBM PC-compatible computers. Early versions were also marketed by IBM as PC-DOS.
      Virtually all the commands of DOS are still usable at the COMMAND PROMPT in Windows. *See also* BAT FILE; COM; EXE FILE; EXTENSION; PATH; WINDOWS (MICROSOFT).

MS-DOS Prompt earlier name for COMMAND PROMPT.

MSIE Microsoft INTERNET EXPLORER.

MSN (**M**icrosoft **N**etwork) an online network established by Microsoft which provides content as well as a connection to the Internet.

MSRP **m**anufacturer's **s**uggested **r**etail **p**rice.

MTBF (**m**ean **t**ime **b**etween **f**ailures) a measure of the reliability of equipment. For example, equipment with an MTBF of 25,000 hours can be expected to run, on the average, 25,000 hours without failing. Some disk drives have an MTBF as high as 800,000 hours (90 years). However, the MTBF is only an average; there is always a risk that any particular piece of equipment will fail sooner.

MUD (**m**ulti-**u**ser **d**omain or **m**ulti-**u**ser **d**imension, formerly **m**ulti-**u**ser **d**ungeon) a type of real-time Internet conference in which users not only talk to each other, but also move around and manipulate objects in an imaginary world.

Originally conceived as multi-user ADVENTURE GAMES, MUDs have developed into a promising format for collaboration and education through the Internet. *Compare* IRC.

multicast *see* IPTV.

multimedia the combination of sound and visual information presented either to inform or to entertain.

Multimedia PC *see* MPC.

MultiMediaCard a type of flash-memory non-volatile storage device similar to CompactFlash but physically smaller, the size of a postage stamp, and often used in digital music players. *Compare* COMPACTFLASH; MEMORY STICK; SECURE DIGITAL CARD; SMARTMEDIA.

multiple inheritance a technique in object-oriented programming whereby an object type is defined to be a combination of two or more pre-existing types. Some programming languages, such as C++, permit this, and others, such as Java, do not. *See* OBJECT-ORIENTED PROGRAMMING.

multiprocessing the use of more than one CPU in a single computer system.

multiprocessor free *see* FREE.

multisession CD a compact disc (CD-ROM) that was not recorded all at once; rather, some files were recorded on it at one time and more files were added later. The directory of a multisession CD occupies more than one block of disc space, and some of the earliest CD-ROM software could not read multisession CDs. *See* CD-ROM and references there.

multitasking the execution of more than one program apparently at the same time on the same computer, even with a single-core CPU. Multitasking makes it possible to print one document while editing another or to perform lengthy computations "in the background" while working on something else on the screen. In reality, the CPU rapidly switches its attention among the various programs (*see* TIMESHARING). If there are multiple CPU cores, then each of them can genuinely run a separate program at the same time as the others, multitasking makes it possible to run more programs than there are cores.

The programs that run concurrently are called *processes* or *tasks*. An important concern is to keep tasks from interfering with each other. For example, two tasks cannot use the same area of memory or the same input-output device, such as a printer, at the same time. For this reason, programs allocate memory and access input-output devices through the operating system rather than directly.

If tasks communicate with each other, it is important to prevent *dead-locks*, in which two tasks are each waiting for the other to do something, so that neither one can make any progress. *See* STARVATION.

The term multitasking is also applied to people attempting to do multiple things at the same time.

multitouch interface Apple's interface for a touchscreen device that can sense touches from more than one finger, allowing you to do things, such as spread two fingers to enlarge the view of a picture that appears on the screen. *See* IOS; IPAD; GESTURE; TOUCHSCREEN; TAP; DOUBLE TAP; PINCH; SPREAD; SLIDE CONTROL; PAN; SWIPE; FLICK; WRIGGLE.

MVS (Multiple Virtual Storage) an operating system for IBM mainframe computers; from the user's point of view, it is almost completely compatible with OS/360. *See* JCL; OS/360; TSO: Z/OS.

mwahahahaha typewritten representation of an evil laugh.

My Computer a FOLDER on the DESKTOP of Microsoft Windows that contains all the disk drives, the Control Panel, and other information about the system.

Ordinarily, folders are directories. The root directory of a disk drive is also a folder. My Computer is a special folder that gives you access to the entire machine.

In Windows Vista and later, My Computer is called simply Computer.

My Documents a FOLDER on the DESKTOP of Microsoft Windows in which the user is invited to store his or her files in the absence of a more elaborate file system. The My Documents folder was created to discourage beginners from storing files in the same folder as the software that created them. In Windows Vista and later, My Documents is called simply Documents.

My Network Places the FOLDER on the Windows DESKTOP that enables the user to BROWSE (examine) the computer resources available through the network, if any. In Windows Vista and later, My Network Places is called simply Network.

MySpace a social networking site launched in August 2003 by founders Tom Anderson and Chris DeWolfe. Often considered to be the first truly popular and widespread social network, as of August 2011 it has roughly 33 million users with the number steadily declining. MySpace has largely fallen out of favor as Facebook has gained popularity, but retains a niche group through MySpace Music. MySpace allows users to create playlists for their pages, and allows artists to directly upload MP3s to be streamed by users, often leading to artists being discovered and offered contracts by the associated record label MySpace Records.

MySQL popular open-source database software. *See* SQL; *www.mysql.com/*.

N

\n in C and related languages, the symbol, within a character string, that indicates starting a new line. Thus, "hello\nworld" is a string which prints out as:

```
hello
world
```

nagware shareware that always opens with a message begging for remuneration. Some nagware is exceptionally persistent and interrupts your work sessions with messages reminding you to register (and pay!). *See* FREE SOFTWARE; SHAREWARE.

nameserver a computer whose job is to translate names into IP ADDRESSES for other computers.

Most computers on the Internet do not contain their own directories of the whole network. Instead, they rely on nameservers to interpret names for them. Nameservers, in turn, obtain information from other nameservers. *See* DNS.

namespace
1. the set of names available for naming things such as files, variables in a program, or computers in a network. If two parts of a program have different namespaces, the same name can be used in both places for different purposes without conflict. *See also* LOCAL VARIABLE; SCOPE.
2. in C#, a section of a program that has its own namespace (definition 1).

NAND gate (Figure 174) a logic gate whose output is 0 if both of the inputs are 1, and is 1 otherwise, thus:

Inputs		Output
0	0	1
0	1	1
1	0	1
1	1	0

A NAND gate is equivalent to an AND gate followed by a NOT gate. NAND gates are important because all the other types of logic circuits can be built out of them. *See* LOGIC CIRCUITS.

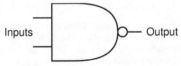

FIGURE 174. NAND gate (logic symbol)

nano- metric prefix meaning ÷1,000,000,000, or 10^{-9}. For example, 1 nanosecond is one billionth of a second. *Nano-* is derived from the Latin word for "dwarf." *See* METRIC PREFIXES.

nanometer (abbreviated nm) a distance of 10^{-9} meter, or a millionth of a millimeter. The wavelength of visible light is measured in nanometers, from violet (350 nm) to red (700 nm). The size of the parts of an INTE-GRATED CIRCUIT is measured in nanometers. For example, a "45-nanome-ter process" is a manufacturing process that can reproduce details as small as 45 nanometers across.

nanosecond a unit of time equal to 10^{-9} second, that is to say, 1/1,000,000,000 second. During one nanosecond, a light wave, electrical field, or radio wave travels about one foot (30.5 cm). The access time of many com-puter memories is less than a nanosecond.

NAP (**n**etwork **a**ccess **p**oint) a location where an Internet service provider or other network connects to a BACKBONE to access the Internet. *See also* MAE.

Napster a company founded in 1999 to provide person-to-person sharing of MP3 music files. Instead of storing files in a central repository, Nap-ster allowed any user to share music files anonymously with anyone else who wanted them.

Napster's file sharing system was shut down by court order in 2001 (*A&M Records v. Napster*). Napster, now part of the RHAPSODY service, provides a service where users can obtain unlimited legal access to over one million songs in return for a monthly subscription fee. Web address: *www.napster.com. See also* DIGITAL MUSIC; GROKSTER; ITUNES; MP3; P2P.

NAS *see* NETWORK ATTACHED STORAGE.

NAT *see* NETWORK ADDRESS TRANSLATION.

native
1. designed for a specific hardware or software environment (rather than for compatibility with something else).
2. consisting of CPU machine instructions rather than instruction codes to be interpreted by a program.

native file format the file format proprietary to an application program; the format in which it normally saves documents or drawings. Most pro-grams can, with the IMPORT command, convert similar file types to their own format. If you want to convert a native file to a more generic file type, use the SAVE AS . . . or EXPORT commands. *Contrast* METAFILE.

native method a computer program compiled in the machine language of the specific computer on which it is being run. For example, a Java program is normally compiled to Java bytecode, but in some cases it might link to a native method that was written in a language such as C++ and compiled into machine language.

native resolution the RESOLUTION of a monitor determined by the available pixels. The sharpest image will occur if the number of pixels generated by the video processor matches the monitor's available pixels. Other resolutions may be available, but the image may be less sharp as interpolation is required to determine the color for intermediate pixels.

natural language a spoken and/or written language used by people to communicate with one another, such as English, Chinese, Spanish, etc. *Contrast* PROGRAMMING LANGUAGE.

natural language processing the use of computers to process information expressed in human (natural) languages.

Getting computers to *understand* English, French, or other human languages is a difficult, largely unsolved problem. It includes SPEECH RECOGNITION, syntactic PARSING to determine sentence structure, semantic analysis to determine meaning, and knowledge representation to encode the meaning into a computer. The challenge of natural language understanding is that human language is far more complicated, and more poorly understood, than early computer scientists realized.

It is much easier to *process* natural-language texts in a way that falls short of full understanding, but still allows some of the meaning to be extracted. In recent years, natural language technology has turned toward INFORMATION EXTRACTION and INFORMATION RETRIEVAL to help manage the huge quantity of natural-language documents now stored in computers.

See also ARTIFICIAL INTELLIGENCE; ELIZA.

natural logarithm logarithm to the base *e* (about 2.718). *See* LOGARITHM.

FIGURE 175. Natural media paint program

natural media actual artists' materials (paint, canvas, etc.) realistically simulated by a computer program (Figure 175). In a natural-media paint program, you can specify the kind of paper or canvas you are working on. The tools available behave very much as their real-world counterparts would act—the chalk smears, the watercolors spread, and markers bleed. The main difference is the ability to combine unlikely media (try to paint watercolors over chalk in real life), and you don't have to wait for anything to dry.

Natural-media programs are very demanding of your hardware; they create huge files and require lots of RAM, fast video boards, and fast CPUs.

navigation finding your way around a complex system of menus, help files, or the WORLD WIDE WEB. This can be a real challenge, but there are a few tricks to help you.

- *Menu navigation.* Learning how to navigate menus requires an adventurous spirit. Make yourself a map (if there's not one already in the manual), as any good explorer would do. Sometimes the logic of grouping certain commands together will not be apparent to you and you'll have to learn some rather arbitrary distinctions. The best defense is to be familiar with your software. If you know that there *is* a command to do whirligigs, but can't remember whether it's under File or Arrange, it's only a matter of a fraction of a second to look under both categories.

  Menus can nest like wooden Russian dolls. One will lead to another in a rather infuriating way. Just remember to take one thing at a time. After making your decisions at each level, click OK. If you've gotten lost in the menus, you can back out at any time by choosing Cancel. Note: if you cancel out, the changes you made will not take place. Be aware that menus can interconnect at lower levels. This means that there *can* be more than one way into the same DIALOG BOX.

- *Help and hypertext files.* Programs for viewing HYPERTEXT files usually have a command called Back that allows you to backtrack to the previous screens. This is similar to Tom Sawyer using a rope to find his way around caves. A frequent frustration is to have a vague memory of a subject you read about yesterday, but can't remember how to get there. Some programs have bookmarks to mark important sections; use them. Also, familiarize yourself with the search capabilities of the hypertext system; it can save you a lot of time. As always, a good index is worth its weight in gold. If the index is too general to be useful, write a complaint to the software vendor. (If enough users complain, something might be done.) In the meantime, you may want to make a few notes on an index card and slip it into the manual.

- *World Wide Web.* The links that make up the World Wide Web can lead you literally in thousands of different directions from any starting point. When searching for information on a particular topic, use one of the standard web search engines such as Yahoo!, Lycos, Google, or Excite (try *www.search.com* to access the major indexes). *See* SEARCH ENGINE to get specific search tips.

  When browsing the WWW for pleasure, you may want to explore a JUMP LIST; most service providers have one. Usually, a web site will contain a page of new links to follow. (This will take care of all the rest of your free time.)

When you find a web page you think you'll want to return to, bookmark it, or add it to your Favorites folder. During the same web-surfing session, you can also use the Back and Forward buttons on your browser. Back returns you to the previous web page; after backing up, you can use Forward to retrace your steps. Your browser maintains a list of where you've been (the HISTORY FOLDER). The most recently visited sites are a mouse-click away under the Go menu.

Navigator web browser developed by Netscape (and often simply called Netscape). *See* NETSCAPE NAVIGATOR.

negative a photographically reversed image; black becomes white, white becomes black, and colors become their complements.

In desktop publishing, white letters on a black background are usually called a REVERSE. A *negative* is the physical film that is the intermediate step between camera-ready copy and a printing plate. *See* INVERT.

FIGURE 176. Negative image

nerd *(slang)* a person who is intensely interested in computers to the exclusion of other human activities (and even basic life skills). Unlike *geek*, *nerd* is usually at least mildly insulting, though among some sets of people it can be a compliment. *Compare* GEEK.

nest to put a structure inside another structure of the same kind. For example, in BASIC, three nested FOR loops look like this:

```
FOR I=1 TO 100
  FOR J=1 TO 100
    FOR K=1 TO 100
    ...statements to be repeated go here...
    NEXT K
  NEXT J
NEXT I
```

Note that indenting is used so that human readers can see how the loops are nested.

.net *see* TLD.

.NET *see* .NET FRAMEWORK.

.NET Framework an application program interface (API) for Microsoft
Windows, introduced in 2001 as a downloadable add-on to Windows
2000 and XP and included in subsequent versions of Windows.

The purpose of the .NET Framework is to reduce the amount of work
programmers have to do, while at the same time increasing reliability
and introducing Java-like portability. Despite the name, networking is
not its main purpose, although networking is included.

The .NET Framework is fully object-oriented. Programmers communicate with the operating system with a rich system of data types
rather than with pointers. For example, if a particular operation requires
a list of strings, the programmer can give it a list of strings, rather than
a pointer to a place where a carefully constructed list of strings has been
stored. The called procedure can verify that a list of strings is indeed
what it received. Thus, a very tedious and error-prone task is
eliminated.

The .NET Framework manages the memory used by each program.
Uninitialized variables and uninitialized pointers—a common source of
erratic behavior in earlier software—are generally ruled out. So are
"resource leaks" (memory or other system resources allocated to a program and never released when the program ends). The software components used by each program are tightly tied together so that none of them
will be replaced accidentally (*see* ASSEMBLY; *contrast* DLL HELL).

Like Java, the .NET Framework normally compiles programs into
bytecode, a concise notation that is converted to machine language when
the program is ready to run.

net neutrality a policy of treating all Internet traffic alike, so that, for
instance, an Internet service provider could not give faster service or
cheaper rates for connections to some Internet sites versus others. This
is increasingly important as many people watch television shows via the
Internet, and many Internet service providers are also in the cable TV
business; they have an incentive to discourage their Internet customers
from connecting to their competitors to watch television.

Supporters of net neutrality argue that the Internet has traditionally
been open equally to all types of traffic, subject only to genuine technical limitations. Opponents argue that ISPs cannot invest in enough
Internet capacity for high-bandwidth television (video) connections
unless they can be assured of reaping the profits from their customers'
pay TV usage.

In 2010 the Federal Communications Commission issued new rules
favoring net neutrality, but those rules were challenged by Verizon and
others. At the time of this writing the case is pending before the U.S.
Court of Appeals for the District of Columbia.

net surfing *see* SURFING.

Net, the a colloquial name for the INTERNET.

NetBEUI (**NetB**IOS **E**xtended **U**ser **I**nterface) a data transmission protocol developed by IBM and Microsoft and widely used in local-area networking. It is usually the preferred protocol for networking Windows systems but does not support routing. *See* PROTOCOL; ROUTER. *Contrast* ATM; IPX/ SPX; TCP/IP.

NetBIOS (**Net**work **B**asic **I**nput-**O**utput **S**ystem) an operating system extension designed by IBM to allow software to access a network. Net-BIOS includes a network protocol that was later extended to form Net-BEUI. *See* NETBEUI; PROTOCOL.

netbook (*net* + *notebook*) a small notebook or laptop computer with little processing power, meant almost exclusively for web browsing, e-mail, and other Internet access. Netbooks are smaller, lighter, and less expensive than laptops or notebooks.

netcafe an INTERNET CAFE.

netcam a camera attached to a computer, used to send images over a network. *Compare* WEBCAM. Physically, webcams and netcams are alike; the difference is in how they are used.

netiquette (**net**work et**iquette**) the conventional practices that make the INTERNET usable. More than just politeness, netiquette involves fundamental respect for the rights of other users who are helping pay the cost of running the network.

    For example, it is unacceptable to post off-topic material in NEWS-GROUPS, be rude during chats, ask people to do your homework for you, or bother them with commercial solicitations. *See also* ACCEPTABLE-USE POLICY; COMPUTER ETHICS; NEWSGROUPS.

netizen (**Internet** **citizen**) a person who is part of the Internet community in CYBERSPACE.

Netscape Navigator a pioneering WEB BROWSER, produced by Netscape Communications Corporation (see their web site at *netscape.aol.com*). In 1998 Netscape was acquired by AOL. *See also* MOZILLA.

network a set of computers connected together. *See* INTERNET; INTRANET; LOCAL-AREA NETWORK; PROTOCOL; WIDE-AREA NETWORK.

network address translation (NAT) the automatic changing of IP addresses by a router or gateway so that several computers can share a single IP address visible to the outside world. This is commonly done in home networks, where the DSL or cable modem has a single IP address. This is a solution to the problem that only about 3 billion IPv4 addresses exist, which is not enough for all the computers in the world.

    The router changes the IP addresses on the data packets as they come in and go out so that each computer can communicate with the Internet. By varying port numbers, it ensures that incoming packets can be matched up with the computers for which they are intended. *See also* PIX.

network attached storage file storage that resides on a separate computer, which owns and manages the files. *See* FILE SHARING. *Contrast* DISK SHARING; STORAGE AREA NETWORK.

neural network a computer program that models the way nerve cells (neurons) are connected together in the human brain. Neural networks enable a computer to train itself to recognize patterns in a strikingly human-like way. Like the human brain, neural networks give only approximate results, but they can do things that no other kind of computer program can do efficiently.

Figure 177 shows how a neural network is set up. Each neuron has several inputs but only one output. Some of the inputs excite (activate) the neuron while others inhibit it, each with a particular strength. The idea is that each output neuron will be activated when one particular kind of pattern is present at the input. In the computer, the neurons and connections are simulated by arrays of numbers.

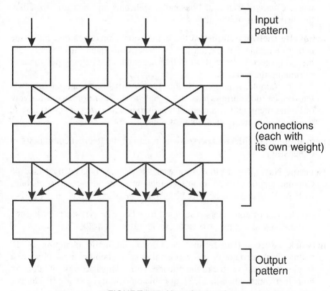

FIGURE 177. Neural network

Training a neural network is like training an animal. Patterns are applied to the input, and a simple algorithm adjusts the weights of the connections to try to get the desired output. After many training runs in which many different patterns are utilized, the neural network "learns" to recognize patterns of a certain kind. Even the programmer need not know exactly what these patterns have in common, because the patterns are analyzed by the neural network itself.

Neural networks are good at recognizing inputs that are vague, ill-defined, or likely to contain scattered variation. For example, a neural network can recognize images of human faces, or patterns of weather data, or trends in stock market behavior. However, a neural network is never 100% reliable, and even simple calculations can be quite slow.

new the command in C++, C#, and Java that calls the CONSTRUCTOR for a class to create a new object of that class. *See* OBJECT-ORIENTED PROGRAMMING.

new hacker's dictionary *See* JARGON FILE.

new media the means of communication that are displacing newspapers and television at the beginning of the 21st century. Chief among them is the World Wide Web or, more generally, the Internet. Some differences between the Web and earlier media include the following:

- *Lack of central control.* Almost anyone can publish almost anything without an editor's or publisher's approval.
- *Audience participation.* Readers of new media often have the ability to communicate with the producers and often post comments for other readers to see.
- *Very low cost of production.* You do not have to own a TV station or newspaper company to express yourself; everyone has a voice. In the 1500s, the printing press had a similar impact. It allowed any educated and reasonably prosperous person to print handbills and give them out. Later, newspapers and magazines arose as means of mass communication through printing.
- *Computer-assisted access.* Computers can help you find material you are interested in and filter out things you do not want to see. (*See* SEARCH ENGINE.)
- *Multimedia.* New media can combine the effects of print, painting, photography, music, motion pictures, and animation while adding new capabilities of their own, such as hypertext. *See* HYPERTEXT.
- *Volatility.* The contents of a web page can be changed at any time; it is possible to rewrite history and deny what you published a few weeks earlier. Libraries need to address this by archiving the World Wide Web for the public good. *See* WAYBACK MACHINE.

One thing everyone agrees on is that the new media are in their infancy and their most common uses fifty years hence will probably involve techniques that have not yet been invented or foreseen.

newbie (*slang*) newcomer (to the Internet, a newsgroup, etc.).

newsfeed a link on a web page that is automatically updated with current information. *See* RSS.

newsgroup a public forum or discussion area on a computer network. All users of the network can post messages, and every user can read all the messages that have been posted. The most famous newsgroups are those distributed worldwide by the Usenet system, covering thousands of topics. *See* USENET.

newspaper columns a word processor mode that specifies a newspaper-like format with text flowing from one column into the next. *Contrast* PARALLEL COLUMNS.

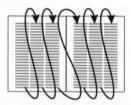

FIGURE 178. Newspaper columns

newsreader a piece of software that enables the user to read Usenet newsgroups. *See* NEWSGROUP.

NFC (**N**ear **F**ield **C**ommunication) wireless transfer of information between two devices that are very close to each other.

NFS (**N**etwork **F**ile **S**ystem) a FILE SHARING protocol originally developed by Sun Microsystems in the mid-1980s and now widely used on UNIX-based systems. *Compare* CIFS.

NIB (describing items for sale) "**n**ew, **i**n **b**ox."

nibble a group of 4 bits, or half of 1 byte.

NIC (**N**etwork **I**nterface **C**ard) the circuit board inside a computer that connects it to a local-area network.

nicad (or NiCd), (**ni**ckel-**cad**mium) a type of rechargeable battery formerly used in laptop computers. Nickel-cadmium batteries are toxic and should not be discarded in ordinary trash. *See also* BATTERY.

Nigerian scam *see* 419 SCAM.

NiMH (**Ni**ckel-**M**etal **H**ydride) a type of rechargeable battery electrically similar to nickel-cadmium (NICAD) but having greater capacity. *See also* BATTERY.

NIST (**N**ational **I**nstitute for **S**tandards and **T**echnology) division of the U.S. Department of Commerce (formerly the National Bureau of Standards) (web page: *www.nist.gov*).

nm *see* NANOMETER.

node

    1. an individual computer (or occasionally another type of machine) in a network.

    2. a connection point in a data structure such as a linked list or tree.

    3. (draw programs) a point on a curve or line that helps define the shape of the line. *See* CUSP NODE; SMOOTH NODE; SPLINE.

non-breaking hyphen a hyphen that does not indicate a place where a word can be broken apart. *See* REQUIRED HYPHEN.

non-breaking space a space that does not denote a place where words can be split apart at the end of a line. *See* REQUIRED SPACE. In T$_E$X, a required space is typed as ~ (TILDE). In Microsoft Word, a non-breaking space is typed by pressing Ctrl-Shift and the space bar together. In HTML, a non-breaking space is indicated by " c" (with no spaces surrounding it), or by use of a "<NOBR>" tag.

non-volatile not erased when turned off. Disks are a non-volatile storage medium; memory (RAM) is volatile.

nondocument mode a type of word processing that produces plain-text (ASCII) files with no special codes for hyphenation, page breaks, fonts, or the like. The most common way of saving a file in nondocument mode is to use the "Save as" menu and choose "text file" or "text only." *See* TEXT FILE.

Nook a line of e-book reader products introduced by the Barnes & Noble bookstore chain in 2009. *See* E-BOOK READER.

NOR gate (Figure 179) a logic gate whose output is 0 when either or both of the two inputs is 1, thus:

Inputs		Output
0	0	1
0	1	0
1	0	0
1	1	0

A NOR gate is equivalent to an OR gate followed by a NOT gate. NOR gates are important because all the other types of logic circuits can be built from them. *See* LOGIC CIRCUITS.

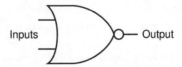

FIGURE 179. NOR gate (logic symbol)

Norton Utilities a set of programs originally written by Peter Norton and now a product of Symantec Corporation, used to provide security, recover erased files, and correct other problems with disks. *See* RECOVER-ING ERASED FILES. Web address: *www.symantec.com/norton.*

NOS

1. (**N**etwork **O**perating **S**ystem) any special operating system or operating system extension that supports networking.

2. (**N**ew **O**ld **S**tock) old but never sold to a customer and still in original packaging; this describes parts for obsolete equipment or the like. *Compare* LNIB.

NOT gate (Figure 180) a logic gate whose output is 1 if the input is 0, and vice versa, thus:

Inputs	Output
0	1
1	0

A NOT gate is also called an *inverter* because it reverses the value of its input. *See* LOGIC CIRCUITS.

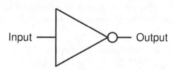

FIGURE 180. NOT gate (inverter)

notebook a computer about the same size as a looseleaf notebook, weighing less than 6 pounds (2.7 kg).

Usage note: The distinction between "laptop" and "notebook" has become blurred; all present-day laptop computers are notebooks by the standards of a few years ago. Many people use "laptop" and "notebook" interchangeably. *See also* PALMTOP; TABLET COMPUTER.

NP-complete problem *see* LIMITS OF COMPUTER POWER.

NPC non-**p**layer **c**haracter, a (simulated) person in an online game who is not controlled by a player.

NPN one of the two types of bipolar TRANSISTORS (*contrast* PNP).

NRFB (describing items for sale) "**n**ever **r**emoved **f**rom **b**ox." *See also* EBAY; MIB.

NSFW Not **S**afe **F**or **W**ork, a warning sometimes given on an online forum when the upcoming content isn't appropriate for a work environment.

NT short for Windows NT. *See* WINDOWS (MICROSOFT).

NTFS the file system used by Windows NT and its successors. *Contrast* CDFS; FAT.

NTSC (**N**ational **T**elevision **S**ystem **C**ommittee) the type of analog color TV signal used in the United States. It was designed to be compatible with a pre-existing black-and-white system. The screen consists of 525 lines, interlaced, and a complete scan takes 1/30 second. Color information is modulated on a 3.58-MHz subcarrier. Regulations mandated the end of NTSC broadcasting in 2009, but NTSC video signals continue to be used for connections between low-cost analog monitors, cameras, and other video equipment, and are delivered by some cable TV systems for use with older TV sets. *Contrast* DIGITAL TELEVISION; HDTV; PAL; SECAM.

nudge to move a selected object in small increments by using the arrow keys instead of the mouse.

null-terminated string a CHARACTER STRING that ends with ASCII code 0. Null-terminated strings are used in the C programming language and in many of the system routines of UNIX and Windows.

Num Lock a key on PC-compatible computers that switches the NUMERIC KEYPAD between two functions: typing numbers or moving the cursor with arrow keys.

number crunching *(slang)* arithmetical calculation, especially for scientific or engineering purposes.

numeric keypad a separate set of keys at the end of the keyboard, containing the digits 0 to 9 and a decimal point key. The digits are arranged in the same way as they are on an adding machine (but upside down from the usual arrangement on a digital telephone). If you have to type large quantities of numeric data, a numeric keypad is quicker to use than the number keys on the regular keypad. Some people prefer a keyboard without a numeric keypad because it lets them place the mouse closer to where they sit. *See also* KEYBOARD.

numerical integration the process of finding the approximate area under a particular curve by dividing the area into many tiny rectangles, adding up the heights of individual rectangles, and then multiplying the sum by their common width. *See* Figure 181. Increasing the number of rectangles leads to a more accurate value but the calculation takes longer. Numerical integration is a good example of a calculation that is practical to do on a computer but not by hand.

    For example, in probability theory it is important to find the area under the bell curve defined by:

$$y = \frac{1}{\sqrt{2\pi}} e^{-x^2/2}$$

This area can be found with the program in Figure 182, which uses a loop to perform a numerical integration.

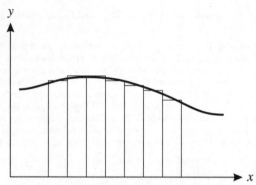

FIGURE 181. Numerical integration

NVIDIA a major manufacturer of graphics processors for personal computers, located in Santa Clara, California (*www.nvidia.com*). The name appears to be a pun on the Latin *invidia* "envy" although it is usually defined as *n* for *numeric* plus *video*.

NVRAM (**n**on-volatile **r**andom-**a**ccess **m**emory) the memory in which information about a computer's configuration is stored; it is either powered by a battery or inherently able to retain data when power is off. *Compare* CMOS RAM, which is an older term. *See also* EEPROM; FLASH MEMORY.

```java
class numerical_integration
{
  /* This Java program finds the area under the standard
     normal probability curve between x=0 and x=b, which is 1.0
     in this example */

  public static void main(String args[])
  {
    double b=1.0;
    double a=0;
    double p=Math.sqrt(2*Math.PI);
    double dx=1/100.0;

    for (double x=dx; x<b; x+=dx)
    {
     double y = Math.exp(-x*x/2);
     a += y;
    }

    double area=a*dx/p;
    System.out.println("Area =" + area);
  }
}
```

FIGURE 182. Numerical integration algorithm

O

OASIS (**O**rganization for the **A**dvancement of **S**tructured **I**nformation **S**tandards) an organization working on the development of e-business standards in areas such as web services (web address: *www.oasis-open.org*).

Ob- *(slang)* "obligatory"; used in newsgroup postings to signify a belated return to the intended topic. *See* TOPIC DRIFT.

obelisk the character †, a symbol used to mark footnotes. *See also* FOOTNOTE. Also called a DAGGER or LONG CROSS.

object
1. a data item that has properties and methods associated with it. *See* OBJECT-ORIENTED PROGRAMMING.
2. one of the parts of a graphical image. *See* DRAW PROGRAM.

object code the output of a compiler; a program written in machine instructions recognizable to the CPU, rather than a programming language used by humans. *Contrast* SOURCE CODE.

object linking and embedding (OLE) (in Microsoft Windows 3.1 and later versions) a method of combining information that is processed by different application programs, such as inserting a drawing or a portion of a spreadsheet into a word processing document. The main document is called the *client* and the document or application that supplies the embedded material is the *server*. OLE supersedes an older feature of Windows called *dynamic data exchange* (DDE).

    OLE can be done in either of two ways. An *embedded* object becomes part of the document that it is inserted into. For example, if you embed a drawing into a word processing document, the whole thing becomes one file, and to edit it, you use the word processor, which will call up the drawing program when you double-click on the drawing to edit it. A *linked* object has a life of its own; it remains a separate file and can be edited separately. When you edit it, the information that is linked from it into other documents is automatically updated. Thus, you can use a word processor to create a report that has links to a spreadsheet, and when you update the information in the spreadsheet, the corresponding information in the report will be updated automatically. *See also* ACTIVEX.

object-oriented graphics graphical images that are represented as instructions to draw particular objects, rather than as light or dark spots on a grid. *See* DRAW PROGRAM.

object-oriented programming a programming methodology in which the programmer can define not only data types, but also methods that are automatically associated with them. A general type of an object is called a *class*. Once a class has been defined, specific instances of that class can be created.

The same name can be given to different procedures that do corresponding things to different types; this is called *polymorphism*. For example, there could be a "draw" procedure for circles and another for rectangles.

Some uses for object-oriented programming include the following:

1. *Graphical objects.* A program that manipulates lines, circles, rectangles, and the like can have a separate "draw" and "move" procedure for each of these types.

2. *Mathematical objects.* In order to work with vectors, matrices, or other special mathematical objects, the programmer has to define not only data structures for these objects, but also operations such as addition, inversion, or finding a determinant.

3. *Input-output devices.* The procedure to draw a line might be quite different on a printer or plotter than on the screen. Object-oriented programming provides a simple way to ensure that the right procedure is used on each device.

4. *Simulation.* In a program that simulates traffic flow, for example, cars, trucks, and buses might be types of objects, each with its own procedures for responding to red lights, obstructions in the road, and so forth. This, in fact, is what object-oriented programming was invented for. The first object-oriented programming language was Simula, introduced in 1967.

5. *Reusable software components.* Object-oriented programming provides a powerful way to build and use components out of which programs can be built. For example, a programmer might use a predefined object class such as "sorted list" (a list that automatically keeps itself in order) rather than having to write procedures to create and sort a list.

Here is an example of object-oriented programming in Java. Imagine a program that manipulates points, lines, and circles. A point consists of a location plus a procedure to display it (just draw a dot). So the programmer defines a class called pointtype as follows:

```java
class pointtype
{
  int x; int y;
  void draw(Graphics g)
  {
    g.drawRect(x,y,1,1);
  }
}
```

The class pointtype is defined to include two integer variables (x and y) and one method (draw). (The class also would include a CONSTRUCTOR—a method called when a new object of that class is created.)

Now variables of type pointtype can be declared, for example:

```
pointtype: a,b;
```

Here the objects a and b each contain an x and a y field; x and y are called *instance variables*. In addition, a and b are associated with the draw procedure. Here's an example of how to use them:

```
a.x = 100;
a.y = 150:
a.draw(g);
```

This sets the x and y fields of a to 100 and 150, respectively, and then calls the draw procedure that is associated with a (namely pointtype. draw). (The g stands for graphics.)

Now let's handle circles. A circle is like a point except that in addition to x and y, it has a diameter. Also, its draw method is different. We can define circletype as another type that includes a pointtype, and it adds an instance variable called diameter and substitutes a different draw method. Here's how it's done:

```
class circletype
{
  pointtype p;
  int diameter;
  void draw(Graphics g)
  {
    g.drawOval(p.x,p.y,diameter,diameter);
  }
}
```

Your program would create a new object of class circletype (call it c), define values for the variables, and then call the method circletype. draw to display the circle on the screen.

It is important to remember that instance variables belong to individual objects such as a, b, and c, but methods (procedures) belong to object types (classes). One advantage of object-oriented programming is that it automatically associates the right procedures with each object: c.draw uses the circle draw procedure because object c is a circle, but a.draw uses the point draw procedure because object a is a point.

The act of calling one of an object's methods is sometimes described as "sending a message" to the object (e.g., c.draw "sends a message" to c saying "draw yourself"). All object-oriented programming systems allow one class to inherit from another, so the properties of one class can automatically be used by another class. For example, there is a standard Java class called Applet which contains the code needed to display an applet on the web. When you write your own applet, it will inherit from (extend) this class, so you don't need to recreate that code yourself. *See also* C++; C#; JAVA; SMALLTALK.

Objective-C an extension of the C programming language that adds OBJECT-ORIENTED PROGRAMMING capabilities. Objective-C is used mainly for Mac OS (Macintosh) and IQS application development. *Compare* C++; C#, and JAVA.

OBO abbreviation for "**or b**est **o**ffer," often used when advertising things for sale on the Internet.

obscenity sexually explicit material that can be prohibited by law. In 1973 the Supreme Court of the United States ruled that material is obscene if the average person, using contemporary community standards, would find that its primary purpose is to stimulate sexual appetite ("the prurient interest"); it depicts sexual behavior defined as offensive by specific laws; and it "lacks serious, literary, artistic, political or scientific value" (*Miller v. California*). *Contrast* INDECENCY. *See also* COMPUTER LAW; PORNOGRAPHY.

OCR *see* OPTICAL CHARACTER RECOGNITION.

octal a way of writing numbers in base-8 notation. Octal numbers use only the digits 0, 1, 2, 3, 4, 5, 6, and 7, and the next column represents multiples of 8. For example, the octal number 023 means 2 eights and 3 ones, or 19. Here are some further examples:

Binary	Octal	Decimal
001 000	10	$1 \times 8^1 = 8$
001 001	11	$1 \times 8^1 + 1 = 9$
001 010	12	$1 \times 8^1 + 2 = 10$
010 001	21	$2 \times 8^1 + 1 = 17$
011 001	31	$3 \times 8^1 + 1 = 25$
100 001	41	$4 \times 8^1 + 1 = 33$
101 010 100	524	$5 \times 8^2 + 2 \times 8^1 + 4 = 340$

Note that each octal digit corresponds to three binary digits.

octet a group of exactly eight bits, regardless of whether eight bits represent a character on any particular computer. *Contrast* BYTE.

octothorpe the character #; originally a map-maker's representation of a village with eight fields (thorpes) around a central square. Also called a POUND SIGN.

ODM (**O**riginal **D**esign **M**anufacturer) a company that produces products for another firm that will sell them under its brand name.

OEM (**O**riginal **E**quipment **M**anufacturer) a company that assembles complete pieces of equipment from parts. In some Microsoft documentation, "OEM" is used as a euphemism for "IBM" in order to avoid naming the competitor directly; but it also refers to other manufacturers.

OEM character set the native character set of the IBM PC. For a chart, *see* IBM PC.

off-by-one error a programming error caused by doing something the wrong number of times (one time too many or one time too few); also called a FENCEPOST ERROR.

Office, Microsoft suite of office applications including Word, Excel, Outlook, and PowerPoint. Microsoft markets specialized versions of Office for home or student use as well as a premium version that includes the database program Access. Details of the various collections vary as Microsoft's marketing targets different users. Microsoft Office is the leading business application software used on microcomputers since the 1990s. Its main competitor is OPEN OFFICE. *See also* GOOGLE DOCS.

offset the distance, in a computer memory, between one location and another. The offset of a data item is its address relative to the address of something else (0 if they are in the same position, 5 if they are 5 bytes apart, and so forth).

offset printing a way of printing on paper by means of ink transferred by a rubber roller from another surface. Offset printing is a cheap way for a print shop to produce hundreds of copies of a laser-printed original.

Ogg Vorbis a format for encoding compressed digital audio that is non-proprietary, with better sound quality than MP3 format. For more information, see *www.vorbis.com*. Contrast MP3.

ohm the unit of measure of electrical resistance. If an object has a resistance of 1 ohm, then an applied voltage of 1 volt will cause a current of 1 ampere to flow. *See* OHM'S LAW.

Impedance is also measured in ohms. Impedance is similar to resistance but is defined in terms of alternating current rather than direct current. *See* IMPEDANCE.

Ohm's law a basic law describing the behavior of electricity. It states that the current that flows through a circuit element is equal to the voltage applied across that element divided by the resistance of that element:

$$I = V/R$$

where I = current, in amperes; V = voltage, in volts; and R = resistance, in ohms. In effect, voltage is the force that drives a current through a resistance.

OLAP (**O**nline **A**nalytic **P**rocessing), performing analysis of multidimensional hierarchical data. An OLAP software tool will typically interact with data that is stored in a large database, but it provides more advanced techniques for processing and viewing the data than are provided by a database query language such as SQL. OLAP tools also provide more flexibility and power than do traditional spreadsheets.

A business typically will store data on a large number of individual transactions in a giant database. An OLAP tool will need to aggregate this data into a form that is useful for decisions. The data is inherently multidimensional, typically including dimensions for the time of the transaction, the location, the type of product, and a dimension for the type of variable (such as revenue, cost, and margin). Each dimension typically has a hierarchy; for example, the time dimension is arranged by year/quarter/month/day; the location dimension can be arranged by country/state/city/store; and the product dimension is arranged into a hierarchy of categories.

To provide effective decision support, an OLAP tool should be able to generate views of the data quickly while supporting multiple users.

For an example of using a spreadsheet to view a limited form of multidimensional data, *see* PIVOT TABLE.

OLE *see* OBJECT LINKING AND EMBEDDING.

OLED (**o**rganic **l**ight-**e**mitting **d**iode) a type of light-emitting diode based on organic polymers instead of semiconductor crystals. *See* LED.

OLPC (**O**ne **L**aptop **P**er **C**hild) a nonprofit organization providing inexpensive laptop computers to children in developing nations (web address: *www.laptop.org*).

OLTP abbreviation for on-line transaction processing.

OMA (**O**pen **M**obile **A**lliance) group that works on standards for mobile communications and computing devices (web address: *www.openmobilealliance.org*).

OMG (**O**bject **M**anagement **G**roup) a consortium of hundreds of computer companies that develop standards for software components to interact with each other. See web address: *www.omg.org*. *See also* CORBA.

on-board included within a piece of equipment. For example, it is common for a motherboard to have an on-board Ethernet interface.

one-way function a function whose inverse is very hard to calculate. A function f is a one-way function if, given x, it is relatively easy to calculate $y = f(x)$, but it is hard to calculate the inverse function (i.e., calculate the value of x if you are given the value of y). One-way functions are used in public key encryption schemes; *see* ENCRYPTION.

onionskin (in animation software) a translucent drawing layer placed on top of a reference image for purposes of tracing, like onionskin paper.

online connected to a computer or available through a computer. For example, online help is information that can be called up immediately on a computer screen rather than having to be looked up in a book.

Usage note: Online is also written with a hyphen when used before a noun, as in *on-line processing*, or as two separate words when used predicatively, as in *The computer is on line*.

In and near New York City but not elsewhere, *on line* means "in a queue," as in *We are standing on line*—the rest of the country says *standing in line*. In this context it is not a computer term and is not written as a single word.

online trading the buying and selling of stocks or other securities through the Internet. Instead of paying a broker to type transactions into a computer, you type them in yourself. Brokerage fees are much lower, and transactions are completed more promptly. Unfortunately, the broker's wise counsel is absent, and fortunes have been lost through speculative day trading. *See* DAY TRADING.

ontology
1. (in database technology, artificial intelligence, and Semantic Web) a classification of kinds of things, with their attributes and relationships. For example, an ontology for keeping records at a school might include students (with names, grade levels, etc.) and classes (each pertaining to a particular semester and containing a set of students).
2. (in philosophy) the study of what kinds of things exit, including questions such as whether minds are distinct from physical objects.

OOBE *see* OUT-OF-BOX EXPERIENCE.

OOC abbreviation for "out of character," used in role playing games and the like to indicate that a person's comment is not part of the imaginary situation. Example: "OOC: That dragon reminds me that I need to feed my pet iguana." *See also* IC; RPG (definition 1).

OOP *see* OBJECT-ORIENTED PROGRAMMING.

OPA (**O**pen **P**atent **A**lliance) a group of companies formed in 2008 to promote development of WIMAX Internet use. Web address: *www.open-patentalliance.com*.

opacity (from *opaque*) inability to be seen through; the opposite of transparency. In a graphical image, objects with low opacity are partly transparent. Many special effects are implemented by creating a new image, with opacity under the control of the user, and superimposing it on the existing image. *See also* ALPHA CHANNEL.

open
1. (in a program) to prepare a file to have data transferred into or out of it. *Contrast* CLOSE.
2. (in an application) to call a file, document, or drawing up from a disk in order to work with it within that application.
3. when selecting a file from a directory or menu, Windows and other systems may launch a specified applications program to work with that file. The application normally launched depends on the file's extension. If you wish to choose another application to launch the file, *see* OPEN WITH.

4. (in electronics) to put a switch into the position that does not allow current to flow. By analogy, cars cannot cross a drawbridge when it is open. *Contrast* CLOSE.

open architecture a computer architecture whose details are fully made public so that other manufacturers can make clones and compatible accessories. The architecture of the original IBM PC is open; that of the original Macintosh is not.

open beta a test of incomplete software that is open to a very large group, often the entire public. See BETA TESTING.

Open Handset Alliance a group of companies that together developed the open-source ANDROID mobile platform (web address: *www. openhandsetalliance.com*)

Open Office OPEN SOURCE SOFTWARE suite whose functionality rivals the industry-leading Microsoft Office suite. Open office comprises programs for word processing, spreadsheets, presentations, graphics, and databases. It is maintained by a worldwide organization of programmers and contributors who provide the software free-of-charge. Some users report that the OpenOffice.org user interface isn't as polished as its commercial rival, however user training and support is available at *www. openoffice.org*.

open source software software whose source code is published so that anyone can submit contributions. This is different from proprietary software such as Microsoft Windows, where the source code is a trade secret and only employees of the manufacturer work on the software's development. Significant examples of open source software include the LINUX operating system, the APACHE web server, the OPEN OFFICE suite, and various GNU products.

open systems interconnection *see* DATA COMMUNICATION.

Open With If you right-click on a file within Windows and choose "Open With" from the menu, you can choose an application that you wish to use to work with that file. For example, if you double-click on a file with extension ".html," the computer will assume that you want to open the file with a web browser so you can view it. If, instead, you wish to edit the file, choose "Open With," and then select a text editor such as Notepad from the list of possible programs.

OpenType a format for type fonts on personal computers developed by Microsoft in the late 1990s as a combination of TrueType and Adobe Type 1. (*See* TRUETYPE FONT; TYPE 1 FONT.) OpenType support is built into Windows 2000 and its successors.

Opera a popular independent web browser created by Opera Software (*www.opera.com*), using W3C standards. *See* BROWSER.

operands the items on which a mathematical operation is performed. For example, in the expression $2 + 3$, the operands are 2 and 3, and the operation is addition.

operating system a program that controls a computer and makes it possible for users to enter and run their own programs.

A completely unprogrammed computer is incapable of recognizing keystrokes on its keyboard or displaying messages on its screen. Most computers are therefore set up so that, when first turned on, they automatically begin running a small program supplied in read-only memory (ROM), or occasionally in another form (*see* BOOT). This program in turn enables the computer to load its operating system from disk, though some small microcomputers have complete operating systems in ROM.

Under the control of the operating system, the computer recognizes and obeys commands typed by the user. In addition, the operating system provides built-in routines that allow the user's program to perform input-output operations without specifying the exact hardware configuration of the computer. A computer running under one operating system cannot run programs designed to be run under another operating system, even on the same computer. For articles on specific operating systems, *see* ANDROID; CMS; CP/M; LINUX; MAC OS X; MS-DOS; MVS; OS/2; OS/360; UNIX; WINDOWS (MICROSOFT); Z/OS.

operations research the mathematical modeling of repetitive human activities, such as those involved in traffic flow, assembly lines, and military campaigns. Operations research makes extensive use of computer simulation.

opt out to choose not to receive mass e-mailings. When giving your e-mail address to an online merchant, look carefully for an opt-out CHECKBOX somewhere on the screen, and be sure to opt out of mailings you do not want to receive.

Many spammers falsely describe their mailing lists as opt-out lists; they ignore requests to opt out, because any reply tells them they have reached a good e-mail address. This is why it's so important to *never* send an email reply in response to spam. It's like being hit on the head once and then asked whether you want to opt out from being hit again. *See* SPAM.

optical character recognition (OCR) the recognition of printed or handwritten characters in an image of a piece of paper. OCR software is commonly used with scanners so that information received on paper will not have to be retyped into the computer. Also, OCR software on tablet computers can recognize handwritten words.

A difficulty is that the computer usually cannot recognize letters and digits with complete certainty, so it has to make intelligent guesses based on the spellings of known words. For example, if you type "chack" an OCR device is likely to read it as "check." Obviously, OCR has difficulty distinguishing l from 1 or O from 0; so do humans if they don't know the context. Information obtained through OCR should be carefully checked for accuracy. *See also* SCANNER.

optical disc any kind of data storage disc that is read by means of light rays (visible, infrared, or ultraviolet). For examples *see* BLU-RAY DISC; CD; DVD.

optical zoom a change in the field view of a DIGITAL CAMERA achieved by changing the focal length of the lens. Unlike digital zoom, optical zoom does not sacrifice resolution (at least if the lens is of high quality). *Contrast* DIGITAL ZOOM.

A lens marked "3× zoom" has a focal length that is three times as long at maximum as at minimum. *See also* FOCAL LENGTH.

option buttons small circles in a dialog box, only one of which can be chosen at a time. The chosen button is black and the others are white. Choosing any button with the mouse causes all the other buttons in the set to be cleared. Because option buttons work like the pushbuttons on older car radios, they are sometimes called *radio buttons*.

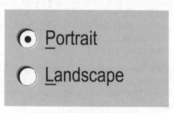

FIGURE 183. Option buttons

Option key a key on the Macintosh keyboard labeled "Opt" that acts as another kind of Shift key, allowing special characters to be typed quickly. *See also* COMMAND KEY; MODIFIER KEY.

OR gate (Figure 184) a logic gate whose output is 1 when either or both of the inputs is 1, as shown in the table:

Inputs		Output
0	0	0
0	1	1
1	0	1
1	1	1

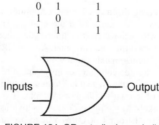

FIGURE 184. OR gate (logic symbol)

An OR gate can have more than two inputs, and the output will be one if any of the inputs is at one. *See also* LOGIC CIRCUITS; COMPUTER ARCHITECTURE.

Oracle a leading producer of database software. Oracle Corporation is headquartered in Redwood Shores, California. Web address: *www. oracle.com*.

Orange Book
1. the official standard for compact discs that can be recorded by the user. *See* CD-ROM.
2. the U.S. government's *Trusted Computer System Evaluation Criteria*, published in 1985 and defining standards for computer security.

ORB (**O**bject **R**equest **B**roker) a system that allows objects to connect to other objects over a network. See CORBA for a description of one set of standards that define how ORBs connect different components.

order of magnitude a factor-of-10 difference in size. If one number is 10 times larger than another, they differ by one order of magnitude. Personal computers have sped up by more than three orders of magnitude—that is, a factor of more than 1,000—since the early days of the IBM PC.
  More formally, the order of magnitude is the exponent in exponential notation. *See* EXPONENTIAL NOTATION.

.org *see* TLD.

orphan
1. the last line of a paragraph if it appears by itself as the first line of a page. Some word processors automatically adjust page breaks to avoid creating orphans. *See also* WIDOW.
2. a computer product that is no longer supported by its manufacturer, or whose manufacturer is out of business. For example, the Amiga is now an orphan computer.

orthogonal
1. meeting at right angles. For example, in three-dimensional space, the *x*-AXIS, *y*-AXIS, and *z*-AXIS are orthogonal. The edges of a rectangular box are orthogonal.
2. usable in all combinations. For example, if the size and color of an object are orthogonal attributes, you can combine any size with any color.
  Orthogonality was an important design goal of ALGOL and the many programming languages that it inspired. For example, if a language contains both arrays and pointers, then for the sake of orthogonality, it should have arrays of arrays, arrays of pointers, pointers to arrays, and pointers to pointers.

OS/2 a multitasking, virtual memory operating system with a graphical user interface for 386 and higher PC-compatible computers. In the late 1980s and early 1990s, OS/2 was an important predecessor of Windows 95, but it is now obsolete.

OS/2 was originally developed by Microsoft in cooperation with IBM. Later it became solely an IBM product, competing against Windows 3.1 and 95.

OS/360 the operating system released with the IBM 360 in the early 1960s, and which formed the basis of many subsequent operating systems (OS/VS2, MVT, MVS, etc.). *See also* JCL; MVS; TSO; z/OS.

OSCAR (**O**pen **S**ystems for **C**ommunication in **R**ealtime) a protocol developed and used by AOL for its instant messaging and presence-information services.

oscilloscope an instrument for viewing sound waves or electrical waveforms.

OSI *see* DATA COMMUNICATION.

out of band outside the defined frequency range or channel for a communication signal; more generally, outside a defined code. For example, characters with numeric values greater than 128 can be described as "out of band" if ASCII characters are expected.

out-of-box experience (*somewhat humorous*) a user's first experience on initially unpacking a product and trying to get it to work, without digging deeply into the instructions. Favorable out-of-box experiences result in satisfied customers.

(Pun on "out-of-body experience" in psychology and spiritualism.)

outdent to mark the first line of a paragraph by letting it extend into the left margin; HANGING INDENT, HANGING TAB; the opposite of INDENT. The entry terms in this dictionary are outdented.

outline

1. a graphical image showing only the edges of an object.

FIGURE 185. Outline (definition 1)

2. a way of representing the main points of a text without giving all the details. People have been making outlines on paper for centuries, but a computer can simplify the process in two ways. First, with a word processor, it is easy to create a document by first typing an outline of it, and then going back and filling in the sections one by one. Second, software has been developed to let you display just the desired parts of an outline while concealing the rest. While you are working on one section, the details of other sections, even if they have already been written, can be removed from the screen.

```
                    I. Animal classification
                        A. mammals
                            1. dogs and wolves
                                a. pets
                                b. wild animals
                            2. cats
                                a. domestic
                                b. large cats
                            3. primates
                        B. birds
```

FIGURE 186. Outline (definition 2)

Outlook popular e-mail and calendar software provided as part of the Microsoft Office suite.

Outlook Express the e-mail software provided with Microsoft Windows and also made available by Microsoft for other operating systems. A more elaborate commercial version is called Outlook.

output the information that a computer generates as a result of its calculations. Computer output may be either printed on paper, displayed on a monitor screen, or stored on disk or tape.

output device a device that shows, prints, or presents the results of a computer's work. Examples of output devices include MONITORS, PRINTERS, and IMAGESETTERS.

overclocking the practice of running a CPU at higher than its rated clock speed. For example, a 2.2-GHz CPU might run successfully at 2.4 GHz.

Overclocking usually yields a small increase in performance and a substantial decrease in reliability. Overclocked CPUs emit more heat, requiring a larger HEAT SINK than when run at their rated speed.

Sometimes, physically identical CPUs are sold with different speed ratings because the manufacturer does not want to make separate types. In this case, the lower-rated ones are less expensive but can be overclocked with no risk of problems.

overflow the error condition that arises when the result of a calculation is a number too big to be represented in the available space. For example, adding $65,535 + 1$ will cause an overflow on a computer that uses 16-bit unsigned integers, because $2^{16} - 1 = 65,535$ is the largest integer representable in that format. (Or, worse, if the computer does not detect overflows, it may simply compute $65,535 + 1 = 0$ without letting you know anything is wrong.) *Compare* UNDERFLOW.

overlaid windows windows that can overlap; when they do, one window hides the parts of others that are behind it (Figure 187). To bring another window to the front, move the mouse pointer so that it is within the window you want to be on top, and then click the button. *Contrast* TILED WINDOWS. *See also* CASCADE.

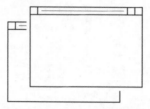

FIGURE 187. Overlaid windows

overwrite to write over information that is already on a disk. For example, if you copy a file called ABC.TXT onto a disk that already has a file with the same name, some operating systems will ask you whether you want the new file to replace the old file (which will lose the information in the old file). If you say no, the new file will not be copied.

own (*slang*) to conquer or defeat an opponent in a game; to break into a computer and control it.

P

P (on a digital camera) programmed autoexposure, a mode in which the camera chooses both the lens aperture and the shutter speed. *Contrast* A; AV; S; TV.

p-p (**p**eak-to-**p**eak) a way of measuring AC voltage. *See* PEAK-TO-PEAK.

P2P
 1. abbreviation for PEER-TO-PEER.
 2. the use of peer-to-peer networking to share files over the Internet.

packet a group of consecutive characters sent from one computer to another over a network. On most networks, all communications are in the form of packets that begin with labels indicating the machine to which they are addressed.

packet radio the transmission of data (in Ethernet-style packets) by radio. It is a popular hobby among radio amateurs ("hams"), and is the basis of practically all wireless data communication today, including WiFi and WiMax. Unlike WiFi and WiMax, amateur radio packet systems are permitted to use shortwave frequencies that travel thousands of miles without repeaters, making amateur packet radio a useful means of communication during natural disasters and other emergencies. *See also* AX.25; PROTOCOL.

 A typical amateur packet system consists of a computer linked by a terminal-node controller (TNC) to a VHF radio transmitter and receiver. The TNC constructs and recognizes packets. The packet radio protocol effectively prevents two systems from transmitting at the same time, and all data are error-checked. Packet systems are often used to run bulletin boards (*see* BBS). Unlike telephone-line BBSs, packet BBSs are inherently multi-user systems because each packet contains a label indicating its sender and receiver. Thus, the computer can keep track of many users concurrently.

 Commercial packet systems often involve portable computer terminals carried by delivery or service personnel. The terminals are linked by radio to a main computer many miles away.

page
 1. information available on the World Wide Web. *See* HOME PAGE; WEB PAGE.
 2. a section of memory that is accessible at one time. *See* VIRTUAL MEMORY.

page fault the situation that arises when the computer needs to access an area of memory that has been swapped out to disk; it is not a malfunction. *See* VIRTUAL MEMORY.

page frame an indication of the edges of the paper displayed by your computer's software. The area around the page frame is called the *pasteboard*.

page layout software software specially designed for creating CAMERA-READY COPY. Page layout programs, such as Adobe InDesign and QuarkXPress, allow the desktop publisher to combine many separate files of different types into a specified design. These special designs, called TEMPLATES or STYLESHEETS, provide a framework to put the individual elements into. Most programs come with a library of predefined stylesheets.

Page layout software also allows more control over typography than most word processors. *See* DESKTOP PUBLISHING; FRAME.

page printer a printer that forms, in its digital memory, a graphical image of the whole page, or requires the computer to do so, before printing it out. Laser printers are page printers, and inkjet printers commonly operate as page printers. *Contrast* LINE PRINTER.

pagination to divide a document into pages for printing.

paint program one type of program for drawing pictures on a personal computer. The user draws with the mouse pointer (or a graphics tablet), and commands are provided for drawing circles, lines, rectangles, and other shapes, as well as for drawing freehand and choosing colors.

Paint programs treat the picture as a grid of pixels (*see* PIXEL; BITMAP). Shadings are easy to produce by manipulating the color of each individual pixel. It is hard to move an element of the picture if it is not where you want it. *Contrast* DRAW PROGRAM.

More sophisticated paint programs are called *photopaint programs* because of their ability to retouch photographs and produce realistic images. *See* PHOTOPAINT PROGRAM.

PAL (**P**hase-**A**lternate-**L**ine) the type of analog color TV signal used in Great Britain and many other countries, now being displaced by digital television, although PAL signals continue to be used for connections between low-cost video monitors, cameras, and the like. The screen consists of 625 lines, interlaced, and a complete scan takes 1/25 second. Color information is modulated on a 4.43-MHz subcarrier. *Contrast* DIGITAL TELEVISION; HDTV; NTSC; SECAM.

palette
1. a set of colors chosen from a much larger set. The whole set of displayable colors is also sometimes called a palette.
2. a floating window containing specialized tools or setting controls.

Palm a line of handheld computers and organizers, beginning with the pioneering Palm Pilot in 1996. Palm, Inc. is located in Milpitas, California; web address: *www.palm.com*.

palmtop a computer that you can hold in one hand while using it. *Compare* PDA.

pan (animation and 3-D software) to move the viewing area left or right to see additional sections of the scene. On a multitouch interface this can be done by sliding your finger along the screen.

Panther version 10.3 of MAC OS X.

Pantone Matching System (**PMS**) a color matching and calibration system designed by the Pantone company. (Web address: *www.pantone.com*.) There are a wide variety of products all keyed to the same numbering system. If you want a certain color, you can specify it by its Pantone number and be assured of consistent reproduction. Some software also utilizes the Pantone system. A competing system is TRUMATCH. *See* COLOR.

paper jam a situation in which paper cannot feed through a printer because it has gotten stuck. A common cause of paper jams is that sheets of paper are stuck together when they enter the printer. *See also* SEPARATOR PAD.

paper sizes In the U.S., standard paper sizes are letter size ($8\frac{1}{2} \times 11$ inches) and legal size ($8\frac{1}{2} \times 14$ inches). (*See also* EXECUTIVE SIZE.)

TABLE 11
PAPER SIZES, ISO

Each size is made by cutting the next larger
size in half.

	mm (exact)	inches (approximate)
A0	841 × 1189	33.1 × 46.8
A1	594 × 841	23.4 × 33.1
A2	420 × 594	16.5 × 23.4
A3	297 × 420	11.7 × 16.5
A4	210 × 297	8.3 × 11.7
A5	148 × 210	5.8 × 8.3
A6	105 × 148	4.1 × 5.8
B0	1000 × 1414	39.4 × 55.7
B1	707 × 1000	27.8 × 39.4
B2	500 × 707	19.7 × 27.8
B3	353 × 500	13.9 × 19.7
B4	250 × 353	9.8 × 13.9
B5	176 × 250	6.9 × 9.8

In much of the rest of the world, ISO standard paper sizes are used. A0 paper (840×1189 mm) has an area of 1 square meter. Each size can be cut in half to make the next smaller one. Thus, the area of a sheet of A4 paper (the best known size) is $\frac{1}{16}$ m². The sizes are shown in Table 10. All sizes have the same height-to-width ratio (1.414:1). B0 paper is 1 meter wide.

Note that A4 paper is usually mailed in C6 or DL envelopes.

These standards are administered by the International Standards Organization (ISO). They were formerly a German industrial standard (**D**eutsche **I**ndustrie-**N**orm) and were known as DIN paper sizes.

parallel

1. conducting electricity along more than one path at the same time (Figure 188). *Contrast* SERIES.

2. transmitting different parts of the same data along more than one wire at the same time. *See* BUS; PARALLEL PORT.

3. using more than one CPU at the same time. A parallel computer executes more than one instruction at the same time.

parallel columns adjacent columns of printed text in which the second column is *not* a continuation of the first; instead, the second column may give notes, comments, or a translation into another language. Many Canadian documents are printed in parallel columns of English and French. *Contrast* NEWSPAPER COLUMNS.

parallel port an output device that lets a computer transmit data to another device using parallel transmission, with 8 bits of data, plus several control bits, sent simultaneously over separate wires. Traditionally microcomputers have used parallel ports to communicate with printers, but newer printers use USB ports instead. *See* IEEE 1284, USB.

FIGURE 188. Parallel circuit (two resistors)

FIGURE 189. Parallel port (with symbol indicating a printer)

parallel printer a printer that connects to a computer's parallel port (rather than, for example, to a USB port or a network cable).

parallel processing computation carried out at the same time on different CPUs, or on a CPU that can execute more than one instruction at the exact same time.

By contrast, most multitasking is accomplished by making a single CPU switch its attention among several tasks. This is called concurrent processing or timesharing.

parameter a symbol that will be replaced in a procedure, function, or method by supplied values when the procedure is called. For example, if max is a function, then in max(x,y), x and y are the parameters. *See* ACTUAL PARAMETER; FORMAL PARAMETER.

parens *(slang)* parentheses.

parent an object that gives its properties to a newly created object (the CHILD). Updating the properties of the parent object affect the children, but changing the properties of the child do not affect the parent. *See* DRAW PROGRAM; INHERITANCE; OBJECT-ORIENTED PROGRAMMING.

parent directory the directory that contains another directory. On most operating systems, a double dot ".." refers to the parent directory of the CURRENT DIRECTORY, while a single dot "." indicates the current directory.

parental controls software options enabling parents to control what web sites their children access. *See* FILTER (definition 3).

parentheses the characters ( ), also called *round brackets*.

Usage note: The singular is *parenthesis.* That is, (is a left parenthesis,) is a right parenthesis, and ( ) is a pair of parentheses. For use, see PRECEDENCE. *Contrast* ANGLE BRACKETS; CURLY BRACKETS; SQUARE BRACKETS.

parity the property of whether a number is odd or even. Often, when groups of bits (1's and 0's) are being transmitted or stored, an extra bit is added so that the total number of 1's is always odd (or, alternatively, always even). This is called the parity of the data.

One incorrectly transmitted bit will change the parity, making it possible to detect the error; the parity would be unchanged only if there were two (or an even number of) incorrect bits. Thus, if errors are frequent, some of them will be detected and the recipient of the information will have some warning that errors are present.

The memory of PC-compatible servers is often parity-checked to detect corrupted bits. With two parity bits per word, it is possible to correct single corruptions, a scheme known as SECDED (single-error-correcting-double-error-detecting).

parsing the analysis, by computer, of the structure of statements in a human or artificial language. For instance, Windows has to parse the command

```
dir b: /p
```

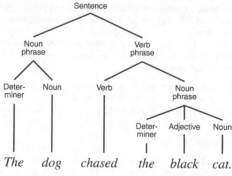

FIGURE 190. Parsing: structure of a sentence

(1) Sentence	→	Noun Phrase + Verb Phrase
(2) Noun Phrase	→	Determiner + Noun
(3) Noun Phrase	→	Determiner + Adjective + Noun
(4) Verb Phrase	→	Verb + Noun Phrase
(5) Determiner	→	*the*
(6) Noun	→	*dog*
(7) Noun	→	*cat*
(8) Adjective	→	*black*
(9) Verb	→	*chased*

FIGURE 191. Parsing: grammar rules used in Figure 190

to determine that di r is the name of the command, b: specifies the files to be shown, and p is another parameter (in this case, it means "pause when the screen is full"). Compilers and interpreters have to parse statements in programming languages. (*See* COMPILER; INTERPRETER.) Programs that accept natural-language input have to parse sentences in human languages.

Parsing is done by comparing the string to be parsed to a *grammar*, which defines possible structures. For example, Figure 190 shows the structure of the sentence "The dog chased the black cat." Figure 191 shows a small part of the grammar of English.

Parsing can be done either *top-down* or *bottom-up*. In top-down parsing, the computer starts by looking for a particular constituent. It consults the grammar to determine what this constituent consists of, and then looks for those constituents instead, thus:

Look for Sentence
Rule 1: Sentence consists of Noun Phrase + Verb Phrase
  Look for Noun Phrase
  Rule 2: Noun Phrase consists of Determiner + Noun
    Look for Determiner

> Accept Determiner *the* from input string
> Look for Noun
> Accept Noun *dog* from input string
> Look for Verb Phrase (etc.)

The process is complete when the input string is empty and all of the elements of a sentence have been found.

In bottom-up parsing, the computer accepts elements from the input string and tries to put them together, thus:

Accept *the*, which is a Determiner
Accept *dog*, which is a Noun
Determiner + Noun make a Noun Phrase
Accept *chased*, which is a Verb
Accept *the*, which is a Determiner
Accept *black*, which is an Adjective
Accept *cat*, which is a Noun
Determiner + Adjective + Noun make a Noun Phrase
Verb + Noun Phrase make a Verb Phrase
Noun Phrase + Verb Phrase make a Sentence

Parsing algorithms must be able to *backtrack* (back up and try alternatives) because the grammar provides alternatives. For example, a noun phrase may or may not contain an adjective, and a word like *leaves* can be a verb or a noun. Further, parsing algorithms usually use *recursion* to handle the recursive structure of human languages. For example, a noun phrase can contain a noun phrase, which can contain another noun phrase, as in *the discoverer of the solution to the problem. See* BACK-TRACKING; NATURAL LANGUAGE PROCESSING; RECURSION.

Part 15 device a radio transmitter that is allowed to operate without a license under the terms of Part 15 of the Federal Communications Commission's regulations (known to lawyers as 47 CFR 15). Examples include cordless telephones, wireless intercoms, and some kinds of wireless computer communication devices (wireless LANs). Because individual Part 15 transmitters are not licensed, there is no way to guarantee that they will not interfere with each other, but spread-spectrum technology makes interference unlikely. By contrast, licensed transmitters can be given exclusive use of a particular frequency in a particular area. *See also* SPREAD-SPECTRUM.

partition a part of a HARD DISK that is treated by the computer as if it were a separate disk drive. Most hard disks consist of only one partition, but multiple partitions are sometimes used with larger drives.

Pascal a programming language developed by Niklaus Wirth in the early 1970s. Pascal is essentially a modernized version of ALGOL, and it has greatly influenced the design of other languages, as well as becoming popular in its own right. *See* TURBO PASCAL for information on a popular version.

```pascal
PROGRAM primecheck;
   {This is Turbo Pascal.}
VAR    n,i,max: INTEGER;
       continue: BOOLEAN;
       status: STRING[13];

BEGIN
  REPEAT
    write('Enter a whole number (type 0 to quit): ');
    readln(n);
    status := ' is prime';
    IF n>2 THEN continue := TRUE
         ELSE continue := FALSE;
    i := 1;
    max := TRUNC(SQRT(n));
       {max   is   the   largest   divisor   that   must   be
       checked to see if n is prime}
    WHILE continue DO
      BEGIN
        i:=i + 1;
        IF (n MOD i)=0 THEN
          BEGIN
            status := ' is not prime';
            continue := FALSE
          END;
        continue := (i < max);
      END; {end of WHILE loop}
    write(n);
    writeln(status);
  UNTIL n=0
END.
```

FIGURE 192. Pascal program

Figure 192 shows a sample program in Pascal. A Pascal program consists of:
- A PROGRAM statement to give the program a name (and, in older versions, to declare input and output files);
- Declarations of global variables;
- Declarations of procedures and functions;
- The keyword BEGIN, the action part of the main program, the keyword END, and finally a period to mark the end.

Procedures and functions, in turn, can contain their own declarations, including more procedures and functions (a kind of nesting that is not permitted in C).

Pascal is not case-sensitive (e.g., A and a are equivalent). In this book, uppercase letters are used for *reserved words* (keywords that cannot be redefined, such as IF, THEN, and ELSE), and lowercase letters for everything else.

Semicolons are used as separators *between* statements. Thus a statement ends with a semicolon only when what follows is the beginning of another statement. This contrasts with C and PL/I, which end every statement with a semicolon regardless of the context.

Comments in Pascal are enclosed in braces, {}, or the symbols (**). A statement does not have to fit on one line; lines can be broken anywhere that blank space is permitted.

Pascal provides four standard data types: real, integer, Boolean, and character. Integer variables can take on only values that are whole numbers or the negatives of whole numbers. Real variables can take on numerical values that include fractional parts, such as 23.432. Boolean variables are logic variables that can have only two possible values: true or false. Char variables can take on single character values.

An assignment statement in Pascal looks like this:

```
x := 3;
```

This statement gives the value 3 to the variable x. Note that the symbol for assignment is :=, not =. The arithmetic operators are + for addition, – for subtraction, * for multiplication, / for floating-point division, div for integer division, and mod for modulo (remainder from division).

See also MODULA-2.

Pascal notation a way of combining words by running them together, all capitalized; ThisIsAnExample. Procedure names in Pascal programs are often formed this way. *Contrast* CAMEL NOTATION. *See* INTERCAPS.

Pascal, Blaise (1623–1662) a French mathematician who, in 1642, built a mechanical adding machine that was one of the early forerunners of calculators and computers.

passive FTP a variation on FTP (file transfer protocol) in which all connections are initiated by the client (the user's PC), not the server. This is necessary because some routers and firewalls, for security reasons, do not allow the server to initiate connections to the client. In that situation, a user can establish an FTP connection but cannot get a list of files and folders. Passive FTP overcomes the problem.

To select passive FTP, type the command passive in a command-line FTP session, or make the appropriate choice in setting up your FTP client software. For example, in Microsoft Internet Explorer, passive FTP is an option under Tools, Internet Options, Advanced.

passive matrix an older type of liquid crystal display that produces lower contrast than newer ACTIVE MATRIX displays.

password a secret sequence of typed characters that is required to use a computer account or system, thus preventing unauthorized persons from gaining access. A special password may be required for privileged access to the protected area of the system (often called "administrator" or "root" or "single-user" access).

If you are using a password to protect your computer:

- Protect your password. Keep it a secret and don't share it.
- Don't choose an obvious password. Use some imagination and forethought. What would be hard to guess? Your password is not your mantra and should *not* express your personality or indicate in any way who you are.
- Don't use a word in any language; some people crack computers by automatically trying every word in a dictionary. Include digits and special characters to make your password hard to guess. *See* DICTIONARY ATTACK.
- Use the initial letters of a memorable phrase or title to create a password. Again, using digits and special characters will help safeguard your password. Alternatively, an old phone number of someone other than yourself (such as Grandma's phone number you memorized as a child) may serve as a good password, provided this is formation is no longer associated with you on any current records.
- Change your password regularly, but not so often you can't keep track of it.
- When you need to provide passwords for multiple systems, distinguish between systems that need high security and those that can tolerate low security. Use a high security unique password for systems that provide access to your valuable personal data such as your e-mail account. When you need to give a password to obtain access to web information where security is not a crucial concern, use the same password for all of these locations (as long as it is different from your high-security passwords). This way you won't have to keep track of a dozen different passwords for a dozen different organizations.
- If you are the administrator for a computer system, be sure to use a different password than the one you use to login for ordinary work, and never remain logged in with privileged access while doing other work.

paste to transfer material from a holding area into the document you are editing. In Windows and Macintosh environments, the keyboard shortcut for *paste* is Ctrl-V. *See* CLIPBOARD; COPY; CUT.

PATA (**p**arallel **ATA**) the original hardware implementation of the ATA hard disk interface, using parallel data transmission through a rectangular 40-pin connector, later expanded to 80 conductors by using the two sides of each hole separately. If no other type·of interface is specified, "ATA" usually means PATA. *See* ATA. *Compare* ESATA; SATA.

patch to correct a defective piece of software by modifying one or more of the files on which it resides, rather than by installing a complete, corrected copy.

patent legal protection for the design of a machine or mechanical process, preventing others from using the same idea without the inventor's permission. Unlike a copyright, a patent protects an idea itself, not just an expression of the idea. In the United States, a patent remains in force for 20 years.

Computer programs were not originally considered patentable, since they were viewed as mathematical discoveries. In 1981, the U.S. Supreme Court ruled that software can be patented (*Diamond v. Diehr*). Software patents have become common, on the ground that software can be an essential part of a machine. Some early U.S. software patents were handled clumsily and appeared to cover techniques that were not actually original. In 2010, the Supreme Court affirmed that a patent could not be issued for a mathematical technique for hedging against the risk of price fluctuation (*Bilski v. Kappos*), but there is still uncertainty about precisely what is patentable. *See also* COMPUTER LAW; COPYRIGHT; TRADE SECRET.

In 2011, Congress passed the Leahy-Smith America Invents Act (Public Law 112-29), intended to speed up the patent process and reduce the need for litigation. Patent priority will now be awarded to the first person to file instead of the first person to invent.

path

1. a designation that specifies how to find a file on a disk that has more than one directory. In Windows, paths have either of two forms. For example,

    \AAA\BBB\CCC

means, "In the root directory there is a directory called AAA. In AAA there is a directory called BBB. In BBB there is a directory or file called CCC."

If the initial backslash is left out, the path starts at the directory currently in use rather than at the root directory. For example, the path

    AAA\BBB\CCC

means, "In the current directory there is a directory called AAA. In AAA there is a directory called BBB. In BBB there is a directory or file called CCC." Paths in UNIX are written the same way but with forward slashes (/ rather than \). *See* MISFEATURE.

2. The set of directories in which the computer will look for an executable file when the user types a command. Some software packages have to be on the path in order to work properly. In Windows, the current directory is always treated as if it were on the path; in UNIX it is not, unless explicitly included as "." (a period). Use the PATH command to change directories on the path.

3. a contour or outline. Objects in a draw program are defined by paths. *See* DRAW PROGRAM; POSTSCRIPT; VECTOR GRAPHICS.

4. a line that defines the movement of an object in an animation.

PC any computer whose architecture is derived, however distantly, from the original IBM PC (IBM Personal Computer) of 1981, and which is considered to be part of the same lineage, in contrast to the MACINTOSH, or others.

Today, *PC* denotes a computer that is built to run Microsoft Windows, although it may equally well run Linux, BSD UNIX, or some other operating system. Despite having adopted a very similar hardware architecture, the Pentium-based Apple Macintosh is not considered to be a PC; instead, it is the PC's arch-rival.

PC 100, PC 133 the special bus used by the Pentium III to communicate with RAM, at 100 or 133 MHz depending on the model.

PC 2001 a specification issued by Intel and Microsoft for the design of LEGACY-FREE personal computers (i.e., computers that run the latest PC operating systems but are not burdened by the need for full compatibility with the original PC hardware). *See* LEGACY-FREE.

PC Card a newer name for PCMCIA expansion cards. *See* PCMCIA; *see also* EXPRESSCARD and note there.

PC compatibility the ability of a computer to run the same software and use the same hardware accessories as the original IBM Personal Computer (PC) or its descendants. PC compatibility began with the manufacture of an IBM-like computer by Compaq in 1983. Today, compatibility depends on conformity to industry standards, such as PC 2001 and its successors, and the original IBM PC has been left far behind.

PCI (Peripheral Component Interface) an improved bus for PC-compatible computers, introduced by Intel in 1992. PCI is faster than EISA and has been expanded to 64 bits to meet the needs of the Pentium processor. PCI-bus computers can use a bus interface unit on the motherboard to connect to EISA or ISA cards, so that the same motherboard has both PCI and ISA slots. *See* BUS.

PCI Express a faster version of the PCI bus introduced by Intel in 2004 as a replacement for both PCI and AGP, with which it is not compatible. It is not truly a bus, but rather a very high-speed serial communication system. *See also* EXPRESSCARD.

PCIe, PCI-E *see* PCI EXPRESS.

PCMCIA (Personal Computer Memory Card International Association) an organization that defines standards for connecting peripherals to miniaturized computers such as notebooks and laptops. The standard ISA, EISA, PCI, and VLB buses are too bulky for laptop computers; the PCMCIA bus (now known as PC Card and CardBus) is a widely accepted standard. See *www.pcmcia.org*. *See also* BUS; CARDBUS; EXPRESSCARD.

PDA (personal digital assistant) a pocket-sized, special-purpose personal computer that lacks a conventional keyboard. PDAs do such things as send and receive fax messages, maintain an electronic address book and telephone directory, and serve as notepads on which files can be created for subsequent processing on a larger computer. *See also* BLACKBERRY; PALM; SMARTPHONE.

PDF (**P**ortable **D**ocument **F**ormat) a file format representing images of printable pages. PDF files are viewable with Adobe Reader.

See ACROBAT; ADOBE SYSTEMS, INC.

peak a way of measuring the voltage of alternating current from zero volts up to the most positive point. The peak voltage of any symmetrical waveform is exactly half of the peak-to-peak voltage. *See also* PEAK-TO-PEAK; RMS.

peak-to-peak a way of measuring the voltage of alternating current from the most positive to the most negative point. For example, the audio output of a microphone is about 0.002 volt peak-to-peak; the "line out" from a piece of audio equipment is about 1 volt peak-to-peak. Peak-to-peak measurement is used mostly with low-level signals that are viewed on oscilloscopes; ordinary voltmeters usually read rms voltage. The peak-to-peak voltage of a sine wave is 2.828 × the rms voltage. *Contrast* PEAK; RMS.

pebi- (Pi) a factor of $2^{50} = 1,125,899,906,842,624$, approximately 1.1×10^{15}. *See* METRIC PREFIXES.

PebiByte 2^{50} bytes. *See* METRIC PREFIXES.

PEBKAC *(humorous)* (**P**roblem **E**xists **B**etween **K**eyboard **A**nd **C**hair) an uncomplimentary way to indicate that a computer problem is the fault of the user. A legendary, and apparently recurrent, PEBKAC consists of the user mistaking the CD-ROM disk tray for a coffee cup holder and eventually breaking it.

peer-to-peer a network architecture in which there is no central server; all computers are equal participants.

pel (**p**icture **el**ement) PIXEL; one of the small dots of which a bitmap image is composed.

pen (in draw or paint programs) a tool used to create lines. Sometimes a similar tool is shown as a pencil. Most programs allow control of the width of the stroke the pen makes, the shape of the nib of the pen, the miter limit, and the shape of the endcaps. *See* Figure 193.

FIGURE 193. Pen tool

Pentium a high-performance 32-bit microprocessor introduced by Intel in 1993 as the successor to the 486. If the original numbering scheme had been continued, the Pentium would have been the 586, hence its name. The Pentium is software-compatible with the 8088 used in the original IBM PC. Subsequent models (Pentium Pro, Pentium II, Pentium III, and many others) have steadily increased in speed (to about 1000 times that of the original 8088) and have introduced fast caches, 64-bit registers, superscalar pipelining, and multiple cores. Today, the Pentium is the most popular microprocessor for general-purpose computing.

per computer (describing a software license) assigned to a specific computer or set of computers. Most software is licensed per computer; that is, the license gives you the right to install each copy on one computer for the use of anyone who wants to use it there. *Contrast* PER SEAT, PER USER.

per device (describing a computer license) PER COMPUTER.

per incident (describing a service plan) charging a fee each time service is requested. Each request is called an incident.

per seat (describing a software license) allowing a specific number of people to use the software at one time.

In some Microsoft documentation, *per seat* means either PER USER or PER DEVICE, even though neither of these is exactly what others have normally meant by *per seat*.

See SEAT. *Contrast* PER COMPUTER, PER USER.

per user (describing a software license) allowing specific people to use the software. For instance, if a software package is licensed for 12 users and installed on a server, then up to 12 user accounts of the server can access the software. *Contrast* PER COMPUTER, PER SEAT.

peripheral a device connected to a computer, such as a printer.

Perl (**P**ractical **E**xtraction and **R**eport **L**anguage) a programming language developed by Larry Wall for writing utilities that perform large amounts of string handling, text file processing, and interaction with the operating system. Like AWK and REXX, which it resembles, Perl is normally interpreted, not compiled. It is designed to minimize the programming effort needed for computations that are relatively simple and quick.

Figure 194 shows a simple Perl program. The overall syntax resembles C. Numbers and strings are interconvertible and are not distinguished; as far as Perl is concerned, 4 == '4'.

Every variable name begins with a character indicating its type: $ for scalars (numbers and strings), @ for ordinary arrays, and % for associative arrays (arrays whose elements are retrieved by keyword rather than by position). Array elements are numbered from 0; the operator $# retrieves the index of the highest element, which is one less than the total number of elements. Lines that begin with # are comments.

```
#!/usr/local/bin/perl
@path         =         split(/:/,$ENV{'PATH'});
$n = 1 + $#path;
print "You have $n directories on your path.\n";
print "They are:\n";
foreach $i (0..$#path) { print "$path[$i] \n"; }
```
FIGURE 194. Perl programming example

Under UNIX, Perl programs are often called *scripts* and begin with the line

```
#!/usr/local/bin/perl
```

so that if the program is passed to UNIX as a SHELL SCRIPT, it will be given to the Perl interpreter for execution.

On the WORLD WIDE WEB, Perl is often used to implement web pages that perform computations. Instead of writing a web page in HTML, the programmer writes a Perl program that generates the HTML from other sources of information, such as database files, calculations, and even the user's menu choices. *See also* AWK; CGI; HTML; REXX.

permalink a permanent link; in a BLOG or online newspaper, a permanent link (URL) to a particular article or page, which will remain usable after the article ceases to be today's news.

permission an attribute of a file that indicates who is allowed to read or modify it. For example, the UNIX command

```
chmod ugo+r-wx myfile.txt
```

sets permissions for the *u*ser, *g*roup, and *o*ther users of file myfile.txt by adding read permission (+r) and removing write and execute permission (-wx). In Windows, with NTFS, you can set permissions on a file or directory by right-clicking on it and choosing Properties, Security.

personal computer a computer designed to be used by only one person, either at home or in a business setting. One of the first personal computers was the Digital Equipment Corporation PDP-8, a minicomputer often used in scientific laboratories in the early 1970s. *See also* IBM PC; MACINTOSH.

personal digital assistant *see* PDA.

PERT (**P**rogram **E**valuation and **R**eview **T**echnique) a method for project planning by analyzing the time required for each step. *See* PROJECT MANAGEMENT.

peta- (P) metric prefix meaning ×1,000,000,000,000,000 (10^{15}). *Peta-* is apparently derived from the Greek word for "to fly" or "to soar." *See* METRIC PREFIXES.

Petabyte 10^{15} = 1,000,000,000,000,000 bytes. *See* METRIC PREFIXES.

PGA

   1. **p**in **g**rid **a**rray, the arrangement of pins on a Pentium or similar microprocessor, making it possible to plug the processor into a socket.

   2. **P**rofessional **G**raphics **A**dapter, an early high-performance graphics system for the IBM PC, marketed in the mid-1980s.

PGP (**P**retty **G**ood **P**rivacy) a public-key encryption system developed by Philip Zimmerman.

phishing a type of fraud carried out by sending out e-mail that pretends to come from a bank or corporation with which the victim has an account. The e-mail message tells the victim to click on a link in order to handle some kind of urgent business. In reality, both the message and the link are counterfeit, and the victim ends up giving his or her password or credit card information to the phisher, or at the very least, visiting a web site that disseminates MALWARE.

   To protect yourself from phishing, do not click on web links that arrive in e-mail. Instead, when you want to contact your bank, type its web address yourself. Some web browsers detect links that are known to be phishing sites, but this is not perfect protection because phishers often change their addresses. *See also* SMISHING.

phone plug a plug of a type originally designed for telephone switchboards, now used on audio equipment. Three sizes are used, each with 2 to 4 conductors. The miniature 3.5-mm 3-conductor phone plug (Figure 195, center) is used for stereo connections to sound cards. *Contrast* RCA PLUG; RJ-11.

FIGURE 195. Phone plugs

phono plug *see* RCA PLUG.

phosphorus chemical element (atomic number 15, symbol P) added to silicon to create an N-type SEMICONDUCTOR.

Photo CD Kodak's proprietary format for storing digitized photographs on CD-ROM, now seldom used.

photo paper

   1. light-sensitive paper used in making conventional photographic prints (not involving a computer).

   2. paper that has a glossy coating, but is not light-sensitive, used in inkjet printers for high-quality printing of photographs.

photograph a continuous-tone image created with a camera, either digital or film. Because photographs closely reproduce what we are able to see with our eyes, we credit them with being more "real" than drawings. Photographs make any document more interesting and convey much more information to the readers than words alone.

You can choose to use photographs from collections of stock photographs, take photographs with a digital camera, or have some of your older photographs scanned in.

It's best to scan the photo at the finished size and at the resolution of the output device (usually your laser printer). The contrast and brightness of the image can be adjusted while scanning it.

You'll notice that photographs can create large files. A $3\frac{1}{2} \times 5$-inch color snapshot, saved as a 300 DPI, 24-bit (millions of colors), uncompressed TIFF file, creates a 3.3-megabyte file that is too large to e-mail conveniently. It's best to save to a compressed file format (e.g., JPEG). Files of black-and-white photos are smaller; they don't have to include as much information.

A photopaint program like Adobe PhotoShop or PhotoShop Elements can be used to improve digital images. Spots and flaws can be removed, distracting elements erased, backgrounds changed, or the overall color balance adjusted. (*See* IMAGE PROCESSING; RETOUCHING.) Then import the digital photo into your page layout or word processing program, or publish it on the World Wide Web. *See* DIGITAL CAMERA. *Contrast* GRAYSCALE.

photopaint program a type of bitmap editing program with special tools and filters for manipulating photographs. You can also create illustrations from scratch with the drawing tools provided. *Compare* PAINT PROGRAM. *Contrast* DRAW PROGRAM.

In many ways, photopaint programs are the professional versions of the limited paint programs that come with operating systems. They are proportionately difficult to learn and master. Be prepared to spend enough time reading the manual and experimenting. *See also* IMAGE PROCESSING.

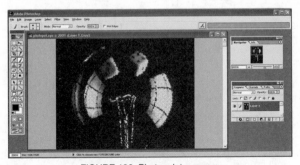

FIGURE 196. Photopaint program

PHP a scripting language often used to generate web pages by computation on the server (*compare* CGI, definition 1; ASP). PHP originated as a set of small, efficient CGI programs to do common tasks, released by Rasmus Lerdorf in 1995. The package was called *PHP Tools,* short for Personal Home Page Tools. Today, *PHP* is said to stand for *PHP Hypertext Processor* (yes, the acronym includes itself; *compare* GNU).

PHP is available free of charge for a wide range of computers. For more information see *www.php.net.*

phreak (or phone phreak) a person who makes a game of defrauding telephone companies by means of fake control signals, stolen credit card numbers, and the like. *See* 2600.

pi the Greek letter π, which stands for a special number that is approximately equal to 3.14159. If the radius of a circle is r, then the circumference is $2\pi r$ and the area is πr^2.

The valve of π can be approximated by the formula

$$\frac{\pi}{4} = 1 - \frac{1}{3} + \frac{1}{5} - \frac{1}{7} + \frac{1}{9} - \frac{1}{11} + \dots$$

The following Java program calculates π to nine-digit accuracy.

```
class picalc {
public static void main(String  arg[]) {
double p=1.0,  double denom=3.0,  double sign=-1.0;
while (denom<1000000000.0) {
p+=(sign*1/denom);
sign*=(-1.0); denom+=2.0;}
System.out.println(4*p),}}
```

pica (in typesetting) a unit of measurement equal to 12 points. There are approximately 6 picas to one inch (2.54 cm).

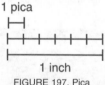

1 pica

1 inch

FIGURE 197. Pica

pick tool a mouse cursor shaped like an arrow that is used to pick up or pick out (select) objects in an image.

pickup roller in a printer, the roller that picks up pieces of paper from the paper tray and drags them through the printer. It usually has a soft, rubbery surface. The pickup roller should be cleaned or replaced if the printer is suffering frequent paper jams from the inability to pick up a piece of paper.

pico- (abbreviated p, pronounced pee-koh) metric prefix meaning ÷1,000,000,000,000 = 10^{-12} = one-trillionth. *Pico-* is derived from a Spanish word that means, among other things, "small quantity." *See* METRIC PREFIXES.

PICS (**P**latform for **I**nternet **C**ontent **S**election) the specifications for META TAGS that label web sites with their content ratings; the standard used by rating systems such as *SafeSurf.*

pictograph
1. a picture that represents an idea. Computer icons are a type of pictograph.
2. a bar graph that uses stacked or stretched symbols instead of plain vertical bars. Although this lends some visual interest to the graph, it can also be confusing if not handled correctly.

pie chart a type of chart that resembles a pie and graphically shows the relative size of different subcategories of a whole. *See* Figure 251 on page 470.

piece fraction a fraction constructed of three characters: small numerals for the numerator and denominator separated by a forward slash or a horizontal bar (½, or $\frac{1}{2}$). *Contrast* BUILT FRACTION; CASE FRACTION. *See* illustration at CASE FRACTION.

pilcrow the symbol ¶, which is used to mark the beginning of a new paragraph when the text is set with continuous paragraphs. The pilcrow can also be used as a footnote symbol. *See* FOOTNOTE.

pin
1. a stiff prong in an electronic connector that conducts current. For example, a VGA video connector has 15 pins; a serial port connector has 9 or 25 pins.
2. a movable stiff wire that presses on the ribbon of a dot-matrix printer under computer control in order to make dots on the paper.

PIN (**P**ersonal **I**dentification **N**umber) a number used as a password by a computer user.

pinch a touchpad or touchscreen gesture that makes an image or object smaller; the opposite of EXPAND (definition 2). To pinch, place two fingers in contact with the screen and bring them closer together.

FIGURE 198. Pinch (gesture on a touchpad or touchscreen).

pinch out spreading two fingers apart on a touchscreen, to zoom in on part of a picture.

ping
1. to send a message to another site on a TCP/IP network and await a response.
2. (slang) to check in with someone; to send someone a brief message asking for a response but not much information.

ping flooding the practice of maliciously disrupting a computer by *pinging* it continuously (i.e., flooding it with test data packets to which it must respond). Also known as SMURFING. *See* DENIAL-OF-SERVICE ATTACK.

pipe
1. a way of stringing two programs together so that the output of one of them is fed to the other as input. For example, the Windows command

```
c:\> dir | sort | more
```

invokes dir (which lists the names of the files on a disk), feeds its output to sort (which puts the items in alphabetical order), and feeds that output to more (which displays it one screenful at a time).
    See also BROKEN PIPE.
2. the character | (the pipe symbol).

pipeline a device within a CPU that enables it to fetch (read) instructions in advance of executing them, so that whenever an instruction is completed, the next instruction is ready to execute. This is a way of partly overcoming the Von Neumann bottleneck. *See also* COMPUTER ARCHITECTURE.

piracy the unauthorized copying of software, which is forbidden by law. *See* COPYRIGHT; SOFTWARE LICENSE.

pitch (typesetting) the number of characters per inch in a particular size and style of type. Fixed-pitch type has every character the same width; proportional-pitch type has some characters wider than others (e.g., *M* wider than *I*), and the pitch can be measured only approximately as the average of many different letters. *See* Figure 104, page 195.

pivot table a multi-dimensional data table that can be rearranged to allow different views of the data. For example, suppose you need to keep track of a budget with two divisions and three spending categories for three months. Here is the original data:

DIVISION	MONTH	CATEGORY	AMOUNT
NORTH	January	EMPLOYEES	564
NORTH	January	SUPPLIES	320
NORTH	January	RENT	40
NORTH	February	EMPLOYEES	602
NORTH	February	SUPPLIES	348
NORTH	February	RENT	40
NORTH	March	EMPLOYEES	620
NORTH	March	SUPPLIES	352
NORTH	March	RENT	40
SOUTH	January	EMPLOYEES	212
SOUTH	January	SUPPLIES	180
SOUTH	January	RENT	20
SOUTH	February	EMPLOYEES	240
SOUTH	February	SUPPLIES	200
SOUTH	February	RENT	20
SOUTH	March	EMPLOYEES	265
SOUTH	March	SUPPLIES	160
SOUTH	March	RENT	20

It would be easier to understand the data if it were arranged in a pivot table, like this:

NORTH

	EMPLOYEES	SUPPLIES	RENT	TOTAL
January	564	320	40	924
February	602	348	40	990
March	620	352	40	1012
TOTAL	1786	1020	120	2926

SOUTH

	EMPLOYEES	SUPPLIES	RENT	TOTAL
January	212	180	20	412
February	240	200	20	460
March	265	160	20	445
TOTAL	717	540	60	1317

Sometimes it helps to rearrange the data. Here are two different ways of doing this:

January

	EMPLOYEES	SUPPLIES	RENT	TOTAL
NORTH	564	320	40	924
SOUTH	212	180	20	412
TOTAL	776	500	60	1336

February

	EMPLOYEES	SUPPLIES	RENT	TOTAL
NORTH	602	348	40	990
SOUTH	240	200	20	460
TOTAL	842	548	60	1450

March

	EMPLOYEES	SUPPLIES	RENT	TOTAL
NORTH	620	352	40	1012
SOUTH	265	160	20	445
TOTAL	885	512	60	1457

****

EMPLOYEES

	NORTH	SOUTH	TOT
January	564	212	776
February	602	240	842
March	620	265	885
TOT:	1786	717	2503

SUPPLIES

	NORTH	SOUTH	TOT
January	320	180	500
February	348	200	548
March	352	160	512
TOT:	1020	540	1560

RENT

	NORTH	SOUTH	TOT
January	40	20	60
February	40	20	60
March	40	20	60
TOT:	120	60	180

Or, you might wish to consolidate all of the spending categories and create a view like this:

ALL CATEGORIES

	January	February	March	TOTAL
NORTH	924	990	1012	2926
SOUTH	412	460	445	1317
TOTAL	1336	1450	1457	4243

Excel contains a wizard that automatically creates pivot tables.

PIX (**P**rivate **I**nternet E**x**change) a type of secure hardware FIREWALL developed in 1994 by John Mayes and Brantley Coile at Cisco Systems. It will translate network addresses, so the internal network can use IP addresses of its own choosing without worrying about clashes with IP addresses in the worldwide Internet. It was one of the first implementations of NAT (network address translation).

pixel one of the individual dots that make up a graphical image. For
example, an XGA color screen in high-resolution mode consists of a
1024 × 768 pixel array. A program can draw pictures on the screen by
controlling the color of each pixel. *See* GRAPHICS.

pixelate, pixelize to transform a bitmap image into rectangular blocks of
uniform color, as if the pixels were much larger than before.

FIGURE 199. Pixelated image

PKCS (**P**ublic-**K**ey **C**ryptography **S**tandards) a set of standards developed
by RSA Laboratories and others. Information on the web is available at
www.rsa.com/rsalabs/pubs/PKCS.

PL/1 (**PL/I**) a powerful programming language developed by IBM in the
early 1960s to accompany its System/360 computer. The name stands for
Programming Language One.
   PL/1 can be described as a combination of ALGOL 60 block structure, FORTRAN arithmetic, and COBOL data structuring. PL/1 is the
language of choice for writing complex programs on IBM mainframe
computers, but it has received little use on other types of machines.

planar
   1. *(adjective)* flat. For example, planar transistors are made of flat
pieces of silicon.
   2. *(adjective)* situated on the motherboard of a computer (e.g., planar
RAM).
   3. *(noun)* motherboard. *See* MOTHERBOARD; *contrast* DAUGHTERBOARD;
DAUGHTERCARD; RISER.

plane
   1. in geometry, all the points on a flat surface. Thus a plane is a two-
dimensional space on which things have length and width but no
thickness.
   2. in computer graphics, one of several images that are superimposed to
produce the final image. For example, many video cards have separate
planes (internal bitmaps) for red, green, and blue. The complete image
is a combination of the images stored on the three planes. *See*
CHANNEL.

platform a piece of equipment or software used as a base on which to build something else. For example, a mainframe computer can serve as a platform for a large accounting system. Microsoft Windows serves as a platform for application software.

plenum-rated (describing cable) suitable for use in places where air circulates, such as above suspended ceilings. (A *plenum* is a place full of air, the opposite of a vacuum.) Plenum-rated cable is fire resistant and does not give off noxious fumes when overheated. *Contrast* RISER-RATED.

plotter a device that draws pictures on paper by moving pens according to directions from a computer. *See* GRAPHICS.

Plug and Play a standard way of configuring PC-compatible computer hardware automatically, developed by Microsoft and a number of other companies in the mid-1990s. Plug and Play hardware is compatible with conventional hardware (ISA, PCI, PCMCIA, USB, etc.) but has additional capabilities. Each card or accessory inserted into a computer contains identifying information that can be read by the BIOS and the operating system. Thus, the computer can see all the installed accessories and can configure itself to use them appropriately.

plug-in an accessory program that provides additional functions for a main application program. Plug-ins have to be loaded at the same time as the main program; they then show up as an option in an appropriate menu. Plug-ins are also added to a web browser to allow it to view additional file formats, such as multimedia shows.

PMS *see* PANTONE MATCHING SYSTEM.

PNA (**P**ersonal **N**avigation **A**ssistant) *see* GEOLOCATION.

PND (**P**ersonal **N**avigation **D**evice) *see* GEOLOCATION.

PNG (**P**ortable **N**etwork **G**raphics) a bitmapped image format that was created to improve on .GIF (and is not patented).

PNP one of the two types of bipolar TRANSISTORS (*contrast* NPN).

PnP abbreviation for PLUG AND PLAY.

podcasting (from *iPod* and *broadcast*, but not confined to the Apple iPod) the practice of preparing audio and video programs like radio and TV broadcasts, but distributing them through the Internet for playback on MP3 players, iPods, and similar devices. *See* IPOD.

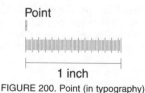

FIGURE 200. Point (in typography)

point

1. in geometry, an exact location; in graphics, a precise location or single PIXEL.

2. a unit of typographical measurement equal to $\frac{1}{72}$ inch. The height of type is usually expressed in points. However, this is not a measurement of the size of the letters, but rather of the wooden blocks on which the metal type was mounted for printing presses. This usually included some space at the top of the tallest capital letters and below the descenders. Therefore, different typefaces of the same point size may actually differ in size. To this day, even digitized typefaces show some of the same idiosyncrasies. A desire to be faithful to the original designs has prevented the type's apparent size from being regularized. *See* LEADING; TYPEFACE; TYPESETTING MISTAKES.

FIGURE 201. 24-point type samples

point-of-sale system a computer used in place of a cash register where merchandise is sold. Besides keeping track of cash, the computer can keep track of inventory and print informative invoices and receipts, and perhaps automatically deduct funds from the customer's account.

point release a minor upgrade of a piece of software, such as the upgrade from version 2.0 to 2.1.

point-to-point protocol *see* PPP; PROTOCOL.

pointer

1. an arrow-like symbol that moves around a computer screen under the control of the user. For example, to execute a command in a windowed operating system, use the mouse to move the pointer to the icon representing that command, and then quickly press the mouse button twice.

2. a data item consisting of an address that tells where to find a desired item. For examples, *see* LINKED LIST; TREE. Pascal, C, and many other programming languages provide a specific data type called a pointer variable that can be used to keep track of data structures that vary in size as the program is executed.

3. a device for pointing to a board or projection screen using a stick or a laser beam.

pointing device a computer peripheral that allows you to control your computer in a graphical user interface (GUI). The most familiar pointing device is a MOUSE, but some people prefer a TRACKBALL or a GRAPHICS TABLET. The pointing device on a LAPTOP is often a TOUCHPAD or a button that works like a miniature joystick. *See also* TOUCHSCREEN.

Polish notation a way of writing algebraic expressions that does not require parentheses to state which operations are done first. It is named in honor of its inventor, Jan Lukasiewicz (1878–1956), whose name most English-speaking mathematicians cannot pronounce. The ordinary algebraic expression

$$4 + (5 - 3) + 2$$

translates into Polish notation as

$$4\ 5\ 3 - + 2 +$$

To evaluate the expression, work through it from left to right until you encounter an operation (a plus or minus), then perform that operation on the numbers immediately to the left of the operator, replace the numbers and the operator with the result of the operation, and keep going in the same manner. Thus,

$$4\ 5\ 3 - + 2 +$$

simplifies to

$$4\ 2 + 2 +$$
$$6\ 2 +$$
$$8$$

This is technically known as reverse Polish notation (RPN); the expression can also be written in the other direction and worked through from right to left. Many calculators and programming language interpreters translate expressions into Polish notation in order to evaluate them. Also, Hewlett-Packard calculators use Polish notation rather than parentheses on the ground that Polish notation is easier to work with once the user becomes accustomed to it.

polygon a closed geometric figure with any number of straight sides. Triangles, squares, pentagons (five-sided), hexagons (six-sided), heptagons (seven-sided), and octagons (eight-sided) are all examples of polygons. Figure 202 shows some regular polygons, in each of which all sides and angles are equal.

FIGURE 202. Polygons

polymorphism the use of different procedures, each with the same name, which are associated with different object types. For example, procedures named draw could be associated with the types point, circle, and square. Calling draw for any particular object then activates the right drawing procedure for that type. *See* OBJECT-ORIENTED PROGRAMMING.

Ponzi scheme *see* PYRAMID SCHEME.

pop to remove the topmost item from a stack. *See* STACK.

POP

1. **P**ost **O**ffice **P**rotocol, a standard protocol for delivering e-mail to personal computers. *See* PROTOCOL.

2. **p**oint **o**f **p**urchase (point of sale). For example, a POP computer is a computer used as a cash register. *See* POINT-OF-SALE SYSTEM.

3. **p**oint **o**f **p**resence, a place where an INTERNET SERVICE PROVIDER can be accessed, such as a local telephone number, for modem access (now almost obsolete).

pop-under ad an advertisement that appears automatically underneath (behind) the WEB PAGE you are viewing. Although pop-under ads are less intrusive than pop-up ads, they are still unwelcome because of the clutter they generate. *See* BANNER AD; MOUSETRAP; POP-UP AD.

pop-up ad an advertisement that appears automatically in a separate window when you access a WEB PAGE. *See* ADWARE. *Compare* BANNER AD; POP-UNDER AD.

pop-up menu *see* PULL-DOWN MENU.

pornography publications or images whose primary purpose is to stimulate sexual appetite. *See also* INDECENCY; OBSCENITY.

Even the most innocent Internet user occasionally stumbles upon pornography. Some pornographers send advertisements to all the e-mail addresses they can obtain or make up (*see* SPAM). (Such e-mail does not indicate that the recipient has been viewing pornographic web pages, even if it says that it does.) Others rig their web pages so that SEARCH ENGINES will lead users to them when they are looking for something else.

Many individuals find pornography strongly addictive. The purpose of pornography is to make money, and the only reason it is given away free is to get people "hooked" so that they will pay for more.

In the United States, most of the pornography on the Internet is legal, but sexually explicit images of children are not, and images of sexual behavior may not be legal, depending on local laws. (*See* COMPUTER LAW; CIPA; OBSCENITY.) Law enforcement is hampered by the difficulty of determining the physical locations of web sites. Note however that because the laws prohibit *distribution* of obscene material, a link to an obscene site can itself be illegal.

There have been various efforts to keep pornography from reaching children and unwilling audiences. The Communications Decency Act of 1996 was struck down because it assumed, incorrectly, that Internet service providers can control the information sent through their computers; replacement legislation has been proposed. Schools and libraries sometimes use "filtering" software to block access to known pornographic web sites, but the filtering process is imperfect.

Pornography is associated with credit card fraud and other crimes. Several Internet pornography vendors have been caught making unauthorized charges to credit card numbers, presumably expecting the victims to be too embarrassed to complain. In some cases the numbers were stolen or made up and belonged to people who had never had any contact with the vendors.

It is naive to describe pornography as "victimless." The most obvious victims are the individuals who become addicted, and whose relationships and even marriages are damaged. The young people hired to pose for pornographic pictures are also victims of exploitation.

port

1. to adapt a program from one kind of computer to another. For example, some PC programs have been ported to the Macintosh.

2. a connection where a computer can be connected to an external device, such as a printer, flash drive, or digital camera. *See* PARALLEL; SCSI; SERIAL; USB.

3. a unique number used by a microprocessor to identify an input-output device.

4. a number identifying the type of connection requested by a remote computer on the Internet. *See* URL.

port replicator a DOCKING STATION for a portable computer that contains serial and parallel ports (and perhaps other ports, such as USB) which substitute for those in the computer itself.

portable

1. able to be carried around. A portable computer is larger than a laptop computer, but is still easily movable.

2. (said of programs) able to run on more than one type of computer or operating system. *Compare* INTEROPERABILITY.

Portable Document File *see* PDF.

portal a web site designed for people to visit when they are looking for links to other sites. Examples include *www.msn.com* and *www.yahoo. com* as well as the home pages of various Internet service providers.

portrait the position in which a sheet of paper is taller than it is wide, like a portrait painting. Most printers print with the paper in portrait orientation. If the printed image can be turned sideways, the result is called *landscape orientation*. *See* Figure 148, page 282.

POS

1. **p**oint **o**f **s**ale. *See* POINT-OF-SALE SYSTEM.

2. **p**rogrammable **o**ption **s**elect, the system for recording the configuration of a computer into CMOS RAM so that the computer can boot successfully. *See* CMOS RAM.

POSIX (usually understood as "**p**ortable **o**perating **s**ystem **i**nterface based on UNIX" though this is not its official definition) an IEEE standard set of operating system functions available to software. The POSIX standard makes it possible to write programs that will run under any POSIX-compliant operating system by simply recompiling them. Windows 95, 98, and Me are partially POSIX-compliant; Windows NT, 2000, XP, Vista, and later versions are more so. POSIX is a trademark of the IEEE. *See* IEEE; INTEROPERABILITY; Z/OS.

post to place a message in a NEWSGROUP, BBS, WEB PAGE, or other public discussion forum.

postfix notation including an operator symbol after the operands. For example, 2 3 + would mean to add the two and three together. *See* POLISH NOTATION; PREFIX NOTATION; INFIX NOTATION.

posting a message placed in a NEWSGROUP, BBS, or other public discussion forum.

PostScript a programming language for controlling laser printers and other graphical output devices, developed by Adobe Systems of Palo Alto, California. A PostScript printer accepts not only characters to be printed but also commands to change the size of type fonts or to draw lines or circles in specific positions. An application designed to work with Post-Script will automatically send PostScript codes to the printer. The user can also write programs in the PostScript language. Figure 203 shows an example. The text following the percent signs is treated as comments, but some of the comments (such as BoundingBox) are used by some types of software. This program is suitable for encapsulation into larger programs; to print it by itself, add the command showpage after the last line.

```
%!PS-Adobe-2.0 EPSF-2.0
%%BoundingBox: 1 800 1 800
% PostScript program to print a gray square
% and the words 'PostScript Example'
/Helvetica-Bold findfont 12 scalefont setfont
newpath
72 720 moveto            % start drawing rectangle
182 720 lineto
182 648 lineto
72 648 lineto
closepath
.75 setgray              % choose 75% gray
fill
0 setgray                % restore color to black
85 700 moveto
(PostScript) show        % print text
85 685 moveto
(Example) show
```

FIGURE 203. PostScript program

PostScript works with a coordinate system with the origin at the lower left-hand corner of the page, with units $1/72$ of an inch long. The program demonstrates the use of the moveto command, the lineto command (which draws a line from the previous point to the indicated point), and the fill command (which fills an area with a desired shade of gray).

Text is printed by enclosing it in parentheses and then using the command show. Before printing, the appropriate font must be selected; fonts can be scaled to different point sizes. PostScript also lets the programmer use variables and define abbreviations and procedures. Figure 204 shows the output of Figure 203.

Many printers expect a Ctrl-D (UNIX end-of-file mark) at the end of every PostScript job. Some software also generates a Ctrl-D at the beginning of the job, to clear out anything that may have previously been sent to the printer.

PostScript was introduced in 1985; Level 2 PostScript, an extended version of the language, was introduced in 1991 and is now the minimum standard. Another revision, called simply PostScript 3, was introduced in 1997. *Encapsulated PostScript* (EPS) is a file format for using the PostScript language to exchange graphics between programs. EPS files must contain a BoundingBox comment, must follow certain other restrictions, and can contain bitmap previews of the image. Notoriously, software that imports some EPS files do not necessarily understand the entire PostScript language; many programs confine themselves to the Adobe Illustrator (AI) subset of EPS.

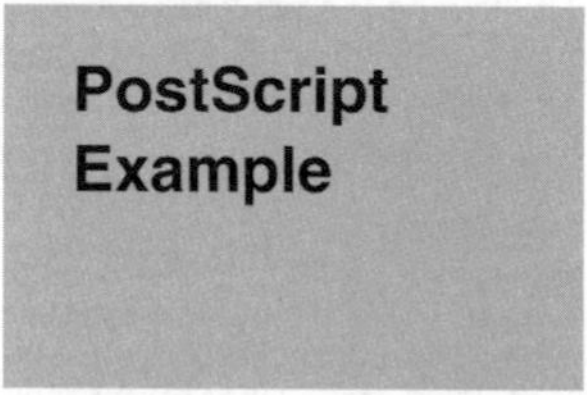

**PostScript
Example**

FIGURE 204. PostScript output (from the sample program)

POTS (**P**lain **O**ld **T**elephone **S**ervice) humorous name for conventional analog telephone lines compatible with all telephones made since the 1920s. Designing modems for POTS lines has been a challenging engineering problem. At present, the highest possible data rate is thought to be about 56 kbps, but other, much lower, rates were thought to be the highest possible rate in past years. *Contrast* CABLE MODEM; DSL; ISDN; T1 LINE.

pound key the key on a telephone marked with the symbol #. It is often used to signal the end of an international telephone number.

pound sign
1. the character #. Also called an OCTOTHORPE.
2. the character £ denoting British pounds.

power cycle to switch off electric power to a device, then switch it on again. This is one way to REBOOT a computer. However, it should be done only in emergencies because many operating systems (including

UNIX and Windows) will lose data if not shut down properly. After turning power off, always wait a few seconds for capacitors to discharge and disks to spin down before turning the power on again.

power line protection measures taken to protect a computer from problems caused by the AC power supplied by the wall outlet. Several things can go wrong:
1. Brief bursts ("spikes") of excessive voltage can damage the computer. These spikes come from lightning or from large electric motors switching off. They are easily absorbed by a surge protector (*see* SURGE PROTECTOR).
2. Power failures cause the computer to shut down or restart suddenly, losing the data that you were working on. A surge protector cannot prevent this. If the problem is frequent, you may want to invest in an uninterruptible power supply (UPS).
3. The computer can emit radio or TV interference through the power line. *See* RFI PROTECTION.

power supply the part of a computer or other electronic equipment that supplies electric power to the other parts. The power supply generally includes stepdown transformers and voltage regulators. *See also* SWITCHING POWER SUPPLY.

The watt and ampere ratings of a power supply represent the maximum that it can deliver; the actual power consumed will depend on the devices attached to it. Correct practice is to use a power supply with the *correct* voltages and *correct or higher* watt and ampere ratings.

PowerPC a family of high-performance 32- and 64-bit microprocessors developed jointly by IBM, Motorola, and Apple to compete with the Intel microprocessors and Microsoft software that were dominating the market. From 1994 to 2006, PowerPC CPUs were used in the Apple Macintosh. Despite the name, the PowerPC microprocessor has never been used in Windows-based PCs.

PowerPoint presentation software sold with Microsoft's Office suite. The user can create an outline version of a talk and then display it one page at a time or one line at a time, and graphics can be included as well. Speaker notes or handouts can also be printed.

PowerToys a set of small Windows utilities distributed free of charge by Microsoft to allow additional customization of the operating system.

PPM (**p**ages **p**er **m**inute) a measure of the speed of a printer.

PPP (**P**oint-to-**P**oint **P**rotocol) a communications protocol often used in DIAL-UP NETWORKING. *Compare* SLIP. *See* PROTOCOL.

PPPoE (**P**oint to **P**oint **P**rotocol **o**ver **E**thernet) a protocol allowing the use of PPP (as would be used in dial-up networking) when the user is connected to the network through an Ethernet port (as would be the case for a user connected to the Internet via a cable modem).

precedence the property of arithmetic operations that determines which operations are done first in a complex expression.

Typically, exponentiations are done first, then multiplications and divisions, and finally additions and subtractions. For example, the Excel expression

```
=5+4*3^2
```

means $5 + 4 \times 9 = 5 + 36 = 41$. You can use parentheses to change the order of the operations when you need to, since any operation in parentheses will be done first. For example,

```
=5+(4*3)^2
```

means $5 + 12^2 = 5 + 144 = 149$.

precision the exactness with which a quantity is specified. For numbers, the precision is the number of significant digits that the computer keeps track of when it carries out arithmetic operations. *See* ROUNDING ERROR. For examples in Java, *see* DOUBLE PRECISION; LONG.

Precision is entirely separate from accuracy. If I weigh 175 pounds and you say that I weigh 150.03535 pounds, your assertion is precise but not accurate.

preferences settings for a computer program to allow for individual differences. The preferences menu is sometimes a rather obscure catchall for adjustments to mouse tracking, the double-click rate, the NUDGE rate, and the brush style. Take the time to become familiar with the "Preferences" settings in your software; sometimes a problem can be quickly solved by making a small adjustment.

prefix notation listing the operator before its operands. For example, + 2 3 means to add two and three. *See* POLISH NOTATION; POSTFIX NOTATION; INFIX NOTATION.

preflight the step just before printing an image or document. During preflight checking, software can detect missing fonts, images too large for the paper, and the like. The name apparently alludes to the preflight checks performed on aircraft just before taking off.

prepend to append at the beginning; to put in front. For example, if you prepend // to a line in a C++ program, that line becomes a comment.

prepress the preparation of material to be printed in quantity on a printing press. Many prepress functions are highly automated and well suited to being performed with computers. For example, there are software packages that take a PostScript file and slightly increase the outline of color areas to create TRAP. The graphic arts industry now uses a digital production system where the printing plates are prepared directly from computer files. *See also* PDF.

press to depress a mouse button and hold it down until the mouse action is completed. *Contrast* CLICK.

FIGURE 205. Press

pretzel *(slang)* nickname for ⌘, the Macintosh command key.

preview a viewing mode that displays the appearance of the finished document or drawing. In order to let you work quickly, many drawing programs show you only an outline of the objects on screen. (This is called WIREFRAME mode.) When you want to see what the final printed piece would look like, you have to use the "Preview" command. Then all of the objects appear with their fills so that you can check whether they are layered correctly.

Most drawing programs will allow you to work in preview mode, but the time spent redrawing the screen after each action can be quite irritating. If it becomes a problem, work in the wireframe view and preview frequently to check your work. Another method is to open two windows containing the same file, one in wireframe and the second in preview.

Most word processors also allow you to preview your document.

primary key a field in a database record with a unique identifier. When sorting a database, the items will be sorted first according to the primary key. Sometimes you also wish to define a secondary key. For example, you may wish to sort a list of club members first by their membership date (the primary key), and then alphabetically by their last name (the secondary key). *See* KEY.

primary mouse button the button used to select objects on a mouse with more than one button. For a right-handed user, this is usually the left mouse button. The SECONDARY MOUSE BUTTON is the button used to call up the action menu.

Left-handed users have the option of reversing the default order for mouse buttons; they can use the right mouse button as the primary button and the left button as the secondary.

primitive a basic element or concept in terms of which larger elements or concepts are formed. For example, in programming languages such as FORTH and Lisp, it is common for programmers to create their own statements by defining them in terms of primitives provided by the language.

print head The part of an INKJET PRINTER that actually contacts the paper in order to print. It contains tiny holes through which ink is sprayed; if some of these holes are clogged, printing will be streaky and the print head should be cleaned as specified in the instructions.

print server a computer through which other computers access a printer over a network. A print server may be an ordinary computer or a small circuit board or box mounted inside or just outside the printer.

print spooler a program that stores computer output in memory so that the user's program can finish creating the output without waiting for the printer to print it. The spooler then sends the stored output to the printer at the proper speed. Print spoolers are built into Windows and UNIX. *See also* SPOOLING; BUFFER.

printer a device for putting computer output on paper or other appropriate media such as transparencies and adhesive labels. *See* ELECTROSTATIC PRINTER; IMPACT PRINTER; INKJET PRINTER; LASER PRINTER; LINE PRINTER; PAGE PRINTER; PICKUP ROLLER; RESOLUTION; THERMAL PRINTER.

private key the key (password, code word) that the recipient of a message uses to decrypt a message that was encrypted with the recipient's PUBLIC KEY. Only the recipient of a message knows his or her own private key. *See* ENCRYPTION.

procedure a SUBROUTINE; a smaller program that is part of a main program. The procedure is executed when the main program calls it.

Procedures eliminate the need to program the same thing more than once. If you know that one task will be performed more than once in your program, it is better to write a procedure to handle the task rather than duplicate the program code when the task is needed again. Also, a large program is easier to understand if it consists of procedures, each with a well-defined purpose. *See* TOP-DOWN PROGRAMMING.

A procedure that returns a value is often called a FUNCTION. In object-oriented languages such as Java, a procedure is called a METHOD.

process a series of instructions that a computer is executing in a multitasking operating system. Many processes execute concurrently. From the user's viewpoint, processes may be programs or parts of programs (such as the editing routine and the printing routine in a word processor that can print while editing). *See* MULTITASKING; UNIX.

process color four-color printing on a commercial printing press, usually used for producing a full-color publication. *See* CMYK. *Contrast* SPOT COLOR.

Processing a programming language derived from JAVA and developed at the MIT Media Lab to make it easy to teach programming to people whose primary interest is computer graphics, including the graphic arts. The syntax is similar to Java, but graphical operations (such as allocating windows and drawing on them) play a very large role in any program and are easy to perform.

processor *see* COPROCESSOR; CPU; MICROPROCESSOR.

profile

1. in any software package or operating system, a file of saved information that contains settings chosen by the user.

2. in Windows, the folder containing information specific to one user, including account information, numerous settings and preferences, e-mail files, the DESKTOP and all the files on it, and the like. *See* DOCUMENTS AND SETTINGS. *See also* ROAMING USER PROFILES.

3. a user's home page on a social networking site, displaying basic biographical information and pictures.

program a set of instructions for a computer to execute. A program can be written in a programming language, such as C or Java, or in an assembly language. *See* APPLICATION PROGRAM; UTILITY.

programmable function key a key on a computer keyboard whose function depends on the software being run. In many cases, programmable function (PF) keys can be defined as equivalent to combinations or sequences of other keys.

programmatically *(adverb)* by means of a computer program. For example, in Windows, the volume level of the speaker can be changed programmatically; that is, software can change it.

programmer a person who prepares instructions for computers.

programming the process of composing instructions for a computer to carry out. A programmer needs to develop a well-defined concept of how to solve a problem. (*See* ALGORITHM.) Then this concept must be translated into a computer language. (*See* PROGRAMMING LANGUAGE.) Finally, the program needs to be typed into the computer, tested, and debugged before being placed into service.

programming language a language used to give instructions to computers. During the 1960s and 1970s, a huge variety of programming languages were developed, most of which are no longer in wide use. Moreover, a substantial amount of programming is now done with special program development tools (e.g., Visual Basic), or in programming languages that pertain to specific pieces of software (e.g., Maple) rather than by simply writing instructions in a general-purpose language.

The following is a rough classification of programming languages. Most of these languages are treated in separate articles in this book.

    1. General-purpose languages for large, complex programs: PL/I, C, C++, Pascal, Modula-2, Ada, Java, C#.

    2. General-purpose languages for smaller programs: BASIC, Visual Basic, Pascal, Python.

3. Mathematical calculation, science, and engineering: Fortran, APL, Maple, and the general-purpose languages named above.
4. Business data processing: COBOL, RPG. Where microcomputers are involved, BASIC, C, and languages associated with specific database products are also widely used.
5. Artificial intelligence and programs of extreme logical complexity: Lisp and Prolog.
6. String handling and scripting: SNOBOL, REXX, Awk, Perl, Python, VBSCRIPT, JavaScript.

Another useful classification is based on the way the program is organized.

1. Sequential languages treat the program as a series of steps, with an occasional GOTO statement as a way of breaking out of the sequence. In this category are Fortran, BASIC, and COBOL (though COBOL also allows programs to be written in a style more like a block-structured language).
2. Block-structured languages encourage structured programming by allowing the programmer to group statements into functional units. (*See* STRUCTURED PROGRAMMING.) This category originated with Algol and now includes Pascal, Fortran 90, Modula-2, C, PL/I, and Ada.
3. Object-oriented languages allow the programmer to define new data types and associate procedures with them. Languages of this type include C++, Java, C#, object-oriented extensions of Pascal, and Smalltalk.
4. Symbolic languages allow the program to examine and modify itself, treating instructions as data. Lisp and Prolog fall into this category.

Usage note: Although names of some programming languages are normally written in all capital letters, names of most languages are not, even if they are acronyms. Usage varies from language to language. With some, usage has shifted over the years. *See also* BASIC (Usage note).

See also ARRAY; BACKTRACKING; COMMENT; EXTREME PROGRAMMING; LOGO; LOOP; OBJECT ORIENTED PROGRAMMING; RECURSION; SOFTWARE ENGINEERING; SORT; STRUCTURED PROGRAMMING; TOP-DOWN PROGRAMMING. For *contrast*, see NATURAL LANGUAGE.

project the set of all files needed to produce the ready-to-use version of a program. Typically, the compiler accepts procedures from several different files and combines them into one executable (EXE) file. *See* MAKE; LINK.

project management the scheduling of a complex project involving many different tasks. A typical task requires some resources and a certain amount of time; it also requires that certain other tasks have already been finished. You may sometimes schedule two tasks to be performed simultaneously if they don't overtax the supply of available resources, but when the tasks are sequential, you must schedule them in the proper order. For example, the engines on the wings of an airplane cannot be installed until the wings have been built. A project manager program takes the information the user enters for each task and then determines how to schedule the tasks. The results are often presented in the form of a diagram called a Gantt chart (*see* Figure 206).

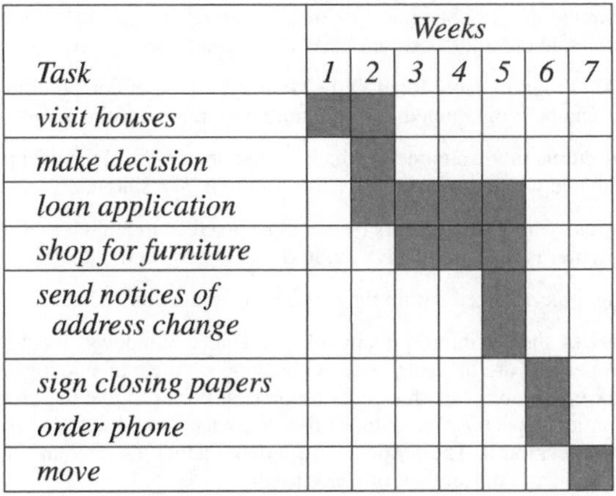

Task	Weeks						
	1	*2*	*3*	*4*	*5*	*6*	*7*
visit houses	■	■					
make decision		■					
loan application			■	■	■		
shop for furniture			■	■			
send notices of address change					■		
sign closing papers						■	
order phone						■	
move							■

FIGURE 206. Project management: Gantt chart
for moving to a new home

Prolog a programming language developed in the early 1970s by Alain Colmerauer at the University of Marseilles and standardized by the ISO in 1995. Prolog is used for writing computer programs that model human thinking. It exemplifies *logic programming,* a kind of programming developed by Robert Kowalski of the University of London.

In ordinary programming, a program describes the steps that a computer is to work through in order to solve a problem. In logic programming, the program gives the computer facts about the problem, plus rules by means of which other facts can be inferred. The computer then applies a fixed procedure to solve the problem automatically.

For example, Prolog can chain together the fact "Atlanta is in Georgia" and the rule "*X* is in the U.S.A. if *X* is in Georgia" to answer the question, "Is Atlanta in the U.S.A.?" In Prolog, the fact and the rule are:

```
located_in(atlanta,georgia).
located_in(x,usa) :-located_in(x,georgia).
```

The question (called a *query*) is typed:

```
?- located_in(atlanta,usa).
```

and is answered "yes."

One of the most important properties of Prolog is its ability to back-track, that is, to back up and try alternative solutions. This is necessary whenever the search starts pursuing a chain of rules that do not lead to a solution.

Prolog is not confined to the simple kind of logic described here. It can implement all types of algorithms, including sorting, numerical computation, and parsing. *See also* ANONYMOUS VARIABLE; ARTIFICIAL INTELLIGENCE; BACKTRACKING; SINGLETON VARIABLE.

PROM (**P**rogrammable **R**ead-**O**nly **M**emory) a type of computer memory that can be programmed once but not reprogrammed. *See also* EPROM.

promiscuous mode a mode in which a computer reads all the data packets on the network, not just those addressed to it. *See* SNIFFER.

prompt a symbol that appears on a computer screen to tell the user that the computer is ready to receive input. *See also* COMMAND PROMPT.

prop an object placed within the scene of an animation.

properties the attributes of any object. Under Windows, menus titled "Properties" are the usual way of changing settings. In Windows, right-click on an object to change its properties. For example, the properties of an icon specify what it looks like and what should happen when the user clicks on it. The properties of a disk include the amount of space available and the amount of space used.

proportional pitch the use of characters with different widths in a single typeface. For example, in proportional-pitch type, *M* is wider than *I*. Compared to a fixed-pitch typewriter or printer, this improves the appearance of the type and makes it more readable. Most books and newspapers are set in proportional type. *See* FIXED-PITCH TYPE. TYPE; TYPEFACE.

proprietary owned by a specific company or individual. A feature of a computer is proprietary if one company has exclusive rights to it.

protocol a standard way of carrying out data transmission between comput-ers. *See* HANDSHAKING; ATM (definition 4); DHCP; FTP; GOPHER; HTTP; IIOP; IMAP; IPV6; IPXSPX; KERBEROS; KERMIT; NETBEUI; POP; PPP; REALAUDIO; SAMBA; SMTP; SOAP; TCP/IP; TELNET; TWAIN; VOIP; X.25.

proxy an item that represents something else. *See also* PROXY SERVER.

proxy server a computer that saves information acquired from elsewhere on the INTERNET and makes it available to other computers in its immedi-ate area. For example, if several users connect to the same WEB SITE through a proxy server, each page of information will be downloaded from that site only once and then provided to all the users.

A disadvantage of proxy servers is that they make it impossible to count HITS accurately.

PS 2
1. an advanced version (Level 2) of the POSTSCRIPT graphics language.
2. Sony Playstation 2, a video game machine.

PS/2 *see* IBM PC.

PS/2 keyboard, PS/2 mouse a keyboard or mouse with a small round connector of the type originally used on the IBM PS/2 but now widely used on other PC-compatible computers.

pseudocode an outline of a computer program, written in a mixture of a programming language and English. Writing pseudocode is one of the best ways to plan a computer program. For example, here is a pseudocode outline of a Pascal program to find the largest of a set of 10 numbers:

```
begin
  repeat
    read a number;
    test whether it is the largest found so far
  until 10 numbers have been read;
  print the largest
end.
```

Here is the program that results from translating all of the pseudocode into genuine Pascal:

```
PROGRAM findthelargest (INPUT, OUTPUT);
VAR num, largest, count : INTEGER;
BEGIN
    count := 0;
    largest := 0;
    REPEAT
      count := count + 1;
      read(num);
      IF num > largest THEN largest := num;
      UNTIL count = 10;
      writeln('The largest number was ',largest)
END.
```

(This program assumes that the largest number will be greater than zero.)

The advantage of pseudocode is that it allows the programmer to concentrate on how the program works while ignoring the details of the language. By reducing the number of things the programmer must think about at once, this technique effectively amplifies the programmer's intelligence.

public domain the status of literature, art, music, or software that was not copyrighted, or whose copyright has expired and not been renewed.

A computer program is in the public domain if it is not covered by any kind of copyright. Few substantial public-domain programs exist, but the term "public domain" is often used incorrectly to describe other kinds of freely copyable software (*see* FREE SOFTWARE). *See also* COPYRIGHT.

public key a publicly revealed password used for encoding private messages to a particular recipient. The recipient then uses his or her own secret PRIVATE KEY to decrypt the message. *See* ENCRYPTION.

public html typical name for the directory in which an individual user's WEB PAGE is stored under UNIX.

pull the process whereby the user retrieves information from a network at the user's request, as in traditional web browsing; *contrast* PUSH (definition 2).

pull-down menu a menu that appears when a particular item in a menu bar is selected. *See also* MENU BAR. *Contrast* ROLL-UP MENU.

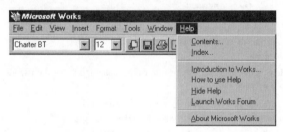

FIGURE 207. Pull-down menu

Puma version 10.1 of MAC OS X.

punched card a stiff paper card on which holes can be punched to encode data that can be read by a computer. In the 1960s, punched cards were the dominant way of feeding programs into computers, but they have now been replaced by interactive keyboards. Punched cards are still used in some voting systems. (*see* CHAD).

IBM punched cards had 80 columns, each with 12 positions to accommodate a rectangular hole, and each card corresponded to one line of a text file. Univac cards had 90 columns, with circular holes. The use of punched cards for data processing actually preceded the invention of the computer by more than 50 years. Herman Hollerith realized that it took several years to process data from the 1880 census. He calculated that, unless a faster method was found, the U.S. Census Bureau would still be working on the results from the 1890 census when it came time to start the 1900 census. Hollerith developed a system in which census data were punched on cards, and machines were used to sort and tabulate the cards. Even earlier, in 1801, a system of punched cards was used to direct the weaving pattern on the automatic Jacquard loom in France.

Punycode an Internet standard for transforming Unicode character strings into ASCII character strings (*see* UNICODE; ASCII). The results are not intended to be readable but merely to create a unique representation from which the original Unicode can be retrieved.

The encoding consists of "xn--" followed by the ASCII characters from the original string (if any), a hyphen, and further ASCII characters whose numerical values indicate changes to be made in order to recover the Unicode. For example, résumé encodes as xn--rsum-bpad.

Punycode is used in order to allow non-ASCII characters in Internet domain addresses.

purge to discard data that is no longer wanted; in an e-mail reading program, to discard messages that have been marked for deletion.

push

1. to place an item on a stack. See LIFO; STACK.

2. to deliver information to a client machine without waiting for the user to request it. Push technology makes the World Wide Web work rather like TV; the user selects a "channel" and views whatever is being sent out at the moment. This contrasts with the way web browsers traditionally work, where the user manually selects information to retrieve from the Web. (*Contrast* PULL.) Push technology is useful for delivering information that has to be updated minute by minute, such as stock market quotes or news bulletins. (*See* RSS.) However, the user demand for push technology is not what had once been expected. Users do not want to give up control of the Internet in order to watch it passively like television.

push technology *see* PUSH (definition 2).

pushdown stack, pushdown store a data structure from which items can only be removed in the opposite of the order in which they were stored. See STACK.

pushing the envelope working close to, or at, physical or technological limits. *See* ENVELOPE.

PvE (**P**layer versus **E**nvironment) a type of game where players overcome challenges given to them by the game itself rather than by other players.

PvP (**P**layer versus **P**layer) a type of game where players compete against each other.

pyramid scheme (Ponzi scheme) a get-rich-quick scheme in which early participants receive money from later participants. For example, you might receive a message containing a list of names. You're expected to send money to the first person on the list, cross the first name off, add your name at the bottom, and distribute copies of the message.

Pyramid schemes are presently common on the Internet, but they are illegal in all 50 states and in most other parts of the world. They can't work because there is no way for everyone to receive more money than they send out; money doesn't come out of thin air. As the number of participants increases, an even greater number of other participants need to be recruited to keep the scheme going, and soon the scheme hits a limit on the number of available people. Pyramid schemers often claim the scheme is legal, but that doesn't make it so. *See also* COMPUTER LAW.

```python
# File plural6.py -M. Covington 2002
# Python function to form English plurals

def pluralize(s):

    "Forms the plural of an English noun"

    # Exception dictionary. More could be added.

    e = { "child"    : "children",
          "corpus"   : "corpora",
          "ox"       : "oxen" }

    # Look up the plural, or form it regularly

    if e.has_key(s):
       return e[s]

    elif s[-1] == "s" \
      or s[-2:] == "sh" \
      or s[-2:] == "ch":
       return s + "es"

    else:
       return s + "s"
```

FIGURE 208. Python program

Python a programming language invented by Guido van Rossum for quick, easy construction of relatively small programs, especially those that involve character string operations. Figure 208 shows a simple Python program that forms the plurals of English nouns.

Python is quickly replacing Awk and Perl as a scripting language. Like those languages, it is run by an interpreter, not a compiler. That makes it easy to store programs compactly as source code and then run them when needed. It is also easy to embed operating system commands in the program.

Python is also popular for teaching programming to non-programmers, since even a small, partial knowledge of the language enables people to write useful programs.

The syntax of Python resembles C and Java, except that instead of enclosing them in braces, groups of statements, such as the interior of a while loop, are indicated simply by indentation.

Powerful data structures are easy to create in Python. These include lists and *dictionaries,* where a dictionary is an array whose elements are identified by character strings. Operations such as sorting, searching, and data conversion are built in.

Free Python interpreters and more information can be obtained from *www.python.org. See also* AWK; INTERPRETER; PERL; STRING OPERATIONS.

Q

QoS Quality of Service

QR code (**Q**uick **R**esponse code) a type of two-dimensional square BAR CODE originally invented by a subsidiary of Toyota for use in a manufacturing process, but now commonly used to label commercial products, advertisements, and signs with information to be decoded by smart phones with cameras. Although it can contain any type of data, a QR code normally contains a web address, and the user can browse to that web address by aiming his smartphone camera at the QR code. *Caution*: By substituting QR codes (using stickers or the like), a prankster can trick people into going to a malicious or fake web site.

FIGURE 209. QR code that says http://www.termbook.com
(the address of this book's web page)

quad-core having four CPU cores. *See* CORE (definition 1).

quantum computing a possible method for creating future computers based on the laws of quantum mechanics. Classical computers rely on physical devices that have two distinct states (1 and 0). In quantum mechanics, a particle is actually a wave function that can exist as a superposition (combination) of different states. A quantum computer would be built with *qubits* rather than bits. Theoretical progress has been made in designing a quantum computer that could perform computations on many numbers at once, which could make it possible to solve problems now intractable, such as factoring very large numbers. However, there are still practical difficulties that would need to be solved before such a computer could be built.

quantum cryptography an experimental method for securely transmitting encryption keys by using individual photons of polarized light. A fundamental principle of quantum mechanics, the Heisenberg uncertainty principle, makes it impossible for anyone to observe a photon without disturbing it. Therefore, it would be impossible for an eavesdropper to observe the signal without being detected. *See* ENCRYPTION.

qubit a **qu**antum **bit**. *See* QUANTUM COMPUTING.

query language a language used to express queries to be answered by a database system. For an example, *see* SQL.

queue
1. a data structure from which items are removed in the same order in which they were entered. *See* FIFO. *Contrast* STACK.
2. a list, maintained by the operating system, of jobs waiting to be printed or processed in some other way. *See* PRINT SPOOLER.

Quicken a popular financial record keeping program produced by INTUIT.

Quicksort a sorting algorithm invented by C. A. R. Hoare and first published in 1962. Quicksort is faster than any other sorting algorithm available unless the items are already in nearly the correct order, in which case it is relatively inefficient (*compare* MERGE SORT).

Quicksort is a recursive procedure (*see* RECURSION). In each iteration, it rearranges the list of items so that one item (the "pivot") is in its final position, all the items that should come before it are before it, and all the items that should come after it are after it. Then the lists of items preceding and following the pivot are treated as sublists and sorted in the same way. Figure 210 shows how this works:

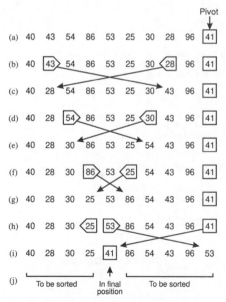

FIGURE 210. Quicksort in action

```java
class quicksortprogram
{
/* This Java program sorts an array using Quicksort. */
 static int a[]  = {29,18,7,56,64,33,128,70,78,81,12,5};
 static int num  = 12; /* number of items in array */
 static int max  = num-1; /* maximum array subscript */

 static void swap(int i, int j)
 {
  int t=a[i]; a[i]=a[j]; a[j]=t;
 }

 static int partition(int first, int last)
 {
 /* Partitions    a[first]...a[last]    into 2   sub-arrays
    using a[first] as pivot. Value returned is position
    where pivot ends up. */

  int pivot = a[first];
  int i = first;
  int j = last+1;

  do
  {
    do { i++; } while ((i<=max) && (a[i]<pivot));
    do { j--; } while ((j<=max) && (a[j]>pivot));
    if (i<j) { swap(i,j); }
  }
  while (j>i);

  swap(j,first);
  return j;
 }

 static void quicksort(int first, int last)
 {
   /* Sorts the sub-array from a[first] to a[last]. */
   int p=0;
   if (first<last)
   {
     p=partition(first,last); /* p = position of pivot */
     quicksort(first,p-1);
     quicksort(p+1,last);
   }
 }

 public static void main(String args[])
 {
   quicksort(0,max);
   for (int i=0; i<=max; i++)
   {
      System.out.println(a[i]);
   }
 }
}
```

FIGURE 211. Quicksort

(a) Choose the last item in the list, 41, as the pivot. It is excluded from the searching and swapping that follow.

(b), (c) Identify the leftmost item greater than 41 and the rightmost item less than 41. Swap them.

(d), (e), (f), (g) Repeat steps (b) and (c) until the leftmost and rightmost markers meet in the middle.

(h), (i) Now that the markers have met and crossed, swap the pivot with the item pointed to by the leftmost marker.

(j) Now that the pivot is in its final position, sort each of the two sublists to the left and in right of it. Quicksort is difficult to express in languages, such as BASIC, that do not allow recursion. The amount of memory required by Quicksort increases exponentially with the depth of the recursion. One way to limit memory requirements is to switch to another type of sort, such as selection sort, after a certain depth is reached. (*See* SELECTION SORT.) Figure 211 shows the Quicksort algorithm expressed in Java.

QuickTime a standard digital video and multimedia framework originally developed for Macintosh computers, but now available for Windows-based systems. The *QuickTime Player* plays back videos and other multimedia presentations and is available as a free download from *www. apple.com/downloads*.

The premium version of QuickTime provides video editing capability as well as the ability to save QuickTime movies (.mov files). *Compare* AVI FILE; MOV.

quit to clear an application program from memory; to EXIT. Most software prompts you to save changes to disk before quitting. Read all message boxes carefully.

R

race condition, race hazard in digital circuit design, a situation where two signals are "racing" to the same component from different places, and although intended to be simultaneous, they do not arrive at exactly the same time. Thus, for a brief moment, the component at the destination receives an incorrect combination of inputs.

radial fill a way of filling a graphical object with two colors such that one color is at the center, and there is a smooth transition to another color at the edges. *See* FOUNTAIN FILL. *Contrast* LINEAR FILL.

FIGURE 212. Radial fill

radian measure a way of measuring the size of angles in which a complete rotation measures 2π radians. The trigonometric functions in most computer languages expect their arguments to be expressed in radians. To convert degrees to radians, multiply by $\pi/180$ (approximately $1/57.296$).

radio a device that receives radio signals. Mobile devices may contain one radio to receive GPS signals, another radio for WiFi signals, and another radio to receive signals from cellphone towers. *See* ELECTRO-MAGNETIC RADIATION.

radio buttons small circles in a dialog box, only one of which can be chosen at a time. The chosen button is black and the others are white. Choosing any button with the mouse causes all the other buttons in the set to be cleared. Radio buttons acquired their name because they work like the pushbuttons on older car radios. Also called OPTION BUTTONS.

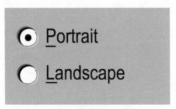

FIGURE 213. Radio buttons

radix the base of a number system. Binary numbers have a radix of 2, and decimal numbers have a radix of 10.

radix sort an algorithm that puts data in order by classifying each item immediately rather than comparing it to other items. For example, you might sort cards with names on them by putting all the A's in one bin, all the B's in another bin, and so on. You could then sort the contents of each bin the same way using the second letter of each name, and so on. The radix sort method can be used effectively with binary numbers, since there are only two possible bins for the items to be placed. For other sorting methods, *see* SORT and references there.

ragged margin a margin that has not been evened out by justification and at which the ends of words do not line up.

> This is
> an example of
> flush-left, ragged-right type.

See also FLUSH LEFT, FLUSH RIGHT.

RAID (**r**edundant **a**rray of **i**nexpensive **d**isks) a combination of disk drives that function as a single disk drive with higher speed, reliability, or both. There are several numbered "levels" of RAID.

RAID 0 ("striping") uses a pair of disk drives with alternate sectors written on alternate disks, so that when a large file is read or written, each disk can be transferring data while the other one is moving to the next sector. There is no error protection.

RAID 1 ("mirroring") uses two disks which are copies of each other. If either disk fails, its contents are preserved on the other one. You can even replace the failed disk with a new, blank one, and the data will be copied to it automatically with no interruption in service.

RAID 2 (rarely used) performs striping of individual bits rather than blocks, so that, for instance, to write an 8-bit byte, you need 8 disks. Additional disks contain bits for an error-correcting code so that any missing bits can be reconstructed. Reliability is very high, and any single disk can be replaced at any time with no loss of data.

RAID 3 (also uncommon) performs striping at the byte rather than bit or sector level, with error correction.

RAID 4 performs striping at the level of sectors (blocks) like RAID 0, but also includes an additional disk for error checking.

RAID 5 is like RAID 4 except that the error-checking blocks are not all stored on the same disk; spreading them among different disks helps equalize wear and improve speed. RAID 5 is one of the most popular configurations. If any single disk fails, all its contents can be reconstructed just as in RAID 1 or 2.

RAID 6 is like RAID 5 but uses double error checking and can recover from the failure of any two disks, not just one.

Caution: RAID systems do not eliminate the need for backups. Even if a RAID system is perfectly reliable, you will still need backups to retrieve data that is accidentally deleted and to recover from machine failures that affect all the disks at once.

railroad diagram a diagram illustrating the syntax of a programming language or document definition. Railroad-like switches are used to indicate possible locations of different elements. Figure 214 shows an example illustrating the syntax of an address label. First name, last name, and City-State-Zip Code are required elements, so all possible routes include those elements. Either Mr. or Ms. is required, so there are two possible tracks there. A middle name is optional, so one track bypasses that element. There may be more than one address line, so there is a return loop track providing for multiple passes through that element. *Compare* BACKUS-NAUR FORM. *See* PARSING.

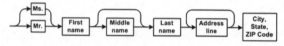

FIGURE 214. Railroad diagram

RAM (**R**andom-**A**ccess **M**emory) a memory device whereby any location in memory can be found as quickly as any other location. A computer's RAM is its main working memory. The size of the RAM (measured in megabytes or gigabytes) is an important indicator of the capacity of the computer. *See* DRAM; EDO; MEMORY.

random-access device any memory device in which it is possible to find any particular record as quickly, on average, as any other record. The computer's internal RAM and disk storage devices are examples of random-access devices. *Contrast* SEQUENTIAL-ACCESS DEVICE.

random-access memory *see* RAM.

random-number generator a computer program that calculates numbers that seem to have been chosen randomly. In reality, a computer cannot generate numbers that are truly random, since it always generates the numbers according to a deterministic rule.

However, certain generating rules produce numbers whose behavior is unpredictable enough that they can be treated as random numbers for practical purposes. Random-number generators are useful in writing programs involving games of chance, and they are also used in an important simulation technique called MONTE CARLO SIMULATION.

range the set of all possible output values from a mathematical function. *Contrast* DOMAIN (definition 1).

rapid prototyping the construction of prototype machines quickly with computer aid. Computerized CAD-CAM equipment, such as milling machines and THREE-DIMENSIONAL PRINTERS, can produce machine parts directly from computer-edited designs.

raster graphics graphics in which an image is generated by scanning an entire screen or page and marking every point as black, white, or another color, as opposed to VECTOR GRAPHICS.

A video screen and a laser printer are raster graphics devices; a pen plotter is a vector graphics device because it marks only at specified points on the page.

raster image processor (**RIP**) a device that handles computer output as a grid of dots. Dot-matrix, inkjet, and laser printers are all raster image processors.

rasterize to convert an image into a bitmap of the right size and shape to match a raster graphics output device. *See* BITMAP; RASTER GRAPHICS; VECTOR GRAPHICS.

RAW in digital photography, unprocessed; the actual binary data from the camera, with, at most, only the processing that is unavoidably done by the camera itself. Although commonly written uppercase (*RAW*), this is simply the familiar word *raw,* meaning "uncooked."

Raw image files contain more detail than JPEG compressed images but are much larger and can only be read by special software.

ray tracing the computation of the paths of rays of light reflected and/or bent by various substances.

Ray-tracing effects define lighting, shadows, reflections, and transparency. Such computations often are very lengthy and may require several hours of computer time to produce a RENDERING (realistic drawing of three-dimensional objects by computer).

RCA plug (also called PHONO PLUG) an inexpensive shielded plug sometimes used for audio and composite video signals (*see* Figure 215); it plugs straight in without twisting or locking. *Contrast* BNC CONNECTOR.

FIGURE 215. RCA plug

RDRAM (**R**ambus **d**ynamic **r**andom **a**ccess **m**emory) a type of high-speed RAM commonly used with the Pentium IV, providing a bus speed on the order of 500 MHz. *Contrast* SDRAM.

RE abbreviation for REGULAR EXPRESSION.

read to transfer information from an external medium (e.g., a keyboard or flash drive) into a computer.

read-only pre-recorded and unable to be changed. *See* ATTRIBUTES; CD-ROM; LOCK; WRITE-PROTECT.

read-only memory computer memory that is permanently recorded and cannot be changed. *See* ROM.

readme (from *read me*) the name given to files that the user of a piece of software is supposed to read before using it. The readme file contains the latest information from the manufacturer; it often contains major corrections to the instruction manual.

real estate (*informal*) space on a flat surface of limited size, such as a motherboard (on which different components consume different amounts of real estate) or even a computer screen. *Compare* SCREEN ESTATE.

real number any number that can be represented either as an integer or a decimal fraction with any finite or infinite number of digits. Real numbers correspond to points on a number line.

Examples are 0, 2.5, 345, -2134, 0.00003, $\frac{1}{3}$, $\sqrt{2}$ and π. However, $\sqrt{-1}$ is not a real number (it does not exist anywhere among the positive or negative numbers). *Contrast* COMPLEX NUMBER.

On computers, real numbers are represented with a finite number of digits, thus limiting their accuracy. *See* ROUNDING ERROR.

In many programming languages, "real number" means "floating-point number." *See* DOUBLE; FLOATING-POINT NUMBER.

real-time programming programming in which the proper functioning of the program depends on the amount of time consumed. For instance, computers that control automatic machinery must often both detect and introduce time delays of accurately determined lengths.

RealAudio a communication protocol developed by Real Networks (*www. realaudio.com*) that allows audio signals to be broadcast over the Internet. The user hears the signal in real time, rather than waiting for an audio file to be downloaded and then played. RealAudio is used to distribute radio broadcasts. *See* INTERNET RADIO; PROTOCOL.

RealPlayer a widely used program for playing RealAudio files, distributed by Real Networks. *See* REALAUDIO.

ream 500 sheets of paper.

reblog to post, in one's own blog, content that was previously posted by another blogger. Reblogging is common on the microblogging site TUMBLR.

reboot to restart a computer (i.e., turn it off and then on again). Many operating systems, including UNIX and Windows, have to be shut down properly before power to the computer is turned off; otherwise, data will be lost. *See* BOOT; CTRL-ALT-DEL; SAFE MODE.

record a collection of related data items. For example, a company may store information about each employee in a single record. Each record consists of several fields—a field for the name, a field for a Social Security number, and so on.

The Pascal keyword record corresponds to struct in C. *See* STRUCT.

In object-oriented languages, the same concept is used in a more general fashion: an OBJECT can include methods as well as data items.

recovering erased files retrieval of deleted files whose space has not yet been overwritten by other data.

In Windows and on the Macintosh, deleted files usually go into a TRASH can or RECYCLE BIN from which they can be retrieved. The disk space is not actually freed until the user empties the trash. Until then, the files can be restored to their original locations.

Even after the trash can or recycle bin has been emptied, the physical disk space that the file occupied is marked as free, but it is not actually overwritten until the space is needed for something else. If you erase a file accidentally, you can often get it back by using special software. As soon as you realize you want to recover a file, do everything you can to stop other programs from writing on the same disk so that nothing else will be written in the space that the file occupied.

recursion the calling of a procedure by itself, creating a new copy of the procedure.

To allow recursion, a programming language must allow for local variables (thus, recursion is not easy to accomplish in most versions of BASIC). Each time the procedure is called, it needs to keep track of values for the variables that may be different from the values they had the last time the procedure was called. Therefore, a recursive procedure that calls itself many times can consume a lot of memory.

Recursion is the natural way to solve problems that contain smaller problems of the same kind. Examples include drawing some kinds of fractals (*see* FRACTAL); parsing structures that can have similar structures inside them (*see* PARSING); sorting (*see* QUICKSORT); and calculating the determinant of a matrix by breaking it up into smaller matrices.

A recursive procedure can be used to calculate the factorial of an integer. (*See* FACTORIAL.) Figure 216 shows a program that does so.

A simple example of recursion involves finding factorials, defined as follows:

1. The factorial of 0 or 1 is 1.
2. The factorial of any larger whole number x is x times the factorial of $x - 1$.

This definition is recursive in step 2, because to find a factorial, you have to find another factorial. It can be translated directly into a recursive computer program (Figure 214). Admittedly, this is not the fastest way to do the computation, but it is a classic example.

```java
class factorial_program {

  /* Java     program     to     find     the     factorial     of     a
     whole number (4 in this example) by recursion */
  static int factorial(int x)
  {
    System.out.println("Now looking for factorial of " + x);
    int z=1;
    if (x<1)
    {
      z=1;
    }
    else
    {
      z=x*factorial(x-1); /* this is the recursive step */
    }
    System.out.println("The factorial of "+x+" is " + z);
    return z;
  }

  public static void main(String args[])
  {
    System.out.println(factorial(4));
  }
}
```

FIGURE 216. Recursion

In the program, the recursion occurs when the function `factorial` calls itself. Note that the `else` clause is crucial. That clause gives a non-recursive definition for the factorial of zero. If it were not there, the program would end up in an endless loop as the function `factorial` kept calling itself until the computer ran out of memory. Any time recursion is used, it is necessary to make sure that there is some condition that will cause the recursion to halt.

Following is an example of the output from this program when the number 4 is given as the input. In practice, you would want to remove the two `println` statements from the function, but they are included here to make it possible to see the order of execution.

```
Now looking for factorial of 4
Now looking for factorial of 3
Now looking for factorial of 2
Now looking for factorial of 1
Now looking for factorial of 0
The factorial of 0 is 1
The factorial of 1 is 1
The factorial of 2 is 2
The factorial of 3 is 6
The factorial of 4 is 24
24
```

Any iterative (repetitive) program can be expressed recursively, and recursion is the normal way of expressing repetition in Prolog and Lisp.

Recycle Bin in Windows, the place where deleted files are stored, corresponding to the TRASH on the Macintosh. You can put a file in the Recycle Bin by dragging it there or by choosing "delete" in Explorer and similar applications. Files in the Recycle Bin still occupy disk space and are retrievable. To reclaim the disk space, empty the Recycle Bin.

FIGURE 217. Recycle Bin

Red Book the Philips/Sony standard format for audio compact discs. *See* CD.

Red Hat a company headquartered in Raleigh, N.C., that sponsors the Red Hat and Fedora distributions of Linux. Red Hat distributions were originally freeware, but the current product, Red Hat Enterprise Linux, is commercially licensed and supported. It is recommended for organizations that need commercial support for Linux. The freeware Red Hat project continues under the name Fedora. For more information see *www.redhat.com. See also* FEDORA. *Compare* DEBIAN, UBUNTU. (It's not related to BLACK HAT or WHITE HAT despite the similar name.)

redirect in HTML, a tag causing the browser to go to another web page without requiring the user to click. This is achieved with an HTML instruction such as:

```
<META HTTP-EQUIV="Refresh" CONTENT="0; URL=www.termbook.com">
```

This means: "Refresh (reload) this page immediately (after 0 seconds) from a different address, namely *www.termbook.com*."

redline to mark a portion of a printed document that has been changed. Redlining is usually a line (originally red) in the margin or a gray shading applied to the marked area. It is used with manuals, laws, regulations, and the like, where changes need to be marked.

redo to reverse the effect of the most recent UNDO command.

redundancy

1. unnecessary repetition; lack of conciseness. Data files can be compressed by removing redundancy and expressing the same data more concisely. *See* DATA COMPRESSION.

2. the provision of extra information or extra hardware to increase reliability. For example, a simple way to protect a message from errors in transmission is to transmit it twice. It is very unlikely that both copies will be corrupted in exactly the same way. *See* ERROR-CORRECTING CODE.

Redundant hardware is extra hardware, such as one disk drive serving as a backup for another. *See also* RAID.

reentrant procedure a procedure that has been implemented in such a way that more than one process can execute it at the same time without conflict. *See* MULTITASKING.

refactoring the process of reorganizing a computer program without changing its functionality. Refactoring a program usually means dividing it up into conceptual units and eliminating repetitious code.

referential integrity in a database, the requirement that everything mentioned in a particular field of one table must be defined in another table. As an example, consider a database with two tables, one listing customers and their addresses, and the other listing orders the customers have placed. A referential integrity requirement might specify that every customer who appears in the order table must also be listed in the customer table.

reflection the ability of a computer program to obtain information about itself. Some computer languages, such as LISP and PROLOG, support extensive reflection; the program can treat itself as data. In Microsoft .NET Framework, the reflection subsystem allows a running program to obtain information about its classes (object types). *See* CLASS.

reflow (rewrap) to rearrange a written text so that the ends of lines come out more even. For example, reflowing will change this text:

```
Four score and seven years ago our
forefathers
brought forth upon this continent a
new
nation, conceived in liberty. . .
```

into this:

```
Four score and seven years ago our
forefathers brought forth upon this
continent a new nation, conceived in
liberty. . .
```

Reflowing changes the total number of lines and thus the positions of the page breaks. *See* WORD WRAP.

refresh
1. to update the contents of a window to show information that has changed; to REPAINT the screen.
2. to RELOAD the contents of a WEB PAGE from the machine on which it resides.
3. to regenerate the display on a CRT screen by scanning the screen with an electron beam. Though it seems to, the screen does not glow

continuously; instead, it is refreshed 30 to 90 times per second, rather like a movie screen.

4. to freshen the contents of a memory chip. Dynamic RAM chips have to be refreshed many times per second; on each refresh cycle, they read their own contents and then store the same information back into the same memory location.

refresh rate the rate at which a CRT screen is repeatedly scanned to keep the image constantly visible; typically 30 to 90 hertz (cycles per second). A faster refresh rate gives an image less prone to flicker. Since LCD displays hold the image in memory, the refresh rate is not critical.

regional settings the settings in an operating system that pertain to the user's location, such as language, currency, and time zone.

register
    1. a collection of FLIP-FLOPS used to store a group of binary digits (bits) while the computer is processing them. (*See* COMPUTER-ARCHITECTURE.)
    2. to inform a manufacturer of a purchase (*see* REGISTRATION, definition 1).
    The word *register* has many other meanings in business and education; only those specific to computers are covered here.

registrar an organization authorized to register TLD. For example, the domain *covingtoninnovations.com* belongs to some of the authors of this book because they have registered it with a registrar.

registration
    1. the act of informing the manufacturer of a product that you have purchased and installed it. Registering software is a good idea because it makes you eligible for customer support and upgrades from the manufacturer.
    2. the alignment of color plates in a multi-color printing job on a printing press. If the colors are not perfectly aligned, there may be MOIRÉS, or there may be unintentional gaps between colors. *See* TRAPPING.
    3. the recording of information in the Windows Registry or similar configuration files. *See* REGISTRY.

Registry the part of Windows that stores setup information for the hardware, software, and operating system. It takes over most of the functions performed by INI files in earlier versions of Windows.
    The information in the Registry is supplied by the Control Panel and the setup routines for particular applications. You can also view the contents of the Registry directly by choosing Run from the START MENU and typing regedit. This is rarely necessary unless unusual problems arise. *See* HIVE.

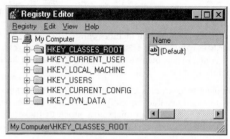

FIGURE 218. Registry Editor (Regedit)

regular expression a way of defining a possible series of characters. Table
12 gives some examples. In UNIX, the grep command searches a file for
character strings that match a regular expression; regular expressions are
also used in several programming languages and in some editors. *See*
AWK; GREP; PERL.

TABLE 12
REGULAR EXPRESSIONS

Expression	Matches
abc	The string abc
a.c	Like abc but with any character in place of b
a*bc	Zero or more a's, followed by bc
a*b+c	Zero or more a's, one or more b's, and c
*	An asterisk
\\	A backslash
[BbCx]	The character B, b, C, or x
[A-E2-4]	The character A, B, C, D, E, 2, 3, or 4
[^A-E2-4]	Any character except A, B, C, D, E, 2, 3, or 4
[Ff]ill	Fill or fill
^abc	abc at beginning of line
abc$	abc at end of line

Regular expressions are efficient to process because the computer can
always tell whether a string matches a regular expression by working
through the string and the expression from left to right, one item at a
time. This is simpler than the methods used to parse Backus-Naur form
or other kinds of syntactic description. *See* BACKUS-NAUR FORM;
PARSING.

relational database a database that consists of tables made up of rows and columns. For example:

Name	City	State
Downing, D.	Seattle	Washington
Covington, M.	Athens	Georgia

The table defines a relation between the things in each row. It says that Seattle is the city for Downing, Athens is the city for Covington, and so on.

One important operation in a relational database is to *join* two tables (i.e., cross-reference information between them). For example, the names in this table could be cross-referenced to another table containing names and salaries; the result would be a table relating name, city, state, and salary.

A database with only one table is called a *flat-file database.* Every relational database has a *query language* for expressing commands to retrieve data. *See* PIVOT TABLE; QUERY LANGUAGE; SQL.

relative address
1. in computer memory, a memory address measured relative to another location. To convert a relative address into an absolute (true) address it is necessary to add the address of the point it is measured from. *Compare* OFFSET.
2. in a spreadsheet program, a cell address that indicates the position of a cell relative to another cell. If this formula is copied to another location, the address will be changed so that it refers to the cell in the same position relative to the new cell. In Lotus 1-2-3 and Microsoft Excel, a cell address is treated as a relative address unless it contains dollar signs. (*See* ABSOLUTE ADDRESS.) For example, if the formula 2*D7 is entered into the cell E9, the D7 in the formula really means, "the cell that is one column to the left and two rows above." If this formula is now copied to cell H15, the formula will now become 2*G13, since G13 is the cell that is one column to the left and two rows above the cell H15.

relative URL a URL for a document in the same directory as the current document. For example, if a web page contains the link <a href="doc1.html"> it will look for the document doc1.html in the same directory as the page containing the link. If you copy both of these files to a different directory or different machine, the link will still work. *Contrast* ABSOLUTE URL.

release
1. the edition or version number of a software product. Most commonly, whole-number increments in the release number (e.g., from 1.0 to 2.0) signify a major upgrade to the program. Fractional increases are for minor upgrades and bug fixes.
2. to let go of the mouse button. *Contrast* CLICK; PRESS.

reload to obtain a fresh copy of information that is already in a computer; an example is reloading a WEB PAGE that may have changed recently, rather than viewing a copy stored in a CACHE on your own computer.

remote located on a computer far away from the user. *Contrast* LOCAL.

Remote Desktop a feature of some versions of Microsoft Windows that allows one computer to serve as the screen, keyboard, and mouse of another; thus, any computer can be operated remotely. This is particularly handy for administering servers that may be located in a different room.

To enable remote access to a computer, go to Control Panel, System, Remote, and turn on remote access. Add one or more user accounts to the Remote Desktop Users security group. If the computers involved are separated by a firewall, make sure port 3389 traffic is allowed between them.

Once you have made a computer accessible, you can "remote in" to it from a second computer by going to Programs, Accessories, Communication, Remote Desktop Connection, and typing its network address. The host computer's desktop will be a window on the screen of the client computer.

Common versions of Windows allow one or two remote users at a time. Server versions can be licensed to allow larger numbers of users.

remoting the spreading of a computational task across multiple computers in different locations.

remove spots a paint program filter that erases spots from digitized photographs and pictures. Technically, it removes all pixel groups below a certain size; image detail may be lost.

render (3-D program) to apply a color, texture, and lighting to a WIREFRAME model.

rendering the technology of drawing three-dimensional objects realistically on a computer. It involves computations of texture and light reflections. Rendering is performed automatically by VRML viewers. *See also* RAY TRACING; VRML.

repaginate to allow a word processor or page layout program to reposition page breaks by working forward from the current cursor position. *See also* REFLOW; WRAP.

repaint to regenerate the display on all or part of a computer screen.

repeat keyword used to define one kind of loop in Pascal. The word REPEAT marks the beginning of the loop, and the word UNTIL marks the end. Here is an example:

```
REPEAT
  writeln(x);
  x := 2*x;
  writeln('Type S if you want to stop.');
  readln(c); {c is of type CHAR}
UNTIL c = 'S';
```

The computer always executes the loop at least once because it does not check to see whether the stopping condition is true until after it has executed the loop. *See* DO. *Contrast* WHILE.

repeater a device that receives signals by network cable or by radio and retransmits them, thereby overcoming limits of cable length or radio range. A repeater can also conserve BANDWIDTH by retransmitting only the data packets that are addressed to sites in its area.

required hyphen a hyphen that does not indicate a place where a word can be broken apart. For instance, if the hyphenated word "flip-flop" falls at the end of the line, then "flip-" can appear on one line, with "flop" at the beginning of the next. But if you type "flip-flop" with a required hyphen, it will not be split up. In Microsoft Word, to type a required hyphen (also called a NON-BREAKING HYPHEN), press Ctrl-Shift and the hyphen key together.

required space a space that does not denote a place where words can be split apart at the end of a line. For instance, you might not want a person's initials (as in "T. S. Eliot") to be split at the end of a line. You should therefore use required spaces between them rather than ordinary spaces. In T$_E$X, a required space is typed as ~ (TILDE). In Microsoft Word, a required space (also called a NON-BREAKING SPACE) is typed by pressing Ctrl-Shift and the space bar together.

resample to change the size of a bitmap image or the SAMPLING RATE of a digital audio file, using interpolation to fill in the intermediate samples (Figure 219). *See also* INTERPOLATION (definition 2).

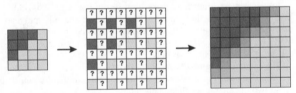

FIGURE 219. Resampling (interpolation) to enlarge an image

reseat to remove an integrated circuit (IC) or a printed circuit board from its socket and reinsert it. This often yields a better electrical connection.

reserve price a secret minimum bid in an auction. Ordinarily, the minimum bid (the lowest price that the seller will take) is announced to would-be buyers. However, auction services such as eBay allow the seller to specify a secret minimum bid, called a reserve price. The amount of the reserve price is not disclosed, but bids below it do not result in a sale. *See* AUCTION; EBAY.

reserved word a word that has a special meaning in a particular programming language and cannot be used as a variable name. For example, in C and its derivatives, if is a reserved word. COBOL has dozens of reserved words. Fortran and PL/I have none, since in these languages it is always possible to tell from the context whether or not a word is a variable name. *See* KEYWORD.

resistance the measure of how difficult it is for electric current to flow through a circuit or component. Resistance is measured in a unit called the ohm. *See* OHM'S LAW.

resize to change the size or dimensions of; to SCALE.

To resize an object interactively with the mouse in most environments, select the object, and then drag one of the HANDLEs in the desired direction. Dragging a corner handle will keep the vertical and horizontal aspects of the object in the same proportion to each other (like reducing or enlarging something on a photocopier). Dragging one of the handles at the midpoint of the BOUNDING BOX will affect only one dimension of the object. This way, you can stretch or shrink the object to the desired shape.

resolution a measure of the amount of detail that can be shown in the images produced by a printer or screen. For instance, many laser printers have a resolution of 600 dots per inch (dpi), which means that they print characters using a grid of black and white squares each 1/600 of an inch across. This means that their resolution is 300 lines per inch when printing line art, or 100 lines per inch when printing halftone shadings (such as photographs), which use pixels in groups of six.

Inkjet printers often have very high resolution (e.g., 2800 dots per inch), which means they control the position of the ink sprayer to a precision of 1/2800 inch. The actual dots of colored ink are much larger than 1/2800 inch in size. However, halftoning is not needed; each dot can be any color or shade of gray.

The human eye normally resolves about 150 lines per inch at normal reading distance, but a person examining a page critically can distinguish two or three times this much detail.

The resolution of a screen is given as the total number of pixels in each direction (e.g., 1024 × 768 pixels across the whole screen). The equivalent number of dots per inch depends on the size of the screen. Present-day video screens resolve about 100 dots per inch; they are not nearly as sharp as ink on paper.

A big advantage of draw programs, as opposed to paint programs, is that they can use the full resolution of the printer; they are not limited to printing what they display on the screen. However, some paint programs can handle very detailed images by displaying only part of the image at a time. *See* DRAW PROGRAM; PAINT PROGRAM; VECTOR GRAPHICS.

resource
  1. anything of value that is available for use. *Resources* can refer to computers on a network, preallocated memory blocks in an operating system, or money in a budget.
  2. a modifiable part of a program, separate from the program instructions themselves. Resources include menus, icons, and fonts.

resource leak *see* LEAK.

restart (in Windows) to REBOOT.

restore to make a window go back to its previous size after being minimized or maximized. In Windows, the restore button is to the right of the minimize button on the title bar and alternates with the maximize (fullscreen) button. Or, right-click the application's icon on the taskbar; the top choice of the pop-up menu is "Restore."
  See also MAXIMIZE; MINIMIZE; WINDOW.

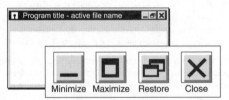

FIGURE 220. Restore button

retouching the alteration of a digital image to change its content, e.g., by removing visible blemishes on the skin of a person in a portrait. *See* PHOTOPAINT PROGRAM. Because they are so easily retouched, digital images are not usable as evidence (in science or in courtrooms) unless their authenticity can be proven. Retouching is different from image processing, which involves applying a uniform transformation to the entire image to enhance the visibility of information already contained in the image.

retrocomputing the hobby of preserving old computer technology, either by maintaining the machines themselves or by emulating them on newer equipment. *See* Figure 221.

FIGURE 221. Retrocomputing: a 1981 computer
emulated under Windows 2000

return

1. the keyboard key that transmits ASCII code 13 (CR), normally the same as the Enter key. *See* CR.

2. to give a value as a result of a computation. For example, in many programming languages, sqrt(2) returns the square root of 2.

Returning a value is not the same as printing it out; returning a value makes it available for further computation, as in sqrt(2)+3.

3. in C and related languages, the statement that causes the computer to exit a function or subroutine and return to the program that called it. For example, return x; means "exit, returning the value of x as the value of the function," and return; means "exit, returning no value."

Return key the key on a computer keyboard that tells the computer that the end of a line has been reached, called this because the Return key on a typewriter returned the typing element to the beginning of a line. On most keyboards the Return key is marked Enter. It may also have a leftward-pointing "return" arrow.

retweet to repost a message on Twitter that came from someone else, so that the people who see your own messages can see it. *Compare* TWEET. *See* TWITTER.

reusable components pieces of software that can be used in other programs. For example, Java classes are reusable; they can be used by programs other than the one for which they were originally created.

reverse (in graphics) to replace white with black and black with white. A reversed block of type can be a dramatic design element—however, legibility can become a factor. A large block of reverse text is difficult to read. Typefaces with hairline strokes do not reverse well. The letters may spread and fill in if the font size is too small. Always evaluate a proof of reverse type carefully.

Type can also be reversed out of a color or a tint. Check that there is enough contrast between the type and the background for the text to be read.

FIGURE 222. Reversed type

reverse engineer to find out how something works by examining and dis-
assembling the finished product.

reverse Polish notation *see* POLISH NOTATION.

revert to reload from disk a previously saved version of a file, losing all
intermediate changes. Revert is therefore a super-undo command. Save
your file before attempting a potentially dangerous command (search
and replace or applying a filter), and you will have the option of revert-
ing to the older file in case something goes wrong.

rewrap *see* REFLOW.

REXX a programming language used to write procedures that contain
operating system commands used on some IBM mainframe operating
systems. *Compare* AWK; PERL.

RF (**r**adio-**f**requency) a frequency in the range that is typical of radio
waves, approximately 0.5 to 2000 megahertz. *Contrast* AF.

RFC
1. (**r**adio-**f**requency **c**hoke) an inductor (coil) designed to keep high-
frequency signals from flowing into power supply lines and other interconnections. *See* RFI PROTECTION.
2. (**R**equest **F**or **C**omment) one of numerous documents defining the
standard for the Internet. All are supposedly unofficial, although most
are followed universally. For example, RFC 822 specifies the format for
E-MAIL messages in transit. RFCs are available online at *www.cis.ohio-
state.edu/hypertext/information/rfc.html* and other sites.

RFI protection protection of electronic equipment from radio-frequency
interference.
Computers use the same kind of high-frequency electrical energy as
radio transmitters. This often causes RFI (radio-frequency interference),
also called EMI (electromagnetic interference). All computers interfere
with nearby radio and TV reception to some extent, and sometimes the
problem is severe. On rare occasions, the opposite happens—a strong
signal from a nearby radio transmitter disrupts the computer, or two
computers interfere with each other. *See* EMC.
Here are some suggestions for reducing RFI:
1. If possible, move the radio or TV receiver away from the computer, and plug it into an outlet on a different circuit.

2. Supply power to the computer through a surge protector that includes an RFI filter (*see* SURGE PROTECTOR).
3. Ground the computer properly (*see* SURGE PROTECTOR).
4. Use high-quality shielded cables to connect the parts of the computer system together. Make sure all cable shields and ground wires are connected properly. This is especially important for the monitor cable and the printer cable. If possible, wind the cable into a coil to increase its inductance.
5. Check that the computer has the appropriate approval from the FCC (Federal Communications Commission). Some computers are not approved for use in residential areas. *See* CLASS A; CLASS B; FCC.

RFID (**r**adio-**f**requency **i**dentification) the use of radio signals to recognize, from a few feet away, a tiny device ("RFID tag") that can be built into price tags, library books, parking permits, ID cards, passports, or the like. RFID tags are even implanted under the skin of dogs for positive identification so that they can be returned to their owners if lost and found.

The RFID tag consists of an antenna and an integrated circuit, but no battery. The antenna picks up enough power from the transmitter that it can energize the integrated circuit and transmit a response, typically just an identifying number. The RFID tag itself contains almost no information; its usefulness comes from a database linking its ID number to other records.

RFP (**R**equest **F**or **P**roposal) an invitation to submit a price quotation, sales pitch, or grant proposal.

Rhapsody a subscription music service (see *www.rhapsody.com*).

ribbon in the redesigned user interface of Microsoft Office 2007, the part of the screen containing tabs providing access to commands.

ribbon bar a row of small icons arranged just below the menu bar of a window. Each icon gives the user access to a frequently used command.

rich text text that contains codes identifying italics, boldface, and other special effects. WORD PROCESSING programs deal with rich text rather than plain ASCII or UNICODE text. *See* RTF. *Contrast* NONDOCUMENT MODE; TEXT FILE.

Rich Text Format *see* RTF.

right-click to CLICK the SECONDARY MOUSE BUTTON (usually the right button). In Windows, right-clicking the mouse will pop up an action menu that includes access to the "Properties" dialog for the selected object.

RIM (**R**esearch **I**n **M**otion) the producer of the BLACKBERRY. Web address: *www.rim.com*.

RIMM (**R**ambus **i**nline **m**emory **m**odule) a memory module similar to a SIMM, but containing Rambus high-speed memory (RDRAM).

Ring 0, Ring 1, Ring 2, Ring 3 levels of privilege for processes running on a Pentium-family microprocessor. Normally, parts of the operating system run at Ring 0 (the maximum privilege level), and everything else runs at Ring 3.

rip
1. (from *raster image processing*) to convert a PostScript or vector graphics file to a bitmap file suitable for a particular output device, such as a color printer.
2. to convert an audio file from audio CD format to a digital format such as MP3.

RISC (**R**educed **I**nstruction **S**et **C**omputer, pronounced "risk") a CPU design with a small number of machine language instructions, each of which can be executed very quickly. The Sun Sparcstation and the PowerPC are historic examples of RISC computers. The opposite of RISC is CISC; an example of CISC is PENTIUM.

   RISC architecture was developed for speed. A RISC computer can execute each instruction faster because there are fewer instructions to choose between, and thus less time is taken up identifying each instruction. However, a larger number of instructions have to be fetched from memory than with a CISC architecture, and RISC machines are often limited by memory speed. *See also* CISC; COMPUTER ARCHITECTURE; POWERPC.

riser a small circuit board inserted perpendicularly into the motherboard, containing slots for cards. *Compare* DAUGHTERBOARD; DAUGHTERCARD. *See also* CARD (definition 2); MOTHERBOARD.

riser-rated (describing cable) suitable for use inside walls and in open areas but not in places where air circulates, such as above suspended ceilings. Riser-rated cable is fire-resistant but can give off noxious fumes when overheated. *Contrast* PLENUM-RATED.

river a series of white spaces between words that appear to flow from line to line in a printed document, like the white patch in the following example. Rivers result from trying to justify type when the columns are too narrow or the available software or printer is not versatile enough. *See* JUSTIFICATION.

> Quo   usque   tandem
> abutere,   Catilina,
> patientia   nostra?
> quamdiu   etiam
> furor iste tuus nos
> eludet?

RJ-11 the 4-pin modular connector used to connect telephones and modems to the telephone line (*see* Figure 223, *right*). One RJ-11 connector can support two telephone lines, one on the inner pair of pins and one on the outer pair.

RJ-45 the 8-pin modular connector used on the ends of 10base-T and 100base-T cables (*see* Figure 223, *left*); it resembles a 4-pin telephone connector but is wider. The color code for wiring RJ-45 connectors is shown in Table 13. *See also* CATEGORY 3 CABLE, CATEGORY 5 CABLE.

FIGURE 223. RJ-45 connector (*left*) and RJ-11 connector (*right*)

TABLE 13
RJ-45 CONNECTOR WIRING FOR
10BASE-T and 100BASE-T NETWORKS

T568A	T568B
1 white-orange	1 white-green
2 orange	2 green
3 white-green	3 white-orange
4 blue	4 blue
5 white-blue	5 white-blue
6 green	6 orange
7 white-brown	7 white-brown
8 brown	8 brown

Pins are numbered from left to right as seen with the plug pointing away from you, contacts up.

Note that one twisted pair (on pins 3 and 6) goes to nonadjacent pins.

Normal cables are T568A or T568B at both ends. A crossover cable is T568A at one end and T568B at the other.

RL abbreviation for "**r**eal **l**ife" in e-mail and online games.

rlogin (**r**emote **login**) the UNIX command that allows you to use your computer as a terminal on another computer. Unlike telnet, rlogin does more than just establish a communication path: it also tells the other computer what kind of terminal you are using and sends it your user name.

RMI (**R**emote **M**ethod **I**nvocation) technique for calling a method in a Java class located on a machine (such as a web server) different from the machine (such as the browser client) on which the current application is running.

rms (**r**oot-**m**ean-**s**quare) the most common method of measuring the voltage of an alternating current; the square root of the mean of the square of the instantaneous voltage. This method of measurement is used because power (wattage) depends on the voltage squared; thus, 120 volts AC rms will light a light bulb to the same brightness as 120 volts DC. With a sine wave, the rms voltage is 0.707 × the peak voltage or 0.353× the peak-to-peak voltage. *Contrast* PEAK; PEAK-TO-PEAK.

roaming user profiles in Windows NT and its successors, a facility that allows each user's desktop, account information, and files to be stored on a server so that they are accessible from any networked PC at which the user logs on. *See* PROFILE (definition 2).

robot
   1. a computer that moves itself or other objects in three-dimensional space under automatic control. Robots are now widely used in manufacturing. *See also* ARTIFICIAL INTELLIGENCE.
   2. *(slang; also bot)* a computer program that performs a human-like communication function such as replying to E-MAIL or responding to messages in a NEWSGROUP. *See also* DAEMON.
   3. a program that searches the World Wide Web, gathering information for indexing in search engines. *See* CRAWLER; SEARCH ENGINE; SPIDER. *See also* META TAG.

robust reliable even under varying or unforeseen conditions. *Contrast* BRITTLE.

Rock Ridge a compatible extension to the ISO 9660 CD-ROM format, allowing longer filenames, commonly used in UNIX systems. On computers that do not support Rock Ridge format, the discs can still be read, and the files still have unique names, but the names are shortened. *Compare* JOLIET FILE SYSTEM.

ROFL online abbreviation for "**r**olling **o**n the **f**loor **l**aughing." *See also* ROTFL.

RoHS (**R**estrictions **o**n **H**azardous **S**ubstances) a directive adopted by the European Community and effective on July 1, 2006, requiring the almost complete elimination of lead, mercury, cadmium, hexavalent chromium, polybrominated biphenyls, and polybrominated diphenyl ethers in electronic equipment sold in Europe. Similar restrictions are being adopted elsewhere.
   The main effect of RoHS is to mandate the use of lead-free solder and to eliminate nickel-cadmium batteries. *See* NICAD; SOLDER.

role-playing game a game in which the player controls a fictional character that is not merely a representation of themselves (*contrast* AVATAR). Computer games that are designated as role-playing usually have design elements in common with table-top games like Dungeons and Dragons, such as the use of "experience points" and "leveling up" to measure characters' increases in power. MUDS, MOOS, and MMORPGS are all role-playing games.

roll-up menu a dialog box that can be "rolled up" to just the size of its title bar to keep it visible but reduce its size when it is not in use. It is very similar in concept to a TOOLBOX.

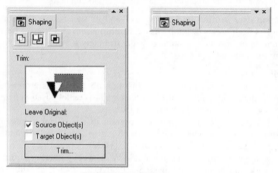

FIGURE 224. Roll-up menu

roller (as part of a printer) *see* PICKUP ROLLER; TRANSFER ROLLER.

rollerball *see* TRACKBALL.

rollover

1. an important change in the date or another gradually increasing number, such as the date rollover from 1999 to 2000.

2. an explanatory note that appears as the mouse cursor is placed onto (*rolls over*) a key word, icon, or graphic even though the mouse has not been clicked. Rollovers are used by operating systems and application programs, but are especially common on web pages.

JavaScript can be used to provide rollover effects on a web page. The following example uses the status line at the bottom of the browser window to include a description of a link when the mouse passes over it:

```
<html><head><title>Mouse Rollover example</title>

<script language='javascript'> <!-- hide

function rollOn(choicedescription) {
  window.status=choicedescription;
}
```

FIGURE 225. Rollover (definition 2)

```
function rollOut() {
  window.status=" ";
}
->
</script></head>
<body>
<h1>Example of a Mouse Rollover, using the status line</h1>
<ul>
<li><a href="#choice1"
     onMouseOver="rollOn('Here is text that describes
          choice 1'); return true;"
     onMouseOut="rollOut(); return true;">
     Choice 1 </a>
<li><a href="#choice2"
     onMouseOver="rollOn('Here is text that describes
          choice 2'); return true"
     onMouseOut="rollOut(); return true;">
     Choice 2 </a>
</ul>
<a name="choice1"><h2>Here is choice 1</h2></a>
Here is some text for choice 1.<br>
<a name="choice2"><h2>Here is choice 2</h2></a>
Here is some text for choice 2.<br>
</body></html>
```

The next example changes the display of the image when the mouse rolls over the links:

```
<html><head><title>Mouse Rollover example</title>

<script language='javascript'> <!-- hide

function rollOn(choicenum) {
if (choicenum==1)
     { document.image1.src="image_for_choice_1.jpg"; }
```

```
else {document.image1.src="image_for_choice_2.jpg"; }
}

function rollOut() {
  document.image1.src="default_image.jpg";
}
-></script></head>
<body>
<h1>Example of a Mouse Rollover with a changing image</h1>
<ul>
<li><a href="#choice1"
    onMouseOver="rollOn(1); return true;"
    onMouseOut="rollOut(); return true;">
    Choice 1 </a>
<li><a href="#choice2"
    onMouseOver="rollOn(2); return true;"
    onMouseOut="rollOut(); return true;">
    Choice 2 </a>
</ul>

<img name="image1" height="200" width="300"
    src="default_image.jpg">

<a name="choice1"><h2>Here is choice 1</h2></a>
Here is some text for choice 1.<br>
<a name="choice2"><h2>Here is choice 2</h2></a>
Here is some text for choice 2.<br>
</body></html>
```

See also HTML; JAVA; JAVASCRIPT; RIGHT-CLICK.

ROM (Read-Only Memory) a computer memory that contains data or instructions that do not need to be changed, such as bootup code or device drivers. The computer can read instructions or data out of ROM but cannot store new data in it. See also CD-ROM; EPROM; PROM.

ROM BIOS see BIOS.

roman the kind of type that books are normally typeset in, as opposed to italics or boldface. The type you are reading now is roman type. See TYPEFACE; SERIF.

root the account name used by the system administrator under UNIX. (From ROOT DIRECTORY.)

root directory the main directory of a disk, containing files and/or subdirectories. See DIRECTORY.

root hub the set of USB ports located inside a computer. See USB.

root-mean-square see RMS.

rootkit a software package that tampers with the innermost kernel of an operating system, concealing its presence and its effects unusually well because it can intercept any attempt to detect it.

Originally, a "root kit" was a set of cracking programs designed to run under the ROOT (system administrator) account of UNIX while leaving no trace of their presence.

Today, most rootkits are for Windows. The only sure way to detect them is to boot an entirely separate operating system, such as a copy of Windows on a CD, and scan the installed Windows kernel to verify its authenticity.

Compare VIRUS. *See also* COMPUTER SECURITY; CRACKER; MALWARE.

rot13 (rotate 13) a type of ENCRYPTION commonly used on the Internet to conceal answers to puzzles and the like. To encode a message, the first 13 letters of the alphabet are swapped with the last 13. Performing the same swap again decodes the message. This is not a secure code, of course, but it provides a way to make things temporarily unreadable.

Qba'g lbh jbaqre jung guvf fnlf?

rotate

1. in draw programs, to turn an object around a specific center. By default, the object rotates around its own center. You can drag this center to wherever you want it to be and then rotate the object around it. Rotation can be done interactively with the mouse, or if you require more precision, you can set the angle of rotation in degrees.

2. a touchpad or touchscreen gesture to rotate an object or image. To perform it, place two fingers in contact with the screen and then move them as if rotating about an axis.

FIGURE 226. Rotate

ROTFL online abbreviation for "rolling on the floor laughing." *See also* ROFL.

round brackets the characters (), more properly called *parentheses*. *Contrast* ANGLE BRACKETS; CURLY BRACKETS; SQUARE BRACKETS.

rounding replacing a number with the nearest number that has a smaller number of significant digits. For example, 2.76 rounded to one decimal place is 2.8. The rule is that if the first digit to be discarded is 5 or greater, the last digit that is kept should be increased by 1. Thus 2.74 → 2.7, but 2.76 → 2.8. *Contrast* TRUNCATION.

An alternative way to do rounding—easier on the computer—is to add 0.5 (or 0.05, or 0.005, etc.) to the number before discarding digits. For example:

$$2.74 + 0.05 = 2.79 \rightarrow 2.7$$
$$2.76 + 0.05 = 2.81 \rightarrow 2.8$$

The addition changes 7 to 8 in the desired cases; then the subsequent digits can simply be discarded.

In C and C++, you can round x to the nearest integer by evaluating floor(x+0.5), where floor finds the integer just below x. You can round x to two decimal places by evaluating floor(100*x+0.5)/100 (unless the result is thrown off by *rounding error*; see next entry).

There is a big difference between rounding a number, which actually changes it, and simply displaying it with a limited number of decimal places. In the latter case, the number itself is not changed, and its original value remains available for further computation.

rounding error a loss of precision that occurs because the computer cannot store the true value of most real numbers; instead, it can store only an approximation of a finite number of digits.

If you wish to write ⅓ as a decimal fraction, you can approximate it as 0.333333333, but it would require an infinite number of digits to express it exactly. The computer faces the same problem except that internally it stores the numbers in binary, and it can lose accuracy in converting between binary and decimal. For example, 0.1 has no exact representation on a computer; if you add the computer's representation of 0.1 to 0 ten times, you will not get exactly 1. To avoid rounding error, some computer programs represent numbers as decimal digits. *See* BINARY-CODED DECIMAL.

Route 128 a highway that skirts the west side of Boston, Massachusetts, passing through the cities of Needham and Waltham. Route 128 has been the home of a number of computer companies, including Digital Equipment Corporation and Lotus.

router a network component that joins several networks together intelligently. A router is often used to link an incoming DSL or cable modem connection to a home network. A router is more powerful than a bridge because instead of just choosing network segments based on previous traffic, a router can look up the best route to a distant site. The Internet relies heavily on routers. *Compare* BRIDGE; HUB; SWITCH (definition 2). *See also* DNS (definition 1).

RPG

1. abbreviation for **r**ole-**p**laying **g**ame.

2. (**R**eport **P**rogram **G**enerator) a programming language developed by IBM in the 1960s in an attempt to simplify programming for business applications.

RPG was often the first programming language taught to trainees because RPG programming can be reduced to a fixed procedure for filling out forms. However, RPG programs are markedly less readable than programs in other languages, and complex algorithms are difficult to express in RPG.

RPM (**r**evolutions **p**er **m**inute) a measure of speed of rotation. For example, many newer hard disks rotate at 10,000 RPM.

RPN *see* POLISH NOTATION.

RS-232 an Electronics Industries Association (EIA) recommended standard for transmitting serial data by wire. This standard is now officially known as EIA-232D. Computer serial ports follow the RS-232 standard.

TABLE 14
RS-232 PIN CONNECTIONS (25-PIN)

(Pin numbers are embossed on the connector.)

Pin	Signal	Direction	Explanation
1	GND	Both	Frame ground—ties together chassis of terminal and modem; often omitted.
2	TxD	To modem	Transmitted data.
3	RxD	To terminal	Received data.
4	RTS	To modem	Request to send—high when terminal is on and able to communicate.
5	CTS	To terminal	Clear to send—high when computer on other end is able to receive.
6	DSR	To terminal	Data set ready—high when modem is on and functioning.
7	SG	Both	Signal ground—reference point for all signal voltages.
8	CD	To terminal	Carrier detect—high when a connection to another computer has been established.
20	DTR	To modem	Data terminal ready—high when terminal is on and functioning. Most modems hang up phone when DTR goes low.
22	RI	To terminal	Ring indicator—high when telephone is ringing.

RS-422, RS-423A two standards, recommended by the Electronics Industries Association (EIA), which define a format for transmitting serial data by wire, intended to replace the older RS-232 format. The new format offers faster data rates and greater immunity to electrical noise.

RS/6000 *see* WORKSTATION.

RSA encryption a public key encryption algorithm named after the initials of its developers (Ron Rivest, Adi Shamir, and Leonard Adleman). The security of the system relies on the difficulty of factoring very large numbers. More information about RSA encryption can be found at *www.rsa.com. See also* ENCRYPTION.

RSN **R**eal **S**oon **N**ow. *(sarcastic)* at an indefinite time in the future, probably much later than promised. *See* VAPORWARE.

RSS (**R**eally **S**imple **S**yndication, or sometimes **R**ich **S**ite **S**ummary), a system that makes it easy to be notified of new information on web sites. The RSS material comes from a special XML file on the web site, and the person who maintains the web site also updates that file when there is new material to announce. Blogs often make their content available this way. The original version of RSS was developed by Netscape in the late 1990s.

RT abbreviation for RETWEET.

RTF (**R**ich **T**ext **F**ormat) a format created by Microsoft for interchange of files between different word processing programs. RTF files consist of ASCII text with codes that indicate formatting and typefaces. For example,

```
{\rtf This is a {\b sample} of {\i RTF.}}
```

is RTF code for:
This is a **sample** of *RTF.*
RTF works somewhat like the lowest-level codes in TEX, but it is designed to be produced by programs, not humans. Many popular word processors can save their files in RTF. *Compare* TEX; *contrast* TEXT FILE.

RTFM (**r**ead **t**he **f**riendly **m**anual) an exhortation to computer users who are unwilling to look things up for themselves. *Compare* RYFM.

rubber stamp a paint program tool that duplicates a selected area of a drawing. *See the illustration at* CLONE TOOL.

Ruby a scripting language for object-oriented programming similar in intent to PERL and PYTHON. Ruby was developed by Yukihiro Matsumoto in 1995. *See www.ruby-lang.org/en.*

rule a procedure defined in advance that will automatically perform a particular action when a certain type of e-mail is received; for example, forwarding all messages from a particular person to another person, or moving all messages on a specific topic into the relevant folder.

ruler a strip at the top (and sometimes the side) of the on-screen work area, marked in units of measurement. Like its physical counterparts, an on-screen ruler is used to help you measure things. Rulers can be found in word processors, drawing programs, and page layout programs. You have the option to display the ruler, or to hide it and give yourself some more working room. You can also have the ruler show units of measurement other than inches (PICAS might be more useful for many applications). A ruler is especially useful when using a high degree of zoom because it helps you keep your orientation.

In a word processor, the ruler is used to set the TABS and margins.

FIGURE 227. Ruler

run to make the computer execute a program. A distinction is often made between *compile time* (the time when the program is compiled; *see* COMPILER) and *run time* (the time when the program is run).

run-length encoding a way of storing data in less than the usual amount of space by using special codes to indicate repeated bytes. *See* DATA COMPRESSION.

run-time error an error that occurs when a program is being executed; an EXCEPTION. For example, a run-time error might occur if division by 0 is attempted or if the subscript for an array is outside the allowable bounds for that array. A run-time error may cause the program to stop execution, or it may be handled by an error-trapping routine (*see* TRAPPING). *Contrast* COMPILE-TIME ERROR.

Run. . . a menu choice under Windows's START BUTTON that allows you to run a program or open a file by typing its filename. For instance, to run myprog.exe from drive A, choose "Run. . ." and type a:\myprog.exe or simply myprog (it isn't necessary to type the extension). This is a common way to run setup programs when installing new software.

running head a small headline that appears at the top or bottom of each page. Running heads are usually there to remind the reader which chapter (or section) he or she is reading. In a dictionary like this one, the running heads tell you the first and last entries on the page spread.

RYFM (**r**ead **y**our **f**riendly **m**anual, pronounced "riff-um") *Compare* RTFM.

S

S (on a digital camera) shutter-priority autoexposure, the mode in which the user sets the shutter speed (exposure time) and the camera chooses the lens opening (f-ratio); same as *TV*. *See* F-RATIO. *Contrast* A; AV; P; TV.

Saas software as a service. *See* CLOUD COMPUTING.

Sad Mac (pre OS X only) the icon of a frowning Macintosh computer that announces the Mac has found a hardware problem and cannot finish booting.

Safari Apple Computer's WEB BROWSER for the Macintosh OS and Windows. The free download is available at *www.apple.com/safari/download*. *Compare* FIREFOX; INTERNET EXPLORER; OPERA.

safe mode a way of running Windows with many special hardware drivers disabled, to work around problems with improperly installed hardware or software. Safe mode is used only for testing and to recover from an improper shutdown. For example, if the computer lost power before it could properly shut down, the next time you use it you should start in safe mode. Then restart the computer so it can shut down and restart normally.

Samba a widely used, free, open-source software package for linking UNIX systems to Windows file and printer sharing, and for achieving various other kinds of interoperability between networks. For details, see *www.samba.org*. The name is derived from SMB (**S**erver **M**essage **B**lock), an important part of the protocol that Samba follows. *See* CIFS; PROTOCOL.

sampling rate the number of times per second that sound waves are sampled and digitized. The highest frequency that can be reproduced is half the sampling rate. High-fidelity audio is usually sampled at 44.1 kHz (44,100 samples per second) in order to reproduce frequencies up to 22.05 kHz, just above the limit of human hearing. Speech can be stored more compactly by sampling at a lower rate, 22.05 or 11.025 kHz.

Another parameter is the number of bits of data stored in each sample. High-fidelity audio requires 16 bits per sample; speech can be reproduced adequately with 8 bits. One minute of sound, sampled at 44.1 kHz with 16 bits per sample, requires about 5 megabytes of disk space (10 megabytes for stereo). *See also* MP3.

SAN *see* STORAGE AREA NETWORK.

sandbox a safe environment to play in; a protective mechanism that prevents a program from accessing or changing memory or disk space outside of its own permitted area. This is a security feature preventing programs from damaging the system they run on. For example, a Java applet loaded from the World Wide Web runs in a sandbox where it is prohibited access to the hard disk on the browser's computer.

sans-serif a typeface that does not have serifs, such as this one. Serifs are small perpendicular marks at the ends of the strokes (*sans* is French for "without"). *See* Figure 228. *Contrast* SERIF. *See also* TYPEFACE.

FIGURE 228. Sans-serif type

SAP a large developer of e-business software, headquartered in Walldorf, Germany. The name stands for the German words for "Systems, Applications, Products." See *www.sap.com.*

SATA (serial ATA) a newer hardware implementation of the ATA (PC **AT A**ttachment) hard disk interface, using serial data transmission through a narrow 7-pin connector, giving greater speed than PATA. SATA disk drives also have a new, narrow 15-pin power connector instead of the traditional 4-pin one. *Compare* ESATA; PATA. *See also* IBM PC.

saturation the intensity of a color. A highly saturated color is vivid and brilliant color; to dull a color (decrease its saturation), you add small amounts of its COMPLEMENT, making it closer to gray. *See* COLOR; HSB.

save to transfer information from the computer's memory to a storage device such as a disk drive. Saving data is vital because the contents of the computer's memory are lost when power is turned off. The opposite process is known as loading, retrieving, or opening.

Save As ...
  1. to save a document or drawing under a different name. The first time you save an untitled work, you will use "Save As ... " instead of "Save."
  2. to save a file in a different format (e.g., to save a CorelDraw file as a Windows Metafile). *See also* EXPORT.

SBC *see* SINGLE-BOARD COMPUTER.

scalable able to be used on a large or small scale without major changes. For example, much of the appeal of the UNIX operating system is its scalability; it can be used on small or large computers with little change in the way it works.

scalable font a font that can be used to print characters of any size. Most printers include scalable fonts; also, TrueType, OpenType, and Type 1 fonts are scalable. The shapes of the characters in a scalable font are stored in the form of vector graphics rather than bitmaps. *See* FONT; VECTOR GRAPHICS.

scalar a quantity represented by a single number, as opposed to a VECTOR, ARRAY, or LIST.

scalar processor a computer that operates on only one piece of data at a time. Most computers are scalar processors. *Contrast* VECTOR PROCESSOR. *See also* SUPERSCALAR PROCESSOR.

scale to change the size of a graphical object without changing its shape. In most draw programs you can scale any object by selecting it and then dragging one of the dots (called HANDLES) that appear at its corners. *Contrast* ASPECT RATIO; STRETCH.

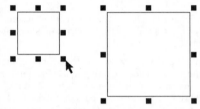

FIGURE 229. Scale

scam *See* 419 SCAM; ADVANCE FEE FRAUD; NIGERIAN SCAM; SPAM; SCAREWARE; PHISHING; COMPUTER SECURITY.

ScanAlert a company that developed technology that could be used to verify that a web site has protection from hackers, and providing Hacker Safe certificates to web pages that passed the tests. However, it still is difficult to verify that a web page is truly safe. In 2008 ScanAlert was acquired by McAfee (web address: *www.mcafee.com*).

scanner
1. a device that enables a computer to read a printed or handwritten page. The simplest scanners give the contents of the page to the computer as a graphic image—a handy way of putting pictures into the computer (*see* DESKTOP PUBLISHING).

There are many nuances involved in scanning artwork. In some ways, it is quite similar to photography and if you are comfortable with a camera, it will make the transition to working with a scanner very smooth. Scanners can adjust the contrast and brightness of the image. Controls for setting the *highlight* and *shadow* area are usually provided. Color images can be color-corrected at the scanning stage.

With appropriate software, scanners can read the letters of typewritten text, transmitting them into the computer as if they were typed on the keyboard (OCR). This process, however, is seldom 100% accurate. You will find it necessary to proofread scanned copy very carefully.
2. Several other kinds of electronic devices are called scanners, including bar code readers (*see* BAR CODE) and devices for scanning the radio spectrum.

scareware a message designed to scare its recipient, often hoping to coax the recipient into taking some action, such as seeking protection from nonexistent malware on their computer by downloading a purported remedy that in reality installs actual malware on their computer.

scattergraph, scatter plot a graph that shows points of data plotted on an *x-y* coordinate system. Also called an *x-y graph.*

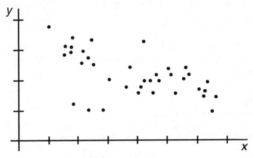

FIGURE 230. Scattergraph

scientific notation *see* EXPONENTIAL NOTATION.

scissors
  1. a tool available in paint programs that allows you to define an area of the picture that you wish to separate from its surroundings. The resulting cutout may be resized (scaled), stretched, rotated, or moved.

   The scissors tool is one of several SELECTION TOOLS available to you. Others include the LASSO, MAGIC WAND, and box selection tools. To save space, these tools may be grouped together in your toolbox and only one may be visible at a time.
  2. icon for "cut the selected item to the Clipboard." *See also* COPY; PASTE.

FIGURE 231. Scissors icon

SCO a software company that sued several companies claiming that it owned a copyright to part of the code in the open-source operating system Linux. Its claims were denied (*SCO v. Novell*).

SCR
  1. (silicon controlled rectifier) an electronic component that functions as a latching switch for direct current. *Compare* TRANSISTOR.

Usage note: The hyphenation *silicon-controlled rectifier* is incorrect. The term means a controlled rectifier made of silicon, not a rectifier controlled by silicon.

2. (as a filename extension) screen saver. In Windows, an `.scr` file is just like an `.exe` file except that it can be installed as a screen saver; the assumption is that it will display graphics. A common way to trick people into running a malicious program is to give it the extension `.scr`, which they won't recognize, instead of `.exe`. *See* EXE FILE; MALWARE.

scratch disk, scratch tape a disk or tape that one can erase and reuse at any time because it does not contain anything that needs to be kept for future use.

screen
1. a computer display; a monitor.
2. a screenful of information.
3. to process a grayscale image for printing by breaking down the various shades of gray into very small dots. *See* HALFTONE.

screen capture *see* SCREEN SHOT; SCREEN SNAPSHOT.

screen estate *(informal)* space on a computer screen, especially when thought of as a limited resource. A program that consumes too much screen estate will be hard to use concurrently with others. *Compare* REAL ESTATE.

screen saver a program that automatically blanks the screen of a computer, or displays a moving picture, when the computer has not been used for several minutes.

The original purpose of screen savers was to prevent "burn-in" (i.e., to keep the screen coating from wearing out in places where bright parts of the image were constantly displayed). Modern screens are less vulnerable to burn-in, and today, screen savers serve mainly to protect the privacy of users who are away from their desks, and to save energy when used in conjunction with monitors that turn themselves off when the screen goes blank. Screen savers also provide entertainment. *See also* GREEN PC; ENERGY STAR.

screen shot, screen snapshot an image of the current screen, saved as a bitmap.

Snapshots of the screen are easy to obtain: on the Macintosh, hold down Command and Shift, then press 3. This places a bitmapped image of the screen in a PICT file in your root directory. In Windows, pressing the Print Screen key puts a copy of the entire screen onto the CLIPBOARD. Holding down Alt while pressing Print Screen saves a bitmap of the active window only.

script
1. a style of type that resembles cursive handwriting (not italics), as shown in Figure 232.

2. a file containing commands to be executed, such as a SHELL SCRIPT or a script of dialing commands for a communication program. *See also* JAVASCRIPT; VBSCRIPT; PERL; PYTHON; CGI.

3. a file or printout containing a copy of information that was displayed on the screen.

Handgloves

Handgloves

Handgloves

FIGURE 232. Script type

scroll
 1. to move information across the screen vertically or horizontally as if the screen were a window or porthole through which you are looking at a larger surface. For example, to see material below what you are presently looking at, scroll downward. *Contrast* FLICK.
 2. *(slang)* to type gibberish rapidly and repeatedly in order to disrupt a discussion in a chat room. (This makes all the real messages scroll by too fast for people to read them.) *See* CHAT ROOM.

scroll bar the bar at the right-hand side and/or bottom of a window that enables you to scroll the window (i.e., look at different areas of the data that the window is displaying), treating the window as a portion of a larger picture. To scroll, click on the arrows at the ends of the scroll bar or use the mouse to move the scroll box along the bar. For an illustration, see WINDOW. *See also* THUMB.

Scroll Lock a key on the PC keyboard that toggles the keyboard between two modes. Almost all software ignores the difference between the two modes, but in Microsoft Excel, the Scroll Lock key switches between two ways of moving through a spreadsheet. With Scroll Lock turned off, the arrow keys move the cursor from cell to cell, all over the screen; the spreadsheet holds still until the cursor actually moves off the screen. With Scroll Lock on, the cursor always stays in the same place on the screen, and the entire spreadsheet moves beneath it.

SCSI (**S**mall **C**omputer **S**ystems **I**nterface, pronounced "scuzzy") a standard way of interfacing a computer to disk drives, tape drives, and other devices that require high-speed data transfer. Up to seven SCSI devices can be linked to a single SCSI port. Thus, a single SCSI adapter can interface a computer to one or more hard disks, a CD-ROM drive, a tape drive, and a scanner (*see* Figure 233).

 SCSI is especially popular with Macintoshes and UNIX workstations but is also used on some PC-compatible computers, where it is supported by device drivers. Almost all SCSI hard disks use the same device driver, with no need for further settings to be made; that makes SCSI hard disks easier to install than any other type. Other SCSI devices such as CD-ROM drives require additional device drivers. This is often done in two layers: an ASPI (Advanced SCSI Programming Interface) device driver for the SCSI system, and various drivers that issue ASPI commands to specific devices.

The cable that comes out of a SCSI port is essentially an 8-bit bus (or 16-or 32-bit if it follows the newer SCSI-2 or SCSI-3 standard). The devices connected to it are daisy-chained with a *SCSI terminator* (a resistor pack) at the end. Each device, including the SCSI port itself, has an address between 0 and 7 inclusive; most addresses are switch-selectable to prevent conflicts.

See also BUS; DEVICE DRIVER. *Contrast* ESDI; IDE.

FIGURE 233. SCSI connectors (two of several common types)

scuzzy *[sic] see* SCSI.

SD card *see* SECURE DIGITAL CARD.

SDHC (**S**ecure **D**igital **H**igh **C**apacity) *see* SECURE DIGITAL CARD.

SDK **S**oftware **D**evelopment **K**it (any of several products).

SDRAM (**s**ynchronous **d**ynamic **r**andom **a**ccess **m**emory) a type of RAM chip whose output is synchronized with the system bus, making data available to the CPU more quickly than with FPM or EDO RAM. SDRAM normally communicates with the CPU at a bus speed of 100 to 133 MHz (200 to 266 for DDR SDRAM). *Contrast* EDO; RDRAM. *See also* DDR.

SDTV **s**tandard-**d**efinition **t**elevision; television with a resolution of about 640 × 480 pixels, or 720 × 480 pixels if the pixels are narrower than they are high. This is the resolution of traditional analog TV, although SDTV can be transmitted digitally. *Contrast* HDTV. *See also* DIGITAL TELEVISION.

search and replace to work through a file, changing every occurrence of a particular sequence of characters into some other sequence of characters. In Macintosh software, this is usually called *Find and Change*. *See* EDITOR. It is a good idea to make a backup copy of a file before performing this operation, since it cannot be easily reversed. If you change every "blue" in the document to "red," and then change every "red" back to "blue," you will find that not only will the original blues be back to blue, but also all of the original reds will have turned to blue.

search engine a computer program that searches through large amounts of text or other data. For example, a search engine for the WORLD WIDE WEB can be accessed at *www.yahoo.com* or at *www.google.com.*

Depending on the search engine, there are generally several ways to search. If you type a phrase such as *golden isles,* the search engine will normally search for all documents that contain *golden* and/or *isles,* giving highest priority to those that contain both words. Alternatively, you can specify that you want only the documents that contain the whole phrase, and you can specify boolean ("and" and "or") relationships between words you are searching for (e.g., "Visa OR MasterCard" versus "Visa AND MasterCard"). There is generally a help button that explains how to perform various kinds of searches. *See also* BOOLEAN QUERY; FULL-TEXT SEARCH.

Some people pay large amounts of money to try to get their web sites listed on search engines. This is unnecessary because every search engine's job is to find all possible web sites by itself, and major search engines gladly accept additional web addresses from anyone who wants to submit them. Search engine operators do not take kindly to attempts to manipulate the system by listing a web site dishonestly to generate more hits (*see* GOOGLEWHACKING; META TAG). *See also* ROBOT (definition 3); SPIDER.

seat
1. *(noun)* a place where a person can use a computer system or software product. The cost of software is often calculated in terms of seats. For example, a multi-user computer that supports five users has five seats; so does a group of five personal computers. *See* LICENSE; PER SEAT.
2. *(verb)* to insert an integrated circuit (IC) or a printed circuit board into a socket.

SECAM (**S**équentiel **C**ouleur **a**vec **M**émoire) the type of analog color TV signal used in France, now being displaced by digital television. *Contrast* DIGITAL TELEVISION; HDTV; NTSC; PAL.

SECDED (**S**ingle **E**rror **C**orrection—**D**ouble **E**rror **D**etection) an error-correcting procedure that can correct a single erroneous bit, and can detect (but not correct) the error if there are two erroneous bits. *See* ERROR CORRECTING CODE; PARITY.

second-generation computers computers made with discrete transistors in the 1950s and 1960s.

Second Life a virtual world created by Linden Research, Inc. Although it is similar in appearance to a game, the designers' goal is to create a virtual world that can be used for real business. Users can customize avatars and their environment; the majority of the world's content is created by users. The free client is available at *www.secondlife.com*.

secondary mouse button the mouse button used to call up the action menu. For a right-handed user, this is usually the right mouse button. *See* RIGHT CLICK. The left mouse button (the PRIMARY MOUSE BUTTON) is used to select objects.

Left-handed users have the option of reversing the default order for mouse buttons; they can use the right mouse button as the primary button and the left button as the secondary.

section sign the symbol § which is used to mark sections of text for reference (usually in legal documents). The section sign can also be used as a footnote symbol. *See* FOOTNOTE.

sector part of a track on a disk. For example, the original IBM PC diskette system partitions the diskette into 40 circular tracks with each track having 8 sectors. *See* DISK; TRACK.

Secure Digital card (SD card) a type of flash-memory nonvolatile storage card that incorporates a cryptographic security system to prevent copyright violations, intended for use in digital music players. SD cards are commonly used in digital cameras, where the cryptographic system is irrelevant. They exist in three sizes, the conventional SD card, the microSD card, and an intermediate size called miniSD. Smaller SD cards can plug into a conventional SD card slot with an adapter. SD card slots can be built so that they also accept MMC cards. *Compare* COMPACTFLASH; FLASH MEMORY CARD; MEMORY STICK; MULTIMEDIACARD; SMARTMEDIA.

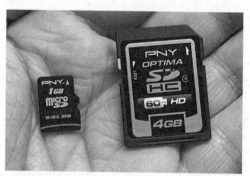

FIGURE 234. SD cards: microSD (left) and conventional

SED (Single **E**rror **D**etection) the ability to detect (but not correct) a single erroneous bit. *See* SECDED; ERROR CORRECTING CODE.

seed

1. a number that is used to start a series of seemingly random numbers. If the seed remains the same, a random-number generator will produce the same "random" numbers (in sequence) every time you use it. To get an unpredictable seed, programs sometimes look at the system clock. In Java, you may enter the seed in the constructor for a random number generator. For example, the statement

```
Random rnumgen=new Random(123);
```

creates a random number generator named *rnumgen* with seed 123. Each time you run this program, the random numbers generated in statements such as

```
int x=rnumgen.nextInt();
```

will always come in the same sequence. Use this constructor

```
Random rnumgen=new Random();
```

to generate a sequence that will be different each time the program is run. *See also* RANDOM-NUMBER GENERATOR.

2. an original host in a BitTorrent system. *See* BITTORRENT.

seek time the average time taken by a disk drive to *seek* (move) from one track to another.

segmentation fault an error in a program causing it to try to access a memory address that does not belong to it.

select to tell the computer you are ready to work with an object. You can select one or more objects at a time (Figure 235). Usually, you select an object by clicking on it with the mouse. To select a group of objects, use MARQUEE SELECT or hold down the Shift key while clicking on individual objects until they are all included in the bounding box.

FIGURE 235. Selecting a group of objects

selection area the selected part of an image. *See* Figure 162, page 306.

selection marquee *see* MARQUEE SELECT.

selection sort algorithm for sorting the elements of an array by first selecting the lowest-valued item, then the next lowest, and so on. In practice,
the lowest-valued item is interchanged with the first item in the part
of the array being searched, and the search is confined to the remainder
of the array from then on.

Selection sort is probably the easiest to remember of the many general-purpose sorting algorithms. The program in Figure 236 implements
selection sort in Java.

```java
class selectionsort
{
  /* This Java program performs a selection sort */

  /* Array to be sorted and number of items in it. */
  static   int   a[]={29,18,7,56,64,33,128,70,78,81,12,5};
  static int n=12;

  public static void main(String args[])
  {

    /* Perform the selection sort */
    for (int i=0; i<=n-1; i++)
    {
      int m=i;
      for (int j=(i+1); j<=n-1; j++)
      {
        if (a[j]<a[m]) { m=j; }
      }
      int y=a[m];
      a[m]=a[i];
      a[i]=y;
    }

    /* Display the results */
    for (int i=0; i<=n-1; i++)
    {
      System.out.println(a[i]);
    }
  }
}
```

FIGURE 236. Selection sort

selection tools (in graphics programs) tools provided to define an area or
choose an object to be worked with. Examples include the POINTER,
LASSO, MAGIC WAND, and SCISSORS.

selvage detachable perforated strips on the edges of some printer paper.

Semantic Web a way of using the WORLD WIDE WEB so that computers can
recognize the nature of the data sent to them; for example, so that a

catalog of items for sale and prices is recognized as such, not just as a set of letters and digits to be displayed at particular places on the screen. The Semantic Web can be thought of as a combination of ordinary web technology and DATABASE technology implemented in XML.

semiconductor a material that is neither a good conductor of electricity nor a good insulator, and whose conduction properties can therefore be manipulated easily.

Semiconductor devices, such as diodes, transistors, and integrated circuits, are the essential parts that make it possible to build small, inexpensive electronic machines.

The most widely used semiconductor material is silicon. Each atom in a silicon crystal contains four outer-level (or valence) electrons. A pure silicon crystal is not a very good conductor because these electrons normally stay bound to their atoms.

An N-type semiconductor region is formed by adding a bit of impurity to the pure silicon. This process is known as *doping*. The impurity added is a material such as phosphorus, in which each atom has five valence electrons. The result is a crystal much like the original one, except that there are now a few extra electrons floating around (one for each atom of phosphorus that was added). The whole crystal is called an N-type region because it contains movable negative charges.

If an impurity with only three valence electrons, such as boron, is added to the silicon crystal, there are not enough electrons to fill all of the available positions within the atoms of the crystal. Each gap is called a *hole*. Even though a hole is nothing but the absence of an electron, it can be thought of as carrying a mobile positive charge. A semiconductor region with an excess of holes is called a P-type semiconductor region.

Electric current can flow in an N-type region in much the same way that it flows in a regular conductor. In a conductor, the current is made up of outer-level valence electrons that are not too tightly bound to their atoms. When a negative voltage is applied to one end of the N-type region and a positive voltage is applied to the other, the loose electrons will be repelled by the negative voltage and attracted by the positive voltage.

Current can flow in the P-type region, but the process is quite different. If a negative voltage is applied to one end of the P-type region, the electrons will be repelled. However, the P-type region does not contain any mobile electrons. What an electron can do is jump into one of the holes. This process creates a new hole where the original electron used to be. We can think of the hole itself as moving toward the negative voltage, carrying a positive charge with it.

A semiconductor diode is formed by joining a P-type region and an N-type region. A transistor consists of a thin layer of one type of semiconductor between two layers of the opposite type. A semiconductor integrated circuit is made by placing many P and N regions on a single chip, so as to form a complex circuit containing many miniature transistors and other circuit elements.

send backward; back one comparable commands that send the selected object down one layer. *See also* ARRANGE; BRING FORWARD; BRING TO FRONT; DRAW PROGRAM; FORWARD ONE; SEND TO BACK; TO BACK; TO FRONT.

send to back; to back comparable commands that send the selected object to the bottom layer. *See also* ARRANGE; BACK ONE; BRING FORWARD; DRAW PROGRAM; FORWARD ONE; SEND BACKWARD; SEND TO FRONT; TO FRONT.

Send to front   Send to back
FIGURE 237. Send to front; send to back

separator pad (separation pad) in any printer or fax machine that takes loose sheets of paper, a stationary pad across which the paper passes when it is being fed in, to introduce friction and help separate the top sheet of paper from the rest.

The separator pad is commonly two or three inches wide and is placed in the middle of the paper path. It should be cleaned or replaced if the printer tends to pick up more than one sheet at a time.

sequential-access device a data-storage device in which it is necessary to read through all preceding records before the computer finds the record it is looking for. Tape storage devices are examples of sequential-access devices. *Contrast* RANDOM-ACCESS DEVICE.

serial method of transmitting data one bit at a time over a single wire. *See* BAUD; RS-232; SERIAL PORT. *Contrast* PARALLEL.

serial-access device *see* SEQUENTIAL-ACCESS DEVICE.

serial bus a system for rapid communication among components of a computer using a minimum number of wires. Successive bits of each byte or word travel along the same wire, rather than along separate wires as in a conventional bus. *See* BUS. For examples, *see* FIREWIRE; USB.

serial mouse a mouse that is attached to a serial port of a computer. *See* MOUSE.

serial port a connection by which a computer can transmit data to another device using serial transmission—that is, one bit at a time. Windows PCs typically have two serial ports labeled COM1 and COM2, one of which may be an internal modem; UNIX systems often identify their serial ports as /dev/ttya and /dev/ttyb. Most serial ports follow the EIA-232D (RS-232) standard. *See* RS-232. *Contrast* PARALLEL PORT; USB.

FIGURE 238. Serial port
(note "10101" symbol indicating a stream of bits)

series connection of two electronic components so that current flows through one and then the other (*see* Figure 239). *Contrast* PARALLEL.

FIGURE 239. Series circuit (two resistors)

serif the short finishing strokes of the letterforms in a roman typeface, present in I F A and absent in IFA (Figure 240). It is thought that the horizontal nature of serifs helps guide the reader's eye along the line of type. *Contrast* SANS-SERIF. *See also* TYPEFACE.

Serif

FIGURE 240. Serif (highlighted on two letters)

server a computer that provides services to another computer (called the *client*). On multitasking machines, a process that provides services to another process is sometimes called a server. For specific examples, *see* CLIENT SERVER; FILE SERVER; WEB SERVER; X SERVER.

server-side application a computer program that runs on a network server rather than on the client PC. For instance, Java servlets are server-side applications; when you view a web page that contains a servlet, the computation is done on the server rather than on your PC. *Contrast* APPLET; CLIENT-SIDE APPLICATION.

service in Windows, a program that runs continuously, unseen by the user, such as a Web or FTP server, or a program with a more mundane function such as updating the system clock; the equivalent of a UNIX DAEMON.

service bureau a business that provides services to computer users, such as high-quality color printing, disk format conversions, or the like.

service pack a set of updates to a software package, delivered together or even delivered with the original software.
   Usage note: The phrase *Windows 7 Service Pack 1* can mean either "Service Pack 1 for Windows 7" or "Windows 7 with Service Pack 1 included."

servlet a Java program that runs on a web server. By contrast, an applet is a Java program running on a web browser client.

session
   1. a period of time during which a person is using a particular computer service, such as a connection to the Internet.
   2. an occasion upon which data is written to a recordable CD-ROM. Multisession CDs have had data written to them at different times.

set
   1. the input of a flip-flop that places it into state 1, as opposed to the *reset* input. *See* FLIP-FLOP.
   2. the command in Windows and UNIX, that stores information in the operating system's environment area (*see* ENVIRONMENT).
   3. in mathematics, a collection of objects of any kind. For example, {2, 4, –425} is a set of numbers, and {{2, 3}, {4, 5}} is a set of sets. *See* INTERSECTION; SET DIFFERENCE; UNION.
   4. a data type in Pascal that consists of a group of values of a specified type.

set difference the set of elements that belong to one set and not to another. For example, the difference between {a, b, c} and {b, c} is {a}.

SETI@home a distributed computer system where users sign up to have their computers analyze pieces of data received from radio telescopes, in a search for extra-terrestrial intelligence (SETI). See *http://setiathome. berekely.edu.*

seven layers *see* DATA COMMUNICATION.

sexting (*sex* + *texting*) sending racy or explicit sexual pictures or text, especially pictures of oneself, by cellular telephone or Internet. This is often done by young people who regret it later, especially when they find that the pictures can be preserved and circulated by other people with whom they are no longer on good terms. *See also* INDECENCY; OBSCENITY; PORNOGRAPHY.

SGML (**S**tandard **G**eneralized **M**arkup **L**anguage) a standard set of codes for marking boldface, italics, etc., in ASCII text files, which became the basis for HTML. *See* HTML; XML.

shadow
1. (or **shadows**) the darkest area in a digitized photograph. Contrast HIGHLIGHT (definition 2).
2. to automatically and constantly copy the contents of memory or a storage device as a backup.

shadow RAM random-access memory (RAM) that holds a copy of the ROM BIOS. The copy is made at boot-up for faster access because RAM is faster than ROM. *See* BIOS; BOOT; RAM; ROM.

share
1. *(verb)* to make a file, folder, or printer available to others through a network.
2. *(noun)* a folder that is shared on a network.

Sharepoint Microsoft software for working groups to share information (web address: *sharepoint.microsoft.com*).

shareware software that is copyrighted but can be distributed free of charge to anyone. Users are asked or required to make a payment directly to the author if they use the program regularly. Shareware is sometimes misleadingly described as "free" (*see* FREE SOFTWARE).

sharp
1. a musical signal that usually indicates raising a note by a half-tone (# is the symbol for sharp).
2. because of its similarity with the ASCII character # (octothorpe or pound sign), certain Microsoft products like C# are described as C-sharp (rather than C-octothorpe).

sharpen a paint program filter that sharpens the focus of a defined area by UNSHARP MASKING. It can improve a slightly blurred image. (Don't expect miracles—the computer cannot compute information that is not in the original picture!) If overused, the sharpen filter can overemphasize small random specks or film grain because it works by increasing the difference between adjacent pixels. *See* PIXELATE; PIXELIZE; UNSHARP MASKING. For technical details, *see* CONVOLUTION.

shell a program that accepts operating system commands and causes them to be executed. For example, when you type a command such as dir, the command is read by the shell.
    The Windows shell is called COMMAND PROMPT or MS-DOS PROMPT and is derived from command.com, which was part of DOS. UNIX users have a choice of shells, such as the C shell (csh), the Bourne shell (sh), and the Korn shell (ksh).

shell script a file of commands to be executed by the SHELL (the command processor of an operating system). Windows .BAT files are shell scripts. In UNIX, a shell script can begin with a line to indicate which of several shells should process it; for example, the line

```
#!/bin/csh
```

identifies a script for the C shell. PERL and other programming language interpreters can be used as shells to execute scripts written in their respective languages.

Shell sort a variation of the insertion sort algorithm (*see* INSERTION SORT) invented by D. L. Shell. A Shell sort is a series of insertion sorts in which each item, instead of being compared with the items next to it, is compared with items a certain number of elements away. On each pass, this number (the *skip count*) becomes smaller until it reaches 1; thus, the last pass is an ordinary insertion sort. The earlier passes take care of large moves that would be time-consuming in a pure insertion sort.

Shergold, Craig a young cancer victim who, in 1989, circulated an appeal for postcards. He no longer wants any postcards, but people wouldn't stop circulating his appeal, which now haunts the Internet, often with altered names and addresses. For more information, see the *Guinness Book of World Records. See also* HOAX.

shift register a REGISTER (definition 1) in which all the bits can be moved one place to the left (or the right) when a particular control signal is pulsed. For example, the register containing 0 0 0 0 1 1 0 1 when shifted left once is 0 0 0 1 1 0 1 0, and when shifted twice is 0 0 1 1 0 1 0 0. For an application, *see* BINARY MULTIPLICATION.

Shockwave a file format for presenting audiovisual shows on the Web, designed by Macromedia, Inc., which produces the software that interprets it. A free Shockwave player is available for users to download from *www.adobe.com*.

shoeshine *(slang)* to move tape back and forth repeatedly like a shoeshine cloth, often done by tape drives that are experiencing media errors.

shortcut

1. in Windows, an ICON that serves as a LINK to a file or icon elsewhere on the same computer. Shortcuts let you put the same program or file into the menu system in more than one place. In Windows shortcut icons are recognizable by an arrow displayed in the corner, and they are represented by files with the extension .1nk in the directory corresponding to the folder in which they reside.

To create a shortcut, find the desired program or folder and right-click it. One of the menu options will be "Create Shortcut." Then cut and paste or drag the new shortcut to where you want it (usually your Desktop). *Contrast* ALIAS (Macintosh).

2. a faster way to access a command without having to pick it from a menu. Shortcuts are often indicated by underlined letters on menus; typing the letter (perhaps while holding down Alt) will take you directly to that menu selection. Some menus also indicate explicit shortcuts (such as Ctrl-S), which you can press at any time, even when that part of the menu is not on the screen.

shouting typing a message (e-mail, text, chat-room, etc.) with the CAPS-LOCK key on, or in ALL-CAPS. THIS IS CONSIDERED SHOUTING. This should be done very sparingly or not at all, as SHOUTING is considered impolite in most circles.

shrinkwrap the clear plastic coating that covers the boxes in which commercial software is sold.

shrinkwrap license a software license that the purchaser supposedly accepts by opening the package. Obviously, if the license is hidden inside the package, there will be some difficulty enforcing it in court. The validity of this "acceptance" has never been fully tested in court. *See also* COMPUTER ETHICS; COMPUTER LAW; EULA; LICENSE.

shrinkwrapped product a product packaged in SHRINKWRAP; a product that is sold in retail stores, not just through mail order catalogs or through personal contact with a specialist.

side effect an effect of a program or subprogram other than simply computing its output from its input. For example, this Java method swaps the two values in a two-element array, and also has the side effect of changing the global variable t:

```
static void swap(int a[]) {
    t=a[0];
    a[0]=a[1];
    a[1]=t;
}
```

Side effects on global variables are usually undesirable because they disrupt variables used by other parts of the program. If t were declared local, the side effect would not occur.

sideload to transfer data between two devices, neither of which is a network server, such as transferring files between a laptop computer and an MP3 player. *Compare* UPLOAD; DOWNLOAD.

SIG
1. a special interest group within various organizations and online services.
2. a SIGNATURE FILE.

sigma
1. the uppercase Greek letter Σ, which stands for the sum of all possible values of an expression. For example,

$$\sum_{i=1}^{3}(i+1)$$

is read "the sum of $i+1$ from $i=1$ to 3" and stands for

$$(1+1)+(2+1)+(3+1).$$

2. the lowercase Greek letter σ, which stands for the standard deviation in statistics.

signature an identification code sent with a message identifying the sender of the message. *See* DIGITAL SIGNATURE.

signature file a file automatically appended to outgoing e-mail and Internet postings, giving the sender's name, e-mail address, and other pertinent information. Many people use their signature file ("sig file") as a means of artistic expression, containing elaborate displays of ASCII GRAPHICS, poetry, or favorite quotes. *See also* STATIONERY.

Users sometimes embarrass themselves by forgetting what is in their signature file. Inside jokes and funny mottoes can be quite out of place on serious correspondence such as job applications.

silicon the chemical element (atomic number 14, symbol Si) most often used to make semiconductor devices. Its electrical properties can be changed by adding small amounts of impurities. *See* INTEGRATED CIRCUIT; SEMICONDUCTOR.

Silicon Creek an area in suburban Atlanta, Georgia, extending from Buckhead to the city of Norcross, home to several important computer companies, including American Megatrends (AMI), Peachtree Software, numerous Internet service providers, and formerly Hayes and Quadram, makers of important early PC peripherals. *Compare* SILICON VALLEY.

Silicon Fen an area surrounding Cambridge, England, which is home to numerous computer and electronics companies and research labs, including a major Microsoft research facility. *Compare* SILICON VALLEY.

Silicon Glen an area in Scotland comprising Glasgow, Edinburgh, and other nearby cities, home to numerous computer companies; over 25% of the PCs sold in Europe are reportedly produced there. *Compare* SILICON VALLEY.

Silicon Sandbar a concentration of computer industry companies located on Long Island, New York. *Compare* SILICON VALLEY.

Silicon Valley the Santa Clara Valley and surrounding area between San Jose and San Francisco, California, including the cities of Cupertino, Sunnyvale, and Palo Alto. It is the home of numerous semiconductor and computer companies, including Google, Hewlett-Packard, Intel, and Apple, as well as Stanford University. This was the original term for a geographic concentration of computer companies. The term was adapted for several other regions (*see* previous entries). *Compare* ROUTE 128.

silver rare chemical element (atomic number 47, symbol Ag) used in electronics because it is a good conductor of electricity.

silver gelatin print *see* GELATIN SILVER PRINT.

silverlight a tool from Microsoft for creating web and mobile applications. See *www.microsoft.com/silverlight*.

SIMM (**s**ingle **i**n-line **m**emory **m**odule) a tiny printed circuit board to which several memory chips are attached. It plugs into a slot on a larger printed circuit board and is handled as if it were a single integrated circuit. *See also* DIMM.

simulation the process of representing the actions of one system by those of another. A computer simulation is a computer program that carries out a step-by-step representation of the actions of something in the real world. For example, a computer model of population growth can simulate the behavior of a real population. A deterministic simulation occurs when the future path of the system is exactly determined by the parameters of the system. A Monte Carlo simulation occurs when probabilities are known and a selection of random numbers is used to guide the system. *See also* EMULATION.

simulcast making the audio of a radio program available on a web page at the same time it is being broadcast on the air, locally. This allows people all over the world to listen to radio stations, even when they are out of the reception area.

sin, sine the trigonometric sine function. If A is an angle in a right triangle, then the sine of A (written as sin A) is given by

$$\sin A = \frac{\text{length of opposite side}}{\text{length of hypotenuse}}$$

The function sin(a) in many programming languages calculates the value of sin A, if A is in radians. For an illustration, *see* TRIGONOMETRIC FUNCTIONS.

single-board computer a complete computer that resides on a single printed circuit board, usually a small one. Single-board computers are often built into industrial equipment. *See also* EMBEDDED SYSTEM.

single-byte font a font that represents each character with a single byte, as in ASCII or EBCDIC, and is therefore limited to 256 or fewer characters. *Contrast* DOUBLE-BYTE FONT; UNICODE.

singleton something that is in a set by itself; the only member of a one-member set.

singleton variable in Prolog, a variable that occurs only once in a fact or rule. Since all variables are local, a singleton variable does not carry information from one place to another, and it should be replaced by an anonymous variable. *See* ANONYMOUS VARIABLE; PROLOG.

SIRI personal assistant software available on the iPhone that understands NATURAL LANGUAGE requests to send messages, make phone calls, and set up appointments.

site license a software license that allows unlimited copying of a computer program for use by a single organization at a specified site. A site license

is often much cheaper than the purchase of multiple copies. *See also*
SOFTWARE LICENSE.

six sigma a high standard in statistical quality control. In statistics σ
(sigma) represents the standard deviation. If a production process is
operating well, then there will be a very small standard deviation in
measured performance. This means that only a small number of parts
will be defective, and the defective parts will be a few standard deviations away from the mean. In theory, if only those parts that are more
than 6 standard deviations away from the mean are defective, then less
than 2 parts per billion would be defective. In practice, the six sigma
standard is taken to mean 3.4 defects per million.

size *see* SCALE.

skew to bend a graphical object as shown in Figure 241. When you skew
an object, you slide one side of its bounding box to the left or to the right.
This will slant it or shift its bottom edge uphill or downhill. Skewing can
be done interactively with the mouse, or, for more precision, the degree
of skew can be specified in a dialog box.

FIGURE 241. Skew

skin a set of graphics and/or computer code that changes the appearance of
a piece of software (Figure 242). For instance, Windows Media Player
can be decorated with skins that change its color scheme, window shape,
and overall appearance. In games with three-dimensional graphics, skins
are also used to personalize the appearance of characters.

FIGURE 242. Skins
(two ways of displaying Microsoft Media Player)

skunk works (*slang*) a group of engineers and programmers who are deliberately isolated from their employer in an attempt to foster creativity and boost morale.

Skype a popular Internet telephony service (web address: *www.skype.com*). Skype users can use their computers to make free voice and video phone calls to each other. For a fee, they can also call conventional telephone numbers. Skype was acquired by Microsoft in 2011. (*See also* VOIP).

slash the character /, as opposed to the backslash \. Note that the slash has a positive slope, going up from lower left to upper right. By contrast the backward slash has negative slope. *Compare* BACKSLASH; BAR; WHACK.

Slashdot a popular web site (*www.slashdot.org*) that provides technologically oriented news for computer enthusiasts. Most of the news stories are contributed by readers. Rob Malda created Slashdot in 1997. It is now owned by OSDN, a subsidiary of VA Software Corporation.

The name was chosen so that "slashdot.org" would be confusing when read aloud ("slash dot dot org").

slave
1. the dependent unit in a pair of linked machines. *Contrast* MASTER (definition 1).
2. one of a pair of IDE hard disks or other devices connected to the same IDE cable. Generally, jumpers have to be set on IDE devices to identify them as master and slave. *Contrast* MASTER (definition 2).

sleep transistor a transistor that cuts off power to an electronic circuit when it is not needed, enabling it to "sleep" and be turned on again electronically.

slide a single image in a graphical presentation. The slide can be textual, pictorial, or graphical. Slides can also contain animations, sounds, music, and video.

slide control a symbol appearing on a touchscreen that will take an action when you slide the symbol by touching it with your finger. For example, after you press the off button on an iPad, a slide control will appear for you to confirm that you really want to turn the device off.

slide sorter an on-screen representation of an entire graphical presentation. The individual slides are shown in rows, very small. It is then easy to reorder the slides, assign special effects and timings to the slides, or select the next slide to work on.

SLIP (**S**erial **L**ine **I**nternet **P**rotocol) an adaptation of TCP/IP for DIAL-UP NETWORKING. *Compare* PPP.

slot a socket in a microcomputer designed to accept a plug-in circuit board. *See* CARD.

SLR (single-lens reflex) a camera that contains a mirror in front of the film or image sensor, so that the viewfinder can use the same lens that will actually take the picture. When a picture is taken, the mirror flips up before the shutter opens.

Unlike most other cameras, SLRs normally have interchangeable lenses, and the user can see exactly what the picture will look like with any lens. *See also* DSLR.

small caps a specially designed alphabet of capital letters that are approximately two-thirds the cap height of the font, LIKE THIS. Text set in small caps has the same visual texture as normal text but gives the emphasis of setting text in all caps. The cross references in this book are set in small caps. *See* C/SC; EVEN SMALLS.

Smalltalk one of the first object-oriented programming languages. It was developed at Xerox Palo Alto Research Center (PARC) in the late 1970s and included a powerful graphical user interface that influenced the design of the Macintosh and Microsoft Windows. *See* GRAPHICAL USER INTERFACE; OBJECT-ORIENTED PROGRAMMING.

smart card a portable card containing a microprocessor and memory. Smart cards can carry identification information for the individual, and they can be used for electronic payment systems. *See also* RFID.

smart pen a pen that keeps track of its movement as the user writes, so it can create a file that can be imported into a computer (and, with handwriting recognition software, be converted into a text file). It also may record sound when you are taking notes in a meeting or class.

smartboard an interactive, electronic whiteboard manufactured by SMART Technologies. Often these capture all notes and diagrams written on the board so that students can access them online later.

FIGURE 243. SmartMedia card

SmartMedia a type of flash memory storage device used in Olympus digital cameras and other portable devices. SmartMedia cards are square with one corner cut off, and the connectors are on the surface (Figure 243). *Compare* COMPACTFLASH; FLASH MEMORY CARD; MEMORY STICK; MULTIMEDIACARD; SECURE DIGITAL CARD.

Confusingly, the name SmartMedia (capitalized and spaced various ways) has also been used by a number of web page development companies.

smartphone a cellular telephone that includes the functions of a PDA (a general-purpose pocket-sized computer), such as web browsing, Wi-Fi wireless access, a camera, and a music player. Popular smartphones include the Apple iPhone and products from several manufacturers using the Google Android operating system. *See* CELLULAR TELEPHONE; IPHONE; ANDROID.

SMB *see* CIFS; SAMBA.

smear a retouching tool available in most PAINT PROGRAMS. The smear paintbrush drags color from one area over another, as if you had run your finger over a chalk picture. The smear paintbrush works with the colors already present in the picture; contrast SMUDGE, which adds random mixed colors to the image.

smiley an icon or representation of a face that is used to give the reader clues of the writer's emotional state or intention. In plain text messages, smileys can be made with regular text characters (*see* EMOTI-CON.) In more modern message systems, colorful, small graphics are used for the same purpose. Some sets of smileys are very extensive and cover a wide range of expressions; some smileys are animated, and some have sound.

FIGURE 244. Smiley icons

smishing a fraud similar to PHISHING in which the message arrives as a cell phone text message (SMS message) and the victim is told to go to a web site, which then asks for credit card numbers or similar information or downloads MALWARE. *See* PHISHING.

smoke test (*slang*) to start up a machine or computer program for the first time and "see if smoke comes out" (i.e., see if it fails catastrophically).

smooth node a point (NODE) that defines the shape of a curve but does not mark a sudden change of direction. (The *control points* lie on a straight line with the node; *see* Figure 245.) *Contrast* CUSP NODE.

SMTP (**S**imple **M**ail **T**ransfer **P**rotocol) a protocol used to transfer electronic mail between computers on the Internet and other TCP/IP networks. *See* IMAP; INTERNET; POP; PROTOCOL.

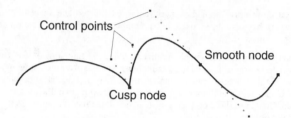

FIGURE 245. Smooth and cusp nodes

smudge a retouching tool available in most PAINT PROGRAMS. The smudge spray can randomly mixes colors in an area. The smudge spray can adds texture to the image; with coarse settings, the effect achieved is rather impressionistic. *Contrast* SMEAR; SPRAY CAN.

smurfing the practice of maliciously disrupting a computer by *pinging* it continuously (i.e., flooding it with test data packets to which it must respond). (*Smurf* is the name of a program often used to do this.) Also known as PING FLOODING. *See* DENIAL-OF-SERVICE ATTACK.

snagless (describing connectors) designed not to catch on other objects when pulled in either direction.

snail mail (*slang*) ordinary postal mail, as opposed to E-MAIL.

snap point (of an object in a draw program) a point that clings to the GRID or user-defined GUIDELINES. Most objects have multiple snap points; generally speaking, they will be at every *node* that defines the shape of the object. *See* Figure 246.

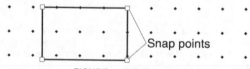

FIGURE 246. Snap points

snap to grid a mode in which a drawing program lines up all objects on a (nonprinting) grid. This makes it easy to line up parts of diagrams that are drawn separately, rather like drawing with a pencil on graph paper.

sniffer a hardware device or computer program for intercepting data packets as they pass through a network either to test the network or to intercept other people's confidential data. *See* FIREWALL.

Snow Leopard version 10.6 of MAC OS X.

snowflake *see* FRACTAL; KOCH SNOWFLAKE.

SOA (**S**ervice **O**riented **A**rchitecture) designing systems based on software units that each provide a specific service (*see* CLOUD COMPUTING).

SOAP (**S**imple **O**bject **A**ccess **P**rotocol) a protocol for executing methods (procedures, functions, subroutines) on a remote computer using XML to encode the data and HTTP to perform the data transmission. SOAP can be used by COM, CORBA, and other kinds of distributed applications. *See* COM; CORBA; HTTP; PROTOCOL; XML.

social engineering manipulating people to reveal confidential information. *See* PHISHING; SCAM.

social networking site a web site where users can build a personalized community (of other users) to socialize with. Common features include a customizable profile, the ability to add other users as friends, the ease of sharing pictures, music, text, and links, and built-in chat and mail features. Social networking sites are becoming one of the most popular methods of contacting friends and organizing gatherings. A very popular example is FACEBOOK. The business social networking site LINKEDIN is primarily for business contacts rather than personal friendship and entertainment.

Social networking sites provide a safer environment than e-mail or the Web as a whole because all members are, at least to a degree, identifiable and accountable. There are, however, privacy concerns, particularly with younger users who may be too eager to share personal information with strangers, and users of all ages can easily be mistaken as to who is seeing their messages.

social responsibility *see* EICC.

socket
1. an electrical connector into which another connector, with pins, can be inserted.
2. a communication path between two computer programs not necessarily running on the same machine. Sockets are managed by a socket DEVICE DRIVER that establishes network connections as needed; the programs that communicate through sockets need not know anything about how the network functions.

Sockpuppet a fake online identity created by another user so that the user talks through another mouthpiece while pretending not to (like a literal sock puppet). Sockpuppets often pop up in forums to defend the original person's arguments or to deliver praise in order to make the user seem more popular.

SODIMM (**S**mall **O**utline **D**ual **I**nline **M**emory **M**odule) a smaller type of DIMM commonly used in laptop and notebook computers. *See* DIMM.

soft brush (in paint programs) a category of tools that includes paintbrushes, airbrushes or spray cans, smear paintbrushes, and clone tools. All of these tools leave soft edges and have transparent strokes. These tools are sometimes grouped together in the toolbox and have similar dialog boxes for their settings.

soft copy computer output that is only viewable on the computer screen. *Contrast* HARD COPY.

soft edge in a graphical image, a boundary between two areas that is diffuse and somewhat blurred. *See* Figure 127, page 232.

soft error an error or defect on a data storage device that is present only intermittently; an error that goes away when the same operation is tried again. *Contrast* HARD ERROR.

soft hyphen a hyphen that is used only when the word falls at the end of a line; sometimes called a DISCRETIONARY HYPHEN. *Contrast* HARD HYPHEN; REQUIRED HYPHEN.

soft page, soft page break an invisible control code that indicates where the text will break at the end of a page. Unlike a HARD PAGE, a soft page break is inserted by the program and will move if the amount of text on the page changes. *See* WRAP.

software programs that tell a computer what to do. The term contrasts with *hardware,* which refers to the actual physical machines that make up a computer system. The hardware by itself is of little value without the software.

Software can be classified into *system software* (*see* OPERATING SYSTEM) and *application software.* For examples of common types of application software, *see* BROWSER; IMAGE PROCESSING, WORD PROCESSING, SPREADSHEET, DATABASE MANAGEMENT. For information on creating software, *see* PROGRAMMING and PROGRAMMING LANGUAGE.

software engineering the art and science of designing and constructing software. The computer industry has learned from bitter experience that large programs cannot be constructed as casually as small ones. Some principles of software engineering include the following:

1. Before starting a project, estimate the amount of labor it will require, based on previous experience. Err on the side of caution. Do not reduce an estimate just because a manager or customer wishes it were lower.
2. Allow adequate time for planning. Decide exactly what is needed, and if possible, write some of the documentation for the finished product before starting to write the program.
3. "Freeze" the specifications when planning is complete. Make sure clients and higher management understand that any further changes will delay completion and raise costs. The only exceptions are changes proposed by the programmers in order to simplify implementation and improve performance.
4. Set priorities. Which is more important, finishing on time or implementing the full set of features? Can the product be

developed incrementally, as a minimal first version followed by upgrades?

5. Use reliable programming techniques, including STRUCTURED PRO-GRAMMING and appropriate use of COMMENTS.

6. Insist that programmers remove errors as soon as they are found; do not leave debugging for later. You cannot build the upper stories if the foundation is not solid.

7. Keep programmers' morale high. Long working hours, although traditional in Silicon Valley, do not increase productivity; few people really work more than eight hours a day no matter how long they are at the office.

8. Do not add personnel to a project that is running late; the time taken to orient the new programmers will delay it further. Instead, find ways to help the current programmers work more efficiently. Shield them from unnecessary meetings, administrative chores, and even telephone calls.

9. Deadline crises are a symptom of incompetent management. A well-managed project gets finished on time without going into "crunch mode." If a manager does not know how long a project will take, that's not the employees' fault. If the time needed cannot be estimated in advance, everyone should realize it rather than relying on wishful thinking.

See also CREEPING FEATURISM; STRUCTURED PROGRAMMING.

software interrupt *see* INTERRUPT.

software license an agreement between the publisher of a computer program and the person who buys a copy of it, allowing the software to be used.

Some licenses specify that when you buy a copy of a program, you do not really own the copy but have merely bought the right to use it in certain ways. Normally, the license allows you to make a working copy of the program, which would otherwise be forbidden by copyright law (*see* COPYRIGHT).

Most licenses allow a single copy of the program to be used on only one machine at a time. It can be copied for backup purposes, and it can be moved from one machine to another, but it cannot be actually in use in two places at once. Thus you are forbidden to load the same program into more than one machine through a network (*see* LOCAL-AREA NET-WORK). However, it is usually permissible for several people to use the same program on a multi-user machine with a single CPU.

A *site license* allows unlimited copying of a program for use by a single organization at a specified site. A site license is often much cheaper than the purchase of multiple copies. Another alternative for schools and colleges is the use of student editions of software; these are less powerful than the commercial versions and are sold at much lower prices.

Often, purchasers of software have no opportunity to examine the license until after they have made the purchase (*see* SHRINKWRAP LICENSE). When dealing with unclear or unreasonable software licenses, users should make a good-faith effort to obey copyright law and to avoid depriving the publisher of income. *See also* ACTIVATE (definition 3); EULA; FREE SOFTWARE.

SOHO abbreviation for "**s**mall **o**ffice, **h**ome **o**ffice." (Soho is also the name of districts in London and New York City.)

Solaris the version of UNIX developed by SUN MICROSYSTEMS.

solder metal which is melted to join other metals without melting them. Most solder consists mainly of tin. Until recently, the solder in electronic equipment was usually 60% tin and 40% lead, but in order to reduce the amount of poisonous lead in landfills, the electronics industry is switching to tin-antimony and other lead-free solders. *See* ROHS.

solid photography the process of creating sculptures or models of objects based on analysis of photographs from multiple angles. *See also* THREE-DIMENSIONAL PRINTER.

solver

1. a computer program that solves equations that may have variables on either side of the equal sign, such as $x = 1 + 1/x$. This contrasts with ordinary calculators, spreadsheets, and programming languages, which can evaluate only expressions that consist entirely of known values.

2. an add-on for Microsoft Excel that can solve some kinds of optimization problems. The user specifies a target cell that is to be maximized or minimized; some cells representing variables that can be changed; and some constraints, such as specifying that the values in certain cells must be less than or greater than specific values.

sort to arrange items in numerical or alphabetical order.

Many different algorithms can be used to sort a group of items. If the number of items is small, it is probably best to use an algorithm that can be represented by a short program. If the number of data items is large, then it is more important to use a faster algorithm, even if it is complicated. Some algorithms assume that the data items have been read into the memory of the computer. However, if there is a very large number of items, it will be necessary to use an algorithm that works when the data items are stored on an auxiliary storage device. Since sorting is such a common operation, many operating systems include built-in sorting algorithms. For examples of specific sorting algorithms, *see* BUBBLE SORT; INSERTION SORT; MERGE SORT; QUICKSORT; RADIX SORT; SELECTION SORT; SHELL SORT.

Sound Blaster a line of popular sound cards for PCs marketed by Creative Labs, Inc., of Milpitas, California. Their web address is *www. soundblaster.com*.

sound card a circuit board that can be added to a computer to enable or improve its ability to record and reproduce sound. Most current motherboards now include the function of a sound card, but higher audio quality can be obtained by adding a separate sound card. Sound cards often include other features such as a MIDI musical instrument interface, a controller for a CD-ROM drive, and an audio amplifier that can drive speakers. *See* Figure 247.

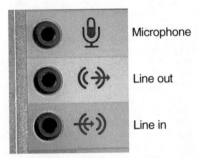

FIGURE 247. Sound card connections

source
1. *see* SOURCE CODE.
2. a place from which information is copied; the opposite of TARGET.
3. one of the three parts of a field-effect transistor (*see* FIELD-EFFECT TRANSISTOR).
4. an audio signal.

source code
1. a computer program written in a programming language, such as C or Java, as opposed to the machine-language OBJECT CODE into which the compiler translates it. *See* COMPILER.
2. the HTML code or other special code that underlies a web page or other presentation. To view a web page as source code means to view the HTML code itself rather than the display that results from it. *See* HTML.

source program a program written in a programming language (e.g., Pascal, C, or C++) and fed into a computer. The compiler translates the program into a machine-language *object program.*

SP1, SP2 abbreviations for *Service Pack 1* and *Service Pack 2*, which denote update packages for various software products.

spaghetti code (*slang*) a disorganized computer program using many GO TO statements, as easy to read as a plate of spaghetti. *Contrast* STRUCTURED PROGRAMMING.

spam unsolicited and unwelcome advertisements sent to people via e-mail or posted in newsgroups. "Spammers" have discovered that they can reach a large audience at low cost on the Internet by posting the same message to all available newsgroups or e-mailing it to all possible addresses.

Spamming is considered seriously unethical for two reasons. First, newsgroups and e-mail would be useless if they routinely contained unwanted material. Second, the cost of transporting e-mail and newsgroup postings is not paid by the sender; it is paid by the recipient's site and other sites along the way. Thus, it is important not to impose expenses on people by sending them unwanted material.

In some places, spamming by e-mail is illegal, and there is a strong movement to prohibit it everywhere. More importantly, almost all Internet service providers (ISPs) flatly prohibit both e-mail and newsgroup spam. The few ISPs that allow spamming are ostracized by other sites, which refuse to accept any data from them.

Experts advise that you should never reply to spam, even to ask to be taken off the mailing list, because that will merely tell the spammer that he has hit a valid address. Even if only a very tiny percentage of recipients buy something from the spammer, it may still be cost-effective to send the spam because the spammer does not have to pay the full cost. Also, some spam is really sent as a devious way to distribute malware.

Spam was named after a Hormel processed-meat product, following a Monty Python comedy act which involved repeatedly saying "spam" to drown out all other dialog. For Hormel's response to the situation, see *www.spam.com*.

See CAN-SPAM; COMPUTER ETHICS; COMPUTER LAW; COMPUTER SECURITY; NETIQUETTE; SPAM FILTER; ZOMBIE.

spam filter a piece of software that distinguishes SPAM from ordinary e-mail. Spam filters are used in most major e-mail systems and can also run on an individual's computer.

The way spam is recognized is kept secret, but it involves analysis of vocabulary, recognition of key phrases, and identification of known spam sites. To try to get around spam filters, spammers misspell the names of products and often include large numbers of irrelevant words. *See* BAYESIAN SPAM FILTER.

spammer a person who sends out SPAM. Spammers are viewed with great contempt by the entire Internet community.

S/PDIF (Sony/Philips Digital Interface) a format for hardware and software for transferring digital audio files, used on CD players and other audio devices.

speaker-dependent, speaker-independent *see* SPEECH RECOGNITION.

special characters characters that cannot be typed directly from the keyboard, but require entering a special code or selection through the

KeyCaps or KEYBOARD VIEWER (Macintosh) or the Character Map (Windows).

Windows software accesses these special characters in many different ways. If you prefer to keep your hands on the keyboard, you can type most special characters by holding down the Alt key and typing a four-digit code on the numeric keypad.

Macintosh users can type special characters by holding down the Option or Ctrl buttons while typing (here the Option key acts like another Shift key). KeyCaps lets you see which typewriter key corresponds to the desired character.

See also EXPERT SET; IBM PC; UNICODE.

specular highlight a bright point of light on a reflective or shiny surface.

speech recognition the use of computers to recognize spoken words. This is a nontrivial task because the same spoken word does not produce entirely the same sound waves when pronounced by different people or even when pronounced by the same person on more than one occasion. The computer must digitize the sound, transform it to discard unneeded information, and finally try to match it with words stored in a dictionary.

Most speech recognition systems are *speaker-dependent*; they have to be trained to recognize a particular person's speech and can then distinguish thousands of words (but only the words they were trained on). *Speaker-independent* speech recognition is less effective. The biggest demand for speech recognition arises in situations in which typing is difficult or impossible, such as equipment for the handicapped, highly portable equipment, and computers that are to be accessed by telephone. Increasingly, speech recognition is used for automated switchboards, voice-activated dialing, GPS driving directions, smartphone applications, etc.

It is easier to recognize DISCRETE SPEECH (speech with pauses between words) than CONTINUOUS SPEECH, but discrete speech is slow and awkward. Hesitation noises ("uh," "um"), coughs, and sneezes are sometimes mistaken for words.

speech synthesis the generation of human-like speech by computer (by computing the pronunciation of each word, not by playing back recordings).

Originally handled by special hardware, speech synthesis is now usually done by means of software running on a personal computer with a sound card. The technology to generate understandable speech has existed since the 1960s, but the speech is not completely natural; the intonation and timing are not perfect, and the voice may be monotonous and robot-like.

Speech synthesis is important in making computers accessible to blind people and delivering computer data by telephone. A speech synthesizer is built into Windows.

spell checker a program that checks the spelling of every word in a document by looking up each word in its dictionary. Many word processors do this as the words are typed. If the word does not appear in the dictionary, the user is alerted to a possible misspelling, and possible corrections are often suggested. Sometimes the correction will be made automatically, but you need to double-check to make sure that the resulting word is correct. For example, if you are writing about a player being elected to the "hall of fame," and you mistakenly type "hall of sfame," it will obviously be a typographical error; but if it autocorrects to "hall of shame," it will be very embarrassing.

A spell checker will not recognize unusual proper names or specialized terms, but it will often allow you to create your own personal dictionary of specialized words you often use. (Be sure not to put misspelled words into it!) Spell checkers are valuable aids to proofreading, but they cannot catch the substitution of one correctly spelled word for another (such as *form* for *from* or *to* for *too*). Thus they do not guarantee that a document is free of spelling errors.

spider a program that explores the World Wide Web; a CRAWLER.

SPIM a SPAM message sent by instant messaging.

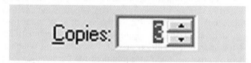

FIGURE 248. Spin button

spin button a dialog box element that allows the user to change numbers rapidly by clicking on the up and down arrows or by typing the desired number directly into the number box.

spindle count in a disk or file sharing system, the total number of actual disk drives (each with a stack of magnetic disks revolving around a single spindle).

splash screen a screen display or small window that appears briefly while a program is starting up, displaying its name, trademark, and version information.

spline a curve that connects a set of points smoothly. Figure 249 shows some examples. For details of computation, *see* B-SPLINE; BÉZIER SPLINE; CUBIC SPLINE.

splog (**spam blog**) a web page masquerading as a blog but in reality is an attempt to entice users to click on links to advertisers.

sploit (*slang; plural **sploitz***) an EXPLOIT; a way of breaching the security of a system.

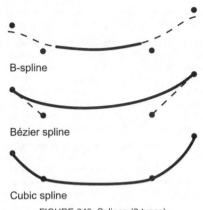

B-spline

Bézier spline

Cubic spline

FIGURE 249. Splines (3 types)

spoofing the act of impersonating a user or a machine. For example, *IP spoofing* is the act of attaching a computer to the Internet using an IP ADDRESS assigned to a different computer, thereby intercepting communications intended for the other machine. *See* PHISHING.

spooling the process of storing computer output before sending it to the printer. *See* PRINT SPOOLER.

spot color the use of a specified color of ink in a printing job. Spot color can be used for emphasis or to add interest to documents. *Contrast* PROCESS COLOR. These terms apply to mass-production printing with a printing press, not to inkjet or laser printers attached directly to computers.

spray can a tool found in various paint programs that leaves a circular pattern of the selected color. To use it, you press and hold down the mouse button and drag the mouse. The center of the spray pattern will be solid, but the edges will feather out to the background color. If you need a dense, solid color, move the mouse slowly; if you want a wispy trace of color, move the mouse rapidly. You can change the size of the spray can's coverage area—usually by changing the brush size.

A similar tool is the AIRBRUSH. Generally, a program will have either an airbrush or a spray can tool, but not both.

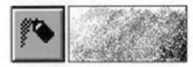

FIGURE 250. Spray can

spread to put two fingers on the screen and spread them apart in a multi-touch interface, typically causing the image on the screen to zoom in.

spread-spectrum a technique of radio transmission in which the frequency changes many times per second in a predetermined but seemingly random sequence. The receiver knows the sequence and follows the frequency changes. Spread-spectrum transmission overcomes interference because two transmitters will never be on the same frequency for more than a moment. Spread-spectrum transmission also provides privacy because the signal is almost impossible to intercept without knowing the sequence of frequency changes. *See* WIRELESS COMMUNICATION.

spreadsheet a table of numbers arranged in rows and columns. Paper spreadsheets were used for business data long before computers were invented. The first computer spreadsheet was VisiCalc, used on the Apple II computer in the late 1970s. Recently the most popular spreadsheet has been Microsoft Excel. Here are some general features of such a program:

1. Data is arranged in rows (labeled with numbers) and columns (labeled with letters). Each location in the spreadsheet is called a cell. You can enter numbers or letters in a cell, as in this example, which records the sales of different types of products at a small store:

	A	B	C	D
1	Item	Price	Quantity	
2	cereal	3.99	10	
3	milk	2.15	25	
4	toothpaste	1.95	7	

2. The computer will do calculations automatically if you enter formulas. For example, to calculate the revenue from the sale of cereal, enter the formula =B2*C2 in cell D2. (The asterisk * represents multiplication; the initial equal sign indicates this is a formula and not a label.

	A	B	C	D
1	Item	Price	Quantity	Revenue
2	cereal	3.99	10	39.90
3	milk	2.15	25	
4	toothpaste	1.95	7	

When a formula is entered, the spreadsheet will display the result of the formula, not the formula itself, in that cell. However, moving the cell pointer to a cell will let you see the formula for that cell at the top of the screen, and you can edit it if needed.

3. A formula in one cell can be copied to other cells. For example, the formula in cell D2 can be copied to cells D3 and D4, which will give the total revenue for the other products:

	A	B	C	D
1	Item	Price	Quantity	Revenue
2	cereal	3.99	10	39.90
3	milk	2.15	25	53.75
4	toothpaste	1.95	7	13.65

The copy command automatically changes formulas when they are copied to new cells. In the preceding example, when you copy the formula =B2*C2 from cell D2 to cell D3, it will become the formula =B3*C3, and in cell D4 it will become =B4*C4. This is because B2 and C2 in the formula in the original cell (D2) were written in the form of a RELATIVE ADDRESS. *See* ABSOLUTE ADDRESS to learn how to prevent the cell addresses from being changed by the copy command.

4. A formula can contain built-in functions, such as a command to sum all cells in a range. Entering Excel formula =SUM(D2:D4) into cell D5 will automatically calculate the column total (cells D2, D3, and D4). Many such functions are included with spreadsheet programs.

5. Spreadsheets are especially valuable because the formulas will be automatically recalculated whenever one of the numbers is changed. For example, if later in the month you update your sales figures, the program will automatically recalculate the revenue for each item, and the total revenue. This makes spreadsheets especially useful for "what-if" analysis. You can design a spreadsheet with many variables, and see how the result changes when one or more of those variables are changed.

6. Spreadsheets can automatically create graphs of your data. For example, Figure 251 shows a pie chart giving the fraction of the sales of each item. Graphs can also illustrate how a variable changes with time, or how two variables are related to each other.

7. MACROS can be used to combine a series of keystrokes into one command, and advanced macros are themselves computer programs that can interact with users and process data.

8. Modern spreadsheets have added many features to improve the appearance of the output. For example, some cells can be displayed in boldface type, or a cell can be emphasized with shading.

9. Originally, spreadsheets were two-dimensional, making them analogous to putting all of your work on one giant piece of paper. Later spreadsheets added three-dimensional capability, which is analogous to keeping your work on different pages in a notebook. Also, modern spreadsheets allow different worksheets to be automatically linked together. For example, you can put your monthly sales figures in 12 different worksheets, and then have those linked to a single spreadsheet with year-end summary data.

See also EXCEL; LOTUS 1-2-3; MACRO.

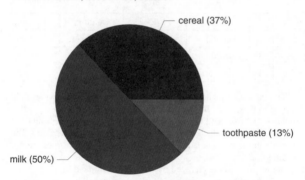

FIGURE 251. Spreadsheets can
create graphs such as this pie chart

sprite a moving element in a graphical display. Most video games use sprites.

spyware software that monitors a computer user's activity without his or her knowledge and reports it to a central location. The purpose of spyware ranges from purportedly benign (enforcing copyrights, displaying targeted advertisements) to very malicious (stealing passwords and credit card numbers).

The most common way to get spyware on your computer is to install it yourself. This happens when you are tricked into installing free software that supposedly does something else, such as improve your computer's performance or enable access to a web site.

Most spyware runs under Microsoft Windows, which formerly allowed web sites to download and install software on your computer automatically (*see* ACTIVEX). Current versions of Windows ask for permission before installing software, but it is very important for the user to be alert and not give this permission inappropriately. Above all, do not click on web site buttons that offer to do anything to your computer, such as check it or "optimize" it.

Software tools for detecting and removing spyware can be found at *www.safer-networking.org* and *www.lavasoftusa.com*. *See also* ADWARE; MALWARE; VIRUS.

SQL (**S**tructured **Q**uery **L**anguage, formerly Sequel) a standard query language used by many programs that manipulate large databases. Here is an example of an SQL query:

```
SELECT NAME, SALARY FROM TABLE1
WHERE SALARY > 35000
```

This means "Give me the name and salary from each row in TABLE1 where the salary is more than 35,000." *See* QUERY LANGUAGE; RELATIONAL DATABASE.

square brackets the characters [ ], also called simply *brackets*. *Contrast* ANGLE BRACKETS; CURLY BRACKETS; PARENTHESES.

SRAM (**S**tatic **R**andom-**A**ccess **M**emory, pronounced "S-ram") a type of computer memory that does not require a periodic refresh signal. SRAM is more expensive than DRAM and is rarely used as the main memory of a computer system, but it is often used for caches, video memory, and microcontroller systems. *See* MEMORY; RAM. *Contrast* DRAM.

SSL (**S**ecure **S**ocket **L**ayer) an encryption system developed by Netscape based on RSA ENCRYPTION. SSL protects the privacy of data exchanged by the web site and the individual user. It is used by web sites whose names begin with https instead of http.

stack
1. a data structure from which items are removed in the reverse order from which they were inserted; also called a *pushdown stack* or *pushdown store*.

For example, when a program calls a subroutine, information about how to return to the main program is usually placed on the stack. If the subroutine then calls another subroutine, information about how to return to the first subroutine is placed on the stack. Since this information is retrieved from the stack in the opposite order from which it was placed there, each subroutine returns control to the right place.

Stacks are very useful for dealing with one operation nested inside another. To *push* a data item is to place it on a stack; to *pop* the stack is to remove an item from it. *See also* LIFO. *Contrast* FIFO; QUEUE.

2. A set of DEVICE DRIVERS loaded in a specific order to implement a function such as TCP/IP.

stacking order the order in which objects are arranged in a drawing program. This order determines which objects overlay others. Commands to reorganize the stacking order (Send to Front, Send to Back, Forward One, Back One) are usually found under an Arrange menu. *Compare* Z-ORDER.

Standard Generalized Markup Language, SGML a standard set of codes for marking boldface, italics, and so on, in ASCII text files, which became the basis for HTML. *See* HTML; XML.

standard input, standard output the input and output streams that a computer program reads and writes when not told to use a file; in CONSOLE MODE, the keyboard and screen.

star the character * (asterisk).

star dot star the WILD CARD character sequence *.*, which matches all Windows filenames.

star key the key on a telephone keypad marked with the symbol *. It is often used to give commands to software at the telephone company.

Start button a button, labeled "Start . . . ", that is normally on the screen whenever Windows is running. By clicking on the Start button, you can access application programs and other functions of the computer through the START MENU.

    If the Start button is not visible, it's probably because the TASKBAR at the bottom of the screen has been reduced to minimum width. Just move the mouse pointer to where it ought to be, and it will appear. By dragging the taskbar with the mouse cursor, you can restore it to normal width and make it readable again.

    You can also display the Start menu at any time by pressing Ctrl-Esc.

FIGURE 252. Start button and start menu (Windows)

Start menu the menu that is called up by the START BUTTON in the corner of the screen under Microsoft Windows. It leads to all the application software that is installed on the computer. To edit or modify the Start menu, open it with the right mouse button rather than the left button.

startup folder a FOLDER under the Windows START MENU containing programs that are to be run automatically when Windows starts up or when a user logs on. There may be a starting folder for "All Users" and another one for the specific user who is logging in.

starvation in MULTITASKING, a situation where a task can never finish because it can never get a necessary resource, such as a large block of memory. The operating system should detect such tasks and do its best to allocate the resources that they need. *See* MULTITASKING.

statement a single instruction in a computer programming language. One statement may consist of several operations, such as $x = y+z/w$ (a division, an addition, and an assignment). *See* PROGRAMMING LANGUAGE.

static
1. in C and related programming languages, a keyword indicating that a variable continues to exist even when the function that defines it is not in use. That is, a static variable remembers its value from one invocation of the function to the next.
2. in C++ and related programming languages, a keyword indicating that a variable exists, or a method can be called, without creating an object of the class to which it is attached, and if several such objects are created, they will share one copy of the static item.
3. (describing electricity) standing still; accumulating as a charge rather than flowing in a circuit. Static electricity accumulating on the human body can damage integrated circuits when a person suddenly touches them. To prevent this, be sure to touch the frame of the computer before touching anything inside it, and use anti-static spray on carpets.
4. (describing audio or video) popping or frying sounds or speckled patterns like those caused by discharges of static electricity interfering with radio or television reception. In the digital world, this kind of static usually results from an insufficient data transmission rate, or corrupted data, rather than from static electricity.

static IP address an IP address that is assigned permanently to a computer. A static IP address is needed for any kind of server that people access through the Internet. *Contrast* DYNAMIC IP ADDRESS.

static RAM *see* SRAM.

stationery
1. paper, envelopes, and so forth on which information is to be printed.
2. a template for e-mail messages including colors and graphics to give it a distinctive appearance, implemented by using HTML.

statistics program a software package for performing statistical calculations.

A statistics program works with lists of numbers instead of single values. It should have built-in commands for calculating the average and standard deviation of the elements of a list, for testing hypotheses about the relationships between variables through methods such as multiple regression, for performing transformations (such as taking the logarithm of each of the elements in a list), and for drawing graphs of the data. Examples of statistics programs include SAS (**S**tatistical **A**nalysis **S**ystem) and SPSS (**S**tatistical **P**rogram for the **S**ocial **S**ciences).

status bar, status line a line of information on the computer screen that indicates the current settings of the software and the current cursor position. The contents of a status line will vary depending on the software used; some programs give different information during the execution of different commands. It is a good idea to get into the habit of noticing what is in the status line. If you do not understand what you see there, take a moment to review the manual.

FIGURE 253. Status line

steganography the concealment of a small message inside a larger file that appears to consist entirely of something else. For example, an encrypted message might be hidden among some slight variations of color at selected points in a picture. Crucially, a person viewing the picture would not know that a message was concealed in it. Messages can also be hidden in inaudible low-level noise superimposed on digitized music.

Steganography goes hand-in-hand with encryption but is not the same thing. Encryption makes a message unreadable by unauthorized persons; steganography hides the very existence of the message. *See also* CRYPTOGRAPHY; ENCRYPTION.

stochastic random; constantly varying; unpredictable; scattered.

storage area network a computer network that shares disk space using DISK SHARING rather than FILE SHARING. *Contrast* NETWORK ATTACHED STORAGE.

store to place a data item into a memory device.

stored program computer a computer that can store its own instructions as well as data. All modern computers are of this type. The concept was originated by Charles Babbage in the 19th century and was developed by John Von Neumann. The ability of a computer to store instructions allows it to perform many tasks without human intervention. The instructions are usually written in a programming language. *See* COMPUTER.

Storm worm a WORM virus introduced in 2007 that linked thousands of computers into a ZOMBIE network.

stream
  1. audio or video content made available by streaming.
  2. (*noun*) in C++, Lisp, and other computer languages, a file or device that can be read or written one character at a time. For example, the screen and keyboard can be treated as streams.

streaming delivering audio or video signals in real time, without waiting for a whole file to download before playing it. *See* REALAUDIO.

stretch to increase or reduce either the vertical or horizontal dimension of an object, thereby changing its overall shape. To use the mouse to stretch a selected object interactively, drag out one of the handles at the mid-points of the BOUNDING BOX. *Contrast* SCALE, which maintains the height-to-width ratio of the object.

FIGURE 254. Stretch

string (character string) a sequence of characters stored in a computer and treated as a single data item. *See* STRING OPERATIONS.

string operations operations that are performed on character string data. Here are some examples from Java, where A represents the string "GEORGE" and B represents "WASHINGTON":
  1. Compare two strings to see if they are the same. For example, A.equals(B) (in other programming languages, A==B or A=B) will be false.
  2. Determine if one string comes before the other in alphabetical order. For example,

  A.compareTo(B)<=0

  will be true (because GEORGE comes before WASHINGTON). In other programming languages this is expressed as A<B. Alphabetical order is determined on the basis of Unicode character codes, so lowercase letters come after uppercase letters (*see* UNICODE).
  3. Join strings together (concatenation). For example,

  A+" "+B

  is
  "GEORGE WASHINGTON" created by joining A, a blank, and B.

4. Calculate the length of a string. For example, A.length() is 6.
5. Select specified characters from any position in string. For example,

```
B.substring(4,7)
```

is the string "ING". The 4 means to start at character 4, which is the character I since the first character (W) is character 0. The 7 means to include all characters up to (but not including) character 7 (which is T).

6. Determine if one string is contained in another string, and if so, at what position it starts. For example,

```
A.indexOf("OR")
```
is 2, since OR starts at character 2 of GEORGE (recall that the first character is character 0). However,

```
B.indexOf("AND")
```

is −1 since the string AND does not occur within the string WASHINGTON.

7. Determine the Unicode value for an individual character. For example, if C is a character variable, then

```
(short)C
```

will give its Unicode value. Here *short* is a type of integer variable.

8. Determine the character associated with a given Unicode value. For example, if K is an integer variable, then

```
(char)K
```

is the character associated with that value.

9. Determine the numerical value of a string that represents a number. Here are two examples (for integers and strings):

```
String x="234";
int z=Integer.parseInt(x);

String x2="234.567";
double z2=(Double.valueOf(x2)).doubleValue();
```

Note the capitalization needs to be exactly as shown.

10. Convert a numeric value into a string. For example,
```
String x=String.valueOf(567);
```
will cause *x* to become the string "567".

striping the practice of spreading consecutive data blocks across different disk drives (e.g., block 1 on disk 1, block 2 on disk 2, block 3 on disk 1 again, and so on). *See* RAID.

struct in C and C#, a data structure consisting of several simpler items grouped together.

A struct is not an OBJECT; that is, a struct cannot have METHODS. Java does not have structs; it uses only classes (object types). C# has both.

See also CLASS; OBJECT-ORIENTED PROGRAMMING.

structured programming a programming technique that emphasizes clear logic, modularity, and avoidance of GO TO statements (which are intrinsically error-prone).

One of the most important barriers to the development of better computer software is the limited ability of human beings to understand the programs that they write. Structured programming is a style of programming designed to make programs more comprehensible and programming errors less frequent. Because it is more a popular movement than a precise theory, structured programming can be defined in several ways, but it usually includes the following;

1. *Block structure.* The statements in the program must be organized into functional groups. For example, of the following two Pascal program fragments, the first is structured, while the second is not:

```
Structured:                 Unstructured:
IF x<=y THEN                IF x>y THEN GOTO 2;
  BEGIN                     z := y-x;
    z := y-x;               q := SQRT(z);
    q :=SQRT(z);            GOTO 1;
  END                       2: z:= x-y;
ELSE                        q:=-SQRT(z);
  BEGIN                     1: writeln(z,q);
    z := x-y;
    q := -SQRT(z)
  END;
WRITELN(z,q);
```

Note that it is much easier to tell what the first example does.

2. *Avoidance of jumps* ("GO-TO-less programming"). It can be proved mathematically that, if a language has structures equivalent to the (block-structured) IF-THEN and WHILE statements in Pascal, it does not need a GO TO statement. Moreover, GO TO statements are often involved in programming errors; the programmer becomes confused as to the exact conditions under which a particular group of statements will execute.

Advocates of structured programming allow GO TO statements only under very restricted circumstances (e.g., to deal with error conditions that completely break out of the logic of a program) or not at all.

3. *Modularity.* If a sequence of statements continues uninterrupted for more than about 50 lines, human beings have a hard time understanding it because there is too much information for them to keep track of. As an alternative, programs should be broken up

into subroutines, even if some of the subroutines are called only once. Then the main program will read like an outline, and the programmer will never need to understand more than about one page of code at a time. (The programmer must know what the subroutines do, but not how they do it.) This principle is sometimes called *information hiding*—irrelevant information should be kept out of the programmer's way. Structured programming was first advocated by E. W. Dijkstra in the early 1970s.

stub
1. a temporary substitute for a part of a computer program that has not yet been written. For instance, if a procedure to read numbers from a file has not yet been written, the programmer might put in a stub that simply gives the same number every time, so that the rest of the program can proceed.
2. a declaration that tells how to call a method or function that is defined elsewhere.

StudlyCaps (*slang*) INTERCAPS. *See also* PASCAL NOTATION.

StuffIt a data compression program for Macintosh and Windows written by Raymond Lau. Like ZIP and WinZip, StuffIt allows several files to be combined into one. StuffIt can also encode and decode BinHex files. A free StuffIt expander program can be downloaded from *www.stuffit.com*. *See* DATA COMPRESSION; ZIP FILE.

style (**of type**) a particular kind of type, either plain, boldface, or italic, belonging to a specified font. *See* FONT; TYPEFACE.

Normal *Bold Italic*
Italic Condensed
Bold Extended

FIGURE 255. Styles of Helvetica type

style sheet a file (in WordPerfect, L^AT_EX, HTML, and other publishing programs) that defines the overall layout and type specifications of a document or web page. *See* CASCADING STYLE SHEETS; DESKTOP PUBLISHING; GRID SYSTEM.

stylus
1. the pen-like part of a graphics tablet (*See* Figure 122 at GRAPHICS TABLET, page 224). They may contain sophisticated electronics to improve accuracy and measure the pressure placed on the tablet by the artist.
2. a sharp, pen-like device used for pressing on the touchscreen of a handheld computer or PDA. The stylus contains no electronic parts; any object that has a non-marking point but is not too sharp will do the job.

subdirectory a disk directory that is stored in another directory. *See* DIRECTORY.

subnet mask a bit pattern, usually written as four decimal numbers, that indicates which parts of an IP address belong to the same network.

   In the IPv4 protocol, the most common subnet mask is 255.255.255.0, which indicates that the first three numbers of the IP address might be the same through the subnet (the local network). A larger network might use 255.255.254.0, which leaves one more bit for identifying individual computers, or ever 255.255.0.0, which indicates that only the first two numbers are the same throughout the subnet. Here 255 (binary 11111111) means "the number in this position is the same throughout the network" and 0 (binary 00000000) means "this number varies from computer to computer."

   More technically, subnet masks are 32-bit binary numbers which are logically ANDed with an IP address to extract the part that identifies the network. Values other than 0 and 255 can extract particular bits while leaving others unused.

   In IPv6, subnet masks work the same way but are much larger and are written in hexadecimal rather than decimal. A common subnet mask is FFFF:FFFF:FFFF:FFFF:0:0:0:0. *See* IPV4; IPV6.

subroutine a sequence of instructions that will be executed when a program calls for it. In most newer programming languages, subroutines are called FUNCTIONS, PROCEDURES, or METHODS. Subroutines may be independently compiled and are assigned to memory with a starting address known as an ENTRY POINT. *See* STRUCTURED PROGRAMMING; TOP-DOWN PROGRAMMING.

subscribe
   1. to request to be included in an e-mail mailing list.
   2. on social networking sites, to choose to view a particular person's public postings.

subscript a number or other indicator used to identify a particular element in an array. In mathematics, subscripts are written below the main line, as in x_1 or a_k. In most computer languages, however, subscripts are usually enclosed by either parentheses or square brackets, as in x[1] or A[k]. *See* ARRAY.

subscripted variable array variable. *See* ARRAY.

subwoofer a speaker that reproduces only very low-frequency sounds, used to supplement the other speakers in an audio system.

suit (*slang*) a manager or salesman; a (male) worker in the computer industry who is neither an engineer nor a programmer and is therefore not allowed to dress casually.

suitcase (Macintosh) a special kind of folder that contains system resources (fonts, sounds, desk accessories). For example, you can manage your fonts by keeping them grouped logically in suitcases. Some prefer to store their fonts in typeface families—others group fonts used for specific projects in separate suitcases.

Sun Microsystems the company that developed SPARC microprocessors, Sun WORKSTATIONS, the SOLARIS operating system, and the JAVA programming language. Sun workstations dominated academic computer networking in the 1990s, before PCs were fully network-capable. During their heyday, most Sun workstations used Sun's proprietary RISC microprocessor called SPARC. In 2010 Sun was acquired by ORACLE.

See *www.oracle.com/us/products/servers-storage/servers*.

superclass a class from which another class in an object-oriented programming language is descended. For example, if your applet program myapplet extends the class Applet, then Applet is the superclass for myapplet. *See* EXTENDS.

supercomputer a computer designed to run markedly faster than ordinary mainframe computers, generally by using parallel processing. Examples are the Cray vector processors and the Intel iPSC parallel processor.

supercookie a COOKIE designed to be very hard to detect once it is present on your hard disk, where it potentially could act as MALWARE.

superior character a superscript; small letters and numbers set above the baseline ^like this^. Used mainly in mathematical typesetting. *See* SUPERSCRIPT. *Contrast* INFERIOR CHARACTER; SUBSCRIPT.

superscalar processor a computer that is in between conventional SCALAR PROCESSOR and VECTOR PROCESSOR architectures; it accepts instructions like those of a scalar processor but has some ability to double them up and do more than one thing at once at runtime. The PENTIUM is an example of a superscalar processor.

superscript a small character written above the baseline, ^like this^. In mathematics, a superscript indicates an exponent, which denotes repeated multiplication. For example, $4^3 = 4 \times 4 \times 4$.

supertwist a newer type of liquid crystal display (LCD) that produces higher contrast than earlier types. An LCD works by twisting light waves to change their polarization. Supertwist displays produce more of a change in polarization than their predecessors.

support ticket *see* TICKET.

surface computing working on a computer screen that is not a traditional monitor; for example, a tabletop that has a built-in touchscreen computer display.

surface mapping the act of applying a surface (complete with color, pattern, shading, and texture) to a 3D wireframe model. *See* RENDER.

surfing *(slang)* the practice of browsing the WORLD WIDE WEB or other information services, much like a surfer riding one wave and then another.

surge protector device that absorbs brief bursts of excessive voltage coming in from the AC power line. These surges are created by lightning or by electric motors switching off.

Surge protectors do little good unless the power line is properly grounded. Always plug the computer into a properly grounded outlet. If possible, do not plug a laser printer into the same outlet strip or extension cord as the computer, because laser printers draw heavy current intermittently.

Many surge protectors also incorporate RFI protectors to help reduce radio and TV interference emitted by the computer into the power line. (*See* RFI PROTECTION.) A surge protector cannot do anything about momentary power failures; for that, you need an uninterruptible power supply.

See also POWER LINE PROTECTION; UNINTERRUPTIBLE POWER SUPPLY.

surround sound a system of sound reproduction where there are speakers in several directions from the listener (Fig. 256). This contrasts with *stereophonic* sound, with just left and right speakers, and *monophonic* sound, with just one speaker (or multiple speakers playing the same signal).

Several systems have been developed for encoding and decoding surround sound in a two-channel stereo signal, and many computer SOUND CARDS now have surround-sound output. *See* 5.1; 6.1; 7.1.

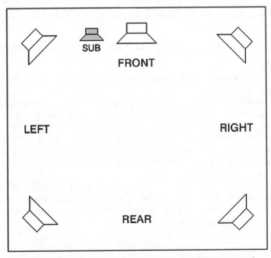

FIGURE 256. Surround sound (5.1 speaker arrangement)

suspend to stop the CPU and input-output devices of a computer while leaving the contents of memory in place, so that it can resume where it left off without rebooting. Unlike a hibernating computer, a suspended computer continues to consume a small amount of battery power. *Contrast* HIBERNATE.

SVG (scalable vector graphics) a markup language for two-dimensional graphics (see *www.w3.org/Graphics/SVG*).

SVGA (Super **VGA**) a video resolution of 800 × 600 pixels. *Contrast* XGA.

swap file a file used for swap space. In Windows, the swap file is hidden and does not normally appear in directory listings (*see* HIDDEN FILE). It can be either permanent, and fixed in size, or temporary, and varying in size. Permanent swap files give faster program execution.

Besides the swap file used by the operating system, there are also swap files used by particular applications, such as Adobe PhotoShop. *See* SWAP SPACE.

swap space disk space that an operating system or program uses as a substitute for additional memory. *See* VIRTUAL MEMORY; SWAP FILE.

swash a capital letter with a decorative flourish. Swashes are best used sparingly.

FIGURE 257. Swash capital letters

.swf (Shockwave file) filename extension used by Macromedia Shockwave. *See* SHOCKWAVE.

swipe sliding your finger across a touchscreen. *See* TRANSITION EFFECT.

switch

1. in electronics, a device for interrupting or rerouting the flow of electric current.

2. in telecommunications and networking, a device for establishing connections between one location and another, doing the work of a telephone operator. For instance, on a computer network, a switch is a device that temporarily creates high-speed paths between different segments as they are needed. It works like a hub but does not add congestion to cables on which the traffic is not actually needed. *See* BRIDGE. *Compare* HUB; ROUTER.

3. in C and its derivatives, a statement for choosing different actions corresponding to different values of a variable. Each section must end with break unless you want execution to continue in the next section. Here is an example in Java:

```
switch (p)
{
case 1:
        System.out.println("First place\n"); break;
case 2:
        System.out.println("Second place\n"); break;
case 3:
        System.out.println("Third place\n"); break;
default:
        System.out.println("Something else\n");
}
```

switched line an ordinary (POTS) telephone line on which you establish connections by dialing; the path actually taken by the signals need not be the same when you call the same number twice on different occasions. *Contrast* DSL; T1 LINE; T3 LINE.

switching power supply a power supply that regulates the voltage of direct current by switching it off and on very rapidly and then smoothing out the variations. Most computer power supplies are of this type. The advantages of a switching power supply are that it does not waste energy and does not require a heavy transformer, since the incoming AC is chopped to give a high frequency that can be handled by a smaller, lighter transformer. The disadvantage is that it produces radio-frequency interference. *See* POWER SUPPLY; RFI PROTECTION.

SXGA (Super XGA) a monitor resolution of 1280×1024 pixels.

symbol font a font containing symbols or ornaments rather than a regular alphabet. Also called a pi font or DINGBATS.

FIGURE 258. Symbol font (Minion Ornaments)

symbolic algebra the manipulation of mathematical symbols (not just their numerical values). For example, we can calculate that $(a + b) \times (c + d) = ac + ad + bc + bd$ without knowing the values of a, b, c, or d.

Symbolic algebra on computers began with the MACSYMA project at MIT in the 1960s. Today, popular symbolic algebra programs for personal computers include MathCad, Maple, Mathematica, and MATLAB. They greatly simplify the formerly tedious process of deriving and manipulating mathematical formulas.

symbolic debugger program that lets you step through a compiled program, interrupting it at any point and examining or changing the values of variables.

"Symbolic" means that programmer-assigned names in the program are recognized. A symbolic debugger analyzes the source code and the object code together, so that even though the program has been compiled, you can work with it as if you were editing the source program.

symbolic programming a kind of programming in which variables can stand for pieces of the program itself (symbolic expressions), not just numbers, strings, or other values. Lisp and Prolog are examples of symbolic programming languages. *See* LISP; PROLOG; SYMBOLIC ALGEBRA.

sync to synchronize the content on two devices; for example, to sync your iPad and desktop computer so they contain the same pictures and music.

synchronization
1. the process of keeping two or more disk drives up to date relative to each other, by copying the latest version of each file to each device. This is a practical problem if you work with more than one computer, such as a laptop and a desktop machine.
2. the act of making an analog video display scan each line at exactly the right time so that the image is displayed correctly.

synchronous occurring in unison with a separate signal. In synchronous data transmission, there are two signals, *data* and *clock*. The clock signal indicates exactly when the *data* line should be read in order to obtain each successive bit.

syntax the set of rules that specify how the symbols of a language can be put together to form meaningful statements. A syntax error is a place in a program where the syntax rules of the programming language were not followed.

syntax diagram a diagram showing how to arrange elements of a language. For an example *see* RAILROAD DIAGRAM.

synthesizer
1. a device or program for generating speech sounds by computer. *See* SPEECH SYNTHESIS.
2. a device for generating musical sounds by computer, usually from MIDI data. *See* MIDI.

Sys Req key the key on IBM mainframe terminals that enables the user to communicate with the communications system itself rather than the application program. The IBM PC AT and all subsequent PCs have a Sys Req key, but little or no software makes use of it.

sysadmin (**sys**tem **admin**istrator) a person who manages a multiuser computer.

systems programmer person who writes the programs needed for a computer system to function (as opposed to the programs that do particular kinds of useful computation). Some of the programs that systems programmers write include operating systems, language processors and compilers, and data file management programs. Systems programming requires considerable knowledge of the particular computer system being used. *Contrast* APPLICATIONS PROGRAMMER.

T

T1 line a special type of telephone line for digital communication only, with a maximum data rate of 1.544 million bits per second. Many Internet sites are connected to each other through T1 lines. *Contrast* DSL; ISDN; SWITCHED LINE; T3 LINE.

T3 line a high-speed digital telephone line with a maximum data rate of 45 million bits per second, 28 times that of a T1 line. Larger Internet sites use T3 lines to link to each other. *Contrast* DSL; ISDN; SWITCHED LINE; T1 LINE.

tab a visual indication of multiple pages in a dialog box (Figure 259). Click on the appropriately labeled tab to get to the desired page.

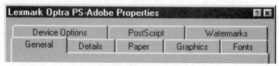

FIGURE 259. Tabs in dialog box

Tab the key on a computer keyboard that is marked with forward and backward arrows (Figure 260). (From *tabulator*, a mechanical device for lining up columns on a typewriter.)

The Tab key advances the cursor to a preset spot; Shift-Tab goes back to the previous tab stop. Most word processors and page layout programs let you set the TAB STOPS where you want them and otherwise provide a reasonable set of defaults, usually every half inch or so.

Always use the Tab key instead of the space bar to align type. When setting proportional type, it is impossible to get columns to line up by adding space characters; you *must* set the tabs.

The Tab key has ASCII code 9 and is equivalent to Ctrl-I. The backward Tab (Shift-Tab) key has no ASCII code.

When entering text into a dialog box, the Tab key often moves the cursor from one field to the next.

FIGURE 260. Tab key

tab-delimited separated by the Tab character (ASCII 9). A tab-delimited file is a text file in which data items are separated by Tab characters, which will usually cause the items to line up in columns when viewed in an editor, although different editors place the columns differently. This is one way of saving the contents of a spreadsheet to a text file that can be read back in without losing the arrangement of the items. *Compare* CSV FILE.

tab stops adjustable markers that indicate the next horizontal position of the cursor when the Tab key is pressed. *See* Figure 261.

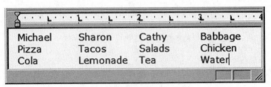

FIGURE 261. Tab stops

tabbed browsing the ability to open more than one page simultaneously in a web browser, with each page appearing as a tab on the screen (but not in a separate window), allowing the user to quickly switch between them.

table an arrangement of data in a database where each row defines a relationship between the items in that row. *See* RELATIONAL DATABASE.

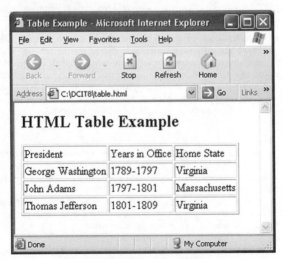

FIGURE 262. Table (in HTML)

table, HTML a set of tabular information displayed with special HTML tags. Here is an example:

```
<html><head><title>Table Example</title></head>
<body>
<h2> HTML Table Example</h2>
<table border>
<tr><td>President</td><td>Years in Office</td>
    <td>Home State</td></tr>
<tr><td>George Washington</td><td>1789-1797</td>
    <td>Virginia</td></tr>
<tr><td>John Adams</td><td>1797-1801</td>
    <td>Massachusetts</td></tr>
<tr><td>Thomas Jefferson</td><td>1801-1809</td>
    <td>Virginia</td></tr>
</table>
</body></html>
```

The `border` attribute automatically sets up a border for the table; the border can be set wider by specifying its width in pixels (`border=3`). If no border is desired, simply delete the `border` attribute.

Each row of the table is enclosed between the `<tr>` and `</tr>` tags, and each data item in the table is enclosed between `<td>` and `</td>` tags. The web browser will automatically line up the items correctly; it doesn't matter where the line breaks in the HTML code occur. Figure 262 shows how this table is displayed.

The table elements do not have to be text; they can also include graphic images and links. Many web designers use tables with invisible borders to organize and align elements of a web page.

tablet computer a computer roughly the size of a book, without a keyboard, used like a PDA or smartphone except for the full-size screen. The touchscreen functions as a keyboard when needed. For prolonged typing, a normal keyboard can be connected. A popular tablet computer is the Apple iPad. Other tablet computers run Microsoft Windows or Google Android operating systems. Many of them have 3G or 4G wireless access to the Internet through the cellular telephone network. *See* IPAD; ANDROID; PAD.

tag

1. a code inserted into a FILE or data structure indicating how something is to be interpreted. Many pieces of software use tags of various kinds for various purposes. HTML commands are often called tags. *See* DATA STRUCTURES; HTML.

2. on Facebook, to associate another user's name with an uploaded picture, either to identify a person in the picture or to cause the person to be notified that the picture has been uploaded.

tag cloud a visual representation of the most frequent words or HASHTAGS on a web page or in a text. More commonly used words are represented larger. This provides a visual way to show what words or topics are most common at any given time.

The figure shows a tag cloud for a short text about computer safety. It was created with *www.wordle.com* and is reproduced by permission.

FIGURE 263. Tag cloud for a short text about computer safety

talent (digital video) hired human actors or voice actors, as opposed to computer-generated characters. *Contrast* ACTOR.

tall paper orientation that is taller than it is wide; also called PORTRAIT or VERTICAL orientation.

tan the trigonometric tangent function.

If A is an angle in a right triangle, then the tangent of A (written as tan A) is defined to be

$$\tan A = \frac{\text{length of opposite side}}{\text{length of adjacent side}}$$

The function tan(A) in many programming languages calculates the value of tan A, with A in radians. *See* TRIGONOMETRIC FUNCTIONS for an illustration.

tangent
1. a line that just touches a circle or other curve.
2. the trigonometric tangent function. *See* TRIGONOMETRIC FUNCTIONS.

tap touching a picture on a touchscreen to cause an action; for example, tapping a key on a virtual keyboard or tapping an icon to start an app.

tape a thin, flexible plastic material with a magnetic coating on which data can be stored sequentially. In the 1970s, tape was a common alternative to disks as a way for computers to store files. Today, tapes are still used for backups. Tapes are much slower than disks; writing a large backup to tape can take hours.

tape drive a device that enables a computer to read and write magnetic tape.

tar file in UNIX, a collection of files made into one file with the tar (**tape archive**) program. (Nowadays, tar files are almost always stored on disk, not tape.) To extract the contents of a tar file, use the command:

```
% tar -xvf filename.tar
```

Unlike ZIP, tar does not compress files; thus, tar files are often compressed with another utility (such as compress, which adds .z at the end of the filename). *See* ZIP FILE.

target
1. the place to which information is copied (e.g., the "target disk" when copying disks); the opposite of *source*.
2. something that is being searched for (as when searching for a word in a document).
3. The *target* attribute in an HTML link can be used to specify where the result of the link will appear. Here is an example where the linked web page will appear in a new window:

```
<a href="test2.htm" target="_blank">link to test2</a>
```

task a PROCESS; one of several computer programs that are executing concurrently.

Task Manager a Windows utility that shows a list of running programs and operating system tasks and allows you to terminate them. You can access it at any time by pressing Ctrl-Alt-Del or by typing taskmgr at a command prompt.

To find out the function of any task, especially if you are concerned that it might be MALWARE, simply search for its name on GOOGLE or another large search engine.

taskbar the area at the bottom of the screen in Windows, containing the START BUTTON and a button for every program that is currently running. It also contains tiny icons for the speaker (volume control), clock, printer (if printing), fax modem (if active), and other specialized programs.

The taskbar normally includes one row of buttons, but you can widen it, shrink it, or move it to a different edge of the screen by dragging it with the mouse. If you can't see the taskbar, look closely to see whether it has been reduced to minimum width or moved to an unusual location.

See also AUTOHIDE.

FIGURE 264. Taskbar (Windows)

TB terabyte. *See* METRIC PREFIXES.

TCL/TK (**T**ool **C**ommand **L**anguage and [graphical] **T**ool **K**it) a programming language developed by John Ousterhout in the tradition of Perl and Awk. As its name suggests, TCL/TK is for building customized tools. It links together pre-existing software and system facilities, including network communication, along with new code to generate easy-to-use programs with a graphical user interface. It is one of the easiest ways to do GUI programming under UNIX, and implementations for Microsoft Windows also exist. TCL/TK is an open-source project, and most implementations of it are distributed free of charge. For more information, see *www.scriptics.com*.

TCO (**t**otal **c**ost of **o**wnership) the complete cost of owning and using a machine during its useful life, including not only the cost of the machine itself, but also maintenance, repairs, and consumable supplies such as ink and paper.

A low-cost inkjet printer can have higher TCO, in the long run, than an expensive laser printer if its ink cartridges are relatively expensive.

TCP/IP (**T**ransmission **C**ontrol **P**rotocol/**I**nternet **P**rotocol) a standard format for transmitting data in packets from one computer to another. It is used on the Internet and various other networks. The two parts of TCP/IP are TCP, which deals with construction of data packets, and IP, which routes them from machine to machine. *See* INTERNET; WIDE-AREA NETWORK.

Tebi- (Ti) prefix meaning $2^{40} = 1,099,511,627,776$. *See* METRIC PREFIXES.

TebiByte (TiB) $2^{40} = 1,099,511,627,776$ bytes. *See* METRIC PREFIXES.

teh a common typing error for *the* that has been adopted as a deliberately comical spelling. *See* LEETSPEAK.

telecommute to work at a job from a home office with the aid of a computer, modem, telephone, fax, and other specialized equipment.

telecompute to use the computer facilities at another location by using a WIDE-AREA NETWORK or a modem link.

Telnet a protocol for using one computer as a terminal on another; only textual communication is supported, not graphics. Telnet is widely used to access UNIX systems remotely. To use it, type telnet or tn at a command prompt, or type a URL such as telnet:abc.xyz.com into your browser. *See also* RLOGIN; TCP/IP.

template a pattern for arranging or matching things:
  1. a plastic card with shapes cut out of it. A programmer using a template card can easily trace out the symbols that are needed in drawing a flowchart.
  2. a particular pattern for a spreadsheet program, a database program, or page layout program that is frequently used. Therefore, storing the template will save you from having to retype the specifications each time.
  3. a regular expression or other pattern to be matched. *See* REGULAR EXPRESSION.

ter Latin for "a third time," used to denote revised CCITT and ITU-T standards. *See* CCITT; ITU-T.

tera- metric prefix meaning ×1,000,000,000,000 (10^{12}, or one trillion) or, in rating computer memories and disks, ×1,099,511,627,776 (= 1024^4). *Tera-* is derived from the Greek word for monster or freak. *See* METRIC PREFIXES.

terabyte an amount of storage capacity approximately equal to one trillion bytes. *See* METRIC PREFIXES.

terminal an input-output device consisting of a screen and keyboard for communicating with a computer.
  The earliest terminals were teletype machines. Today, personal computers are sometimes used as terminals on larger computers. *See* DATA COMMUNICATION; DOWNLOAD; MODEM; REMOTE DESKTOP; TELNET; UPLOAD.

terminal-node controller *see* PACKET RADIO.

Terminal Services the subsystem of Windows that supports REMOTE DESKTOP and TELNET access from other computers. *See* REMOTE DESKTOP; TS-CAL.

terminator a connector containing resistors to absorb reflected signals in a cable. Terminators are usually required on SCSI cables and on coaxial network cables.

TeX (pronounced "tekh") a computer typesetting program used by the American Mathematical Society and many book publishers and educational institutions. T_EX was designed and first implemented by D. E. Knuth of Stanford University. It was used to typeset this book.
  Unlike most desktop publishing systems, T_EX does not attempt to show you the appearance of the finished document on the screen as you edit it (though screen previews can be generated). Instead, you type a document with codes in it that indicate boldface, italics, special characters (e.g., \int for an integral sign), and the like (Table 15).

TABLE 15
TₑX NOTATIONS USED IN MATHEMATICAL FORMULAS

∞	\infty
$\pm$	\pm
$\times$	\times
$\div$	\div
$\prime$	^\prime
$\circ$	^\circ
$\leq$	\leq
$\geq$	\geq
$\in$	\in
$\subset$	\subset
$\subseteq$	\subseteq
$\rightarrow$	\rightarrow
$\Rightarrow$	\Rightarrow
α, β	\alpha, \beta (etc.)
Γ, Δ	\Gamma, \Delta (etc.)
a^{bcd}	a^{bcd}
a_{bcd}	a_{bcd}
$\dfrac{xyz}{abc}$	{xyz}\over{abc}
$\sqrt{xyz}$	\sqrt{xyz}
$\displaystyle\sum_{i=1}^{n} a_i$	\sum_{i=1}^{n} a_{i}
$\displaystyle\int_{a}^{b} f(x)dx$	\int_{a}^{b} f(x) dx

The rationale is that correct typesetting relies on distinctions that are too subtle to see on a computer screen. A user who wants an en dash rather than an em dash should say so with explicit codes rather than trying to make a mark that appears the right length on the screen. Likewise, large-scale aspects of design should be automated; you should be able just to give the title of a chapter, and let the computer take care of numbering the chapter and putting the title in the right place on the page.

Most TₑX users access TₑX through LᴬTₑX, a package of ready-to-use document designs and command shortcuts that make the system easier to use. *See* LATEX.

TₑX is generally considered the most sophisticated computer typesetting system, as well as (for an experienced user) one of the easiest to use. It sets a standard that other desktop publishing systems try to emulate.

Usage note: The logo TₑX is easily produced from within TₑX or LᴬTₑX. Otherwise, it is usually typed "TeX."

Texas Instruments (TI) a manufacturer of semiconductors and computers, headquartered in Dallas, Texas. Jack S. Kilby developed the first working integrated circuit ("silicon chip") at TI in 1958, making it possible to miniaturize electronic equipment to a degree far beyond earlier expectations. Currently, TI produces computers, calculators, and a wide variety of related components and other electronic devices. Web address: *www.ti.com*.

text (verb) to send a TEXT MESSAGE.

text box an area within a window where the user can type or edit characters.

Save as...   readme

FIGURE 265. Text box

text editor an editor for text files. *See* EDITOR.

text file a file containing only characters (in ASCII, EBCDIC, or Unicode) plus end of line marks (*see* CR, LF), without any way of indicating the style, size, or color of type or any other special effects. In Windows, the Notepad program is an editor for text files. *Contrast* RICH TEXT.

text message a short message often typed on a cellular telephone, to be read by the recipient immediately, or soon after it is sent. Abbreviations are often used (*see* the list under CHAT ROOM) *See also* INSTANT MESSAGING.

text to columns a procedure to split the data currently in a single spreadsheet column so that it spans adjacent columns. For example, if the text "100, 200" appears in column A, then splitting the text using the comma as the delimiter will put "100" in column A and "200" in column B. This feature is particularly helpful when pasting data off a web page into a spreadsheet.

text wrap *see* REFLOW; WORD WRAP.

texting sending a TEXT MESSAGE.

texture mapping the act of applying a texture to the surface of a 3D wireframe model.

thermal printer a printer that prints by heating spots on the paper with an array of tiny, fast-acting heating elements. Thermal printers are among the least expensive printers and are often used in calculators and point-of-sale terminals. They require special paper that may discolor with age.

thickwire the thicker type of Ethernet coaxial cable. *See* 10BASE-5.

thin client a computer terminal with some computational power built in; a networked computer that relies on the server not only to store files, but also to do nearly all the computing while the client manages the graphical user interface. *See* TERMINAL. *Contrast* DISKLESS WORKSTATION, which does its own computing.

thinking outside the box *(jargon)* thinking outside presumed limits; thinking creatively.

thinnet thinwire Ethernet. *See* 10BASE-2; ETHERNET.

thinwire the thinner type of Ethernet coaxial cable. *See* 10BASE-2.

third-generation computers the first generation of computers made with integrated circuits.

third party someone other than the maker of a machine and the END USER. For example, third-party software is software that does not come from the manufacturer of the computer, nor is it developed by the user. Most software today is third-party software.

thread
1. a series of messages in a discussion forum, each responding to the previous one. *See* NEWSGROUP.
2. a task or process in a computer program that uses MULTITASKING. For example, a word processor might have one thread to accept keystrokes from the keyboard, and another thread, running concurrently, to keep the screen updated. The Java programming language is designed to facilitate the creation of programs with more than one thread.

threaded discussion an online discussion where users can post comments. Users can reply to a previous post, which may have been a reply to an earlier post. This keeps the replies organized in a hierarchical pattern so readers can easily follow the thread of one discussion.

threaded interpretive language a programming language in which programs are stored almost exclusively as lists of addresses of subroutines. *See* FORTH.

threadjacking the act of deliberately switching the topic of a forum thread; intentional TOPIC DRIFT. An example would be a thread on cooking being threadjacked by someone posting Michelle Obama's shortbread cookie recipe with a long ramble on politics, switching the thread from its original purpose (recipes) to a new discussion (politics).

three-dimensional graphics the process of representing three-dimensional images on a two-dimensional computer screen. This ability is especially important in CAD and in games. For example, imagine that you are designing a house, and your computer program lets you simulate walking through the different rooms. The computer needs to keep track of three-dimensional coordinates of the points of the house, and it needs to know which points are connected with lines, which planes should be filled in (as in a wall) or left open (as in a door). To allow the user to view the image from different points, the computer needs to be able to translate or rotate the points as directed. Particularly in a game setting, the computer needs to redraw the entire screen very quickly to maintain the illusion of rapid motion.

A simple kind of image is a wireframe view, which shows only the basic structure of an object, not the details of surfaces. This type of image is particularly helpful when designing pieces that need to fit together.

Three-dimensional images can be transmitted to other computers using the VRML language. *See* VRML.

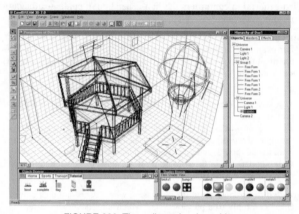

FIGURE 266. Three-dimensional graphics

three-dimensional mouse a handheld joystick-like device that allows movement in three dimensions by rotating, pulling, or pushing along at least three axes.

three-dimensional printer a device analogous to a computer printer that makes three-dimensional objects instead of marks on paper. Three-dimensional printers typically work by spraying thin layers of plastic, one after another, to form the desired shape. The result is a ready-to-use plastic object, such as a prototype of a machine part. *See* RAPID PROTOTYPING.

three-dimensional transistor a type of FIELD EFFECT TRANSISTOR with a silicon channel that sticks up like a fin and is contacted by the gate on three sides. This design, put into production by Intel in 2011, increases performance by improving the ability of the transistor to block current when in the off state.

three-finger salute *(slang)* Ctrl-Alt-Del.

three-tier architecture a database system with a user interface running on a microcomputer, a database engine running on a mainframe computer or other powerful enterprise-wide computer, and a layer of MIDDLEWARE that connects these two tiers. *See* UML.

thumb the box on an elevator bar (scroll bar). The position of the thumb gives a graphical representation of the window's current position in the document or list. If you are near the top of the document, the thumb is near the top of the bar; if you are near the bottom of the document, the thumb is near the bottom of the bar. The thumb can be dragged with the mouse to scroll rapidly around the page.

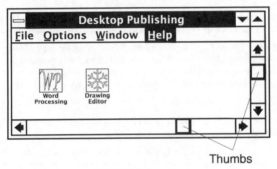

FIGURE 267. Thumbs

thumb drive *see* USB FLASH DRIVE.

thumbnail (from the artists' term *thumbnail sketch*) a small image of a graphics file displayed in order to help you identify it.

Thumbs.db a system file in which Windows stores thumbnail representations of graphics. Windows may create a Thumbs.db file in any directory (folder), and the file can be deleted without harm, since it will be re-generated if needed.

THX on-line abbreviation for "thanks."

TIA online abbreviation for "thanks in advance."

tick marks short lines that cross another line to mark the increments of measurement in a graph.

ticket a record of a problem that is being diagnosed or repaired. Originally a slip of paper, a ticket is now usually a record maintained online, and "open a ticket" means "make a request for technical assistance."

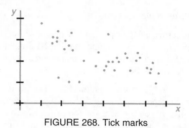

FIGURE 268. Tick marks

tickler a program that examines the computer system's date and alerts the user about scheduled events.

tiered data plan a DATA PLAN with rates that vary depending on the usage (so higher rates apply for heavy usage, such as downloading movies).

TIFF (Tag Image File Format) a format for storing bitmapped images on disk, developed by Aldus, Microsoft, and several other companies. TIFF files can store very large images with millions of colors, using several kinds of data compression. *Compare* GIF; JPEG. *See also* BITMAP.

Tiger version 10.4 of MAC OS X.

tight type set so closely that the letters almost touch. *See* LETTERSPACING for illustration. *See also* KERNING; TRACKING.

tilde the character ~. Under UNIX and in many web addresses, the tilde indicates the home directory of a particular user; for example, ~smith is the home directory of the user named smith.

tile
1. to cause windows to divide the screen into sections without overlapping one another (Figure 269). *Contrast* CASCADE; OVERLAID WINDOWS.
2. to print a large page (larger than your printer can handle) by having the page broken up into a series of regular-sized sheets, which can then be fastened together.
3. to create a pattern with a simple design by repeating it over and over. Many draw and paint programs have a library of tile designs; you can also design your own.

tiled windows windows that divide the screen into sections without overlapping one another. *Contrast* CASCADE; OVERLAID WINDOWS.

timeout failure of an operation because it has exceeded the allowable time. This usually means that something else went wrong first, such as loss of a network connection. *Contrast* TTL.

Times Roman a highly legible typeface designed by Stanley Morison in 1931 for *The Times* of London. Times Roman and its many varieties (Times New Roman, Dutch 801, and others) reproduce well at low

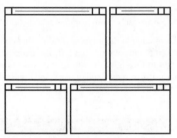

FIGURE 269. Tiled windows

resolutions, and this probably led to its current popularity as a laser printer font. This book is set in Adobe Times Roman. *See* TYPEFACE.

timesharing a technique developed in the 1960s for running more than one program on the same computer at the same time, so that, for example, the computer can serve many users at different terminals simultaneously.

Timesharing is based on the idea that a computer spends most of its time waiting for things to happen. Almost all input-output devices (printers, disks, etc.) operate much more slowly than the CPU itself; the extreme case is a terminal or console where the computer may spend minutes or hours waiting for someone to type something. In a timesharing system, more than one program is loaded into memory at once, and when the computer is unable to proceed with one program, it jumps to another.

In practice, the computer does not stay on one program more than a fraction of a second even if there is nothing to wait for: to do so would prevent other, possibly shorter, programs from being executed. Also, programs that are not executed are frequently "rolled out" of memory (i.e., copied to disk) to make memory space available to programs that are actually running.

Modern operating systems such as UNIX and Windows use timesharing to run multiple programs concurrently. *See* MULTITASKING.

tint a shade of a color; usually expressed as a percentage of a solid color. *See* Figure 270.

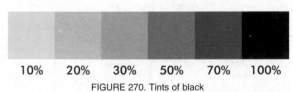

| 10% | 20% | 30% | 50% | 70% | 100% |

FIGURE 270. Tints of black

title (on a web page) descriptive text that defines the title of a web page and displays it in the browser's status bar. *See* WEB PAGE TITLE.

title bar the horizontal bar at the top of a window that contains the application program's icon and name at the left, the name of the open file (if appropriate), and to the right, the trio of window control buttons (MINIMIZE, RESTORE [or full-screen], and CLOSE). *See* Figure 271. In Windows, clicking on the application program's icon will pop up a menu to control the window.

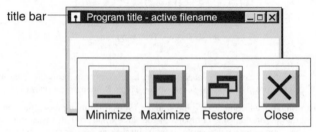

title bar

FIGURE 271. Title bar and set of possible buttons

TLA **t**hree-**l**etter **a**cronym; **t**hree-**l**etter **a**bbreviation. A significant obstacle to progress in the computer industry is the fact that there are only 17,576 TLAs, of which some, such as UGH, do not make good trademarks.

TLD (**t**op-**l**evel **d**omain) (TLD) the last part of a web or e-mail address, such as *.com, .uk,* or the like.

Top-level domains are administered by registrars ultimately licensed by ICANN (*see* ICANN). Some TLDs are administered by only one registrar, and some, such as *.com,* are shared by many.

There are three basic types of TLDs. First, the original set, dating from the early days of the Internet:

.com	commercial entities
.edu	university-level educational institutions
.gov	the U.S. government
.int	international organizations (such as the ITU and United Nations)
.mil	U.S. military sites
.net	network service providers
.org	non-profit organizations

These are used mostly in the United States, although, except for *.mil,* they can be assigned anywhere. Other early TLDs, such as *.uucp* and *.bitnet,* stood for connections to other networks, and are no longer used.

At the end of the 1990s, several registrars began using *.com, .net,* and *.org* indiscriminately for all types of sites. In 2000, ICANN authorized an additional set of international TLDs, as follows:

.aero	aeronautical industry sites
.asia	pan-Asia and Asia Pacific
.biz	business sites of all types
.cat	Catalan linguistic community
.coop	cooperatives (customer-owned businesses)
.info	sites of all types
.jobs	human resource management
.mobi	mobile products and services
.museum	museums
.name	individual persons
.pro	licensed professionals (lawyers, etc.)
.tel	contact data
.travel	travel industry
.xxx	xxx rated entertainment

Confusion can arise because two website with different TLDs can have the same name (for example, *www.whitehouse.com* and *www. whitehouse.org* are not connected to the official White House web page, which is *www.whitehouse.gov*).

Meanwhile, an official set of country code TLDs (ccTLDs) was adopted and maintained. For a complete listing of the ccTLDs, *see* the tables on page 580 to 582. Note that the code for the United States, *.us,* is seldom used.

Most of these ccTLDs are used only in the country to which they belong, but some, such as *.tv* and *.ws,* have been resold for use elsewhere—a source of income for small countries, and confusion for everyone else. *See also* CCTLD; GTLD; ICANN.

In 2008 ICANN announced it would start considering a significant expansion of the number of TLDs by considering proposed new names from other organizations.

tn *see* TELNET.

tn3270 *see* TELNET.

TNC **t**erminal-**n**ode **c**ontroller. *See* PACKET RADIO.

TNX abbreviation for *thanks*, sometimes written TNXE6 or TNX1E6 to signify "thanks a million" (*see* EXPONENTIAL NOTATION).

to back; send to back comparable commands that send the selected object to the bottom layer. *See also* ARRANGE; BACK ONE; BRING FORWARD; DRAW PROGRAM; FORWARD ONE; SEND BACKWARD; SEND TO FRONT; TO FRONT.

to front; bring to front comparable commands that send the selected object to the top layer. *See also* ARRANGE; BACK ONE; BRING FORWARD; DRAW PROGRAM; FORWARD ONE; SEND BACKWARD; SEND TO BACK; TO BACK.

toggle to switch something back and forth from one state to another. For instance, in some editors, the Ins key "toggles" insert mode; that is, it turns insert mode on if it is off or off if it is on.

token

1. the special message that is passed around a TOKEN-RING NETWORK to enable the computers to take turns transmitting.

2. one of the items in a set, whether or not distinguishable from the others. For example, the list {a,a,b,c,c} contains five tokens but only three types. *Contrast* TYPE (definition 3).

3. a basic meaningful unit of a language. For example, the one-line BASIC program

```
10 PRINT "The square root of 2 is ";SQR(2)
```

consists of ten tokens:

| 10 | PRINT | "The square root of 2 is " | ; | SQR | (| 2 |) |

(Some people do not count the spaces as tokens.) Breaking the input into tokens is the first step in processing any computer language.

token-identical absolutely identical, not just similar; the same instance of the same object. For example, the capital of the United States is token-identical with the city of Washington; they are the same thing, described two different ways. *Contrast* TYPE-IDENTICAL.

token-ring network a type of network in which the computers are connected together in a ring. A special message, called the *token,* is passed from one machine to another around the ring, and each machine can transmit only while it is holding the token. IBM marketed a token-ring network for the PC family of computers. *See* LOCAL-AREA NETWORK.

tokenize to break a character string into the smallest units that are significant in a language (*see* PARSING; TOKEN, definition 3).

toner the black powder that is used by laser printers and photocopy machines to create the image on paper. It consists of tiny particles of easily melted plastic. If you spill toner where it isn't wanted, make sure it doesn't become hot before cleaning up; if the tiny particles melt, they will stick permanently to any surface.

toner cartridge replaceable assembly in a laser printer that contains the toner (a powdery ink) that will be used to make marks on the paper. Most toner cartridges also contain other parts that are likely to wear out (e.g., the electrophotographic drum), and replacing the cartridge replaces quite a bit of the inner workings of the laser printer. (This contributes to the cost of the toner cartridge.) Some types of toner cartridges are recyclable and refillable; however, the quality of refilled cartridges is not always equal to that of new ones.

tool a specialized version of the mouse cursor that gives the cursor new abilities and properties. For example, in a paint program, the brush tool will have a special shape, size, and color—any pixels touched by the "brush" will change to the brush color.

toolbox a collection of icons that represent frequently used commands. A toolbox may be displayed across the top or side of the screen or you may be able to relocate it by dragging it with the mouse. The more complicated paint programs sometimes have several toolboxes, with similar tools grouped together. *See* DOCK.

FIGURE 272. Toolbox

top-down programming a technique of programming by defining the overall outlines of the program first and then filling in the details.

The top-down approach is usually the best way to write complicated programs. Detailed decisions are postponed until the requirements of the large program are known; this is better than making the detailed decisions early and then forcing the major program strategy to conform to them. Each part of the program (called a *module*) can be written and tested independently. *See also* STUB.

topic drift the tendency of the topic of an online discussion to shift while the title of the messages remains the same, because everyone is replying to an existing message and therefore automatically keeping the same title. After a while, a THREAD titled "Windows Vista setup" may actually be discussing chili recipes. Topic drift can be particularly amusing when reading a newsgroup frequented by individuals with wide-ranging interests. *See* LURK; NEWSGROUP; THREAD.

topology the mathematical study of how points are connected together. If an object is stretched or bent, then its geometric shape changes but its topology remains unchanged.

The topology of a computer network is the pattern of connections between the machines in the network. Figure 273 illustrates some common topologies: a ring network, a star network, and a bus network. *See* LOCAL-AREA NETWORK.

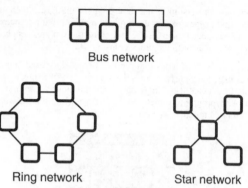

Bus network

Ring network　　　　　　**Star network**

FIGURE 273. Topologies of computer networks

torrent a file ready to be downloaded by the BitTorrent method. *See* BITTORRENT.

touch interface *see* MULTITOUCH INTERFACE.

touchpad a substitute for a MOUSE on a laptop or notebook computer (Figure 274). The user uses a finger to make strokes on a rectangular touch sensor. Just as with a mouse, the direction and length of the strokes is significant, but not their absolute position.

FIGURE 274. Touchpad (on a laptop computer)

touchscreen a computer screen that is sensitive to touch, so that the user can point to things on it by touching the screen itself, without using a mouse. Touchscreens are commonly used on tablet computers, pocket-sized computers, and smartphones. *See also* GESTURE. *Compare* TOUCHPAD.

trace
1. to execute a program step by step, observing the results of each step.
2. (in a draw program) to create a path or outline around the contours of a bitmapped shape. It is necessary to trace bitmaps to convert them into VECTOR GRAPHICS. Tracing can be done by a separate utility program or from within the drawing program.

track
1. one of the concentric circles in which data is recorded on a disk (Figure 275), or one of the parallel strips in which data is recorded on tape.
2. a music selection on a CD-ROM.
3. a video selection on a DVD.
4. a portion of a MIDI file that specifies the performance details of a single instrument.

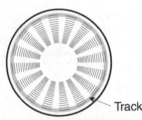

FIGURE 275. Track

trackball a computer pointing device similar in function to a mouse. Instead of rolling the mouse around the desktop, the user rotates the ball on the trackball in the direction desired. The trackball unit itself does not move, which is an advantage if there is not enough desktop space to conveniently operate a mouse.

FIGURE 276. Trackball

tracking letterspacing (spacing between letters in words). *See* LETTERSPAC-ING for an illustration.

tracking cookie a COOKIE that sends reports listing what web pages you visit back to the source of the cookie. Unlike other cookies that may improve your web browsing by storing your preferences for viewing certain web pages, the tracking cookies are solely for the benefit of advertisers and are often installed on your machine without your knowledge.

tracking protection limiting the web pages with which a browser will share certain information, to help protect your privacy.

tractor feed a mechanism that uses toothed gears to pull the paper forward in a dot-matrix computer printer. The teeth fit into the feed holes in the side of the paper.

trade secret a piece of information (usually about the design or manufacturing of a product) that is kept secret because it gives the maker an advantage over competitors. A famous trade secret is the formula for Coca-Cola.

The security of a trade secret depends on successfully keeping outsiders from knowing it. Patents, by contrast, are openly disclosed to the public, with a prohibition against unauthorized use.

The internal workings of most software packages are trade secrets, but it is somewhat unclear whether software licenses can actually prevent people from analyzing the working of machines that they own. *See also* PATENT; REVERSE ENGINEER.

transfer rate the rate at which data is transferred from one place to another; a measure of the performance of disk drives, modems, and other peripheral devices.

transfer roller in a laser printer, the roller that transfers the toner particles from the DRUM to the paper. *See* DRUM.

transistor an electronic device that allows a small current in one place to control a larger current in another place; thus, transistors can be used as amplifiers in radio and audio circuits, and as switches in logic gates (*see* NOT GATE; NOR GATE; OR GATE; NAND GATE; AND GATE). This article deals with bipolar transistors, the most common kind. *See also* FIELD-EFFECT TRANSISTOR.

A bipolar transistor is made by sandwiching a thin layer of one kind of semiconductor material (P-type or N-type) between two layers of the opposite type (N-type or P-type, respectively). Thus, an NPN transistor is a P layer between two N layers; a PNP transistor is the opposite. (*See* SEMICONDUCTOR.) The circuit diagram symbols for NPN and PNP transistors are shown in Figure 277. The middle section of a transistor is called the base, and the other two sections are the emitter and collector.

Figure 278 shows how an NPN transistor works. (A PNP transistor works the same way with all polarities reversed.) The emitter is connected to ground (0 volts), and the collector is connected to +5 volts through some type of load. Electrons try to flow from emitter to collector, but with 0 volts on the base, they can't get through because the base-collector junction is like a reverse-biased diode (*see* DIODE).

But if the base were to become full of electrons, it would no longer behave like P-type material, and the base-collector junction would no longer block electron flow. We can get electrons into the base by pulling them in from the emitter. Thus if we apply a positive voltage to the base in order to forward-bias the base-emitter junction, the base-collector junction will become free to conduct. A small flow of electrons through the base controls a much larger flow of electrons through the collector.

In computers, transistors act as switches. The current flowing through the base controls the current flowing through the collector, turning it on or off under external control. *See also* ELECTRONIC CIRCUIT DIAGRAM SYMBOLS; INTEGRATED CIRCUIT; LOGIC CIRCUITS.

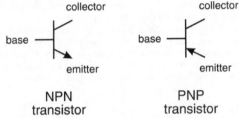

FIGURE 277. Transistors (circuit diagram symbols)

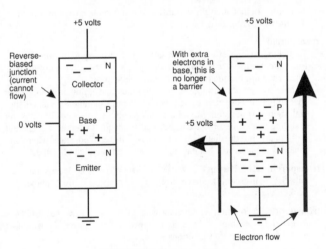

FIGURE 278. Transistor action

transition effect (in video editing and presentation software) a method of changing the scene from one view to another. Transition effects can give visual interest to a presentation by introducing an element of motion to the graphics. In video editing, they can help establish a change in location, or indicate the passage of time. There are literally hundreds of transition effects, and the exact terminology varies from program to program. Basically, there are four major types of transition effects:

1. *Dissolve.* Gradually replaces the first image with the second, either superimposing the pictures in mid-transition (like a double exposure) or replacing the image pixel-by-pixel or in larger blocks.

2. *Swipe.* The first image is seemingly wiped off, revealing the second image underneath. Swipes can go from left to right, right to left, up, or down, and the speed and the sharpness of the swipe edge can usually be controlled.

3. *Fade.* The image either darkens to black or lightens to pure white.

4. *Fly-in.* An image element moves in suddenly from off-screen.

    It is wise to use transition effects sparingly. Not every editing cut or slide change merits special attention; in fact, overuse of distracting transitions will annoy and possibly confuse the audience.

translator

    1. a program that exchanges data between application programs. *See also* EXPORT; FILTER; IMPORT.

    2. a program that attempts to translate one human language into another. *See* NATURAL LANGUAGE PROCESSING.

transparent

    1. lacking visible effect. For instance, if a print-spooling program is transparent, all other software works just as if the print-spooling program were not installed. This is a desirable feature.

    2. able to be seen through. Some graphics and paint programs have special features or filters to help you render transparent objects. Of special interest is the ability to adjust the opacity of objects or bitmaps via a sliding scale; the object can be totally opaque to totally transparent with many intermediate gradations. The in-between state where the image is recognizable but can be seen through is called ghosting.

transparent GIF a bitmap file whose background color is clear. A transparent GIF will seem to have irregular borders and float above the background.

transposition a common typing error where the order of two keystrokes is reversed. For example, "the" may be typed as "hte." A SPELL CHECKER is useful for catching transpositions.

trap

    1. to detect an abnormal situation and take action. *See* TRY.

    2. the area of overlap allowed between different colors of ink in a color printing job on a printing press. A slight amount of trap will prevent unintentional gaps between the two areas of color. Trap is needed only in processes that are patches of opaque ink, such as silkscreen or newspaper printing presses, but not on computer printers. *See* TRAPPING (definition 2).

trapping

1. the act of detecting and responding to events that would ordinarily interrupt the operation of the computer. For instance, some programming languages provide "error trapping," which means that when the program attempts to do something impossible (such as divide by zero or read a file that doesn't exist), control will be transferred to an error-handling routine supplied by the programmer. If no error trapping were provided, the program would simply end with an error message that might puzzle the user. In BASIC, trapping is activated by statements such as ON ERROR. For a Java example, *see* TRY.

2. the technique of aiding the REGISTRATION of color plates in a printing job by creating slight areas of overlap where two colors meet. *See* TRAP (definition 2).

Some software is capable of creating the trap automatically (*see* DESKTOP PUBLISHING; PREPRESS). At other times, the designer will have to overlap design elements intentionally to ensure full coverage, even with a slight misregistration.

Trapping is only necessary when preparing CAMERA-READY COPY for a printing press; there are no registration problems when printing directly from your computer to a color printer.

Trash the place where deleted files are stored on the Macintosh, corresponding to the RECYCLE BIN under Windows. The space occupied by the files does not become available until you empty the Trash. Until then, you can get the files back if you need them.

Traveling Salesman Problem the mathematical problem of finding the shortest route that connects n points, given the distances between the points. As far as is known, this problem can be solved only by exhaustive search, which can take a gigantic number of steps. *See* LIMITS OF COMPUTER POWER.

tray (in Windows) a small area on the screen at the right of the taskbar (*see* Figure 279). The tray holds the system clock display as well as icons for volume control and other device drivers such as printers, video card, and virus checkers.

FIGURE 279. Tray (in Windows)

tree

1. a branching structure in which information is stored: for example, a system of directories and subdirectories (*see* DIRECTORY) or a branching diagram of a web site.

2. a data structure similar to a linked list, except that each element carries with it the addresses of two or more other elements, rather than just one. *See* LINKED LIST.

Trees are a very efficient way of storing items that must be searched for and retrieved quickly. Suppose, for example, that you want to store the following names in a computer:

Jones	Voss
Steinfeld	Marino
Alexander	Zhang
Bateman	Rodriguez

The names can be arranged into a tree by using the following two-step procedure:

1. Use the first name on the list as the root of the tree.
2. To find where to put each subsequent name, start at the root of the tree. If the name you are dealing with precedes the root name alphabetically, follow the left pointer; otherwise follow the right pointer. Proceed in this way until you come to an empty pointer; attach the new name to it.

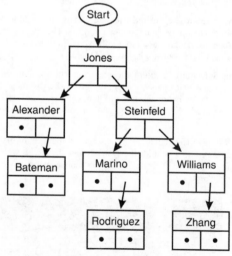

FIGURE 280. Tree (for binary search)

The result is the tree shown in Figure 280. Step 2 in this procedure can be used to locate names already in the tree in a minimum of steps (in this case, no more than four steps even though there are eight names in the list). The algorithm that results is not quite as good as a binary search, but it is much better than having to work through the whole list. Furthermore, as with linked lists, new nodes can be added at any time without requiring that existing nodes be moved.

trending (presumably short for *trending upward*): gaining in popularity at the moment. This is said of topics on Twitter and other words or topics whose frequency of mention can easily be measured. *See* HASHTAG.

trialware software that you are allowed to use free for a limited period of time, but you must purchase it if you wish to continue using it when the trial period is over. See *www.trialware.org*.

trigonometric functions the mathematical functions that relate an angle to the lengths of the sides of a right triangle (Figure 281), defined thus:

$$\sin\theta = \frac{\text{length of opposite side}}{\text{length of hypotenuse}}$$

$$\cos\theta = \frac{\text{length of adjacent side}}{\text{length of hypotenuse}}$$

$$\tan\theta = \frac{\text{length of opposite side}}{\text{length of adjacent side}} = \frac{\sin\theta}{\cos\theta}$$

If θ is small, $\sin\theta \approx \tan\theta \approx \theta$ (measured in radians).
See also ARC COSINE; ARC SINE; ARC TANGENT; COS; SIN; TAN.

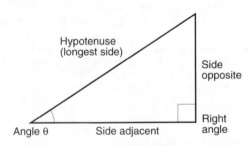

FIGURE 281. Triangle for defining trigonometric functions

Trojan horse a computer program with a hidden destructive function, such as erasing the disks on a specified date. Trojan horses are often distributed as counterfeit "new" versions of shareware products.

Knowingly distributing a destructive computer program is a crime under common law and under specific laws of various states. *See also* VIRUS.

troll

1. a message that is posted in an online forum solely in order to stir up as many replies as possible. Trolls often contain deliberate misinformation or insults. (From *troll,* a fishing term.)

2. a person who posts inflammatory material in an online forum for the purpose of starting an argument. "Please don't feed the trolls" means "Please don't reply to inflammatory messages."

TrueType font an outline font format originally developed in 1991 by Apple as a competing format to PostScript fonts. TrueType fonts are sets of mathematical descriptions of the letterforms as B-spline curves. What this means in practical terms is that it is possible to SCALE or size the type to practically any point size. (*See* VECTOR GRAPHICS.) A common competing type format is Adobe's Type 1 font format. *See also* OPENTYPE.

There is a slight difference in the TrueType formats for Macintosh and PC platforms; conversion utilities can convert one to the other.

Trumatch a color matching and calibration system developed and distributed by Trumatch, Inc., New York, New York. Web address: *www. trumatch.com.*

truncation the act of cutting off part of something; specifically:

1. dropping digits of a number that are to the right of the decimal point. For example, truncating 6.45 gives 6, and truncating 737.984 gives 737. In Pascal this operation is symbolized by trunc; in BASIC, by INT; in Java, by floor; in Excel by rounddown. *Contrast* ROUNDING, which is finding the nearest whole number (such as 738 for 737.984).

2. cutting off part of an image or a printed word when not enough space is available to print it.

try in C++ and related programming languages, a command that marks an operation that may fail. A block of code is introduced by try if it might cause an EXCEPTION (an error condition) for which the programmer wishes to specify an action. For example:

```
/* This is Java */
try
{
  theURL = new URL(urlbase,n0);
  /* more statements can go here */
}
catch (MalformedURLException e)
{
  System.out.println("Bad URL: "+theURL);
  /* more statements can go here */
}
```

```
finally
{
    System.out.println("All done.");
}
```

The code within the `try` block will attempt to locate the specified URL. If successful, the program will proceed with the additional statements in the `try` block; if the URL is not valid, then it will execute the `catch` block (which displays a message for the user). Then, whether or not the exception occurred, the `finally` block will execute.

The advantage of this approach is that it saves the programmer from having to write separate `if-then` statements for each possible error that can occur. Instead, any error that arises in the `try` block can be processed by the `catch` block later on. This makes programs easier to read because the code for handling exceptional situations is clearly separated from the code for normal situations.

Also, the `finally` block provides a way to guarantee that certain statements will execute before leaving the `try-catch-finally` structure, no matter how this is done; even a `goto` or `return` statement will not get around it.

TS-CAL (Terminal Services—Client Access License) a license allowing more than the minimum number of users to access a Windows server through REMOTE DESKTOP. Without TS-CALs, depending on the version of Windows, only one or two users can access the computer at a time.

TSO (Time Sharing Option) the part of OS/360 and related IBM operating systems that supports timesharing terminals. TSO commands correspond to the various statements in JCL; for example, the `allocate` command corresponds to the JCL DD statement. *See* JCL.

TTFN, TT4N online abbreviations for "ta ta (i.e., good-bye) for now."

TTL
   1. (Transistor-Transistor Logic) a type of digital INTEGRATED CIRCUIT that requires an accurately regulated 5-volt power supply. Although TTL has largely been replaced by CMOS circuitry, the original TTL voltage levels are still widely used on input-output devices. *Contrast* CMOS.
   2. (through the lens) description of a light meter or viewfinder that uses the main lens of a camera, the same lens with which pictures are taken. *Compare* SLR.
   3. (time to live) a counter included in data transmitted via a network (such as IP data packets), indicating when the data (such as a client request) is to be discarded if it has not been sent successfully. TTL fields are intended to prevent "immortals" from circulating forever.

TTL monochrome monitor the type of monitor used with the original IBM monochrome display adapter (MDA) in the early 1980s. *See* MONITOR.

TTYL online abbreviation for "talk to you later."

Tumblr a social networking and microblogging website, *www.tumblr.com*, where users share primarily pictures with commentary. Founded in 2007, Tumblr emphasizes an easy-to-use interface that encourages reblogging and keeps an open record of how many people have reblogged the same entry. (*See* REBLOG.) Posts can be text, videos, audio, and links, but Tumblr posts are mainly images.

tune to improve the performance of a system by adjusting numerical parameters such as the size of the swap file, the time delays allowed for certain operations, and the like.

tunnel a private, secure link between two distant places that connects two local-area networks. For example, a company with two main offices may establish a tunnel between them using dial-up modems, leased telephone lines, or a secure (encrypted) connection over the Internet.

turbo the higher-speed mode on a computer that offers a choice of clock speeds. (Originally from *turbocharger,* a device for increasing the power of an automobile engine.)

Turbo Pascal an extremely popular Pascal compiler written by Anders Hejlsberg and introduced by Borland International in 1984, contributing greatly to the popularity of Pascal on microcomputers. Later versions included extensions for object-oriented programming. *See also* C++; DELPHI.

Turing machine an imaginary machine conceived by Alan Turing in the 1930s to help identify the kinds of problems that are potentially solvable by machines.

The machine is a kind of simple computer. It consists of a long string of paper tape and a machine through which the tape can be fed. The machine can do four things: it can move the tape one space, it can place a mark on a space, it can erase a mark, or it can halt. Turing's thesis states that this simple machine can solve any problem that can be expressed as an algorithm (if it has an unlimited supply of paper tape). As you might imagine, in practice it would be difficult to give instructions to a Turing machine so that it could solve a particular problem. The Turing machine is important theoretically, however, because it provides an indication of what kinds of problems computers can solve and what kinds they can never solve. *See* CHURCH'S THESIS.

Turing test a test proposed by Alan Turing in 1950 to determine whether machines have achieved human-like intelligence. According to the Turing test, a machine is intelligent if, under certain specified conditions, it is indistinguishable from a human when you carry on a conversation with it by teletype. For a critique, *see* ARTIFICIAL INTELLIGENCE; ELIZA. *See also* CHURCH'S THESIS.

turnkey system a computer system that is ready to perform a particular task with no further preparation ("just turn the key and it does it"). A turnkey system is sold as a complete package from a single vendor.

turtle a pointer that moves around the screen leaving a trail (when its "tail" is down) as it goes and that is used to draw pictures in LOGO and related computer languages. Originally, the turtle was a small robot that rolled around on a large piece of paper, drawing a line.

Turtle graphics is a form of vector graphics. The turtle cannot be told to go to a particular position; it can only be told to turn through a particular angle and go a particular distance. *See* VECTOR GRAPHICS. For an example of turtle graphics programming, *see* LOGO.

TÜV (**T**echnischer **U**berwachungs-**V**erein, "technical supervision union") a German organization that certifies that electronic equipment meets applicable safety standards and complies with government regulations.

TV

1. (.tv) top-level-domain country code for Tuvalu, an island in the South Pacific, often used by television stations elsewhere.

2. (for "time value," on a digital camera) shutter-priority autoexposure. *See* S. *Contrast* A; AV; P.

TWAIN a protocol for delivering graphical images from a scanning or imaging device to application software. The name is said to stand for "**t**echnology **w**ithout **a**n **i**nteresting **n**ame."

TWAIN strives to reduce the number of device drivers needed by providing a standard communication format. For more information about TWAIN, see *www.twain.org*. *See also* PROTOCOL.

tweet

1. (noun) a message of up to 140 characters posted on the microblogging site Twitter.

2. (verb) to post a short message on Twitter.

See TWITTER.

twiddle *(slang)* to make small changes in settings.

twip (from "twentieth of a point") a unit of distance equal to 1/1440 inch or 1/20 point, used in Windows graphics and RTF. *Compare* POINT (definition 2).

twisted pair a pair of unshielded wires twisted together, providing a cheap and relatively noise-free way to transmit signals. The two wires carry equal and opposite signals. Any electrical noise that they pick up will be the same (rather than opposite) in the two wires, and the circuitry on the receiving end can be designed to ignore it. Category-3, -5, and -6 cables are twisted pairs. *Contrast* COAXIAL CABLE.

Twitter a microblogging service based on short messages of up to 140 characters, or "tweets" (web address: *www.twitter.com*). Founded in March 2006 by Jack Dorsey, Evan Williams, and Biz Stone, Twitter quickly grew in popularity and now is one of the most popular blogging websites. The concise nature of tweets makes them easy to quickly post, read, and respond. Tweets of common subjects are often grouped by hashtag (*See* HASHTAG). Popular subjects are also tracked so users can see what is TRENDING (rising in popularity) at the moment. *See also* MICROBLOGGING; TWEET; RETWEET.

two-tier architecture *see* CLIENT-SERVER. *Contrast* THREE-TIER ARCHITECTURE.

type

1. letters printed or displayed by a computer. *See* TYPEFACE.

2. a kind of data item, such as integers, floating-point numbers, character strings, and pointers. *See* DATA STRUCTURES and entries for particular programming languages.

3. one of the distinguishable items in a set. For instance, the list {a,a,b,c,c} contains five tokens but only three types. *Contrast* TOKEN (definition 2).

4. (in Windows and other operating systems) the command that causes the contents of a text file to be displayed. For example,

```
type letter.txt
```

causes the file LETTER.TXT to be displayed on the screen. The equivalent UNIX command is cat.

Type 1 font an outline font format developed by Adobe Systems. Type 1 fonts are sets of mathematical descriptions of the letterforms as BÉZIER splines. In practical terms this means that it is possible to SCALE or size the type to practically any point size. (*See* VECTOR GRAPHICS.) TRUETYPE fonts are a competing format to Type 1 fonts. *See also* OPENTYPE.

type-identical alike, but not the same, such as two instances of the same word in different places in a text, or two copies of the same data in different places in memory. *Contrast* TOKEN-IDENTICAL.

typeface a particular design of lettering, in a consistent weight and style. Most of the typefaces used on computer printers today fall into the following categories (*see* Figure 282):

1. *Roman type, proportionally spaced, with serifs.* This kind of type originated with the stone engravers of ancient Rome. "Proportionally spaced" means that different letters are different widths (e.g., *M* is wider than *I*); serifs are the marks at the ends of the strokes (e.g., the horizontal marks at the top and bottom of *I*). Times Roman is a popular roman typeface; it was designed by Stanley Morison for the London *Times*.

Roman type is the most readable kind of type and is used for the text of most books. Blocks of roman type should never be underlined; use *italics* instead (or **boldface** in some situations).

Roman type usually includes some characters that are not on a typewriter, such as the dash (—) and distinct opening and closing quotation marks (" "). Be sure to use these where appropriate. *See* TYPESETTING MISTAKES.

2. *Sans-serif type, proportionally spaced.* A popular typeface of this kind is Helvetica. Sans-serif type is better for short captions, posters, or labels, but can be tiring to read for long periods.

3. *Fixed-pitch, typewriter-like typefaces.* Courier and similar fixed-pitch typefaces are used when all characters must be the same width in order to line up properly, such as in computer program listings (for an example, *see* COBOL), financial tables, and documents that were laid out for a fixed-pitch printer.

4. *Novelty typefaces* such as Zapf Chancery. These should be used very sparingly to make dramatic-looking titles or mastheads.

See also DESKTOP PUBLISHING; FONT; LEADING; PITCH; POINT; SERIF.

Times Roman
ABCDEF abcdefghijklmnopqrstuvwxyz
1234567890 @#$%&*( ).,:;!?

Helvetica
ABCDEF abcdefghijklmnopqrstuvwxyz
1234567890 @#$%&*( ).,:;!?

Courier
ABCDEF abcdefghijklmnopqrstuvwxyz
1234567890 @#$%&*( ).,:;!?

Apple Chancery
ABCDEF abcdefghijklmnopqrstuvwxyz
1234567890 @#$%&( ).,:;!?*

FIGURE 282. Typefaces

typesetting mistakes common errors in the use of type on computers, arising because most computer users do not know the practices of the printing industry.

To avoid blunders, notice the differences between typesetting and typing on a typewriter or less sophisticated word processor:

– opening and closing quotation marks are different characters ("like this");

– a dash (—) is not the same as two hyphens (- -);

– underlining is rarely used—where you would underline on a typewriter or handwriting, use *italics* (or possibly **boldface**) in type.

With proportionally spaced type, letters are not all the same width. Accordingly, you can't measure width by counting characters, nor can you rely on the space bar to bring you to the exact position of something in the previous line. Always align columns with the Tab key, not the space bar.

Don't use justified type all of the time. Flush-left type with a ragged right margin is easier to read if the columns are narrow; with narrow columns, justification puts excessive space between words. *See* JUSTIFI-CATION; RIVER.

Don't use more than one or at most two fonts in a document (italics, boldface, and different sizes count as a single font). Multiple-font documents are almost always ugly. Odd typefaces (such as Old English) are very hard to read.

Make sure your document is not missing any essential features, such as adequate margins or page numbers. If in doubt, find a well-designed document or book and imitate it.

Use appropriate features of your software. When you type a footnote, use the footnote instruction if there is one, rather than just moving the cursor to the foot of the page. That way, if you change the layout later, the software will probably still handle the footnote correctly.

Finally standardize. Don't face each document as an original design problem. Develop a standard format that you like, and stick with it.

U

u typewritten representation for the Greek letter μ (mu), abbreviation for *micro-* (1/1,000,000).

ubiquitous in use everywhere. For example, "ubiquitous web protocols" are protocols such as HTTP and FTP that are available to practically all computer users. *See* PROTOCOL.

Ubuntu a Linux distribution based on Debian, with even easier installation and greater interoperability with Microsoft Windows. Ubuntu is highly recommended for Windows/Linux dual-boot systems.

Ubuntu was originated by South African entrepreneur Mark Shuttleworth. Its name is Zulu for "humanitarianism." For more information, or to download Ubuntu, see *www.ubuntu.com*. *See also* DEBIAN; LINUX.

uC (more properly μC, where μ is the Greek letter mu) abbreviation for MICROCONTROLLER.

UCM (**U**se **C**ase **M**aps) a visual representation of the requirements of a system, using a precisely defined set of symbols for responsibilities, system components, and sequences. UCMs have been applied to the development of telecommunications and other complex systems.

UCMs can be created with a free software tool (Use Case Maps Navigator, available at *www.usecasemaps.org/tools/ucmnav*) which ensures that the UCM has the correct syntax and also can be used to generate an XML listing of the system requirements. *See also* USE CASES.

UDDI (**U**niversal **D**escription, **D**iscovery and **I**ntegration) a framework for describing WEB SERVICES so other Internet users can find them. See *www.uddi.org*.

UDDRP, UDRP (**U**niform **D**omain Name **D**ispute **R**esolution **P**olicy) a process established by ICANN to allow trademark holders to wrest control of domain names away from domain name poachers. An arbitration panel decides if the domain name holder obtained the domain name in bad faith to violate a trademark.

UI *see* USER INTERFACE.

U/lc (**u**pper and **l**owercase) MIXED CASE. Also written *c/lc* (caps and lowercase). U/lc is the normal method of setting type. *Contrast* CAPS.

ulimitcheck *see* LIMITCHECK.

ULSI (**U**ltra **L**arge **S**cale **I**ntegration) the manufacture of integrated circuits containing more than one million gates. *See* INTEGRATED CIRCUIT.

ULV **U**ltra **L**ow **V**oltage.

UML (Unified Modeling Language) a language used for the visual representation of software systems (and other types of systems). Much of UML was developed at Rational Software, and it was adopted as a standard by the Object Management Group (OMG) in 1997. UML includes standard notation for representing classes and their attributes and associations, and it includes state transition, interaction, component, and deployment diagrams.

Figure 283 shows an example of a UML class diagram for a program that keeps track of the movement of boats. Each class is enclosed in a rectangle, with the name of the class at the top. The middle part of the rectangle lists attributes (or variables) for the members of that class.

For example, boats have a name represented as a string, x and y position coordinates and vx and vy velocity components, all of which are double-precision numbers. The bottom part of the class lists the operations (or methods) of that class.

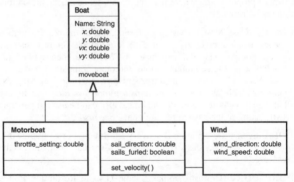

FIGURE 283. UML class diagram

In this example, two specific types of boats (sailboats and motorboats) inherit from the class Boat. Inheritance is indicated by an open arrow. Another class is the wind. The line connecting the wind and sailboat class indicates an interaction between those two classes since the operation that sets the velocity of the sailboat needs to know the wind direction and speed.

Figure 284 shows an example of a UML deployment diagram for a three-tier system where customers use a browser to connect over the Internet to the web server. The web server is, in turn, connected to the corporate mainframe database.

UML is designed for the development of complicated systems, so a complete design will include many different UML diagrams. UML diagrams can be created by hand or with a specialized software drawing tool.

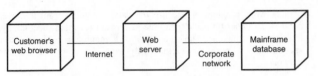

FIGURE 284. UML deployment diagram

unboxing (in Microsoft .NET Framework) the opposite of BOXING; the automatic conversion of simple objects back into value types, such as numbers and structs, after an operation for which BOXING was needed.

UNC (**U**niform **N**aming **C**onvention) the standard way of identifying shared resources (disks, directories, or printers) on Microsoft networks. UNC names have the form

$$\backslash\backslash computer\backslash resource$$

or

$$\backslash\backslash computer\backslash resource\backslash path$$

For example, if computer zeta shares its drive C under the name cdrive, then file c:\MyDoc\letter.doc on that machine is accessible through the network as

$$\backslash\backslash zeta\backslash cdrive\backslash MyDoc\backslash letter.doc.$$

Under Windows 2000 and later versions, URLs (**U**niform **R**esource **L**ocators) can be used as an alternative to UNC paths. The example just given would be *file://zeta/cdrive/MyDoc/letter.doc* in URL form.

underflow in computation, a situation that arises when a number is too small to be represented in the chosen format; it may then be incorrectly represented as 0.

For example, on an 8-digit fixed-point calculator, the computation $1 \div 1,000,000,000$ would cause an underflow because the result, 0.000000001, could not be distinguished from zero.

On most computers, that particular computation would rarely cause a problem, since computers normally use a binary form of EXPONENTIAL NOTATION, but there are limits on the size of the exponent; for example, a computer might not be able to represent 2^{-1024} because the exponent would have too many binary digits. While small inaccuracies due to underflow are usually insignificant, certain types of calculations may be affected, particularly when computations involve small differences between large numbers and/or the stability of an interactive process that is intended to converge upon a solution. *Compare* OVERFLOW.

underrun an unexpected lack of data. When recording a CD-R or DVD-R, the drive must run at a fixed speed throughout the recording process. If the computer cannot deliver data to it fast enough—because of a network problem or because the data is coming from a slower device—an underrun occurs, and the disc is not recorded successfully. The cure is to make sure no other software is running, record at a lower speed, and, if necessary, temporarily take the computer off the network.

undo a command that allows the computer user to reverse the effects of the most recent operation. If "Undo" is DIMMED (printed in gray), it is not possible for your program to undo a command (perhaps you have performed an intermediate step—or perhaps the most recent command was a complex operation that cannot be undone). For this reason, it is wise to save different versions of the file as you work so that you will have a recent version to REVERT to in case of disaster. *See also* REDO.

undocumented not described in the literature (documentation) provided by the manufacturer of a product.

Some computer programs rely on undocumented features of the machine on which they run. The risk of using undocumented features is that they may not be the same in future versions of the program or machine.

Undocumented features exist for several reasons. Some are accidental omissions from the documentation. Others represent incompletely tested features that will be made reliable and documented in future versions. Still others may be kept secret in order to give the vendor a competitive advantage in making add-on products. *See also* DOCUMENTATION.

unerase *see* RECOVERING ERASED FILES.

unfriend on social networking sites such as Facebook, to remove someone from your list of friends so that they will no longer see your postings. This can be done discreetly, without any notification being sent to the person being unfriended.

ungroup (in vector graphics) to cause a grouped object to be broken down into its component objects. It is necessary to ungroup to change the attributes of a single object or to change its shape.

unhandled exception an error condition, such as inability to write on a file, that was detected while running a program that provided no specific way of handling it. This is a common error message in the .NET Framework, and if the cause is not obvious, it reflects a programmer's error. *See* EXCEPTION; .NET FRAMEWORK.

Unicode a system for representing characters using up to 20 bits, allowing for 1,048,576 different characters, enough to represent all the written languages of the world, including Japanese and Chinese. This contrasts with the 128 or 256 characters possible in ASCII and similar systems.

The Unicode standard is not yet complete. Originally, Unicode characters were 16 bits, as in the UTF-16 format described later, and only

65,536 characters were possible. Unicode version 3 goes beyond this limit and defines over 90,000 characters. Complete information is available at *www.unicode.org*.

The first 128 Unicode character codes are the same as ASCII, including end-of-line marks (*see* CR, LF). In various programming languages and editors, Unicode character codes are written as u+xxxx or \uxxxx, where xxxx stands for a series of hexadecimal digits; thus, the letter A, ASCII hexadecimal 41, is Unicode U+0041. Figure 285 shows examples of Unicode characters.

There are several kinds of Unicode text files. The most important are:

- UTF-8—Same as ASCII for codes up to 127; thus, a UTF-8 file can also be an ASCII file. Higher-numbered codes are represented by sequences of up to 4 bytes.
- UTF-16 big-endian—Each character occupies 2 bytes (16 bits), high-order byte first. The file begins with hexadecimal FE FF (a nonprintable code to identify the file format) or with any Unicode character. Codes higher than 16 bits are represented by pairs of 16-bit sequences.
- UTF-16 little-endian—Just like UTF-16 big-endian, except that each pair of bytes has the low-order byte first, and the file begins with hexadecimal FF FE (representing the value FEFF) or with any Unicode character. This is the Unicode system normally used in Microsoft Windows.

Unicode is used internally by Microsoft Windows, Mac OS X, the Java and C# programming languages, and many newer software packages. However, the characters that you will actually see on your machine are limited by the fonts installed.

Hint: When you open a UTF-16 file in an ASCII text editor on a PC, you generally see characters separated by blanks ("l i k e   t h i s"—the blanks are really ASCII 0). The remedy is to use a Unicode editor, such as Windows Notepad, and save the file as ASCII.

See also ASCII; BIG-ENDIAN; LITTLE-ENDIAN; PONYCODE.

Character	ASCII	Unicode
$	hex 24	U+0024
A	hex 41	U+0040
π	none	U+03C0
א	none	U+05D0

FIGURE 285. Unicode characters

uniform fill one solid color or tint that fills a graphical object. *Contrast* FOUNTAIN FILL.

FIGURE 286. Uniform fill

uninitialized variable a VARIABLE in a computer program that has not been given a value. It contains random data depending on its exact location in memory and the programs that have run previously. Commonly, a program containing this kind of error will run correctly most of the time (when the variable happens to contain a reasonable value) but will fail at unpredictable times.

Some compilers automatically initialize all variables to zero or signal an error when an uninitialized variable is used. *See* INITIALIZE (definition 1).

uninterruptible power supply (UPS) a power supply that uses batteries to continue providing electricity to a computer for a few minutes in the event of a power failure. This makes it possible to shut down the computer in an orderly way without losing data.

A UPS is not the same as a SURGE PROTECTOR. The surge protector absorbs momentary (millisecond-long) spikes of *excess* voltage; the UPS protects against the *absence* of voltage for minutes or hours. Most UPSes include surge protection, but not vice versa.

The batteries in a UPS deteriorate with age. A UPS that has been in use for two or three years generally has much less capacity than when it was new.

Usage note: The spelling *uninterruptable* is also widely used. Both spellings, with *-ible* and *-able*, are consistent with the word's Latin etymology.

union a data item that can hold values of more than one type. *See* VARIANT.

uniprocessor free *see* FREE.

universal serial bus *see* USB.

UNIX an operating system, or family of operating systems, developed at Bell Laboratories in the early 1970s as a replacement for an earlier system called *Multics*. UNIX is noteworthy because, although developed by a small team of about four people, it is in many ways superior to operating systems developed by large teams at tremendous expense (e.g., OS/360). The Macintosh operating system (MAC OS X) is based on UNIX, as is LINUX.

The main features of UNIX include the following:
1. *Highly modular, structured design.* The entire system is defined in terms of a relatively small number of subroutines; UNIX can be implemented on any machine by implementing those routines.

Furthermore, the operation of the whole system is based on a relatively small number of principles carried through very consistently; there is little arbitrary detail for the user to learn.

2. *Extensibility.* In many operating systems, users can create commands of their own that execute sequences of ordinary commands stored on files. UNIX, however, provides a full-fledged programming language for this purpose (the "shell"), with `if`, `while`, and `case` statements similar to those of Pascal, as well as extensive facilities for string handling.

3. *Input-output redirection.* Any program invoked by a command can be told to take its input from, and/or write its output onto, a file rather than the user's terminal. For example,

```
sort <alpha >beta
```

tells the `sort` program to take its input from `alpha` and write its output onto `beta`. UNIX also supports *pipes*, which allow one program to transmit its output directly into the input of another program. *See* PIPE.

Many UNIX commands, called *filters*, read a file and output a copy of it that has undergone some simple transformation, such as removing repeated lines. Powerful operations can be accomplished by stringing filters together through pipes.

4. *Tree-structured directories.* In all earlier operating systems, a user's files were kept in a single list called a DIRECTORY. In UNIX, however, directories are handled like files, and a user can have an unlimited number of them, each of which must be listed in a higher directory until the main ("root") directory is reached. This makes it possible to arrange files into logical groups—for example, to put all files related to a particular project into a single directory. Tree-structured directories are a virtual necessity if one user is to keep track of more than a few dozen files.

The following are some common UNIX commands:

cc	Compile a C Program. (*See* C.)
cp	Copy a file onto a file or into a directory.
diff	Display the differences between two text files.
grep	Search a file for lines matching a pattern.
ls	List contents of a directory.
mkdir	Create a directory.
lpr	Print a file.
rm	Remove (delete) a file.
rmdir	Delete a directory (which must be empty).
cat	Copy file from standard input to standard output.
chmod	Change file permissions.

See also /DEV; /ETC; /HOME; /USR.

unlock *see* LOCK.

unsharp masking a method of sharpening an image by subtracting from it a blurred copy of itself. This was once done with photographic plates but is more easily done digitally, and most paint programs provide an unsharp masking filter. *See also* IMAGE PROCESSING and cross-references there.

FIGURE 287. Unsharp masking

unsubscribe
1. to request to be removed from an e-mail mailing list.
2. on social nerworking sites, to choose to stop viewing a particular person's public postings.

uP (more properly **µP**, where µ is the Greek letter mu) abbreviation for MICROPROCESSOR.

uplevel pertaining to a later version of a product. For example, many Windows 2000 programs are compatible with uplevel versions of Windows, such as Windows 7 and 8. *Contrast* DOWNLEVEL.

uplink
1. a connection through which signals can be transmitted to a satellite. *Compare* UPLOAD.
2. a connection from one hub to another hub. *See* HUB.

upload to transmit a file to a central computer from a smaller computer or a computer at a remote location. *See* FTP. *Contrast* DOWNLOAD; SIDELOAD.

UPnP (**U**niversal **P**lug a**n**d **P**lay) technology for standardizing connections between different devices. For information see the UPnP forum at *www. upnp.org*.

uppercase capital letters, such as A, B, C, as opposed to a, b, c (lowercase) or A, B, C (small caps). The term "uppercase" goes back to the early days of letterpress printing. The metal type was kept in divided drawers called cases; the capital letters were traditionally kept in the upper case, and the small letters in the lower.

UPS *see* UNINTERRUPTIBLE POWER SUPPLY.

upstream (describing data transmission) in a direction from the client to the server, or from the peripheral to the main computer. *Compare* UPLOAD. *Contrast* DOWNSTREAM.

upward compatibility the situation in which a computer program or accessory works not only on the machine for which it was designed but also on newer models. For instance, programs written for the IBM PC in 1981 will still run (considerably faster) on present-day Pentium machines. Thus we say that the Pentium is upward compatible with the processor in the PC. *Contrast* DOWNWARD COMPATIBILITY.

urban legend a story that is told by highly educated people as if it were true, but cannot be confirmed. Typically, it happened to a "friend of a friend" (i.e., a person who is almost, but not quite, identifiable), and it involves some improbable but highly amusing misadventure. The term was coined by Jan Harold Brunvand, who has written several books on the subject. The Internet is one of many means by which urban legends circulate. *See also* HOAX. Some of these legends are debunked at *www.snopes.com*

URL (Uniform Resource Locator, Universal Resource Locator) a way of specifying the location of publicly available information on the Internet, in the form:

   protocol://domain address:port number/filename?query

Not all parts of this are needed in all cases. An example is:

   http://www.termbook.com

which connects you to this book's web page.

   The protocol indicates what kind of connection is desired, such as HTTP for web pages or FTP for file transfers. The domain address identifies the machine to which you are connecting. The port number, usually unnecessary, can distinguish between different services running on the same machine with the same protocol. The filename is the name of the resource (usually a file or program), and the query contains additional information to be passed to the server, such as a database request.

   With the FTP protocol, a username and password can be included thus:

ftp://username:passward@www.example.com/directoryname/filename

This is a common way to access a web server in order to transfer files to and from it. However, the username and password are transmitted without encryption and can be read by anyone intercepting data packets on the network.

U.S. International a Windows keyboard layout that makes it easy to type a variety of foreign languages with an ordinary U.S. English key board. (Keyboards specially labeled for this layout are also made.)

In Control Panel, Region and Language, select U.S. International layout, and the keyboard will work as shown in Fig. 288. If you make more than one layout available at the same time, a tool will appear on the screen for selecting between them as you work.

In the U.S. International layout, the right-hand Alt key becomes the Alt Gr key, for selecting alternate characters (the ones shown on the right side of each key in the illustration). The keys ' ` " ^ ~ are "dead keys"— they are used to put an accent mark on the following letter, but only if it is a combination that is actually used (you can't put an accent on *x*, for example). To type any of the dead-key characters by itself, press the key and then the space bar.

U.S. legal the size of paper used for legal documents in the United States, $8\frac{1}{2} \times 14$ inches. *See* PAPER SIZES.

U.S. letter the size of paper used for business letters in the United States, $8\frac{1}{2} \times 11$ inches. *See* PAPER SIZES.

USB (**U**niversal **S**erial **B**us) a standard way of connecting peripherals to computers, designed to replace serial, parallel, SCSI, and other kinds of ports. USB 1.0 provides a data rate of 12 million bits per second (Mbps), slower than its rival, Firewire (IEEE 1394), but cheaper to implement. USB 2.0 ("Hi-Speed USB") achieves 480 Mbps and is fully compatible with the previous version. Only four wires are required, two for data signals, one for power, and one for ground. USB 3.0 promises speeds of up to 5 Gbps, reduced power consumption, and backward-compatibility.

The maximum cable length is 5 meters (16 feet). Any USB port can be expanded into many ports by using a USB hub, and long cable runs can be achieved by inserting a hub every 5 meters (5.5 yards).

Unlike parallel, serial, and SCSI ports, USB ports allow devices to be plugged in and unplugged while the computer is running. Also, USB ports provide a limited amount of electric power to external devices, so that in many cases the peripherals do not need their own power connectors. USB ports are even used to power lights and speakers.

Figure 289 shows the USB "trident" logo, which represents a branching cable; the USB type A connector, which plugs into the computer; and the type B connector, which plugs into a peripheral device (although many peripherals use type A connectors instead).

USB was developed by Intel and other companies starting in 1997. For more information see *www.usb.org*.

Windows U. S. International keyboard layout

Hold down Alt Gr to type additional characters.   Press ` ´ " ˆ ~ before a letter to add an accent mark.

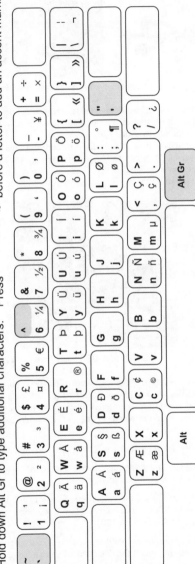

FIGURE 288. U.S. International keyboard layout

FIGURE 289. USB: symbol, type A connector, type B connector

USB flash drive a small, keychain-sized FLASH MEMORY device with a USB
interface (Fig. 290), treated by the computer as if it were a disk drive;
also called a *thumb drive* or a *jump drive*.

USB flash drives have practically replaced diskettes as a handy way
to transport data. They can be carried in one's pocket and plugged into
any computer for immediate access. The next step will be to build a CPU
into the device so that it becomes a complete computer.

FIGURE 290. USB flash drive

USB hard disk a HARD DISK that connects to the USB port of a computer.
USB hard disks are usually portable, with their own enclosures and
power supplies, and are convenient backup devices since they can be
attached to the computer when needed and stored in a safe place the rest
of the time.

USB root hub the interface between a MOTHERBOARD and a set of USB ports.

USB storage device a data-storage device that connects to a USB port; a
USB FLASH DRIVE or USB HARD DISK.

USC (United States Code), the collection of laws of the United States of
America, available online at *uscode.house.gov*. For example, 17 USC
1201 means Title 17, Section 1201.

use cases a description of events that occur as a user interacts with a system. Ivar Jacobson, one of the designers of UML, introduced the concept,

although there are disagreements over whether developing use cases helps the process of system development. See *www.pols.co.uk/usecasezone*.

Usenet

1. a set of thousands of NEWSGROUPS (discussion forums) distributed via the Internet (formerly distributed through the Usenet wide-area network). Newsgroups have descriptive names such as sci.astro.amateur and are arranged into hierarchies (classifications), of which the main ones are:

comp.	for computer science and technology;
sci.	for other academic topics (including humanities);
soc.	for cultural interest groups;
rec.	for hobbies and sports;
alt.	for trial newsgroups and "alternative" topics.

Usenet has no headquarters; the messages are copied back and forth among numerous servers. However, in recent years, the number of servers has declined greatly, and many users prefer to access the newsgroups through *groups.google.com* (Google Groups).

2. a wide-area network for UNIX machines that formerly exchanged files by modem through the UUCP ("UNIX-to-UNIX copy") command. Usenet addresses were of the form *psuvax!ugacc!aisun1!mcovingt* (which means "user mcovingt on machine aisun1, which can be reached through ugacc, which can be reached through psuvax"). Usenet has been supplanted by the INTERNET.

user-friendly easy for people to use.

In the days when computers were operated only by specialists, little attention was paid to making programs user-friendly. However, when computers became more popular, it became very important to write programs that could be used easily by nonspecialists.

The most important requirement for making a program user-friendly is that the program should fit the task—that is, it should be suitable for the job it is supposed to do, and should take advantage of what the user already knows about how to do the work. Also necessary are clear, understandable documentation and good online help.

Other features that can help make a program user-friendly are menus that clearly list the available choices and command names that are easy to remember. However, a program should not contain so many on-screen explanatory messages that it becomes cumbersome to use for people who have already learned how the program works. *See also* INTUITIVE.

user interface the way a computer program communicates with the person who is using it. There are three important types of user interfaces:

1. *Command languages.* This is a common way of giving instructions to operating systems; for instance, in DOS or VAX/VMS, the user can obtain a list of files by typing the command dir. Command

languages work well only if they are used constantly so that the user never forgets the commands.

2. *Menus.* The user chooses an item from a displayed list. Menus are ideal for software that is seldom used, but experienced users may find them too slow.

3. *Graphical environments.* The user performs operations by selecting icons (pictures) with a mouse. Environments of this type can be highly productive. For examples, *see* MACINTOSH; WINDOWS (MICROSOFT); GRAPHICAL USER INTERFACE. A drawback is that there is no simple way to describe how something is done; you almost have to see someone else do it. By contrast, commands in a command language can be written down on paper and even embedded in computer programs.

/usr in UNIX, a directory that formerly contained users' files (hence the name) and now contains installed software and parts of the operating system. Users' files are now usually stored in subdirectories of /home.

UTF-8, UTF-16 *see* UNICODE.

utility a program that assists in the operation of a computer but does not do the main work for which the computer was bought. For instance, programs that compress data or defragment disks are utilities (*see* DATA COMPRESSION; FRAGMENTATION; NORTON UTILITIES). By contrast, word processors, financial programs, engineering programs, and other programs that do actual work for the user are called *application programs.*

UTP (**u**nshielded **t**wisted **p**air) a cable consisting of pairs of wires twisted together and insulated but not provided with a metallic shield. *See* TWISTED PAIR. *Contrast* COAXIAL CABLE.

UUCP (**UNIX**-to-**UNIX** **cop**y) a command to transfer files from one computer to another. It has largely been superseded by FTP. *See* FTP. The Usenet network was sometimes called the UUCP network. *See* USENET.

uuencode a UNIX utility program that makes it possible to send binary files through electronic mail systems that only accept text files. A uuencoded file consists of printable characters arranged in lines of reasonable length. The *uudecode* program regenerates the original binary file from it. *See also* BASE64; BINARY FILE; TEXT FILE.

UV protector a clear filter that protects a camera lens from dust and dirt and excludes ultraviolet (UV) light, supposedly resulting in a slightly sharper picture. If the UV protector is of low optical quality, it can easily degrade the picture rather than improving it.

UXGA (**U**ltra e**X**tended **G**raphics **A**rray) a monitor resolution of 1600 by 1200 pixels.

V

vacuum tube an electronic component consisting of electrodes placed inside an evacuated glass tube. Vacuum tubes work by using electric and magnetic fields to control the movements of electrons that have been emitted by one of the electrodes.

A CRT (cathode ray tube) television or monitor screen is one example of a vacuum tube. The vacuum tubes originally used in computers performed the same type of functions that semiconductor diodes and transistors perform now. A vacuum tube diode consists of two electrodes: a cathode, which emits electrons, and an anode, or plate, which collects electrons. The diode conducts electricity only when a positive voltage is applied to the cathode. A vacuum tube triode contains an electrode called the grid, located between the cathode and the plate. The flow of electrons from the cathode to the plate is controlled by the electric field of the grid. (Similarly, the current flow from the emitter to the collector in a transistor is controlled by the voltage applied to the base.) Vacuum tube triodes can be used for amplification and logic functions.

An early electronic digital computer, the ENIAC, contained 18,000 vacuum tubes. The disadvantages of vacuum tube computers are that they are very big, they consume a great deal of power, and they generate a lot of heat. Also, it is necessary to constantly replace burned-out tubes. *See* COMPUTERS, HISTORY OF.

value-added reseller someone who buys computers, improves them in some way (e.g., by installing ready-to-use software of a specific type), and then sells them as complete working systems. *See also* TURNKEY SYSTEM.

vampire tap a cable-piercing connector used with thickwire Ethernet (10base-5) coaxial cables. *See* 10BASE-5; COAXIAL CABLE.

vanilla *(slang)* plain, without extra features; for example, one might speak of "vanilla" command line T$_E$X as opposed to T$_E$X with graphical development environment. This term comes from the widespread misconception that vanilla ice cream is unflavored, a mistake that can only be made if one judges ice cream by its color and not its taste. *See also* FLAVOR.

vaporware software that is announced by a vendor but never actually reaches the market.

var in VB, JavaScript, and C#, the keyword that marks variable declarations.

VAR *see* VALUE-ADDED RESELLER.

variable a symbol in a programming language that represents a data item, such as a numerical value or a character string, that can change its value during the execution of a program. *See also* ANONYMOUS VARIABLE; DATA STRUCTURES; DATA TYPES; SINGLETON VARIABLE.

variable pitch varying width of characters in a typeface; the I, for instance, will be much narrower than the W. Also called PROPORTIONAL PITCH. *See* Figure 104, page 195, at FIXED-PITCH TYPE.

variant (also called *union*) a data type that can take on values corresponding to more than one other type.

VAX popular line of minicomputers produced by Digital Equipment Corporation in the 1970s and 1980s. VAX stood for **V**irtual **A**ddress Extension (i.e., hardware support for virtual memory).

VAX/VMS the most widely used operating system for Digital Equipment Corporation VAX computers (now obsolete).

An unusual feature of VAX/VMS was the way it kept previous versions of files. If you created a file called XXXX.YYY, it would be known as XXXX.YYY;1. If you then edited it, you would create XXX.YYY;2, and XXXX.YYY;1 would still exist. Whenever you did not specify a version number, you would get the latest version of the file.

VB.NET *see* VISUAL BASIC.

VBScript a Microsoft product for adding executable commands to a web page using a language based on Visual BASIC. For another example of a web page scripting language, *see* JAVASCRIPT.

VDT (**v**ideo **d**isplay **t**erminal) a computer screen. *See* MONITOR.

vector a quantity with both magnitude (length) and direction. For example, "one mile due northeast" describes a vector. Vectors can also be described with coordinates. For example (4, 10) describes a vector in two-dimensional space, and (12, 15, −4) describes a vector in three-dimensional space.

vector graphics a method of creating pictures on a computer by telling it to draw lines in particular positions. The lines may be displayed on a screen or plotted on paper. An advantage of vector graphics is that a picture can be enlarged or reduced without loss of sharpness, since the picture is not made of a fixed number of pixels. *Contrast* BITMAP GRAPHICS. *See also* DRAW PROGRAM; PAINT PROGRAM.

vector processor a computer that can perform an operation on an entire array of numbers in a single step; also known as an *array processor.* Cray supercomputers are vector processors. They have machine instructions that can (for example) add each entry of array A to the corresponding entry of array B and store the result in the corresponding entry of array C. *Contrast* SCALAR PROCESSOR; SUPERSCALAR PROCESSOR.

version problem difficulty arising if you are not careful about updating a file on more than one computer. If you make some changes to the file on your desktop, and other changes to the previous version of the file on your laptop, you won't have any version of the file incorporating all of the changes. *See* BRIEFCASE.

FIGURE 291. Vector graphics displayed as wireframe

vertical paper oriented so that it is taller than wide; also called PORTRAIT or TALL orientation.

VGA the video system introduced by IBM on the PS/2 computers in 1987, the basis of current PC graphics. *VGA* originally stood for **V**ideo **G**ate **A**rray (an ASIC on the PS/2 motherboard) but nowadays is usually interpreted as **V**ideo **G**raphics **A**dapter.

The VGA provided a maximum resolution of 640×480 with 16 colors. It also supported all the video modes of the earlier IBM video adapters (MDA, CGA, and EGA). *See also* SVGA; XGA.

VGA connector the DB-15 connector commonly used for analog video output from computers since the late 1980s, used not only with the original VGA but also with its many derivatives (SVGA, XGA, etc.). *See* Fig. 292. *Contrast* DVI (definition 1).

FIGURE 292. VGA video connector

video
1. the signals sent from a computer to its monitor screen.
2. moving pictures displayed on a computer. *See* DVI (definition 1); MPEG; QUICKTIME.

video adapter *see* VIDEO CARD.

video capture the process of digitizing moving television images and storing them in a computer. Unlike a FRAME GRABBER, a video capture card records moving video, not just still pictures.

video card a plug-in circuit board that enables a computer to display information on a particular type of monitor (screen).

video chat an informal conversation using NETCAMS to enable chatters to see one another. *Compare* VIDEOCONFERENCING.

video memory the memory on a video card in which a computer keeps track of the present contents of the screen.

videoconferencing the use of video cameras and computer networking to enable participants to converse and see one another.

videomail e-mail consisting of a video presentation, often a message recorded by the sender with his NETCAM.

viewer a program for viewing graphics files in a particular format. Most WEB BROWSERS can interface to separate viewers that support additional kinds of graphics. By extension, a program for playing sounds is sometimes called a viewer. *See also* ACROBAT.

vignette a rounded image with edges that shade gradually into the background. Many paint programs have a filter that produces a vignetted effect upon any image.

FIGURE 293. Vignette

viral (as in "this video went viral") spreading among human beings like an infectious virus. When a piece of Internet content (a picture, a video, etc.) becomes very popular in a short time due to people passing it along to their friends, usually by social networks, it is said to have "gone viral." The exponential spread of their popularity is similar to how a virus infection starts off small and quickly gains ground.

viral marketing advertising designed to spread from one person to another, in the manner of a virus. Effective viral marketing campaigns are interesting conversation pieces that people with no commercial interest in promoting the product will discuss and propagate. On the Internet, viral marketing usually takes the form of videos and interactive web sites.

virtual in computer science, referring to a system that can act as, or fulfill the function of, another system. *See* the next five entries.

virtual keyboard a keyboard that appears as an image on a touch-screen.

virtual machine a computer that does not physically exist but is simulated by another computer. In IBM's VM/ESA operating system, the computer simulates multiple copies of itself.

A Java applet is run by a Java virtual machine, which is part of a web browser that executes Java bytecode. *See* JVM.

virtual memory a way of extending the effective size of a computer's memory by using a disk file to simulate additional memory space. Typically, the operating system keeps track of which memory addresses actually reside in memory and which ones must be brought in from disk when they are referred to. Virtual storage is divided into units called *pages,* and the operation of bringing in a page from disk is called a *page fault.*

virtual private network (VPN) a network where data is transferred over the Internet using security features preventing unauthorized access.

virtual reality the simulation of a person's entire environment (sights, sounds, movements, etc.) by computer. Most commonly this is done by displaying a realistic picture (*see* THREE-DIMENSIONAL GRAPHICS) and allowing the user to manipulate objects by clicking on them with the mouse. *See* VRML.

Truly realistic virtual reality is more a goal than an existing technology, but some computer games achieve a limited kind of realism by having the user wear a special helmet and gloves and/or stand on a special platform.

virtual storage
1. storing data in THE CLOUD.
2. same as VIRTUAL MEMORY.

virtualization the process of using a VIRTUAL device (for example, using VIRTUAL STORAGE).

virus a computer program that automatically copies itself, thereby "infecting" other disks or programs without the user knowing it, and then plays some kind of trick or disrupts the operation of the computer.

Viruses have existed as academic pranks since the 1960s, but 1987 saw the first malicious viruses, apparently the work of disgruntled programmers trying to sabotage their competition.

Nowadays, most virus infections result when the user of a computer is tricked into running a malicious program by opening it as a file. To avoid viruses, never open a file that arrives unexpectedly in e-mail, even if it appears to be from someone you know and trust (*see* WORM VIRUS). Always run antivirus software; keep your antivirus software up to date; and always install software from the manufacturer's original disks rather than from copies made on a potentially infected machine.

Knowingly spreading a computer virus is a crime under common law and under specific laws in various states. *See also* ANTIVIRUS SOFTWARE; MACRO VIRUS; SPYWARE; TROJAN HORSE; WORM VIRUS.

virus protection software a computer program that offers protection from VIRUSes by making additional checks of the integrity of the operating system. No vaccine can offer complete protection against all viruses. Also known as ANTIVIRUS SOFTWARE.

Visicalc the first computer spreadsheet program, developed for the Apple II in the late 1970s by Dan Bricklin and Bob Frankston. *See* SPREADSHEET.

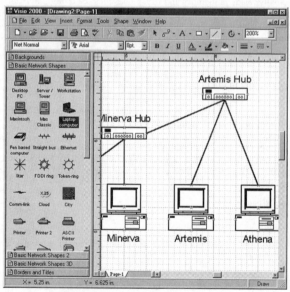

FIGURE 294. Visio graphics software

Visio a widely used software package for creating business and technical diagrams. Unlike earlier graphics software, Visio recognizes the ways in which symbols interact with their environment. Each symbol, or "Smart-Shape," can be programmed to behave in specific ways as it is moved or resized. For example, in an electronic circuit diagram, when you stretch the symbol for a resistor, the stretching affects only the connecting lines on the ends; the symbol itself remains the proper shape. Thus, drafting can be done quickly, and Visio helps keep a complex diagram properly connected together as parts of it are rearranged. In 2000, Visio Corporation was purchased by Microsoft. Their web address is *www.microsoft. com/office/visio*.

vision, computer the use of computers to recognize objects in images (not just store, retrieve, and manipulate the images themselves). Computer vision is surprisingly difficult to implement. Some of the main challenges are: *edge detection* (finding the boundaries of objects); *perspective* (interpreting a two-dimensional image as three-dimensional); *color constancy* (adapting to variations in the color of light, including light reflected from other nearby objects); and *shape constancy* (recognizing the same shape from different angles).

Computer vision has found some industrial applications where the number of objects to be recognized is small and the positioning and light are constant, such as identifying objects that pass by on an assembly line and sounding an alarm when one of them is missing or looks abnormal.

See also IMAGE PROCESSING.

vision, human the ability to see. Computer displays rely on many special properties of human vision, among them the following:
  1. The eye blends together images that are less than $\frac{1}{30}$ second apart. For flicker-free viewing, the computer must scan the screen at least 30 and preferably more than 70 times per second.
  2. Movements that are made in steps lasting $\frac{1}{30}$ second or less appear to be continuous. A moving image is actually a series of still images presented in very rapid succession.
  3. Colors can be simulated by mixing other colors. For example, yellow on a computer screen does not contain any yellow light; instead, it is a mixture of red and green light. *See* COLOR.

Working with a computer screen can be tiring to the eyes, especially if the display is blurry or glare is a problem, but no permanent harm results. Eyeglasses designed for the proper working distance can make computer work much easier. *See* EYEGLASSES, COMPUTER. *See also* SOLID PHOTOGRAPHY.

vision, machine *see* VISION, COMPUTER.

visit the occurrence of one web browser requesting documents (WEB PAGES) from a site during a short period of time. A single visit to a web site may generate several HITS.

Vista *see* WINDOWS (MICROSOFT).

Visual Basic one of the first successful *interactive development environments* for Windows programming, introduced by Microsoft in 1991. Programmers can lay out the program's windows graphically (Figure

295) and write BASIC code to specify what happens when each button is clicked or other events occur. Any part of the layout or code can be changed at any time. Unlike in earlier Windows programming environments, the programmer need not write any general code to initialize windows, handle events, or interact with the operating system.

The current version is called *Visual Basic .NET* or *VB.NET* and uses the .NET Framework for fully object-oriented programming. Similar products for other programming languages include Microsoft's Visual C++ and Visual C# and Borland's Delphi and Kylix (for Pascal), JBuilder (for Java), and C++ Builder.

See also EVENT-DRIVEN PROGRAMMING; .NET FRAMEWORK; OBJECT-ORIENTED PROGRAMMING.

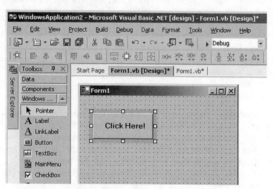

FIGURE 295. Visual Basic

visual chat a CHAT ROOM or similar online conversation where, in addition to chat handles (names), users are represented by graphics.

Visual Studio development environment provided by Microsoft for Visual Basic, C++, C#, and other languages.

visualization

1. in scientific computing, the science and art of making information visible through graphs, charts, and animation.

2. in audio playback programs, a way of creating visual images that move with the sound being played, such as waveforms, spectra, or abstract effects.

VLSI (very large-scale integration) the manufacture of integrated circuits (silicon chips) containing 10,000 or more logic gates. *See also* INTEGRATED CIRCUIT; ULSI.

VM *see* JVM; VIRTUAL MACHINE.

VM/CMS *see* CMS; VM/ESA.

VM/ESA (**V**irtual **M**achine/**E**nterprise **S**ystems **A**rchitecture) an operating system for large IBM mainframe computers, such as the 370, 3081, and 390, based on the idea of one computer simulating multiple copies of itself. VM/ESA was formerly known as VM/SP. (*See also* MVS; TSO.)

voice chat an audio conversation or conference with multiple participants, transmitted by computer network. *Compare* VIDEOCONFERENCING.

voice mail messages that are received by telephone, recorded, and played automatically when the recipient requests them. Voice mail systems are computer-controlled; messages are saved in digital form.

voice recognition
  1. the recognition of spoken words by a computer. *See* NATURAL LANGUAGE PROCESSING.
  2. the identification of people by computers that recognize the distinctive characteristics of their voices. *See* BIOMETRICS.

void in C and related programming languages, a keyword that means "no data type" and declares a function or method that returns no value or a pointer to an unknown type.

VoIP (**V**oice **o**ver **I**nternet **P**rotocol) the transmission of voice telephone conversations through the Internet or through IP networks. Several protocols are used for this purpose. *See* INTERNET TELEPHONY; PROTOCOL; SKYPE.

voken (**v**irtual t**oken**) an advertisement that appears over the contents of a browser window, but not in a window of its own. *Compare* POP-UP AD.
  The voken can move around the screen, rotate, and blink to attract attention. A moving voken can trick you into clicking on it—thus going to the advertiser's site—when you meant to click on something else, but it got in the way.

volatile not permanent; erased when turned off. The memory (RAM) of a computer is volatile; that is, it goes blank when power is removed. Flash memory and disks are non-volatile. In some programming languages, a variable is declared volatile if it can be changed by something outside the program.

volt the unit of measure of electric potential. If a potential of 1 volt is applied to a resistance of 1 ohm, then a current of 1 ampere will flow through the resistance. (*See* OHM'S LAW.)

volume
   1. an individual diskette, disk, or tape.
   2. the perceived loudness of a sound. The volume control on a sound card may be a knob on the card itself, a setting made in software, or both.

volume serial number an identifying number assigned to a disk or tape by Windows or other operating systems. Volume serial numbers ensure that the computer will know when the disk or tape in a drive is changed.

Von Neumann architecture a type of computer design in which programs and data are stored in a single kind of memory. *Contrast* HARVARD ARCHITECTURE. *See* COMPUTER ARCHITECTURE.

Von Neumann, John (1903–1957) mathematician who worked on one of the earliest computers and developed the concept of storing programs in memory.

voxel (from *volume cell*) one of the cubes into which a three-dimensional space is divided, like a PIXEL but in three dimensions.

VPN abbreviation for VIRTUAL PRIVATE NETWORK.

VRAM (**v**ideo **r**andom **a**ccess **m**emory) RAM that is specially designed for use in video cards. Commonly, it can be read and written simultaneously so that the generation of the display is not interrupted when the CPU needs to place data in it.

VRML (**V**irtual **R**eality **M**arkup **L**anguage or **V**irtual **R**eality **M**odeling **L**anguage) a programming language developed by Mark Pesce and Tony Parisi to describe three-dimensional objects for graphical display. A VRML program describes a "world" of virtual objects that a person can walk or fly through. The computer draws the objects as they are seen from a specified position, which can be constantly changing. Objects can respond to mouse clicks.

   Figure 297 shows a sample program written in VRML 1.0 (1996). It depicts a sphere and three blocks in front of a large black panel. In the language, a "separator" is an object composed of one or more primitive shapes. Figure 296 shows this scene as viewed from two different angles with a VRML BROWSER (viewing program). More sophisticated VRML programs can provide very realistic views of scenery and buildings. The successor to VRML is X3D.

FIGURE 296. VRML example, displayed two ways

```
#VRML V1.0 ascii

Separator {
    Separator {
        # Black panel
        Transform { translation 0 0.1 -0.5 }
        Material { diffuseColor 0 0 0 }
        Cube { width 1.2 height 0.65 depth 0.5 }
            }
    Separator {
        # Ball
        Transform { translation 0 0.2 0 }
        Material { diffuseColor 1 0.7 0.3
                   specularColor 0.3 0 0 }
        Sphere { radius 0.1 }
            }
    Separator {
        # Middle block
        Material { diffuseColor 0.6 0.6 1.0 }
        Cube { width 0.2 height 0.2 depth 0.2 }
            }
    Separator {
        # Block
        Transform { translation 0.3 0 0 }
        Cube { width 0.15 height 0.2 depth 0.2 }
            }
    Separator {
        # Block
        Transform { translation -0.3 0 0 }
        Cube { width 0.15 height 0.2 depth 0.2 }
            }
        }
```

FIGURE 297. VRML programming example

VSN *see* VOLUME SERIAL NUMBER.

VT-100 a computer terminal made by Digital Equipment Corporation that had a major impact on the computer industry in the early 1980s. It provided convenient control codes for positioning the cursor, clearing the screen, and selecting normal, bold, or underlined type. This makes it possible to implement full-screen, personal-computer-like software on an asynchronous terminal. Most implementations of Telnet can emulate the VT-100.

W

W3C *see* WORLD WIDE WEB CONSORTIUM.

WAI (**W**eb **A**ccessibility **I**nitiative) part of the World Wide Web Consortium dedicated to increasing Web accessibility. Since 1999, it has published guidelines for web sites to help designers improve usability. In addition to helping users with physical disabilities, increasing the accessibility of a web site makes it easier to view the site on devices like phones.

wall transformer a small transformer, often including other power-supply components, that plugs into a wall outlet (Figure 298).

Wall transformers keep high-voltage AC completely outside the equipment being powered. Because of this, only the wall transformer, not the rest of the equipment, has to pass fire safety certifications. For this reason, they are very popular with manufacturers.

Most wall transformers are designed to burn out harmlessly when overloaded; there is no replaceable fuse. A dead wall transformer is a common cause of inoperative equipment.

It is very important not to substitute wall transformers unless you are sure that the replacement delivers the same voltage with the same polarity (arrangement of + and – connectors) and the same or greater maximum current (amperes, milliamperes). Equipment can be damaged by using the wrong power supply.

FIGURE 298. Wall transformer ("wall wart")

wall wart *(slang)* a WALL TRANSFORMER.

wallpaper a picture or pattern displayed as a background in a windowed operating system.

WAN *see* WIDE-AREA NETWORK.

WAP
1. *see* WIRELESS ACCESS POINT.
2. (**W**ireless **A**pplication **P**rotocol) an open global specification for wireless devices to interact with information providers. See *www.wapforum.org*.

war dialing (*slang*) the practice of using an autodial modem to dial many telephone numbers in succession (e.g., 000-0000 to 999-9999) to see if a computer answers any of them. If so, attempts are made to break into the computer. If a human being answers, he or she hears a tone, or nothing at all. The practice was popularized by the movie *Wargames* (1983).

war driving (*slang*) the practice of driving or walking around town with a laptop computer, to see if it can connect to anyone's wireless network. *Compare* WAR DIALING.

warez pirated software, usually traded over the Internet on peer-to-peer networks. *See* PIRACY.

warm boot, warm start *See* BOOT.

warp to digitally manipulate an image so that it appears twisted or stretched (Figure 299).

FIGURE 299. Warp effect

watermark
   1. a pattern visible when paper is held up to light; it is pressed into the paper during manufacturing. For example, U.S. government stationery has the Great Seal of the United States in its watermark.
   2. a faint pattern or second image added to a digital image for identification or other purposes.
   3. an invisible code placed in a digital image to identify it. *See* INVISIBLE WATERMARK; STEGANOGRAPHY.

Watson computer developed by IBM that beat human experts in the television game show *Jeopardy* in 2011. *See* ARTIFICIAL INTELLIGENCE.

watt unit for measuring the rate at which electrical power energy is usually being consumed. One watt is equivalent to one joule per second. Wattage depends on both voltage and current, as follows:

```
watts = volts × amperes
```

For example, a 5-volt, 10-ampere power supply delivers 50 watts. The power can also be found from the formula I^2R, where I is the current and R is the resistance in the circuit. The amount of AC power going into the power supply is somewhat greater, depending on the inefficiency of the supply.

watt-hour the amount of energy consumed by using energy at the rate of one watt for one hour. One watt-hour equals 3,600 joules. In the United States, electricity costs about 10 cents for 1,000 watt-hours (one kilowatt-hour).

.wav the filename extension for digitized sound wave files under Microsoft Windows.

wave file a file containing a digital representation of sound waves. *See* SAMPLING RATE; SOUND CARD; WAV.

wavetable synthesis a technique for synthesizing musical instrument sounds by computer using stored information about the waveforms produced by real instruments. *Contrast* FM SYNTHESIS.

Wayback machine a service providing archived copies of many web pages from previous times. Because web pages often change, there would be a serious risk that much history would be lost if this archiving service did not exist. Web address: *www.archive.org. Compare* CACHE.

WCF (**W**indows **C**ommunication **F**oundation) part of the .NET FRAMEWORK that allows developers to create services that can interact with other systems.

Web the WORLD WIDE WEB.

WEB a programming tool developed by D. E. Knuth to make it easier to create modular programs. WEB is a more abstract form of the Pascal (or, in later versions, C) programming language. The programmer is free to define procedures in any order and write blocks of code to be inserted into larger blocks written later. Heavy use of comments is encouraged and listings are printed elegantly with reserved words in boldface.

Web 2.0 a vague name for a number of new ways of using the WORLD WIDE WEB, especially those that involve SOCIAL NETWORKING and audience participation. "Web 2.0" is not the name of any specific technical standard.

web address a string of characters that identifies a file accessible through the WORLD WIDE WEB, such as:

http://www.CovingtonInnovations.com/christian.html

The web address specifies protocol (usually *http*), the domain address of the site (such as *www.CovingtonInnovations.com*), and, optionally, a directory path and filename. *See* PROTOCOL; URL.

web browser *see* BROWSER.

web log *see* BLOG.

web page a file of information made available for viewing on the WORLD WIDE WEB and seen by the user as a page of information on the screen.

web page design the production of WEB PAGES for others to view. Many web pages are badly designed. Here are some guidelines for designing a good one:

1. Decide on the purpose of your web page. What information do you want to communicate? What's important and what's not? Focus on conveying your message rather than showing off your repertoire of special effects.

2. Plan for maintainability. How soon will something have to be changed? Can frequently changed information be placed in separate files that are easier to update?

3. If you want people to visit your web site repeatedly, put something useful there, such as reference information, links to other sites, or free software.

4. Do not draw attention to the wrong things. The most important part of your message should be the most visually prominent. Unimportant graphics that blink or move can be very annoying.

5. Remember that you do not have a captive audience. People are not going to sit through time-consuming graphics or animations if what they really want could have been delivered more quickly.

6. Remember that some people still use older browsers. You probably don't want to limit your audience to people who have this month's version.

7. Use dark type on a white background for anything the reader may need to print out. Some browsers cannot print out light type on a dark background.

8. Attach links to informative words, not the word "here." Instead of "Click <u>here</u> to learn about our new software," just say "<u>New software</u>."

See HTML.

FIGURE 300. Web page

web page title the descriptive text that appears in the browser's title bar at the top of its window. The title text is not part of the web page text and cannot be modified by other markup tags. The web page title is used as the name when the user creates a BOOKMARK.

web search the act of searching the WORLD WIDE WEB with a SEARCH ENGINE.

web server a computer that is attached to the Internet and contains web pages (HTML files) that can be viewed using a web browser. Every web page resides on a web server somewhere. The web server has to be connected to the Internet continuously, and it runs an HTTP server program such as Apache or Microsoft's IIS. The web server may also need to run special software (such as a CGI script) in response to a client's request. *See* WEB PAGE; WORLD WIDE WEB.

web services programs running on computers connected to the Internet that can interoperate with programs on other computers, using XML as a standard way of formatting data to be communicated. Standards for web services are being developed by OASIS. *See also* .NET FRAMEWORK.

web site a file or related group of files available on the WORLD WIDE WEB.

webcam A camera attached to a computer that distributes a live image to the WORLD WIDE WEB. *Compare* NETCAM. Physically, webcams and netcams are alike; the difference is in how they are used.

webcast (**web** broad**cast**) an event intended to be viewed simultaneously by numerous people connecting to the same web site. Webcasts often feature celebrity interviews, open-forum discussions, or product announcements. If too many people "tune in" at the same time, however, the server or network can be overloaded. *Compare* INTERNET RADIO; IPTV; PODCASTING.

webinar (**web** sem**inar**) a presentation or meeting held through the World Wide Web, using real-time video and audio communication enabling people at different locations to participate.

webliography (**web** bib**liography**) a list of web-based documents on a specific subject.

webmaster the person who has principal responsibility for maintaining a site on the WORLD WIDE WEB and updating some or all of the WEB PAGES.

weight the boldness (heaviness) of a style of type. For example, **this is heavy-weight type** and this is ordinary-weight type. Some fonts provide several different weights (light, medium, demibold, bold, and extra bold). *See* Figure 301.

Light
Normal
Bold
Extra Bold

FIGURE 301. Weight (of typefaces)

weld (in vector graphics) to join two or more objects so that the resulting single object has the outline of the group of objects.

WEP (**W**ired **E**quivalent **P**rivacy) a relatively weak encryption system built into WI-FI and related 802.11b wireless networking systems. The original version of WEP used a 40-bit key (sometimes described as a 64-bit key) and is not considered highly secure. Newer versions use a 128-bit key and are considerably better.

Despite possible limitations, even 40-bit WEP is definitely better than nothing, since without it, all data sent through the network would easily be readable by an eavesdropper outside the building. *See* COMPUTER SECURITY; WIRELESS NETWORK.

whack (slang) the backward slash character \.

WHATWG (**W**eb **H**ypertext **A**pplication **T**echnology **W**orking **G**roup) a group of people working on new developments in web pages and HTML features (web address: *www.whatwg.org*).

wheel (from "big wheel") a user who has some system administration privileges; on a UNIX system, a user who is a member of the group named wheels, reserved for system administrators.

Whetstone a standard benchmark program for testing computer speed. *See* MIPS.

Whidbey code name used for the 2005 version of Microsoft Visual Studio before its release. *See* VISUAL STUDIO.

while the keyword, in Pascal, C, and related languages, that causes a LOOP to execute over and over until a condition becomes false. Here is an example in Java:

```java
/* This is Java; C, C++, C# are very similar */
int i=5;
while(i>0)
{
    System.out.print(i + "...");
    i--;
}
System.out.println("Finished");
```

The computer tests whether the condition i>0 is true, and if so, executes the statements within the loop. Then it tests the condition again and does the same thing. When the condition becomes false, execution continues after the loop. Thus, these lines cause the computer to print:

```
5...4...3...2...1...Finished!
```

The Java statement i-- (which means subtract 1 from i) and its Pascal equivalent i:=i-1 are vital here. Without it, i would always remain greater than 0 and the program would run forever.

If the condition of a while loop is false at the beginning, the statements in the loop are never executed. *See also* DO. *Contrast* REPEAT.

Whistler internal code name that denoted Windows XP and Windows .NET Server before their release. *Compare* CAIRO; CHICAGO; LONGHORN; MEMPHIS.

white balance in a digital camera, compensation for the color of the light source. For instance, pictures taken by incandescent light will require a different white balance than those taken by sunlight because incandescent light is redder. *See also* COLOR TEMPERATURE.

white hat someone who is in favor of COMPUTER SECURITY and has some expertise in the field; one of the "good guys," like the characters in old Western movies who wore white hats. *Contrast* BLACK HAT. The term *white hat* is also used by CRACKERS who claim to have beneficent motives (*see* ETHICAL HACKING).

white noise sound consisting of random oscillations with equal amounts of energy at all frequencies. The effect is a hissing sound, often used in computer sound effects. This is analogous to white light, which is a mixture of all visible wavelengths.

white paper a brief technical report, often introducing a new technology.

white space
1. characters that, when printed, do not put ink on the paper: spaces, tabs, newlines, form feeds, and the like.
2. unused frequencies in the television broadcast portion of the electromagnetic spectrum. Several companies have proposed using these frequencies for wireless Internet transmission.

whiteboard a common feature of VIDEOCONFERENCING software that, like a real whiteboard, provides a surface on which all users may write comments or draw diagrams that are then visible to all members of the group.

whitelist list of e-mail senders whose messages are accepted. *Contrast* BLACKLIST and GRAYLIST.

Wi-Fi a set of widely used product compatibility standards for wireless 802.11 networking. *See* 802.11. *Contrast* WIMAX.

wide LANDSCAPE or horizontal orientation. *Contrast* PORTRAIT or TALL.

wide-area network (WAN) a set of widely separated computers connected together. For example, the worldwide airline reservation system is a wide-area network. The Internet is a set of interconnected wide-area networks. *Contrast* LOCAL-AREA NETWORK.

widget a small software application on a web page (named after a term used in economics for a generic manufactured product).

widow the first line of a paragraph when it appears by itself as the last line of a page. Some word processors automatically adjust page breaks so that there are no widows. *See also* ORPHAN.

Wii a video game console released by Nintendo that distinguishes itself with a wireless handheld controller. The wireless controller captures movement in a way that can be used in games; for example, swinging the controller may mean the character in the video game swings his sword.

wiki (pronounced "weekee" or "wicky") a multi-user BLOG or set of web pages where all users can add content and edit the content of others. The term comes from Hawaiian *wiki* ("quick").

Wikipedia a multilingual, free encyclopedia in WIKI format that is written collaboratively by thousands of volunteers from around the world. Web address: *www.wikipedia.org*.

wild card a symbol that matches any other string. For instance, the Windows command

```
dir ab*.exe
```

means "display a list of files whose names begin with ab and end with .exe." The symbol * is a wild card and stands for the middle part of the filename, whatever it may be.

WiMax (**W**orldwide **I**nteroperability for **M**icroware **Ac**cess) a set of wireless networking standards for long-distance (50-km, 31-mile) wireless networking, based on IEEE standard 802.16. The purpose of WiMax is to solve the LAST MILE problem by eliminating the need for cables to individual buildings. *Contrast* WI-FI, which usually has a range the size of a building or less. *See also* OPA.

Win key, Winkey (pronounced "win key") the Windows key. A key marked with the Microsoft Windows logo and found on some PC keyboards (Figure 302). It provides a shortcut to some Windows menus but is not strictly necessary because all functions of Windows are accessible without it. *See* WINDOWS (MICROSOFT).

Win32 the 32-bit core of Windows 95 and its successors. Programs written for Win32 will run under all of these Windows operating systems.

FIGURE 302. Win key

Win32s a subset of Win32 that could be installed as an extension to Windows 3.1, making it possible to run many Windows 95 programs.

Winchester disk any hard disk designed for use in microcomputers. "Winchester" is an early industry code name, not a brand name. *See* HARD DISK.

window a rectangular area of the screen set aside for a special purpose. On the Macintosh, in Microsoft Windows, and in other similar operating systems, the screen is divided into windows for different pieces of software. The user can control the size, shape, and positioning of the windows. The *active window* is the one in which you are currently typing.

Figure 303 shows the main parts of a window in Microsoft Windows. To move the window, place the mouse pointer on the title bar, hold down the left button, and move the mouse. To change the size of the window, do the same thing but with the pointer on the left, right, or bottom border of the window. To close the window, click once on the *close box* (the box with the × symbol) or double-click on the control menu button. *See also* DIALOG BOX; ICON; MAXIMIZE; MENU BAR; MESSAGE BOX; MINIMIZE; PULL-DOWN MENU; SCROLL BAR; THUMB; TITLE BAR.

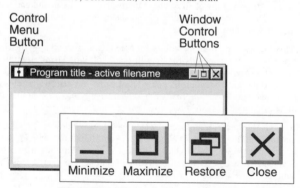

FIGURE 303. Window (in Microsoft Windows)

Windows (Microsoft) a family of operating systems whose lineage is shown in Figure 306, produced by Microsoft Corporation of Redmond, Washington.

Windows originated in 1983 as a GRAPHICAL USER INTERFACE that ran under DOS to provide windowing and mouse support for graphics software. The idea of the graphical user interface had been invented by Xerox's Palo Alto research center and popularized by Apple's Macintosh. In 1990, **Windows 3.0** introduced the ability to multitask DOS programs, thereby giving Windows an advantage over DOS even for non-graphical uses.

Separately, Microsoft and IBM collaborated on a 32-bit multitasking operating system for the 80386, 486, and Pentium, but the collaboration broke up and produced two separate products, IBM OS/2 and Microsoft **Windows NT**, the direct ancestor of present-day Windows versions. Internally, Windows NT resembles UNIX, and UNIX software is relatively easy to port to it. *See also* POSIX.

Windows 95, **98**, and **Me** (Millennium Edition) were transitional products that moved toward the Windows NT architecture while maintaining a high level of compatibility with DOS, including DOS device drivers and programs that access the hardware directly.

Windows 2000, **XP**, **Vista**, **7**, and their successors are derived directly from Windows NT. The user interface of Windows changed little from Windows 95 to Windows 2000. In Windows XP it was redecorated with no real change in functionality. Windows Vista features a redesigned user interface (*see* AERO) substantially influenced by Mac OS X. Windows 7 is a minor upgrade from Vista, and Windows 8 is slated to introduce a new user interface influenced by Apple's IOS. *See also* METRO.

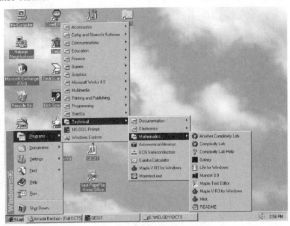

FIGURE 304. Windows menus

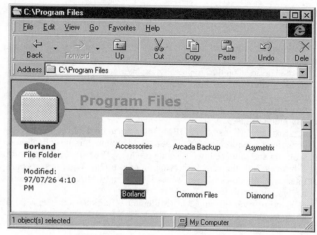

FIGURE 305. Windows user interface

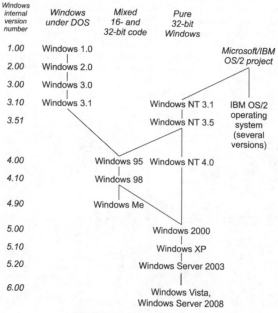

FIGURE 306. Windows versions

Compared to Windows XP, Vista introduced significant internal improvements in security and efficiency. In particular, Vista normally asks permission for any change to the machine configuration, making it hard for viruses or malware to make changes without the user's knowledge. Because of improved security, Windows Vista and Windows 7 are less tolerant of software that violates some long-standing (Windows-NT-era) security recommendations, and many older device drivers no longer work. Older application software (from Windows 95 or later) seldom has problems.

Windows is used mainly on 32-bit Pentium-family processors, but several 64-bit versions exist. Versions of Windows NT were produced for the DEC Alpha, MIPS R4x00, and PowerPC CPUs. (*See* ALPHA.) Versions of Windows XP support AMD64 (x64) and Itanium (IA-64) CPUs. Windows Vista and Windows 7 are available in 64-bit versions for the x64 but not the Itanium.

See also COMMAND PROMPT; DEVICE DRIVER; MULTITASKING; OS/2; UNIX.

Windows-1252 a character set created by IBM and Microsoft for the IBM PC. It is a superset of ASCII.

Windows 9x abbreviation for "Windows 95 and 98."

Windows accelerator a graphics card that can move or overlay windows on its own without having the CPU completely redraw each window. *See* SVGA.

Windows Messenger *see* LIVE MESSENGER.

Winmodem a modem that relies on a CPU running Microsoft Windows to do part of the signal processing traditionally done by the modem itself. *See* MODEM.

Wintel *(slang)* **Win**dows–**Intel** (i.e., PC-compatible).

wireframe a drawing displayed in outline form. Displaying a wireframe is much faster than displaying the full image, and details are visible in it that may be obscured in the finished product. Many 3-D and draw programs give you a choice of editing a wireframe image or an image displayed in finished form.

See illustration at VECTOR GRAPHICS. *See also* THREE-DIMENSIONAL GRAPHICS.

Wireless-A a 54-Mbps, 5-GHz wireless protocol now largely superseded by Wireless-G. *See* 802.11.

wireless access point the hub of a wireless network; the central transmitter and receiver, with antennas, attached to a wired network.

Wireless-B the first widely popular WI-FI wireless communication standard, giving 11 Mpbs at 2.4 GHz. *See* 802.11.

wireless cloud the irregularly shaped area in which a WIRELESS NETWORK is usable. Because radio waves fade out gradually with increasing distance and penetrate some kinds of obstacles better than others, the size and shape of the wireless cloud depends both on the environment and on the equipment at both ends of the link. Better antennas or greater height give greater range. A would-be intruder with a special antenna can access a wireless network from ten times the normal distance.

wireless communication the transfer of electromagnetic signals from place to place without cables, usually using infrared light or radio waves.

Communication by infrared light is practical only over short distances in unobstructed places with a clear line of sight. For example, infrared light is used by TV remote controls and occasionally to link a keyboard or mouse to a computer. It does not pass through walls.

Radio waves travel freely in all directions and penetrate obstacles. As Figure 307 shows, every transmitter fills a large area with its signal. Since only a finite range of frequencies is available, transmitters often interfere with each other. Unlicensed transmitters are limited to very low power and short range (*see* PART 15 DEVICE); more powerful transmitters require regulation and licensing. Spread-spectrum technology provides an especially efficient way to share frequencies (*see* SPREAD SPECTRUM).

Radio signals are inherently non-private. There is no physical way to keep them from being received, voluntarily or involuntarily, by receivers other than the intended one. Private information should not be transmitted by radio unless it is encrypted to keep it secret. *See* ENCRYPTION; WEP; WIRELESS NETWORK.

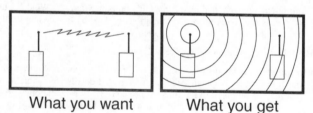

What you want   What you get

FIGURE 307. Wireless communication

Wireless-G a widely used WI-FI wireless communication standard, giving 54 Mpbs at 2.4 GHz and compatible with Wireless-B equipment. *See* 802.11.

wireless keyboard a keyboard connecting to a computer with a wireless signal, rather than being plugged into it.

Wireless-N a widely used WI-FI wireless communication standard, giving 100 Mpbs at 2.4 GHz and compatible with Wireless-B and Wireless-G equipment. *See* 802.11.

wireless network, wireless LAN a LOCAL-AREA NETWORK (LAN) in which computers communicate via radio waves rather than through cables. *See* 802.11; BLUETOOTH; WI-FI; WIRELESS COMMUNICATION.

Radio waves do not stop at property lines, and many wireless networks have severely inadequate security. Many home networks do not have WEP or any other kind of ENCRYPTION because the owner has never turned encryption on; neighbors have been known to enjoy the free Internet access.

Four types of attack are possible: *freeloading* to use the network or Internet connection without permission; *eavesdropping* to pick up the owner's data, including passwords sent to systems elsewhere; *intrusion* to tamper with the owner's system; and *jamming* to prevent the use of the network, or degrade its performance, by deliberately transmitting radio waves that interfere with it. *See* COMPUTER SECURITY; WAR DRIVING; WEP; WIRELESS CLOUD.

In some places, access to wireless networks is provided to the public free of charge. This is presently the case in many Starbucks coffee shops and in some downtown areas; anyone with an 802.11b-equipped computer can access the Internet through the wireless network. *See also* 1G, 2G, 3G, 4G; WIMAX.

Wireless Pre-N a marketing term used to describe equipment that attempted to follow the WIRELESS-N standard before that standard was officially released.

wizard

1. a utility that automates certain common tasks in application software. Wizards are useful for setting up frequently used documents or performing tedious tasks. For example, after collecting information from the user about the company name and address, a word processor wizard can construct a letterhead for that company.

Wizards differ from template documents in that they collect specific information from the user and create a unique document that can be used as a template. *See also* SCRIPT.

2. any of various utilities for creating or distributing windowed software. The term *wizard* does not mean anything specific here.

3. an expert computer user; one who is gifted in solving problems or has acquired a vast store of useful knowledge about computers and software.

WLAN (**w**ireless **l**ocal-**a**rea **n**etwork) *see* WIRELESS NETWORK.

WMA (**W**indows **M**edia **A**udio) a format for compressing music stored as computer files; an alternative to the MP3 format.

WML (**w**ireless **m**arkup **l**anguage) an extension of XML aimed at wireless devices.

w/o online abbreviation for "without."

WOFF (**w**eb **o**pen **f**ont **f**ormat) a standard format for downloading fonts to be used on web pages. developed in 2009. (See *www.w3.org/ FontsWOFF-FAQ.html.*)

WOO a MOO (interactive environment or game) on the World Wide Web. *See* MUD; MOO.

woot in LEETSPEAK, a victory exclamation that has achieved widespread usage. Also spelled *w00t*.

word a group of bits equal in size to one CPU register. The number of bits in a word depends on the type of computer being used. A word on the original IBM PC is 16 bits long.

Word Microsoft's word processing program, which is available for Windows and Macintosh OS X operating systems. *See* MICROSOFT.

word processing the process of using a computer to prepare written documents (letters, reports, books, etc.). The boundary between word processing and *desktop publishing* is not sharp, but in general, word processing is the preparation of clearly worded, readable text, and does not include elaborate design or typography.

Word processing makes it easy to change or correct a document and then print it out without introducing new errors. More importantly, word processing lets you turn a rough draft into a finished report with no retyping and no wasted effort. You can start with a rough, fragmentary outline of what you want to say, then fill in the pieces in any convenient order. You don't have to finish page 1 before writing page 2. Many writers find this very convenient; you can get a document almost finished while waiting for information that you will fill in at the last minute, and if you have to produce many similar documents (letters, for instance), each one can be a slightly altered copy of the previous one.

Many word processors include spelling and grammar checkers. Take their advice with a grain of salt; they don't understand English perfectly, and they don't know what you are trying to say. A spelling checker simply looks up each word in a dictionary and complains if it can't find it; it does not catch substitutions of one correctly spelled word for another, such as *to* for *too*. Grammar checkers catch some common errors, but they also complain about some combinations of words that are not ungrammatical. There is no substitute for careful reading by a human being.

Almost all current word processors have all the features needed for office work and student term papers. Not all of them handle mathematical formulae, chemical symbols, foreign languages, or long footnotes; if you will be typing academic or technical material, choose software that meets your specific needs. The most versatile academic word processor (but definitely not the easiest to use) is TEX, from Stanford University. *See* DESKTOP PUBLISHING; LATEX; TEX; TYPESETTING MISTAKES.

word wrap the process of breaking lines of text automatically so that the typist does not have to press Enter at the end of each line. Word wrap is one of the great conveniences of word processing. In general, in a word processor, you should only press Enter where you want to begin a new paragraph; otherwise, just keep typing, and the computer will automatically break the text into lines that fit the margins. *See* REFLOW. *Contrast* WRAP.

wordle *see* TAG CLOUD.

WordPerfect a popular word processing program available for both PCs and Macintosh computers. It is noted for its ability to handle a wide variety of document formats, including footnotes, legal citations, and foreign language characters.

WordPress popular OPEN SOURCE SOFTWARE for creating a BLOG, available from *www.wordpress.org*. WordPress is highly customizable. The software can be used to set up a blog on your own web server; WordPress also provides web log service similar to BLOGGER, LIVEJOURNAL, or XANGA.

wordspacing the spacing between words, sometimes called INTERWORD SPACING. *Contrast* LETTERSPACING.

WordStar a word processing program marketed by MicroPro in the 1980s; the first popular word processor for microcomputers.

workaround an improvised method of avoiding a problem, typically by avoiding the use of a defective part of a system. For example, if the Tab key on a keyboard does not work, one possible workaround is to use Ctrl-I instead—on many but not all systems, it transmits the same code.

workgroup
1. a group of people who work together on a single project.
2. a group of computers that are treated as a small unit of a larger network.

workstation a computer at which one person works; a desktop computer. In the 1990s, workstation meant a powerful microcomputer typically used for scientific and engineering calculations. Nowadays, there is no distinction between workstations and other relatively well-equipped personal computers.

World Wide Web (WWW) a loosely organized set of computer sites that publish information that anyone can read via the Internet, mainly using HTTP (Hypertext Transfer Protocol). Each screenful (*page*) of information includes menu choices and highlighted words through which the user can call up further information, either from the same computer or by linking automatically to another computer anywhere in the world. *See* HYPERLINK. Thus, the information is arranged in a web of tremendous size, and the links are created by the author of each page. *See* BROWSER; HTML; INTERNET.

World Wide Web Consortium (abbreviated W3C) a group of member organizations founded in 1994 that works to develop standards and otherwise enhance the World Wide Web (web address *www.w3.org*).

WORM (**w**rite **o**nce, **r**ead **m**any times) any storage medium that allows a computer to save information once, and then read that information, but not change it, such as a CD-R.

worm virus a destructive computer program that spreads through the Internet or a LAN by transmitting itself to other computers from the infected one. For example, some worm viruses spread by e-mailing themselves to everyone in the victim's ADDRESS BOOK.

WOT (**w**eb **o**f **t**rust) a tool for determining if a web page in safe, based on user experiences (web address: *www.ntywot.com*).

WPA (**W**i-**F**i **P**rotected **A**ccess), system for encrypting data on a wireless network that provides improvements over WEP because the encryption keys are changed regularly.

WPF (**W**indows **P**resentation **F**oundation) part of the .NET FRAMEWORK used by developers to create user interfaces and write the code needed to handle events, such as clicking on a button.

wrap
  1. to manipulate the margins of text so that they follow the outline of a graphic. *See* Figure 308.
  2. *See* WORD WRAP.

FIGURE 308. Wrapping text around a graphic

wriggle shaking motion of an icon on an IOS device. This happens after you have been pressing the icon for a few seconds, and it makes it possible for you to move or delete the icon.

write to record digital information onto a storage device.

write-protect to set a disk or tape so that the computer will not write or erase the data on it.

WRT with respect to, with regard to.

WSDL (**W**eb **S**ervices **D**escription **L**anguage) an extension of XML describing how computers can work with WEB SERVICES.

WSVGA (**W**idescreen **S**uper **VGA**) a monitor resolution of 1024 × 600 pixels.

WSXGA (**W**idescreen **S**uper **XGA**) a monitor resolution of 1440 × 900 pixels.

WTB online abbreviation for "want to buy."

WUXGA (**W**idescreen **UXGA**) a monitor resolution of 1900 × 1200 pixels.

WVGA wide VGA (800 or more pixels wide by 480 pixels high). *See* VGA.

WWW WORLD WIDE WEB.

WXGA (**w**idescreen **XGA**) a monitor resolution of 1280 × 720 pixels or slightly more.

WYSIWYG acronym for "what you see is what you get." With a word processing program, this means that the appearance of the screen is supposedly an exact picture of how the document will look when printed. A disadvantage is that formatting codes are invisible and subtle alignment errors may be hard to see, whereas in an editor with explicit codes, they would be obvious. *See* TEX; TYPESETTING MISTAKES.

X

x-axis the horizontal axis in an *x-y* coordinate system. *See also* Y-AXIS; Z-AXIS.

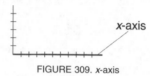

FIGURE 309. *x*-axis

x-height the height of the *body* of the lowercase letterforms (such as the small x of a typeface). Some typefaces make x half as high as X; some make it 40% as high; and some make it 60% as high.

A typeface with a large x-height looks larger than a typeface of the same point size with a small x-height. *See also* FONT; TYPEFACE.

FIGURE 310. x-height

X-OFF, X-ON codes that, respectively, turn off and on the transmission of data from a computer to a terminal. Many computers accessible by Telnet are programmed so that if the person at the terminal presses Ctrl-S (X-OFF), the computer will stop transmitting until the person presses Ctrl-Q (X-ON).

X server the process that manages the screen, keyboard, and mouse in the X Window System. *See* X WINDOW SYSTEM.

X terminal a terminal that is actually a small computer capable of running the X Window System. The terminal functions as an X server, managing the screen, keyboard, and mouse, while all other computation is done on the remote computer. *See* X WINDOW SYSTEM.

X Window System ("X Windows" for short) a software package for UNIX systems that allows programs to display text and graphics in windows and respond to a mouse (*see* WINDOW). X Windows software was developed at MIT and is distributed free. It is built into all major Linux distributions.

X Windows relies on multitasking. A process called an *X server* manages the screen, keyboard, and mouse; other processes call on the X server when they want to use these devices.

X.25 an ITU-T (formerly CCITT) standard protocol that defines a standard way of arranging data in packets. Each packet contains information indicating which computer sent it and which computer should receive it. *See* PACKET. X.25 has been adapted for amateur packet radio, and the adapted version is called AX.25. *See also* PROTOCOL.

X3D a graphics system for describing objects in space; intended as a successor to VRML. See *www.web3d.org/x3d/specifications*.

x64 a 64-bit extension of the Pentium (32-bit) CPU architecture originally developed by AMD for the Athlon 64 processor, and then adopted by Intel; the two companies' versions, which are compatible but may differ slightly, are known as AMD64 and EM64T respectively. Unlike IA-64 (Itanium), x64 is completely compatible with unmodified Pentium software; programmers can take advantage of the additional 64-bit instructions if they wish. Thus, x64 extends the Pentium the same way the Pentium extended the earlier 80286.

x86 abbreviation for 8086/286/386/486, the series of microprocessors used in all PC-compatible computers, including the Pentium but not the PowerPC. *See* MICROPROCESSOR.

x86-64 earlier name for X64.

XA *see* CD-ROM XA.

Xanga a web site (*www.xanga.com*) with a web log service (see BLOG) that is especially popular with teenagers. "Xanga" is pronounced "zang-uh." *Compare* BLOGGER; LIVEJOURNAL; WORDPRESS.

XBRL (Extensible Business Reporting Language) a language for business financial data using XML-style tags. For more information, see *www. xbrl.org*.

xerography a dry process that produces duplicate documents by combining electrostatic and photographic techniques. Originally called "electrophotography," it was developed by Chester Carlson in 1938 (and later patented). The Greek word "xerox" means "dry." *See also* LASER PRINTER.

XGA (Extended Graphics Array) a super VGA card marketed by IBM for the PS/2. The original XGA, introduced in 1991, offered 1024×768-pixel images. Today XGA denotes any monitor or projector that can display 1024×768-pixel images. *See* SVGA.

XHTML a newer formulation of HTML as an extension of XML. In XHTML tag names must be in lowercase and include a closing tag. For example, the code for including an image can be written <img src = "photo1. jpg"></img>, or else <img src = "photo1.jpg"/ >. See also *www.w3.org/ TR/xhtml1*.

XMCL (**E**xtensible **M**edia **C**ommerce **L**anguage) an XML-based language designed to support the business of delivering digital content (music, etc.) over the Internet. Although much content on the Internet is free, other content will only be available if there is a mechanism allowing the content creators to receive reasonable payment for their work. XMCL provides a standard way to transmit data needed for this process. For more information, see *www.xmcl.org*.

XML (**E**xtensible **M**arkup **L**anguage) a language similar to HTML, but designed for transmitting complex data structures of any type, not just web pages. XML is a subset of SGML adopted as a standard by the W3C in 1998. XML is designed to be easier to use than SGML while providing richer features and better implementation of LOGICAL DESIGN than HTML.

In an XML document, the beginning and end of elements of the document are marked with tags, such as <from> and </from> to mark the beginning and end of the part of a memo that indicates who the memo is from. Note that the notation for tags follows the same format as HTML. However, XML does not define a set of tags as does HTML. Instead, it is extensible because different users can extend the language definition with their own set of tags.

When an XML document uses these tags, a document type definition (DTD) is needed to define the elements. The DTD may be included in the XML document itself, or it may be in a separate document that can be used by all documents in the same document class.

Below is an example of an XML document that we could use to store data about people we might want to recruit for computer jobs in our company. In this example, the document type definition (DTD) is included at the front of the document.

This example creates a document type called RECRUITLIST, which consists of elements called RECRUITS. Because the DTD contains a plus sign after the declaration of RECRUIT, a document can have one or more recruits. Each RECRUIT can consist of four elements: NAME, ADDRESS, DEGREE, and ACCOMPLISHMENT. Each recruit must have exactly one NAME and one ADDRESS. The asterisk after DEGREE means that a recruit can have zero, one, or more degrees. The element NAME consists of three elements: FIRSTNAME, LASTNAME, and NICKNAME. The question mark after the definition of NICKNAME means that a name may contain zero or one nickname. Following the document type definition, this sample shows two particular recruits.

```
<?xml version="1.0" encoding="UTF-8"?>
<!DOCTYPE RECRUITLIST [
<!ELEMENT RECRUITLIST (RECRUIT+)>
<!ELEMENT RECRUIT (NAME,ADDRESS,DEGREE*,ACCOMPLISHMENT+)>
<!ELEMENT NAME (FIRSTNAME,LASTNAME,NICKNAME?)>
<!ELEMENT FIRSTNAME (#PCDATA)>
<!ELEMENT LASTNAME (#PCDATA)>
```

```
<!ELEMENT NICKNAME (#PCDATA)>
<!ELEMENT ADDRESS (STREET+,CITY,STATE,ZIP)>
<!ELEMENT STREET (#PCDATA)>
<!ELEMENT CITY (#PCDATA)>
<!ELEMENT STATE (#PCDATA)>
<!ELEMENT ZIP (#PCDATA)>
   <!ELEMENT DEGREE (SCHOOL, YEAR, TYPE)>
<!ELEMENT SCHOOL (#PCDATA)>
<!ELEMENT YEAR (#PCDATA)>
<!ELEMENT TYPE (#PCDATA)>
   <!ELEMENT ACCOMPLISHMENT (#PCDATA)>
]>

<RECRUITLIST>
<RECRUIT>
<NAME>
   <FIRSTNAME>Bill</FIRSTNAME>
   <LASTNAME> Gates</LASTNAME>
   <NICKNAME> Trey </NICKNAME>
</NAME>
<ADDRESS>
   <STREET>One Microsoft Way</STREET>
   <CITY>Redmond</CITY>
   <STATE>Washington</STATE>
   <ZIP>98052</ZIP>
 </ADDRESS>
 <ACCOMPLISHMENT>Founded Microsoft</ACCOMPLISHMENT>
 <ACCOMPLISHMENT>Completed two years of Harvard
   </ACCOMPLISHMENT>
</RECRUIT>
<RECRUIT>
  <NAME>
   <FIRSTNAME>Donald</FIRSTNAME>
   <LASTNAME>Knuth</LASTNAME>
  </NAME>
  <ADDRESS>
   <STREET>353 Serra Mall</STREET>
   <CITY>Stanford</CITY>
   <STATE>California</STATE>
   <ZIP>94305</ZIP>
  </ADDRESS>
  <DEGREE>
   <SCHOOL>Case Institute of Technology</SCHOOL>
   <YEAR>1960</YEAR>
   <TYPE>B.S.</TYPE>
  </DEGREE>
  <DEGREE>
   <SCHOOL>California Institute of Technology</SCHOOL>
```

```
   <YEAR>1963</YEAR>
   <TYPE>Ph.D.</TYPE>
 </DEGREE>
 <ACCOMPLISHMENT>Created TeX</ACCOMPLISHMENT>
 </RECRUIT>
</RECRUITLIST>
```

If we run this document through an XML-validating parser, we can verify that it is a valid XML document. A valid XML document must contain a closing tag for each opening tag, the elements must be correctly nested inside each other, and all of the elements specified in the DTD must be present in the specified sequence. However, the XML parser will not process the data; that must be done with an application designed to work with this type of document. XML is intended for a broad array of applications, including presentation of web documents and storage and transfer of database information. For more information, see *www.w3.org/XML*.

XOR gate (exclusive-**OR** gate) a logic gate whose output is 1 when one but not both of its inputs is 1, as shown in this table.

Inputs		Output
0	0	0
0	1	1
1	0	1
1	1	0

The XOR function is interesting because if you XOR one bit pattern with another, you get an obscure pattern; but if you then XOR that pattern with one of the original patterns, you get the other original pattern. XOR gates are useful for encryption, hashing, and in RAID systems, and various other applications. *See* Figure 311. *See also* COMPUTER ARCHITECTURE; LOGIC CIRCUITS.

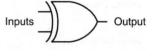

FIGURE 311. XOR gate (logic symbol)

XP

1. version 5.1 of Microsoft Windows. *See* WINDOWS (MICROSOFT).
2. abbreviation for EXTREME PROGRAMMING.

XrML (**E**xtensible **R**ights **M**arkup **L**anguage) an XML-based language for specifying rights and conditions associated with digital content or services. For more information, see *www.xrml.org*. *See also* COPYRIGHT.

XSEDE (Extreme Science and Engineering Discovery Environment) a network of powerful computers available for scientific research, supported by the National Science Foundation (web address: *www.xsede. org*).

XT the second model of IBM PC, introduced in 1983. The PC XT had eight expansion slots instead of the original five and it included a 10-megabyte hard disk. The microprocessor was a 4.77-MHz 8088 with an 8-bit bus, just as in the original PC.

XUL (pronounced "zool") Extensible User-interface Language, an XML-based language for defining graphical user interface elements such as buttons and dialog boxes. For more information, see the web site at *developer.mozilla.org/en/docs/XUL*.

Y

Y online abbreviation for "why?"

y-axis the vertical axis in an *x-y* coordinate system (Figure 312). In traditional mathematical representation, the *y*-axis value increases as you move up. However, on computer graphics systems, the *y* coordinate often is zero at the top of the screen, and increases as you move down. *See also* X-AXIS; Z-AXIS.

FIGURE 312. *y*-axis

Yahoo a popular SEARCH ENGINE for the WORLD WIDE WEB, accessible at *www.yahoo.com*. Yahoo also offers other Internet services. *Compare* GOOGLE.

Year 2000 Problem (Y2K Problem) the problem caused by software that represents the year date as two digits (such as 99 for 1999) and thus did not recognize that 2000 comes after 1999. Instead, the software interprets 00 as 1900. This causes mistakes in calculations that involve the date. Dates were originally represented as two digits in the 1960s for two reasons: computer memories were expensive and limited, and punched cards could hold only 80 characters.

The panicky predictions that massive computer failures would occur on January 1, 2000 proved to be false, but much of the effort made to update software was necessary or beneficial for other reasons.

Yellow Book the book that originally defined the Philips/Sony standard for recording data on CD-ROMs.

YKYBHTLW abbreviation for "you know you've been hacking too long when," as in "YKYBHTLW you start to dream in C++." In this expression, *hacking* means "programming," not "attempting computer crime." *See* HACKER.

YMMV online abbreviation for "your mileage may vary" (i.e., your results may be different).

yotta- metric prefix meaning ×1,000,000,000,000,000,000,000,000 (10^{24}). *See* METRIC PREFIXES.

You've Got Mail the familiar audio announcement used by AMERICA ONLINE software to announce the arrival of e-mail. It is derived from "you have mail," a text message often displayed to users logging into UNIX.

YouTube a popular video sharing site (*www.youtube.com*) where users can upload and watch video clips of all types. Since 2006, YouTube has been owned and maintained by Google. Although many videos are home-made, be aware of copyright issues before posting television or movie clips or music videos. *See* COPYRIGHT.

Z

z-axis the direction toward and away from the viewer in a three-dimensional coordinate system. *Compare* X-AXIS; Y-AXIS.

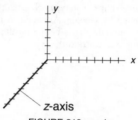

FIGURE 313. z-axis

In computer graphics, the x-axis is always horizontal and the y-axis is always vertical; the z-axis points toward the viewer. In mathematics books, however, the axes are often drawn as if the paper were lying on a flat desk with the z-axis pointing toward the ceiling; thus, in printed diagrams the z-axis often points straight up.

z-buffer (3D program) an editing buffer that allows the program to keep track of objects that are hidden from view by other objects.

z-order the arrangement of elements of an image from front to back. Z-order determines which items are in front of others.

Z80 an 8-bit microprocessor produced by Zilog, Inc., and used in microcomputers that ran the CP/M operating system in the 1970s and early 1980s. *See* MICROPROCESSOR.

zero day flaw a software vulnerability that has been exploited by malicious hackers on or before the day the software creators become aware of the problem.

zetta- metric prefix meaning ×1,000,000,000,000,000,000,000 (10^{21}). *Zetta* is apparently a nonsense word. *See* METRIC PREFIXES.

ZIF socket (**z**ero **i**nsertion **f**orce socket) a socket into which an integrated circuit can be inserted without pressure. It has a lever to open up the holes for easy insertion. The lever is then moved to tighten the connectors once the IC is in place.

Zip drive a 100, 250, or 750-megabyte removable-cartridge disk drive made by Iomega Corporation of Roy, Utah.

ZIP file a file containing files and/or directories compressed with WinZip (web address: *www.winzip.com*), an earlier program called PKZIP, or the built-in ZIP compression feature of Windows. (ZIP files are not related in any way to Iomega Zip drives.)

zombie a computer infected by a VIRUS that makes it perform some action on behalf of the virus author, such as distributing SPAM or carrying out a distributed DENIAL-OF-SERVICE ATTACK, without the knowledge of the computer owner. *See* DDOS.

zool *[sic] see* XUL.

zoom

1. (in graphics editing) to magnify a small area of a document on the screen. The amount of zoom is usually expressed as a percentage and displayed in a status line. To *zoom in* is to increase the magnification; to *zoom out* is to return to normal view (Figure 314).

FIGURE 314. Zoom (definition 1)

2. (in photography) to change the focal length, and hence the magnification of the camera lens (Figure 315). OPTICAL ZOOM changes the spacing of the lens elements to form a larger image, revealing more detail. DIGITAL ZOOM takes the existing pixels and spreads them farther apart (*see* RESAMPLE); the digitally enlarged image does not contain any more detail than it did before zooming. A lens marked "3× zoom" has a focal length that is 3 times as long at maximum as at minimum. *See also* FOCAL LENGTH.

FIGURE 315. Zoom (definition 2)

z/OS the newest operating system in the OS/360 lineage for IBM MAINFRAME COMPUTERS, combining MVS with UNIX compatibility. This allows the newest Internet technology to be combined with long-established mainframe data processing systems. *See* MVS; OS/360; POSIX.

Zuckerberg, Mark founder of Facebook in 2004 while a computer programming student at Harvard. He led Facebook's expansion to other colleges and then to the general public and continues as its CEO. He was named 2010's Person of the Year by *Time* Magazine due to the influence Facebook has had on daily life. There were controversies over the original ownership of the company that resulted in two lawsuits that were settled out of court. A partly fictionalized version of Facebook's founding and the surrounding controversies and lawsuits became the basis for the critically acclaimed 2010 film *The Social Network*.

GREEK LETTERS

α (alpha) the opacity of a layer in a graphical image. *See* ALPHA.

γ (gamma) a measure of the contrast of photographic film or the nonlinearity of an electronically obtained image. *See* GAMMA.

μ (mu) abbreviation for *micro-* (one-millionth). *See* METRIC PREFIXES.

μC abbreviation for *microcontroller*.

μP abbreviation for *microprocessor*.

π (pi) the ratio of the circumference of a circle to its diameter, approximately 3.14159. *See* PI.

The Greek Alphabet

A	α	alpha
B	β	beta
Γ	γ	gamma
Δ	δ	delta
E	ε	epsilon (ε in some typefaces)
Z	ζ	zeta
H	η	eta
Θ	θ	theta (ϑ in some typefaces)
I	ι	iota
K	κ	kappa
Λ	λ	lambda
M	μ	mu
N	ν	nu
Ξ	ξ	xi
O	o	omicron
Π	π	pi (ϖ in some typefaces)
P	ρ	rho (ρ in some typefaces)
Σ	σ	sigma (ς at ends of words)
T	τ	tau
Υ	υ	upsilon
Φ	φ	phi (φ in some typefaces)
X	χ	chi
Ψ	ψ	psi
Ω	ω	omega

VISUAL DICTIONARY OF CHARACTERS AND SYMBOLS

Many symbols fall into more than one category. For the Greek alphabet, see page 574. For symbols used in diagrams, *see* ELECTRONIC CIRCUIT SYMBOLS and FLOWCHART.

Computer Keyboard Symbols

^	circumflex, hat
~	tilde
`	grave accent, backquote
′	upright quotation mark, apostrophe
'	left quotation mark
'	right quotation mark, apostrophe
"	double quotation mark
@	at sign
#	pound sign, crosshatch, octothorpe
$	dollar sign
%	percent sign
&	ampersand
+	plus sign
–	minus sign, hyphen
_	underscore mark
=	equal sign
*	asterisk
/	slash
\	backslash
|	vertical bar, pipe
< >	less than/greater than *or* angle brackets
( )	parentheses, round brackets
[ ]	square brackets
{ }	braces, curly brackets
¬	not sign (EBCDIC)

Note: In ASCII, ' is equivalent to ′ and ` is equivalent to '.

"Emoticons" used in e-mail

:)	smiling face (happiness, amusement)
:(	frowning face (sadness, disappointment)
-)	tongue in cheek
;-)	winking
=:-O	scared or surprised
^.^;	distressed (with drops of sweat)

Commercial and Scientific Symbols

@	at, price each
#	identifying number or pounds (weight)
%	percent (per hundred)
°/oo	per mil (per thousand)
°	degrees
ℓ	liters (obsolete; use L instead)
Ω	ohms
μ	micro- (millionths)
©	copyright
$	dollars, pesos
¥	yen
£	pounds (currency)
€	Euro sign

English Punctuation Marks

.	period
,	comma
:	colon
;	semicolon
!	exclamation mark
?	question mark
-	hyphen
–	en dash, minus sign
—	em dash
. . .	ellipsis dots
'	upright single quotation mark, apostrophe
"	upright double quotation mark
'	left single quotation mark
"	left double quotation mark
'	right single quotation mark, apostrophe
"	right double quotation mark
*	asterisk (first footnote)
†	dagger (second footnote)
‡	double dagger (third footnote)
§	section mark
¶	paragraph mark (pilcrow)
•	bullet (to mark list items)

Accents

á	acute accent
a̋	double acute accent
à	grave accent
â	circumflex
ä	umlaut or dieresis
ã	tilde
ā	macron (long vowel mark)
ă	breve (short vowel mark)
č	wedge (hachek)
ç	cedilla

Other Foreign Characters

„ "	German quotation marks
« »	French quotation marks (guillemets)
¿	Spanish inverted question mark
¡	Spanish inverted exclamation mark
ß	German ss (estsett)
Æ æ	AE digraph
Œ œ	OE digraph
Å å	A with circle (Scandinavian)
Ø ø	O with slash (Scandinavian)
Ł ł	Barred L (Polish)
İ i I ı	Dotted and dotless I (Turkish)

Arithmetic and Algebra

$=$	equals
$\neq$	does not equal
$\approx, \doteq$	is approximately equal to
$>$	is greater than
$\geq$	is greater than or equal to
$<$	is less than
$\leq$	is less than or equal to
$+$	addition
$-$	subtraction
$\times, \cdot$	multiplication
$\div, /$	division
$\sqrt{}$	square root
$\sqrt[n]{}$	nth root
$!$	factorial
$|x|$	absolute value of x
∞	infinity
$\propto$	is proportional to
Δx	change in x
$\int$	integral
∂	partial derivative

Mathematical Logic

$\forall x, (x)$	universal quantifier ("for all x...")
$\exists x$	existential quantifier ("there exists an x...")
$-p, \neg p, \sim p$	negation ("not p")
$p \wedge q, p \ \& \ q$	conjunction ("p and q")
$p \vee q$	disjunction ("p or q")
$p \underline{\vee} q$	exclusive-or ("p or q but not both")
$p \rightarrow q, p \supset q$	implication ("if p then q")
$p \leftrightarrow q, p \equiv q$	equivalence ("p if and only if q")
$p \vdash q$	from p one can derive q

Set Theory

$\{a, b, c\}$	set whose members are a, b, and c
$\emptyset$	empty set
$\cup$	set union (elements in one or both of two sets)
$\cap$	set intersection (elements shared by two sets)
$\backslash$	set subtraction (elements in one set and not the other)
$\in$	is an element of
$\subset$	is a subset of
$\subseteq$	is a subset of or equals

COUNTRY CODES FOR TOP-LEVEL DOMAINS

.ac	Ascension Island	.ch	Switzerland (Confœderatio Helvetica)
.ad	Andorra		
.ae	United Arab Emirates	.ci	Cote d'Ivoire
.af	Afghanistan	.ck	Cook Islands
.ag	Antigua and Barbuda	.cl	Chile
.ai	Anguilla	.cm	Cameroon
.al	Albania	.cn	China
.am	Armenia	.co	Colombia
.an	Netherlands Antilles	.cr	Costa Rica
.ao	Angola	.cu	Cuba
.aq	Antarctica	.cv	Cape Verde
.ar	Argentina	.cx	Christmas Island
.as	American Samoa	.cy	Cyprus
.at	Austria	.cz	Czech Republic
.au	Australia	.de	Germany (Deutschland)
.aw	Aruba	.dj	Djibouti
.az	Azerbaijan	.dk	Denmark
.ba	Bosnia and Herzegovina	.dm	Dominica
.bb	Barbados	.do	Dominican Republic
.bd	Bangladesh	.dz	Algeria
.be	Belgium	.ec	Ecuador
.bf	Burkina Faso	.ee	Estonia
.bg	Bulgaria	.eg	Egypt
.bh	Bahrain	.eh	Western Sahara
.bi	Burundi	.er	Eritrea
.bj	Benin	.es	Spain (España)
.bm	Bermuda	.et	Ethiopia
.bn	Brunei Darussalam	.fi	Finland
.bo	Bolivia	.fj	Fiji
.br	Brazil	.fk	Falkland Islands (Malvinas)
.bs	Bahamas		
.bt	Bhutan	.fm	Micronesia
.bv	Bouvet Island	.fo	Faroe Islands
.bw	Botswana	.fr	France
.by	Belarus	.ga	Gabon
.bz	Belize	.gd	Grenada
.ca	Canada	.ge	Georgia
.cc	Cocos Islands	.gf	French Guiana
.cd	Congo	.gg	Guernsey
.cf	Central African Republic	.gh	Ghana
.cg	Congo, Republic of	.gi	Gibraltar

.gl	Greenland	.lc	Saint Lucia
.gm	Gambia	.li	Liechtenstein
.gn	Guinea	.lk	Sri Lanka
.gp	Guadeloupe	.lr	Liberia
.gq	Equatorial Guinea	.ls	Lesotho
.gr	Greece	.lt	Lithuania
.gs	South Georgia and the	.lu	Luxembourg
	South Sandwich Islands	.lv	Latvia
.gt	Guatemala	.ly	Libyan Arab Jamahiriya
.gu	Guam	.ma	Morocco
.gw	Guinea-Bissau	.mc	Monaco
.gy	Guyana	.md	Moldova
.hk	Hong Kong	.mg	Madagascar
.hm	Heard and McDonald	.mh	Marshall Islands
	Islands	.mk	Macedonia (former
.hn	Honduras		Yugoslav Republic)
.hr	Croatia/Hrvatska	.ml	Mali
.ht	Haiti	.mm	Myanmar
.hu	Hungary	.mn	Mongolia
.id	Indonesia	.mo	Macau
.ie	Ireland	.mp	Northern Mariana
.il	Israel		Islands
.im	Isle of Man	.mq	Martinique
.in	India	.mr	Mauritania
.io	British Indian Ocean	.ms	Montserrat
	Territory	.mt	Malta
.iq	Iraq	.mu	Mauritius
.ir	Iran	.mv	Maldives
.is	Iceland	.mw	Malawi
.it	Italy	.mx	Mexico
.je	Jersey	.my	Malaysia
.jm	Jamaica	.mz	Mozambique
.jo	Jordan	.na	Namibia
.jp	Japan	.nc	New Caledonia
.ke	Kenya	.ne	Niger
.kg	Kyrgyzstan	.nf	Norfolk Island
.kh	Cambodia (Kampuchea)	.ng	Nigeria
.ki	Kiribati	.ni	Nicaragua
.km	Comoros	.nl	Netherlands
.kn	Saint Kitts and Nevis	.no	Norway
.kp	North Korea	.np	Nepal
.kr	South Korea	.nr	Nauru
.kw	Kuwait	.nu	Niue
.ky	Cayman Islands	.nz	New Zealand
.kz	Kazakhstan	.om	Oman
.la	Laos	.pa	Panama
.lb	Lebanon	.pe	Peru

.pf	French Polynesia	.tg	Togo
.pg	Papua New Guinea	.th	Thailand
.ph	Philippines	.tj	Tajikistan
.pk	Pakistan	.tk	Tokelau
.pl	Poland	.tm	Turkmenistan
.pm	St. Pierre and Miquelon	.tn	Tunisia
.pn	Pitcairn Island	.to	Tonga
.pr	Puerto Rico	.tp	East Timor
.ps	Palestinian Territories	.tr	Turkey
.pt	Portugal	.tt	Trinidad and Tobago
.pw	Palau	.tv	Tuvalu
.py	Paraguay	.tw	Taiwan
.qa	Qatar	.tz	Tanzania
.re	Reunion Island	.ua	Ukraine
.ro	Romania	.ug	Uganda
.ru	Russian Federation	.uk	United Kingdom
.rw	Rwanda	.um	U.S. Minor Outlying
.sa	Saudi Arabia		Islands
.sb	Solomon Islands	.us	United States
.sc	Seychelles	.uy	Uruguay
.sd	Sudan	.uz	Uzbekistan
.se	Sweden	.va	Holy See (Vatican City
.sg	Singapore		State)
.sh	St. Helena	.vc	Saint Vincent and the
.si	Slovenia		Grenadines
.sj	Svalbard and Jan Mayen	.ve	Venezuela
	Islands	.vg	Virgin Islands (British)
.sk	Slovak Republic	.vi	Virgin Islands (U.S.)
.sl	Sierra Leone	.vn	Vietnam
.sm	San Marino	.vu	Vanuatu
.sn	Senegal	.wf	Wallis and Futuna
.so	Somalia		Islands
.sr	Suriname	.ws	Western Samoa
.st	Sao Tome and Principe	.ye	Yemen
.sv	El Salvador	.yt	Mayotte
.sy	Syrian Arab Republic	.yu	Yugoslavia
.sz	Swaziland	.za	South Africa
.tc	Turks and Caicos Islands	.zm	Zambia
.td	Chad (Tchad)	.zw	Zimbabwe
.tf	French Southern		
	Territories		

For explanation, and for international top-level domains such as *.com, see* TLD.

HOW TO STAY SAFE
ON THE INTERNET

1. Choose passwords that nobody can guess. Your password must not be a word in any language (spelled forward or backward), nor a birthday, telephone number, or other information that a person could associate with you.

2. Do not believe everything that appears on your screen. Remember that e-mail messages and web sites are very easy to fake. Fake web sites for banks are particularly common. Do not connect to any password-protected site (bank, e-mail, etc.) through a link that is e-mailed to you; instead, type the web address yourself.

3. Do not click on a file, document, or link that appears in an e-mail from a stranger, no matter what it claims to be. Instead, find out who sent it to you and whether it is legitimate.

4. Never give your password to anyone who asks for it, no matter how official they sound. Computer administrators *never* need your password.

5. Never leave a computer logged in to a password-protected site while you are away from it.

6. In public places, do not connect to wireless networks that you don't know anything about. A network called "Free Local Wi-Fi" is often a scam, a link to a single virus-infected computer.

7. Keep current antivirus software on your computer, but don't expect it to do your thinking for you. Most viruses trick you into giving them permission to install themselves. Some web sites falsely tell you that you have a virus so that you will give them permission to make changes to your computer, and then they give you a virus. Do not let a web site do anything to your computer ("clean" or "optimize" or "customize" it) unless you are 100% sure it is trustworthy.

8. Do not put information on the Internet that would be seriously damaging if made public. Whatever you post to the Web or Facebook can and will be preserved by other people and forwarded to people you didn't anticipate. Even e-mail is not secure enough for truly confidential information.

9. Do not spread misinformation and gossip. Use *www.google.com* and *www.snopes.com* to check facts before you pass along information. Remember that if an e-mail says, "pass this along to all your friends," it is almost certainly a hoax, or at least badly out of date, and you do not know who originally wrote it. Reliable information is found on web sites whose authors will take responsibility for what they are saying.

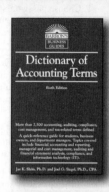
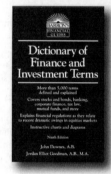